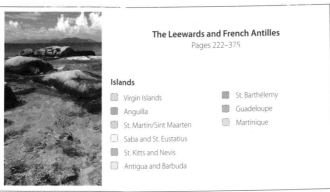

The Leewards and French Antilles
Pages 222–375

Islands

- Virgin Islands
- Anguilla
- St. Martin/Sint Maarten
- Saba and St. Eustatius
- St. Kitts and Nevis
- Antigua and Barbuda
- St. Barthélemy
- Guadeloupe
- Martinique

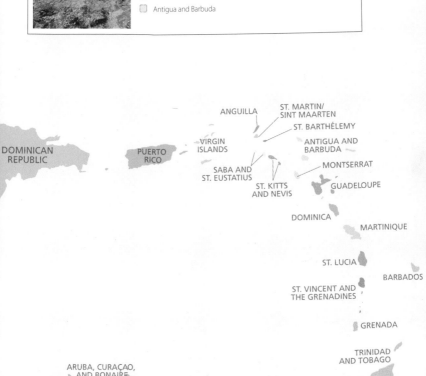

DOMINICAN REPUBLIC

PUERTO RICO

VIRGIN ISLANDS

ANGUILLA

ST. MARTIN/ SINT MAARTEN

ST. BARTHÉLEMY

ANTIGUA AND BARBUDA

SABA AND ST. EUSTATIUS

ST. KITTS AND NEVIS

MONTSERRAT

GUADELOUPE

DOMINICA

MARTINIQUE

ST. LUCIA

BARBADOS

ST. VINCENT AND THE GRENADINES

GRENADA

TRINIDAD AND TOBAGO

ARUBA, CURAÇAO, AND BONAIRE

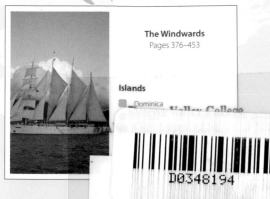

The Windwards
Pages 376–453

Islands

- Dominica

EYEWITNESS TRAVEL

CARIBBEAN

EYEWITNESS TRAVEL

CARIBBEAN

DK

LONDON, NEW YORK,
MELBOURNE, MUNICH AND DELHI
www.dk.com

Managing Editor Aruna Ghose
Editorial Manager Ankita Awasthi
Design Managers Sunita Gahir, Kavita Saha
Project Editor Shikha Kulkarni
Project Designer Anchal Kaushal
Editors Divya Chowfin, Jayashree Menon, Souvik Mukherjee
Designers Sonal Bhatt, Neha Gupta, Kaberi Hazarika
Senior Cartographic Manager Uma Bhattacharya
Cartographer Zafar-Ul-Islam Khan
DTP Coordinator Azeem Siddiqui
Senior Picture Researcher Taiyaba Khatoon
Picture Researcher Sumita Khatwani

Contributors
Christopher Baker, James Henderson, Skye Hernandez, Lynda Lohr, KC Nash, Don Philpott,
Theresa Storm, Lynne Morgan Sullivan, Polly Thomas

Photographers
Demetrio Carrasco, Nigel Hicks, Linda Whitwam

Illustrators
Chapel Design & Marketing Ltd., Chinglemba Chingtham,
Aurgho Jyoti, Arun Pottirayil, Mark Arjun Warner

Printed in Malaysia by Vivar Printing Sdn. Bhd.

First published in the UK in 2009
Dorling Kindersley Limited, 80 Strand, London WC2R 0RL

14 15 16 17 10 9 8 7 6 5 4 3 2 1

Reprinted with revisions 2011, 2014

Copyright © 2009, 2014 Dorling Kindersley Limited, London
A Penguin Random House Company

MIX
Paper from
responsible sources
FSC™ C018179
www.fsc.org

The information in this
DK Eyewitness Travel Guide is checked regularly.

Every effort has been made to ensure that this book is as up-to-date as possible at
the time of going to press. Some details, however, such as telephone numbers,
opening hours, prices, gallery hanging arrangements and travel information are
liable to change. The publishers cannot accept responsibility for any consequences
arising from the use of this book, nor for any material on third party websites, and
cannot guarantee that any website address in this book will be a suitable source of
travel information. We value the views and suggestions of our readers very highly.
Please write to: Publisher, DK Eyewitness Travel Guides, Dorling Kindersley,
80 Strand, London WC2R 0RL, UK, or email: travelguides@dk.com.

Front cover main image: Colorful tropical fish on a coral reef, Grand Cayman

◀ Aerial view of Turtle Cove Marina, Grand Turk

Contents

How to Use
this Guide **6**

Souvenir mask, Puerto Rico

Visiting the
Caribbean

The Caribbean
at a Glance

Yachts in Christiansted Harbor,
St. Croix, US Virgin Islands

The Greater
Antilles

Palm Beach in Grand Anse Bay, Grenada

Musée Victor Schoelcher in Pointe-à-Pitre,
Guadeloupe

The Leewards and
French Antilles

The
Windwards

The Southern
Caribbean

Moko Jumbie stiltwalkers at the Carnival,
Trinidad and Tobago

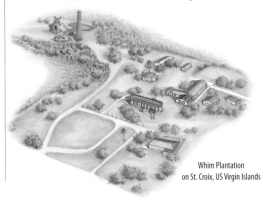

Whim Plantation
on St. Croix, US Virgin Islands

HOW TO USE THIS GUIDE

This guide helps you get the most from your visit to the Caribbean. It provides detailed practical information and expert recommendations. *Visiting the Caribbean* maps the area and provides tips on practical considerations and travel. The *At a Glance* section introduces the region's history and culture, with an overview of the best

activities available. The isles are divided into four main groups, each broken down into individual island chapters. These begin with a map, followed by descriptions of local sights and top beaches. Information about outdoor activities, hotels, restaurants, nightlife, and practical details is found at the end of each chapter.

Island by Island

The map on the inside front cover shows the four main divisions and the 22 different Caribbean island entities dealt with in this guide.

1 At a Glance Map
Each section starts with a map color coding the various islands covered in separate chapters.

2 Introduction to an Island
Some isles with particular characteristics get a more in-depth introduction to their geography, history, and culture.

Captions briefly describe some of the important sights on the island.

3 Area Map
For easy reference, sights in each island nation are numbered on the map, in the same order that they are described in the chapter.

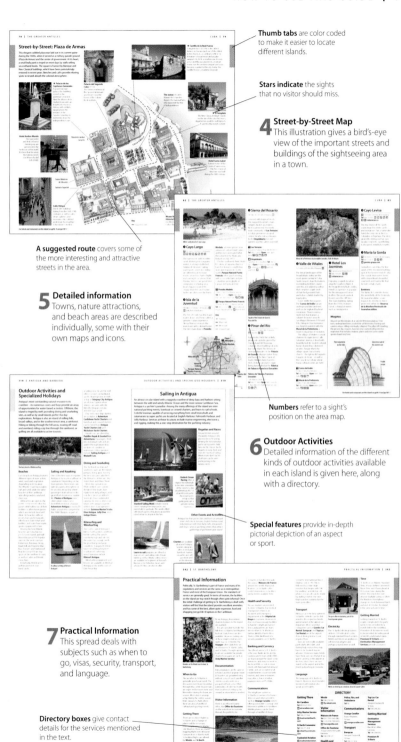

Thumb tabs are color coded to make it easier to locate different islands.

Stars indicate the sights that no visitor should miss.

4 Street-by-Street Map
This illustration gives a bird's-eye view of the important streets and buildings of the sightseeing area in a town.

A suggested route covers some of the more interesting and attractive streets in the area.

5 Detailed information
Towns, nature attractions, and beach areas are described individually, some with their own maps and icons.

Numbers refer to a sight's position on the area map.

6 Outdoor Activities
Detailed information of the different kinds of outdoor activities available in each island is given here, along with a directory.

Special features provide in-depth pictorial depiction of an aspect or sport.

7 Practical Information
This spread deals with subjects such as when to go, visas, security, transport, and language.

Directory boxes give contact details for the services mentioned in the text.

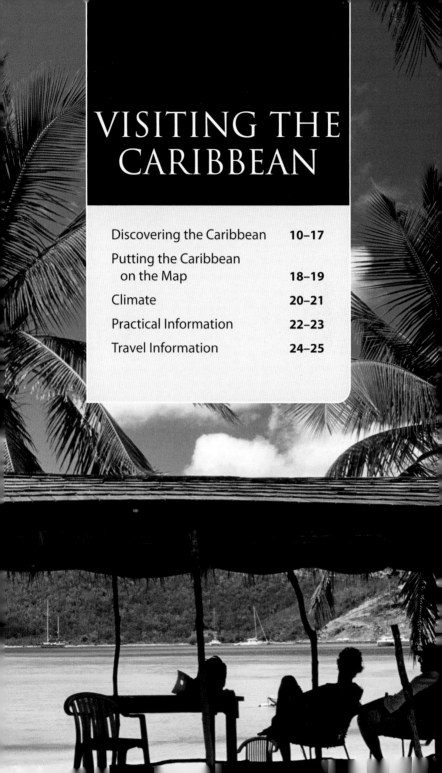

VISITING THE CARIBBEAN

DISCOVERING THE CARIBBEAN

The Caribbean is vast and comprises dozens of widely-dispersed islands, so attempting to visit the entire region in one trip is an impossible task. Consequently, the following tours concentrate on the most beguiling and rewarding islands. To start with there are one- and two-day itineraries of each of the Greater Antilles' capital cities – Havana, San Juan, and Santo Domingo. Next are two week-long tours designed to guide you to the best of Western Cuba and Jamaica. Millions of visitors choose to visit the Caribbean by cruise ship, so there is an itinerary of a typical route around the Southern Caribbean. Finally, for the more adventurous, there is a 7- or 14-day sailing itinerary of the Leewards Islands.

A Week in Jamaica

- Watch hummingbirds eat from your hand at Rockland Bird Sanctuary outside **Montego Bay**.
- Laze on the white sands of **Negril**, then snorkel or scuba dive; at night dance to reggae.
- Visit the **Great Morass Royal Palm Reserve** and **YS Falls** en route to **Treasure Beach**.
- Explore Devon House and the Bob Marley Museum while passing through **Kingston**.
- Take in the views as you ascend into the **Blue Mountains** en route to **Port Antonio**.
- Admire the coastal vistas as you drive to **Ocho Rios**.
- Commune with the ghosts of the past at **Rose Hall and Greenwood Great Houses**.

English Harbour, Antigua
Beautiful views of this protected harbor and Nelson's Dockyard can be enjoyed from Shirley Heights.

7-Day Cruise of the Southern Caribbean

- Roam **English Harbour and Nelson's Dockyard** on **Antigua**.
- Marvel at the majesty of **St. Lucia's** volcanic spires – **The Pitons**.
- Hike amid cool rainforest at **Grand Etang Forest Reserve** on **Grenada**.
- Watch Atlantic rollers crash ashore at **Bathsheba**, on the east coast of **Barbados**.

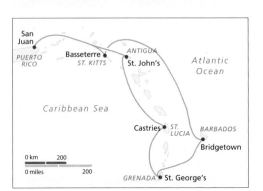

◄ Beach at the Great Harbor, Jost Van Dyke, Virgin Islands

Atlantic Ocean

The Leewards

Western Cuba

Jamaica

Caribbean Sea

Southern Caribbean

Locator Map

7 or 14 Days Sailing the Leewards

- Snorkel the waters off **Jost Van Dyke**, BVI, and look for rays and marine turtles.

- Explore the colonial ruins of Brimstone Hill Fortress on **St. Kitts**.

- Shop for duty-free items in Phillipsburg, on **St. Maarten**.

- Hike The Quill, on **St. Eustasius**, to roam the rainforest in an extinct volcanic crater.

- Dine on divine dishes and party on **St. Barthélemy**.

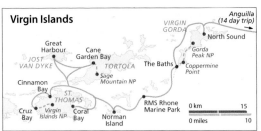

Virgin Islands

Anguilla (14 day trip)

VIRGIN GORDA

North Sound

Great Harbour
Cane Garden Bay
JOST VAN DYKE
TORTOLA
The Baths
Gorda Peak NP
Coppermine Point
Cinnamon Bay
Sage Mountain NP
ST. THOMAS
Cruz Bay
Virgin Islands NP
Coral Bay
Norman Island
RMS Rhone Marine Park

0 km 15
0 miles 10

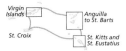

Virgin Islands
Anguilla to St. Barts
St. Croix
St. Kitts and St. Eustatius

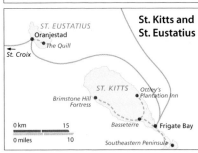

St. Kitts and St. Eustatius

ST. EUSTATIUS
Oranjestad
The Quill
St. Croix

ST. KITTS
Ottley's Plantation Inn
Brimstone Hill Fortress
Basseterre
Frigate Bay
Southeastern Peninsula

0 km 15
0 miles 10

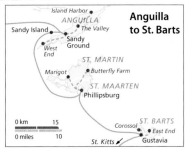

Anguilla to St. Barts

Island Harbor
ANGUILLA
The Valley
Sandy Island
Sandy Ground
West End
ST. MARTIN
Marigot
Butterfly Farm
ST. MAARTEN
Phillipsburg
ST. BARTS
Corossol
East End
St. Kitts
Gustavia

0 km 15
0 miles 10

Havana
Museo Ernest Hemingway
Las Terrazas
Cayo Levisa
Soroa
CUBA
Valle de Viñales
Pinar del Río
Península de Zapata
Boca de Guamá
Cienfuegos
Playa Girón
Trinidad

0 km 100
0 miles 50

Key

══ A week in Jamaica

∿∿ 7-Day Cruise of the Southern Caribbean

══ 7 or 14 Days Sailing the Leewards

- - Sailing the Leewards (overland route)

══ A Week in Western Cuba

A Week in Western Cuba

- Stroll the cobbled colonial plazas of **Habana Vieja**.

- Enjoy a zipline ride in Las Terrazas and explore the orchid garden at **Soroa** in the **Sierra del Rosario**.

- Marvel at the magnificent scenery of the **Valle de Viñales**.

- Immerse yourself in the bucolic countryside tilled by ox-drawn ploughs en route to **Cienfuegos**.

- Wander the quaint colonial-era streets of **Trinidad** and shop for hand-stitched lace and fine artwork.

2 Days in Havana

Cuba's capital has a vast array of memorable sights, including a variety of architecture and cobbled colonial plazas, plus the Plaza de la Revolución.

- **Arriving** José Martí International Airport is located about 15 miles (25 km) southwest of the city center. Separate terminals serve international, US, and domestic airlines. The terminals are not linked by public transport, and there are no buses or trains connecting the airport to the city. Taxis are the sole means of transport.

Havana's oldest fortress, Castillo de la Real Fuerza

Day 1
Morning A couple of days in Havana will only scrape its surface, but do devote at least one day to Habana Vieja – the city's colonial core. Start early at **Plaza de San Francisco** *(p76)* and take a peek inside the basilica. Continue to **Plaza Vieja** *(pp76–7)* to admire its eclectic architectural styles and attractions, such as the **Casa del Conde Jaruco** *(p77)* in the southeast corner. Follow the **Calle Mercaderes** *(p76)* west, stopping en route at the **Maqueta de la Habana** *(p76)*, before arriving at **Plaza de Armas** *(pp78–9)*. Visit the **Castillo de la Real Fuerza** *(p79)* and the Museo de la Ciudad, then take a break for refreshments at one of the cafés in this square.

Afternoon After visiting **Plaza de la Catedral** *(p76)*, follow Calle Empedrado west to the Cuban section of the **Museo Nacional de Bellas Artes** *(p80)*, which has a world-class collection spanning four centuries. Stroll one block to the **Museo de la Revolución** *(p80)* for an immersion in recent history; don't miss the *Granma*, the vessel that brought Fidel Castro and his Rebel Army from Mexico to launch the revolution.

Day 2
Morning Begin by admiring the grandiose buildings around **Parque Central** *(p80)*, including the Gran Teatro and the imposing **Capitolio** *(p81)*. Then ramble down the tree-shaded **Prado** *(p80)* and savor the vibrant life along the **Malecón** *(p80)*, the sinuous seafront boulevard that delivers you to the **Hotel Nacional** *(p80)*. Step inside this building to admire its lavish Moorish lobby; the garden patio is a delightful place to enjoy a snack and a mojito.

Afternoon Walk to the **Hotel Tryp Habana Libre** *(p81)*, a high-rise Modernist gem with magnificent art in its lobby. Next, take a taxi to **Cementerio Colón** *(p81)*, full of extravagant marble tombs and mausoleums. End your day at **Plaza de la Revolución** *(p81)*, Cuba's political center since the 1950s, and be sure to photograph the iconic giant image of Che Guevara. For a fantastic bird's-eye view of Havana, take the elevator to the top of the tower located behind the statue with the Museo de José Martí at its base.

> **To extend your trip…**
> Journey out of town to the **Museo Ernest Hemingway** *(p81)*, the Nobel Prize-winning author's former home in San Francisco de Paula.

2 Days in Santo Domingo

The cosmopolitan capital city of the Dominican Republic boasts a well-preserved colonial center, plus a wealth of more modern attractions.

- **Arriving** Las Américas Airport is located 12 miles (20 km) east of downtown Santo Domingo and is linked by expressway. Shuttle buses operate to downtown, and taxis are available for the 20-minute journey.

Day 1
Morning Roaming the Zona Colonial is richly rewarding. Start by visiting **Fortaleza Ozama** *(pp168–9)*, begun in 1502 and the oldest extant European building in the Americas. Next, stroll along **Calle Las Damas** *(p168)*, stopping to visit the **Panteón de la Patria** *(p168)* and the charming **Hostal Nicolás de Ovando** *(p168)*. Immerse yourself in colonial history in the **Museo de las Casas Reales** *(p168)* before settling down to lunch on **Plaza España** *(p168)*.

Afternoon Cross the square to the **Museo Alcázar de Colón** *(p168)*, former home of Christopher Columbus's son, Diego. Delight in the beauty of the amber gemstones on display at the **Museo Mundo de Ambar**

(p168), then head to **Parque Colón** *(p169)* and the **Catedral Primada de América** *(p171)*, started in 1514.

Day 2

Morning View the statue of national hero Juan Pablo Duarte in **Parque Duarte** *(p169)*, then step inside the Iglesia y Convento de los Padres Dominicos to admire the stone zodiac wheel. Walk west to the **Museo Memorial de la Resistencia Dominicana** *(p169)*, dedicated to the resistance against Rafael Trujillo's dictatorship. Passing through the old city walls, you'll arrive at **Parque Independencia** *(p170)*, where Duarte's remains are interred in the Altar de la Patria.

Afternoon Walk three blocks to the northwest to reach the Neo-Classical extravagance that is the **Palacio Nacional** *(p170)*, the presidential palace. Fans of modern art should head to the **Galería de Arte Candido Bidó** *(p170)* to delight in this late artist's colorful paintings. Next, take a taxi to **Faro a Colón** *(p170)* and be awestruck by the mammoth monument to Christopher Columbus.

> **To extend your trip…**
> Take a day excursion to **Boca Chica** *(p172)* and spend the day lazing on the beach and snorkeling in turquoise waters.

1 Day in San Juan

Old San Juan, the compact jewel of Puerto Rico's vibrant capital city, teems with castles, cobbled plazas, and intriguing museums.

- **Arriving** Luis Muñoz Marín Airport is 3 miles (5 km) southeast of downtown San Juan, to which it is linked by taxi service; at rush hour, traffic jams can make this a 45-minute journey. Isla Grande Airport is closer to Old San Juan and serves domestic airlines.

Morning The best place to start your exploration is Plaza del Inmigrante; from here, follow **Paseo de la Princesa** *(p199)* via the old Puerta de San Juan gate to **Plazuela de la Rogativa** *(p199)*. Admire the Modernist sculpture of the torch-lit procession that saved the city in 1797, then continue to the imposing **Fortaleza San Felipe del Morro** *(p199)*. After exploring the bastions and museum, retrace your steps to **Plaza del Quinto Centenario** *(p198)* to visit the **Museo de las Américas** *(p198)*, replete with exhibits of the American cultures. In **Plaza de San José** *(p198)*, enjoy the quaint **Museo de Pablo Casals** *(p198)*, dedicated to the Spanish-born cellist who lived here, before heading to one of

A gazebo in Parque Duarte, a colonial plaza in Santo Domingo

the nearby cafés for a light lunch and refreshments.

Afternoon Stroll down **Calle del Cristo** *(p198)*, stopping to sample the lovely ambience of the **El Convento** hotel *(p198)* and the Neo-Classical Catedral de San Juan Bautista. Next, turn east and follow Calle San Francisco past **Plaza de Armas** *(p198)* to roam the ancient battlements, barracks, and tunnels of **Castillo San Cristóbal** *(p200)*.

> **To extend your trip…**
> Spend a morning exploring the **Museo de Arte de Puerto Rico** *(p201)*, then laze the afternoon away on the beach in **Condado** *(p201)*.

The picturesque Paseo de la Princesa following the city walls, San Juan

A Week in Western Cuba

- **Airports** Arrive and depart Havana's José Martí International Airport.

- **Transport** Public transport is extremely limited. Foreign visitors are barred from regional buses, but the Víazul tourist bus system links Havana to Las Terrazas and Viñales, plus Cienfuegos and Trinidad. For more freedom to explore at your own pace, hire a car upon arrival in Cuba for the duration of the tour. In Havana, the HabanaBusTour runs a circuit of the entire city, providing a hop-on, hop-off service that stops at more than 40 tourist sites.

- **Booking ahead** Sierra del Rosario: Guided excursion at Las Terrazas.

Day 1: Havana
Havana (pp78–81), the vibrant capital of Cuba, has lots to offer. You could spend a week here and not exhaust its possibilities. To make the most of your time, pick a day from the city itinerary on p12.

Day 2: Sierra del Rosario
Only a 90-minute drive from Havana, the pine-scented heights of the Sierra del Rosario immerse you in nature and prove a delight for both hikers and birders. First stop is **Las Terrazas** (p82), a sustainable rural community established on the slopes around a lake. Many artists live here, including the renowned painter Lester Camper; his studio is open to visitors. Ecological activities abound, so consider a birding excursion, a horseback ride, or a hike to a colonial-era coffee estate or to cascades. Nearby **Soroa** (p82) is set in a deep vale: its steep slopes are laced with hiking trails and graced by the Orquideario, an orchid garden that is not to be missed. A 15-minute hike to the Saltón waterfall is invigorating and well worth it.

Day 3: Viñales
The emerald **Valle de Viñales** (p83) rewards visitors with the most dramatic scenery in Cuba. Framed by soaring flat-topped limestone formations called *mogotes*, the broad vale is tobacco-growing country, where oxen plough the cinnamon soils into furrows. The views are best enjoyed from the visitor center atop a *mogote* on the road to the town of Pinar del Río. Allow a full day for exploring, and do not miss the Mural de la Prehistoria, a depiction of evolution painted onto the face of a *mogote*. Also worth a look is the **Cueva del Indio** (p83), a flooded underground cave that can be explored by boat. Viñales village exudes a 19th-century colonial charm, but it erupts with energy at night, with live music at the Casa de la Cultura.

> **To extend your trip...**
> After visiting Viñales, take the ferry to **Cayo Levisa** (p83) to relax for one or two days on one of the best white-sand beaches in Cuba.

Day 4: Pinar del Río and Cienfuegos
Take the road south to **Pinar del Río** (p82) to reach the Autopista, Cuba's only freeway. The drive east to **Cienfuegos** (p85) will take about 5 hours, so break the journey in two by stopping at the **Museo Ernest Hemingway** (p81), the author's former home on the outskirts

Visitors on a boat exursion to see the Cueva del Indio

of Havana. Founded in 1819 by French settlers from New Orleans, Cienfuegos has a unique ambience. Wander around Parque Martí to savor the mood, and don't leave without dining at the Mughal-inspired **Palacio de Valle** (p85).

Days 5 and 6: Trinidad
Follow the Circuito Sur along the Caribbean coast to reach **Trinidad** (pp86–7). A UNESCO World Heritage Site, this hill town was founded in 1514 and grew wealthy from sugar and slave trading. Today Trinidad is a perfectly preserved colonial gem, and the joy lies in walking along its many cobbled streets. The main sights surround Plaza Mayor and include the **Museo Romántico** (p86), the **Iglesia Parroquial de la Santísima Trinidad** (p87), and the **Iglesia y Convento de San Francisco** (p86). The town is a center for arts and crafts, including hand-sewn lacework, so allow time for shopping. At night, head to **La Casa de la Trova** (p86) for traditional music and dance.

Day 7: Península de Zapata and Havana
Head back to Cienfuegos, then drive to Havana via the **Península de Zapata** (p84). Stop at Playa Girón to visit the **Museo Playa Girón** (p84), recalling the CIA-sponsored 1961 invasion of the Bay of Pigs; and at **Boca de Guamá** (p84) to see crocodiles.

Horse grazing near the lake at Las Terrazas

A Week in Jamaica

- **Airports** Arrive and depart Montego Bay's Sangster International Airport, 3 miles (5 km) east of town.

- **Transport** Private shuttles service downtown and Ocho Rios. You'll need to hire a car for touring the island; reserve one in advance and pick it up on arrival.

- **Booking ahead** Black River: Guided excursion with Black River Safaris; Port Antonio: Bamboo raft ride.

Cruise ship docked at Ocho Rios harbor

Day 1: Montego Bay

A day is just enough to explore **Montego Bay** *(p136)*. Start with a stroll along Gloucester Avenue, also known as the Hip Strip, which leads downtown, then spend some time around Sam Sharpe Square. Finally, relax – either at **Aquasol Beach & Theme Park** *(p136)* or on **Doctor Cave Beach** *(p136)*, which is good for snorkeling.

Day 2: Negril

Start the day with a stop at **Rocklands Bird Sanctuary** *(p136)*, where it is possible to hand-feed hummingbirds. Next, enjoy some of Jamaica's most beautiful coastal scenery as you drive to **Negril** *(p138)*. Dedicate the afternoon to lazing on the white sands and to snorkeling or even scuba diving – Negril has superb coral formations. Plan on a late night at a reggae nightclub.

Day 3: Great Morass, Black River, and Treasure Beach

Explore the wetlands of the **Great Morass and Royal Palm Reserve** *(pp138–9)*, which are accessed by boardwalks. Then drive via Savanna-la-Mar to **Black River** *(p140)* to view crocodiles on a mangrove boat trip with Black River Safaris. Further east, you'll pass through an arid zone studded with cacti before arriving at **Treasure Beach** *(pp140–41)*. This laid-back fishing village is perfect for idling and even going fishing with the locals.

Day 4: St. Elizabeth and Kingston

Head back to Black River, then turn inland for the parish of **St. Elizabeth** *(p141)*, stopping at **YS Falls** *(p141)* to splash in natural pools and cascades. Pass through **Bamboo Avenue** *(p141)*, a bamboo glade, on your way to **Mandeville** *(p141)* a charming hill town and a gateway to the southern plains that lead to the sprawling capital of **Kingston** *(p142)*.

Day 5: Blue Mountains and Port Antonio

Wander the grounds of **Devon House** *(p142)*, then head to the **Bob Marley Museum** *(p142)*, devoted to Jamaica's most famous son. Next, take the scenic route up and over the **Blue Mountains** *(pp144–5)* via Irish Town and Newcastle

Lush terrain and rolling landscape of the Blue Mountains

(the views are stupendous); be extremely cautious on the switchback road, as there are lots of narrow, sharp bends and potholes. Beyond the summit, descend to the sleepy town of **Port Antonio** *(p146)*.

Day 6: Firefly and Ocho Rios

Enjoy a lazy bamboo-raft ride on the Rio Grande before continuing your scenic drive along the north coast. Stop at Noël Coward's former home, **Firefly** *(p148)*, then drive on to the beach resort town of **Ocho Rios** *(pp148–9)*. For dinner, visit **Margaritaville** *(p149)*, a great place for food and evening entertainment.

Day 7: Montego Bay

The lush north coast is blessed with natural wonders. Clamber up **Dunn's River Falls** *(p149)*, then admire a tropical paradise at **Cranbrook Flower Forest** *(p150)*. For a sense of plantation history, continue to either **Rose Hall Great House** *(p137)* or **Greenwood** *(p137)*; both are stuffed with reminders of the slave era. Continue along the coast back to **Montego Bay** *(p136)*.

> **To extend your trip...**
> Head into **Cockpit Country** *(p151)*, about 36 miles (60 km) southeast of Montego Bay. The spectacular limestone formations of this wild region are ideal for hiking and horseback riding.

7-Day Cruise of the Southern Caribbean

- **Airports** Arrive and depart Luis Muñoz Marín Airport.
- **Transport** Cruise companies offer free shuttles from the airport to the ship; alternatively, hire a taxi.
- **Booking ahead** Cruises need reserving well in advance, especially in winter. St. Kitts: Lunch at Ottley's Plantation Inn.

Day 1: San Juan

Most cruise ships depart in the evening from the cruise dock in Old San Juan. If you arrive early, explore the city (see p13).

Day 2: At sea

Relax, taking advantage of the ship's amenities.

Day 3: Antigua

Awake to find the ship docked at **St. John's** (p312). Book one of the ship's excursions or explore the town on foot, taking in the **Anglican Cathedral** (p312) and the **Museum of Antigua and Barbuda** (p312). After lunch, hire a car or taxi to tour the island, which should take about 1 hour. Visit the main sites, such as the **English Harbour and Nelson's Dockyard** (p314), **Betty's Hope** (p313), and wind-swept **Devil's Bridge** (p313).

Day 4: St. Lucia

Arrive in **Castries** (p396), St. Lucia's capital. One of the most scenic Caribbean isles, **St. Lucia**

(pp394–409) deserves thorough exploration, so join a cruise excursion or hire a car or taxi. Head south to **Soufrière** (p397), a fishing town set in a bay beneath twin volcanic spires called **The Pitons** (p397), then continue to the southeastern tip of the island for the **Vieux Fort and East Coast** (p397). Nature lovers might like to stop at the **Mankote Mangrove Swamps** (p397) or **Latille Gardens** (p397).

Day 5: Grenada

The mountainous "Isle of Spice" is clad in rainforest. Step ashore at **St. George's** (p426) and explore the town's historic sites, then join an excursion or hire a taxi and head into the mountains to the **Grand Etang Forest Reserve** (p427), where you can spot mona monkeys.

Day 6: Barbados

Bridgetown (p440), the Bajan capital, is full of historic buildings. Spend half a day discovering it on foot, being sure to visit the Parliament Buildings. Later, hire a car or taxi and go to the Atlantic coast to watch breakers crashing ashore at **Bathsheba** (p443). Return via the **Barbados Concorde Experience** (p441) and explore the interior of the famous supersonic airplane.

Day 7: St. Kitts

Once a major sugar-producing isle, tiny **St. Kitts** (pp294–309) retains many historic sites from the era. Step back in time at **Romney Manor Plantation** (p297) and **Brimstone Hill Fortress** (pp296–7). **Ottley's**

Plantation Inn (p306) is a lovely spot to lunch before returning to the capital city of **Basseterre** (p296), with time to explore the National Museum.

Day 8: San Juan

Back in Puerto Rico, fly home or explore the city (see p13).

> **To extend your trip...**
> Hire a car and explore **Puerto Rico** (pp194–221) on day trips to the **El Yunque National Forest** (p208) and **Arecibo Observatory** (p202).

7 or 14 Days Sailing the Leewards

This 14-day itinerary explores two distinct regions of the Caribbean. A 7-day tour of the main sailing paradise – the Virgin Islands – can be combined with a further 7 days exploring the northern Leeward Islands (Sep–Dec and May–Jul, when the Anegada Passage linking the regions can be crossed safely).

- **Airports** Arrive at Cyril E. King Airport, which is served by direct flights from the USA.
- **Transport** Taxis are available at the airport.
- **Booking ahead** Yacht charters must be reserved in advance.

Day 1: St. Thomas–St. John, U.S. Virgin Islands

Enjoy a leisurely sail to **Cruz Bay** (p230), on St. John, where you can swim in crystal-clear waters and explore sites such as The Battery. Nature lovers might wish to explore the **Virgin Islands National Park** (p230), where a visitor center has exhibits on local ecology.

Day 2: St. John, U.S. Virgin Islands

Sail around the island of St. John and anchor at **Cinnamon Bay** (p231); go ashore to hike the Cinnamon Nature Trail, which leads to the ruins of a sugar

One of the huge boulders that scatter the landscape at Bathsheba, Barbados

For practical information on travelling around the Caribbean, see pp24–5 plantation. In the afternoon, head to **Coral Bay** *(p230)*, where the Emmaus Moravian Church is of historic importance. Enjoy dinner at the **Skinny Legs Bar & Grill** *(p252)*.

Day 3: Jost Van Dyke–Cane Garden Bay, Tortola, BVI

Take a quick cruise to scenic Great Harbour, on the south side of **Jost Van Dyke** *(p244)*, and have lunch at **Foxy's Bar** *(p241)*, a legendary bar-restaurant fronting calm turquoise waters beneath forested peaks. After beach-combing and snorkeling, sail on to **Cane Garden Bay** *(p244)*, on Tortola's north shore.

Day 4: Tortola–Norman Island, BVI

Rent a car for a driving tour of **Tortola** *(pp238–9)*; be sure to hike to the top of **Sage Mountain National Park** *(p238)*. In the afternoon, sail on to the popular anchorage of The Bight, off tiny Norman Island, said to be the setting for Robert Louis Stevenson's *Treasure Island*.

Day 5: RMS Rhone Marine Park–The Baths, Virgin Gorda, BVI

Norman Island is a good base for exploring **RMS Rhone Marine Park** *(p241)*, a world-famous dive site where the Royal Mail Steamer *Rhone* sank in 1867; now coral-encrusted, it lies just 20 feet (6 m) down. Continue to **The Baths** *(p240)*, where soft-contoured boulders form grottos of jade-colored waters that are perfect for snorkeling.

Day 6: Virgin Gorda, BVI

Spend the morning on **Virgin Gorda** *(pp240–41)*. Drive to the ruined copper mines at Copper-mine Point and visit **Gorda Peak National Park** *(p241)* to hike through rare Caribbean dry forest. Sail on to **North Sound** *(p245)* to spend the night.

Day 7: St Thomas or Anguilla

Leave early to end your trip with the full-day return to St. Thomas via the **Outer Islands** *(pp240–41)*. Alternatively, extend your trip (Sep–Dec and May–Jul, conditions permitting) to include

Large yachts and sailing boats at Gustavia Harbor, St. Barts

the northern Leeward Islands. Depart early to sail the 85 miles (142 km) across the Anegada Passage to the beautiful island of **Anguilla** *(pp256–65)*. Anchor in the evening at well-protected **Sandy Ground** *(p258)*.

Day 8: Anguilla

Explore this tiny, flat island by rental car. Start by driving to the **West End** *(pp258–9)*, lined with gorgeous beaches; then head east via **The Valley** *(p258)* to discover the old Wallblake House plantation home. Continue through the historic villages of the **East End** *(p259)* and the colorful fishing com-munity of **Island Harbor** *(p259)*. Next, sail to Sandy Island, a protected anchorage that is ideal for late-afternoon snorkeling.

Day 9: St. Martin/St. Maarten

Leave for **St. Martin/St. Maarten** *(pp266–79)*, a 3-hour cruise away. French in the north and Dutch in the south, this is one of the Caribbean's most diverse islands. Engage in some duty-free shopping in the Dutch port of **Philipsburg** *(p268)*, followed by an island tour that includes the charming French capital of **Marigot** *(p269)* and the **Butterfly Farm** *(p270)*.

Day 10: St. Barthélemy

Sail to sophisticated **St. Barts** *(pp332–43)*. This French island, with stunning scenery, chic restaurants, and trendy boutiques, is small enough to explore in a day by rental car.

First, explore the town of **Gustavia** *(p334)* on foot, then drive to the **East End** *(p335)* to marvel at the cape-cusped coves. Continue to **Corossol** *(p335)* for some local charm and watch villagers weave straw baskets.

Day 11: St. Kitts

Sail north to **St. Kitts** *(pp294–309)* and anchor in **Frigate Bay** *(p298)*, with its lively bars and restaurants. In the afternoon, tour this scenic island by rental car, taxi, or minibus. Stop to explore **Basseterre** *(p296)*, a pretty town replete with Victorian buildings; **Brimstone Hill Fortress** *(pp296–7)*, a massive complex with superb views; and **Ottley's Plantation Inn** *(p306)*, the perfect spot for dinner. Alternatively, explore the **Southeastern Peninsula** *(pp298–9)* and go snorkeling at **Major's Bay** *(p299)*.

Day 12: St. Eustatius

Head to the volcanic isle of **St. Eustatius** *(pp280–93)*, also known as "Statia," and anchor off **Oranjestad** *(p286)*, the capital city that seems to be caught in an 18th-century timewarp. Don't miss the **St. Eustatius Historical Foundation Museum** *(p286)*, which offers guided walking tours of the town. Take a hike to the summit of Mount Mazinga, an extinct volcano also known as **The Quill** *(p289)*. The crater is clad in rainforest protected as The Quill National Park. End your day with dinner at **The Old Gin House** *(p292)*.

Day 13: St. Croix

Your journey 121 miles (195 km) northwest to **St. Croix** *(pp232–3)* will take all day, so start around dawn to arrive by early evening. Anchor off Christiansted and perhaps dine at **The Buccaneer Hotel** *(p232)*, set in a former sugar mill.

Day 14: St. Croix–St. Thomas

Spend the morning roaming **Christiansted** *(p232)*, with its well-preserved 18th-century buildings. After an early lunch, set off for St. Thomas to end your sailing adventure.

Putting the Caribbean on the Map

Sweeping in a great arc some 2,000 miles (3,218 km) long, from the western tip of Cuba to the Leewards in the east, then south to the top of South America, and westward along Venezuela's north coast, the chain of island nations comprising the Caribbean wrap around the Caribbean Sea like a shepherd's crook. The Greater Antilles to the northwest include the larger islands: Cuba, Jamaica, Hispaniola, and Puerto Rico. To their east, the smaller islands of the Lesser Antilles form a barrier against the Atlantic Ocean. Together they encompass a dazzling diversity, from semiarid deserts to fern-choked rainforests; limestone plateaus to soaring volcanos; and coral reefs to mountains.

Key

= Highway

= Major road

- - = International border

For map symbols see back flap

Climate of the Caribbean

All the Caribbean islands lie within the tropics and the climate is like an endless summer, although the weather patterns vary from isle to isle. Temperatures are fairly constant year-round, but seasonal temperatures in the Greater Antilles vary more than in the Lesser Antilles. The trade winds blow throughout the year and keep temperatures within tolerable levels, especially on east-facing shores. Variations in altitude affect the climates of the islands: temperatures decline with increasing elevation, and higher mountains form rain shadows on their leeward sides, eastern shores thus receiving more rain than the western sides. Rainfall varies from about 10 inches (25 cm) per year on Bonaire to 350 inches (900 cm) in parts of Dominica.

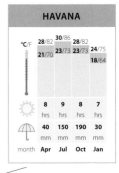

HAVANA			
°C/F			
28/82	30/86	28/82	
21/70	23/73	23/73	24/75
			18/64
8 hrs	9 hrs	8 hrs	7 hrs
40 mm	150 mm	190 mm	30 mm
month Apr	Jul	Oct	Jan

Turks and Caicos has an average of 350 days of sunshine a year.

Cuba's summers can be torrid, especially in the eastern provinces.

Jamaica can be cold atop the highest peaks of the Blue Mountains.

Hurricanes

The Caribbean islands are located within a hurricane belt. These tropical storms, which evolve over warm ocean water and revolve around a low-pressure center, are characterized by very high winds and rainfall and can cause huge devastation. The hurricane season lasts from June to November, with a peak in September, but this does not at all mean that all islands are affected every year. The southernmost islands rarely get hit by forceful hurricanes.

KINGSTON			
°C/F	33/91	32/90	
31/88			30/86
24/75	24/75	23/73	21/70
09 hrs	09 hrs	07 hrs	08 hrs
64 mm	74 mm	188 mm	69 mm
month Apr	Jul	Oct	Jan

0 kilometers 200
0 miles 200

Cienfuegos in Cuba struck by a powerful hurricane

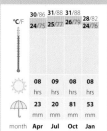
Large boulders in the arid landscape of Aruba

SANTO DOMINGO

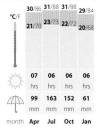

°C/F				
	30/86	**31**/88	**31**/88	**29**/84
	21/70	**23**/73	**22**/72	**20**/68
☀	**07** hrs	**06** hrs	**06** hrs	**06** hrs
☂	**99** mm	**163** mm	**152** mm	**61** mm
month	**Apr**	**Jul**	**Oct**	**Jan**

Puerto Rico's wettest part is El Yunque, with an average of over 200 inches (508 cm) of rain annually.

ROSEAU

°C/F				
	29/84	**31**/88	**32**/90	**32**/90
	20/68	**20**/68	**22**/72	**22**/72
☀	**08** hrs	**08** hrs	**07** hrs	**08** hrs
☂	**61** mm	**274** mm	**198** mm	**132** mm
month	**Apr**	**Jul**	**Oct**	**Jan**

The Dominican Republic has several distinct climates and a pronounced rainy season in the summer months.

ST. THOMAS

°C/F				
	30/87	**32**/89	**32**/89	**29**/85
	23/74	**26**/78	**24**/76	**22**/72
☀	**07** hrs	**08** hrs	**08** hrs	**09** hrs
☂	**70** mm	**62** mm	**136** mm	**47** mm
month	**Apr**	**Jul**	**Oct**	**Jan**

Average monthly maximum temperature

Average monthly minimum temperature

Average daily hours of sunshine

Average monthly rainfall

WILLEMSTAD

°C/F				
	30/86	**31**/88	**31**/88	**28**/82
	24/75	**25**/77	**26**/79	**24**/76
☀	**08** hrs	**09** hrs	**08** hrs	**08** hrs
☂	**23** mm	**20** mm	**81** mm	**53** mm
month	**Apr**	**Jul**	**Oct**	**Jan**

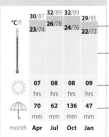

Aruba is arid but the temperature stays moderate thanks to a constant ocean breeze.

PRACTICAL INFORMATION

Virtually every Caribbean isle relies on tourism and provides visitors with a broad range of amenities up to international par. However, in more remote areas tourist facilities may be limited. It is relatively easy to island hop, although advance planning is essential. Most islands have their own tourist offices, which can assist in itinerary planning and give information on hotels, restaurants, attractions, and other activities. There are plenty of travel and tour agencies in the islands, and an effective approach is to book local excursions using their offices, usually based in the major hotels.

When to Go

Any time of year is good for visiting the Caribbean. However, June through November is hurricane season, and July and August are torrid months that can make touring away from the beach quite tiring. December to April is the best period to visit, when the climate is warm without being unbearable, and there are cultural events on most isles.

Getting There

The best way to get to the Caribbean is by air, although cruises can be a leisurely way to explore the area. Prices soar during the peak season from December to April. The ferry is also an option between some islands. Refer to the respective islands for more details.

Documentation

Entry requirements vary widely among the island nations, so always check before you travel. For most countries, visitors need to have a valid passport and a return ticket, as well as a tourist visa (typically good for 30- to 90-day stays), usually issued by the travel agency. Trinidad and a few other islands require that visas be issued in advance. Canadian citizens can enter the Turks and Caicos without a passport, although valid ID together with a birth certificate is mandatory. Special restrictions apply to US citizens wishing to visit Cuba. Most islands require those who visit for business or as a journalist to apply for a special visa in advance. All US citizens returning to the United States by air are required to present a valid passport for re-entry, and since 1 June 2009 those re-entering the country by land or sea must have a passport book (full passport), passport card (credit-card-sized mini passport), or a Global Entry Trusted Traveler Program card, issued to pre-vetted frequent border crossers. The only exception to these new Western Hemisphere Travel Initiative requirements is travelers on closed-loop cruises, who do not require a passport. For further details of WHTI-compliant documents, contact the **US Customs and Border Protection Agency**, the **US Department of Homeland Security** or the **US Department of State**.

Customs and Duty-Free

Besides personal belongings, tourists are allowed to carry up to 2 liters (67 fl.oz) of alcohol and two cigarette cartons to most Caribbean isles. Certain drugs require a prescription. Local and Caribbean customs are on guard for drug trafficking.

US Customs allows $800 worth of goods duty-free, including 1 liter (33 fl.oz) of alcohol, 200 cigarettes, and 100 non-Cuban cigars, plus an unlimited amount of original art. Visitors who travel to the US Virgin Islands plus another Caribbean island may bring back $1,600 worth of goods duty-free. No Customs declaration is required when traveling between Puerto Rico and the US. The UK permits £390 worth of goods, plus 200 cigarettes or 50 cigars, plus 2 liters (72 fl.oz) of wine, and 1 liter (36 fl.oz) of spirits.

Avoid buying items made from endangered species such as tortoise shell, black coral, or reptile skin. These are covered under the Convention on International Trade in Endangered Species (CITES) and anyone in possession can be fined.

Visitor Information

The **Caribbean Tourism Organization** represents the entire region and has headquarters in London and New York. All the island nations have official tourism promotion boards that provide maps, literature, and other information. Most have offices in the UK and North America, as well as local offices on the respective islands.

Health and Security

The islands vary greatly in terms of safety and medical facilities. Private clinics are preferable to public hospitals. Malaria is prevalent on many islands, and the region has experienced an epidemic of dengue fever in recent years; check for recommended inoculations before traveling.

Visitors need to guard against pickpockets and mugging in most large Caribbean cities. Traffic is one of the biggest dangers as locals often drive without due regard for the law. Riptides (dangerous undertows) claim many lives among inattentive swimmers. On beaches, avoid seeking shade under coconut palms, as falling fruit is a real hazard. Women should avoid lonely beaches. Due to security concerns, Haiti has not been covered in this guide.

Banking and Currency

A wide variety of currencies are in use throughout the Caribbean. Many English-speaking islands use the East Caribbean dollar; the French-speaking isles use the euro; and Aruba uses the Aruban florin. The US dollar is accepted almost everywhere and many businesses also accept euros. Banks are ubiquitous, although ATMs often run out of cash. Most hotels are also happy to change foreign currency.

Communications

Hotels usually charge high fees for phone calls. It is wise to buy a phone card for use with public phones. Every island has them and the cards can be bought in stores and gas stations. If you plan to use your cellphone, check that your carrier network is compatible with the island(s) you wish to visit. Internet is available throughout the Caribbean (though it is expensive in Cuba) and there is no shortage of Internet cafés. Many hotels have Wi-Fi access, either complimentary or available for a fee.

Transport

Getting around can be a challenge, depending on the island. Bus service on most small islands is by crowded minivans. Tourist taxis offer efficient, albeit pricey service from major hotels in big cities; elsewhere locals prefer cheaper shared taxis. For details on car rentals, refer to the Practical Information pages for each island.

Shopping

The Caribbean is a cornucopia of crafts and every island has its own distinct style. Cuba, especially, has some of the most profound art, while the Dominican Republic is a great place to pick up Haitian art. Beautiful wood carvings are a specialty on every isle, as are jewelry, straw hats, and baskets, sold at beach stalls and markets and where haggling over the price is half the fun. Cigars and rum, hammocks, and *guayaberas* (on Spanish-speaking isles) are other local treasures. Cruise ports specialize in duty-free items such as perfumes and watches. It is advisable not to buy items made from animals, or coral and seashells.

Languages

Cuba, Puerto Rico, and the Dominican Republic speak Spanish; English is spoken on Britain's former colonies; while French and Dutch are the *lingua franca* of the islands with ties to those nations. Virtually every island also has its own local patois, vernacular Creole languages, that creatively merge a form of the colonial "mother tongue" with words adopted from African languages.

Electricity

Most islands of the Greater Antilles operate on 110 volts, as in the US, but even here many outlets use 220 volts. In the Lesser Antilles, 220 volts is common, as in Europe, and North American travelers may need adaptors for their appliances. Power outages are common throughout the region; take a flashlight.

Time

The Caribbean islands span two time zones. The Dominican Republic and islands to the east are in the Atlantic Standard Time Zone, 4 hours behind Greenwich Mean Time. Islands to the west are on Eastern Standard Time, 5 hours behind GMT. Some islands use Daylight Saving Time, with beginning and ending times varying for each nation.

Etiquette

Most islands are conservative and nudism and topless bathing are not permitted. However, the French islands are renowned for being more liberal and even other conservative islands have all-inclusive naturalist resorts. Bathing suits should not be worn away from the beach.

The Spanish-speaking islands especially retain macho traditions and, except in Cuba, the taboo against homosexuality remains ingrained in most island cultures. Caribbean men feel virtually obliged to pay compliments to women passing by, although it is not always expressed in good taste. No reaction is seriously expected, and women would be wise to totally disregard such comments. The best way to put an end to unwanted flirtation is to say that you are married.

Barring business meetings, fine-dining restaurants and nightclubs, a jacket or formal evening dress is not needed. Many resort restaurants demand proper shoes (no toes showing and no trainers), especially for men.

Recommended Hotels and Restaurants

In the hotel and restaurant listings for each island, look out for venues labeled as DK Choice. These have been highlighted in recognition of an exceptional feature – a stunning location, breathtaking views, inviting atmosphere and service, excellent amenities, or a combination of these.

DIRECTORY

Visitor Information

Caribbean Tourism Organization
80 Broad Street, Suite 3302, New York, NY 10004. **Tel** 212 635 9530. 22 The Quadrant, Richmond, London TW9 1BP. **Tel** 020 8948 0057. W caribbeantravel.com

Documentation

US Customs and Border Protection Agency
W cbp.gov

US Department of Homeland Security
W dhs.gov

US Department of State
travel.state.gov
W getyouhome.gov

TRAVEL INFORMATION

The Caribbean covers a huge region and trying to explore the many diverse islands in one go is a challenge. Most islands have airports served by direct or non-stop international flights while many smaller islands are served by smaller planes from regional hubs. There are many luxurious Caribbean cruises which stop at several islands. Apart from cruises, traveling between many of the islands by sea is difficult, as only a few are linked by ferry. Bus services vary. Modern air-conditioned buses link major tourist destinations on larger islands, but most islanders rely on crowded minibuses. Driving offers the most flexibility in terms of speed and accessibility, but it can be hair-raising with bad road conditions.

Runway at the small airport of St. Barthélemy

Arriving by Air

Taking a plane to the Caribbean islands is the best way to get here. International long-haul flights from North America and Europe serve most of the islands, although visitors may need to connect in major regional hubs such as San Juan or St. Thomas. The major North American carriers with Caribbean service include **Air Canada**, **American Airlines**, **Delta**, **JetBlue**, **Spirit Airlines**, **United Airlines**, and **US Airways**. Three Caribbean airlines **Air Jamaica**, **Caribbean Airlines**, and **LIAT** also have international service to the region, while **Cubana** serves Cuba from Canada and Europe. From Europe, some international airlines fly via the US, although Air France, **British Airways**, Iberia, **KLM**, and **Virgin Atlantic** operate direct flights, as do LIAT and Air Jamaica. Many charter airlines also fly to the Caribbean.

Small passenger planes are a staple form of getting around within the islands. American Eagle links major airports within Puerto Rico, and Cubana and **AeroDomca** provide domestic service within Cuba and the Dominican Republic, respectively. Dozens of charter companies offer scheduled flights aboard 4- to 16-passenger aircraft linking key tourist destinations within individual islands or island groups.

Visitors can also island-hop between the small isles of the Lesser Antilles by one of several small Caribbean carriers. For more details, refer to specific islands.

Airports

There are some 30 major Caribbean airports that receive international flights, plus dozens of other airports and airstrips for domestic flights. Most Caribbean airports are small and the aircrafts are not connected directly to a terminal. Hence, visitors will have to walk on the tarmac from the plane to the terminal.

Cruises

The Caribbean is a top year-round destination for cruise ships. More than 20 cruise lines offer a vast range of ships and itineraries. The ships sail at night and berth at their next port of call before dawn, permitting visitors to explore ashore by day. Cruise companies sell a wide range of group-oriented shore excursions, but it is often cheaper and more fun to make your own arrangements ashore. Special theme cruises are a popular option. More details are available from **Cruise Lines International Association**.

A huge cruise liner moored at Pointe-à-Pitre, Guadeloupe

Passengers getting off a ferry boat in Puerto Rico

Ferries and Sailboats

Ferries link Puerto Rico to both the Dominican Republic and the US Virgin Islands, which are connected by ferry to the British Virgin Islands. Trinidad and Tobago are also connected by ferry. Sailboat charters are a popular way of exploring the islands. Yachts can be chartered with or without crews on virtually every island, although it is wise to book your sailing vacation in advance from a reputable company such as the **Caribbean Yacht Rental** or **Ed Hamilton**.

Driving

Traveling by car is the most practical and flexible way of exploring all but the smallest isles. Car rentals are widely available, and major international rental companies have franchises on most islands. Driving in the Caribbean can be challenging. Hazards include poorly paved and pot-holed roads, stray animals on the road, and local drivers who have no concern for the safety of other road users. It is advisable not to drive at night. Cars drive on the left side of the road on most Caribbean islands except Bonaire, St. Eustatius, Aruba, the Dominican Republic, Guadeloupe, Curaçao, Cuba, Martinique, Puerto Rico, St. Martin/Sint Maarten, and Saba.

Package Deals and Organized Tours

Air fares can vary greatly from season to season, between airlines and ticket whole-salers, and according to time of year. The further in advance you buy your ticket, the cheaper it usually is. Air-hotel packages are available for every island. These inclusive vacations tend to be cheaper than independent travel. Most major airlines offer inclusive packages, as do many companies in Europe and North America.

If you are interested in a beach vacation, there are special tours that may appeal to visitors. Most islands offer a variety of watersports and there are several package deals. Popular themed vacations include birding, hiking, cycling, scuba diving, and sportfishing. For more details, refer to specific islands.

Driving through the rainforest, Puerto Rico

DIRECTORY

Arriving by Air

AeroDomca
W aerodomca.com

Air Canada
W aircanada.com

Air Jamaica
W airjamaica.com

American Airlines
W aa.com

British Airways
W britishairways.com

Caribbean Airlines
W caribbean-airlines.com

Cubana
W cubana.cu

Delta
W delta.com

Jet Blue
W jetblue.com

KLM
W klm.com

LIAT
W liat.com

Spirit Airlines
W spirit.com

United Airlines
W united.com

US Airways
W usairways.com

Virgin Atlantic
W virgin-atlantic.com

Cruises

Cruise Lines International Association
910 SE 17th Street., Suite 400 Fort Lauderdale, FL 33316. **Tel** 754 224 2200. W cruising.org

The Cruise Line
Cruise Line House, 109–111 High Street, Hurstpierpoint, West Sussex, UK. **Tel** 0800 008 6677. W cruiseline.co.uk

Ferries and Sailboats

Caribbean Yacht Rental
Tel 888 622 1195.
W caribbeanyachtsrental.com

Ed Hamilton
Tel 800 621 7855.
W ed-hamilton.com

THE CARIBBEAN AT A GLANCE

Best Beaches

The Caribbean's greatest appeal is the unequaled beauty of its beaches. While it is almost impossible to make a mistake when choosing a sun-and-sand destination, there are distinct differences among the islands and their beaches. The Atlantic Ocean batters the eastern shores of most of the 7,000 islands and cays between North and South America, making their windward coasts rugged with huge breaking waves and a surfer's dream. The leeward coasts are washed by the gentle Caribbean Sea and are favored by swimmers, snorkelers, and divers. The sand too varies from soft and white to black and coarse.

Punta Cana
Is part of the 21-mile (34-km) Coconut Coast on the eastern end of the Dominican Republic. Hundreds of swaying palms tower over fine white sand and dozens of all-inclusive resorts provide all comforts and offer a variety of activities.

Grace Bay *(see p120)* on Turks and Caicos has 12 miles (19 km) of uninterrupted beach scattered with upscale resorts.

TURKS
AND CAICOS

CUBA

Playa Ancón

CAYMAN
ISLANDS

DOMINICAN
REPUBLIC

JAMAICA

Seven Mile Beach in Negril, Jamaica, has been one of the Caribbean's most popular stretches of sand since the 1960s, when hippies discovered it. Though overdeveloped, it is innately beautiful.

Caribbean   Sea

ARUBA, CURA
AND BONAI

Seven Mile Beach in Grand Cayman is a well-groomed beach on the island's west coast. Although lined with busy shops, restaurants, and resorts, this stretch of sand gives an impression of spaciousness and unspoiled nature.

Best of the Rest

Good beaches line both sides of virtually every island but top ratings go to beaches with the best water conditions, sand quality, availability of shade, facilities, and ease of access.

Playa Ancón *(see p88)*, Cuba, is a lovely white strip of sand on the secluded stretch of Caribbean Sea facing Ancón peninsula.

Great Bay Beach in Sint Maarten is a white sand beach along the bay, with Philipsburg's main shopping street running parallel to it.

◀ Aerial view of Isla Palominas, Puerto Rico

Luquillo *(see p208)* in Puerto Rico offers light golden sand, calm waters, and ample amenities making it a popular beach for families. As a certified Blue Flag Beach, the area adheres to strict environmental standards, guarantees good water quality, and provides facilities for disabled travelers.

Honeymoon Beach, St. John, USVI, is among Caneel Bay's seven spectacular beaches. Its powdery soft sands can only be reached by foot or boat.

Pink Beach in Barbuda is an 8-mile (13-km) strip of pink-hued sand along an isolated stretch of the island's coast.

The Baths *(see p240)*, Virgin Gorda, has some bizarre-shaped natural features, with giant boulders scattered along the water's edge, creating tranquil pools and striking grottos.

ST. MARTIN/
SINT MAARTEN

ANGUILLA

ERTO
ICO

VIRGIN
ISLANDS

SABA AND
ST. EUSTATIUS

ST. KITTS AND NEVIS

ANTIGUA AND
BARBUDA

GUADELOUPE

DOMINICA

MARTINIQUE

ST. LUCIA

BARBADOS

ST. VINCENT AND
THE GRENADINES

Grand Anse Beach

GRENADA

Man O'War
Bay

TRINIDAD
AND TOBAGO

Pigeon
Point

0 kilometers   300

0 miles   300

Shoal Bay in Antigua has visitors lounging on its shaded shimmery-white sand and snorkeling in the calm waters.

Anse Chastanet on St. Lucia is one of the world's most popular beaches, especially among divers, for its excellent diving sites.

The beaches of Tobago offer a near Robinson Crusoe-type holiday. Pigeon Point is a long coral beach. Man O'War Bay is known for its beautiful natural harbor and long stretch of sand.

Grand Anse in Grenada stretches over 2 miles (3 km) in length. Its powdery white sands extend far offshore making it broad as well. Most of the island's best hotels are within walking distance of this beach strip.

Beachlife

Each island enjoys a unique heritage, yet all Caribbean residents share a common modern-day culture based on year-round sunshine and close proximity to the sea. Daily life revolves around the beach, which becomes livelier at night and during special events, and visitors pick up this tropical rhythm with ease. By law, most beaches are public up to the high-water mark, and beachfront property owners allow access. Lifeguards keep watch at popular spots, but in other areas, swimmers are responsible for their personal safety. Police often patrol and signs warn of strong water currents.

Catamaran, Saline Bay, St. Vincent and the Grenadines

Horse-riding along the beach and into the nearby countryside is a popular and relaxing way to tour the coasts of many islands. Riders of all skill levels can participate in beach rides and most include a cooling canter into the surf. Several tour operators also offer romantic sunset rides along the shore.

Beach volleyball is one of the most popular sports in the islands. The annual Caribbean Beach Volleyball Championships are held each fall on different islands, drawing players and fans from around the world.

Sport Activities

Volleyball, scuba diving, surfing, yachting, and other watersports dominate the tourist activities during the day. Calm water on leeward beaches is ideal for swimming and snorkeling, while the windward coasts are best for surfing. Scuba divers favor islands with offshore reefs.

Parasailing is a fun activity available on many beaches. Participants sit in a sling seat attached to a specially-designed parachute, which is hoisted skyward by a boat. Paragliding is also popular on islands with mountains and steady trade winds, such as the Dominican Republic.

Naturist resorts exist on some islands but in general nudity is outlawed on most public beaches and topless sunbathing is not common. Wearing wet or uncovered swimsuits in restaurants and shops is unacceptable, even near the beach.

Children's packages at all-inclusive resorts usually include building sand castles, treasure hunts on the beach, or going for nature walks.

Leisure Activities

The highlight of a vacation is an early morning leisurely stroll along the beach with long afternoons spent in the shade napping, reading, and picnicking on soft white sand or exploring rocky coastlines. Beachfront resorts supply towels, umbrellas, and lounge chairs for guests while waterside huts have rentals for day visitors.

The Caribbean Sea is known for its turquoise color and crystal-clear visibility.

Typical thatched umbrellas, found on most beaches, provide welcome shade from the tropical sun.

Shopping on the beach is a fine way to spend the day. Vendors set up shop on the busiest beaches to sell sarongs, towels, and souvenirs, as well as swimsuits. Whether locally produced or imported, these will all bring back a flavor of the Caribbean.

Beach food, beach bars, and snack shacks specialize in rum-based drinks, ice-cold beer, and seafood sandwiches. On many islands, roti is a popular light meal made of fish, shrimp, chicken or mutton wrapped in flat bread, thinner than naan or pita.

Beach parties take place on most weekends. Except for small private gatherings, visitors are almost always welcome to join the fun. Full-moon parties are often hosted at beachfront bars, especially during festive events.

Popular Diving and Snorkeling Spots

With long stretches of spectacular coral reefs and scores of diverse sites, the Caribbean offers superlative diving and snorkeling. The remarkable marine habitats are a trove of underwater treasures where crystal-clear waters allow visitors to experience profuse marine life viewing combined with the thrill of exploring mysterious Spanish galleons and the wrecks of World War II vessels. Visitors can also island-hop to mix and match a range of incredibly varied and exciting activities, from mingling with stingrays off Grand Cayman to exploring underwater volcanic craters off Dominica.

An outlet renting diving and snorkeling equipment, Curaçao

Wreck Diving

Sunken ships hold a special allure for divers as they attract a wealth of marine life. Often, cannons and other artifacts can still be seen, while World War II warships are fascinating to explore. Wrecks are scattered all along the Caribbean island chain.

Superior Producer, an overloaded freighter that sank in 1977, rests at a depth of 107 ft (32 m), off Curaçao's southwest coast. Divers can also view this artificial reef at night, lit by the glow of cup corals and tiny hunters.

Hilma Hooker wreck, lying 98 ft (30 m) below the waters off Bonaire, was seized in 1984 with marijuana on board. It sank after lying unclaimed for months and now hosts plenty of marine life such as sea anemones.

Snorkeling

Snorkeling is a great way to experience the underwater world without leaving the water surface and all that is needed is a face mask, breathing tube, and flippers for propulsion. It is perfect for exploring coral reefs that lie close to the surface. Unlike scuba diving, snorkeling requires no training. Several islands have good snorkeling sites, including Antigua, Bonaire, the Grenadines, and the Virgin Islands.

Stingray City *(see p106)*, located in the waters off the northwest corner of Grand Cayman, is shallow enough for snorkelers to enjoy feeding and swimming with stingrays.

The Baths *(see p240)*, in the British Virgin Islands, is a great place for snorkelers to glimpse exotic marine life in pools and grottoes amid enormous boulders. It is important to exercise caution during a north swell, which can be tumultuous.

For more details on specific diving and snorkeling spots, refer to the Outdoor Activities pages for each island

Best Sites

① Jardines del Rey, Cuba
② Stingray City, Cayman Islands
③ Bloody Bay Marine Park, Cayman Islands
④ HMS *Endymion*, Turks and Caicos
⑤ The Baths, Virgin Islands
⑥ Buck Island Reef National Monument, Virgin Islands
⑦ *M.V. Talata* wreck, St. Kitts
⑧ Soufrière Marine Reserve, Dominica
⑨ *Hilma Hooker* wreck, Bonaire
⑩ *Superior Producer* wreck, Curaçao

Scuba and Snuba

Scuba diving lets divers explore far below the surface, but requires special training and the use of specialized gear, including canisters of compressed air for breathing. Snuba (SNorkel + scUBA) tethers the canisters to floating rafts, connecting swimmers by air lines without heavy restrictive gear.

Dominica has a number of dive sites along its west coast. With an abundance of marine creatures, the Scott's Head and Soufrière Bay areas are popular diving sites.

Bloody Bay Marine Park *(see p111)* in the Cayman Islands combines dozens of dive sites ranging from those at a mere 6 ft (2 m) depth to others along a wall that plummets to more than 1,640 ft (500 m).

Snuba Diving is the best way to explore Aruba's coral-laden wrecks. At Antilla divers can encounter exquisite marine life around a partially submerged German World War II freighter and a Lockheed Lodestar plane teeming with sea fans and sponges.

Divers preparing to go into the water

Who can Dive?

A PADI (Professional Association of Diving Instructors) or NAUI (National Association of Underwater Instructors) certificate is required for most dives. Dive operators offer both one- and two-tank dives and certification courses. Experienced divers can take night dives, plus advanced courses that include rescue diving. Novices can take "resort courses" – introductory lessons usually followed by a dive. Many all-inclusive resorts have their own dive shops.

Top Sailing Islands

Antigua, the Grenadines, the British Virgin Islands (and the USVI) top the list of islands with the best conditions for sailing and numerous beautiful islets to visit. The Virgin Islands are blessed with dramatic scenery and are also more developed, while the Grenadines have the quiet charm of an earlier era. Antigua is a base for both small and large-crewed yachts, while St. Martin/Sint Maarten and Guadeloupe are also popular sailing destinations.

Sightseeing catamaran at Heritage Quay, St. John's, Antigua

Antigua

Antigua has a centuries-long sailing history, ever since it was the center of British maritime power in the region during the colonial era. The annual Antigua Sailing Week is one of the world's top five regattas and is the highlight of the Caribbean yachting calendar. Five days of tough international competitions attract sailors from all over the world as well as boats of every type.

Sailing events involve fun both on the water and on land. During regattas, the islands have a buzzing nightlife featuring live music, games, drinks, and food. It is a great chance to mix with locals.

Sailing Regattas

Carriacou Regatta Festival, an important summer sailing event

Grenadines: Carriacou Regatta Festival (Jul/Aug) Boats from all over take part in the biggest sailing festival of the Southern Caribbean, which began as a local boat race.

Antigua: Sailing Week (Apr/May) A top sailing event with local and international participation.

Grenadines: Bequia Easter Regatta (Mar/Apr) First run in 1967, it includes races for all classes of boats.

Sint Maarten: Heineken Regatta (Mar) This sailing event strives for a "Clean Regatta".

Historic Redcliffe Quay in St. John's, Antigua, was once home to warehouses storing supplies for the British navy and local merchant ships.

For more on sailing see pp244–5, p319, p419, and p493

The Tobago Cays, a collection of tiny isles surrounded by stunning coral reefs, is a popular destination for day sailing trips from the other Grenadine islands.

The Grenadines

The sailing here is preferred by sailors who find the British Virgin Islands a little overdeveloped. The isles are known for their superb sailing conditions with constant trade winds, island-hopping opportunities, and many regattas.

Sailors often drop anchor in one of the natural anchorages provided to protect the coral reefs surrounding the isles. They use their own dinghies or take watertaxis to come ashore to explore the islands.

The Virgin Islands

The British and the US Virgin Islands, separated by the Sir Francis Drake Channel, have the most developed marina facilities. Owing to the layout of the islands, the anchorages are closer and the isles offer sheltered sailing as well as great island-hopping opportunities.

Monohull yachts are perfect for cruising and are typically used when sailing long distances. A variety of well-maintained yachts, including catamarans, motor yachts, crewed yachts, and bareboats are available for hire.

Bars and Restaurants at most anchorages offer a place for sailors to relax with cool refreshing drinks and barbecued dishes. Popular hangouts in the British Virgin Islands include Foxy's bar at Jost Van Dyke, Rhymer's Restaurant at Cane Garden Bay on Tortola, and the Bath and Turtle on Virgin Gorda.

Tortola, the largest of the British Virgin Islands, is considered a major sailing hub in the Caribbean. Yachts for day trips to the offshore cays of Anegada, and the Baths at Virgin Gorda, depart from the island's several marinas.

Popular Watersports

The Caribbean is a paradise for vacationers who enjoy watersports ranging from exhilarating Jet Ski rides over the waves to tranquil kayaking trips into coastal lagoons. Many individual islands are renowned for certain specific sports, such as Barbados for surfing and the Dominican Republic for kiteboarding. Every all-inclusive hotel offers non-motorized equipment, usually with instructions, while commercial vendors have outlets for motorized watersports on most beaches.

Water boats for hire lined up on Palm Beach, Aruba

Riding the Waters

Active vacationers are spoilt for choice when it comes to watersports, with specific activities varying according to local weather conditions and facilities. Although surfing is restricted to certain areas where high waves roll ashore, easier lessons for beginners are also available. Placid aqua-bikes and thrilling banana-boat rides are great family activities, while kayaking is a good way to get close to wildlife.

Surfing is a popular sport, and many islands offer world-class surfing. Rincón, on the west coast of Puerto Rico, is the setting for many world championship competitions.

Banana boats, inflatable pontoons towed at high speed, offer a bumpy ride and are lots of fun, though passengers can expect the "banana" to tip over.

Aqua-bikes are available at many popular beach resorts. These tricycles are kept afloat by huge tires, and steered by a pair of riders who constantly work the pedals.

Jet Skis, powerful scooters that skim across the water at high speed, are a potential risk to nearby swimmers and many resorts have banned or confined them to special areas.

Kayaking through mangroves and lagoons is a great way to explore the indigenous flora and fauna of the Caribbean islands.

For more details on watersports, refer to the Outdoor Activities pages for each island

Sportfishing

The Caribbean and Atlantic waters teem with game fish such as sailfish, marlin, tuna, wahoo, and barracuda. Almost every island offers excellent sportfishing opportunities.

Bottom fishing for snapper, grouper, and jack is a popular sport. Visitors can try fly-fishing for bonefish in the inshore shallows.

Charters, catering to sportfishers, are available for half- and one-day trips. Most islands offer deep-sea fishing, with the types of fish varying according to season.

Wind Powered

The year-round trade winds, usually on the windward side of the Caribbean islands, create ideal wind and wave conditions for kiteboarding, sailing, and windsurfing, drawing a number of experts. With a bit of tuition, amateurs can also easily enjoy these sports.

Windsurfing is a favorite activity at almost every beach resort and many hotels include this sport in their charges.

Hobie Cats are relatively small and easy-to-maneuver sailcrafts preferred by most resort-goers with limited sailing experience.

Paragliding involves flying either solo or in tandem, tethered by harness to a parachute towed by a speedboat. It offers a bird's-eye view of the coastline.

Riptides

Dangerous undertows or riptides claim many lives each year. They can occur on beaches where incoming waves bring ashore more water than the backwash can drain. The excess water pours back to sea via narrow, fast-moving channels that can pull unwary swimmers out to sea. Riptide locations change unpredictably. If caught, it is vital to swim parallel to the shore.

Crashing waves at Bathsheba, Barbados

Kiteboarding is essentially a form of surfing where the rider's feet are strapped to a mini surfboard, while a waist harness is attached to a giant kite. Sweeping above the waves, aficionados perform exhilarating aerial acrobatics.

Hiking in the Caribbean

Geology differs throughout the Caribbean chain, with the terrain varying from flat and barren to mountainous and forested, depending on whether the island is a coral formation or the result of a volcanic eruption. Hikers are treated to spectacular vistas with a vast range of foliage, wildlife, and archaeological sites. There are numerous nature reserves and national parks with well-maintained trails. Tour operators on the islands arrange guided hikes for visitors at all levels of fitness, though experienced hikers may prefer self-guided excursions.

Waterfall at Asa Wright Nature Centre, Trinidad

Hiking Options

Most islands have trails with a gradual incline that are suitable for hikes of 2 hours or less. Nearly all trails passing through national parks are paved, beginning at a visitors' center, and meander among labeled native plants or historic sites. However, experienced hikers can enjoy the more challenging treks such as the one leading to Guadeloupe's La Soufrière summit.

Pico Duarte, Dominican Republic, is the highest mountain in the Caribbean *(see p177).* Experienced climbers can cover the distance to the top in about a 3-day round-trip, accompanied by mules that carry their gear.

Best Hiking Trails

Easy Trails

1 Arikok National Park, Aruba, 21 miles (33.8 km) of marked trails
2 Barre de l'Isle Forest Reserve, St. Lucia, 1 mile (1.6 km)
3 The Baths, Virgin Gorda, BVI, 0.5 mile (0.8 km)
4 Lake Trail, Grand Etang National Park, Grenada, 2.5 miles (4 km)
5 Reef Bay Trail, St. John, USVI, 2 miles (3.2 km)

Moderate Trails

1 Blue Mountains hike, Jamaica, 7 miles (11 km)
2 Chaconia Trail, Asa Wright Nature Centre, Trinidad 2 miles (3.2 km)
3 El Yunque trails, Puerto Rico 36 miles (58 km)

4 Hooiberg (Haystack Mountain), Aruba, 562 steps at 541 ft (164 m)
5 Parc Naturel, Basse-Terre, Guadeloupe, 180 miles (290 km) of marked trails
6 Pic du Paradise, St. Martin 4 miles (6.4 km)

Challenging Trails

1 Adventure Trail, Asa Wright Nature Centre, Trinidad 19 miles (31 km)
2 Edmund Forest Trail, St. Lucia 7 miles (11 km)
3 La Soufrière summit, Guadeloupe 5 miles (8 km)
4 Mount Qua Qua, Grenada 3 miles (4.8 km)
5 Pico Duarte, Dominican Republic 14.5 miles (23.3 km)
6 Valley of Desolation, Dominica 5.5 miles (8.9 km)

Morne Trois Pitons National Park, Dominica, has many hikes from the easy Trafalgar Falls to the more difficult Valley of Desolation trail. Some trails are not as well maintained, so a guide is recommended.

For more on hiking see p213, p237, p289, p303, and pp388–9

Blue Mountains, Jamaica, covering 28 miles (45 km) east to west, offer some of the best hiking on the island *(see pp144–5)*. The most rewarding is the 6-hour hike to the Blue Mountain Peak.

El Yunque National Forest, Puerto Rico, has various dirt and paved trails *(see p208)*. The El Yunque Trail reaches a peak overlooking the Atlantic Ocean from 3,500 ft (1,067 m).

Arikok National Park, Aruba, has a number of easy to moderate marked trails *(see p483)*. The trek up the 620-ft (188-m) Mount Jamanota is steep but short, and offers fantastic views from the summit.

The Baths, Virgin Gorda, BVI, is more of a rock scramble than a hike *(see p240)*. It provides an afternoon of exploration through dramatic landscapes riddled with caves, tunnels, and giant boulders along the sea.

Reef Bay Trail, St. John, USVI, is one of the most popular in the Caribbean. The trail runs downhill from Centerline Road to Genti Bay Beach, past a natural pool inscribed with petroglyphs.

Golf in the Caribbean

Golf has been a popular sport in the Caribbean for the past century. A new hybrid grass has eliminated many problems related to maintaining greens in the tropics. As a result, more courses are being laid out and many of the older ones have been updated to meet the expectations of today's player. Year-round sunshine guarantees an ideal vacation for golfers of all levels; while international championships draw big-name players to the best courses. Vacation packages are widely available, but independent travelers can schedule their own tee times through most pro shops. Professional coaching is available to beginners.

Fidel Castro at a golf course in Havana, Cuba, in 1961

Tryall Club, **Jamaica**, offers a demanding 18-hole golf course tempered by breathtaking views. Designed by Ralph Plummer, the championship course incorporates the natural challenges of the Caribbean Sea and Flint River. It also hosts various international tournaments.

Sandy Lane, Barbados *(see p449)*, has three courses with a total of 45 holes. Known by the quirky names Green Monkey, Old Nine, and the Country Club, each course has tropical land-scaping, perfectly accentuated by natural seascapes.

Casa de Campo, Dominican Republic *(see p181)*, has three renowned courses designed by Pete Dye. The seven-hole Teeth of the Dog is considered one of the best in the Caribbean.

Other Courses

The Manchester Country Club in Jamaica was built more than one hundred years ago, with magnificient views from the course's 2,200 ft (660 m) elevation. Favorites include the Nick Faldo-designed Legacy Course at Roco Ki Golf Club in the Dominican Republic, the Royal St. Kitts Golf Club, and CuisinArt Golf Club, Anguilla, designed by Greg Norman.

Coamo Springs, Puerto Rico, an 18-hole course with amazing mountain views, is designed by Ferdinand Garbin.

Provo Golf Club, Turks and Caicos, is known for its 18-hole course that blends with the limestone outcroppings.

For more details on golf courses, refer to the Outdoor Activities pages for each island

Top Golf Courses

① The North Sound Club
② Manchester Country Club
③ Tryall Club
④ White Witch Golf Course
⑤ Provo Golf Club
⑥ Casa de Campo
⑦ Roco Ki Golf Club
⑧ Coamo Spings
⑨ Carambola Golf & Country Club
⑩ CuisinArt Golf Club
⑪ Royal St. Kitts
⑫ Empress Josephine Golf Course
⑬ Sandy Lane
⑭ Tierra del Sol

Best Golf Courses

The Caribbean golf courses often have panoramic views of the sea, intriguing landscaping, and natural water hazards such as creeks, streams, and gullies. The larger islands offer a selection of celebrity-designed courses, with more being built.

Tierra del Sol Golf Course, Aruba, is designed by Robert Trent Jones II. Gallons of desalinated water are used to keep the grass lush on the 18-hole course on this arid island.

Water bodies on island courses come in the form of lakes, ponds, rivers, and the ocean lending a scenic appeal to the Caribbean courses.

The greens are usually well maintained and the grass is cut very short to allow the ball to roll a longer distance.

Carambola Golf & Country Club, USVI, has an outstanding 18-hole golf course designed by Robert Trent Jones Sr. for philanthropist Laurance Rockefeller. It has a tropical forest in the backdrop.

The North Sound Club, Grand Cayman, located at Crystal Harbor, was designed by Roy Case to complement the terrain.

Empress Josephine Golf Course, Martinique, is an 18-hole course designed by Robert Trent Jones Sr. on an exceptional location.

White Witch Golf Course, Jamaica, named after Rose Hall Plantation's owner, has spectacular ocean views.

Sports

The Caribbean's diverse heritage is reflected in the wide variety of sports played here, though the popularity of each game varies between islands. Vibrant passions range from the love of cricket among the English-speaking isles to the frenzied craze for baseball in Spanish-speaking Cuba and the Dominican Republic. However, almost all residents adore soccer, while dominoes is practically a national pastime. Many of the islands have produced world-class athletes who have found international success at the Olympics.

Children playing cricket in a local park, Jamaica

Cricket

The popularity of cricket extends from St. Kitts and Nevis to powerhouse nations Jamaica and Trinidad. Although each isle has its own team, the region is represented in international Test cricket as the West Indies team. The game has inspired art, music, and endless debate and made players such as Sir Garfield Sobers and Brian Lara iconic figures.

Kensington Oval in Bridgetown, Barbados, was built in 1882 and is known as the Caribbean mecca of cricket. The stadium also hosted the final match of the ICC Cricket World Cup in 2007.

Cheering fans, drinking, dancing, and singing, are the highlights of any Caribbean sporting event. The atmosphere is similar to that of a carnival, with families setting up picnics in the viewing galleries.

Regional cricket teams, such as the Antigua Hawksbills, play with local and international sides in tournaments that have corporate sponsors and offer big amounts in prize money.

Cricket on the beach clearly indicates the islands' obsession with cricket. Often playing scratch matches with makeshift bats, balls, and wickets, youngsters hone their skills in less than perfect, albeit lovely settings. Locals happily welcome strangers into their game.

Baseball

US marines introduced baseball to the Spanish-speaking islands in the 19th century. Although Cuba and the Dominican Republic vie with each other to be the best in the world, Puerto Rico also has well-known players. The islands supply US league clubs with talented players.

Cuba beat USA in 2013 in the first friendship series between the two teams since 1996. This latest friendship series has strengthened the case for baseball to be reinstated as an Olympic sport for the 2020 Games.

Tigres del Licey, a professional baseball team of the Dominican Republic, celebrates victory over Águilas Cibaeñas. The team was founded in 1907 and has won many titles since then.

Other Sports

Along with cricket, golf, and baseball, dozens of other sports are played in the Caribbean. These range from cycling to soccer and Jamaica even has a bobsled team, despite the lack of snow or ice. Almost every island nation has a Ministry of Sports and visitors can participate in many of the events.

Soccer is a universal favorite throughout the Caribbean and it is easy to find a game being played somewhere. Although national competitions take place in stadiums, less serious games are played on the sands and soccer fields in the villages.

Boxing is part of the school curriculum in countries such as Barbados and Trinidad. Cuba has produced dozens of Olympic medal winners, but smaller isles have had their own successes too.

Dominoes

The most popular non-active pastime in the Caribbean is dominoes. Played with gusto, it is a source of competition among all the islands. Usually limited to men, this game is generally played in the open under the shade of trees or on the street, and accompanied by shots of rum. On most islands, players slam down their pieces with a loud crack.

Playing dominoes, Cuba

Athletics is where Caribbeans have made a big impact on the international arena. Usain Bolt, Melanie Walker, and Dayron Robles are the latest to join the long star-list.

Family-Friendly Islands

The natural attractions of the Caribbean make it a perfect destination for children. There are sand castles to be built, waves to be surfed, reefs to be snorkeled, and rainforests to be explored. Each island offers its own unique set of experiences, with a variety of family-oriented activities ranging from water parks, dolphin encounters, and whale-watching to zip lines and animal habitats. Anguilla, Jamaica, Curaçao, Dominica, Turks and Caicos, St. Martin/ Sint Maarten, and the Dominican Republic are the islands with the best child-friendly resorts and destinations.

Turks and Caicos are the first choice for families looking for the ultimate island adventure. Children particularly enjoy the dune buggy excursions and the action-packed water park.

Jamaica has many attractions for families, such as Dolphin Cove, Caliche Rainforest, Luminous Lagoon, Island Village, and Dunn's River Falls, although children might need a hand negotiating these.

CUBA

CAYMAN ISLANDS

Activities at the resorts

Many resorts have created environments where families can enjoy a wide range of activities without ever leaving the property. Large chains such as Beaches, Breezes, and Club Med even create special programs just for little ones, older children, and teens. It is worth doing some research before booking, as some resorts have no special facilities for children or are more aimed towards adults.

Playgrounds for children incorporate many special features, such as this pirate ship, which will bring out the swashbuckler in most kids.

Pools, such as the one at Beaches Resort and Spa in Turks and Caicos, make many resorts ideal places for family vacations.

The Beach is a big draw, so opt for a resort right on the sands, such as Dreams Punta Cana in the Dominican Republic.

Party venue at Sonesta Maho Beach Resort, Sint Maarten, is ideal for great family outings as well as private parties.

The Dominican Republic's Cabarete Beach on the north coast attracts families with all types of watersports. Also popular are the Manati Park dolphin and sea lion shows, the Ocean World Adventure Park, as well as the Punta Cana Ecological Park petting zoo.

Anguilla's Dolphin Discovery invites families to swim with dolphins and learn about their habitat and behavior. Children of all ages can enjoy exploring the "hands-on" coral tide pool as well as a jungle bird exhibit.

St. Martin/Sint Maarten have many highlights, including the Sint Maarten Park and Zoo and Butterfly Farm. Other entertainment venues are movie theaters, bowling alleys, and skating rinks.

DOMINICAN
REPUBLIC

PUERTO
RICO

VIRGIN
ISLANDS

ST. BARTHÉLEMY

SABA AND
ST. EUSTATIUS

ANTIGUA AND
BARBUDA

ST. KITTS
AND NEVIS

GUADELOUPE

MARTINIQUE

ST. LUCIA

C a r i b b e a n   S e a

ST. VINCENT AND
THE GRENADINES

BARBADOS

GRENADA

ARUBA, CURAÇAO,
AND BONAIRE

TRINIDAD
AND TOBAGO

| 0 km | 200 |
| 0 miles | 200 |

Dominica's stunning Trafalgar Falls are reached by a short walk on a well-marked trail, while more airborne adventures can be found on the Wacky Rollers Adventure Park's zip lines. River tubing on the Layou River is another popular activity.

Curaçao's Sea Aquarium allows visitors to swim with stingrays. Other attractions are Seaworld Explorer semi-submarine, Dolphin Academy, and Christoffel National Park.

Flora and Fauna

The biologically-rich Caribbean is sculpted to show off the full potential of the tropics with a potpourri of terrains and ecosystems. Most of the major islands are mountainous and buried in tropical forests cut through by rivers that slowly snake across coastal wetlands. Others are desert-dry plateaus studded with cacti. Almost every isle is ringed by coral reefs. Birds and butterflies are prolific, as are reptiles, although mammal species are relatively few – just 90 species, of which 40 are endemic, such as the endangered solenodon, a giant shrew found in Cuba.

Limestone mogotes dominating Valle de Viñales, Cuba

Montane Forests
The densest tropical forests occur on the windward slopes, which receive moisture-laden trade winds. Mists enshroud cloud forest at higher elevations, above which pine forests thrive in cool alpine air. Mosses and epiphytes adorn the branches.

Lowland Forests
Rainforests cloak many of the plains and lower mountain slopes. These complex ecosystems harbor much of the region's wildlife. *Jutias*, an endangered rodent, and iguanas inhabit the understory, while parrots cavort in the treetops. Various palms rise from the plains, including coconut palms.

The Hispaniolan woodpecker is endemic to Hispaniola, comprising Haiti and the Dominican Republic. Like all woodpecker species, it nests in tree trunks.

Puerto Rico's coquí frog is among the tiniest of the 162 Caribbean frog species.

Montane cloud forest has endemic trees such as mountain mahogany, a member of the tea family unique to Saba. The trees are usually covered with epiphytes.

The streamer tail hummingbird of Jamaica is one of the 18 hummingbird species found here.

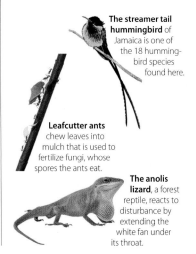

Leafcutter ants chew leaves into mulch that is used to fertilize fungi, whose spores the ants eat.

The anolis lizard, a forest reptile, reacts to disturbance by extending the white fan under its throat.

Environment Under Threat

Pollution of the air, soil, and waterways threatens many of the Caribbean's delicate environments and endemic species of flora and fauna. Deforestation has been a great concern on many islands, although countries such as the Dominican Republic have legislated in favor of protecting their forests, including mangrove systems of vital importance. Most islands have established special reserves aimed at protecting environments critical to the survival of specific endemic species, but coral reefs are increasingly threatened by global warming.

Deforestation, a major threat to the environment of the Caribbean islands

Wetlands and Coasts

Wetlands are some of the area's most diverse ecosystems. Lakes and coastal lagoons are vital staging posts for migrating birds, notably waterfowl. Mangrove swamps are particularly rich in bird and endemic species such as arboreal crabs and crab-eating raccoons.

Dry Forests

Dry forests cover the terrain in the rain shadow – usually the southwestern lee of mountains. Deciduous flora sheds its leaves during seasonal drought, making wildlife easier to spot. Some areas are so arid that the predominant flora is cacti and scrub.

Raccoons, an endangered species, have official conservation status throughout the Caribbean.

Iguanas are camouflaged green for a life in the trees, or brown when living on the ground. Males turn orange during the mating season.

Roseate spoonbills, egrets, flamingos, herons, and other wading birds and waterfowl inhabit the water bodies.

Royal poincianas or *flamboyáns* burst into vermilion bloom in spring. This drought-resistant tree is common on almost every isle.

Mangroves, which thrive in alluvial silt, form a vital nursery for marine creatures and birds, such as the frigate bird.

Bats, comprising more than half of Caribbean mammal species, play a vital role in sustaining the ecosystem.

Marine Wildlife

From starfish and stingrays in turquoise shallows to swordfish and manta rays cruising the ocean deep, the Caribbean is a cornucopia of marine life. The coral reef environment is especially rich, where scuba divers can admire an ever-changing kaleidoscope of creatures varied in size and color. The wildlife includes many species unique to the Caribbean's marine habitats. Dolphins are ubiquitous, as are sharks, while migrating whales add an extra thrill in warm-water bays and the passages between many islands.

Scuba diver exploring a coral reef in Bonaire

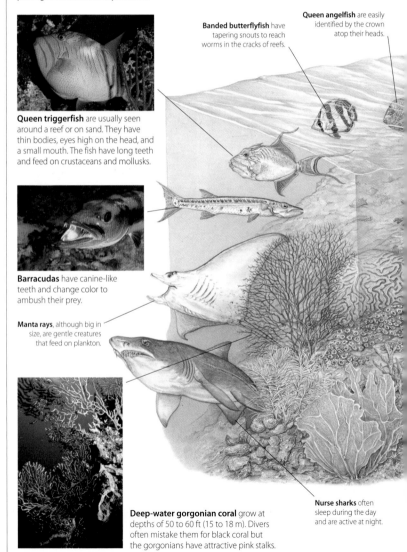

Banded butterflyfish have tapering snouts to reach worms in the cracks of reefs.

Queen angelfish are easily identified by the crown atop their heads.

Queen triggerfish are usually seen around a reef or on sand. They have thin bodies, eyes high on the head, and a small mouth. The fish have long teeth and feed on crustaceans and mollusks.

Barracudas have canine-like teeth and change color to ambush their prey.

Manta rays, although big in size, are gentle creatures that feed on plankton.

Nurse sharks often sleep during the day and are active at night.

Deep-water gorgonian coral grow at depths of 50 to 60 ft (15 to 18 m). Divers often mistake them for black coral but the gorgonians have attractive pink stalks.

Green moray eel is the largest of the Caribbean eels and grows up to 6 ft (2 m). It has big powerful jaws and feeds on small fish and mollusks. It lives in crevices in the reef, and is reclusive during the day but active at night.

Queen parrotfish are spotted easily but tend to shy away from divers. They grow up to 15 inches (38 cm) and feed on algae.

Octopuses have an excellent sense of vision, smell, and touch. They can change color instantly.

Nassau groupers are found near the entrances of caves or behind sea fans between 40 and 100 ft (12 and 30 m) deep. They like to ambush their prey.

Sharknose gobys are small, active fish cleaners found near the ocean floor.

Spiny lobsters are nocturnal feeders, lurking at the back of caves during the day.

Coral Reefs

Coral reefs form a habitat for both animal and plant life. They support several species, from anemones and sponges to sea urchins and fish. These fragile ecosystems are threatened by pollution and global warming; Caribbean reefs have diminished by 80 percent in the past decade.

Endangered Marine Turtles

Six species of marine turtles inhabit the Caribbean waters – from the tiny loggerhead to the massive leatherback. Although protected by law, marine turtles are threatened by ocean pollution, illegal hunting, stealing of eggs, and loss of beach habitat. Females nest on the beaches but only a fraction of their eggs survive to adulthood.

Loggerhead sea turtles

Top Spots for Wildlife

While tourism in the region depends on resort-based vacations, visitors can readily explore the magnificent wildlife, ranging from manatees and curly-tailed lizards to the ivory-billed woodpecker – the Holy Grail of Caribbean birds. Most islands have taken vigorous steps to safeguard their beaches, reefs, and forests, and the varied national parks, reserves, and wildlife centers are ideal for visitors who appreciate nature and are keen to contribute to its conservation. Every isle has its own endemic species. The wide spectrum of birds provides for spectacular photography. Whale sightings are virtually assured in the winter months.

Humpback whale leaping out of the water, not an uncommon sight

① Cuba: Gran Parque Natural Montemar

Cuba's Zapata Biosphere Reserve displaying a diversity of ecosystems and habitats

Cuba's most important wetland area *(see p84)* is known for its large flocks of flamingos. It protects 171 species of birds, 31 of reptiles, and 12 of mammals, a primitive fish called the manjuarí, as well as crocodiles, caimans, and the world's smallest bird, the zunzuncito.

Zunzuncito, the smallest warm-blooded vertebrate, has been nicknamed bee hummer owing to its tiny size.

Land crabs typically inhabit the marshes. Every spring, millions emerge from the swamps surrounding the Bay of Pigs to breed in the nearby sea.

Flamingos inhabit the salt water lagoons of Península de Zapata. Their pink color is believed to be obtained from a particular insect's larvae that they consume.

③ Dominican Republic: Lago Enriquillo

This lake *(see p179)* has the Caribbean's largest population of American crocodiles, which bask in cool marshy waters along the north shore, and on the salty mudbanks of Isla Cabritos. Rhinoceros iguanas can also be spotted.

American crocodiles belong to the same family as the endemic Cuban crocodile, but are considered to be less aggressive.

Iguanas are found crawling about the island. These leathery giant lizards live in both wet and dry ecosystems and like to bask in the sun.

⑧ Barbuda: Frigate Bird Sanctuary

A pair of frigate birds during mating season

Amid the mangroves of tiny Man O'War Island in Codrington Lagoon *(see p316)* can be found one of the Caribbean's largest frigate bird colonies. During the mating season which lasts from September to April, the males inflate their vermilion chests as the females soar overhead. These birds obtain much of their food by stealing it from other sea birds, a habit which lends them their nickname: man o'war. Their nests are just above the water's edge and can be observed from close.

Top National Parks

① Gran Parque Natural Montemar
② Marshall's Pen Great House
③ Lago Enriquillo
④ Los Haitises National Park
⑤ El Yunque National Forest
⑥ Bahía Fosforescente
⑦ Sandy Point National Wildlife Refuge
⑧ Frigate Bird Sanctuary
⑨ The Parrot Conservation and
   Research Centre
⑩ Barbados Wildlife Reserve
⑪ Grand Etang National Park
⑫ Asa Wright Nature Centre
⑬ Washington Slagbaai National Park

---

⑩ Barbados: Barbados Wildlife Reserve

This reserve (see p444) protects a Noah's Ark-load of endemic and exotic species, including brocket deer and green monkeys.

A pair of green monkeys in the Barbados Wildlife Reserve

The caiman can tolerate both salt and fresh water, and is therefore the most common of all crocodile species.

Agoutis are forest-dwelling, rabbit-sized rodents related to the guinea pig. They live mostly on fallen fruits and nuts.

Brocket deer are shy creatures who live either alone or in pairs. Due to their small size and nocturnal behavior, they are not easily observed.

---

⑫ Trinidad: Asa Wright Nature Centre

Covered by rainforest, this reserve (see p463) provides habitat to a wide variety of birds including at least 13 species of hummingbirds. From a comfortable balcony, visitors may observe endemic as well as exotic birds such as the chestnut woodpecker and the white-bearded manakin.

Hummingbirds are little nectar-drinking birds. Exotic varieties include this white-chested emerald and blue-chinned sapphire.

Conservation is promoted through education and research. The center also provides expertly guided trails and tours.

National Parks with Endangered Species

The Caribbean islands have set up a wide range of national parks and wildlife centers that protect the habitat of endangered species of birds, mammals, amphibians, and reptiles.

Washington Slagbaai National Park in Bonaire (see p487) has endemic bird species like the endangered yellow-shouldered parrot and the Caribbean or brown-throated parakeet.

The Parrot Conservation and Research Center in the Botanical Gardens of Roseau (see p382), Dominica, educates visitors about the endangered sisserou and jaco parrots that are bred here.

Sandy Point on St. Croix is a nesting site for rare leatherback turtles, one of the world's six marine turtle species.

Music of the Caribbean

Music is everywhere in the Caribbean. Pouring out of buses, shops, and bars, Jamaican reggae is a constant soundtrack, while soca provides the pulsing backbeat to the many annual carnivals. Sunsets, too, would not be the same without the tinkling tones of that quintessential Caribbean sound, the steel pan. And like the islands themselves, the various musical genres here vary enormously. Whilst everyone can hum along to a Bob Marley classic, discovering lesser-known styles such as zouk or merengue provides an insight into the heart of Caribbean culture.

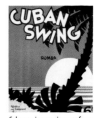

Cuban swing music cover from 1937 for a rumba dance tune

Soca is an evolution of calypso, credited to the late Ras Shorty I by most people. A faster, syncopated version of calypso, suitable for dancing rather than listening, it is the ultimate sound of the Caribbean carnivals.

Salsa to merengue, most Caribbean music is tuned for dancing.

Reggae evolved from a slowing of the ska beat in the 1970s and its best-known exponent is Bob Marley, with a string of albums with the Wailers. Reggae crooners have been eclipsed by the faster dancehall.

Diverse Caribbean Music

Each island is represented by different genres of music. Cuba's popular dance music, son, combines Spanish guitar and African rhythms.

Singers and Musicians

Caribbean music has spawned countless stars over the years and the musicians constitute some of the most talented names in the world. Calypso stalwarts include Mighty Sparrow and the late Lord Kitchener (Trinidad and Tobago), while reggae singers and DJs from Jamaica, such as Sean Paul and Damian Marley, have scored international hits. Ricky Martin and Marc Anthony (Puerto Rico) are the stars of Latino music, while Cuba has produced the Buena Vista Social Club (*son*) and Barbados is the birthplace of R&B singer Rihanna.

Bob Marley, Jamaica's king of reggae, is still celebrated as a master singer and songwriter and as a musical ambassador.

Monty Alexander, a virtuoso pianist, is at the forefront of the Caribbean's burgeoning jazz scene.

Calypso lyrics with their lilting tunes may sound a bit laid-back. However, they uncover a biting social commentary, humor, and some very mischievous double entendre. Trinidad and Tobago's Mighty Sparrow is a very well-known calypso artiste.

Merengue, hailing from the Dominican Republic, is as much a dance style as it is a musical genre. Fast and lively, its Latin-style two-step beat is ideal for dancing with a partner and the twirls and dips are integral.

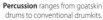

Percussion ranges from goatskin drums to conventional drumkits.

Steel Pan, said to be the only "new" instrument of the 20th century, was invented in oil-rich Trinidad after World War II. The top panels of barrels once used to store crude oil are shaped to form notes, which are beaten by players, known as pannists, to create a distinctive metallic sound.

Zouk, the music of the French Caribbean, particularly Martinique and Guadeloupe, is a derivative of the Haitian cadence genre and sounds like an African version of Trinidadian soca. It is mainly party music.

The guitar is an essential accompaniment providing the all-important bassline.

Machel Montano is the biggest name in the Caribbean soca. His live shows are legendary high-energy affairs.

Celia Cruz was the Caribbean's most successful salsa singer. She is credited with taking Cuban music to the world.

Beenie Man's combination of humor and lyrical skill has ensured his place as one of Jamaica's top dancehall DJs.

Festivals and Events

The Carnival, an elaborate spectacle celebrated in most of the Caribbean, was originally portrayed by African slaves as an irreverent parody of their masters' pre-Lenten masquerade balls. Some events are traditionally still held before Lent, while others take place in July, August, or December. Sailing festivals bring visitors from all over the world for exciting activities and parties. There are also events unique to particular isles, like Tobago's Heritage Festival, or Carriacou's Big Drum festival, and a number of music festivals.

Masked dancers at the Dominican Republic Carnival

Carnival
Carnival is the mother of all Caribbean celebrations. The Trinidad festival, an exuberant blend of music, costumed parades, and massive fêtes, has inspired other carnivals.

Trinidad Carnival, following Caribbean traditions, features J'ouvert, a pre-dawn jump-up.

Costumes are elaborate as various groups flaunt their leaders for the Carnival King and Queen titles.

Blue Devils (Jab Jabs) take over the Paramin area of Trinidad, dancing and demanding payment from onlookers.

Moko Jumbies, as these towering stilt-dancers are known, stride through the streets on Carnival days. They have their origins in traditional African rituals.

Grenada Carnival is celebrated differently in each parish. Various versions of the traditional characters, including Short Knees, Wild Indians, and Jab Jabs, come out on the streets on Carnival days.

Crop Over Festival, Barbados, was originally a harvest festival that celebrated the reaping of the sugarcane crop after a long season of hard work by the plantation slaves. It is now one of the most popular summer highlights.

Music Festivals

Music festivals have sprung up in many islands and performances by well-known local and international stars have made them extremely popular.

St. Lucia Jazz Festival, established in 1992, is one of the best music festivals in the Caribbean.

Merengue Festival, held in the Dominican Republic during late July or early August, features merengue dance and music.

Reggae Sumfest, held in Montego Bay, Jamaica, highlights the best of reggae and dancehall entertainers with new stars and veterans.

Best of the Rest

Many islands have opted for summer carnivals such as Vincy Mas of St. Vincent and the Grenadines. Jamaica's Carnival, breaking all religious ties, is held during Lent and culminates at Easter. St. Kitts, St. Croix, and Montserrat have lively Carnival celebrations at the year end.

Fête des Cuisinières is held in early August, in Point-à-Pitre on Grande-Terre. The festival celebrates the masters of Creole cuisine with a 5-hour banquet that is open to the public.

Antigua Sailing Week hosts international and local sailing enthusiasts. The keenly contested races on the ocean are coupled by fun, food, and partying on land during the week-long celebrations.

Buccoo Goat Races are held on the island of Tobago on Easter Tuesday. This is part of a tradition dating back to 1925. People place bets on the rigorously trained and well-groomed animals.

Major Festivals

Some of the important Caribbean festivals are given below:

Mustique Blues Festival (January/February)

Bob Marley Week, Jamaica (early February)

Festival Casals, Puerto Rico (mid-February to early March)

Trinidad Carnival (Monday and Tuesday before Ash Wednesday)

Holders Season, Barbados (March/April)

Antigua Sailing Week (late April–early May)

St. Lucia Jazz Festival (late April–early May)

Reggae Sumfest, Jamaica (July)

Crop Over Festival, Barbados (late July–early August)

Merengue Festival, Dominican Republic (late July–early August)

Grenada Carnival (August)

World Creole Music Festival, Dominica (October)

Diwali, Trinidad and Tobago (October/November)

Flavors of the Caribbean

The Caribbean owes its varied cuisine to the diverse groups of people who settled in the area over the centuries, combining ingredients they found here with those they brought from elsewhere. First the Amerindians, then the Europeans and their African slaves, followed by people from India, China, and the Middle East, contributed to the region's cultural mix. Each island's cuisine differs according to its ethnic make-up and colonial history, but they have much in common, such as assorted rice-and-pea combinations, seafood, okra dishes, and stews.

Nutmeg, cinnamon, and allspice

European Tastes

Many islands were fought over by European powers, and some had a succession of colonial rulers. The French brought delicate pastries and rich sauces, as well as dishes like stuffed crab back, snails in garlic, and frogs' legs. The British influence is strongest in Barbados – one Christmas specialty is Scottish Jug, made with pigeon peas, cornflour, and salted meat, supposedly based on haggis. From Spain came *pastelles*, *empanadas* (spicy patties), and *escovitch* (pickled and fried fish), while Trinidad's *bacalhau* and *buljol*, both made with salt cod, are Portuguese in origin. Pastries and desserts often combine European culinary styles and local ingredients, such as Christmas rum cake and coconut crème pie.

Preparing conch for a beachside restaurant, Turks and Caicos

Amerindian Heritage

Native Amerindians gave the world their staples of corn, beans, squash, and potatoes. The Taínos of the Greater Antilles smoked and grilled their meat and fish over wood and fragrant leaves. Such grills were known as *barbacoas*, which is the root of the word we now use for the same process – barbecue.

Custard apple Banana Grapefruit Pineapple
Watermelon Coconut Mango
Papaya
Selection of luscious, ripe tropical fruits of the Caribbean

Caribbean Dishes and Specialties

Rice-and-peas is one of the staples on every island, but the ingredients and tastes differ – in Cuba for example, *moros y cristianos* is made with black beans and white rice, and gets much of its flavor from pork; in Trinidad and Tobago, pigeon peas or red beans are used and the dish is flavored with several kinds of herbs and often with coconut milk; the same dish has added hints of nutmeg and other spices in Grenada. Every island has several must-taste dishes, but a sampling of the best known would include curry crab and dumpling in Tobago; jerk chicken or pork in Jamaica; roasted breadfruit and fish in St. Vincent and the Grenadines; *farci* (stuffed crab) in Guadeloupe and *stoba di cabritu* (goat stew) in Curaçao.

Raw giant shrimps

Pastelles are made of corn-meal stuffed with a spicy meat or vegetable filling and steamed in banana leaves.

Colorful, bustling street market in St. George's, Grenada

Memories of Africa

During the time of the slave trade, many new dishes arrived along with the millions of people who were forcibly brought to the Caribbean from West Africa. Produce included okra, plantains, fufu, yams, and ackee. Dishes from Africa included spicy stews like *callaloo*. Jamaica's "jerk" has become popular all over the world, and is believed to have its roots in a fusion of Amerindian barbecue methods with African and Spanish herbs and spices: allspice (also known as Jamaican spice or pimento) is a key ingredient. Cheap and plentiful produce that was used to feed the slaves, such as salt fish and breadfruit, has also become part of the repertoire of island cuisine.

Asian Flavors

Indentured servants from India, and immigrants from China,

added Asian spices and methods of cooking to the mix. Among the well-known dishes is Trinidad's roti – curried meat and vegetables wrapped in a soft flatbread and often accompanied by hot mango or golden apple chutney. Many Indo-Caribbean dishes are

Hot peppers for sale at a market in Pointe-à-Pitre, Guadeloupe

vegetarian: split pea *daal*, curried potato and garbanzos, eggplant and tomato *choka* (roasted with garlic). There are also divine sweets made of flour or milk and flavored with rose-water, cardamom or ginger. Chinese food is widely available, but is particularly good in Trinidad, and considered a special treat by many locals, who do not know how to cook it.

ON THE MENU

Ackee and salt fish (Jamaica)
Delicate yellow ackee fruit looks like scrambled egg and blends well with tasty salt fish for this breakfast specialty.

Bake and Shark (Trinidad)
Popular beachside treat of deep-fried shark wrapped in a fried (not baked) flatbread.

Callaloo (Most islands)
Thick soup made with okra, spinach, crab or salted meat.

Coo coo (Barbados)
Seasoned cornmeal dish eaten with fried or stewed flying fish.

Feroce
(Guadeloupe and Martinique)
Mashed, spiced avocados with cassava flour and salt fish.

Pepperpot (Most islands)
A fiery stew of vegetables and meat. An Amerindian seasoning, cassareep, gives this long-simmered dish its distinctive dark color and exotic taste.

Sancocho is a hearty, festive dish from the Dominican Republic, combining seven types of meat and vegetables.

Arroz con Gandules, Puerto Rico's national dish, is made with salt pork or ham, rice, and pigeon peas, and seasoned with saffron.

Majarete, a rich and creamy corn dessert, is flavored with coconut milk, vanilla essence, and cinnamon.

Best Wedding and Honeymoon Islands

Romance is synonymous with the Caribbean, and its dazzling beaches, lush tropical gardens, historic plantations and forts, and beautiful vistas with a backdrop of mountains sloping into a turquoise sea are all desirable settings for destination weddings. Resorts and local governments are happy to oblige with an impressive array of locations and services for elegant or casual ceremonies and receptions. Even better, couples do not have to travel far to enjoy a perfect honeymoon at one of the many romantic resorts. Top islands for weddings and honeymoons include Antigua, Barbados, Jamaica, St. Kitts and Nevis, and St. Lucia.

A wedding gazebo with floral decorations in Antigua

Antigua

With a number of ideal romantic settings, Antigua would certainly feature in a top-10 list of wedding destinations. June has been designated the Month of Romance on the island, which hosts a Celebrity Destination Wedding each year. From beaches and hilltop vistas to intimate, posh five-star hotels, the island's exotic locales create indelible memories.

Blue Waters resort's trademark is the wedding gazebo placed on a narrow strip of land jutting into the sea. Their five-bedroom Rock Cottage Villa provides the perfect spot for an intimate reception.

Sandals Grande Antigua is one of the leading honeymoon resorts in the world. The lush tropical grounds and beautiful Dickenson Bay Beach provide the ideal backdrop to a luxurious honeymoon at a *rondavel* (traditional African-style house).

Barbados

On this island, couples have a wide choice of venues, from beaches, botanical gardens, clifftops to plantation great houses, private yachts, and elegant resort settings. For something unique, there are wedding safaris into the forests, a submarine for ceremonies, and a high-flying helicopter wedding.

The Flower Forest, St. Joseph, has a picturesque hillside setting overlooking the island's east coast, amid 50 acres (20 ha) of colorful tropical plants.

Sandy Lane Resort allows for great ceremonies and receptions, but this resort is better known for its honeymoon packages that include luxury ocean view rooms, spa treatments, candlelight dinners, champagne, and excellent service.

The Fairmont Royal Pavilion offers a lush environment and luxury trimmings. Couples wed on the lovers' paradise deck overlooking the sea.

For more details, refer to the individual islands

Jamaica

The north coast locations of Negril, Ocho Rios, Port Antonio, and Montego Bay have almost perfect weather and outstanding world-renowned resorts, making it easy to plan a wedding. Among the top resorts known for this are the Ritz-Carlton, the Caves, Strawberry Hill, Tryall Club, and Sandals Royal Plantation.

Strawberry Hill Resort, perched on the Blue Mountains, features a main house and 12 Georgian-style cottages surrounded by botanical gardens that are perfect for relaxed honeymoons.

Sandals Montego Bay Resort, on the longest private white-sand beach on the island, has its own wedding chapel, while the Bay Roc Estate Beachfront Villas are perfect for honeymoons.

St. Kitts and Nevis

This island is ideal for weddings and honeymoons mainly because many former plantations have been converted into inns and hotels, which give it a unique flavor. Historic sites, such as Brimstone Hill Fortress and Romney Manor, and natural wonders, such as Black Rocks and Mount Liamuiga, offer scenic marriage locales.

Ottley's Plantation Inn is a popular site for weddings. The stone-walled restaurant and pool area and the great house with its lawn sloping down to the sea create a lovely backdrop for elegant ceremonies.

Nisbet Plantation on Nevis has a real old-world charm, with stucco cottages, wicker-furnished rooms, and resident vervet monkeys. Couples marry on the white-sand beach and celebrate in the gourmet Great House restaurant.

St. Lucia

Designated as the world's leading honeymoon destination during the World Travel Awards, this island has both natural beauty as well as high-end resorts that attract newlyweds. One of the favorite wedding locations is the Sugar Beach Resort.

Gros Piton and Petit Piton, the towering volcanic cones on the southwest coast, are among the most distinguished landmarks in the Caribbean, giving an unusual wedding backdrop.

Anse Chastanet resort provides intimate wedding experiences in a spectacular scenic location. Among the setting choices are a treehouse, a colonial plantation, a waterfall, and even a coral reef.

Getting Married

With spectacular features ranging from tropical beaches, waterfalls, and gardens to historic locations, the Caribbean is, for many, the dream destination for a wedding. While it may seem like a simple affair, a wedding still involves a legal ceremony as well as arranging various suppliers for photography, wedding cakes, flowers, and entertainment. So it is best to plan well in advance and study the chosen location's rules and regulations, or hire the services of a wedding planner, before enjoying an exotic wedding experience on a beautiful Caribbean island.

A wedding on one of the beaches of St. Lucia

A wedding ceremony at Ottley's Plantation Inn, St. Kitts

Legalities

The Caribbean is a polyglot collection of island nations and protectorates, each with its own regulations and requirements regarding marriage. Every island has different residency require-ments ranging from over a month in the French islands of Martinique, St. Barths, Guadeloupe, and St. Martin, to none in Antigua, Barbados, the Cayman Islands, and the Dominican Republic. When going for the license, expect to produce passports and birth certificates of the couple getting married, as well as any divorce decrees or death certificates if there were previ-ous spouses. Most documents must be either originals or certified copies. The Spanish-language islands, including Cuba and the Dominican Republic, as well as the French islands, expect documents to be translated to their native languages. St. Eustatius and Sint Maarten require that documents be translated into Dutch, and offer local contacts who can handle the documents. Two companies that offer document trans-lations are **Gemini Translation Services** and **MEJ Personal Business Services**.

Other requirements vary from island to island, for example, the number and type of witnesses needed so check this out beforehand.

Types of Weddings

The Caribbean offers an idyllic setting for a tropical wedding, with colorful flowers, lush vegetation, superlative beaches, and turquoise seas. Couples can choose from an incredible array of locales to create their picture-perfect ceremony and reception.

Beach weddings are popular with couples seeking a casual atmosphere, as well as the beautiful backdrop of the aquamarine sea and azure sky. Some splendid beaches include Magens Bay in the US Virgin Islands, Jalousie Plantation in St. Lucia, Grace Bay Beach in Turks and Caicos, and Jumby Bay in Antigua.

Historic-site weddings use painstakingly restored plan-tation great houses, museums, sugar mills, and military sites as dramatic backdrops for ceremonies and receptions. Antigua, St. Kitts and Nevis, Barbados, and St. Lucia offer some of the best sites.

Nature weddings are set against backdrops of specta-cular waterfalls or vistas, or are located in gorgeous botanical gardens. St. Lucia, Nevis, and Dominica are among those offering unique sites.

Villa weddings held in luxurious private villas offer the advantages of having a home-like setting, often with either a spectacular view or private beach.

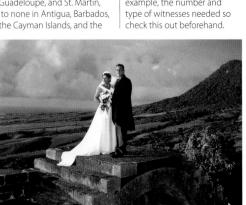

Exchanging vows at the historic site of Brimstone Hill, St. Kitts

For more details on Getting Married, refer to the Practical Information pages for each island

An unusual way to celebrate a wedding is a cruise ceremony that takes place either on the ship or on a beach in one of the ports. Some wedding planners specialize in making arrangements in ports and offer an array of special services.

Nautical weddings are another unique way to get married, and are popular with boating enthusiasts who charter one of the luxury yachts or catamarans available throughout the islands. Antigua, Sint Maarten, the US and British Virgin Islands, and Barbados have the best selections due to their extensive marinas and facilities catering to the yachting crowd.

Websites with detailed information on planning a Caribbean wedding include **Isledo Caribbean Wedding Resource**, **Island Hideaways**, **No Frills Wedding**, **Caribbean Weddings**, **Islandbrides.com The Beach Wedding Guide**, **Luxe Destination Weddings**, and **The Wedding Experience**.

Music bands are arranged by hotels

Waterfall wedding arranged by Tropic Isle Weddings

Hotel packages

One of the easiest and often most cost-effective ways to arrange a wedding in the Caribbean is by using the special packages offered by many hotels and resorts. Packages include a room for the couple and the services of the hotel's wedding planner, and extras such as cakes, decorations, musicians, and a photographer. These also offer some of the best reception options since spacious restaurants are located right on-site. The Sandals chain is the "wedding hotel," offering packages from designers such as Preston Bailey. Other luxury favorites include Anse Chastenet in St. Lucia, Hilton Rose Hall Resort & Spa in Jamaica, and Canouan Resort at Carenage Bay in the Grenadines.

Wedding Insurance

Weddings, especially in a foreign land, often require significant outlays for deposits along with lots of uncertainties. Many couples opt for wedding insurances, which cover the loss of deposits because of severe weather, vendor no-shows, and transportation cancellations, as well as providing reimbursement if the wedding dress, tuxedo or rings are lost in travel, or for non-recoverable costs should sudden illness strike the bride, groom or close family members. Among such insurance companies are **Wed Safe** and **Wedding Protector Plan**.

WEDDING GUIDE

Caribbean Weddings
W caribbeanweddings.com

Gemini Translation Services
Tel 0117 986 9578 (UK).
W tlcuk.biz

Islandbrides.com The Beach Wedding Guide
W islandbrides.com

Island Hideaways
Tel 800 832 2302 (US). 0808 234 5122 (UK). 703 378 7840 (International).
W islandhideaways.com

Isledo Caribbean Wedding Resource
W isledo.com

Luxe Destination Weddings
W luxedestinationweddings.com

MEJ Personal Business Services
Tel 886 557 5336 (US).
W mejpbs.com

No Frills Wedding
Tel 866 460 2545 (St. Kitts).
W nofrillswedding.com

The Wedding Experience
Tel 866 223 9672 (US).
W theweddingexperience.com

Wed Safe
Tel 877 723 3933 (US).
W wedsafe.com

Wedding Protector Plan
Tel 888 342 5977 (US).
W protectmywedding.com

Architecture

The Caribbean pre-Columbian architecture is limited to ceremonial plazas, best seen in Puerto Rico. During their rule, the Spanish built massive fortresses, ornate colonial churches and mansions that still dominate the Greater Antilles' urban centers. The greatest architectural legacy of the Dutch-, English-, and French-speaking isles is in plantation homes and simple, quaint urban dwellings influenced by European trends of the time. In recent years, the major cityscapes have changed significantly due to the growth of contemporary architecture, especially in the financial districts.

The courtyard – a typical feature of Spanish colonial architecture

Sloping roof made with terra-cotta tiles.

Balconies with slender wooden columns.

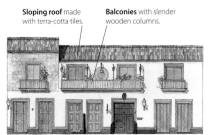

Calle Obispo has a number of buildings with wooden balconies and courtyards, reflecting Spanish influence.

Bohíos are quintessential rural dwellings, with thatched roofs and timber or adobe walls.

The campaniles are asymmetrical.

The rippling façade is adorned by pilasters.

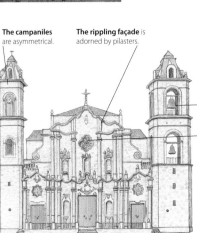

The bells are said to have been cast with a dash of gold to enhance their musical tone.

The vitral over the main entrance resembles a rose.

Catedral de la Habana shows the Baroque style imported from Europe in the late 17th century, and is remarkable for its grandiose façade, famously described by Cuban writer Alejo Carpentier as "music set in stone".

Cuba

Cuba has a spectacular amalgam of architectural styles spanning Mudéjar-style palaces and 19th-century French Rococo structures, while Art Deco and Art Nouveau exteriors from the 1920s fuse with the 1950s Modernist style.

Mediopunto, or stained-glass windows, evolved in the mid-18th century as protection against the tropical sun.

Edificio Bacardí *(1930)* is a superb example of the Art Deco style. Its pink granite and limestone façade is embellished with terra-cotta motifs.

Puerto Rico

Enclosed by massive walls, colonial Old San Juan has more than 800 historic structures, while modern San Juan teems with Art Deco and contemporary buildings.

Castillo San Cristóbal *(see p200)* was completed in 1783. It is one of the largest Spanish fortresses of its day and exemplifies colonial military architecture featuring multiple lines of defense.

Tibes Indigenous Ceremonial Center *(see p206)* features pre-Hispanic *bateyes* (ceremonial plazas) that were used for games and are ringed by granite boulders etched with petroglyphs.

Trinidad

The English-speaking island of Trinidad has a rich architectural legacy. The island's somber 19th-century colonial buildings are in sharp contrast to the crop of towering contemporary structures, and religious shrines reflecting the island's eclectic potpourri of cultures.

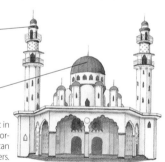

Two minarets, 80 ft (25 m) tall, flank the mosque.

Nicholas Towers (2003), a 21-story blue glass tower, is one of Port of Spain's tallest buildings.

The dome is 40 ft (12 m) in diameter and is typical of Muslim architecture.

Jinnah Memorial Mosque, St. Joseph, built in 1954, is named after Pakistan's first governor-general. The hexagonal mosque, can accommodate up to 1,000 worshippers.

Martinique

Martinique shows off its French roots with a cosmopolitan flavor enhanced by numerous late 19th-century buildings of pre-cast metal. Chic contemporary structures contrast with colonial forts, stone churches, and quaint humble cottages.

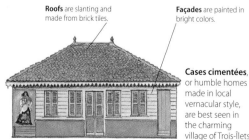

Roofs are slanting and made from brick tiles.

Façades are painted in bright colors.

Cases cimentées, or humble homes made in local vernacular style, are best seen in the charming village of Trois-Îlets.

The Bibliothèque Schoelcher *(see p362)*, by architect Henri Pick, was built in Paris for the 1889 World Exposition before being dismantled and moved to Fort-de-France to serve as a library.

HISTORY OF THE CARIBBEAN

First inhabited by Amerindian tribes, the islands of the Caribbean were later conquered by the Spanish, English, French, and Dutch, who all competed for control of the isles. Once slaves were introduced, the decimated civilizations blended with the African and European cultures. After independence many islands forged their own paths but still maintain ties with their former colonizing nation.

The Caribbean islands began to be inhabited around 7,000 years ago when various Arawak tribal communities started migrating north from South America's Orinoco basin region. Island-hopping in giant *canoas* (dugout canoes), they eventually settled on all the islands.

Arawak communities lived in clan villages led by *caciques* (chieftains). They gathered shellfish, hunted wild animals, and lived well off the sea. They were also skilled slash-and-burn farmers who grew *maíz* (corn) and yuca, a starchy edible root used to make flour for cassava bread. They wove *henequen* (sisal) and wild cotton into *hamacas* (hammocks), and inhaled the smoke of a plant called *cohiba* through a *tabaco* (hollow tube) to induce hallucinations. The Arawaks worshiped *zemís* (spirit gods), which were depicted in rock paintings and carvings in sacred caverns, and on ceremonial ball-courts called *bateyes*.

By the time Christopher Columbus (Cristóbal Colón) arrived in 1492, the larger westerly islands of the Caribbean were inhabited by the Taíno, who had achieved a high degree of social organization.

Engraving of an Indian tribal leader of Cuba greeting Christopher Columbus

By the 15th century, these relatively peaceful farmers and hunter-gatherers, living on today's Puerto Rico and Hispaniola, were being harassed and enslaved by the more warlike Caribs, who were now migrating north through the islands.

		1493 On his second voyage, Columbus establishes Nueva Isabela, the first settlement in the New World, on Hispaniola	
5000 BC First Arawak tribes begin moving north from Orinoco Basin, South America	AD 1000 Caribs start driving out the Taíno		1503 First African slaves transported to Hispaniola

5000 BC   **AD 1460**   **1520**

1000 BC Taíno tribes settle in the Greater Antilles

The Caribs, a fierce warlike tribe

1492 Christopher Columbus sets out on his first voyage of exploration

Etching showing Christopher Columbus landing on Hispaniola

The Conquistadores

Columbus's arrival on his first voyage to the New World spelled doom for the native population. Between 1492 and 1504, he made four voyages and mapped the Caribbean islands from Trinidad to Cuba. He died in Valladolid in 1506 clinging to his belief that these were the islands of Japan and the East Indies. In his wake came gold-hungry Spanish conquistadores who settled the major islands, enslaving the natives to mine gold. Within a few decades, the indigenous peoples were almost entirely wiped out by overwork, brutal massacres, and European diseases; the Spanish began importing African slaves in 1503 to supply the need for forced labor. The Spanish also used Hispaniola, Puerto Rico, and Cuba as bases for exploring the New World. Hernán Cortés conquered Mexico in 1520 and Aztec gold treasures began to be plundered by the Spanish. Soon Colombian emeralds and Inca wealth were added to Europe-bound fleets and led to the development of Santo Domingo, Havana, and San Juan.

Engraving showing the city of Santo Domingo being attacked by Francis Drake

The Age of Pirates

The wealth lured pirates, who began to prey upon Spanish ships and ports by the mid-16th century. Sailing with large fleets, these swashbuckling sea captains blazed a terror trail. In 1555, French pirate Jacque de Sores sacked Havana, and in 1586 privateer Francis Drake led a 20-ship fleet against Santo Domingo in a month-long raid.

Portrait of Francis Drake

This led to the construction of impressive forts, such as Havana's Castillo de la Real Fuerza and St. Kitts' Brimstone Hill, to guard against future attacks.

Pirate attacks increased in the 17th century as Spain attempted to enforce a trade monopoly. The restrictions fostered resentment in France, England, and the Netherlands, leading to wars with Spain and each other for control of the region. European nations issued licenses to privateers for state-sanctioned piracy against the Spanish. The infamous "buccaneers" began life hunting wild boar on a tiny island off Hispaniola. Driven off by the Spaniards, they turned to piracy, captured Spanish ships, and grew powerful. They were officially welcomed to Jamaica's Port Royal, and under Henry Morgan they wreaked havoc throughout the Caribbean and Central America. In 1697, Spain and England signed the Treaty of Ryswyck and committed to ending privateering and piracy.

1623 The English establish their first Caribbean colony, on St. Kitts

1634 The Dutch colonize the southwest Caribbean islands

1697 Spain and England sign the treaty of Ryswyck to end piracy

580   1640   1700

1635 Guadeloupe and Martinique are colonized by the French

1655 English Admiral Penn seizes Jamaica from the Spanish

Welsh pirate, Henry Morgan (1635–88)

African slaves laboring on a sugar plantation, an engraving by Theodore de Bry, 1596

Sugar and Slavery

During the early 17th century, the rest of the Lesser Antilles' islands were colonized by England, France, and the Netherlands. The Dutch dominated early colonization, founding the Dutch West India Company in 1621. They promoted Caribbean trade in defiance of a Spanish monopoly. Constant wars for possession ensued and some islands changed hands more than 20 times. Spain encouraged tobacco and sugar cultivation, fostering a booming economy to satisfy Europe's growing demand for sugar. Other European nations followed suit, and sugar dominated the islands' economy.

The phenomenal growth of the sugar industry was made possible by African slave labor. African men, women, and children were captured and packed aboard ships for the harrowing Middle Passage to the New World, where most were auctioned to planters. Many slaves fell sick and died en route. Britain alone shipped more than three million Africans to the Caribbean between 1662 and 1807. By the late 18th century, slaves outnumbered the white population by ten to one. The slave trade was so lucrative that rival European powers warred for control.

Plantation slaves toiled in the cane fields with little respite from flogging or worse punishments. Slave masters suppressed rebellions with force. By the end of the 18th century, slave uprisings grew in size and frequency – in 1804, a rebellion in France's Saint-Domingue led to the creation of the world's first black republic, Haiti. Plantations were in decline, however, and in 1834 Britain abolished slavery (but introduced Indian indentured labor to Jamaica and Trinidad); the French did so in 1848. Slavery on the Spanish islands continued until 1886, and contributed to Cuba's brutal wars of independence.

Independence

Each Caribbean island evolved its distinct Creole culture that crystallized into nationalist independence movements. The United States, concerned by the violent events in Cuba and Puerto Rico (the Dominican Republic, the third major Spanish possession, had won independence in 1844), declared war on Spain in 1898. The short Spanish-American War ended with Spain's defeat and Cuba and Puerto Rico were ceded to the US. Puerto Rico was retained by the US as a "Commonwealth." In 1903, the US granted

Slave rebellion led by Toussaint L'Ouverture in 1794

1775 Trade embargo on British West Indies enforced by the US till 1783

1845 Indentured laborers from India begin arriving in British colonies

1898 US intervenes i Cuba's independenc war; seizes Puerto Ric

1775 **1815** **1855** 1

1784 France cedes St. Barthélemy to Sweden

1807 England bans slave trading

1834 Britain grants emancipation to slaves in its colonies

freedom to Cuba, which witnessed a boom-and-bust economy under a series of corrupt US-backed governments that ended in 1959, when Fidel Castro toppled dictator General Batista and the island became a Communist nation.

The Danes sold their Virgin Islands to the US in 1917, while Aruba, Curaçao, Bonaire, St. Eustatius, Saba, and Sint Maarten were incorporated as autonomous constituents of the Netherlands. The French possessions were also integrated as full departments of France, with full rights.

In 1958, an attempt to forge the British-ruled islands into an independent Federation of the West Indies foundered. Jamaica and Trinidad and Tobago became independent states within the British Commonwealth in 1962, followed by Barbados in 1966. Next came independence for Dominica (1978), St. Lucia (1979), St. Vincent (1979), Antigua and Barbuda (1981), and St. Kitts and Nevis (1983). Anguilla, Montserrat, Cayman Islands, British Virgin Islands, and the Turks and Caicos still remain dependencies or British Overseas Territories.

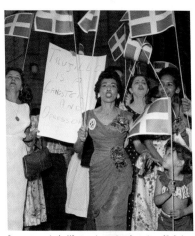

Demonstrators in the US protesting against the regime of Rafael Trujillo in the Dominican Republic

The Caribbean Today

Most islands have overcome their colonial legacy and have evolved as major tourist destinations. Jamaica was the birthplace of the all-inclusive resorts, which now dominate in the Dominican Republic. The Dominican Republic has now emerged from three decades of brutal dictatorship

Poster of Fidel Castro and "Che" Guevara

(1930–61) under Rafael Trujillo, and is one of the leading Caribbean destinations for tourism.

In Cuba, Fidel Castro handed power to his brother Raúl in 2008, and in 2011 the most significant reforms in decades were approved. However, the nation continues to chart a unique socialist path in the face of a US trade embargo. In January 2010 a devastating earthquake struck Haiti, killing more that 230,000 people. Jamaica's capital, Kingston, was rocked when an anti-drug offensive led to gunfights that claimed dozens of lives in May 2010. Nevertheless, the trend today is towards greater political stability and development with each island presenting its unique culture, blending African, European, and other influences into a fascinating combination.

Cyparis, sole survivor of Mont Pelée eruption

1961 US imposes trade embargo on Cuba

1962 Trinidad and Tobago gain independence

1965 25,000 US Marines quell labor unrest in the Dominican Republic

Hurricane George (1998), Greater Antilles

2008 Hurricane Ike devastates Grand Turk, Haiti, and Cuba

1935

1975

2020

02 Mont Pelée erupts Martinique; St. Pierre is destroyed

1958 Federation of British West Indies established but fails four years later

1959 Fidel Castro seizes power in Cuba and begins a Communist revolution

1983 US Marines invade Grenada to topple a leftist government

2010 A huge earthquake hits Haiti, leveling Port-au-Prince and killing 230,000 people

2012 Partial relaxation of the US trade embargo on Cuba

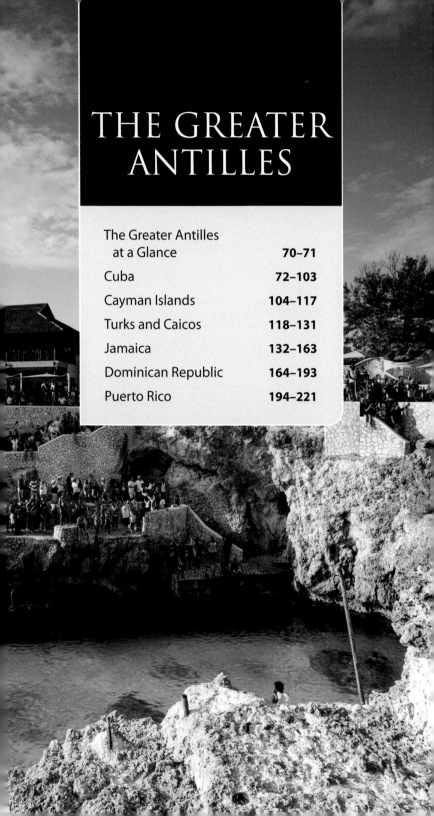

THE GREATER ANTILLES

The Greater Antilles at a Glance

The larger nation states of the Greater Antilles offer the greatest diversity in the Caribbean due to their size. Spanish-speaking Cuba, the Dominican Republic, and Puerto Rico each boast remarkable early-colonial cities crammed with cathedrals and castles; of these Havana is particularly enthralling. All three islands have sensational beaches, rugged mountains, and world-class hotels, as does English-speaking Jamaica. The relatively tiny Cayman Islands and Turks and Caicos have splendid beaches, fantastic diving, and unique wildlife.

Locator Map

Havana

Matanzas

Colón

Pinar del Rio

Santa Clara

Ciego de Avila

Nueva Gerona

Trinidad

CUBA
(See pp72–103)

Camagüey

Las Tunas

Holgu

Santiago de Cuba

CAYMAN ISLANDS
(See pp104–17)

JAMAICA
(See pp132–63)

Montego Bay

Ocho Rios

Kingsto

Cuba, the largest island in the Caribbean, is steeped in history and a land of immense beauty. Habana Vieja, the core of the capital city, Havana, has the finest collection of colonial buildings in the Americas.

Jamaica is the land of reggae music and spectacular beaches. The craggy Blue Mountains, fabulous Blue Lagoon, famous resorts, sandy beaches, and vibrant towns with festive nightlife make it one of the most popular islands with visitors.

◀ The beautifully located Rick's Cafe, Negril, Jamaica

The Turks and Caicos sit atop an underwater plateau with walls that plunge to the bottom, making it a world-class diving and snorkeling destination. Rich marine life, nature reserves that protect scores of bird species, historic buildings, lively nightlife, and excellent hotels make these islands a major tourist attraction.

Puerto Rico is a unique island fusing Latin and American cultures with dramatic landscapes, boutique hotels, and exciting activities ranging from golf to surfing. The capital, San Juan, boasts cobbled streets lined with magnificent colonial buildings.

TURKS AND CAICOS
(See pp118–31)

ntánamo

Puerto Plata

DOMINICAN REPUBLIC
(See pp164–93)

Santiago de los Cabelleros

HAITI

Santo Domingo

La Romana

San Juan

Arecibo

Ponce

PUERTO RICO
(See pp194–221)

Barahona

0 km   100
0 miles   100

The Dominican Republic, one of the most geographically diverse islands in the region, provides innumerable opportunities for adventure and ecotourism. Mangrove swamps, alpine wilderness, cascading waterfalls, spectacular beaches, and colonial buildings add to the charm of the island.

A PORTRAIT OF CUBA

Cuba is typified by images of the hot sun, sugarcane fields, tall palms, and clear blue sea. This largest Antillean island is indeed all these things, but it is also a nation with a deep-rooted, complex culture where old traditions and modernism co-exist. Dance and music are the soul of this exhilarating and vital island.

Tourism in this Caribbean nation has boomed and attracts more than three million visitors annually, mainly from Europe and Canada. Despite setbacks since the collapse of the Soviet Union in 1991, Cuba has developed its hotel and tourist infrastructure in keeping with international standards. While most travelers come to relax on the spectacular beaches and swim in the jade-colored seas, the real Cuba is to be found in the centuries-old cities and countryside, where peasant farmers still live in simple thatched houses shaded by royal palms. Creaking ox-drawn carts trundle past tobacco plantations, and lime green sugarcane fields sway in the lee of dramatic lime-stone formations, epitomized by the knoll-like *mogotes* of Valle de Viñales. Forested mountains and the largest Caribbean swamps teem with exotic wildlife, drawing both birders and hikers. Cuba's coral reefs are extremely beautiful, earning accolades from divers.

Lifestyle

Cubans are gregarious and sociable, a blend of ethnic diversity – part Asian, part Spanish, and part African. Life is lived on streets as women pull their *sillones* (rocking chairs) onto the sidewalks to gossip, while men play dominoes, smoke cigars, and share shots of aguardiente (cheap white rum). They have a passion for music and dance – the sensual undercurrent of daily life. The streets are abuzz with the sounds of *son* and salsa, reflecting their instinct for gaiety despite material hardship. Santería, the mix of Catholicism and African beliefs, plays a significant part in many people's lives and it is common to wear beads in the color of one's personal *orisha* (god).

A rhumba singer entertaining passersby on Havana's Callejón de Hammel, a street with colorful murals

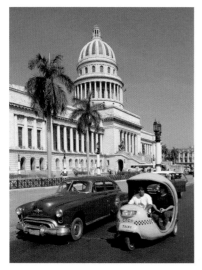
Classic Cuban car in front of El Capitolio, Havana

Vibrant, bustling Havana, a city of two million people, is filled with nightclubs simmering with sentimental allure. The modern city is adorned with buildings spanning Art Deco to Art Nouveau, while in Habana Vieja (Old Havana) the previously crumbling but now restored Baroque and Neo-Classical cathedrals and cobbled plazas are made even more surreal by the omnipresent 1950s automobiles trundling down the narrow streets to radios blaring rhumba. UNESCO has recognized the cultural and architectural importance of Old Havana, which is one of Cuba's nine World Heritage Sites.

History and Politics

Cuban heritage is steeped in struggle. The people take profound pride in their rich, often traumatic history, and monuments to the wars of Independence and the Revolution that swept away the corrupt US-backed regime of Fulgencio Batista are found in every city. For five decades Cuba has been Communist under the leadership of Fidel Castro, who stepped down in 2008 in favor of his brother Raúl Castro. Fidel Castro's larger-than-life presence is everywhere – along with that of Che Guevara – in billboards and media exhortations. Cubans are divided between those who support the socialist system and those who chaff at the restrictions on liberty. Nationalist pride that derives from the nation's freedom from US control is tempered by the dictates of a paternalistic government on which they are entirely dependent. In 2012, Cuba received its first American goods shipment in over 50 years, following a partial relaxation of the US embargo.

Culture and the Arts

Part of Cuba's appeal is its unique blend of Communism and Caribbean culture. Cabarets recall the Mafia heyday of the 1950s, while *casas de la trova* (clubs showcasing live music) keep alive traditional forms of music, such as the *son*. The Ballet Nacional de Cuba, managed by reputed ballerina Alicia Alonso, is one of the top ballet companies of the world.

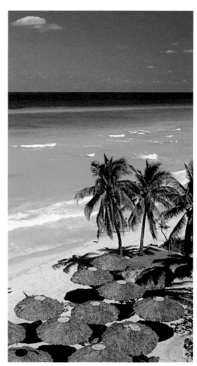
Varadero, one of Cuba's most popular beaches

Exploring Cuba

Cuba's north coast bustles with thriving resorts edged by white sands and coral reefs. Its southern coast is less developed and is a haven for crocodiles and other wildlife. Two mountain ranges dominate the west and east, while the Sierra Escambray rises over the center. In the lowlands, ox-drawn carts trundle past sugarcane fields, and dramatic limestone formations loom over lush tobacco fields. Havana, the capital city, is full of bustle and entertainment, teeming with architectural gems. Trinidad is caught in a time-warp, while Santiago de Cuba is a center for Afro-Cuban rhythms.

Locator Map

Varadero
All-inclusive hotels line the spectacular beach running the length of the long peninsula.

Habana Vieja
The castles, palaces, cathedrals, museums, and cultural venues of the capital's colonial core have been restored to their former splendor.

Trinidad
Set on a hill, with a fine beach close by, Trinidad has a restored, fully pedestrian center.

Sights at a Glance

1. Havana pp76–81
2. Cayo Largo
3. Isla de la Juventud
4. Sierra del Rosario
5. Pinar del Río
6. Valle de Viñales
8. Cayo Levisa
9. María la Gorda
10. Varadero
12. Península de Zapata
13. Cienfuegos
14. Santa Clara
15. Cayo Santa María
16. Trinidad pp86–7
17. Valle de los Ingenios
18. Topes de Collantes
19. Playa Ancón
20. Camagüey
21. Jardines del Rey p89
22. Playa Santa Lucía
23. Guardalavaca
24. Holguín
25. Bayamo
26. Santiago de Cuba
27. Baracoa

Featured Hotels and Resorts
7. Hotel Los Jazmines
11. Mansión Xanadú

0 kilometers 75
0 miles 75

Key

▭▭ Highway
▬ Major road
▭▭ Minor road
⊢⊢ Railroad
⋯⋯ Ferry route
▭▭ International border

Iglesia y Convento de San Francisco, Trinidad

Jardines del Rey

This series of offshore cays is fringed by snow-white sands and surrounded by turquoise waters. Cayo Coco is the major beach resort.

Getting Around

Cuba is a large island and the easiest way of exploring end to end is by rental car. All major cities are linked by air and train. Air-conditioned tourist buses connect important cities and beach resorts, but inter-city buses serving locals no longer accept tourists. High-speed hydrofoils run from Isla de la Juventud to Batabanó in Havana province. Tourist taxis operate throughout Havana, in the beach resorts, and at other tourist centers. Buses in and around towns are generally uncomfortable; locals also tend to rely on *bicitaxis* (bicycle rickshaws) and horse-drawn carts.

Baracoa

The oldest city in Cuba, Baracoa is famous for its cocoa. Located on a curved bay, it provides beautiful views.

Green tobacco fields in Valle de Viñales, Pinar del Río province

For keys to symbols *see back flap*

❶ Havana

One of the great historical cities of the world, Havana is a lively, vibrant capital full of architectural jewels in a medley of styles. The city is worth the trip to Cuba in its own right. Encompassing the colonial city that lay within the now largely demolished, original city walls, Habana Vieja (Old Havana) was declared a UNESCO World Heritage Site in 1982. This historic heart has regained its splendor after ongoing restoration; its castles, convents, museums, and cobbled plazas mesmerize visitors. Mementos of Havana's 20th-century heyday are concentrated in Vedado, the municipal center, and the residential Centro Habana.

View of the Catedral de San Cristóbal from Plaza de la Catedral

🏛 Plaza de la Catedral

Calles San Ignacio & Empedrado. 🔌 Museo de Arte Colonial: Calle San Ignacio 61. **Tel** (7) 862 6440. **Open** 9am–5pm daily. 🐾 🚻 🔌 🚾 without a fee.

This exquisite and intimate square was once a terminus for the Zanja Real, the royal aqueduct constructed to supply water to ships in the adjoining harbor. A plaque marks the spot now. The cobbled plaza is dominated by the Baroque profile of the **Catedral de San Cristóbal**, completed by Jesuits in 1777, with asymmetrical bell towers to each side. The Neo-Classical nave with eight side chapels is austere, as is the simple altar.
 In the 18th century, Spanish nobles built their palaces around the square. Most noteworthy is the Casa del Conde de Bayona, today housing the **Museo de Arte Colonial**, full of period furnishings. Mulatta women, dressed in colorful colonial costume, stroll the plaza and pose for photos beneath the shaded arcades. Just off the

northwest corner, is La Bodeguita del Medio bar-restaurant, where Ernest Hemingway was once a regular visitor.

🏛 Calle Mercaderes

Linking Plaza de Armas to Plaza Vieja. Maqueta de la Habana: Calle Mercaderes 114. **Tel** (7) 866 4425. **Open** 9am–6:30pm daily. 🐾 🗹 🔌 🚾 without a fee.

This narrow cobblestoned street is lined with restored colonial structures and boasts a mix of museums, restaurants, and boutiques. Not to be missed, the **Maqueta de la Habana**,

The tree-shaded Calle Mercaderes

housed in one of the buildings here, is a 1:500 scale model of Habana Vieja. The 17th-century Casa de la Obra Pía is a fine example of colonial architecture.

🏛 Calle Obispo

🔌 Farmacia Taquechel: Calle Obispo 155. **Tel** (7) 862 9286. **Open** 9am–6pm daily. 🔌

Habana Vieja's liveliest street, sloping west from Plaza de Armas (see pp78–9) to Parque Central, is the pedestrianized Calle Obispo, which bustles with commercial activity just as it did in colonial days. At its west end, El Floridita is where Ernest Hemingway famously downed daiquiris; today his bronze likeness rests an elbow at the bar. His room (No. 511) at Hotel Ambos Mundos (see p97) is preserved as a museum. Another interesting site is **Farmacia Taquechel**, an old pharmacy with apothecary jars lining the shelves.

🏛 Plaza de San Francisco

Calle Oficios. 🔌 Basílica Menor de San Francisco de Asís: Calles Oficios y Amargura. **Tel** (7) 862 9683. **Open** 9am–5:30pm Mon–Fri, 11:30am–7pm Sat. 🐾 🗹 🔌 🚾 without a fee.

Next to the modern cruise-ship terminal, this airy cobbled square once opened onto the colonial waterfront. At its heart, the marble Fuente de los Leones, guarded by lions, is modeled on a fountain in the Alhambra in Spain. To the north is the restored Neo-Classical Lonja del Comercio, the former commerce exchange, crowned by a winged statue of Mercury. Dominating the square, the **Basílica Menor de San Francisco de Asís** dates back to the 1580s, although it was rebuilt in 1730. In 1762, the British seized Havana and began worshipping in the church. Today it is a concert hall and the adjoining convent is a museum of religious art.

🏛 Plaza Vieja

Calles Mercaderes & Brasil. 🔌 "Old Square" began as Plaza Nueva (New Square) in 1587 and served as Havana's

Façade of the colonial Casa del Conde de Jaruco, Plaza Vieja

main market place and
bullfight arena. Buildings from
four centuries surround the
plaza, which has been restored,
complete with a fountain
replicating the original. **Casa
del Conde de Jaruco**, built
between 1733 and 37 on the
southeast corner, features
colonial details, including
mediopuntos (half-moon
stained-glass windows). The
Palacio Cueto is an astonishing
Art Nouveau building,
currently being converted
into a hotel.

Ecclesiastical Quarter
S of Plaza Vieja. Convento de Santa
Clara: Calle Cuba 610. **Tel** (7) 861 3335.
Open 9am–5pm Mon–Fri.
Iglesia de Nuestra Señora de la Merced:
Calle Cuba 806. **Tel** (7) 863 8873.
Open 8am–noon & 3–5:30pm daily.
Casa-Museo José Martí: Calle
Leonor Pérez 314. **Tel** (7) 861 3778.
Open 9am–5pm Tue–Sat.

Southern Habana Vieja was in
colonial days a major ecclesi-
astical center and has many
convents and churches. The
charming 17th-century
Convento de Santa Clara is an

outstanding example of colonial
architecture. A part of it is today a
posada-style hotel. The **Iglesia de
Nuestra Señora de la Merced**,
with a lavish interior and frescoed
dome ceiling, is popular with
followers of both the Catholic and
Santería(Afro-Cuban) religions.

Casa-Museo José Martí,
almost a religious shrine to
Cubans, is the birthplace of
Cuba's foremost national figure,
José Martí (see p80). The simple
home of the hero is now a
museum. Visitors can view
paintings, furniture, and some
of his written works.

Havana City Center

Key

Street-by-Street area
see pp78–9

Street-by-Street: Plaza de Armas

This elegant cobbled plaza was laid out in its current guise during the 1600s, when it served as a military parade ground (Plaza de Armas) and the center of government. At its heart, a small leafy park is ringed on most days by stalls selling secondhand books. The square is framed by Baroque and Neo-Classical buildings, which have been painstakingly restored in recent years. Benches and cafés provide relaxing spots to sit and absorb the colonial atmosphere.

Palacio del Segundo Cabo (1776)
The former residence of the Spanish lieutenant-governor is now the home of the Cuban Book Institute.

★ Palacio de los Capitanes Generales
A grand Baroque palace, this building served as the governor's mansion. Now the Museo de la Ciudad, it provides an insight into Havana's history with exhibits ranging from the remains of the Espada Cemetery to mementos from the independence wars.

Hotel Ambos Mundo
The typewriter and desk of Ernest Hemingway are preserved in the bedroom at this hotel. It is here that he wrote the famous novel, *For Whom the Bell Tolls* (1940).

Plaza de la Catedral
(see p76)

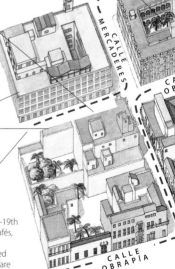

Former Ministerio de Educación

Farmacia Taquechel

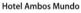

Calle Obispo
Lined with buildings dating from the 16th–19th centuries as well as cafés, shops, galleries, and museums, this cobbled pedestrian thoroughfare is the district's liveliest.

★ **Castillo de la Real Fuerza**
Completed in 1582, this is the oldest fortress in Havana (and one of the oldest in the Americas, according to UNESCO). It features a broad moat and angular ramparts. In 1634, a weathervane known as La Giraldilla was placed on a lookout tower over the western rampart and soon became a symbol of the city. Today, the Castillo houses a maritime museum.

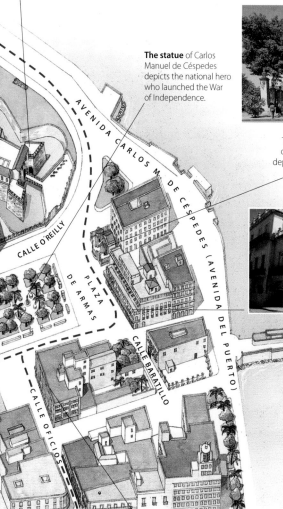

The statue of Carlos Manuel de Céspedes depicts the national hero who launched the War of Independence.

★ **El Templete**
The Neo-Classical temple stands on the site of the city's first mass, depicted on a wall-to-wall triptych. A sacred ceiba stands outside.

Hotel Santa Isabel
Former home of the Count of Santovenia, this Neo-Classical structure was built during the 18th century.

| 0 meters | 60 |
| 0 yards | 60 |

Museo Nacional de Historia Natural has excellent exhibits on Cuba's flora and fauna.

Key

— Suggested route

🏛 Fábrica de Tabacos Partagás

Calle Industria 520. **Tel** (7) 863 5766. **Open** 9–11am & noon–3pm Mon–Fri. **Closed** public hols. 🎟 for a fee. 📷

This four-story, 19th-century cigar factory has a Spanish-style industrial façade with pilasters and a Baroque roof-line. It was founded by Jaime Partagás Ravelo, a Catalan businessman. Visitors can take in aromatic tobacco scents and witness the hand-rolling of premium cigars for export.

🏛 Capitolio
See p81.

🌳 Parque Central

Paseo de Martí at Calle Neptuno. ♿ This spacious park, the informal center of the city, serves as the major gateway between Habana Vieja and the modern districts to the west. Designed in 1877, the park has a statue of José Martí in its center. Gracious structures surround the park, including the Hotel Inglaterra and Hotel Plaza, notable for their elegant 19th-century façades. Most striking is the Gran Teatro de la Habana, a Baroque confection adorned with statues.

🏛 Museo Nacional de Bellas Artes

Palacio de Bellas Artes, Trocadero e/ Zulueta y Monserrate. Centro Asturiano: San Rafael y Zulueta. **Tel** (7) 861 0241. **Open** 10am–6pm Tue–Sat, 10am–2pm Sun. **Closed** public hols. 📷 🎟 ♿ ✉ 📷 **W** museonacional.cult.cu

Havana's National Fine Arts Museum displays an astonishingly rich trove in two buildings. The **Palacio de Bellas Artes** is

given over to Cuban art, with sections that are devoted to colonial and 20th-century works. The **Centro Asturiano**, on the other hand, houses international works, including those of European masters, plus a collection of Egyptian, Greek, and Roman antiquities.

Hawker Sea Fury F50 airplane inside the Museo de la Revolución

🏛 Museo de la Revolución

Calle Refugio 1 e/ Zulueta y Monserrate. **Tel** (7) 862 4091. **Open** 10am–5pm daily. 📷 🎟 ✉ without payment. 📷 📷

Housed in the extravagantly eclectic former presidential palace inaugurated in 1920, the Museo de la Revolución dramatizes the Cuban struggle for independence, from the colonial era to the current day. Most exhibits depict the revolution that toppled

dictator Fulgencio Batista. To the rear, the Granma Memorial displays military hardware related to the Bay of Pigs invasion in 1961 (see p85).

🏛 Prado

Between Parque Central and Malecón. ♿

Officially named Paseo de Martí, this tree-shaded boulevard was redesigned in 1927 by French architect Forestier and features a raised walkway adorned with bronze lions, wrought-iron lampposts, and marble benches. The many Neo-Moorish buildings include the Hotel Sevilla, from 1908. Nearby, Havana's main wedding venue, the beautiful Neo-Baroque Palacio de los Matrimonios, has an ornately stuccoed interior.

🏛 Malecón

Between Prado and Río Almenderes. 📷

The sinuous seafront Malecón boulevard is Havana's main thoroughfare. It is lined with fanciful buildings and, in the Vedado district, high-rise hotels. Highlights include the Monumento al Maine, a memorial to sailors killed when the USS Maine exploded in the Havana harbor on February 15, 1898.

🏨 Hotel Nacional

Calles O & 21. **Tel** (7) 836 3564. 📷 **W** hotelnacionaldecuba.com

Overlooking the Malecón, this gem of an Art Deco building opened in 1930. It features a lavish Moorish interior, while cannons stud the lawns. Considered Havana's finest hotel, its illustrious guest list includes Churchill, Sinatra, Ava Gardner, and Hemingway.

José Martí (1853–95)

Born in Havana in 1853, José Martí became a nationalist in his youth and was imprisoned by the Spanish for treason at 16. He was later exiled and, after settling in New York, led the campaign for Cuban independence. A prodigious writer and philosopher, he also championed the cause of social justice. In 1895 he returned to Cuba with General Máximo Gómez to lead the War of Independence. On May 19 the same year, he was killed in action at Dos Ríos.

Statue of José Martí

The tree-lined Prado, also known as Paseo de Martí

🛏 Hotel Tryp Habana Libre

Calles L & 23. **Tel** (7) 834 6100. 🚗 ♿
🌐 meliacuba.com

A Havana landmark, this modernist high-rise hotel atop La Rampa opened as the Havana Hilton in 1958. A spectacular mural, *Carro de la Revolución*, adorns the *porte cochère* entrance, and the atrium lobby features modernist art pieces.

🏛 Cementerio Colón

Zapata y Calle 12. **Tel** (7) 832 1050. **Open** 8am–5pm daily. 🚗 📷 for a fee. ♿ 📹 without payment.

Havana's vast cemetery covers 135 acres (56 ha) and was arranged in a strict grid in the

1870s. It has been named a National Historic Monument for its spectacular mausoleums in eclectic styles, from Neo-Classical to Avant-Garde. At its core is the Capilla Central, a chapel with lavish frescoes.

🏛 Plaza de la Revolución

Paseo between Av. Carlos M. de Céspedes & Av. Rancho Boyeros. 7

This monumental plaza has been Cuba's political and administrative center since it was laid out in the 1950s as Plaza Cívica. It is the main center for political rallies. The façade of the Ministerio del Interior is adorned with a seven-story high steel sculpture of Che Guevara. Dominating the plaza,

the Memorial José Martí features a marble statue of the national hero backed by a star-shaped tower with the Museo de José Martí at its base. Behind the memorial are the main government headquarters.

🏛 Museo Ernest Hemingway

Calle Vigía y Steinhart, San Francisco de Paula. **Tel** (7) 891 0809. **Open** 10am–5pm Mon–Sat, 10am–1pm Sun. 🚗 📷 📹 without payment. 📷

Ernest Hemingway's former home, Finca Vigía, is maintained as the author left it, with his possessions in situ. Visitors, not allowed to enter inside, can look through the open windows and door.

Capitolio

The most imposing Neo-Classical structure in Havana, El Capitolio was inaugurated in 1929 by the dictator General Gerardo Machado. An imitation of the Washington DC Capitol, Cuba's former congressional building served as seat of government until 1959. Now closed for renovation in advance of use, once again, as the home of Cuba's National Assembly, the building is still worth seeing from the outside. The interior and exterior will be restored to their former glory.

VISITORS' CHECKLIST

Practical Information
Paseo de Martí esq. San José.
Closed for renovations.

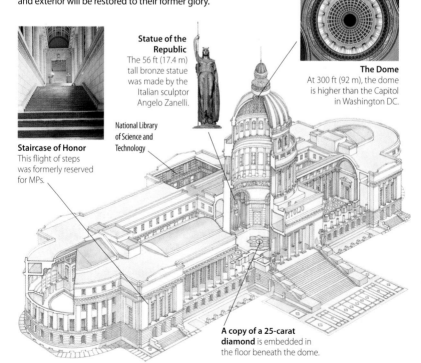

Statue of the Republic
The 56 ft (17.4 m) tall bronze statue was made by the Italian sculptor Angelo Zanelli.

The Dome
At 300 ft (92 m), the dome is higher than the Capitol in Washington DC.

National Library of Science and Technology

Staircase of Honor
This flight of steps was formerly reserved for MPs.

A copy of a 25-carat diamond is embedded in the floor beneath the dome.

White sandy beach of Cayo Largo

❷ Cayo Largo

112 miles (180 km) S of Havana.

This narrow isle, with its white sands shelving into turquoise waters, is a long-established holiday destination. Sailing, watersports, and horse-riding are offered by all-inclusive resorts served by charter flights and overnight excursions from Havana. Visitors can spend time swimming or relaxing on a beach. Iguanas patrol the craggy shoreline, and marine turtles are often seen by divers.

❸ Isla de la Juventud

94 miles (150 km) S of Havana.
daily from Batabanó.

The "Isle of Youth" has few major tourist draws, and hence offers a genuine Cuban experience. Sleepy Nueva Gerona is the main town with colonial homes. The isle's main draw is **Presidio**

Modelo, a former prison, now a museum, where Fidel Castro and his men were jailed after they attacked the Moncada Barracks in July 1953.

On the southwest shore, Hotel El Colony at Siguanea Bay is a base for diving to coral formations and shipwrecks. To the south, **Parque Natural Punta Francés** offers good viewing, with a crocodile farm and pre-Columbian petroglyphs at Cuevas de Punta del Este.

▥ Presidio Modelo
3 miles (5 km) E of Nueva Gerona.
Tel (46) 32 5112. **Open** 9am–4pm Tue–Sat, 9am–noon Sun.

✹ Parque Natural Punta Francés
25 miles (40 km) S of Nueva Gerona.
Tel (46) 32 7101. ℹ Ecotur, Calles 24 esq, 47 Nueva Gerona. from Ecotur.

Key
— Highway
— Major road
— Minor road
— Unpaved road

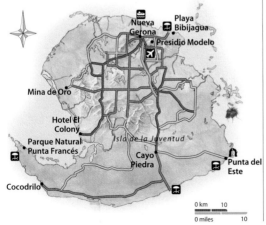

❹ Sierra del Rosario

54 miles (87 km) W of Havana. ⓣ

Covered with tropical forests, this rugged mountain chain delights birders and hikers. At its eastern end, the lovely rural community of **Las Terrazas** is Cuba's premier ecological center. Nearby Soroa is known for its **Orquideario** (orchid garden) and the Saltón waterfall.

✹ Las Terrazas
Autopista Habana-Pinar del Río Km51.
Tel (48) 57 8600. **Open** 9am–5pm daily.

❂ Orquideario
Carretera de Soroa Km8. **Tel** (48) 52 3871. **Open** 8:30am–4:30pm daily. ❂ compulsory. ♿ without payment.

Façade of the Palacio de Guasch, Pinar del Río

❺ Pinar del Río

109 miles (175 km) SW of Havana.
190,000.

Founded in 1669, the orderly provincial capital is graced by Classical and Art Nouveau columns. Most buildings of note line Calle Martí. The Museo de Ciencias Naturales, in the **Palacio de Guasch**, displays native flora and fauna. The Neo-Classical Teatro Milanés dates back to 1835. Visitors can watch cigars being hand-rolled at the **Fábrica de Tabacos Francisco Donatién**.

Fábrica de Tabacos Francisco Donatién
Calle Maceo Oeste 157.
Tel (48) 77 3069. **Open** 9am–noon & 1–4pm Mon–Fri, 9am–noon Sat–Sun.

❽ Cayo Levisa

🚉 155 miles (250 km) W of Havana.
Tel (48) 75 6501. 🏨 🍴 🏖 🛶 🤿 ⛴
👤 🌐 **cubanacan.cu**

This tiny island off the north coast, ringed by white sands and mangroves, has a namesake hotel, the only one in the Los Colorados archipelago. The isle is geared for diving and has spectacular coral reefs. Sportfishing is also good, notably for marlin.

❾ María la Gorda

🚉 193 miles (310 km) SW of Havana.
Tel (48) 77 8131. 🏨 🏖 👤
🌐 **gaviota-grupo.com**

Sunbathers can enjoy the fine sands of this renowned bathing-spot at the far west end of Cuba. The crystal-clear waters teem with extraordinarily beautiful coral reefs and marine life that includes whale sharks.

Environs
The Bahía de Corrientes forms the underbelly of the Península de Guanahacabibes, a rare tropical dry deciduous forest protected within the **Reserva de la Biosfera Península de Guanahacabibes**.

Mural de la Prehistoria by Leovigildo González, Valle de Viñales

❻ Valle de Viñales

127 miles (205 km) W of Havana. 🚌

The lyrical landscapes of the broad Viñales Valley are the most quintessential in Cuba. Giant *mogotes*, karst formations resembling beehives, stand over this and adjoining valleys that comprise a quilt-work of thatched peasants' huts and tobacco fields shaded by royal palms.

Caves riddle the *mogotes*. The **Cueva del Indio** has an underground lake and river, and can be explored by boat excursions. There is even a nightclub that features a cabaret show in Cueva de San Miguel. Between 1959 and 1962, Mogote Dos Hermanos was brightly painted with the **Mural de la Prehistoria**, a modern depiction of evolution.

The village of Viñales is a rural charmer. Its main street, Calle Salvador Cisneros, is lined with beautiful red-tile-roofed colonial homes fronted by columned arcades. Parque Martí, the village square, has a lovely church – the Iglesia del Sagrado Corazón de Jesús – as well as the Casa de la Cultura, where many cultural events are held.

🗻 **Cueva del Indio**
3 miles (5 km) N of Viñales.
Tel (48) 79 6280. **Open** 9am–5pm daily. 🏞 🅿 🎁

🗻 **Mural de la Prehistoria**
3 miles (5 km) W of Viñales.
Tel (48) 79 6260. **Open** 8am–7pm daily. 🏞 ♿ 🅿

❼ Hotel Los Jazmines

🏨 Carretera de Viñales Km25.
Tel (48) 79 6205. 🅿 ♿
🌐 **cubanacan.cu**

Enjoying a superb location atop the southern flank of the magnificent Viñales Valley, Hotel Los Jazmines is popular for the unsurpassed views it offers. The pool sundeck hovers over the cliff-face. The main building, dating from the 1930s, features classic colonial elements such as *mediopuntos*.

Mogotes

Mogotes are the remains of an ancient limestone plateau. Over eons, underground rivers eroded the soft limestone, forming vast caverns whose ceilings eventually collapsed. The pillars left standing, the present-day *mogotes*, have become covered with protective vegetation that includes endemic plants and even some reptile species found only here.

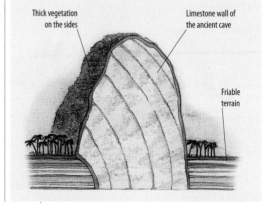

Thick vegetation on the sides

Limestone wall of the ancient cave

Friable terrain

For hotels and restaurants on this island see pp96–9 and pp100–1

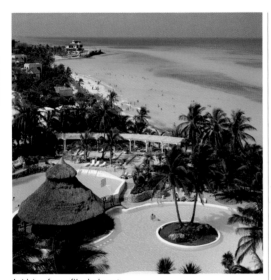

Aerial view of some of Varadero's resorts

⑩ Varadero

🚆 90 miles (145 km) E of Havana.
✈️ 🏊 🚣 ⛴️

One of Cuba's top resort areas
occupies the 12-mile (19-km)
pencil-thin Península de
Hicacos, lined by stunning
white beaches along its Atlantic
seaboard. Once a private
playground for Cuba's elite,
today Varadero is the island's
main tourist destination; still off-
limits to the majority of Cubans.
The dozens of all-inclusive
hotels here all offer watersports,
with scuba diving being the
main draw. The Varadero Golf
Club (see p95) is Cuba's first
18-hole course. Visitors can
enjoy swimming with dolphins
at the **Delfinario**.

Environs
Most visitors to Varadero take
excursions to nearby sites,
including **Matanzas**, a historic
port city with a cathedral, plaza,
and theater, and the **Cuevas de
Bellamar**, which feature
fascinating dripstone formations.
The **Museo Municipal Oscar
María de Rojas**, in the town
of Cárdenas, dates back to
1900 and is among the oldest
museums on the island. It has
an eclectic collection of shells,
butterflies, colonial weapons,
and stuffed animals.

🐬 **Delfinario**
Autopista Sur Km11. **Tel** (45) 66 8031.
Open 9am–5pm daily. 🐬 extra
charge to swim with dolphins.
📷 without payment.

⑪ Mansión Xanadú

🏌️ Carretera Las Americas.
Tel (45) 66 8482. 🍴 🅿️
🌐 **varaderogolfclub.com**

US billionaire Alfred Irénée
du Pont owned much of
Varadero in the 1920s, and
built this grand marble-and-
mahogany villa atop the cliffs.
It is now a deluxe hotel with an
elegant restaurant and bar.

⑫ Península de Zapata

125 miles (202 km) SE of Havana
🏢 ✅

This vast peninsula, with the
Caribbean's largest swamp,
is protected in the Gran
Parque Natural Montemar.
Crocodiles and flamingos are
among the wildlife that can be
seen here. **Boca de Guamá**, the
main tourist center of the area,
has a crocodile farm. Playa Larga
has a good beach and its namesake hotel makes a good base
for exploration.

Environs
North of the Boca de Guamá is
Central Australia, former sugar
factory and Fidel Castro's
headquarters during the 1961
Bay of Pigs invasion. It now
houses the intriguing **Museo
Memorial Comandancia de la
FAR**, the displays of which recall
the invasion. The main landing
of the CIA-backed counter-
revolutionaries occurred at
Playa Girón, a beach where the
Museo Playa Girón exhibits
military hardware.

🐊 **Boca de Guamá**
Carretera Playa Larga Km16. **Tel** (45)
91 5551. **Open** 7am–7pm daily. ♿
🅿️ 🖥️ 📷

🏛️ **Museo Memorial
Comandancia de la FAR**
Australia. **Tel** (45) 91 2504. **Open**
9am–5pm Tue–Sun. 🎫 ✅ ♿
📷 without payment.

Boat ride through a lake, Boca de Guamá, Península de Zapata

Statue of Sleeping Beauty at La Reina cemetery, Cienfuegos

⓭ Cienfuegos

150 miles (242 km) E of Havana.
🏔 160,000. ✈ 🚇 🚌

This provincial capital, in a bay on Cuba's south coast, was founded in 1819. Its well-preserved historic core is replete with buildings of note, centered around spacious Parque Martí. The Neo-Classical Teatro Tomás Terry and the Catedral de la Purísima Concepción, dating from 1870, are not to be missed. Nearby, the **Cementerio La Reina**'s Neo-Classical marble tombs are fascinating. The graceful Paseo del Prado crosses the historic center and leads to the Punta Gorda district, tipped by the **Palacio de Valle** – a Mughal-inspired mansion built in 1917, that now houses a restaurant.

Vase, Museo de Artes Decorativas

Environs
The **Jardín Botánico Soledad**, located 9 miles (15 km) from Cienfuegos, is one of Latin America's foremost botanical gardens with a special area dedicated to cacti. Just southeast of here rises the Sierra Escambray with several trails leading to waterfalls and coffee estates.

🏛 **Palacio de Valle**
Calle 37 Y2. **Tel** (43) 55 1003.
Open 10am–11pm daily.

🌿 **Jardín Botánico Soledad**
Calle Central 136, Pepito Tey. **Tel** (43) 54 5115. **Open** 8am–5pm daily.
Closed public hols. 🎫 📷 🏛

⓮ Santa Clara

170 miles (274 km) E of Havana.
🏔 220,000. 🚌

A sprawling industrial and university city, Santa Clara is famous for a single historical event: in 1958 it was here that the final battle that led to dictator Batista's ouster took place. The **Monumento Tren Blindado**, a re-creation of a troop train derailed by Che Guevara's guerrillas on December 28, 1958, is worth a visit. At the **Monumento Ernesto Che Guevara**, a bronze statue of the "heroic guerrilla" stands atop a plinth featuring bas-reliefs and inscriptions. Below the plinth is the Museo de Che, with displays of his life and role in the revolution.

The main square, Parque Leoncio Vidal, has some fine colonial buildings, including the Neo-Classical Teatro de la Caridad and the **Museo de Artes Decorativas**, with its period furnishings from the 17th–20th centuries.

Environs
North of the city, the **Vuelta Arriba** region is a scenic center of tobacco production. In its midst, **Remedios** is a sleepy colonial town that bursts to life during Christmas festivities, when competing teams host a fireworks battle.

🏛 **Monumento Tren Blindado**
Carretera Camujuani. **Tel** (42) 20 2758.
Open 9am–5:30pm Mon–Sat. 🎫 ♿

🏛 **Monumento Ernesto Che Guevara**
Av. de los Desfiles. **Tel** (42) 20 5878.
Open Museo de Che: 9:30am–5pm Tue–Sun. ♿

🏛 **Museo de Artes Decorativas**
Calle Martha Abreu y Luis Estévez.
Tel (42) 20 5368. **Open** 9am–6pm Mon, Wed & Thu, 1–10pm Fri–Sat, 6–10pm Sun. 🎫 📷 ♿

⓯ Cayo Santa María

🏖 220 miles (354 km) E of Havana.
🎣 🏖 🤿

This beach-fringed isle off the coast of Villa Clara province, at the western end of the Jardines del Rey (see p89), is accessed by a 30-mile (48-km) long *pedraplen* (causeway). Several deluxe hotels have been built, and more are planned here and on neighboring Cayo Las Brujas. Fishing and scuba diving are prime draws while the mangroves lining the inner shore are good for bird-watching.

Bay of Pigs Invasion

The long narrow Bahía de Cochinos (Bay of Pigs) was the setting for the landing of 1,400 CIA-trained anti-Castro Cuban exiles on April 16, 1961. Fidel Castro took charge of the defense. After three days of intense fighting that involved US and Soviet tanks, the US withdrew its air support and the abandoned invaders were defeated. After 20 months in prison, the captured exiles were exchanged for medicines.

POWs captured by Castro's men board a plane for Miami

⑯ Trinidad

Founded by Diego Velázquez in 1514, this city was declared a UNESCO World Heritage Site in 1988. From the 1600s to the 1800s, Trinidad was a major center for the sugar and slave trades, and the fine buildings in the heart of the city reflect the wealth of the leading landowners of the time. A long period of isolation from the 1850s until the 1950s protected the city from any radical change. The historic center has been restored, and the original cobblestone streets and pastel-colored houses give the impression that time and life here have scarcely moved on since colonial times.

★ Iglesia y Convento de San Francisco
The church bell tower offers fine views, while the monastery houses the Museo de la Lucha Contra Bandidos (Museum of the Fight Against Counter-Revolutionaries).

★ Museo Romántico
Formerly the Palacio Brunet, this mansion is now a museum exhibiting colonial furnishings of the wealthy.

Nuestra Señora de la Popa

CALLE HERNÁND ECHERRI

CALLE PIRO GUINART

Key
— Suggested route

Canchánchara
This typical *casa de infusiones*, housed in an 18th-century building, is known for its namesake cocktail *canchánchara*, made from rum, lime, water, and honey. Live music is played here.

0 meters   100
0 yards   100

Plazuela del Jigüe, named for its acacia tree (*jigüe*), was the site of the first mass in Trinidad, in 1514.

Ayuntamiento y Cárcel, the old town hall and jail, has a portion of wall exposed to show the original stone-and-lime masonry.

Iglesia Parroquial de la Santísima Trinidad

With an austere façade, the church of the Holy Trinity was built in 1894 replacing another church. The interior has an impressive carved wooden altar with inlaid wood.

Casa de la Música

The Casa de los Conspiradores, today an Italian-run art gallery and restaurant, was the meeting place of the secret society, La Rosa de Cuba.

CALLE LUMUMBA

La Casa de la Trova
Located on Plazuela de Segarte, this is a popular venue for traditional live music and hosts music sessions in the afternoon and evening.

PLAZA MAYOR

CALLE JAVIER

LE MARTÍNEZ VILLENA

CALLE SIMÓN BOLÍVAR

Museo de Arquitectura Colonial
Housed in the restored Casa de los Sánchez Iznaga, this museum displays Trinidadian architecture.

 Casa de la Cultura

★ **Palacio Cantero**
This early 19th-century Neo-Classical gem houses the Museo Histórico Municipal, which recounts local history. Its tower has fine views over the city.

Valle de los Ingenios against the backdrop of the Sierra Escambray

⓱ Valle de los Ingenios

6 miles (10 km) E of Trinidad. 🚌
🍴 daily at Hacienda Iznaga.

This broad fertile valley is named for the numerous *ingenios* (sugar mills) located here during the late 18th and 19th centuries. The sweeping cane fields still remain but the sugar mills are mostly relics. **Manaca Iznaga** is an exception where the estate owner's mansion is now a restaurant. The 147-ft (45-m) high seven-story tower allows great views. Nearby, Sitio Histórico Guaímaro is being restored as a museum; the estate house has splendid murals. Take in the view at **El Mirador**, a hilltop lookout east of Trinidad.

🚌 Manaca Iznaga
Iznaga, 9 miles (14 km) E of Trinidad.
Tel (41) 99 7241. **Open** 9am–5pm daily. 🚻 ♿ ✏

El Mirador
3 miles (5 km) E of Trinidad.
Open 8am–5pm daily. 📷

⓲ Topes de Collantes

14 miles (21 km) NW of Trinidad.
ℹ Hotel Los Helechos, (41) 54 0231.
🚶 through Gaviota Tours. ✏ 🚶

The pristine alpine forests of the Sierra Escambray can best be experienced at the Topes de Collantes mountain retreat, 2,625 ft (800 m) above sea level. The Kurhotel solarium here is used as a recuperative clinic. Hikes lead to Salto de Caburní and its 250-ft (75-m) waterfall,

and to the Hacienda Codina coffee estate, with an orchid garden and medicinal mud pools. The **Museo de Arte Cubano Contemporáneo** displays modern works by famous artists.

🏛 Museo de Arte Cubano Contemporáneo
Topes de Collantes. **Open** 8am–8pm daily. 📷

⓳ Playa Ancón

🚌 6 miles (10 km) S of Trinidad.
🏖 🚶 ♿ 🛥 🚶

Lining the tendril-thin Ancón peninsula, this lovely white beach is lapped by warm turquoise waters. Gorgeous coral reefs tempt divers, most notably at Cayo Blanco, a 20-minute boat ride away. La Boca, a village with a rocky beach at the neck of the peninsula, is popular with Cubans.

⓴ Camagüey

165 miles (265 km) E of Trinidad.
🚇 320,000. ✈ 🚌 🚌 ℹ Infotur, Ignacio Agramonte International Airport, (32) 26 5807. 📅 Jornadas de la Cultura Camagüeyana (early Feb).

Surrounded by pastures, Cuba's third-largest city is known for its *tinajones* – large earthenware jars once used for collecting and storing water. The large historic center was laid out in an irregular fashion – an apparent attempt to confuse pirates – and is rich in colonial plazas.

Palm-shaded Parque Ignacio Agramonte is pinned by an equestrian statue of Ignacio Agramonte, a local independence hero, and by the Catedral de Nuestra Señora de la Candelaria, built in 1757.

The cobbled and colorful Plaza San Juan de Díos is ringed by quaint examples of vernacular architecture, plus the Iglesia de San Juan de Díos. Life-size figures of real-life residents adorn the restored **Plaza del Carmen**. The triangular Plaza de los Trabajadores draws visitors to the Casa Natal de Ignacio Agramonte (birthplace of Agramonte) and the Baroque Iglesia de la Merced, which contains a Holy Sepulcher, cast from silver coins. The acclaimed Ballet de Camagüey performs at the **Teatro Principal**, built in Neo-Classical style.

Teatro Principal
Calle Pedro Valencia 64. **Tel** (32) 29 3048. **Open** 9am–5pm daily (ballet shows usually from 8pm). 📷 ♿

Ceramic statue alongside real-life resident at the Plaza del Carmen, Camagüey

For hotels and restaurants on this island see pp96–9 and pp100–1

㉑ Jardines del Rey

Sprinkled like diamonds off the north coast of Ciego de Ávila and Camagüey provinces, the 400 or so isles of the Archipiélago del Jardines del Rey (King's Garden) stretch for almost 300 miles (500 km). Covered in mangroves and scrub, almost all are uninhabited except by wild pigs, iguanas, and waterfowl, while flamingos, spoonbills, and ibis dot the shallows that separate the cays from the mainland. Lovely beaches line the Atlantic shores and are slated to receive dozens of new hotels in the future. Current development is limited to Cayo Coco and Cayo Guillermo, served by their own international airport.

VISITORS' CHECKLIST

Practical Information
133 miles (215 km) NE of Trinidad.
Infotur, Aeropuerto Jardines del Rey, Cayo Coco, (33) 30 9109; Cubatur Cayo Coco, (33) 30 1436.

Transport

Cayo Coco
With 14 miles (22 km) of fine sugary beaches, the watersports here are a major attraction and the diving on offer is superb.

Cayo Guillermo
This small cay has a number of hotels plus a marina. The inshore mangroves serve as a nesting site for seabirds. Playa Pilar has huge sand dunes.

Cayo Romano is the largest island in the archipelago.

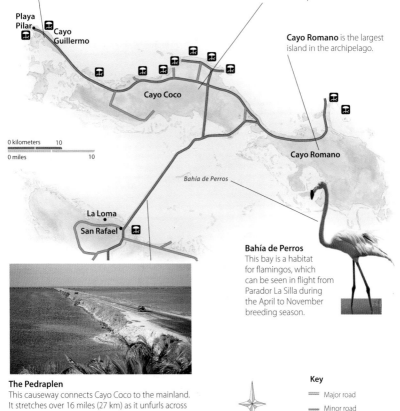

Playa Pilar • Cayo Guillermo

Cayo Coco

Cayo Romano

Bahía de Perros

La Loma •
San Rafael •

0 kilometers 10
0 miles 10

Bahía de Perros
This bay is a habitat for flamingos, which can be seen in flight from Parador La Silla during the April to November breeding season.

The Pedraplen
This causeway connects Cayo Coco to the mainland. It stretches over 16 miles (27 km) as it unfurls across Bahía de Perros.

Key
— Major road
— Minor road

For keys to symbols *see back flap*

㉒ Playa Santa Lucía

338 miles (544 km) E of Havana.

This gorgeous beach resort stretches along 13 miles (21 km) of barren shoreline. Turquoise waters feature beautiful coral reefs and scuba diving is the main draw. Playa Los Cocos, at the western end of Santa Lucía, is a ramshackle fishing village with the most spectacular beach.

㉓ Guardalavaca

450 miles (724 km) E from Havana.

Cuba's third largest beach resort area is being expanded; with new all-inclusive hotels appearing at the western end while the original mid-1980s resort overlooks Playa Guardalavaca. Separating them, Bahía de Naranjo has wildlife-rich nature trails plus an aquarium with dolphin and sea lion shows. Not far away, **Chorro de Maíta** is the largest pre-Columbian necropolis unearthed in the Caribbean. It has skeletons in situ, and an *aldea taína* – a reconstructed pre-Columbian village.

Artifact, Museo
Provincial de Historia

🏠 Chorro de Maíta
3 miles (5 km) E of Guardalavaca. **Tel** (24) 43 0421. **Open** 9am–5pm daily. 🖼 🚻 ✉ without payment.

Blue waters and sandy beach, Guardalavaca

Green and tranquil Parque Céspedes in Bayamo

㉔ Holguín

460 miles (740 km) SE of Havana.
345,000. ✈ 🚌 🚍 🚕
Romerías de Mayo (May 3).

Full of leafy colonial squares, this large city is an industrial center. Holguín was freed from Spanish rule in 1872 by General Calixto García, whose birthplace is east of Parque Calixto García. To the plaza's north, the **Museo Provincial de Historia** features pre-Columbian exhibits. Catedral de San Isidro, completed in 1720, stands over Parque Peralta, and Plaza San José boasts a fine church and colonial houses. About 458 stairs lead to the top of Loma de la Cruz, which has great views.

Environs
An hour's drive east of Holguín is **Sitio Histórico de Birán**, Fidel Castro's birthplace at Finca Manacas, which is open to visitors. Gorgeous valley views can be enjoyed from **Mirador del Mayabe**, 6 miles (10 km) southeast of town, which has an *aldea campesino* (re-created farmer's village).

🏛 Museo Provincial de Historia
Calle Frexes 198. **Tel** (24) 46 3395. **Open** 8am–5pm Tue–Sat, 8am–noon Sun. **Closed** public hols. 🖼 🚻 ✉ without payment.

🏛 Sitio Histórico de Birán
Finca Manacas. **Tel** (24) 28 6114. **Open** 9am–4pm Tue–Sat, 9am–noon Sun. **Closed** public hols. 🖼 🎦 ✉ without payment.

㉕ Bayamo

423 miles (680 km) SE from Havana.
220,000. ✈ 🚍 🛈 Infotur, Plaza del Himno, (23) 42 3468.

Founded in 1513, Cuba's second oldest city was devastated by fire in 1876, during the Ten Years' War. Parque Céspedes, the main square, is overlooked by interesting buildings, including **Casa Natal de Carlos Manuel de Céspedes**, birthplace of the man behind Cuba's quest for independence, and the lovely church, Iglesia Parroquial Mayor de San Salvador.

Environs
To the south lies the rugged **Sierra Maestra** mountain chain, and hikes to the 6,476-ft (1,974-m) Pico Turquino are possible from San Rafael.

Casa Natal de Carlos Manuel de Céspedes
Calle Maceo 57. **Tel** (23) 42 3864. **Open** 9am–5pm Tue–Sat, 9am–1pm Sun. 🖼 🎦 🚻

For hotels and restaurants on this island see pp96–9 and see pp100–1

㉖ Santiago de Cuba

535 miles (862 km) SE from Havana.
470,000. Infotur,
Parque Céspedes, (22) 66 9401.
Carnival (Jul 26).

Santiago, the most African of
Cuban cities, and the second
largest, is lively and exciting:
Santiagueros are passionate
about music and dance,
especially during Carnival.
Founded by Diego Velázquez in
1514, it has a gently sloping
historic core, overlooking
a huge flask-shaped bay.
At its heart, the bustling
Parque Céspedes is
surrounded by fine
buildings: the
Ayuntamiento (town
hall); the mostly
20th-century Neo-
Classical Catedral de
la Asunción; and the
Casa de Diego
Velázquez, the
original governor's 1522
mansion superbly maintained
as the **Museo de Ambiente
Histórico Cubano**. Hotel Casa
Granda's patio *(see p98)* is a
marvelous spot for a mojito and
has fine views over the plaza.

Calle Heredia is lined with
historic buildings. Not to be
missed are the Casa de la Trova
for traditional music, the Museo
del Carnaval, and the **Museo
Municipal Emilio Bacardí
Moreau**, with vast, eclectic
displays ranging from Egyptian
mummies to modern art.

Sprawling in a half-moon
around the historic core,

Detail of Maceo's statue, Plaza
de la Revolución

Santiago's 20th-century districts
are full of sites honoring the city's
title of "Cradle of the Revolution."
The Museo Histórico 26 de Julio,
in Cuartel Moncada, where Fidel
Castro launched the revolution
on July 26, 1953, is near the
massive equestrian statue of
independence hero Antonio
Maceo that towers over Plaza
de la Revolución. The Avenue
Juan Gilberto Gómez connects
the plaza to Cementerio de
Santa Ifigenia, a monumental
cemetery with José
Martí's *(see p80)* tomb.

Environs
Basilica El Cobre, a
hilltop basilica with
a statue of the
Virgen del Cobre,
draws pilgrims from
all over. East of
the city, **Parque
Baconao** spans
310 sq miles (800 sq
km) with quiet beaches, artists'
communities, and an aquarium.
Santiago bay is guarded by the
imposing 1637 **Castillo del
Morro**. Soldiers dressed in period
costumes fire a cannon at sunset.

🏛 **Museo de Ambiente
Histórico Cubano**
Calle Felix Peña 602. **Tel** (22) 65 2652.
Open 9am–4.45pm Mon–Thu & Sat;
2–4.45pm Fri; 9am–12.45pm Sun.
without payment.

🏛 **Museo Municipal Emilio
Bacardí Moreau**
Calle Pío Rosado. **Tel** (22) 62 8402.
Open 9am–6pm Tue–Sat;
9am–1pm Sun.

Polymitas

Endemic to the
Baracoa region, the
polymita is a snail
with a colorful
shell. Each
snail's shell is as
distinct as a
thumbprint, with whorled
patterns in various combinations of reds, yellows, blues,
greens, blacks, and white.

Patterned
polymita shells

㉗ Baracoa

98 miles (157 km) E from Santiago de
Cuba. 80,000. Infotur,
Calle Maceo 129, (21) 64 1781.
Semana de la Cultura (Apr).

Cuba's first settlement was
founded in 1511 and is unusual
for its rickety, centuries-old
wooden homes. It is set on a
broad bay framed by lush
mountains. The best view over
town is from Hotel El Castillo
(see p96), in the 18th- century
Castillo de Seboruco fortress.
The Catedral de Nuestra Señora
de la Asunción, on Parque
Independencia, exhibits a cross
said to have been left by
Christopher Columbus in 1492.

Environs
West of Baracoa is the 1,885-ft
(575-m) high **El Yunque** (the Anvil).
This flat-topped formation lures
birders and hikers with spectacular
views. Its lush rainforests are part
of a UNESCO Biosphere Reserve
protected within Parque Nacional
Alejandro Humboldt.

Panoramic view of the city of Baracoa with El Yunque in the background

Outdoor Activities and Specialized Holidays

Guided excursions are the best way of discovering Cuba's extraordinary wilderness areas and wildlife. Mountains offer rainforest hikes, including to the summit of Pico Turquino, Cuba's highest peak, while lowland ecosystems include mangroves, swamplands, and dry forest. Beach resorts provide a spectrum of watersports, including scuba diving, which is a major draw.

The palm-shaded Playas del Este, Havana

Beaches

Cuba has endless stretches of superb beaches ranging from taupe to gold and snow-white. Most beach resorts are on the north coast, with the heaviest concentration of hotels at Varadero; and at Cayo Santa María, Cayo Coco, and Cayo Guillermo in the Jardines del Rey, where the spectacular white sands of Cayo Sabinal await development. Farther east, Playa Santa Lucía and Guardalavaca's Playa Mayor appeal to budget travelers, while deluxe all-inclusive resorts are the forte of Guardalavaca's Esmeralda, Yuraguanal, and Pesquero beaches. Marea del Portillo in the far east serves

Scuba Diving

Cuba is a paradise for scuba divers, thanks to crystal-clear waters, with temperatures ranging from 70–85° F (23–30° C), and spectacular coral reefs, Spanish galleons and other sunken wrecks, including Soviet vessels and aircrafts. There is an abundance of premium dive sites along both the north and south coasts, and all beach resorts have dive centers. Many all-inclusive tourist hotels have their own dive facilities with professional staff.

Cueva de los Peces is a cenote or "blue hole" full of different kinds of fish.

María la Gorda is a good venue for spotting whale sharks in the Bahía de Corrientes, which also has many dolphins and a garden of black corals.

La Costa de las Piratas has tranquil waters and 56 dive sites off Punta Francés.

Isla de la Juventud offers a variety of sites for both beginners and experienced divers. Huge coral parapets, sponges, and wrecks of the Spanish galleons are highlights of the area.

Punta Perdiz, in the Bay of Pigs, is a spectacular wall dive.

Map labels: Havana, Varadero, Archipiélago de Saba, Mariel, Matanzas, Los Colorado Archipiélago, Viñales, Jovellanos, Sag, la G, Reme, San Cristobal, Batabanó, Jaguey Grande, Colón, Pinar del Río, Golfo de Batabanó, Playa Larga, Santa Clara, Isabel Rubio, San Luis, Cienfuegos, Nueva Gerona, Júcaro, Trinidad, Cayo Largo

Key

— Major road

— Minor road

budget travelers with two all-inclusive hotels, while Playa Siboney is a big lure for families from nearby Santiago de Cuba.

The south coast is mostly swampy and has fewer beaches. Exceptions include Playa Ancón and undeveloped Playas del Este and Playa Blanca on Isla de la Juventud. Playa Sirena stands out among Cayo Largo's sublime beaches. In the far west, Cayo Levisa has some excellent sands. Havana has lovely beaches at Playas del Este, which is a great place to meet locals.

Fishing

Fishing enthusiasts will be in their element in Cuba. Most beach resorts have marinas from where sportfishing vessels set out to catch tuna, swordfish, and marlin. In Havana, the Marina Hemingway is the venue for the annual Ernest Hemingway International Marlin Fishing Tournament, which takes place in June. Cuba's fresh-water lakes are stocked with prize-winning sized bass: try Embalse Zaza, in Sancti Spíritus province. Tarpon and bonefish draw anglers to Las Salinas (Gran Parque Natural Montemar) and the Jardines de la Reina, off the south coast of

Ciego de Ávila and Camagüey, where specialized live-aboard boats cater to package tours. On Cayo Largo, the **Villa Marinera** has a lodge which overlooks flats that are good for bonefishing.

Fly-fishing at Cayo Santa María

Scuba Diving in the Caribbean Sea is one of the most rewarding activities with the coral reef scenery providing the most exciting backdrop to the spectacular fish varieties found here.

DIVE CENTERS

Avalon Dive Center
Tel (53) 89 5497.
W cubandivingcenters.com

Barracuda Diving Center
Tel (53) 61 3481.

Centro Internacional de Buceo
Tel (48) 77 1306.
W gaviota-grupo.com

Club Octopus International Diving Center
Tel (45) 98 7294.
El Colony Tel (46) 39 8181.

Scuba Diving Center Acua
Tel (45) 66 8063.

Archipiélago de Camagüey

San Rafael
Morón
onico Ciego Esmeralda
de Ávila
aro Nuevitas
Camagüey Manatí
Gibara
Guáimaro Puerto Guardalavaca
Padre
Las Holguín
Santa Cruz Amancio Tunas Mayarí Moa
del Sur
Jiguani Cueto
Jardines de la Baracoa
Reina features Bayamo
220 miles Niquero Guantánamo
(350 km) of Pilón El Cobre San Antonio
coral reef. There Santiago del Sur
are numerous de Cuba
marine turtles
and sharks.

Santa Lucía has a large coral reef close by and is blessed with numerous diving choices and many shipwrecks. Shark-feeding can also be witnessed.

0 kilometers 100

0 miles 100

Boats on the beach of Cayo Coco, Jardines del Rey

Watersports

All the tourist beach resorts offer a range of watersports including parasailing and rent sailcrafts such as Hobie Cats, Jet Skis, and banana boats. Larger sailcraft can be hired from almost 20 **Marlin Marinas** nationwide. Visitors wishing to charter their own yacht or catamaran for cruising the Jardines de la Reina can do so through **Charter Partner and Plattensail** in Cienfuegos. All the best resorts have wind-surfing, a popular option, especially at large all-inclusive hotels, where the activity and tuition are usually included in the price.

Boat Excursions

Almost all the holiday resorts have boat excursions, with Varadero providing the most options. Seafari Cayo Blanco

Hikers on a trail, accompanied by a guide

uses state-of-the-art catamarans to take visitors to nearby cays. Sunset sailing trips are also available at Varadero, Cayo Largo, Cayo Santa Maria, Playa Ancón, Cayo Coco, and Playa Santa Lucía, as well as Guardalavaca. Several venues have a "Jungle Tour" exploration of the mangrove ecosystems, but the jet-skis used are potentially damaging to the local ecology.

Hiking and Birding

Organized hiking trails used to be limited to the Sierra del Rosario, around Topes de Collantes, and the Sierra Maestra, where the arduous 2-day ascent to the summit of Pico Turquino rewards intrepid hikers with vast views and the ultimate high. More trails are being developed, along with programs for birders and other ecotourists.

Cuba offers fabulous bird-watching. The Península de Zapata, with its bird-rich wetlands and *salinas*, is a particularly good area for birders. Guided trips are available here and in the Reserva Guanahacabibes, Sierra Escambray, and Refugio Ecológico Los Indios on Isla de la Juventud. In the east, Parque Nacional Alejandro Humboldt, and El Saltón, in the eastern foothills of the Sierra Maestra, are good for birding. Flamingos can be seen at Cayo Coco. For more information contact **Gaviota Tours** and **Ecotur**.

Caving

Cuba is riddled with caverns, although the Valle de Viñales area is the only region currently promoting caving. Boat trips are offered inside Cueva del Indio, but the adventurous guided explorations of Cuevas de Santo Tomás, with 28 miles (45 km) of chambers, are more thrilling. Pre-Columbian petroglyphs can be seen in Cuevas de Punta del Este in Isla de la Juventud, and in caves that stipple Parque Nacional Cuguanas in Sancti Spíritus province. To visit either, you will need to join a guided excursion through EcoTur.

Tour boat exploring the cave at Cueva del Indio

Cycling

Bicycles are the main form of transport for millions of Cubans, and cycling is an excellent way to meet locals and enjoy the landscapes at a leisurely pace. Many visitors bring their own bicycles on vacation, but bikes can also be rented from **Cubania** in Havana. Puncture repair shops are numerous, but it is advisable to bring plenty of spare parts as they may be hard to source locally. Extreme care should be taken on Cuba's dangerous roads; always wear a helmet. Bikes should always be left in supervised places and locked. **Cubalinda** and **Cubania** offer guided bicycle tours. **WowCuba**, based in Canada, specializes in organized group bicycle tours to Cuba, as does **Exodus** in the UK.

Golf

Cuba currently has only two golf courses, although several others are planned in key beach resort areas such as Guardalavaca and Cayo Coco. The **Club de Golf Habana** is a 9-hole course. The 18-hole **Varadero Golf Club** has oceanfront fairways and greens, plus a pro shop.

Signage of Varadero Golf Club

Horse-Riding

Trekking on horseback is a delightful way to explore the countryside, where many Cubans still rely on horses to get around. In Havana, horse-riding is available at Parque Lenin and Playas del Este.

Most resorts and hotels in Cuba offer organized horse-riding excursions along the beach and into the nearby mountains. **Sitio La Güira** is a basic equestrian center on Cayo Coco. Other popular sites for horse-riding include the **Hacienda La Vega**, a working cattle ranch, and the nearby **Finca Dolores**.

Spas

Many beach resorts and hotels have spa facilities offering massage as well as various other treatments. Spa facilities in Cuba tend to be relatively sparse by Western standards and are focused on recuperative health treatments rather than pampered enjoyment. The country's two main spas are **San Diego de los Baños Spa** in Pinar del Río province, and **Baños de Elguea** in the province of Santa Clara.

Tennis

There are no dedicated tennis centers in Cuba, but many hotels in the beach resorts have their own courts for guests' use, and non-guests can often use the facilities for a fee. In Havana, **Club Habana** has squash and tennis courts exclusively for foreigners, as does the Hotel Occidental Miramar (*see p97*).

Horse-riding along a sandy white beach, Jardines del Rey

DIRECTORY

Fishing

Villa Marinera
El Pueblo, Cayo Largo.
Tel (52) 82 7715.

Watersports

Charter Partner
charterpartner.com

Marlin Marinas
Marina Darsena, Carretera de las Morlas Km31, Varadero. **Tel** (45) 66 7550.
Marina Hemingway, Av. 5 y 248, Santa Fe, Havana.
Tel (7) 204 5088. Marina Tarará, Via Blanca Km19, Tarará, Havana.
Tel (7) 796 0242.
Marina Trinidad, Playa Ancón. **Tel** (41) 99 6205.
nauticamarlin.com

Plattensail
platten-sailing.de

Hiking and Birding

Ecotur
Calle 13 No. 18005 between 182 and 5ta Ave, Playa, Havana.
Tel (7) 273 7949 (ext 104).
ecoturcuba.tur.cu

Gaviota Tours
Av. del Puerto 102 e/ Justiz y Obrapia, Havana.
Tel (7) 869 5774.
gaviota-grupo.com

Cycling

Cubalinda
Tel (7) 832 4493.
cubalinda.com

Cubania
Tel (7) 207 9888.
cubaniatravel.com

Exodus
Tel 866 338 8735.
exodus.co.uk

WowCuba
Prince Edward Island, Canada (head office).
Tel (902) 368 2453 (Canada); (7) 799 0759 (Havana).
wowcuba.com

Golf

Club de Golf Habana
Carretera de Vento Km8, Capdevila, Havana.
Tel (7) 649 8918.

Varadero Golf Club
Carretera Las Morlas, Varadero.
Tel (45) 66 7788.
varaderogolfclub.com

Horse-Riding

Finca Dolores
2 miles (3 km) W of Trinidad.
Tel (41) 99 6481.

Hacienda La Vega
Playa Ingles, Cienfuegos.
Tel (43) 55 1126.

Sitio La Güira
Cayo Coco.
Tel (33) 30 1208.

Spas

Baños de Elguea
Villa Clara.
Tel (42) 68 6298.

San Diego de los Baños Spa
San Diego de los Baños.
Tel (48) 54 8812.

Tennis

Club Habana
5ta Av. 188 y 192, Flores, Havana.
Tel (7) 204 5700.

Where to Stay

BARACOA: Hotel El Castillo $
Historic
Calle Calixto García, Loma el Paraíso
Tel *53 21 645165*
W hotelelcastillocuba.com
This hotel, located in a converted hilltop fortress, has modestly furnished rooms with modern amenities. Superb views, and a good restaurant on site.

BARACOA: Villa Maguana $
Beach
Carretera Baracoa-Moa Km20
Tel *53 21 641204*
W villamaguana.com
Villa Maguana has spacious wooden fourplex cabins in a landscaped setting. Overlooks a small cove with a beach.

BAYAMO: Royalton $
Historic
Calle Maceo 53
Tel *53 23 422290*
Dating from the 1940s, this refurbished hotel is located on the main plaza. Offers simple rooms with modern bathrooms.

CAMAGÜEY:
Hotel E Islazul Gran $
Chain
Calle Maceo 64 between Gral. Gómez e Ignacio Agramonte
Tel *53 32 292093*
W islazul.cu
Set in the heart of town, this pleasant hotel is furnished with antique reproductions. Has two restaurants and a piano bar.

CAMAGÜEY:
Hotel Islazul Colón $
Chain
Calle República 472
Tel *53 32 254878*
W islazul.cu
Situated on a busy street, this 19th-century hotel offers heaps of charm, a fine restaurant, and an atmospheric bar.

CAYO COCO: Hotel Tryp Cayo Coco $$
Beach Resort
Cayo Coco, Ciego de Ávila
Tel *53 33 301300*
W trypcayococo.ca
A sprawling all-inclusive resort with well-equipped rooms, three pool complexes, and non-stop entertainment. Family-friendly.

CAYO COCO: Meliá Cayo Coco $$
Beach Resort
Cayo Coco, Ciego de Ávila
Tel *53 33 301180*
W meliacuba.com
Deluxe all-inclusive adults-only resort with watersports, tennis, a spa, and several restaurants and bars to choose from. Beach- or lagoon-view rooms.

CAYO GUILLERMO:
Iberostar Daiquirí $$
Beach Resort
Cayo Guillermo, Ciego de Ávila
Tel *53 33 301650*
W iberostar.com
This is an elegant beachfront all-inclusive, with comfortable rooms. Lots of facilities, nightly entertainment, and watersports.

CAYO LARGO: Sol Cayo Largo $$
Beach Resort
Cayo Largo del Sur
Tel *53 45 248260*
W meliacuba.com
One of the best options on Cayo Largo – a colorful all-inclusive resort centered on a huge pool complex. Rooms with lovely four-poster beds. Choice of restaurants.

CIENFUEGOS: Hotel Jagua $
Chain
Calle 37 between 0 & 2
Tel *53 43 551003*
W gran-caribe.com
This hotel with modernist 1950s styling has functional rooms with bay views. Restaurants include the recommended Palacio del Valle.

CIENFUEGOS: Hotel La Unión $
Historic
Calle 31 Esq. A 54
Tel *53 43 551020*
W hotellaunion-cuba.com
Small colonial-era hotel in the heart of the old city. Decor features antiques and stained glass. On-site facilities include a gym and a spa.

GUARDALAVACA:
Blau Costa Verde Beach $$
Beach Resort
Playa Pesquero
Tel *53 24 433510*
W blau-hotels-cuba.com
This modern all-inclusive resort has bright rooms with rattan furnishings. Activities include badminton, archery, volleyball, and watersports. Large pool.

GUARDALAVACA:
Riu Playa Turquesa $$
Resort
Playa Yuraguanal
Tel *53 24 433540*
W riu.com
This huge, stylishly furnished upscale all-inclusive resort has seven swimming pools, as well as a plethora of sports and entertainment facilities, including watersports.

HAVANA:
Hotel Habana Riviera $
Chain
Paseo & Malecón, Vedado
Tel *53 7 836 4051*
W habanarivierahotel.com
An icon of the mafia heyday, this hotel is adorned in 1950s style. The modestly elegant rooms have ocean views. Facilities include a cigar shop and a nightclub.

HAVANA: Hotel Los Frailes $
Historic
Calle Teniente Rey 8, between Mercaderes & Oficios, Habana Vieja
Tel *53 7 862 9383*
W hotellosfrailescuba.com
At the "Monk's Hotel," located in a former French Navy captain's house, the staff wear habits and the furnishings echo the monastic theme. Enjoy the chamber quartet playing in the bar. Close to many restaurants.

Classically furnished twin room at the Hotel La Unión, Cienfuegos

HAVANA: Hotel Telegrafo $
Historic
Prado 408, corner Neptuno,
Centro Habana
Tel *53 7 861 1010*
W hoteltelegrafo-cuba.com
The eclectic furnishings at this
hotel combine colonial and con-
temporary themes. The bedrooms
have lively color schemes and
modern bathrooms.

HAVANA:
Hotel Ambos Mundos $$
Historic
Calles Obispo 153 & Mercaders,
Habana Vieja
Tel *53 7 860 9530*
W hotelambosmundos-cuba.com
Modest three-star hotel with
its claim to fame being that
Hemingway wrote a novel here.
Features include a lively piano
bar and an antique elevator.

HAVANA: Hotel Conde de
Villanueva $$
Historic
Calle Mercaderes 202, Habana Vieja
Tel *53 7 862 9293*
W hotelcondedevillanueva.com
Charming, well-located hotel
in a converted 18th-century
colonial mansion. Offers
windowless rooms situated
around a patio. There is a cigar
store and lounge upstairs.

HAVANA: Hotel Florida $$
Historic
Calle Obispo 252, Habana Vieja
Tel *53 7 862 4127*
W hotelfloridacuba.com
Regal upscale hotel that abounds
with antiques. The handsome
rooms surround an atrium patio
with a checkerboard marble
floor. Has an excellent restaurant
with 19th-century styling.

HAVANA: Hotel Habana
Libre Tryp $$
Modern
Calle L 23, Vedado
Tel *53 7 834 6100*
W meliacuba.com
Landmark high-rise hotel with
lofty views. Several stylish and
spacious refurbished rooms;
a full gamut of services, as well
as a rooftop nightclub.

HAVANA: Hotel Iberostar
Parque Central $$
Modern
Calle Neptuno between Paseo de
Martí & Zulueta, Habana Vieja
Tel *53 7 860 6627*
W hotelparquecentral-cuba.com
This hotel's unbeatable location
is matched by superb service and
elegant furnishings. Has three
excellent restaurants.

HAVANA: Hotel Marqués
de San Felipe y Santiago
de Bejucal $$
Historic
Calles Oficos 152 & Amargura,
Habana Vieja
Tel *53 7 864 9191*
W habaguanexhotels.com
Spectacularly renovated 18th-
century mansion on one of
Havana's main squares. Chic,
tastefully decorated rooms with
all amenities.

HAVANA:
Hotel Meliá Cohiba $$
Luxury
Paseo between 1ra & 3ra, Vedado
Tel *53 7 833 3636*
W meliacuba.com
Havana's principal business
hotel, this high-rise building
promises excellent service.
The rooms have contemporary
decor and marble bathrooms.
Extensive facilities, including a
nightclub and six restaurants.

HAVANA:
Hotel Meliá Habana $$
Modern
Av. 3ra between 76 & 80, Miramar
Tel *53 7 204 8500*
W meliahabana.com
Modern shorefront hotel
popular with business travelers.
The elegant rooms feature
marble-clad bathrooms. There
is a business center, as well as
a choice of restaurants.

DK Choice

HAVANA: Hotel Nacional
de Cuba $$
Historic
Calle O & 21, Vedado
Tel *53 7 836 3564*
W hotelnacionaldecuba.com
This 1930s grande-dame hotel
is touted by Cuban tourism as
Havana's finest, boasting lots
of famous guests, heaps of
character, including a Moorish-
inspired lobby, and superb
views over the Malecón. The
bedrooms have been tastefully
renovated, the cabaret sizzles,
and the patio bar is the place to
go for a mojito and cigar.

HAVANA: Hotel Raquel $$
Historic
Calle Amargura 103, Habana Vieja
Tel *53 7 860 8280*
W hotelraquel-cuba.com
Neo-Classical, Jewish-themed
hotel, where the bedrooms
have wrought iron furniture.
The beautiful marble-clad lobby
has a stunning stained-glass
atrium ceiling.

One of the elegant event rooms at the Hotel
Nacional de Cuba, Havana

HAVANA: Hotel Santa Isabel $$
Historic
Calle Baratillo 9, Habana Vieja
Tel *53 7 860 8201*
W hotelsantaisabel.com
Furnished throughout with
antiques, this is an intimate
former Neo-Classical palace.
Has a patio bar-restaurant.

HAVANA: Hotel Terral $$
Boutique
Malecón Corner Lealtad, Centro
Habana
Tel *53 7 860 2100*
W habaguanexhotels.com
An excellent option, Hotel Terral
plays on a maritime theme, with
everything stylishly modern.
A tiny bar-restaurant faces
the Malecón.

HAVANA: Occidental Miramar $$
Modern
Av. 5ta between 72 & 76, Miramar
Tel *53 7 204 3584*
W occidentalhotels.com
A huge contemporary hotel
popular with tour groups and
businessfolk. Has a huge pool
and several restaurants.

HAVANA: Hotel Saratoga $$$
Luxury
Prado 603, corner Dragones,
Habana Vieja
Tel *53 7 868 1000*
W hotel-saratoga.com
A rebuilt late colonial-era hotel
with elegant contemporary
furnishings. Stylish mezzanine
bar and excellent restaurant.

HOLGUÍN: Hotel Pernik $
Chain
Av. Jorge Dimitrov & Plaza de la
Revolución
Tel *53 24 481011*
W islazul.cu
Soviet-style prefab hotel with
modest rooms. Has a tennis
court, an Internet café, and an
occasional open-air disco.

The pleasant pool area at the Hotel La Moka, Las Terrazas

LAS TERRAZAS: Hotel La Moka $
Boutique
*Autopista Habana-Pinar Km51,
Pinar del Río*
Tel *53 48 578600*
W lasterrazas.cu
Set amid woods, this delightful
hotel blends in with its
surroundings. Stay in a spacious
colonial-themed room with
floor-to-ceiling windows.

MAYARÍ:
Villa Pinares de Mayari $
Mountain Resort
Pinares de Mayari
Tel *53 24 503308*
W gaviota-grupo.com
Rustic mountain resort with
cozy cabins, a huge restaurant
offering simple meals, plus hiking
and eco-tours.

PINAR DEL RÍO:
Rancho La Guabina $
Boutique
Carretera Pinar a Luís Lazo Km9.5
Tel *53 48 757616*
Small, intimate hotel on a horse-
breeding ranch, featuring
charming decor in cross-
ventilated rooms and cabins.
Lovely restaurant.

PLAYA ANCÓN:
Brisas Trinidad del Mar $$
Beach Resort
Península Ancón, Trinidad
Tel *53 41 996507*
W hotelescubanacan.com
A quasi-colonial-themed
beachfront resort centered on a
large freeform pool. Has a range
of colorful and spacious rooms
with modern bathrooms.

REMEDIOS: Hotel E Barcelona $
Historic
*José A. Peña 67 between La Pastora
y Antonio Maceo*
Tel *53 42 395144*
W hotelescubanacan.com
A twin to Hotel E Mascotte, this
reasonably priced option offers
cozy rooms furnished with
colonial antique reproductions
and a sun terrace.

REMEDIOS:
Hotel E Mascotte $
Historic
Máximo Gómez 114
Tel *53 42 395144*
W hotelescubanacan.com
Comfortable colonial-era hotel
refurbished with pleasant decor
and modern bathrooms. Has a
good restaurant on site.

SANCTI SPÍRITUS:
Hostal E del Rijo $
Historic
*Honorato del Castillo 12 corner
Máximo Gómez*
Tel *53 41 328588*
W hotelescubanacan.com
Delightful remake of a 19th-
century Neo-Classical mansion,
the rooms in Hostal E del Rijo
feature beamed ceilings and
wrought-iron details.

SANCTI SPÍRITUS:
Hotel E Plaza $
Historic
Independencia 1m Plaza Sánchez
Tel *53 41 327102*
W hotelescubanacan.com
Offers rooms of varying sizes
with elegant furnishings. Has
an excellent restaurant and
Internet services.

SANTA CLARA:
Villa La Granjita $
Chain
Carretera de Malezas Km1.5
Tel *53 42 218190*
W hotelescubanacan.com
Sprawling property with nicely
furnished octagonal cabins,
an excellent buffet restaurant,
and a nightclub. Popular with
tour groups.

SANTA CLARA:
Villa Los Caneyes $
Chain
Av. Eucaliptos & Circunvalación
Tel *53 42 218140*
W hotelloscaneyes.com
Villa Los Caneyes has a woodsy
setting, spacious duplex
octagonal cabins, a spring-water
pool, and a buffet restaurant.

SANTIAGO DE CUBA:
Hotel Casa Granda $
Historic
*Calle Heredia 201, corner
San Pedro*
Tel *53 22 653021*
W hotelescubanacan.com
Grande-dame hotel with a
superb location on Parque
Céspedes. The comfy rooms
have modern bathrooms.
Patio bar and nightly cabaret.

SANTIAGO DE CUBA:
Hotel E San Basilio $
Boutique
*Calle San Basilio 403 between
Calvario & Carnicería*
Tel *53 22 651702*
W hotelescubanacan.com
Lovely budget option converted
from a townhouse mansion, with
antique reproductions adding
to the charming ambience.
Small restaurant and bar.

SANTIAGO DE CUBA:
Hotel San Juan $
Chain
*Carretera de Siboney Km1.5,
Vista Alegre*
Tel *53 22 687200*
W islazul.cu
Reasonably priced hotel with
simple rooms in villa blocks. Has
an attractive pool and sundeck,
and cabaret.

SANTIAGO DE CUBA:
Villa Horizontes El Saltón $
Chain
Carretera Filé, Tercer Frente
Tel *53 22 566326*
W hotelescubanacan.com
Rustic mountain spa resort
with modestly furnished
rooms. Has facilities for hikes
and horseback rides, and there
is a lovely waterfall.

DK Choice

SANTIAGO DE CUBA:
Meliá Santiago de Cuba $$
Luxury
Av. de las Américas y Calle M
Tel *53 22 687070*
W meliacuba.com
This eye-popping high-rise hotel
is located close to the historic
center of the city. It offers deluxe
rooms with contemporary
decor and large floor-to-ceiling
windows that have wonderful
views of the city and mountains.
After a day of sightseeing, the
rooftop bar is a great place to sit
and watch the sunset. Excellent
restaurants, sauna, outdoor
pools, art gallery, and nightclub
with live entertainment. Friendly
and helpful staff.

SOROA: Villa Horizontes Soroa $
Chain
Carretera a Soroa Km 8, Candelaria
Tel *53 48 523556*
W hotelescubanacan.com
A lovely and airy complex of
cabins and villas in a peaceful,
wooded hillside setting.
Comfortable rooms.

TRINIDAD: Hotel E La Ronda $
Historic
Calle José Martí 263
Tel *53 41 996133*
W hotelescubanacan.com
Located in the heart of town,
Hotel E La Ronda offers pleasant
rooms and is a few minutes' walk
from restaurants and main sights.

**TRINIDAD: Hotel Iberostar
Grand Trinidad** $$
Luxury
Calle José Martí 262
Tel *53 41 996070*
W thegrandcollection.com
Deluxe hotel under Spanish
management, lavishly appointed,
with an excellent restaurant,
a cigar lounge, billiards room,
and Wi-Fi

**VARADERO:
Mercure Cuatro Palmas** $
Modern
Av. 1ra between 60 & 64
Tel *53 45 667040*
W mercure.com
Perennially popular hotel with a
lively party atmosphere, excellent
facilities, and entertainment.

**VARADERO: Motel Punta
Blanca** $
Boutique
Carretera de Kawama final
Tel *53 45 662410*
W islazul.cu
Three modernist 1950s villas
have been converted into this
peaceful hotel. Offers functional,
simple rooms. Well located, at
the western end of the beach.

DK Choice

**VARADERO: Blau
Varadero Hotel** $$
Modern
Carretera Las Morlas Km15
Tel *53 45 667545*
W blauvaradero.ca
State-of-the-art upscale hotel
inspired by Mayan architectural
styles. This all-inclusive resort
has a huge pool complex, a
wonderful spa, chic furnishings,
and marble-clad bathrooms.
The food is excellent, with lots
of variety. Beautiful white-sand
beach in front of the hotel.

VARADERO: Mansion Xanadú $$
Historic
Carretera Las Américas
Tel *53 45 668482*
W varaderogolfclub.com
Mansion Xanadú is housed in
an extravagant former private
mansion with marble floors
and antique mahogany fixtures.
Great restaurant and golf course.

**VARADERO:
Blau Marina Varadero** $$$
Beach Resort
Punta Hicacos final
Tel *53 45 669966*
W blau-hotels-cuba.com
Huge all-inclusive resort, where
the suites feature beautiful decor
on a nautical theme. There is a
children's section, a choice of
restaurants, watersports facilities,
and live entertainment.

VILLA CLARA: Villas Las Brujas $
Beach
Cayo Las Brujas, Villa Clara
Tel *53 42 350199*
W villalasbrujas.com
Simple bamboo furnishings in
wooden clifftop cabins. Has a
seafood restaurant overlooking
a lovely beach. There is a marina
nearby for scuba divers.

**VILLA CLARA: Iberostar
Ensenachos** $$
Beach Resort
Cayo Santa María, Villa Clara
Tel *53 42 350301*
W iberostar.com
Top-of-the-line luxury all-inclusive
resort boasting heaps of marble.
All rooms have concierge service
and English colonial styling.

**VILLA CLARA: Meliá Cayo
Santa María** $$
Beach Resort
Cayo Santa María, Villa Clara
Tel *53 42 350200*
W meliacuba.com
This deluxe all-inclusive resort
boasts lavish accommodations
with king-sized canopy beds,
a choice of bars and restaurants,
and watersports facilities.

**VIÑALES: Hotel Horizontes
Rancho San Vicente** $
Chain
Carretera P. Esperanza Km33
Tel *53 48 796201*
W hotelescubanacan.com
Charming hotel amid dramatic
landscapes, with rustic cabins
around a swimming pool.
Delightful restaurant. The on-site
spa offers mud treatments.

VIÑALES: Hotel La Ermita $
Chain
Carretera La Ermita Km1.5
Tel *53 48 796250*
W hotelescubanacan.com
Attractive property atop a
mogote with fine views. Simple
furnishings. Open-air poolside bar.

VIÑALES: Hotel Los Jazmines $
Chain
Carretera a Viñales Km23
Tel *53 48 796205*
W hotelescubanacan.com
Iconic hotel with stupendous
views. The newer annexe rooms
are more comfortable. Has an
Olympic-sized pool.

Centered around a fountain, the lobby area at the Iberostar Grand Hotel Trinidad is a lovely place to sit

Where to Eat and Drink

CAMAGÜEY: La Campaña de Toledo $
Traditional Cuban
Plaza San Juan de Díos
Tel *53 32 286812*
Heaps of Colonial charm in this venerable restaurant, with rustic furniture and well-worn terra-cotta floors. Well known for its traditional beef roast.

CIENFUEGOS: El Lagarto $
Traditional Cuban
Calle 35 4B, La Punta
Tel *53 43 519966*
The best *paladar* (owner-managed eatery) in town, this private bayside venue, part of Villa Lagarto, serves huge portions of Cuban staples, including lobster. Excellent service.

**CIENFUEGOS:
Restaurante 1869** $
International
Hotel Unión, Calle 31 & Av. 54
Tel *53 42 551020*
Restaurante 1869's eclectic menu features *seviche* (raw fish with citrus juice) and grilled sirloin. Elegant dining room with antique furnishings.

**CIENFUEGOS:
Palacio del Valle** $$
Traditional Cuban
Calle 37 between 0 & 2
Tel *53 43 551003*
Its unique Mughal architecture is reason enough to visit this superb restaurant serving seafood. Also has a garden restaurant as an airy alternative.

GUARDALAVACA: El Ancla $
Seafood
Playa Mayor
Tel *53 24 430381*
El Ancla is a good-value restaurant perched atop a coral outcrop. Of the many dishes on offer, the *corvina al ajillo* (garlic sea bass) is consistently good.

HAVANA: Doña Eutemia $
Traditional Cuban
Callejón del Chorro 60, Habana Vieja
Tel *53 7 861 1332*
This popular *paladar*, steps from Plaza de la Catedral, serves good Cuban dishes in a cozy setting. Reservations recommended.

HAVANA: La Paella $
Spanish
Calle Oficios 53, Habana Vieja
Tel *53 7 867 1037*
Welcoming Spanish bodega-style eatery serving classic Iberian dishes, including *paella* (for a minimum of two people).

HAVANA: Los Nardos $
Traditional Cuban
Paseo de Martí 563 between Brasil & Dragones
Tel *53 7 863 2985*
In a run-down townhouse, Los Nardos serves up scrumptious garlic shrimp, lobster enchiladas, and more. Fantastic ambience.

HAVANA: Atelier $$
Nouvelle Cuban
Calle 5 511 between Paseo & 2, Vedado
Tel *53 7 836 2025*
Top *paladar* combining striking artwork, a romantic atmosphere, and well-conceived and executed nouvelle Cuban fare.

HAVANA: Café Laurent $$
Nouvelle Cuban
Calle M 257 between 19 & 21, Vedado
Tel *53 7 831 2090*
Well-managed *paladar* in a former penthouse with a warm, friendly feel. Creative dishes based on rabbit, duck, and lobster.

HAVANA: Don Cangrejo $$
Seafood
Av. 1ra between 16 & 18, Miramar
Tel *53 7 204 5002*
This oceanfront restaurant in a former modernist mansion serves excellent seafood and is famed for its after-dinner poolside nightclub.

HAVANA: El Aljibe $$
Traditional Cuban
Av. 7ma between 24 & 26, Miramar
Tel *53 7 204 1583*
Airy thatched restaurant popular with tour groups. Do not miss the all-you-can-eat servings of delicious roast chicken in orange-garlic sauce.

HAVANA: La Casa $$
Nouvelle Cuban
Calle 30 865 between 26 & 41, Nuevo Vedado
Tel *53 7 881 7000*
La Casa is a well-run *paladar* in a 1950s modernist home, serving sumptuous portions of creative nouvelle cuisine, along with beers and cocktails.

HAVANA: La Terraza de Cojímar $$
Seafood
Calle 152 161, Cojímar
Tel *53 7 766 5151*
Enjoy the popular *paella* and other seafood dishes at this former oceanside haunt of Ernest Hemingway, famously referenced as the Terrace in his seminal book *The Old Man and the Sea*.

Place settings at La Paella, a Spanish-style restaurant, Havana

HAVANA: La Torre $$
Cuban
Calle 17 155 between M & N, Vedado
Tel *53 7 832 2451*
Go for the views from Havana's tallest restaurant, atop Edificio Focsa, and enjoy tasty Cuban classics and nouvelle dishes. Excellent service.

HAVANA: Le Chansonnier $$
Nouvelle Cuban
Calle J 257 between 13 & 15, Vedado
Tel *53 7 832 1576*
Le Chansonnier is a *paladar* known for its artsy renovation of an early 20th-century mansion. Serves mouthwatering French-inspired nouvelle cuisine, though the service can be hit-and-miss.

HAVANA: Mediterraneo Havana $$
Italian
Calle 13 406 between F & G, Vedado
Tel *53 7 832 4894*
This Italian-run *paladar* in a beautifully restored mansion delivers delicious Italian-Cuban nouvelle fare that never fails to impress. Great service.

HAVANA: El Floridita $$$
Seafood
Calle Obispo 557 corner Monserrate, Habana Vieja
Tel *53 7 8671300*
Flamboyant retro ambience pervades this former haunt of Ernest Hemingway. Serves excellent surf 'n' turf and is *the* place in Havana for a daiquirí.

HAVANA: La Cocina de Lilliam $$$
Nouvelle Cuban
Calle 48 1311, Playa
Tel *53 7 209 6514*
Catapulted to fame when former US president Jimmy Carter dined here in 2002, this *paladar* delivers some of the most creative Cuban dishes in town.

DK Choice

HAVANA: La Guarida $$$
Nouvelle Cuban
Calle Concordia 418, Centro Habana
Tel *53 7 866 9047*
Reminiscent of a Parisian bistro, Cuba's most famous *paladar* occupies a dramatically deteriorated townhouse made famous as the setting for the movie *Fresa y Chocolate*. Consistently superb nouvelle Cuban cuisine, such as honey-mustard chicken, is served by proficient and friendly staff. Reservations advised.

Photos and interesting artworks adorn the walls at La Guarida, Havana

HOLGUÍN: Taberna Pancho $
Traditional Cuban
Av. Dimitrov, Rpto. Pedro Díaz
Tel *53 24 481868*
Warm and atmospheric *taberna* serving draft beer to go with delicious Cuban dishes such as garlic shrimp, as well as simple chicken and pork dishes.

SANCTI SPÍRITUS: Mesón de la Plaza $
Traditional Cuban
Av. Máximo Gómez 34
Tel *53 41 28546*
Mesón de la Plaza is themed as a Spanish bodega, with cowhide chairs and rough-hewn tables. The house dish is *garbanzo* (chickpeas) with bacon and pork sausage.

SANTIAGO DE CUBA: El Barracón $
Traditional Cuban
Av. Garzón corner Prudencio Martínez
Tel *53 22 661877*
Themed after 19th-century runaway slaves, complete with life-size figures, and wrought-iron and rough-hewn chairs, El Barracón offers a menu heavy on meat dishes.

SANTIAGO DE CUBA: Restaurante La Fontana $$
Italian
Av. de las Américas
Tel *53 22 687070*
Open-air Italian restaurant in the Hotel Meliá Santiago de Cuba, serving pizzas and seafood dishes. Excellent service.

SANTIAGO DE CUBA: Restaurante Salón Tropical $$
Nouvelle Cuban
Calle Fernández Marcané 310 between 9 & 10
Tel *53 22 641161*
Popular *paladar* with rooftop dining. On the menu are tasty dishes such as chicken fricassée and unusual pizzas.

SANTIAGO DE CUBA: Restaurante Zunzún $$
Traditional Cuban
Av. Manduley 159, Rpto. Vista Alegre
Tel *53 22 641528*
A charming state restaurant housed in a former centenary mansion with patio seating. Enjoy Cuban staples while musicians entertain.

TRINIDAD: Restaurante Plaza Mayor $
Buffet
Calles Zerquera and Villena
Tel *53 41 996470*
This state restaurant serves a superb and varied buffet that can be enjoyed while troubadours entertain. It is very popular with tour groups, so avoid peak hours.

TRINIDAD: Paladar Vista Gourmet $$
Traditional Cuban
Callejón de Galdós between Muñ & Callejón de Gallegos
Tel *53 41 996700*
This is a superb rooftop *paladar* with spot-on service, live music, and a choice of buffet and à la carte menus.

VARADERO: Casa de Fondue $
International
Av. 1ra corner 62
Tel *53 45 667747*
Cuba's only fondue restaurant, this place uses Cuban as well as imported cheeses, and also offers grilled lobster and meat dishes. Warm ambience.

VARADERO: Restaurante Las Américas $$$
International
Carretera Las Américas
Tel *53 45 667388*
Located in Mansion Xanadú, and amid extravagant Baroque decor, this restaurant serves creative French-inspired fare such as seared goose liver, and shrimp in sherry vinaigrette.

Practical Information

Following a boom in tourism over the past decade, Cuba now has modern services on par with most of the other Caribbean destinations. There are some weak links, however, and advance planning is essential. Visitors need to be flexible, and patience is required to deal with Cuba's all-encompassing bureaucracy. Refunds are rarely given when things go wrong, and state-run tourism entities and individual tourism workers are adept at extracting extra money from visitors.

Relaxing in the sun at Guardalavaca beach, Cuba

When to Go

Any time of year is good for visiting Cuba, although July and August have torrid rainfall and September to November are prime hurricane months. The best period to visit is from December to April, when it is pleasant. Rain can occur year-round, but is concentrated from June to November, when hotel and car rental rates drop. Many key festivals are held in Havana from November to December, including the Festival Internacional del Nuevo Cine Latinoamericano and the jazz festival.

Getting There

Charter and regular scheduled flights arrive from Europe, Canada, and Central and South America. Cuba has nine international airports, but most visitors land at either Havana's José Martí International Airport (HAV) or the Juan Gualberto Gómez Airport at Varadero (VRA). **Virgin Atlantic** has twice-weekly flights from Gatwick to Havana. **Cubana** flies from Europe. **Air Canada** serves Cuba from gateways in Canada. **Avianca**, **AeroMexico**, and **Copa** fly from Central America, and **Air Jamaica** links Jamaica with Cuba. There are special flights from USA for eligible licensed travelers. There is no ferry service to Cuba.

Documentation

Visitors must have a valid passport, onward ticket, proof of travel insurance, and a tourist visa *(tarjeta de turista)*, issued by your airline upon airport check-in. Visas are valid for 30 days (Canadians receive 90 days), and can be extended. Individuals subject to US law are barred from visiting Cuba except on "people to people" tour programs. Certain US residents (such as journalists and Cuban-American families) can get permission from the **US Department of the Treasury**.

Visitor Information

Official **Cubatur** offices in the United Kingdom and Canada provide brochures. Travel agencies and websites are good for details on specific activities. **Infotur** has offices in major cities and Cuban tour companies have information desks in all hotels and sell organized excursions. A huge amount of information about Cuba is available on the Internet. All websites originating in Cuba are state-run and care should be taken if making bookings online. The US websites are barred from accepting online bookings relating to Cuba travel.

Health and Security

All hotels have a doctor or nurse on duty, or on call 24 hours a day. Special clinics treat visitors, while **Asistur** provides varied assistance to travelers in distress. Cuba is generally a safe place to visit. However, petty theft is endemic. Snatching and mugging are frequent in run-down Havana areas. Keep valuables in hotel safes.

Banking and Currency

Cuba's currency is the *peso*, but all tourist transactions are in *convertible pesos* (designated as CUC$), which can be exchanged for foreign currency at Cadeca exchange bureaux (a surcharge applies for converting US dollars), often located near shops. Euros can be used in Cayo Coco, Varadero, and Cayo

Tourist information office on a Havana street

Colorful papier-mâché dolls on display in a Cuba stall

Largo. Non-US credit cards are accepted for many tourist transactions. All beach resorts and major cities have state-owned banks serving foreigners.

Communications

Public phones are plentiful and reliable, and work with prepaid phone cards that can be purchased at hotels and post offices. Calls from hotels are expensive. **Cubacel** provides cellular service, but activating your personal phone is expensive. To call outside Cuba, dial 0, then 9 followed by the country code. To call Cuba from abroad, dial the international access number, then 53 and the local number. Laptops can be brought into Cuba but may need to be registered on arrival. Most hotels have Internet access and there are cybercafés in most cities.

Transport

The state-owned car rental companies, such as **Rex**, have desks at all hotels. Cars are not well maintained and customer service is not very efficient. Reservations are essential in high season. Tourist taxis are available at all hotels and resorts. Many drivers prefer to negotiate a fare rather than use meters. **Víazul** runs air-conditioned coaches between Havana, key cities, and tourist destinations. Inter-city buses cater only for locals and not tourists. Cuba's railway system links Havana to Pinar del Río and Santiago de Cuba. Visitors can opt for bicycle rickshaws, popular in Havana.

Shopping

All tourist hotels and ARTex shops sell cigars, rum, and other typical Cuban souvenirs. Many of the best bargains are found at street crafts markets, where you can buy from the artisans. Look out for wooden statues, papier-mâché dolls, paintings, and antique model cars. Havana's Fería de la Artesanía market and Trinidad are great places to shop.

Language

Spanish, the official language of Cuba, is spoken with a local inflection, which can be difficult to understand. Tour guides and most service staff in hotels speak English.

Electricity

Electric current is 110-volt, but 220-volt current is also found (and usually marked as such). Most outlets use the US two-prong plugs. The system is unreliable and blackouts (apagones) are common.

Time

Cuba is on Eastern Standard Time, 5 hours behind Greenwich Mean Time. Daylight saving is in effect from March to October.

Getting Married

Getting married in Cuba is bureaucratic and requires that all necessary documents be translated into Spanish and notarized. Contact the **Consultoria Jurídica** in Cuba for more information.

A bicitaxi (bicycle rickshaw) in Havana

Exploring the Cayman Islands

This British overseas territory comprises three tiny islands – Grand Cayman and its sister islands, Little Cayman and Cayman Brac. Located in the western Caribbean, they cover a total land mass of 100 sq miles (259 sq km). The islands are actually coral-encrusted summits of a submarine mountain range. Deservedly, the trio is world-renowned for its stunning beaches and scuba diving. Unspoilt and unhurried, lying 90 miles (145 km) northeast from the busier Grand Cayman, the sister islands are ideal for divers, nature lovers, and those seeking tranquility.

Locator Map

Grand Cayman
The largest of the three islands, Grand Cayman is also the most developed, particularly its western districts. The eastern districts serve good Cayman cuisine.

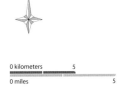

❹ ❸ **HELL**
BOATSWAIN'S BEACH AND CAYMAN TURTLE FARM
West Bay
Head of Barkers
Salt Creek
❷ **STINGRAY CITY**
Rum Point
Water Cay
North Side
Old Man Bay
Cayman Kai
Seven Mile Beach
WEST BAY RD
North Sound
Welch Point
NORTH SIDE RD
Boby Cay
QUEEN ELIZABETH II BOTANIC PARK ❻
FRANK SO
❶ **GEORGE TOWN**
BODDEN TOWN RD
Frank Sound
S SOUND RD
RED BAY RD
PEDRO ST. JAMES NATIONAL HISTORIC SITE
Pease Bay
Breakers
South Sound
Prospect Point
Savannah ❺
Bodden Town
Bodden Bay

0 kilometers   5
0 miles   5

Aerial view of the coastline, Grand Cayman

Sights at a Glance

❶ George Town
❷ Stingray City
❸ Hell
❹ *Boatswain's Beach and Cayman Turtle Farm p107*
❺ Pedro St. James National Historic Site
❻ Queen Elizabeth II Botanic Park
❼ Little Cayman
❽ Cayman Brac

For hotels and restaurants on this island see p114 and p115

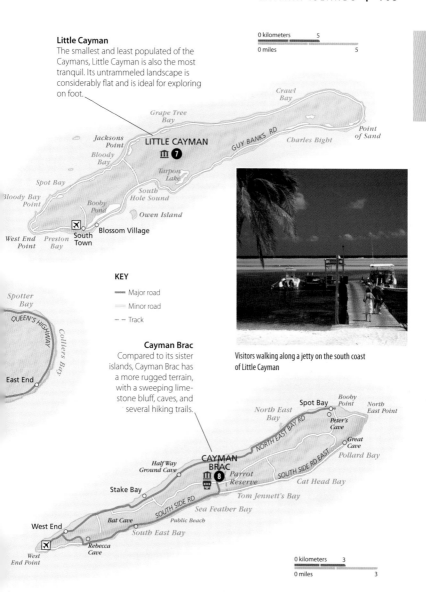

Little Cayman
The smallest and least populated of the Caymans, Little Cayman is also the most tranquil. Its untrammeled landscape is considerably flat and is ideal for exploring on foot.

KEY

— Major road
═ Minor road
-- Track

Cayman Brac
Compared to its sister islands, Cayman Brac has a more rugged terrain, with a sweeping limestone bluff, caves, and several hiking trails.

Visitors walking along a jetty on the south coast of Little Cayman

Getting Around

All international flights to the Cayman Islands arrive at the Owen Roberts International Airport on Grand Cayman. Cayman Airways has regular flights to the sister islands (40 minutes from Grand Cayman). There is no ferry service between the islands. Renting a car or taking a guided tour is the best way to explore the islands. Several tour companies located in Grand Cayman run day trips to the sister islands. There are plenty of taxis available at airports and the drivers are willing to take visitors around.

Entrance of the popular Bat Cave, Cayman Brac

For keys to symbols *see back flap*

❶ George Town

West coast of Grand Cayman.
🚟 27,000. ✈ 🛈 Pavilion Building
on Cricket Square, George Town, 345
949 0623. 🎉 Pirates' Week (Nov).

With a steady stream of cruise
ships docking at the port,
George Town, the capital of the
Cayman Islands, is a busy place
all year round. It takes about an
hour to casually stroll the streets
lined with duty-free shops and
restaurants – the city's major
attractions. The **Cayman Islands
National Museum**, located in
the Old Courts Building, one of
the few surviving 19th-century
structures, has exhibits that
document the islands' past,
including a replica of a hand-
made catboat from the 1920s.

🏛 **Cayman Islands National
Museum**
3 Harbour Drive. **Tel** 345 949 8368.
Open 9am–5pm Mon–Fri, 10am–2pm
Sat. 🔲 📷 💻 🌐 **museum.ky**

Cayman Islands National Museum
in George Town

❷ Stingray City

5 miles (8 km) NE of George Town,
Grand Cayman. 📷 🔲 nearly all dive
and watersports operators offer
guided trips.

A 12-ft (4-m) dive site in the
clear, turquoise waters of North
Sound, Stingray City is world-
famous for its Atlantic southern
stingrays. A perfect paradise for
snorkelers and divers, this is the
only place in the world where
they can swim with, touch, and
hand feed wild stingrays. The
rays were first spotted here in
the early 1980s by fishermen
cleaning their catches in the

Visitors enjoying the shallow waters of Stingray City, Grand Cayman

shallow, protected sound. Dive
operators saw this as an
economic opportunity and
began to offer trips to divers.
Nearby is "The Sandbar," a
shallow sandbank, where non-
divers can also experience close
encounters of the marine kind.
On disembarking the boat into
the waist-deep waters of the
Sandbar, visitors are surrounded
by rays and yellowtail snappers.
Rays are gentle and it is
possible to touch their velvety
white underbelly, but the tail
should be avoided because of
its barb. Dive operators show
how to shuffle along the sea
bed to avoid stepping on a barb
and feed the rays chunks of
squid by making a fist with the
thumb tucked in. The rays have
no teeth, but visitors will feel
quite a strong suction as the ray
hoovers the tidbit.
There have been concerns
that some operators mishandle
the rays in the name of photo
opportunities. It is best to just

enjoy the beauty of their
movement and the tickle of
their fins as they swim past.

❸ Hell

7 miles (11 km) N of George Town,
Grand Cayman. 🛈 Post Office, 345
949 3358. ♿

In the village of the same name
in West Bay, Hell is a small site
featuring 1.5-million-year-old
jagged shards of jet-black
ironshore (limestone coral
and dolomite). Many theories
abound about how the place
got its name. It is popularly
believed that the name
originated after a local official
exclaimed, "This is what hell
must look like." The name stuck
and the site is now a great
tourist attraction, with a hell-
themed post office where
visitors can send postcards
from Hell. The place can be
crowded as it is a stop for
cruise ship tours.

Atlantic Southern Stingrays

These massive creatures are broad, flattish, cartilaginous fish
closely related to sharks. They are the most common of the
stingray family and are frequent visitors to Stingray City. Female
southern stingrays can grow up to 6 ft (2 m) across while males are
smaller. Rays are constantly on the prowl for food – crabs, shellfish,
and worms – and they hunt
by smell, not sight, and suck
the food into their mouth
where it is crushed by hard
cartilage plates. In the wild,
they find their food by
flapping their wing-shaped
fins over the sea bed so that
sand moves around and any
small creatures hiding there
are revealed.

An Atlantic southern stingray foraging
for food along the sea floor

❹ Boatswain's Beach and Cayman Turtle Farm

This 23-acre (9-ha) marine theme park is a great place to spend at least half a day. Pronounced "Bo-suns" Beach, the marine park offers a wonderful opportunity to learn about the unique flora and fauna of the Cayman Islands. The highlight is snorkeling with fish and other marine life in the huge saltwater lagoon. Boatswain's Beach is also the home of the Cayman Turtle Farm, which breeds the rare green sea turtles.

VISITORS' CHECKLIST

Practical Information
786 Northwest Point Road, West Bay, Grand Cayman. **Tel** 345 949 3894. **Open** 8am–5pm Mon–Sat (also some Sun). 🐾 🚻 ♿ 🚫 ⬜ 📷 🖥 turtle.ky

Transport
🚌

Caribbean Bird Aviary and Iguana Exhibit
This free-flight aviary houses many colorful bird species indigenous to the Cayman Islands and the greater Caribbean.

Breaker's Lagoon
This swimming pool is the largest in the Cayman Islands and is perfect for relaxing and cooling off.

Shoreline Nursery is a protected reef and a safe haven for disabled fish that cannot survive in the wild.

Turtle Tank

Entrance

Education Center

Boatswain's Lagoon
Visitors can wade into this saltwater lagoon to see the marine life or watch through the underwater viewing panel.

Breeding Pond
Huge green sea turtles breed in this large artificial pond rimmed by a sandy beach.

Touch Tanks
Under staff supervision, visitors can get to hold one of the sea turtle yearlings and also get a photograph taken.

Everyday items on display at Pedro St. James National Historic Site

❺ Pedro St. James National Historic Site

5 miles (8 km) E of George Town, Grand Cayman. 🚍 ℹ️ Pedro Castle Road, Savannah, 345 947 3329.
Open 9am–5pm daily.
Closed Christmas Day. 🚫 📷 ♿ not on upper floors of the Great House. 🖥️ 🏠 🌐 pedrostjames.ky

Located high above Pedro Bluff, Pedro St. James is the oldest building on the Cayman Islands. William Eden, a wealthy Englishman, used Jamaican slave labor to construct this magnificent three-story stone building in 1780. In 1831, the first Cayman government was formed in this building. The building later suffered damage from hurricanes, fire, and even lightning, but in 1992 the government decided to restore it. Guides are dressed in period costumes and a tour of the house shows a display of its period furniture with mahogany floors and staircases, timber beams, and gabled framework. The visitors' center features an excellent 3-D multi-sensory theater, where, in 20 minutes, visitors can experience 200 years of Cayman history. There are breathtaking views from the house and the site is also a popular location for weddings, concerts, and parties. A memorial commemorates the devastating Hurricane Ivan of 2004.

❻ Queen Elizabeth II Botanic Park

15 miles (24 km) E of George Town, Grand Cayman. 🚕 ℹ️ 345 947 3558.
Open 9am–5:30pm daily.
Closed Christmas and Good Friday.
🚗 ♿ golf carts to assist people with limited mobility are available with advance reservation. 🖥️ 🏠
🌐 botanic-park.ky

This 65-acre (26-ha) park showcases more than half of the plant species native to the Cayman Islands, as well as birds and wildlife, including the rare, endemic blue iguanas. The park offers visitors a short walk through the lovely 3-acre (1-ha) Floral Color Garden, which features hundreds of species of tropical and subtropical plants laid out colorfully. Adjoining the garden is a picturesque lake that attracts aquatic birds including the rare West Indian whistling duck. Located nearby is the Heritage Garden with its traditional ornamental and medicinal plants, which Caymanians used for various ailments. The garden also has a pretty traditional Cayman house dating back to 1900 and a collection of fruit trees.

"Iguana right of way" sign

A path near the entrance, Woodland Trail, gives people the opportunity to view the natural landscape, which covers almost 40 acres (16 ha) of the park. Visitors get a chance to see the blue iguana roaming freely in this stretch. The park is also home to 56 species of butterflies and a garden of orchids.

❼ Little Cayman

89 miles (143 km) NE of Grand Cayman. 🛫 200. ✈️

A mere 10-sq-mile (25-sq-km) island, Little Cayman is the smallest of the three Cayman islands and is inhabited by only a few residents. Nature rules this laid-back, one-road island, where iguanas and birds outnumber humans. The island is a popular day trip from Grand Cayman for travelers who mainly come here for solitude or exceptional diving. Bloody Bay Wall in Bloody Bay Marine Park *(see p111)* offers the Caribbean's finest drop-offs and is known all over the world.

East of the tiny airport sits Blossom Village, the only town on the island, where visitors can stop at a restaurant. Close by is the Booby Pond Nature Reserve, a 206-acre (83-ha) RAMSAR site, a nesting ground for 20,000 red-footed boobies as well as the magnificent frigatebirds and waterbirds. The **National Trust House** at Blossom Village offers viewing platforms with telescopes to observe the birdlife. Just across the reserve

The traditional Cayman house inside Queen Elizabeth II Botanic Park

For hotels and restaurants on these islands see p114 and p115

Corals and seafans growing on Bloody Bay Wall, Little Cayman

is **Little Cayman Museum** that has displays of the island's history. Tarpon fishing and bird-watching is great at Tarpon Lake. Point of Sand, at the eastern tip, has a pretty little beach. The East End Point Lighthouse here overlooks Cayman Brac. Offshore lies Owen Island, a tiny white beach cay, which is ideal for picnics and kayaking.

National Trust House
558 South Church St., Blossom Village.
Tel 345 749 1121. **Open** 9am–5pm
Mon–Fri. 📷 w **nationaltrust.org.ky**

🏛 **Little Cayman Museum**
Blossom Village. **Tel** 345 948 1033.
Open 3–5pm Thu & Fri.

❽ Cayman Brac

90 miles (144 km) NE of Grand Cayman. 🌄 2,100. ✈ ℹ Cayman Islands Department of Tourism, Brac Office, West End Community Park, 345 948 1649; District Administration, Stake Bay, 345 948 2222.
w **itsyourstoexplore.com**

Brac, the Gaelic word for bluff, is a suitable name for this Cayman isle which has the most dramatic topography of the group, dominated by a limestone cliff reaching up to 146 ft (44 m) on its eastern tip. The island has several caves and many trails to explore. A 3-hour hike from Spot Bay leads to an old lighthouse from where there are splendid views of the

ocean. Halfway down the trail is Little Cayman Brac Outlook (a large rock), where bird enthusiasts can see nesting brown boobies.

Another interesting hike is south off Bight Road. This is the 310-acre (125-ha) National Trust Parrot Reserve and Nature Trail, which protects the endemic Cayman Brac parrot, other birds, plants, and native trees. On South Side Road is the Bat Cave, which is home to fruit bats. Farther down the same road, visitors can also see Rebecca's Cave, the historic site where the islanders took shelter during the worst hurricane ever in 1932. It contains the grave of Rebecca Bodden, a baby girl who died in the cave during the storm. Just beside the cave starts the challenging Salt Water Pond trail, which takes hikers from the south to north

coast. At the end of this hike is Salt Water Pond, a sanctuary for a tern colony. Apart from bird-watching, hikers can visit the beautiful **Cayman Brac Heritage House** on North East Bay Road. Local artisans display their work here. Nearby, at Stake Bay is the island's first museum, **Cayman Brac Museum**, opened in 1983. It has exhibits on ship-building and displays on the islanders' lifestyles during the 1930s. The island is undergoing serious reconstruction after being severely damaged in Hurricane Paloma that struck the island in 2008.

Cayman Brac Heritage House
North East Bay. **Tel** 345 948 0563.
Open 9:30am–1pm, 2–5pm Mon–Fri,
10am–3pm Sat. 📷 ♿ 📷

🏛 **Cayman Brac Museum**
Stake Bay. **Tel** 345 948 2222.
Open 9am–noon, 1–4pm Mon–Fri;
9am–noon Sat. 📷 📷 📷

Brown boobies at Little Cayman Brac Outlook on the way to the lighthouse

Blue Iguanas

The Queen Elizabeth II Botanic Park is home to the Blue Iguana Habitat, the center for the National Trust's Blue Iguana Recovery Program. Just two decades ago, the endemic Grand Cayman blue iguana was facing extinction. With an ultimate repopulation goal of 1,000, the Habitat, along the park's Woodland Trail, is the captive breeding ground for these critically endangered reptiles. The blue iguana grows up to 5 ft (2 m) long and can live up to 69 years. Males and females differ in colors. While the coloration of male iguanas can vary from dark grey to turquoise blue, females are olive green to pale blue. They are primarily herbivorous and their diet mainly consists of fruits, plants, and flowers. The National Trust runs daily blue iguana safaris with a 2-hour guided tour that takes visitors behind the scenes of the breeding facility.

The unique blue iguana

Outdoor Activities and Specialized Holidays

The Cayman Islands are renowned for activities that focus on the sea, particularly scuba diving and snorkeling. All three islands have scores of superb diving and snorkeling sites. Non-divers can also experience marine wonders from a submarine with a glass viewing chamber. All the different types of watersports are available in Grand Cayman, as are day-sails aboard a variety of boats. The islands also offer excellent bird-watching opportunities with seven bird sanctuaries on Grand Cayman, as well as great hiking and fishing.

The exquisite Seven Mile Beach, Grand Cayman

Beaches

This tri-island nation is blessed with plenty of white-sand beaches, all of which are public. The crown jewel is Grand Cayman's Seven Mile Beach, a spectacular beach. The crescent of white sand is lined with high-end hotels and condos, beachside restaurants, and watersport operators who offer plenty of activities. On the north tip of Grand Cayman, Cayman Kai has huts, hammocks, beach volleyball, and a good bar and grill. Rum Point's Beach, with calm, shallow water, is a bevy of action and the weekend favorite with the locals.

Little Cayman's secluded Point of Sand on the eastern tip is a great picnicking spot and offers sweeping views of Cayman Brac. On the northern shore, Jacksons Point provides a perfect setting for shore diving and snorkeling.

Although Cayman Brac's shoreline is predominantly limestone, there are a few good beaches including Public Beach and the beach in front of Brac Reef Beach Resort *(see p114)* on West End Point.

Watersports

A large number of the islands' watersports centers are located at major hotels and on the most popular beaches. On Grand Cayman, they offer a full array of watersports and rentals that include ocean kayaks,

Tour boat leaving the beach, Grand Cayman

waverunners, Hobie Cats, aqua bikes, parasailing, water skiing, banana boat rides, and paddleboats.

The reef-protected shallows, stretching for 4 miles (7 km) off East End, are the best location for windsurfing of all levels. Other good spots are found at North Sound and along the west coast. **Red Sail Sports** at Morritt's Tortuga Resort rents equipment, and is the only operator that offers lessons to beginners.

Watersports on Little Cayman and Cayman Brac are primarily non-motorized. Most resorts provide kayaks, windsurfing boards, and other gear.

Day-Sails and Boat Trips

For a day out on the Caribbean Sea, there are a gamut of options available in Grand Cayman. **Atlantis Submarines** offers underwater trips over the coral reefs, either in their submarine or the unique observatory that descends several feet below the surface.

Visitors can party with the **Pirates of the Caymans** on the *Jolly Roger*, a two-thirds-size replica of Columbus's *Niña*. The afternoon pirate adventure and sunset cruises include an open bar. Sailing excursions on a luxury catamaran are available with Red Sail Sports. **Sail Cayman** offers a range of sailing options. Travelers can paddle through tranquil lagoons and protected mangroves on a guided eco-adventure expedition organized by **Cayman Kayaks**. **Cayman Glass Bottom Boat** operates a speed-boat with a huge window at its base that helps occupants view a larger area. Located in George Town, the National Trust organizes guided boat tours through the Central Mangrove Wetlands that cover a large part of Grand Cayman.

Diving off the Cayman Islands

Home to some of the best dive sites in the Caribbean, the Cayman Islands have been continually named among the world's top-five dive and snorkel destinations. The three islands feature pristine walls, shallow reefs, several shipwrecks, a variety of marine life, and more than 250 dive sites. Bloody Bay Wall, offshore Little Cayman, is a diver's mecca. Stingray City, off Grand Cayman, provides the rare opportunity to get up close and personal with dozens of Atlantic southern stingrays.

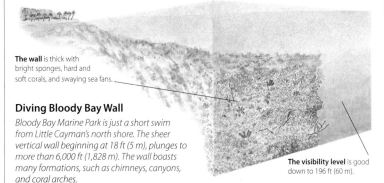

The wall is thick with bright sponges, hard and soft corals, and swaying sea fans.

The visibility level is good down to 196 ft (60 m).

Diving Bloody Bay Wall

Bloody Bay Marine Park is just a short swim from Little Cayman's north shore. The sheer vertical wall beginning at 18 ft (5 m), plunges to more than 6,000 ft (1,828 m). The wall boasts many formations, such as chimneys, canyons, and coral arches.

Schoolmaster snappers, with distinctly yellow fins, are found just above the reefs. These fish are usually wary of divers.

Yellow tube sponges are common in the Cayman Islands, as are red rope, strawberry, and orange vase sponges.

Diving off the other two islands

Grand Cayman has around 130 dive sites, some just a short distance from the shore. Cayman Brac's 50-plus dive sites include four wrecks, the most famous being the 330-ft (100-m) Russian-built warship, M.V. Captain Keith Tibbetts, sunk in 1996.

Stingray City *(see p106)*, in North Sound off Grand Cayman, offers a wonderful opportunity to swim with, or wade among, stingrays flocking here to feed.

DIVE OPERATORS

Diving Spots
W divecayman.ky

Ocean Frontiers
W oceanfrontiers.com

Pirates Point
W piratespointresort.com

Reef Divers
W bracreef.com

Lost world of Atlantis, off Cayman Brac, is an underwater attraction created by local sculptor J. Foots. This replica of the mythological city, with more than 100 sculptures, is popular with divers.

Visitors looking out of Atlantis XI submarine, Grand Cayman

Submarine Rides

A great way to explore Grand Cayman's renowned coral reef and marine life, including tropical fish, is a trip on one of the island's submarines.

Atlantis Submarines offers rides aboard the *Atlantis XI* to depths of 100 ft (30 m). Their *Seaworld Observatory* semi-submarine is a floating observatory just 5 ft (2 m) below the ocean's surface. Its wall-to-wall glass viewing chamber offers spectacular views of the reefs and wrecks.

Another shallow option on Grand Cayman is the glass-hulled **Nautilus**, which takes visitors around the Caymans' waters to see the marine life.

Bird-Watching

In peak season, up to 200 native and wintering bird species can be seen on the Cayman Islands. Grand Cayman has seven protected bird sanctuaries, including the Queen Elizabeth II Botanic Park *(see p108)*, Colliers Pond, and the Majestic Reserve. The National Trust's Governor Michael Gore Bird Sanctuary in Bodden Town is home to about one-third of the islands recorded avian species. It also features an elevated walkway over a freshwater pond. A bird blind and interpretive signs make sighting the 60 species of water and wading birds easy. The **National Trust** offers weekly bird-watching tours to various sites. There are five seabird colonies on the sister islands. These are home to the redfooted booby, brown booby, the magnificent frigate bird, white-tailed tropicbird, and summer visitor – the least tern. Nature Cayman arranges free bird-watching tours with nature guides.

Booby Pond Nature Reserve in Little Cayman is home to the largest breeding colony of red-footed boobies in the Western Hemisphere and the only breeding colony of frigate birds on the Cayman Islands.

Cayman Brac has a 180-acre (73-ha) parrot reserve where visitors may get a glimpse of one of the 350 endangered Brac parrots. Other good birding sites include the East Point bluff, with nesting brown boobies. The Westerly Ponds, Salt Water Pond, and the marshes are inhabited by waterbirds and other seasonal birds. Visitors can also see fruit bats hanging upside down in the Bat Cave *(see p109)*.

Brown boobies, Lighthouse Footpath, Cayman Brac

Hiking

Grand Cayman's most popular hike is the 2-mile (3-km) long Mastic Trail. The woodland has a variety of habitats ranging from wetland to dry forest, including trees that are unique to the Cayman Islands. Wildlife here also includes indigenous species as well as other animals such as butterflies, frogs, lizards, and hermit crabs. Guides for independent hikers are available at the National Trust, which also organizes weekly guided hikes. The trail is not suitable for children under six, the elderly, and the infirm.

Hiking trails are mapped in the Nature Tourism brochures, available at the airport. Hikers will come across ceramic interpretive signs and ecology panels on beach walks, woodland trails, and flora and fauna. Free guided hikes are also offered on the island.

On Cayman Brac, people enjoy walking along the 146-ft (44-m) bluff *(see p109)* from where a variety of birds can be spotted. The isle is peppered with trails including the Salt Water Pond hike and the well trodden Lighthouse Footpath on the eastern tip.

On Little Cayman, there are more than a dozen secluded beaches perfect for strolling, lagoons, mangrove forests, salt ponds, and wetlands to explore. The West End is home to the

View from a rugged limestone bluff, Cayman Brac

historic Salt Rock Nature Trail that once linked Blossom Village to the Salt Rock dock.

Fishing

Prized gamefish such as blue marlin, tuna, wahoo, and mahimahi can be caught year-round. Light tackle and fly-fishing for bonefish and tarpon challenge anglers, especially in the flats off Little Cayman. The **Cayman Islands Angling Club** arranges fishing tournaments and welcomes visitors. The islands have plenty of guides that offer half- and full-day deep-sea, bone, tarpon, and reef fishing. On Grand Cayman,

Fishing in a lagoon, Cayman Brac

Captain Ronald Ebanks of **Fly Fish Grand Cayman** organizes flyfishing and light tackle trips, as does **Fish Bones Guided Fly Fishing**. **Bayside Watersports** provide all types of fishing, from casting for bonefish and tarpon in the flats to wrestling marlin out at sea. **Cool Breeze Boat Charters** is a reputed fishing concessionaire on Cayman Brac.

Golf

The 9-hole championship **Britannia Golf Club**, which can also be played as an 18-hole executive course, is one of only three Caribbean golf courses designed by golf legend Jack Nicklaus. The links-style course has all the natural challenges of a traditional seaside layout, including grassy mounds, rolling dunes, carries over water, and oversized bunkers. The other golf course on Grand Cayman is the 9-hole **Blue Tip** at the Ritz-Carlton (see p114). Designed by well-known

Landscaped grounds, Britannia Golf Club, Grand Cayman

golf course designer Greg Norman, it is only open to guests of the Ritz-Carlton. There are no golf courses on the sister islands.

Horse-Riding

Guided horse-rides along scenic trails or on one of Grand Cayman's many beautiful beaches are offered by **Pampered Ponies** or **Spirit of the West**. Private rides are also available. To make the ride more memorable, visitors can canter into the surf on horseback or sign up for an early morning or sunset ride.

(see p114)

DIRECTORY

Watersports

Red Sail Sports
Grand Cayman.
Tel 345 623 5965.
W redsailcayman.com

Day-Sails and Boat Trips

Cayman Glass Bottom Boat
Grand Cayman.
Tel 345 928 9449.
W aquaventures cayman.com

Cayman Islands Submarines
Grand Cayman.
Tel 345 949 7700.
W caymanislands submarines.com

Cayman Kayaks
Grand Cayman.
Tel 345 926 4467.
W caymankayaks.com

Pirates of the Caymans
Grand Cayman.
Tel 345 945 7245.
W jollyrogercayman. com

Sail Cayman
Grand Cayman.
Tel 345 916 4333.
W sailcayman.com

Submarine Rides

Nautilus
Grand Cayman.
Tel 345 945 1355.
W nautilus.ky

Bird-Watching

National Trust
Grand Cayman.
Tel 345 729 1121.
W nationaltrust.org.ky

Fishing

Bayside Watersports
Morgans Harbour, West Bay, Grand Cayman.
Tel 345 949 3200.
W baysidewatersports. com

Cayman Islands Angling Club
Grand Cayman.
Tel 345 945 3131.
W fishcayman.com

Cool Breeze Boat Charters
Cayman Brac.
Tel 345 924 2887.
W coolbreezefishing. com

Fish Bones Guided Fly Fishing
Grand Cayman.
W fish-bones.com

Fly Fish Grand Cayman
Coconut Place, West Bay Road, Grand Cayman.
Tel 345 947 3146.
W flyfishgrandcayman. com

Golf

Blue Tip
The Ritz-Carlton, Grand Cayman.
Tel 345 815 6500.

Britannia Golf Club
Grand Cayman.
Tel 345 745 4653.
W britannia-golf.com

Horse-Riding

Pampered Ponies
Grand Cayman.
Tel 345 916 2540.
W ponies.ky

Spirit of the West
Grand Cayman.
Tel 345 916 6488.
W seahorses.ky

Where to Stay

The pool area at The Alexander Hotel, Cayman Brac

CAYMAN BRAC:
The Alexander Hotel $$
Resort
Southside Road, West End
Tel *345 948 8222*
W alexanderhotelcayman.com
The Alexander is a clean and friendly colonial-themed resort with sophisticated modern furnishings. Fantastic seafood buffet. Close to the beach.

CAYMAN BRAC:
Brac Reef Beach Resort $$
Beach Resort
Southside Road, West End
Tel *345 948 1323*
W bracreef.com
Family-run resort featuring warm, basic decor. Facilities include a scuba diving center, bicycles, tennis courts, and a fitness room. The restaurant serves island classics.

GRAND CAYMAN:
Morritt's Grand Resort $
Apartments
2289 Queens Highway, East End
Tel *345 947 7449*
W morritts.com
Comfortable condo apartments, with a great location on Seven Mile Beach. Noteworthy features include an infinity pool with ocean views and diving facilities.

GRAND CAYMAN: Plantation
Village Beach Resort $
Apartments
323 West Bay Road
Tel *345 949 4199*
W plantationvillage.com
Large beachfront condo complex with homey decor and varied floor plans. Good snorkeling and watersports facilities.

GRAND CAYMAN: Compass
Point Dive Resort $$
Resort
346 Austin Conolly Drive, East End
Tel *345 947 0000*
W compasspoint.ky
One-, two-, and three-bedroom fully-equipped condominiums with ocean views. Facilities include kayaks, bicycles, kite-boarding instructors, and diving.

DK Choice
GRAND CAYMAN:
Holiday Inn Resort Grand
Cayman $$
Resort
278 Crighton Drive,
Crystal Harbour
Tel *345 949 3100*
W hiresortgrandcayman.com
Undoubtedly one of the most sophisticated resorts in the Caymans, the Ramada Grant boasts minimalist contemporary styling, with turquoise, white, and chocolate color schemes, and state-of-the-art amenities. It hosts a dive shop, jet-ski and bicycle rental, plus tennis courts. Close to Stingray City.

GRAND CAYMAN:
The Retreat at Lookout $$
Boutique
521 Lookout Road, Bodden Town
Tel *705 719 9144*
W retreatatlookout.com
Attentive care from its live-in owners is the hallmark of this quaint B&B. There are relaxing rockers on the long shaded porch. Great base for exploring the island. Excellent breakfasts.

GRAND CAYMAN:
Shangri-La B&B $$
Boutique
1 Sticky Toffee Lane, West Bay
Tel *345 526 1170*
W shangrilabandb.com
Renowned as the island's best B&B, this is a comfortable family-run guesthouse with plantation-style furnishings. Children under 12 not allowed.

GRAND CAYMAN:
Aqua Bay Club $$$
Beach Resort
West Bay Road
Tel *345 945 4728*
W aquabayclub.com
Elegant and cozy all-suites resort, which offers impeccably clean, huge self-catering units with cell phone access and free Wi-Fi.

Price Guide
Prices are based on one night's stay in high season for a standard double room, inclusive of service charges and taxes.

$	up to $100
$$	$100–300
$$$	over $300

GRAND CAYMAN: Grand
Cayman Beach Suites $$$
Luxury
747 West Bay Road, Seven Mile Beach
Tel *345 949 1234*
W grand-cayman-beach-suites.com
Loaded with activities, this deluxe resort adjoins the Britannia golf course and offers spa facilities, tennis, watersports, dive center, and catamaran trips. The suites are spacious and colorful.

GRAND CAYMAN:
The Meridian $$$
Luxury
917 West Bay Road, Seven Mile Beach
Tel *345 945 4002*
W meridian.ky
This six-story resort hotel offers one- and two-bedroom apartments with ocean views and plantation furnishings. It also has a floodlit swimming pool.

GRAND CAYMAN:
The Ritz-Carlton $$$
Luxury
West Bay Road, Seven Mile Beach
Tel *345 943 9000*
W ritzcarlton.com
The Ritz-Carlton on Caymans delivers the luxury and service for which the brand is renowned. Five restaurants, 24-hour room service, tennis facilities, and a golf course are all on site.

LITTLE CAYMAN:
Paradise Villas $$
Beach Resort
Guy Banks Road
Tel *345 948 0001*
W paradisevillas.com
Intimate one-room oceanfront villas, each with front and back porches and well-equipped kitchenettes. Relax in hammocks located at the water's edge.

LITTLE CAYMAN:
Southern Cross Club $$
Beach Resort
Guy Banks Road
Tel *619 563 0017*
W southerncrossclub.com
Southern Cross Club is a laid-back resort with its own dive boat. It offers delightful oceanfront bungalows set amid palm trees, with lovely plantation furnishings.

Where to Eat and Drink

CAYMAN BRAC: La Esperanza $$
Caribbean
La Esperanza hotel, Stake Bay
Tel *345 948 0591*
This nautically themed restaurant is known for its jerk chicken and Key lime pie.

GRAND CAYMAN: Heritage Kitchen $$
Caribbean
11 Boggy Sand Road, West Bay
Tel *345 916 0444* **Closed** *Mon & Tue*
Enjoy the best of home-style island fare at this friendly, casual restaurant serving generous portions of fish fritters, coconut fish, and fish tea.

GRAND CAYMAN: Rackam's Waterfront Bar & Grill $$
Seafood
North Church Street, George Town
Tel *345 945 3860*
This trendy restaurant has open deck seating where it serves up its signature fish 'n' chips and conch fritters with glasses of cold beer. Guests can snorkel off the restaurant's ladder.

GRAND CAYMAN: Agua Restaurant & Lounge $$$
Seafood
Galleria Plaza, Seven Mile Beach
Tel *345 949 2482*
Elegant Italian-owned seafood restaurant offering up such treats as Peruvian *seviche* (raw fish with citrus juice) and couscous-crusted wahoo.

GRAND CAYMAN: Blue by Eric Ripert $$$
Seafood
The Ritz-Carlton, West Bay Road, Seven Mile Beach
Tel *345 943 9000* **Closed** *Sun & Mon*
In the suave Ritz-Carlton, this is Cayman's only Five Diamond restaurant, serving great seafood. Try the baked snapper stew.

GRAND CAYMAN: Deckers $$$
Caribbean
West Bay Road, Seven Mile Beach
Tel *345 945 6600*
Relaxed yet elegant restaurant named for its double-decker bus incorporated into the bar/lounge. Do not miss the "all-you-can-eat lobster" meals every Tuesday and Saturday.

GRAND CAYMAN: Edoardo's $$$
Italian
Coconut Place, West Bay Road, Seven Mile Beach
Tel *345 945 4408*
A local favorite, this friendly Italian restaurant serves delicious fresh mussels, seafood linguine, and a to-die-for banana toffee pie.

GRAND CAYMAN: Grand Old House $$$
International
South Church Street, George Town
Tel *345 949 9333*
Romantic restaurant in a former great house with a seaside veranda and piano music. Great surf 'n' turf and award-winning wine list.

GRAND CAYMAN: Osetra Bay Restaurant & Lounge $$$
Fine Dining
Morgan's Lane, West Bay
Tel *345 325 5000* **Closed** *Sun dinner*
In a breathtaking setting, the extremely sophisticated Osetra Bay serves world cuisine with a Caribbean flair, and there is also a champagne lounge.

GRAND CAYMAN: Ragazzi Ristorante $$$
Italian
Buckingham Square, West Bay Road, Seven Mile Beach
Tel *345 945 3484*
The preferred spot for relaxed Italian dining. Cayman's only wood-burning brick oven turns out delicious thin-crust pizzas.

Price Guide
Prices are based on a two-course meal for one, including tax and service charges and half a bottle of wine.

$	up to $15
$$	$15–40
$$$	over $40

GRAND CAYMAN: The Brasserie $$$
Seafood
171 Elgin Avenue, George Town
Tel *345 945 1815* **Closed** *Sat & Sun*
A warm ambience and sustainable cooking are the highlights of this contemporary brasserie. Creative dishes include chipotle-braised oxtail tacos.

DK Choice

GRAND CAYMAN: The Cracked Conch $$$
Fine Dining
North West Point Road, West Bay
Tel *345 945 5217*
The Cracked Conch is a stylish and airy contemporary restaurant with plush booths. The chef creates delectable Caribbean fare such as crispy calamari with cardamom-marinated carrots, and honey-jerk-glazed tuna with tomato sorbet. A huge prow-shaped deck overhangs the sea.

GRAND CAYMAN: The Wharf Restaurant & Bar $$$
Seafood
43 West Bay Road, Seven Mile Beach
Tel *345 949 2231*
Seashore terrace restaurant. Try the signature basil and pistachio Chilean sea bass. Visitors flock for tarpon fish feeding at 9pm nightly.

LITTLE CAYMAN: Hungry Iguana Restaurant $$$
International
Guy Banks Road
Tel *345 948 0001*
The only oceanfront dining on Little Cayman, Hungry Iguana serves everything from curry to pizza. Huge sports bar and *prix-fixe* theme nights.

LITTLE CAYMAN: Pirate's Point $$$
Caribbean
Pirate's Point Resort, Guy Banks Road
Tel *345 948 1010* **Closed** *mid-Aug–Oct*
Owner Gladys Howard, a Cordon Bleu-trained chef, serves a fixed-price buffet dinner with traditional Cayman dishes.

Attractive decor and comfortable booths at The Cracked Conch, Grand Cayman

Practical Information

Thanks to a flourishing tourism industry and an equally prosperous banking sector, Caymanians enjoy one of the highest standards of living in the world. With the Cayman Island dollar (CI$) worth more than the US dollar, the islands are an expensive destination. The largest and most developed of the islands, Grand Cayman attracts the maximum number of visitors. Though Hurricanes Ivan (2004) and Paloma (2008) dealt a severe blow, the islands have since recovered.

Taxis outside Owen Roberts International Airport, Grand Cayman

When to Go

December to April is when most people visit the Cayman Islands. The year-round temperature ranges between 70–90° F (21–32° C). The dry season lasts from November to April, while the rainy season runs mid-May through October. August to October are prime hurricane months. The islands' unique Hurricane Guarantee covers any cancellations made prior to arrival and offers compensation if vacation time is cut short because of inclement weather.

Getting there

All international flights arrive at Grand Cayman's Owen Roberts International Airport. Scheduled flights to Grand Cayman are available on **Air Canada**, **Air Jamaica**, **American Airlines**, **British Airways**, **Delta**, **United Airlines**, **US Airways**, and **Spirit Airlines**. **Cayman Airways** is the national flag carrier, offering flights from the US. A host of charters also provide non-stop flights from US cities.

Inter-island daily service from Grand Cayman to the sister islands is provided by Cayman Airways and its affiliate Cayman Airways Express. Charter flights can be booked with **Island Air**. There is no ferry service.

Documentation

A valid passport is required, along with a return ticket. British, Canadian and US nationals do not need a visa to enter the Caymans, but many other countries, including several Caribbean states, do. The **Immigration Department** website has details of countries requiring and those exempted from visas. A departure tax is included in the airline ticket.

Visitor Information

The **Cayman Islands Department of Tourism** has its head office in Grand Cayman and a branch in Cayman Brac. **District Administration** has information on the sister islands. The **Tourism Attraction Board** and **Sister Islands Tourism Association** also provide useful information.

Health and Security

The Caymans are one of the Caribbean's safest destinations, with a low crime rate. However, petty theft and pickpocketing does occur, and it is advisable to keep valuables in the hotel safe. The islands are hassle-free, with no street or beach vendors.

The government's **Cayman Islands Hospital** and the private **Chrissie Tomlinson Memorial Hospital** have modern facilities and are well-equipped to deal with emergencies. The state-run **Faith Hospital** is in Cayman Brac, while Little Cayman has the **Little Cayman Clinic**. Medical insurance is mandatory.

Banking and Currency

The Cayman Islands has its own currency, the CI dollar (CI$), but the US dollar is accepted everywhere and there is a fixed rate of exchange. Major credit cards and traveler's checks are widely accepted. ATM machines are available all over Grand Cayman. There is only one on Cayman Brac and one on Little Cayman. The latter has just one bank that opens only on Mondays and Thursdays from 9:30am–2:30pm.

Communications

International Direct Dialing is available from most hotels on the Cayman Islands. The area code is 345, followed by a seven-digit local number. Public phones are available throughout the islands. Prepaid calling cards and mobiles for hire can be found at **Lime Cable & Wireless** offices. **Digicel** also provides mobile service. Internet access is available at

A fully equipped fire engine, Grand Cayman

airports, most hotels, and some restaurants. Cyber cafés are found in most larger towns.

Transport

Visitors must be at least 21 years to drive and have a temporary driving permit issued at any car rental firm. Vehicles can be hired from **Coconut Car Rentals** on Grand Cayman; **CB Rent-A-Car** at the Cayman Brac airport; and from **McLaughlin Car & Moped**

Duty-free shop, George Town, Grand Cayman

Rentals, the only car rental firm in Little Cayman, although scooters can also be rented from **Scooten! Scooters!** Driving is on the left. Main roads are paved and in good condition.

Taxis are readily available at all resorts and airports. There is a taxi stand in George Town.

Daily public bus service on Grand Cayman runs from 6am until midnight depending on the route and the day.

Shopping

Shops selling duty-free goods are found on all the islands. Traditional crafts made of leather, thatch, wood, and shell are the best locally-made buys, as are the local art and food products. Look out for Caymanite (an indigenous semi-precious stone) art and jewelry. The **Cayman Craft Market** is a good place to buy local products.

Language

English is the official language of the Cayman Islands.

Electricity

The electrical system on the Cayman Islands delivers 110 volts at 60 cycles. US-style plugs are used. European appliances will require adaptors and transformers.

Time

The Cayman Islands are on Eastern Standard Time (EST), 5 hours behind Greenwich Mean Time (GMT). The islands do not observe daylight savings.

Getting Married

Visiting couples can marry the day they arrive. It is possible to arrange for a marriage official and apply for a non-resident's marriage license, granted by the Governor, in advance. Contact the **Passport and Corporate Services Office**.

DIRECTORY

Getting there

Air Canada
w aircanada.com

Air Jamaica
w airjamaica.com

American Airlines
w aa.com

British Airways
w britishairways.com

Cayman Airways
Tel 345 949 2311.
w caymanairways.com

Delta
w delta.com

Island Air
w islandair.ky

Spirit Airlines
w spirit.com

United Airlines
w united.com

US Airways
w usairways.com

Documentation

Immigration Department
Tel 345 949 8344.
w immigration.gov.ky

Visitor Information

Cayman Islands Department of Tourism
Tel 345 949 0623 (Grand Cayman). Tel 345 948 1649 (Cayman Brac).
w caymanislands.ky

District Administration
Cayman Brac. Tel 345 948 2222. w itsyoursto explore.com

Sister Islands Tourism Association
Cayman Brac. Tel 345 916 4874. w sita.ky

Tourism Attraction Board
Tel 345 949 6999.
w tab.ky

Health and Security

Cayman Islands Hospital
Grand Cayman.
Tel 345 949 8600.
w hsa.ky

Chrissie Tomlinson Memorial Hospital
Grand Cayman.
Tel 345 949 6066.

Faith Hospital
Cayman Brac. Tel 345 948 2243.

Little Cayman Clinic
Little Cayman.
Tel 345 948 0072.

Police and Fire
Tel 911.

Communications

Digicel
w digicelcayman.com

Lime Cable & Wireless
w lime.com

Transport

CB Rent-A-Car
w cbrentacar.com

Coconut Car Rentals
w coconut.ky

McLaughlin Car & Moped Rentals
Little Cayman.
Tel 345 948 1000.

Scooten! Scooters!
Tel 345 916 4971.
w scootenscooters. com

Shopping

Cayman Craft Market
George Town, Grand Cayman.

Getting Married

Passport and Corporate Services Office
George Town, Grand Cayman.
Tel 345 943 7678.

Exploring Turks and Caicos

A group of islands, Turks and Caicos lie southeast of The Bahamas and northeast of Cuba. Providenciales, the westernmost isle, has the lion's share of beach resorts, spread along Grace Bay. Most of the island's 30,000 inhabitants live on Providenciales. The capital, Cockburn Town, is located on Grand Turk, the easternmost isle. Lightly-populated North, Middle, East, and tiny South Caicos are mostly scrub-covered and teem with birds. Flat as pancakes, the isles sit atop an underwater plateau with walls that plunge to the bottom of near fathomless ocean trenches.

West Caicos Marine National Park
This park protects iguanas and birdlife. It is also a world-renowned scuba diving venue with great wall dives, tunnels, and pelagic sealife.

North, Middle and East Caicos Nature Reserve
Spanning three Caicos islands, this nature reserve protects the habitat of manatees, iguanas, flamingos, and scores of other bird species.

The luxurious Grace Bay Club, Providenciales

Getting Around

The Turks and Caicos have a total land area of 166 sq miles (430 sq km) scattered across 10,000 sq miles (26,000 sq km) of ocean. The isles are connected by a few ferry services and scheduled, small plane charters. A bridge connects North and Middle Caicos. Providenciales is served by tourist taxis and cars. Minivans offer a communal taxi service on Grand Turk and on the smaller isles, where scooter and bicycle rentals are offered, although Grand Turk is small enough to walk around town.

Hobie Cats lined up on the cottony sands of Providenciales

For hotels and restaurants on this island see p128 and p129

Sights at a Glance

❶ Providenciales
❷ Grace Bay
❸ West Caicos Marine
   National Park
❹ North Caicos
❺ Middle Caicos
❻ South Caicos
❼ Grand Turk
❿ Salt Cay

Featured Hotels and Resorts

❽ Grand Turk Inn
❾ Salt Raker Inn

Quiet Blue Horizon Resort in Middle Caicos

0 kilometers 20
0 miles 20

Grand Turk
Administrative center of the islands, it has the most number of historic buildings, as well as delightful inns and a lively nightlife.

*barra
ch*
ambarra
*orimers
Point*

*Drum
Point*

East Caicos

ve

*Belle Sound
Nature Reserve* ❻ SOUTH
CAICOS
Cockburn
Harbor

*Turks Island
Passage*

❼ GRAND TURK
Flamingo Beach
❽ GRAND TURK INN
Pillory Beach
SALT RAKER ❾ Cockburn Town
INN *White Sand
Beach*

*Little
mbergris
Cay*
Big Ambergris Cay

SALT CAY ❿
Balfour Town

*Cotton
Cay*
East Cay

Salt Cay
The saltpans here offer tremendous birding. Humpback whales frolic off the north shore, and can be seen from a close distance.

Colorful houses along the seafront of Cockburn Town, Grand Turk

Key
═══ Minor road
--- Ferry route

For keys to symbols *see back flap*

The sprawling Caicos Conch Farm, eastern Providenciales

❶ Providenciales

Second westernmost isle of Turks and Caicos. 🏝 30,000. ✈ 🚢 *i* Stubbs Diamond Plaza, 649 946 4970. 🏄 Big Blue Unlimited, 649 946 5034. 🪁 Kite Flying Competition (Mar); Music and Cultural Festival (Jul–Aug).

This ox-jaw-shaped isle is renowned for the crescent of never-ending beach at Grace Bay. "Downtown" is the island's business center and has a few shops and offices.

The isle tapers east from Northwest Point, that is pinned by a lighthouse and reached by rough sandy trails. The entire west shore is protected within Northwest Point Marine National Park and Pigeon Pond and Frenchman's Creek Nature Reserve, sheltering wetlands, mangroves, tidal flats, and offshore reefs. Chalk Sound National Park, along the south shore, has beautiful blue waters. For a fine view, head to South Rock, where rock slabs are carved with mariner's markings from the 18th and 19th centuries. At the island's eastern tip, **Caicos Conch Farm** raises edible mollusks and introduces visitors to the lifecycle of the queen conch.

Excursion boats depart from near the farm for snorkeling and party cruises, and to a string of tiny cays off the east coast, including Little Water Cay, crawling with iguanas. Pine Cay is a private jewel and setting for The Meridian Club *(see p128)*, an all-inclusive family resort with sports facilities that range from Hobie Cats to the resort's

own yacht. Wrapped in snowy sands and turquoise waters, Parrot Cay, to the northeast of Providenciales, hosts an eponymous resort *(see p128)* with deluxe rooms decked out in minimalist decor, and a fine-dining restaurant. Guest quarters are a blaze of whites and feature romantic canopy beds. Its luxurious COMO Shambhala spa, on a 2-mile (3-km) long beach, is a perfect place to relax.

Caicos Conch Farm
Leeward Hwy. **Tel** 649 946 5330. **Open** 9am–4pm Mon–Fri, 9am–2pm Sat & hols. 🅿 📷

❷ Grace Bay

📷 N coast of Providenciales. 🚢 🏄 ⚓

This stupendously beautiful bay, curling along the north shore for 12 miles (19 km), is lined with talcum-white sands

Watersports at the excellent Grace Bay

shelving into shallows and some of the best snorkeling spots on the island. This is all protected within the 6,500-acre (2,630-ha) Princess Alexandra Land and Sea National Park, along with iguanas, ospreys, and a variety of marine life.

The beach, tufted with wispy grasses peeping up from sand dunes, is lined with upscale hotels and has plenty of watersports, but there are a lot of quiet spots too.

Among the most deluxe hotel options on Grace Bay, the Andalusian-style Grace Bay Club *(see p128)* is acclaimed for its Anacaona restaurant *(see p129)*. Sprawling over 11 acres (4 ha), the all-suite resort offers tennis and watersports among many other facilities.

❸ West Caicos Marine National Park

15 miles (24 km) SW of Providenciales. 🚢 hire a boat in Providenciales, or join an excursion.

A tiny island of 9 sq miles (23 sq km), West Caicos is inhabited by iguanas, lizards, and birds. In the 1890s, the isle's Yankee Town was the center for salt extraction. Its ruins, including railroads and old buildings, still stand. Near the town, at Lake Catherine Nature Reserve, bird-watchers can spot flamingos while divers can explore the West Caicos wall that plunges to a 7,000 ft (2,133 m) abyss.

An angler with a bonefish,
a popular catch

Bonefish

An easily spooked, bottom-feeding habitué of shallow inshore waters, this relative of the herring has silvery flanks, well-camouflaged against the sandy bottoms. It grows to 10 pounds (4 kg) and is one of the most feisty of an angler's quarries. Once hooked, bonefish typically race off and put up an uncanny fight. It is also known as the phantom and can be caught year-round with a license.

a sisal plantation, it is now a habitat for several bird species, including flamingos.

Fishing boats docked at Cockburn Harbour,
South Caicos

❹ North Caicos

12 miles (19 km) NE of Providenciales. 🏙 1,500. ✈ 🚢 between Providenciales and North Caicos, 6:30am–5:30pm Mon–Sat, 8:30am–4:30pm Sun, 649 946 5406. 🎉 North Caicos Extravaganza (Jun), Festarama Festival (Jul).

With its dense and lush vegetation, North Caicos is the most beautiful of all the Turks and Caicos islands. A short distance from Kew village in the north, Wades Green Plantation recalls the days when sisal and cotton were grown, and ancient cannons still stand sentinel on Fort George Cay nearby. Hotels are concentrated at Whitby Beach, the best of several ultra-white sands, while a boat ride delivers visitors to East Bay Islands National Park, where iguanas and marine turtles can be seen.

Birders flock to Cottage Pond (see p123), a sinkhole with jade waters, to see ducks and grebes; and to the appropriately named Flamingo Pond to observe flamingos. Just offshore is Three Mary Cays Sanctuary (see p123), which is a habitat for ospreys.

❺ Middle Caicos

15 miles (24 km) E of North Caicos. 🏙 300. ✈

This sparsely populated isle was once a major center of the Lucayan Amerindian civilization, remains of which can be seen at the Armstrong Pond Village Historical Site, one of the many

pre-Columbian sites here. This, and some plantation ruins, are accessible via the well-signed Middle Caicos Reserve and Trail System. Stalactites and stalagmites can be admired in **Conch Bar Caves National Park**, a haven for bats. The remote Vine Point and Ocean Hole Nature Reserve, on the south coast, is named in part for its massive blue hole and thrills divers and birders. Mudjin Harbor Beach, near the main settlement of Conch Bar, is framed by dramatic cliffs cusping sheltered coves. Bambarra Beach offers superb snorkeling and hosts the annual Valentine's Day Cup, a sailboat race using scale models handcrafted by local artisans.

Environs

Located about 2 miles (3 km) east of Middle Caicos is the unpopulated **East Caicos**, once

❻ South Caicos

15 miles (24 km) SE of Middle Caicos. 🏙 1,200. ✈ 🚗 🎉 South Caicos Regatta (May).

This diminutive and arid isle, almost entirely lacking in resorts, combines superb wall dives and excellent bonefishing in the jade-blue Bell Sound Nature Reserve and Admiral Cockburn Nature Reserve. Pink flamingos flock around the briny salinas ponds, within sight of the down-at-heels town of **Cockburn Harbour**. The town was severely damaged by Hurricane Ike in 2008. Every May, the streets of Cockburn Harbour burst into life for the South Caicos Regatta, which includes speedboat races, beauty pageants, float parades, and donkey races.

Entrance of the Conch Bar Caves National Park, Middle Caicos

Post office building in Cockburn Town, Grand Turk

❼ Grand Turk

120 miles (195 km) E of Providenciales. 🏝 3,700. ✈ 🚢 ℹ Front Street, 649 946 2321. 🎣 Grand Turk Heineken Game Fishing Tournament (Jul).

The small, semi-arid Grand Turk is an unlikely outpost for Turks and Caicos' capital, **Cockburn Town**. Strolling the streets of its charming historic center casts a time-warp spell. Bermudan-style limestone-and-clapboard structures line the sand-blown streets. Built of ships' timber, 19th-century Guinep House hosts the **Turks and Caicos National Museum**, with especially fine exhibits from the Molasses Reef shipwreck dating from 1513.

The town overlooks coral-tinged Pillory Beach, one of a string of beaches lining the windward shore. Locals believe that Christopher Columbus made his first New World landfall here on October 12, 1492. The offshore reef is protected within Columbus Landfall Marine National Park. The leeward shore is also sprinkled with long, lonesome beaches with soft powdery sands. Two of the most beautiful beaches are Flamingo Beach, in the north, and White Sand Beach, in the south. Between them, South Creek National Park protects precious mangroves.

🏛 **Turks and Caicos National Museum**
Front Street. **Tel** 649 946 2160. **Open** 9am–1pm Mon–Wed, 1–5pm Thu (also all cruise-ship days). 🅿 ♿ ground floor only. 📷 🌐 tcmuseum.org

❽ Grand Turk Inn

📧 Cockburn Town, Grand Turk. **Tel** 649 946 2827. 🌐 grandturkinn.com

Tucked behind a white picket fence, this lovingly restored former Methodist manse in traditional vernacular style is an architectural charmer. The suites of this adults-only inn are accessed by a wrought-iron staircase and are furnished with a combination of antique and contemporary pieces, all with stunning views over the ocean and white sandy beach.

❾ Salt Raker Inn

📧 Cockburn Town, Grand Turk. **Tel** 649 946 2260. ✏ 🌐 hotelsaltraker.com

Originating in the 1850s as a shipwright's home, this two-story, white-and-blue structure in Bermudan style has a marvelous oceanfront setting.

It is a tempting place to relax over lunch in the garden restaurant and to listen to live music on Friday evening.

❿ Salt Cay

8 miles (13 km) SW of Grand Turk. 🏝 200. ✈ 🚢 bi-weekly ferry between Grand Turk and Salt Cay. 🌐 saltcay.org

An arid, arrow-shaped speck of an isle, Salt Cay is named for the salt ponds initiated in the 17th century with windmills to pump water from the sea. Many of the warehouses, homes, and other limestone structures built by Bermudan salt traders have been restored, making tiny Balfour Town an adorable capsule of vernacular industrial architecture. Most locals get around by bicycle or golf cart; cars are virtually unknown.

The salt ponds are one of the Caribbean's premier sites for spotting ospreys and wading birds. In winter, hump-back whales gather in the warm waters southeast of Salt Cay and are easily seen close to shore.

Environs
In 1790 a storm claimed HMS *Endymion*, a British man-o'-war that sank south of Salt Cay. Today, the wreck of the 44-gun frigate is a world-renowned diving site (*see p125*) and draws divers keen to explore among its remains and the unspoilt habitat that surrounds it.

Humpback Whales

These gentle leviathans of the deep gather every January to March to breed and give birth in the warm, shallow waters of the Silver and Mouchoir Banks, southeast of Salt Cay. Despite their massive bulk, up to 50 ft (15 m) long, they often leap clear of the water. Calves are fully functional at birth and feed on up to 150 gallons (570 liters) of protein-rich milk a day. By April the whales migrate north to their feeding grounds in the North Atlantic.

Humpback whale calf with its mother in the ocean waters

Birding in the Turks and Caicos

These islands are renowned for their waterfowl and seabirds, and more than 190 bird species can be seen, including cuckoos, doves, and warblers. About 275 sq miles (712 sq km) of habitat are protected, notably within the North, Middle and East Caicos Nature Reserve, designated an International Ramsar Site and spanning scrub forests, 12 types of wetland, mangroves, and intertidal flats on the southern halves of North, Middle, and East Caicos islands. This site is home to about 61 waterfowl species.

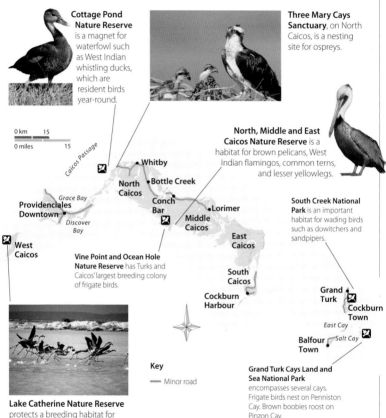

Cottage Pond Nature Reserve is a magnet for waterfowl such as West Indian whistling ducks, which are resident birds year-round.

Three Mary Cays Sanctuary, on North Caicos, is a nesting site for ospreys.

North, Middle and East Caicos Nature Reserve is a habitat for brown pelicans, West Indian flamingos, common terns, and lesser yellowlegs.

South Creek National Park is an important habitat for wading birds such as dowitchers and sandpipers.

Vine Point and Ocean Hole Nature Reserve has Turks and Caicos' largest breeding colony of frigate birds.

Grand Turk Cays Land and Sea National Park encompasses several cays. Frigate birds nest on Penniston Cay. Brown boobies roost on Pinzon Cay.

0 km   15
0 miles   15

Caicos Passage

Whitby
North Caicos
Bottle Creek
Grace Bay
Providenciales Downtown
Discover Bay
West Caicos
Conch Bar
Middle Caicos
Lorimer
East Caicos
South Caicos
Cockburn Harbour
Grand Turk
Cockburn Town
East Cay
Balfour Town
Salt Cay

Key

— Minor road

Lake Catherine Nature Reserve protects a breeding habitat for flamingos and other wading birds. The flamingos thrive on brine shrimp which inhabit this lagoon, once used as a salt pan.

TOUR COMPANIES

Big Blue Unlimited
Tel 649 946 5034.
W bigblue.tc

Salt Cay Tours:

Tel 649 244 1407.
W saltcaytours.com

Frigate Birds

Frigate birds are gregarious sea-going birds that roost atop mangroves. Extremely light birds with huge wing-spans, these kleptoparasites harry other seabirds to steal their food with the aid of their long, hooked bills. They also hunt fish from the ocean surface. Their iridescent black-green feathers lack water-proof oils and the birds risk drowning if they land in the sea.

A male frigate bird inflating its gular sac

Outdoor Activities and Specialized Holidays

Snorkeling and scuba diving are the big draws, offering an exhilarating way to explore the Turks and Caicos' phenomenal underwater life. In winter, whale-watching is excellent, and almost every isle offers a rich birdlife, easily seen along the many hiking trails that lace the islands. Many beaches have watersports such as windsurfing, Hobie Cats, and kayaking. Apart from these activities, visitors also have a choice of a relaxed pampering session in any of the islands' luxurious spas.

Grace Bay, one of the best beaches in Turks and Caicos

Beaches

Most visitors to the Turks and Caicos come to feel the soft sun-soaked sand between their toes. All the isles have lovely beaches, but by far the best is Grace Bay (see p120), on Providenciales. Curving gently along 12 miles (19 km) of shore, it has plenty of hotels, cafés, and watersport outlets, as well as sections where visitors can stroll in solitude and peace. Farther west, Wheeland Beach is more remote, with fewer hotels. Locals like to head to the otherwise deserted Malcolm Road. For a Robinson Crusoe-type escape, rent a boat and seek a secluded beach on Pine Cay or Dellis Cay.

Whitby Beach runs along the northern shore of North Caicos and shelves gently into reef-protected jade-colored shallows. It runs west to Pumpkin Bluff Beach, where snorkelers can explore an ancient wreck. Seemingly endless Long Bay Beach, on South Caicos, is virtually deserted, with rough surf often pounding ashore. Grand Turk is blessed with options. On the leeward side, Governor's Beach fringes Cockburn Town and extends north to Pillory

Beach, but outshining both are intimate White Sands Beach and the never-ending Flamingo Beach, on the windward shore. Tiny Salt Cay also boasts the lovely North Beach.

Spas

The Turks and Caicos islands, especially Providenciales, are a spa lover's mecca. Most of the top spas are associated with deluxe hotels. Anani Spa, at Grace Bay Club (see p128), specializes in Euro-Asian spa treatments. Parrot Cay's COMO Shambhala Spa (see p128) offers Asian-inspired holistic therapies, plus yoga on an Oriental pavilion

The luxurious Anani Spa at Grace Bay Club, Providenciales

overhanging the island's wetlands. Thalasso Spa, at Point Grace (see p128), is a European-style spa with treatment rooms that have lovely ocean views. **Spa Turkoise**, at Grand Turk Cruise Center, is handy for cruise passengers seeking a beach-front massage.

Boat Excursions

Taking to sea on a sailboat is a great way to break the routine of lazing on Grace Bay Beach. Some catamarans can be boarded right off the beach; others depart from Leeward Marina. **Sail Provo** offers a broad menu of half-day snorkeling and sunset cruises, plus the joy of an overnight luxury charter. The romance of the past comes alive aboard the *Atabeyra*, a traditionally rigged trading schooner operated by **Sun Charters**, which offers a pirate cruise plus a nocturnal cruise.

Sail Provo catamaran, Phoenix, on an excursion off Providenciales

Whale-Watching

The arrival, each January, of humpback whales to the Mouchier Banks, south of Grand Turk, provides for spectacular close-up encounters. Whale-watching trips take place in the Turks Island Passage (between South Caicos and Grand Turk) and in the warm, shallow waters off Salt Cay. **Oasis Divers** offers whale-watching excursions, from January to April, as do **Salt Cay Divers**, which let participants actually swim with the whales.

Diving Sites in the Turks and Caicos

Turks and Caicos offers some of the best diving in the world for walls, whales, and wrecks. The crystal clear waters are warm with average temperatures of 73–84° F (23–29° C). There are plenty of shallow dives, but the isles excel for breathtaking wall dives and for wrecks, such as the HMS *Endymion*. Providenciales is blessed with great diving sites, while Grand Turk and Salt Cay have a wall that begins from the shallow waters close to the shore with magnificent corals and marine life.

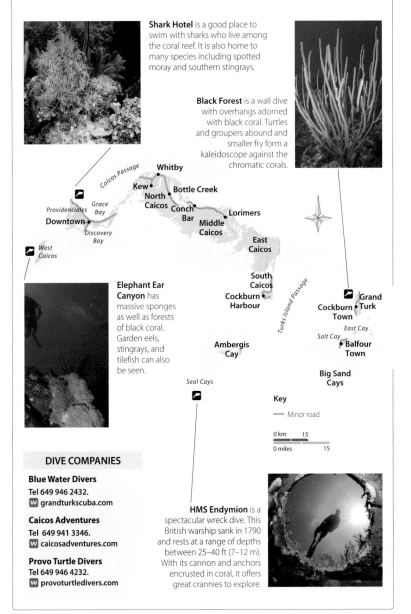

Shark Hotel is a good place to swim with sharks who live among the coral reef. It is also home to many species including spotted moray and southern stingrays.

Black Forest is a wall dive with overhangs adorned with black coral. Turtles and groupers abound and smaller fry form a kaleidoscope against the chromatic corals.

Caicos Passage
Whitby
Kew
Bottle Creek
North Caicos
Grace Bay
Conch Bar
Lorimers
Providenciales
Middle Caicos
Downtown
Discovery Bay
East Caicos
West Caicos
South Caicos
Cockburn Harbour
Grand Turk
Cockburn Town
East Cay
Salt Cay
Balfour Town
Ambergis Cay
Turks Island Passage
Big Sand Cays
Seal Cays

Elephant Ear Canyon has massive sponges as well as forests of black coral. Garden eels, stingrays, and tilefish can also be seen.

Key

— Minor road

0 km   15
0 miles   15

DIVE COMPANIES

Blue Water Divers
Tel 649 946 2432.
W grandturkscuba.com

Caicos Adventures
Tel 649 941 3346.
W caicosadventures.com

Provo Turtle Divers
Tel 649 946 4232.
W provoturtledivers.com

HMS Endymion is a spectacular wreck dive. This British warship sank in 1790 and rests at a range of depths between 25–40 ft (7–12 m). With its cannon and anchors encrusted in coral, it offers great crannies to explore.

Hikers on one of the popular trails in Grand Turk

Hiking

Several islands have trails that wind through mangroves and wetland ecosystems, with fabulous birding opportunities. On Little Water Cay off Providenciales, the 509-ft (155-m) North Shore Trail and the South Shore Trail, a 675-ft (206-m) long route, provide good access to both habitats. Iguanas can often be spotted during the hikes.

Middle Caicos has the best hiking, thanks to the 10-mile (16-km) long Middle Caicos Reserve and Trail system, that runs along the scenic north shore and passes colonial plantations and lagoons with flamingos. Stay on the trails, and bring plenty of water and insect repellent. For more information, contact **Turks and Caicos National Trust**.

Horse-Riding

Wild horses roam several islands, but opportunities for horseback riding are limited. **Provo Ponies** will take visitors cantering along Long Bay Beach. On Grand Turk, **Chukka Caribbean** also offers a "Horseback Ride 'n' Swim".

Golf

Provo Golf Club, the only one in Providenciales, is a par-72 course designed by well-known golf course architect, Karl Litten. It is acclaimed as one of the top Caribbean courses. Its rugged layout features fairways that ripple through limestone formations framed by Caribbean pine and studded by palm-shaded lakes. The 18-hole **Turks and Caicos Miniature Golf Club** in Long Bay is fun

for the entire family. Visitors can take a break with cool drinks and snacks at the club's restaurant.

Tennis

Most resort hotels in Providenciales have tennis courts, and non-guests are usually welcome for a fee. The Provo Golf Club has two tennis courts open to the public but only by reservation. Club Med Turkoise has noteworthy facilities for its guests. There are four hard courts and private instructors as well. Options for tennis on other islands are limited.

Caving

The islands are filled with limestone outcrops and are riddled with caves, although few are accessible and most are underwater. The most extensive system open for viewing is Conch Bar Caves National Park on Middle Caicos (see p121). Guides are available for exploring the winding caverns stippled with stalagmites and stalactites and etched with pre-Columbian petroglyphs. Nearby, the less extensive Indian Cave has a vast cavern crawling with strangler fig roots. This cave also has many legends that local guides love to tell. Both caves are partially paved.

Visitors on a horse-riding trip along with guides, Grand Turk

Boats waiting for fishing tours in Providenciales harbor

Fishing

The shallow waters of the Caicos Banks form a 2,000-sq-mile (5,179-sq-km) habitat for the elusive, hard-fighting bonefish *(see p121)*, an ultimate test of anglers' patience and skill. Tarpon can also be caught in the mangrove lagoons and are known as "silver rockets" for a good reason. Local guides are available on all the isles to punt visitors across the clear waters to the best fishing spots. Reputable operators for bonefish trips include **Bonefish Unlimited** and **Silver Deep**. Visitors can also wade off the beach into fish-full flats on most isles, sometimes right in front of the hotels.

The streaming currents beyond the fringing reefs are virtual highways for migrating sailfish, tuna, wahoo, and marlin. The summer months are the best time to fish for marlin. Providenciales and Grand Turk have the best spots and facilities for deep-sea fishing. Half- and full-day charters are also provided by Silver Deep. Prices vary depending on the size of the group. All equipment, licenses, food, and drinks are included in the packages that are offered by most fishing operators on the islands.

Watersports

Non-motorized watersports, such as windsurfing and aqua-bikes, are free for guests at most resort hotels. Scudding across Grace Bay, one of Providenciales' few beaches that offers water-sports, is a special thrill. Private beach concessionaires, such as **Dive Provo** and Sail Provo also rent kayaks, boards, and Hobie Cats. For more information, contact **Abuv-It-All** and **Ocean Vibes** for snorkeling. **Captain Marvin's** provides an exhil-arating birds'-eye view of the isles by parasail. **Snuba Turks & Caicos** offers snuba, a cross between scuba and snorkeling.

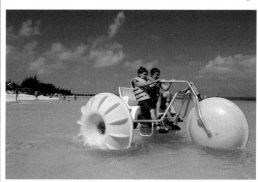

Children on an aqua-bike ride in shallow beach waters

DIRECTORY

Spas

Spa Turkoise
Tel 649 332 1171.
🇼 spaturkoise.net

Boat Excursions

Sail Provo
Tel 649 946 4783.
🇼 sailprovo.com

Sun Charters
Tel 649 231 0624.
🇼 suncharters.tc

Whale-Watching

Oasis Divers
Tel 649 946 1128.
🇼 oasisdivers.com

Salt Cay Divers
Tel 649 241 1009.
🇼 saltcaydivers.tc

Hiking

Turks and Caicos National Trust
Tel 649 941 5710.
🇼 tcinationaltrust.com

Horse-Riding

Chukka Caribbean
Tel 649 332 1339.
🇼 chukkacaribbean.com

Provo Ponies
Tel 649 241 6350.
🇼 provoponies.com

Golf

Provo Golf Club
Tel 649 946 5991.
🇼 provogolfclub.com

Turks and Caicos Miniature Golf Club
Tel 649 941 4653.

Fishing

Bonefish Unlimited
Tel 649 431 1393.
🇼 bonefishunlimited turksandcaicos.com

Silver Deep
Tel 649 946 5612.
🇼 silverdeep.com

Watersports

Abuv-It-All
Tel 649 241 1687.
🇼 windsurfingprovo.tc

Captain Marvin's
Tel 345 945 6975.
🇼 captainmarvins.com

Dive Provo
Tel 954 351 9771.
🇼 diveprovo.com

Ocean Vibes
Tel 649 941 8605.
🇼 oceanvibes.com

Snuba Turks & Caicos
Tel 649 333 7333.
🇼 snubaturksand caicos.com

Where to Stay

GRAND TURK: Manta House $
Boutique
Duke Street
Tel *649 243 2666*
W grandturk-mantahouse.com
A lovely family-run B&B that
specializes in diving vacations.
There is a choice of delightfully
furnished rooms or bungalows,
including one with a full kitchen.

GRAND TURK: Salt Raker Inn $
Historic
Duke Street
Tel *649 946 2260*
W saltrakerinn.com
This is a relaxed and charming
19th-century inn run by friendly
owners. It has cozy furnishings,
and the upstairs rooms boast
lovely sea views. Live music.

GRAND TURK:
Turks Head Mansion $$
Historic
Duke Street
Tel *649 946 2066*
W turksheadmansion.com
This restored 19th-century
mansion is furnished with
antiques and nautical miscellany.
Many rooms have lovely garden
patios. Gourmet meals on offer.

MIDDLE CAICOS:
Blue Horizon Resort $$
Beach Resort
Mudjin Harbor
Tel *649 946 6141*
W bhresort.com
A secluded family-friendly resort
with spectacular seascapes.
Stay in airy, modestly furnished
Caribbean-style cottages with
self-catering.

NORTH CAICOS:
Pelican Beach Hotel $
Beach
Whitby Beach
Tel *649 946 7112*
W pelicanbeach.tc
Intimate and serene beachfront
property with room service, but
without telephones and TVs. Use
of bicycles included. Closed from
mid-August to mid-October.

PROVIDENCIALES:
Caribbean Paradise Inn $
Beach
Grace Bay Road, Grace Bay
Tel *649 946 5020*
W caribbeanparadiseinn.com
A 5-minute stroll from the
beach, this inn offers a homey
intimacy that is rare for Grace Bay.
The pleasing decor includes rattan
furnishings. Acclaimed restaurant.

Beautiful interior of a pavilion at
Amanyara, Providenciales

DK Choice

PROVIDENCIALES:
Amanyara $$$
Boutique
Northwest Point
Tel *649 941 8133*
W amanresorts.com
Beautiful architecture sets this
stunning Balinese-inspired
deluxe resort apart. Amanyara
enjoys a spectacular setting
atop a headland overlooking
sugar-white sands. Guests sleep
in elevated pavilions and villas
with walls of glass. The restaurant
overhangs an infinity lake.

PROVIDENCIALES:
Blue Haven Resort $$$
Luxury
Marina Road, Leeward
Tel *649 946 9900*
W bluehaventci.com
In a sensational end-of-the-island
setting adjoining a marina. Huge
condo suites have state-of-the-
art kitchen facilities. Enjoy the
infinity pool, watersports, and spa.

PROVIDENCIALES:
Gansevoort $$$
Luxury
Grace Bay Road, Grace Bay
Tel *649 941 7555*
W gansevoorthotelgroup.com
Featuring urban-chic decor and
walls of glass, this hotel has a hip
beachfront bistro lounge and a
spa. Yoga classes.

PROVIDENCIALES:
Grace Bay Club $$$
Luxury
Grace Bay Road, Grace Bay
Tel *649 946 5050*
W gracebayresorts.com
This sprawling Andalusian-style
resort is acclaimed for its
restaurant and stunning guest

Price Guide

Prices are based on one night's stay in
high season for a standard double room,
inclusive of service charges and taxes.

$	up to $100
$$	$100–300
$$$	over $300

---

rooms with gleaming marble
floors. There is also a spa and
tennis facilities.

PROVIDENCIALES:
Parrot Cay $$$
Boutique
Parrot Cay
Tel *649 946 7788*
W comohotels.com
Set on its own isle, Parrot Cay
fronts a gorgeous beach
and attracts celebrity guests.
The luxurious rooms, suites and
villas have minimalist decor.

PROVIDENCIALES:
Point Grace $$$
Luxury
Grace Bay Road, Grace Bay
Tel *649 941 7743*
W pointgrace.com
This exclusive resort with classical
plantation styling has sumptuous
suites and penthouses in three-
story units. Excellent dining and
pampering service.

PROVIDENCIALES:
Seven Stars Resort $$$
Luxury
Grace Bay Road, Grace Bay
Tel *649 941 7777*
W sevenstarsgracebay.com
A deluxe all-suite resort housed
in four six-story structures with
contemporary plantation-style
furnishings. Spa, tennis facilities,
and a fine-dining restaurant.

PROVIDENCIALES:
The Meridian Club $$$
Boutique
Pine Cay
Tel *649 946 7758*
W meridianclub.com
Guest rooms and private
cottages have a soothing
ambience at this unpretentious
old-world, all-inclusive family
resort. No TVs or telephones.

SALT CAY: Pirates Hideaway $
Boutique
Victoria Street
Tel *649 244 1407*
W saltcay.tc
Just steps away from the beach,
this delightful guesthouse has
charming arty decor in its two
suites and four-bedroom house.
Landscaped pool and sun deck.

Where to Eat and Drink

GRAND TURK: The Sandbar $
Seafood
Duke Street
Tel *649 243 2666* **Closed** *Sat*
This small, casual beachfront
restaurant is popular with locals.
Enjoy grilled grouper sandwiches,
fish 'n' chips, and lobster
quesadillas on a shaded deck.

GRAND TURK: Guanahani $$$
International
Pillory Beach
Tel *649 946 2135*
A lovely beach setting at Bohio
Dive Resort. International dishes
on the menu include sushi,
pad Thai, and pecan-encrusted
mahi mahi.

PROVIDENCIALES:
Bugaloo's Conch Crawl $
Caribbean
Five Cays Settlement, Grace Bay
Tel *649 941 3863*
A simple laid-back beach bar
with a magical view. Specialties
on offer include fish fingers and
coconut cracked conch. Live
music on weekends.

PROVIDENCIALES:
Baci Ristorante $$
Italian
Turtle Cove Marina
Tel *649 941 3044*
Enjoy authentic Italian food on
a romantic terrace at the Turtle
Cove Marina. Menu highlights
include veal served four ways,
hearty pasta dishes, and brick-
oven pizzas.

PROVIDENCIALES:
Somewhere Café & Lounge $$
Café
Grace Bay Road, Grace Bay
Tel *649 941 8260*
Hip and laid-back café offering
simple salads, fish sandwiches,
rib-eye steaks, and Tex-Mex dishes.
The rooftop lounge is a great
place to sit and admire the sunset.

DK Choice

PROVIDENCIALES:
Anacaona $$$
Caribbean/European
Grace Bay Road, Grace Bay
Tel *649 946 5050*
The Grace Bay Club's chic
signature restaurant, Anacaona
sits over the sands, with
alfresco tables tiered beneath
picturesque open-sided
thatched *palapas*. The interior
has glistening wooden floors
and black chandeliers. The fine
Euro-Caribbean fusion menu on
offer includes low-calorie and
vegan options. The lobster
dishes are a must. A dress code
applies. Open for dinner only.

PROVIDENCIALES:
Coco Bistro $$$
Caribbean/Fusion
Grace Bay Road, Grace Bay
Tel *649 946 5369* **Closed** *Mon*
In a garden setting beneath a
large palm grove, Coco Bistro
serves island-inspired seafood
with European and Asian accents.
Try the crispy conch wontons.

PROVIDENCIALES:
Coyaba Restaurant $$$
Caribbean/Fusion
Grace Bay Road, Grace Bay
Tel *649 946 5186* **Closed** *Tue*
This smart restaurant offers
superb fusion dishes on its daily
changing menu. The desserts
are reason enough to visit – do
not miss the chocolate fondant.

PROVIDENCIALES:
Hemingway's on the Beach $$$
Caribbean
Grace Bay Road, Grace Bay
Tel *649 946 5199*
A lovely, peaceful poolside spot
lit by torches, Hemingway's is
known for its seafood dishes
and jerk chicken. Barbecue every
Tuesday and live jazz on Fridays.

Price Guide	
Prices are based on a two-course meal for one, including tax and service charges and half a bottle of wine.	
$	up to $15
$$	$15–40
$$$	over $40

PROVIDENCIALES:
Lemon Café $$$
Mediterranean
The Village at Grace Bay,
Grace Bay Road, Grace Bay
Tel *649 941 4059*
This chic restaurant serves
delicious fare – spicy chorizo,
grilled octopus, classic moussaka,
and rib roast – on a pleasant
patio. Seasonal opening hours.

PROVIDENCIALES: Magnolia
Wine Bar & Restaurant $$$
International
Turtle Cove, Grace Bay
Tel *649 941 5108* **Closed** *Mon*
Romantic open-air restaurant in
the Miramar Resort. The excellent
chicken and vegetable spring
rolls and sesame-crusted seared
tuna are not to be missed.

PROVIDENCIALES: Opus $$$
Seafood
Grace Bay Road, Grace Bay
Tel *649 946 5885*
Savor fresh fusion seafood at this
elegant candlelit restaurant in the
Ocean Club Resort. Live music.

PROVIDENCIALES:
Parallel 23 $$$
International
The Regent Palms,
Grace Bay Road, Grace Bay
Tel *649 946 8666*
White-upon-white elegance
with indoor or outdoor seating
and an exciting fusion menu
that focuses on fish and seafood.
Good steak, too. Huge wine list.
Dress code.

PROVIDENCIALES: Seven $$$
Seafood
Grace Bay Road, Grace Bay
Tel *649 339 3777*
Relaxed yet elegant restaurant
in the Seven Stars Resort. Try the
lobster with papaya risotto or
the steamed lemongrass shrimp.

SALT CAY: Island Thyme Bistro $
Café
North District
Tel *649 946 6977* **Closed** *Wed*
This colorful hangout with a
terrace overlooking the Salinas
serves delicious bargain-priced
seafood and international
classics. Pizza night every Friday.

Grand entrance to the Seven Stars Resort, Providenciales

Practical Information

Providenciales has witnessed an investment boom during the past decade, and its tourist infrastructure is world class, with a focus on deep-pocket vacationers, while budget travelers prefer Grand Turk for its laid-back charm. North, Middle, East, and South Caicos have relatively limited tourist infrastructure and hotel options, and advance planning is essential. The infrastructure of the islands has been restored since the region was devastated by Hurricane Ike in 2008.

One of the banks at Cockburn Town, Grand Turk

When to Go

These breeze-swept isles are pleasant year-round, although the best weather is from December to April, when there is hardly any rain and the temperatures are near perfect. The mid-summer months can be torrid, while the weather can get sticky during the hurricane season that runs from June to November. Cultural events are mostly in winter, but rates are also higher than in summer.

Grand Turk International Airport, near Cockburn Town

Getting There

Charter and regular scheduled flights arrive at Providenciales International Airport from North America. There are a few direct flights from North America to Grand Turk International Airport. Private charter planes connect all the other islands to Grand Turk and Providenciales. **US Airways**, **Delta**, and **American Airlines** fly to Providenciales from six US gateways. **British Airways** serves Providenciales once a week via the Bahamas, which is also served by **Bahamasair**. **Air Canada** has direct flights

from Montreal, Ottawa, and Toronto to Providenciales. Charter flights from Canada are also provided by **WestJet**.

Documentation

No visas are required for stays of up to 90 days. All visitors must have a valid passport and a ticket for onward travel.

Visitor Information

The **Turks and Caicos Islands Tourist Board** has offices in the US, Canada, and the UK that provide information. Within the Turks and Caicos, it has offices on Grand Turk and on Providenciales (at the airport and at Turtle Cove Marina). Hotel tour desks can also give advice on organized excursions and entertainment. Most companies have websites that give more specific details.

Health and Security

There are public clinics on each island, and a general hospital on Grand Turk, but many may not meet the standards that most people are used to. Private clinics such as **Grace Bay Medical Centre** and **Cockburn Town Medical Centre** are preferred. Some all-inclusive resorts have a nurse on staff. Providenciales also has a hyperbaric chamber. Theft and crime affecting tourists is rare in Turks and Caicos, but it is best to keep valuables in a hotel safe, and to avoid wearing expensive jewelry when out and about.

Public phone, on the islands

Banking and Currency

The US dollar is the official currency of Turks and Caicos, which also issues its own crown and quarter. Traveler's checks in US dollars are accepted in most hotels, taxi services, and restaurants in Providenciales, and can be cashed at local banks. However, cash and credit cards are preferred on other islands, where banks may be fewer. Most major credit cards are accepted. There is no limit on the amount of money that visitors may bring to the islands.

Communications

The Turks and Caicos has an efficient telephone system operated by **Digicel**, **Islandcom**, and **LIME**, which have public phones throughout the islands. Prepaid phone cards can be bought at many stores. Calls from hotels incur a hefty surcharge. To call abroad from the Turks and Caicos, dial 011 and the country code, then the area code and number. To call Turks and Caicos from North America, dial 1, then 649 and the local number; from the UK, dial 00 for international access, then 649 and the local number. Calls within the islands require only the seven digit number. Most hotels offer Internet access. There are Internet cafés on all the islands.

Transport

Holders of an International Drivers license and citizens of the UK, USA, and Canada are permitted to drive on their own license for up to 30 days. Reputable rental companies are **AVIS**, **Hertz**, and **Grace Bay Car Rentals**. Hotels can also arrange for car rentals. Scooters can be rented from companies such as **Tony's Car Rental** on Grand Turk. The company also hires out bicycles. It is advisable to wear helmets.

Minivans operate taxi services on all islands and can be used for touring. Rates can be expensive so be sure to negotiate an agreed fare before setting off. The concierge or front desk staff of most hotels will help visitors call for a taxi from a reputable company.

Shopping

Most hotels have boutiques selling swimwear, cigars, rum, and local craft items such as conch shell jewelry and the island's trademark rag dolls. Select locations, including the airport departure lounge and downtown plazas on Providenciales, sell duty-free cameras, china, crystal, liquor, and perfumes. The Turks and Caicos has no sales tax. A receipt

Colorful souvenir shops in Grand Turk

is needed for conch shell items; the Turks and Caicos is one of the few countries in the world where conch shells can legally be purchased and exported, though restrictions apply.

Time

Turks and Caicos is on Eastern Standard Time (EST), 5 hours behind Greenwich Mean Time (GMT). Daylight Savings is in effect the first Sunday of March through the first Sunday of November.

Language

English is the official language in the Turks and Caicos, spoken by everyone, although many locals speak with a distinct dialect. Many speak a patois

version, while the many Haitians working here speak their own French-derived Creole patois.

Electricity

Turks and Caicos operates on 110 volts. Outlets use US two-prong plugs. Most large hotels have their back-up generators to supply power during occasional outages.

Getting Married

A 24-hour minimum residency on the island is required and visitors need to apply for a marriage license in person through the **Registrar of Marriages**. A nominal fee is charged. Documents such as passport, birth certificate, and proof of single status is mandatory. Licenses are issued at the **Registrar Office** in Provo.

DIRECTORY

Getting There

Air Canada
W aircanada.com

American Airlines
W aa.com

Bahamasair
W bahamasair.com

British Airways
W britishairways.com

Delta
W delta.com

US Airways
W usairways.com

WestJet
W westjet.com

Visitor Information

Turks and Caicos Islands Tourist Board
Tel 649 946 4970 (Providenciales), 649 946 2321 (Grand Turk).
W turksandcaicos tourism.com
W turksandcaicoshta. com W visittci.com

Health and Security

Emergencies
Tel 911.

Police
Tel 649 941 5891 (Providenciales), 649 946 2299 (Grand Turk).

Cockburn Town Medical Centre
Cockburn Town, Grand Turk. Tel 649 941 2900.

Grace Bay Medical Centre
Neptune Plaza, Providenciales. Tel 649 941 5252, 649 231 0525 (emergencies).

Communications

Digicel
W digiceltci.com

Islandcom
W islandcom.tc

LIME
W lime.com

Transport

AVIS
Tel 649 946 4705.
W avis.tc

Grace Bay Car Rentals
Tel 649 941 8500.
W gracebaycarrentals. com

Hertz
Tel 649 941 3910.
W hertztci.com

Tony's Car Rental
Tel 649 946 1879.
W tonyscarrental.com

Getting Married

Registrar Office
Providenciales.
Tel 649 946 2800.

Registrar of Marriages
Front Street, Grand Turk.
Tel 649 946 2801.

A PORTRAIT OF JAMAICA

Jamaica is the quintessential Caribbean island. Its extraordinary natural beauty encompasses white sand beaches, tumbling cascades, and the misty Blue Mountain range with its terraced plantations of premium coffee. The electrifying music scene provides a cultural depth and has helped in making Jamaica famous.

Jamaica has an amazing natural abundance – a reality that did not escape the island's various colonizers. First to settle were the Amerindians from the South American mainland, who farmed and fished here until the arrival of Christopher Columbus in 1494. He claimed the island on behalf of Spain, setting in motion the establishment of the plantation economy which the British made more efficient when they captured Jamaica in 1655. The parting gift of the Spanish was to release the slaves working in the plantations. Heading into the uncharted terrain of Cockpit Country, the freed slaves, known as Maroons, became a thorn in the side of the plantocracy, using guerrilla tactics to win two armed campaigns against

British forces. A peace treaty was eventually signed and Maroon villages still exist as separate enclaves to this day. For the rest of the island's African population, however, life remained unimaginably harsh. Uprisings against the British continued to be brutally suppressed and matters only slowly started to improve after the Emancipation Act of 1833.

Politics

After Jamaica became independent in 1962, two main political parties emerged, the largely right-wing Jamaica Labour Party (JLP), and the more left-wing People's National Party (PNP). The former was the first party to lead an independent Jamaica. The PNP came to

Ocho Rios beach with a cruise ship in the background

A Rastafarian at his stall of local arts and crafts, Ocho Rios

power under the radical Michael Manley during the turbulent 1970s, an era characterized by violent clashes between party supporters during elections. The 1980s were dominated by the JLP but by 1992, the PNP returned led by P.J. Patterson, the country's first black prime minister. In 2006, the PNP's Portia Simpson-Miller became Jamaica's first female prime minister. She lost the title to the JLP when a snap election was called the following year, but regained it in 2012.

Economy

During the early 20th century, the economy was given a boost by the nascent banana and tourism industries. Agriculture now accounts for just six percent of the GDP, with key crops including sugar and bananas. Though sugar production is steadily declining due to competition from South American mechanized farms and the banana industry has been practically crippled by the World Trade Organization's removal of preferential tariffs to European Union markets, the island still earns US$20 million from banana exports. Coffee is another important export, with the annual average export of beans worth around US$20 million; about 85 percent of Jamaica's coffee is shipped to Japan, with the other 15 percent going to the UK, USA, and other countries, where it often sells for up to US$40 per pound. Tourism is the main economic earner, however, with the industry fetching US$2 billion in 2012. The tourist infrastructure is concentrated along the north coast, with the three big resorts of Montego Bay, Negril, and Ocho Rios receiving most visitors.

Jamaica Today

The nation's capital city, Kingston, best encapsulates Jamaica's edgy reputation and life is undeniably harsh in the impoverished ghettos here. However, Kingston also has brilliant restaurants and nightlife. Music in Jamaica is vibrant and exciting. Besides the inimitable Bob Marley, there are innumerable international stars in the field of dancehall and reggae in Jamaica. In 2008, the island received a massive boost when its athletics team dominated the Beijing Olympics. In Beijing 2008, and at the London Olympics in 2012, Usain Bolt won the 100m and 200m races (as well as the 4x100m relay), upholding his title as the fastest man in the world. In 2010 a crackdown on drug lords resulted in mayhem in Kingston, and 72 deaths.

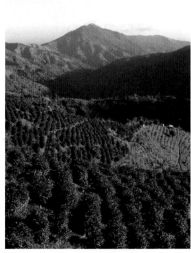
Plantations of premium coffee on the slopes of the Blue Mountains

Exploring Jamaica

Jamaica's ample proportions allow for a varied landscape. To the west are the lavish beaches and grand limestone cliffs of Negril. Popular ports of call for cruise ships, Montego Bay and Ocho Rios in the north are also the island's nightlife hubs, while Port Antonio in the east has an old-world charm. For a taste of the "real Jamaica", head to Kingston, a fascinating city overlooked by the Blue Mountains, and within easy driving distance of great hiking.

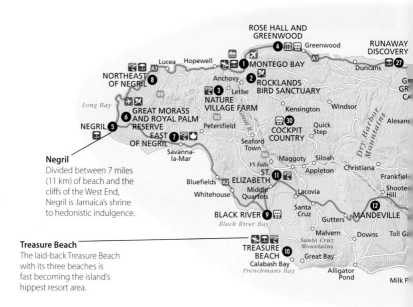

Negril
Divided between 7 miles (11 km) of beach and the cliffs of the West End, Negril is Jamaica's shrine to hedonistic indulgence.

Treasure Beach
The laid-back Treasure Beach with its three beaches is fast becoming the island's hippest resort area.

Sights at a Glance

1. Montego Bay
2. Rocklands Bird Sanctuary
3. Nature Village Farm
4. Rose Hall and Greenwood
5. Negril
6. Great Morass and Royal Palm Reserve
7. East of Negril
8. Northeast of Negril
9. Black River
10. Treasure Beach
11. St. Elizabeth
12. Mandeville
13. *Kingston p142*
14. Hellshire
15. Port Royal
16. *Blue Mountains Tour pp144–5*
17. Port Antonio
18. Frenchman's Cove and the Blue Lagoon
19. Winnifred Beach
20. Long Bay
21. Reach Falls
22. Firefly
23. Oracabessa
24. Ocho Rios
25. Dolphin Cove and Dunn's River Falls
26. Cranbrook Flower Forest
27. Runaway and Discovery Bays
28. Green Grotto Caves
29. Bob Marley Centre & Mausoleum
30. Cockpit Country

0 kilometers   20

0 miles   20

For hotels and restaurants on this island see pp156–9 and pp160–61

Boats lined along the edge of a lagoon in Ocho Rios

Key

═══ Highway

═══ Major road

═══ Minor road

─── Railroad

Blue Mountains
Shrouded in mist, the cool and craggy Blue Mountain peaks are dotted with farms growing some of the best coffee in the world.

Kingston
With plenty in the way of culture and nightlife, Kingston also offers days out to the former pirate capital of Port Royal and Hellshire Beach, for fresh fish.

Getting Around

Most flights tend to land in Montego Bay, which has easy access to Negril and Ocho Rios. To go to Port Antonio or Treasure Beach, it is easier to fly to Kingston. Internal flights are restricted to the odd service between Montego Bay and Kingston/Negril by charter airlines, though the new highway which runs the length of the north coast makes driving to Ocho Rios or Negril from Montego Bay far easier than flying. The best option for getting around the island is to hire a car or a local driver, as buses can be chaotic with no set schedules.

Display of exquisite Jamaican wood carvings at a roadside craft stall

For keys to symbols *see back flap*

❶ Montego Bay

NW Coast. 🗺 110,000. ✈ 🚌 ⛴
🛈 18 Queens Drive; 876 952 4425.
ⓦ **montego-bay-jamaica.com**

Enclosed by a cradle of hills with stunning views of the western coastline, Montego Bay's lovely beaches are the main reason for its enduring popularity. A favorite stopover for cruise ships and the destination for most international flights to Jamaica, it is a busy place, with the center of activity concentrated along the length of Gloucester Avenue, rechristened the Hip Strip. Working south to north, the first point of interest along the Strip is **Aquasol Beach & Theme Park**, a handsome crescent popular with locals, with a go-kart track, excellent watersports facilities, and tennis courts.

Bars, restaurants, and gift shops line most of the avenue between Aquasol and the Strip's only green space, a grassy park with great views down the coast. Past the tacky façades of the Margaritaville and Blue Beat bars is the entrance to the famed white sand and crystal-clear water of **Doctor's Cave Beach** and, some 720 ft (220 m) beyond, Cornwall Beach.

The Strip tails off where Gloucester Avenue becomes Kent Avenue, and the seafront is once again visible; there is a fine slip of beach and great snorkeling offshore. Downtown Montego Bay provides a refreshing antidote to the schmaltz of Gloucester Avenue, and though most visitors do not venture past the southern end of the avenue, there are a couple of sights to look out for. Across the road at the end of the Strip is Fort Street, which threads past the chaotic Gully fruit and vegetable market to Sam Sharpe Square, named after one of Jamaica's national heroes and distinguished by its central fountain. In the northwest corner, next to the cut-stone Cage built by the British as a lock-up for runaway slaves, is a sculpture of Sam Sharpe preaching to his followers. Just around the corner the **Montego Bay Civic Centre** houses a small museum on local history, which has more information about Sam Sharpe.

Doctor bird, Rocklands Bird Sanctuary

🏖 **Aquasol Beach & Theme Park**
Gloucester Av. **Tel** 876 979 9447.
Open daily; hours vary. 🅿 ⓵ 🅿 🖵

🏖 **Doctor's Cave Beach**
Gloucester Av. **Tel** 876 952 2566.
Open 8:30am–sunset daily. 🅿 🅿 🖼
ⓦ **doctorscavebathingclub.com**

🏛 **Montego Bay Civic Centre**
St. James Street. **Tel** 876 952 5500.
Open 9am–5pm Mon–Thu,
9am–4pm Fri. 🅿

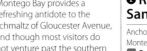

❷ Rocklands Bird Sanctuary

Anchovy, 5 miles (8 km) SW of Montego Bay. **Tel** 876 952 2009.
🚌 **Open** 9am–5:30pm daily.
🅿 🅿

Just off the B8 Highway and past the Lethe turnoff at Anchovy, Rocklands Bird Sanctuary is a low-key attraction that offers bird-lovers one of Jamaica's most unforgettable experiences. The former home of the celebrated ornithologist Lisa Salmon (d. 2000), it is a favored spot for a multitude of birds that come here to feed each day. Buses from Montego Bay to Savanna-la-Mar run past the approach road, but it is a steep and difficult walk up to the sanctuary. No direct route taxis to Rocklands are available and it is advisable to charter one from Montego Bay.

On arrival, visitors are given a feeder of sugar-water. The objective is to entice the diners – mostly different kinds of hummingbirds, including the doctor bird – to descend and perch on the people's hands to drink the water, the whirr of their wings vibrating musically in the air. Other species of birds can also be spotted here, including banaquits, the greater Antillean bullfinch, and the gorgeous black-throated blue warbler. To get so close to these elusive and beautiful creatures is an incredible experience. An interesting nature walk through thick vegetation is also included in the entry fee.

❸ Nature Village Farm

6 miles (10 km) SW of Montego Bay.
Tel 876 468 9966. Ⓣ from Montego Bay (no route taxi service to Lethe).
Open 9am–6pm Mon–Fri, 10am–7pm Sat, 11am–7pm Sun.

From the main coast road, the B8 Highway threads into the hills southwest of Montego Bay – a lush, green, and peaceful alternative to the

Sailing on the crystal-clear waters of Montego Bay

For hotels and restaurants on this island see pp156–9 and pp160–61

Sam Sharpe and the Christmas Rebellion

The Christmas Rebellion of December 1831 was perhaps the most significant uprising of African slaves in Jamaica's history. Though the slave trade had been outlawed in 1807, plantation culture still held sway here, with thousands of Africans working in the sugar estates quite unaware of the legislation. It was in the planters' interests to maintain this ignorance and they made great efforts to suppress the inevitability of emancipation. However, Sam Sharpe, a house slave working in Montego Bay who had taught himself to read by way of his position as deacon of a Baptist church, learned of the activities of abolitionists in Britain, and preached in his sermons that freedom was close. The news spread like wildfire, and talk of insurrection intensified as Christmas approached. By December 27, non-violent protests had developed into full-scale rebellion, with western Jamaica ablaze as some 160 estates were razed to the ground. The British response was brutal, with 1,000 slaves shot dead and another 300 – including Sharpe – hanged by the neck. The death-knell of slavery had been sounded, however, and the uprising was the first step on the road to complete abolition in 1838.

Sam Sharpe monument, Montego Bay

Antique piano on display at Greenwood Great House

Great River on the outskirts of Lethe, near Nature Village Farm

sun-bleached glare of the coast. To make the best of the surroundings, it is a good idea to turn off for **Lethe** and follow the signs to the secluded and serene Nature Village Farm. Inside the property, sweeping lawns and football pitches lead down a hillside to the banks of the Great River, overhung by lianas and towering stands of bamboo. There are several places to take a dip and it is also possible to go on a relaxing tube ride down the river on huge rubber rings. Visitors can enjoy a meal or drink at the open-air restaurant overlooking the water.

❹ Rose Hall and Greenwood

Rose Hall: 10 miles (16 km) E of Montego Bay. **Tel** 1-888 767 3425.
Open 9am–6pm daily.
rosehall.com
Greenwood: 12 miles (19 km) E of Montego Bay. **Tel** 876 953 1077.
Open 9am–6pm daily.
greenwoodgreathouse.com

Understandably, Jamaica does not make too much of an issue about its colonial past, but the era of plantation slavery comes to the fore east of Montego Bay in the form of two palatial great houses that have been opened up as tourist attractions, both of which are signposted from the main coastal highway. Buses along the highway pass the entrances to Rose Hall and Greenwood.

Closest to Montego Bay is Rose Hall Great House, the former home of the "White Witch" Annie Palmer. She came to Rose Hall as the wife of its owner, John Rose Palmer, and soon unleashed a reign of terror. Her wicked deeds are made much of by the tour guides. The supposedly haunted house has been slickly refurbished in period style, with lavish furnishings and antiques. The tours start from the gift shop which has displays of old photographs.

Far more atmospheric, Greenwood Great House is also a more handsome structure, commanding amazing coastal views and filled with original fittings and curiosities. The house once belonged to relatives of the renowned British poet, Elizabeth Barrett Browning. Today it has a large and rare collection of musical instruments as well as a library.

Austere façade of the infamous Rose Hall Great House

Hotels and restaurants lining the beach at Negril, a popular resort area

❺ Negril

52 miles (83 km) SW of Montego Bay. 🚗 4,200. ✈ 🚌 from Montego Bay along Norman Manley Boulevard, and from Savanna-la-Mar along Sheffield Road. ℹ Negril Chamber of Commerce, Vendors Plaza, West End Road; 876 957 4067. 🅦 negril.com

Perhaps the most popular of Jamaica's three main resort areas, Negril is split between its 7 miles (12 km) of picture-perfect white sand, backed by the wide Norman Manley Boulevard, and the limestone cliffs that make up the island's extreme western tip. Both cliffs and beach are lined with hotels, restaurants, and the ever-busy bars that have helped to give the area its reputation for nightlife and loud music; rarely a high-season weekend goes by without a huge stageshow taking place, and visitors can dance in the sand to live reggae most nights of the week.

With its clear warm waters, sheltered by a reef and almost mirror calm, the beach is one of the Caribbean's best. However, the beauty of the place also means crowds of people, including vendors selling everything from hair braids or glass-bottom boat rides to ganja (cannabis). Hotels set up loungers and umbrellas on the sand for the use of their guests, but there are plenty of bars and restaurants that also offer beach facilities. For a quieter environment, it is best to head east along the sand toward Long Bay beach park, where the buildings thin out and the hustle also diminishes accordingly.

Ranged along pockmarked limestone cliffs that sheer off into 13-ft (4-m) deep, crystal-clear waters studded with lovely reefs, the **West End**, south of downtown Negril, is a world away from the beach. It is relatively quieter, although still home to some seriously upscale hotels, as well as a multitude of places geared towards budget travelers. The swimming is fantastic, and restaurants and hotels have stairs down the cliffs and ladders to get in and out – but it can be challenging when the water is choppy.

The West End also provides the perfect spot for watching the sun set, with bars offering happy hour, live music, and cliff-diving displays, during which divers plunge into the sea from amazingly high cliffs.

❻ Great Morass and Royal Palm Reserve

Sheffield Road, 2 miles (5 km) E of Negril. **Tel** 876 364 7407. 🚌 **Open** 9am–6pm daily. 🅿 ✅ ♿ 🖥

Running inland from Norman Manley Boulevard and covering some 9 sq miles (24 sq km), the Great Morass is Jamaica's second-largest wetland. It can be accessed by bus or route taxi from Negril to Savanna-la-Mar, but is a long walk away from the nearest stop. It is best to take a chartered taxi.

The Great Morass is a peaty, reed-covered expanse that provides a habitat to a number of

Boardwalk across the wetlands at Royal Palm Reserve

rare animals and plants, including the many trees around which the Royal Palm Reserve has been created. With wooden boardwalks that lead right out onto the morass, the air alive with the chirping of crickets, cicadas, frogs, and with every inch of surface covered in thick greenery, it is a great place for a walk. Also a good spot for bird-watching, the reserve has a couple of observation towers and more than 50 species of birds to look out for. Visitors can try their luck at fishing as well.

❼ East of Negril

Sheffield Road trundles inland from Negril's main roundabout toward the dusty market town and parish capital of Savanna-la-Mar. There is not much to see in the town, so it is best to turn off the main road before getting into "Sav" proper. Signposts lead visitors to **Roaring River Park**, just outside the small community of Petersfield. Set in a former plantation, the park has a series of deep limestone caverns to explore.

However, the real draw is the **Blue Hole Garden**, just a 5-minute drive farther down the road, where a deep blue spring-water pool overhung

Horse-riding at Rhodes Hall Plantation, northeast of Negril

with greenery makes it a magical place for a swim.

🏞 Roaring River Park
5 miles (8 km) N of Savanna-la-Mar. Note: take a guided tour from Negril; it is advisable to ignore unofficial guides.

🏞 Blue Hole Garden
5 miles (8 km) N of Savanna-la-Mar. **Tel** 876 401 5312. **Open** 8am–6pm daily.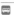

❽ Northeast of Negril

Northeast of Negril, the coastal highway swings past a few diverting attractions. The first is **Rhodes Hall Plantation**, a 550-acre (220-ha) coconut and

vegetable plantation that offers horse-riding both inland and along the beach. There is a crocodile reserve and bird sanctuary on-site. Visitors also have the opportunity to snorkel or enjoy a dip in the mineral spring infinity pool. A short distance beyond, **Dolphin Cove Negril** covers 23 acres (9 ha) outside Lucea. Visitors can swim with dolphins, pet stingrays, and watch thrilling shark shows. Both destinations can be reached either by bus or shared taxi.

Inland from the coast, in the heart of the Dolphin Head Mountains, lies **Mayfield Falls**. There are 22 mini-cascades along a greenery shrouded river. It is a good idea to take a guided walk up the river, which has lots of deep swimming pools, and get a snack or drink, or change into swimwear at the base. At the end of the tour, visitors are led back through pastures lined with fruit trees and clusters of bamboo. The falls can be hard to find, but all the local taxi drivers know the way there.

Rhodes Hall Plantation
8 miles (13 km) NE of Negril.
Tel 876 957 6422. 🏷 💻
W rhodesresort.com

Dolphin Cove Negril
Point, Lucea. **Tel** 876 974 5335.
Open 8am–5pm daily. 🏷 ✉
W dolphincoveja.com

🏷 Mayfield Falls
Glenbrook, 15 miles (24 km) northeast of Negril. **Tel** 876 792 2074. 🏷 🏷 🏷
🏷 **W** mayfieldfalls.com

Hedonistic Negril

First "discovered" in the 1970s, hippies descended on Negril to laze on the beaches in a ganja-wreathed haze. Many are still drawn here by Negril's reputation, which has been built around intemperance. In fact, one of the biggest hotels here goes all out to advertize its deliberately risqué ethos of raunchy pool parties and skinny dips under the stars. The place certainly has a debauched quality to it, and hordes of people come here for the wild partying. Drugs, too, remain part of the fabric, with "special" (magic mushroom) tea on the menu at the occasional restaurant and more than a whiff of marijuana in the evening air. These days, though, the area's most bacchanalian aspect is its nightlife, with a string of lively bars along the beach offering dancing on the sand any day of the week.

A party in one of Negril's hotels

A Jamaican crocodile soaking in the sun on the banks of Black River

❾ Black River

46 miles (73 km) S of Montego Bay.
🚶 4,300. 🚌 🚕 between Savanna-la-Mar and Treasure Beach.
🍴 Fri & Sat.

Weatherbeaten Black River may be the largest town in the parish of St. Elizabeth, but that is not saying much given the region's bucolic feel. Spreading back from the coastline and centered around its bustling market and commercial main street, it is certainly not a tourist hotspot, though it does have a couple of interesting buildings along the waterfront. The most notable among these is the elaborate Invercauld, built in 1894 during Black River's heyday as one of the island's main ports.

The main reason people come here, though, is to take a boat safari up the Black River Great Morass, a wetland populated by Jamaican crocodiles. Boats leave from the depot at both sides of the main town bridge, and meander upstream through the peaty river, passing thick clumps of twisted mangrove that provide a habitat for many bird and marine species. The crocodiles are used to visitors, and many of them have been named by the boat captains. **Black River Safaris** offers crocodile viewing trips from Black River.

For an even quieter retreat, head west of Black River to **Font Hill Beach Park**, a privately-owned beach with white sand.

Black River Safaris
1 Crane Road, Black River.
Tel 876 965 2513.
Open 9am–4pm Mon–Sat. 🛥️

🏖️ **Font Hill Beach Park**
Main Road, 2 miles (3 km) W of Black River. **Tel** 876 462 9011.
Open 9am–5pm daily. 🛥️ 🍴

❿ Treasure Beach

56 miles (90 km) SE of Montego Bay.
🚌 from Mandeville and Black River.
🚕 hotels can arrange taxi transfers from Montego Bay or Kingston airports. 🌐 **treasurebeach.net**

In direct contrast to the glitz and concrete of the north coast, the string of peaceful fishing villages that make up the relaxed and laid-back Treasure Beach offer a more authentic island experience than the resorts. Tourism has developed sustainably here, with the community getting tangible benefits from the industry, both by being directly involved – most of the hotels and restaurants are owned by locals – and by way of initiatives such as the BREDS foundation. A non-profitmaking organization funded largely by visitor donations, BREDS has, among many other things, created an emergency medical response unit for the community and purchased an ambulance. They have also equipped schools with computers and fishermen with much-needed radios.

Beautifully situated between the sea and the arid flatlands that spread out below the Santa Cruz Mountains, Calabash Bay is the heart of the community. Here, the very hip Jake's hotel (see p159) provides a focus for most of the activities, with a smattering of places to eat and stay close by. To the north, Frenchman's Bay offers great opportunities for swimming and bodysurfing. The scenic beach is ideal for sunbathing too. This place is home to more accommodations, and eating, and drinking options. South of Calabash and Frenchman's bays; and separated from them by pastureland and the Great Pedro Pond, is Great Bay, with another fine beach and a thriving fishing industry.Though the sand here is brown rather than white, the waters are clear and extremely clean, and the odd wave makes a refreshing change to the millpond-like northern shore.

It is easy to while away an entire holiday dividing time between the beaches, but it is

Colorful fishing boats on the sands at Treasure Beach

For hotels and restaurants on this island see pp156–9 and pp160–61

well worth arranging for a boat trip along the coast to the unique **Floyd's Pelican Bar**. Built on stilts stuck into a sandspit offshore of Parottee Point near Black River, this ramshackle wooden, thatch-roofed bar is a one-of-a-kind experience. Guests can paddle around the shallows, snorkel in the surrounding waters, or just sit in the bar and have a meal or a beer, enjoying the sunset, which is especially atmospheric here.

⓫ St. Elizabeth

60 miles (100 km) SE of Montego Bay.
Ⓣ

Characterized by bauxite-rich deep red earth and rolling cattle pastures, St. Elizabeth is one of Jamaica's most beautiful parishes. It is not swamped with tourist attractions, but there are a few places worth visiting by way of a driving tour from Treasure Beach.

The tunnel of bamboos in the Bamboo Avenue, parish of St. Elizabeth

From Black River, a signposted road threads north, affording lovely views across the plains toward the Santa Cruz Mountains. After about 12 miles (20 km), the quaint little village of **Middle Quarters** announces itself through a crowd of women selling bags of the spicy and delicious pepper shrimp that the area is known for. Just past here, the signposted road to the left leads towards YS, a huge cattle farm that is also home to the lovely **YS Falls**, surrounded by lush pastures and jungle-covered hills. Reached via a short tractor-trailer ride through the fields, the falls – seven cascades of varying sizes tumbling out of the greenery – are an absolute delight. Several of these end in deep pools which are great for swimming, although some are too rocky. There is a spring-water swimming pool near the snack shop, which is ideal for kids. When water levels allow, tubing along the river is a lot of fun, and there are also three zipwires that allow visitors to whoosh through the tree canopy and over the water.

Beyond YS, the road gets even narrower. Once through the tiny community of Maggotty, the route turns onto Highway

The seven cascades at YS Falls, St. Elizabeth

B6 for the **Appleton Rum Estate**, which is surrounded by endless fields of sugarcane. Appleton is the oldest producer of rum in Jamaica; the estate dates back to 1655 although distilling began only in 1749. Its rums are considered by many to be the island's best. The tour inside the factory complex takes guests through the whole production process, from the selection of the sugarcane to the bottling of the rum, and ends with a chance to sample all 17 of their brands, so it is worth noting that the estate offers transportation for its visitors from their hotels.

The scenic route back follows the B6 Highway south of Maggotty, and turns right at Lacovia along **Bamboo Avenue**, where thick overhanging strands of bamboo create a tunnel-like effect. Just a short distance from here, the route ends at Middle Quarters.

🏞 YS Falls

3 miles (5 km) N of Middle Quarters.
Tel 876 997 6360. **Open** 9:30am–3:30pm Tue–Sun. 🎟 🛶 tubing and canopy tour on payment. 📷
Ⓦ ysfalls.com

Appleton Rum Estate

8 miles (13 km) NE of Middle Quarters.
Tel 876 963 9215. **Open** 9am–4pm Mon–Sat. 🎟 🛒 🍴 📷
Ⓦ appletonestate.com

⓬ Mandeville

65 miles (104 km) SE of Montego Bay.
🏙 50,000. 🚌 from Montego Bay.
🍴 daily.

The capital of Manchester, Mandeville is one of Jamaica's most beautiful spots, set among hills and vegetation some 2,000 ft (600 m) above sea level. It was established by the Duke of Manchester – once governor of Jamaica – and named for his son, the Viscount of Mandeville, in 1816. The town showcases Jamaican architecture – a classic Georgian style using local materials: the Mandeville Court House, built in 1820, has a portico supported by Doric columns; also noteworthy are the Manchester Parish Church, the Mandeville Jail and Work-house (now the Police Station), and the Mandeville Hotel.

Visitors enjoying ice cream at Devon House, Kingston

⓭ Kingston

119 miles (190 km) SW of Montego Bay. 🔼 937,000. ✈ ℹ Jamaica Tourist Board, 64 Knutsford Boulevard; 9am–4:30pm Mon–Fri; 876 929 4926. 🎨 Kingston on the Edge Urban Art Festival (Jun).

Spreading inland from a large natural harbor and cradled to the north by the peaks of the Blue Mountain range, Kingston is Jamaica's cultural and commercial center. The city is loosely divided into New Kingston and Downtown. At the heart of New Kingston is Knutsford Boulevard, which holds the manicured **Emancipation Park** at its southern end, with fountains, a jogging track, and Laura Facey Cooper's *Redemption Song*

sculpture. Roughly parallel to Knutsford, Hope Road swings past some of the classic Kingston sights. Shady gardens surround the splendid **Devon House**, built by the nation's first black millionaire. The complex is a popular place to head for an ice cream or a snack, a tour of the house, or just to relax on the park benches. Farther along Hope Road, Rasta flags and mural-painted walls enclose the **Bob Marley Museum**. Set in his former home, it is a surprisingly low-key tribute to Jamaica's most famous son, with displays of gold and platinum discs, stage clothing, and a wall papered with newspaper reports of his exploits. His kitchen and bedroom remain

as he left them, while in a room at the back, bullet-holes testify to a failed assassination attempt in 1980. At the northern end of Hope Road, it is worth making time for a stroll around **Hope Botanical Gardens**, set in a former sugar estate and filled with rare trees and plants.

Downtown is home to banks, offices and, on its fringes, some of the country's roughest ghettos. Right on the waterfront, behind the grassy lawns and swaying palms of Ocean Boulevard, the **National Gallery** houses the best collection of home-grown art in the country.

🏠 **Devon House**
26 Hope Road. **Tel** 876 929 6602.
Open 9:30am–5pm Mon–Sat.
🎨 🕐 ♿ garden only. 🏪 📷
W **devonhousejamaica.com**

🏛 **Bob Marley Museum**
56 Hope Road. **Tel** 876 978 2929.
Open 9:30am–4pm Mon–Sat.
🎨 🕐 ✉ 📷 🏪 📷
W **bobmarleymuseum.com**

🌺 **Hope Botanical Gardens**
Hope Road. **Tel** 876 970 3505.
Open 6am–6pm daily. ♿ 📷

🏛 **National Gallery**
12 Ocean Boulevard. **Tel** 876 922 1561.
Open 10am–4:30pm Tue–Thu,
10am–4pm Fri, 10am–3pm Sat. 📷
📷 📷 📷 W **natgalja.org.jm**

Kingston

① Emancipation Park
② Devon House
③ Bob Marley Museum

0 meters 500
0 yards 500

⑭ Hellshire

10 miles (16 km) SW of New Kingston.
🚇 85,000. 🚌

On the other side of the harbor from Kingston, and reached by the toll highway to the huge dormitory suburb of Portmore, the Hellshire Hills are an arid, cactus-strewn expanse jutting down into the Caribbean Sea. The main reason to come here is for a swim at **Fort Clarence Beach**, a stretch of white sand that is popular with Kingstonians, or to have a plate of fried fish at the neighboring fishing village of Hellshire, known islandwide for its outstandingly good seafood. Here, ramshackle restaurants line the sand, selling fried fish served with vinegary pepper sauce and bammy or cornbread fritters. It is a thoroughly Jamaican scene during the weekends when huge speakers blast out reggae and local families descend on the beach.

Past Hellshire, the **Two Sisters Caves** are a series of deep caverns in the limestone made accessible by wooden walkways and stairs. Guides explain the caves' history and point out an Amerindian petroglyph on one of the walls.

🏯 **Fort Clarence Beach**
Main Road, Hellshire. **Open**
10am–6pm Mon–Fri, 9am–6pm
Sat–Sun. 🈳 🈲 🖵 Note: showers and changing rooms on-site.

🏯 **Two Sisters Caves**
Main Road, Hellshire. **Open** 9am–6pm
Wed–Sun. 🈳 🖵

Interior of a restaurant with brightly colored murals, Hellshire

Cannons in the courtyard of Fort Charles

⑮ Port Royal

5 miles (8 km) S of New Kingston.
🚇 4,300. 🚌

A series of small cays joined together to form a breakwater between Kingston's harbor and the open ocean, the thin strip of road running along the Palisadoes takes visitors to Port Royal. This atmospheric fishing village, with a colorful past of piracy and naval might, was scarred by a catastrophic natural disaster. A thriving town under the British, it suffered a massive earthquake in 1692 that destroyed most of the place and killed thousands of people, effectively putting an end to its importance.

Port Royal still holds several of the original British-built fortifications, the largest of which is **Fort Charles**, the first of five bastions built here from bricks that had served as ballast on British ships. The Maritime Museum in the courtyard has a small but fascinating collection of artifacts dredged up from the ruins of the original town. Back toward the main square, visit the graveyard of St. Peter's Church; one of the tombs is of Lewis Galdy, who was swallowed by the earth during the earthquake, and miraculously regurgitated seconds later. Another activity here is to take a boat to Lime Cay, a tiny island with white sands and clear waters.

🏯 **Fort Charles**
Tel 876 967 8438. **Open** 9am–4:45pm daily. **Closed** Good Fri & Christmas Day. 🈳 🈲

Pirates of Port Royal

When the British took Jamaica from Spain in 1655, they established a huge fort at the tip of the Port Royal peninsula to guard Kingston's harbor Nelson himself was stationed here and set about employing the services of pirates to help their meager forces defend Jamaica. More palatably referred to as privateers, the pirates enthusiastically went about the business of plundering treasure-laden Spanish ships sailing between Europe and their New World colonies. The

Sir Henry Morgan, pirate and later lieutenant-governor

huge profits they made saw Port Royal boom. Notorious as a haven for piracy and debauchery, it was condemned by the church as the "wickedest city in Christendom". However, the pirates' days ended when Britain signed a peace treaty with Spain in 1670. Having made his name plundering the Spanish colony of Panama in the name of the British king, Sir Henry Morgan was chosen as the Crown's lieutenant-governor to persuade his fellow privateers into a life of peace. His most famous captures were that of "Calico" Jack Rackham and his female accomplices, Mary Read and Anne Bonney. Rackham was executed, his body packed into a cage and left on a cay as warning to others.

For hotels and restaurants on this island see pp156–9 and pp160–61

⑯ Blue Mountains Tour

With its highest peak reaching 7,402 ft (2,256 m), Jamaica's largest range – the Blue Mountains –stretches for 28 miles (45 km) from east to west, its lower canopy of soapwood, dogwood, and Caribbean cedar interspersed with coffee plantations and its upper slopes covered with stunted montane rainforest. From Papine and Kingston, there are two main tour routes. The road divides at The Cooperage, with one fork heading towards Holywell Recreational Park, taking in coffee plantations and a glitzy hotel en route, and the other to Gordon Town and Mavis Bank, where jeeps can be hired to get to the start of the hiking trail to Blue Mountain Peak.

Jamaican oriole, one of the many birds found in the Blue Mountains region

① The Cooperage
This nondescript junction is named for the Irish coopers who made rum barrels here in the 19th century.

② Irish Town
Home to the famed Strawberry Hill Hotel, where Bob Marley convalesced after being shot in 1976.

③ Craighton Coffee Estate
This Japanese-owned coffee plantation is centered around the pretty Great House, where guided tours are available.

④ Newcastle
This colonial-era former British military base, now a training ground of the Jamaica Defence Force, is closed to visitors.

Tips for Drivers

Starting point: Papine.
Length: A full day to see both the Holywell and Mavis Bank sides of the mountains.
Driving conditions: Drive slowly, use the horn on hairpin bends, and avoid the hills if it is raining, as landslides are fairly common.

Map labels:
Wakefield
Green Hills
Section
Silver Hill
Cinch
Botan
Garde
⑥
⑤
▲ Catherine's Peak 5,060 ft
④
Redlight
St. Peters
Westp
③
②
Content Gap
Yallahs River
Gordon Town
Guava Ridge
①
Kingston
Papine
Flamstead

⑤ Holywell Recreational Park
The main visitor center for the Blue and John Crow Mountains National Park, with designated trails through the cloud forest, cabins to stay in, and spectacular views down to Kingston.

⑨ Abbey Green
With whispering eucalyptus trees usually shrouded in mist, Abbey Green is the start of the trail to Blue Mountain Peak. It is home to lodges that serve as bases for the peak climb.

⑧ Mavis Bank
This tiny mountain town is home to the tourable Blue Mountain Coffee Processing Plant and has fabulous views.

⑦ Clydesdale and Cinchona
The former coffee plantation of Clydesdale is the starting point for the hike to the dilapidated but beautiful botanical gardens at Cinchona.

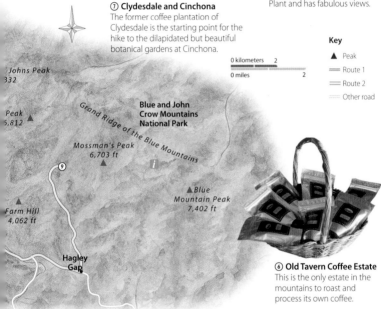

Key

▲ Peak
═══ Route 1
═══ Route 2
---- Other road

0 kilometers 2
0 miles 2

Johns Peak
332

Peak
5,812 ▲

Grand Ridge of the Blue Mountains

Blue and John Crow Mountains National Park

Mossman's Peak
6,703 ft ▲

ℹ

▲Blue Mountain Peak
7,402 ft

⑨

Farm Hill ▲
4,062 ft

Hagley Gap

⑥ Old Tavern Coffee Estate
This is the only estate in the mountains to roast and process its own coffee.

Drying in the sun

Picking coffee berries

Roasting in processors

Sorting the beans

Blue Mountain Coffee

Widely acknowledged as one of the best in the world, Blue Mountain coffee is grown at 2,000–5,000 ft (609–1,524 m). The unique climate and rich soil produces the distinctively delicious beans. Once ripe, beans are hand-picked and transported to the processing factory at Mavis Bank. They are first floated to remove inferior beans, then washed in holding tanks to remove the outer section. After being dried in the open air, or in drums if it is raining, the beans are rested for ten weeks before finally being hulled, sorted into grades, roasted, and packed.

⓱ Port Antonio

61 miles (98 km) NE of Kingston.
🚗 13,000. 🚌 🚐 🛥️ Port Antonio
International Marlin Tournament (Oct).
W **portantoniotravel.com**

A quiet little town that grew
around its deep twin harbors,
Port Antonio owes its origins as
a tourist spot to actor Errol
Flynn (1909–59). Having run
aground here aboard his private
yacht, Flynn took a liking to the
Portland area, buying Navy
Island just offshore and a hotel
that used to stand on the
Titchfield peninsula – the
western tip of Port Antonio's
East harbor. By the 1950s, he
was well-known for inviting a
string of celebrities, including
Bette Davis and Ginger Rogers
to Jamaica to stay and go
rafting on the Rio Grande.

Although little remains to
be seen of the Flynn legacy
today, the area does retain
a sense of faded glamor,
especially in the palatial
resorts east of town. Port
Antonio still has a certain
shabby charm, with a few
colonial-era buildings with
typical overhanging verandas
along its main street. There is
a bustling fruit and vegetable
market and the Port Antonio
Court House, housed in a
grand old Georgian building.

Facing Navy Island is the Port
Antonio Marina, now known
as the Errol Flynn Marina. The
marina offers world-class
facilities, including waterfront
paths for promenading,

Frenchman's Cove, one of Jamaica's best beaches

manicured lawns, a slip of white-
sand beach, and an upscale
restaurant. Unfortunately,
Navy Island is officially closed
to visitors, though local fishermen still take people to its
lovely beaches for a swim
and to snorkel.

⓲ Frenchman's Cove and the Blue Lagoon

5 miles (8 km) E of Port Antonio.
Tel 876 993 7270. 🚕
Open 9am–5pm daily. 🏖️
W **portantoniotravel.com**

The coastline east of Port
Antonio is one of the most
beautiful in the country.
Watered by frequent rain
showers that bounce off the
Blue Mountains, the jungle-like
tangle of ferns, flowers, and
palms cascade down the
inland side of the coast road.

The turquoise waters offshore
are spectacular, with the
odd palm-covered island just
adding to the perfection.
Local hoteliers have long tried
to capitalize on the Portland
area's natural attractions by
developing it as a tourist resort.
However, the lack of decent
roads means it is still relatively
unspoilt, with just a handful
of hotels, including the
impressive, turreted Trident
Castle, and a sprinkling of
beautiful guesthouses.

Just a short distance from
Port Antonio, a weather-
beaten sign marks the
entrance to Frenchman's Cove,
perhaps the most beautiful
of Jamaica's beaches, a perfect
horseshoe of sand enclosed
by jungle-clad hills and with
a refreshingly cool, sandy-
floored river running into
the bay beneath Frenchman's
Cove Resort.

The twin harbors of Port Antonio on Jamaica's northeast coast

For hotels and restaurants on this island see pp156–9 and pp160–61

A short way farther east along the main road, past San San Beach, signposts indicate the turnoff for the Blue Lagoon. At this almost circular pool of unknown depth, chilly spring-water mixes with the warm seawater to amazing effect, making the pretty lagoon an unforgettable place to swim and snorkel. The location was also made famous by the 1980 movie, *The Blue Lagoon*, starring Brooke Shields and Christopher Atkins. Visitors are, however, advised to be wary of the local "guides" who may ask for non-existent entrance fees. A good way to visit is on a bamboo raft trip from Frenchman's Cove.

Peaceful blue waters lapping Winnifred Beach

🄳 Winnifred Beach

5 miles (8 km) E of Port Antonio at Fairy Hill.

Laid-back Winnifred Beach is a rarity in Jamaica. This spectacular white-sand cove has still not fallen victim to development and thus retains its pristine quality. At the moment, only forested cliffs border this curve of soft, powdery sand.

People can walk down to the beach from the main road, just opposite the Jamaica Crest Resort. The only buildings breaking the view are the odd shacks selling food and drink alongside the not-so-functional changing facilities. There is a small reef, which is ideal for snorkeling; equipment can be rented at the beach.

This lovely place is as popular with locals as it is with visitors. However, the regulars are in

Water cascading into the clear pool of Reach Falls

the midst of a dispute with the government, whose redevelopment plans could irrevocably alter the character of Winnifred Beach.

🄴 Long Bay

12 miles (19 km) E of Port Antonio.

The wide beach of Long Bay, a glorious 1-mile (2-km) stretch of yellow sand and crashing waves, has only a few hotels and restaurants overlooking the water. Tourism has developed over the years with young Europeans coming here to relax and go surfing. Currents can be dangerous, so take local guidance before swimming. It is usually safe though, and the waves make an invigorating change to most of Jamaica's beaches. This windswept shore has also become popular in recent years for kiteboarding, thanks to its consistent swells and dependable trade wind. Visitors can negotiate sea trips with the local fishermen who draw their small craft up onto the sands.

🄵 Reach Falls

6 miles (9 km) E of Long Bay.
Open 8:30am–4:30pm Wed–Sun.

Beyond Long Bay, the coast road sweeps spectacularly below cliffs and around the calm reaches of Manchioneal Bay before turning inland again. A signposted road to the right winds upwards through the rainforest to the beautiful Reach Falls that cascade from Drivers River. The green pools at the bottom of the fall are at least 4 ft (1.2 m) deep with crystal-clear water and pebbled floor.

The surrounding area has been developed by the government and now has changing facilities, a visitors' center, and refreshment outlets. However, the falls have suffered a little from development, losing their unspoilt quality. Still, the deep main pool is beautiful and visitors can also follow the river upstream to seek out underground caves and more swimming spots nearby.

Palm trees and the inviting sea at Long Bay

㉒ Firefly

43 miles (69 km) NW of Kingston.
Tel 876 725 0920. 🚌 **Open**
9am–5pm Mon–Thu & Sat. 🖼️ 🖥️

Sitting pretty above the village of Port Maria, Firefly was the Jamaican home of the well-known English playwright, actor, and songwriter Noël Coward (1899–1973) and his partner, Graham Payn (1918–2005), who both lived here until Coward's death. The simple 1950s house, a retreat from his first Jamaican home Blue Harbour which became overrun with houseguests, has been left as it was. Photographs on the walls show the famous visitors to his residence, from Sophia Loren and Audrey Hepburn to Queen Elizabeth II. Perhaps best known for such quintessentially English ditties as "Mad Dogs and Englishmen", Coward also wrote many plays, some of them in this house. However, the main attraction is the fabulous view that Firefly affords of the coastline below, with Cabarita Island in the foreground.

Statue of English novelist and songwriter Noel Coward at Firefly

㉓ Oracabessa

60 miles (95 km) NW of Kingston.
🏙️ 4,300. 🚌 **W** oracabessa.com

A nondescript little place, Oracabessa was the center of banana export until the 1900s. However, the town's claim to fame is that it drew the atten-tion of author Ian Fleming, who built a house and wrote most of

The privately-owned James Bond Beach, Oracabessa

his James Bond novels here. Today, the house is part of the exclusive Goldeneye hotel *(see p158)* and is closed to non-guests. However, the 007 connection remains with the **James Bond Beach**, just down the coast from Goldeneye. It was opened in the mid-1990s by Jamaican-born impresario Chris Blackwell, who produced most of Bob Marley's albums and also owns 70 acres (28 ha) of Oracabessa beachfront.

🏖️ **James Bond Beach**
Old Wharf Road. **Open** 9am–6pm
Tue–Sun. 🖼️ 🏊 Note: changing rooms, toilets, and watersports on-site.

The 007 Connection

The tiny town of Oracabessa may seem an unlikely inspiration for a fictional world of spies, villains, and fantastical gadgets, but that is just what it offered to Ian Fleming. He fell in love with the place during a visit to Jamaica in 1943. Following the footsteps of his friend, Noël Coward, who built two homes just down the coast, Fleming created Goldeneye as a retreat from the bleak English winter and visited Jamaica regularly. Friends such as Graham Greene, Truman Capote, and Evelyn Waugh came to stay and lap up the sybaritic routine of sundowners and snorkeling. It was not until his wife became pregnant in 1952 that Fleming settled down to writing. Naming his hero after an author of a book on birds of the West Indies, and using Jamaica as the setting for *Doctor No* and *The Man with the Golden Gun* (both were eventually filmed here), Fleming was entranced by the island that inspired him to write, "Would these books have been born if I had not been living in the gorgeous vacuum of a Jamaican holiday? I doubt it".

㉔ Ocho Rios

54 miles (86 km) N of Kingston.
🏙️ 16,300. ✈️ 🚌 ⛴️ 🛈 TPDCO
Information Office, Ocean Village Plaza, Main Street; 876 974 2582.
W ochorios.com

Very much on the beaten track, Ocho Rios has grown up around the tourist industry and these days its principal sources of income are the cruise ships whose massive bulk overshadows the harbor most days of the week. Built around a wide bay with a sweeping arc of hotel-lined beach, Ocho Rios is well-geared to meet the limited time

Ian Fleming's former home is now part of the Goldeneye hotel

constraints of cruise passengers, with several attractions that can easily be seen in half a day. Buses and minibuses arrive and depart at the terminal on Main Street and route taxis cover all the main local roads.

The chief attraction is Island Village, at the far west end of Main Street. It is a slick collection of shops, restaurants, and bars with a private beach. Also here is **Margaritaville**, a restaurant and bar that provides family-friendly fun during the day – there is a rooftop hot tub, a two-story waterslide, and a freshwater pool with a swim-up bar. After dark, Margaritaville transforms into a nightclub with a sophisticated Afro-Cuban vibe.

Other than **UDC Beach**, the main attractions overlook the town at Murphy Hill, where the restful **Shaw Park Botanical Gardens** sit some 550 ft (167 m) above sea level. The gardens have beautiful views of the town, and are home to rare plants and trees, as well as a pretty waterfall. Just down the road is **Coyaba River Garden**, offering equally striking views. It is more compact, with paths threading past pools and streams. It also has a small museum dedicated to local history. The garden has a

waterfall in which visitors can take a quick splash.

🎭 Margaritaville
Island Village. **Tel** 876 675 8800.
🌐 📷 **w** **margaritaville caribbean.com**

🏊 UDC Beach
Main Street. **Open** 9am–5pm daily.
🌐 📷 Note: changing facilities, lifeguards, and watersports on-site.

🌺 Shaw Park Botanical Gardens
Shaw Park Road. **Tel** 876 974 2723.
Open 8am–5pm daily. 🌐 ♿ 💻 **w** **shawparkgardens.com**

🌿 Coyaba River Garden
Shaw Park Road. **Tel** 876 383 1281.
Open 8am–5pm daily. 🌐 ♿ 💻 📷 **w** **coyabagardens.com**

㉕ Dolphin Cove and Dunn's River Falls

Dolphin Cove: 2 miles (3 km) W of Ocho Rios. **Tel** 876 974 5335.
Open 8:30am–5:30pm daily. 🌐 📷 for Dolphin Cove. ♿ limited. 📷 💻
📷 Dunn's River Falls: **Tel** 876 974 2857. **Open** 8:30am–4pm daily.
🌐 ♿ limited. 📷 💻 📷
w **dolphincovejamaica.com**
w **dunnsriverfallsja.com**

Practically opposite one another on the coast road west of Ocho Rios, are the well-known

Preparing for a dolphin encounter at Dolphin Cove

Dunn's River Falls and Dolphin Cove, the latter a kind of mini-theme park which provides the opportunity to swim with dolphins, stingrays (with barbs removed), and nurse sharks.

The entrance fee charged at Dolphin Cove gives visitors a run of the complex, including a walking trail where handlers let people get up close to macaws, snakes, iguanas, and goats. It also covers snorkeling in the bay and the use of glass-bottom kayaks. Dolphin, shark, and stingray encounters cost extra.

Just up the road is Dunn's River Falls, a magnificent cascade of multiple tiers, encircled by interesting ferns and foliage, and ending in the sea. Guides lead easy and invigorating climbs up the falls. While the surrounding land has undergone extensive development, the falls themselves remain spectacular, as does the white-sand beach at their base. There is also a lively reef offshore and it is possible to rent snorkel gear.

Both Dunn's River and Dolphin Cove can get a little crowded on cruise ship days.

A short distance east, opposite Reynold's Pier, a road leads uphill to **Mystic Mountain**. This adventure theme park is a must for thrill-seekers with its zipline, rainforest tram, and bobsled ride.

🎢 Mystic Mountain
Tel 876 974 3990. **Open** 7:30am–5pm daily. 🌐 🌐 📷
w **rainforestbobsledjamaica.com**

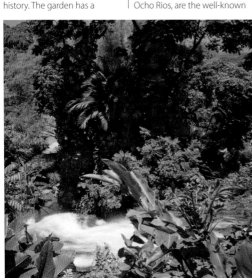
The serene Shaw Park Botanical Gardens, Ocho Rios

Footbridge leading into the lush green Cranbrook Flower Forest

㉖ Cranbrook Flower Forest

18 miles (29 km) W of Ocho Rios. **Tel** 876 770 8071 or 610 6509. Open 9am–5pm daily.

The perfect antidote to Ocho Rios, the Cranbrook Flower Forest offers 130 acres (53 ha) of beautifully landscaped gardens and a thriving forest, all threaded with paths. Shaded by palms and planted with all kinds of beautiful tropical blooms, from heliconias, philodendrons, birds of paradise, hibiscus, and begonias to an amazing display of orchids, the flower gardens are exquisite.

The other highlight is the River Head Adventure Tour which begins at the entrance lawns. It is a lovely walk through the unspoilt tropical forest along the bank of the Little River. The trail leads up to where the river rises from a spring to form a 20-ft (6-m) wide intensely blue natural pool. Elsewhere on-site, visitors can fish for tilapia, picnic on the lawns surrounding the central building, a restored sugar mill, or go bird-watching or take part in an adrenaline-filled canopy tour.

The lush grounds makes this a popular place for weddings and it is possible to rent just the location or have Cranbrook make all the arrangements. There is also a small gift and snack shop near the entrance.

㉗ Runaway and Discovery Bays

25 miles (40 km) W of Ocho Rios.

Unlike Ocho Rios or Montego Bay, the neighboring towns of Runaway Bay and Discovery Bay are made up of a string of huge all-inclusive resorts that line the coast, interspersed with a few roadside restaurants and a couple of good beaches.

Runaway Bay has the Cardiff Hall Public Beach, a handsome strip of white sand that is popular with the locals. There is no entry fee, nor are there any facilities to speak of except for a small bar and a snackshop. Located on Discovery Bay is the **Puerto Seco Beach**, which has a strip of pristine white sand and all the facilities. It is relatively deserted on weekdays.

Puerto Seco Beach
Main Road, Discovery Bay.
Open 9am–5pm daily.
Note: lifeguards and changing facilities on-site.

㉘ Green Grotto Caves

22 miles (35km) W of Ocho Rios.
Tel 876 973 2841.
Open 9am–4pm daily.
greengrottocavesja.com

On the main road between the Runaway and Discovery Bays, Green Grotto Caves is an extensive network of limestone caverns with a subterranean lake and plenty of impressive stalactites and stalagmites. Guided tours take visitors through the history of the caves, which were used by Amerindians as a place of worship and later as a hideout by Spanish troops.

Although it makes a great half-hour trip, the entry fee is rather inflated. There is a pond outside where visitors can fish for tilapia.

One of the limestone caverns in the vast Green Grotto Caves

The Rasta-colored meditation rock at the Bob Marley Mausoleum in Nine Mile

❷ Bob Marley Centre & Mausoleum

25 miles (40 km) SW of Ocho Rios. **Tel** 876 843 0498. 🚌 infrequent rural buses run to Nine Mile. 🚕 **Open** 9am–4pm daily. 🅿 🔲 ♿ 🔲 📷

High in the St. Ann hills amid a gorgeous landscape of rich red earth and grassy cattle pastures, the Bob Marley Mausoleum is located in the hamlet of Nine Mile, where Marley was born and spent his early childhood before moving to Kingston at the age of 13. Encircled by a high fence and with Rasta red, gold, and green flags flapping in the wind, the compound is centered around the tiny wooden shack where the Marleys lived when Bob was aged between 6 and 13 years. The mausoleum itself is a simple white-washed building hold-ing Marley's marble tomb. Incense burns and the stained-glass windows filter colors on to the stone, creating a moving atmosphere.

Located on the property is a vegetarian restaurant as well as a gift shop which sells CDs and various Marley memorabilia. There is also a Rasta-colored "meditation stone" where Marley used to rest his head while contemplating.

Chukka Adventures (*see p155*) takes visitors to the mausoleum either in a jeep or on an old-time country bus. Each year on February 6, Marley's birth anniversary, the village comes alive with a huge concert as part of a week-long tribute to Jamaica's best-known musician.

❸ Cockpit Country

36 miles (58 km) E of Montego Bay. 🚌 minibuses run to Windsor but services are infrequent. 🚹 Southern Trelawny Environmental Agency, 876 610 0818. 🌐 **stea.net**

A vast wilderness covering some 500 square miles (1,294 sq km), the largely uninhabited Cockpit Country is one of Jamaica's most ecologically important areas. Home to innumerable rare plants and animals, it is characterized by the bizarre karst topography of conical hillocks separated by deep sinkholes in the limestone. The best place to appreciate the Cockpit's serene remoteness is **Windsor**, a tiny hamlet on the northern fringes of the area and gateway to the nearby Windsor Caves, a bat colony carpeted with pungent guano.

There are also hiking trails into the Cockpit's fringes from Albert Town, some 10 miles (16 km) south of Windsor, where the Southern Trelawny Environmental Agency offers caving and hiking tours.

A good base for exploring is Good Hope, an 18th-century great house with a spectacular setting and views over Cockpit Country. Good Hope estate can be explored by horse and carriage, and has a zipline. Visits are arranged via Chukka Adventures (*see p155*).

Bob Marley performing at a concert

Bob Marley

Born on February 6, 1945, to Cedella Malcom, a 17-year-old farmer's daughter, and 51-year-old Norval Marley, a white Jamaican former soldier, Bob Marley remains the biggest reggae star in the world. Having grown up in the country, Marley moved to Kingston with his mother after the break-up of her marriage. They lived in the government yard where he met Peter Tosh and Bunny Livingstone, with whom he formed the Wailers as a teenager. They were noticed by Chris Blackwell of Island Records and were introduced to the world. Their first Island album, *Catch a Fire*, was an instant success, and 11 more followed. However, Livingstone and Tosh became increasingly disillusioned with Blackwell and with Marley's dominance in the band and left the group to pursue solo careers. In 1980, Marley was diagnosed with cancer and died on May 11, 1981, in Miami. The tradition continues through the music of his sons Damian "Junior Gong", Ziggy, Ky-Mani, Stephen, and Julian Marley.

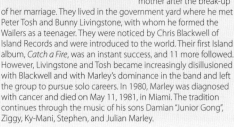

Ruins on the grounds of an old great house, Cockpit Country

Outdoor Activities and Specialized Holidays

Jamaica has an excellent tourist infrastructure and offers a large variety of outdoor activities to its visitors. Besides the obvious pursuits, from world-class golf courses and fantastic beaches to spas and watersports, there are also some unusual options. To give the island an edge over its neighbors, many activities have been designed especially for cruise ship passengers. Alongside boat tours and Jet Skis, horseback rides, and hikes, visitors can also glide down a river on a bamboo raft, swing through treetops, and take a ride on a dogsled.

Visitors at the Mahogany Beach, Ocho Rios

Beaches

Jamaica's top beaches are located along the island's north coast. Sheltered by reefs and boasting powdery white sands straight out of the brochures, they are everything visitors would expect from a Caribbean shoreline. The finest of these beaches, however, have been snapped up by developers and are either incorporated into hotel complexes (therefore off-limits for non-guests) or are privately owned attractions with showers, changing rooms, and an entrance fee.

Along the south coast, owing to past volcanic eruptions, the shore features brown and sometimes decidedly black beaches rather than splendid white sands. Although the movement of the water may give it a murky appearance at the shoreline, a little farther out it is possible to find a perfectly clear blue sea that provides excellent swimming.

Diving and Snorkeling

While Jamaica's reefs may not be the best in the Caribbean, having suffered damage from storms and human carelessness by way of dropped anchors and coastal pollution, there are still some lovely spots for diving and snorkeling. The best snorkeling and diving is along the north coast between Negril and Ocho Rios, where visibility is at a peak, and an almost continuous reef runs parallel to the coast. On these excursions, visitors can observe the fire, elkhorn, and brain corals, and a host of colorful marine life. Several wreck dives are also available, including submerged planes used in ill-fated ganja smuggling operations. All the main resorts have dive sites and operators who rent out snorkeling equipment. The latter is also available from the several watersports outlets on the beaches. Some of the main operators in Jamaica include the **Negril Scuba Centre**, **Resort Divers**, and **Lady G'Diver**.

River Rafting

Gliding along calm waters surrounded by riverbanks swathed in greenery remains a spectacular way to see the island. River rafting was first popularized by Errol Flynn (*see p146*), who noticed farmers transporting their goods along the Rio Grande by bamboo raft and thought it might make a pleasurable jaunt. Although there is no organized rafting center in Port Antonio, raft captains offer trips to interested visitors. The Martha Brae River, west of Montego Bay, is the next best spot. While lacking the towering mountain scenery of the Rio Grande, it is a beautiful trip through the lush Trelawny countryside. **Rafting on the**

Rafting on the Martha Brae River

Horse-riding in the water at Chukka Cove, near Ocho Rios

Martha Brae offers tours on a 30-ft (9-m) bamboo raft, with a trained raft captain. Whitewater rafting can be done on the Great River – when water levels allow. Rafting trips are provided by **Caliche River Rafting Tours**.

Boat Cruises

From Negril, Ocho Rios, and Montego Bay, boats offering day trips for visitors cruise up and down the coastline. Most are catamarans, complete with bathrooms, bars, and nets over the hulls for sunbathing. The trips tend to include an open bar, as well as a stop for snorkeling. Some boats also offer shorter sunset cruises or evening trips that include dinner. These could be the party-hard booze cruise type, so do check before booking. **Cool Runnings Boat Tours**, **Wild Thing Watersports**, and **Dreamer Catamarans** offer boat cruises.

Watersports

All of the main beaches in Ocho Rios, Montego Bay, and Negril have watersports outlets offering everything from rental of scuba equipment to non-motorized options such as kayaking and sailing in Sunfish boats. The motorized activities include Jet Skiing, parasailing, waterskiing, glass-bottom boats, and banana boat rides. The **Garfield Diving Station** offers Jet Skiing and glass-bottom boat rides.

Horse-Riding

Alongside gentle horse-rides through the countryside, Jamaica's stables have also developed beach rides. Visitors may take a short amble through the bush to the seashore, de-saddle their mount, change into swimming gear, and climb back on for an exhilarating trot through the water. The rides offered by Chukka Caribbean Adventures (see p155) and **Hooves** have the horses walking through deep water, but Montego Bay's **Half Moon Equestrian Centre** takes it a step further and has the horses swim, a magical experience. The latter also offer riding lessons.

Hiking

Jamaica's thick forests offer many pleasant hikes through spectacular scenery. The best of the walks are located in the misty Blue Mountains (see pp144–5), where visitors can amble along the easy trails within Holywell Recreational Park or go for more challenging routes such as the uphill trek to Cinchona Botanical Gardens. The island's ultimate hike, however, is the Blue Mountains Peak trail, a 6-hour walk through forest that changes from montane rainforest to stunted elfin growth, overhung with ferns and surrounded by miniature orchids and epiphytic plants.

Bird-Watching

Jamaica provides for some great bird-watching, most notably in the Blue Mountains, Cockpit Country (see p151), the Royal Palm Reserve near Negril (see p138), and the Black River (see p140). Of the 280-odd species recorded on the island, 21 birds are found nowhere else in the world, a level of endemism not found on any other Caribbean island. Spectacular humming-birds can be seen up close at Rocklands Bird Sanctuary in St. James (see p136). Jamaica's national bird, the streamertail hummingbird, the Jamaican woodpecker, and the 2-inch (5-cm) long vervain humming-bird, the second-smallest bird in the world, are a few species to look out for. Tour companies such as the **Sun Venture Tours** provide birding trips. Some hotels, such as Mockingbird Hill (see p159), offer packages.

Hiking through the spectacular forests of the Blue Mountains

Caving

Much of Jamaica is covered with soft sedimentary limestone, eroded by water over centuries to create thousands of caves. Many of these, such as the Roaring River and Two Sisters, are open to the public as show caves, with electric lights and walkways. However, most caves remain untouched. Of these undeveloped ones, Windsor Caves in Cockpit Country *(see p151)* are the easiest to access. Cockpit Country also has the deepest of the island's sinkholes – deep pits with sheer edges that are descended by way of ropes and pulleys. Guided tours and trips are provided by **Cockpit Country Adventure Tours** and **Jamaican Caves Organization**.

Golf

Jamaica has 12 golf courses, which host local and international tournaments all year round. Recognized as some of the best courses in the world, and designed by some well-known golf course architects,

Golf course at the Half Moon Club, Montego Bay

including Robert Trent Jones Sr. and Jr., Jamaica's links boast spectacular locations by the sea. Montego Bay has no less than five premier courses around town. Ocho Rios is second best. Smaller courses are found in both Negril and Kingston. Useful information is available from the **Jamaica Golf Association.**

Spas

No high-class resort in Jamaica is complete without its spa, and several smaller places also offer massages and beauty treatents. Many spas are beautifully located, with massage rooms right on the water, cooled by sea breezes, and with a soundtrack of waves. Alongside massages, larger spas such as the **Oasis Spa**, the Aveda Concept Spa at The Caves hotel *(see p158)*, Half Moon hotel's Fern Tree Spa *(see p157)*, and the Driftwood Spa at Jake's hotel *(see p159)*, offer the full range of beauty, body, and facial treatments, as well as manicures and pedicures.

DIRECTORY

Diving and Snorkeling

Lady G'Diver
Port Antonio, Portland.
Tel 876 995 0246.
W ladygdiver.com

Negril Scuba Centre
Negril Escape Hotel, West End Road, Negril.
Tel 876 877 7517.
W negrilscubacenter.com

Resort Divers
Ocho Rios & Runaway Bay. **Tel** 876 881 5760.
W resortdivers.com

River Rafting

Caliche River Rafting Tours
Montego Bay.
Tel 876 940 6558.
W whitewater raftingmontegobay.com

Rafting on the Martha Brae
Gloucester Avenue, Montego Bay.
Tel 876 940 6398.
W jamaicarafting.com

Boat cruises

Cool Runnings Boat Tours
121 Main Street, Ocho Rios. **Tel** 876 376 4310.
W coolrunnings catamarans.com

Dreamer Catamarans
Montego Bay.
Tel 876 979 0102.
W dreamer catamarans.com

Wild Thing Watersports
Norman Manley Boulevard, Negril.
Tel 876 957 9930.

Watersports

Garfield Diving Station
Ocho Rios, St. Ann.
Tel 876 544 4354.
W garfielddiving.com

Horse-Riding

Half Moon Equestrian Centre
Half Moon Hotel, Ironshore, Montego Bay.
Tel 876 953 2286.
W horsebackriding jamaica.com

Hooves
61 Windsor Road, St Ann's Bay. **Tel** 876 383 0659.
W hooves-jamaica.com

Bird-Watching

Sun Venture Tours
Kingston 10.
Tel 876 960 6685.
W sunventuretours.com

Caving

Cockpit Country Adventure Tours
Albert Town, Trelawny.
Tel 876 610 0818.
W stea.net

Jamaican Caves Organization
W jamaicancaves.org

Golf

Jamaica Golf Association
80 Knutsford Boulevard, Kingston 5.
Tel 876 755 3593.
W thejga.com

Spas

Oasis Spa
Couples Sans Souci Hotel, Ocho Rios.
Tel 876 994 1206.
W couples.com

"Soft" Adventure Tours

Jamaica provides a variety of alternatives to spending a day on a beach. Popularly known as "soft" adventures, these refer to fun but safe activities and range from river tubing to horseback rides in the sea. More unusual adventures include a swing through the treetops attached to a harness and a zipwire, an aerial bobsleigh run, open gondola rides up the hillside, or a dogsled tour. Most of these activities take place at sites along the north coast and the trips include pickups and drop-offs at hotels in Montego Bay, Ocho Rios, and Negril.

Land Adventures

Popular land-based tours include safaris aboard zebra-striped, open-top jeeps or old-time country buses into the heart of Jamaica's rugged interior, or up to the Bob Marley Museum. Downhill mountain-bike rides are also offered by different agencies.

Dogsled tours involve riding in modified buggies on wheels, pulled by an enthusiastic team made up of mostly rescue dogs.

Canopy tours provide for an exciting adventure. From a series of wooden platforms built into the rainforest canopy, soar through the trees by way of an intricate system of harnesses, pulleys and carabiners attached to horizontal traverses.

ATV Safaris include a lesson on handling these rugged four-wheel buggies or all-terrain vehicles, after which visitors can meander through the countryside, negotiating a few gullies and hills.

Sea Trek is a great way to get up close to the reefs and marine life. Walk on the seabed, breathing through a spaceman-like helmet.

Water Adventures

Visitors are never far from the sea in Jamaica, and even horseback rides here involve a dip in the ocean. Rafting down the island's rivers is a pleasant way to spend half a day. Guided ocean safaris aboard dinghies weave around the coast, stopping for swimming or snorkeling.

River Tubing and Kayaking are exhilarating ways to see Jamaica's rivers. Paddle downstream sitting in a huge rubber ring, or tackle gentle whitewater in a kayak. Sections of tame rapids keep things lively.

TOUR OPERATORS

Chukka Caribbean Adventures
Montego Bay.
Tel 876 953 6699.
W chukkacaribbean.com

Rain Forest Aerial Trams
Ocho Rios.
Tel 1-866 759 8726.
W rainforestrams.com

Where to Stay

**BLACK RIVER: Ashton Great
House and Hotel** $
Historic
Luana
Tel *876 965 2036*
W theashtongreathouse.com
Exuding serenity and aged charm,
this is a large house house
in the country, with modestly
furnished rooms and waxed
wooden floors and stairs.

DK Choice

**BLUE MOUNTAINS:
Strawberry Hill** $$$
Boutique
Irish Town
Tel *876 944 8400*
W islandoutpost.com
One of Jamaica's best hotels,
this stunning mountain
retreat has beautifully designed
wooden cottages that offer the
height of comfort and balconies
with spectacular views. There is
a picturesque infinity pool, an
Aveda spa, a sauna, and a top-
rated restaurant.

FALMOUTH: Time 'n' Place $
Boutique
Trelawny Parish
Tel *876 843 3625*
W mytimenplace.com
A charming and rustic family-run
hotel with thatched cottages
on the sands. The open-air
restaurant and bar is a popular
venue for fashion shoots.

KINGSTON: Mikuzi $
Boutique
5 Upper Montrose Road, New Kingston
Tel *876 978 4859*
W mikuzistudios.com
A budget option in a lovely old
house. The individually styled
rooms range from backpacker
units to elegant apartments.

KINGSTON: Altamont Court $$
Modern
1 Altamont Terrace, New Kingston
Tel *876 929 4498*
W altamontcourt.com
A friendly hotel in the heart of
town, close to restaurants and
clubs. With smart decor, as well
as a pool, Jacuzzi, and sun deck.

KINGSTON: Courtleigh $$
Modern
*85 Knutsford Boulevard,
New Kingston*
Tel *876 936 3570*
W courtleigh.com
Rooms range from plush doubles
to luxury suites at this family-run
upmarket option. All have lovely
views and mahogany furniture.

**KINGSTON: Knutsford
Court Hotel** $$
Modern
16 Chelsea Avenue, New Kingston 5
Tel *876 929 1000*
W knutsfordcourt.com
Focusing on both business
and leisure travelers, this clean,
well-run hotel has an elegant
Georgian decor. Pool and gym.

**KINGSTON:
The Spanish Court** $$
Modern
1 St. Lucia Avenue, Kingston 5
Tel *876 926 0000*
W spanishcourthotel.com
Chic, retro furnishings highlight
this upscale hotel in the city
center Close to restaurants.

KINGSTON: Terra Nova Hotel $$
Modern
17 Waterloo Road, Kingston 10
Tel *876 926 2211*
W terranovajamaica.com
The Terra Nova is a venerable
city-center hotel with a classy
Edwardian decor and a choice
of fine-dining restaurants. It is
popular with business travelers.

Price Guide
Prices are based on one night's stay in
high season for a standard double room,
inclusive of service charges and taxes.

$	up to $100
$$	$100–300
$$$	over $300

KINGSTON: Pegasus $$$
Luxury
81 Knutsford Boulevard, New Kingston
Tel *876 926 3961*
W jamaicapegasus.com
High-rise business hotel with
extensive facilities, including
a jogging track, a tennis court,
and an Olympic-sized pool.

**MONTEGO BAY:
Altamont West** $
Boutique
33 Gloucester Avenue
Tel *876 939 9378*
W altamontwesthotel.com
A chic little place, tastefully
furnished in Jamaican plantation
style. Rooms have hair dryers and
irons, and there is an on-site spa.

**MONTEGO BAY:
Coyaba Beach Resort** $$
Luxury
Main Road, Ironshore
Tel *876 953 9150*
W coyabaresortjamaica.com
Intimate and elegant, this family-
run hotel has its own private
beach and tastefully furnished
rooms. Coyaba is known for its
excellent service.

**MONTEGO BAY:
Doctor's Cave Beach Hotel** $$
Beach
Gloucester Avenue
Tel *876 952 4355*
W doctorscave.com
A popular beach hotel with
simply furnished rooms and
facilities such as a pool, a
Jacuzzi, and a games room.
Friendly service.

Luxury cottages set in gorgeous surroundings at Strawberry Hill, Blue Mountains

MONTEGO BAY: El Greco $$
Beach
11 Queen's Drive
Tel *876 940 6116*
W elgrecojamaica.com
Peaceful clifftop hotel with beach
access via an elevator. The villa
apartments have full kitchens
and are perfect for families.

MONTEGO BAY:
Sandals Montego Bay $$
Resort
Kent Avenue
Tel *877 308 8204*
W sandals.com
This is a couples-only all-inclusive
resort on a private beach. The
non-stop fun and activities
include nightly entertainment.
Well-appointed rooms.

DK Choice

MONTEGO BAY:
Half Moon $$$
Resort
Main Road, Rose Hall
Tel *876 953 2211*
W halfmoon.com
Set in beautiful surroundings,
this luxury resort exudes all the
class of old-time Jamaica. Guests
can enjoy watersports, tennis,
a world-renowned golf course,
and spacious landscaped
grounds. Choose between
standard rooms or villas.

MONTEGO BAY: Round Hill
Hotel & Villas $$$
Luxury
John Pringle Drive
Tel *876 956 7050*
W roundhill.com
Exclusive hilltop boutique hotel
with a plantation theme and a
beach club. The rooms and villas
were styled by Ralph Lauren.
Jackets are required for dining.

MONTEGO BAY:
Secrets Saint James $$$
Resort
Freeport
Tel *876 953 6600*
W secretsresorts.com
A super-chic bayfront resort
boasting elegant plantation-era
furnishings and a huge range
of facilities, including seven
gourmet restaurants.

NEGRIL: The Yellow Bird $
Beach
Norman Manley Boulevard
Tel *876 957 4252*
W theyellowbird.com
A great budget option with
simple yet nicely appointed
beachfront cottages and rooms,
some with shared bathrooms.

NEGRIL: Charela Inn $$
Beach
Norman Manley Boulevard
Tel *876 957 4277*
W charela.com
This hotel owes its enduring
appeal to its location, tasteful
furnishings, and good service.

NEGRIL: Citronella $$
Resort
West End Road
Tel *757 228 3246*
W citronellajamaica.com
Set amid lovely clifftop gardens,
Citronella's thatched two- and
three-bedroom cottages offer
plenty of comforts. The open-air
restaurant overlooks the sea.

NEGRIL: Country Country $$
Beach
Norman Manley Boulevard
Tel *876 957 4273*
W countryjamaica.com
Spacious and comfortable pastel-
hued cottages are equipped with
hair dryers, refrigerators, and
kettles. There is also a romantic
beachfront restaurant and bar.

NEGRIL: Idle Awhile $$
Beach
Norman Manley Boulevard
Tel *876 957 9666*
W idleawhile.com
An upscale beachfront option
with gorgeous furnishings,
private verandas, and all modern
conveniences. The six suites have
kitchens, too. Beach restaurant.

NEGRIL: Jackie's on the Reef $$
Beach
Lighthouse Road
Tel *876 957 4997*
W jackiesonthereef.com
Health-oriented hotel renowned
for its yoga programs. Built out
of coral stone and set atop a cliff,
it offers serene, airy rooms.

NEGRIL: Negril Tree
House Resort $$
Resort
Norman Manley Boulevard
Tel *1 800 790 5264*
W negriltreehouse.com
A spa resort with tropical-style
rooms in bungalows and two-
story units. Facilities include a
beach bar and watersports.

NEGRIL: Nirvana on the Beach $$
Resort
Norman Manley Boulevard
Tel *941 708 0203*
W nirvananegril.com
Nirvana offers creatively
decorated wooden cottages
and suites in secluded gardens
dotted with hammocks. Rates
include a cook/housekeeper.

Stylish seating area at Half Moon,
Montego Bay

DK Choice

NEGRIL: Rockhouse $$
Boutique
West End Road
Tel *876 957 4373*
W rockhousehotel.com
Rockhouse has a wonderful
cliffside setting and lush
gardens. The thatched cabins
have stylish designer touches
and ladders straight to the
sea. There is an infinity pool
and a restaurant overhanging
the ocean.

NEGRIL: Rondel Village $$
Resort
Norman Manley Boulevard
Tel *876 957 4413*
W rondelvillage.com
Functional self-catering rooms
are housed in two-story
octagonal villas set in lush
gardens. Two pools, outdoor
Jacuzzis, and a full-service spa.

NEGRIL: Samsara Hotel $$
Resort
West End Road
Tel *876 957 4395*
W negrilhotels.com
Samsara is a clifftop hotel with
simple, colorful decor. The on-site
restaurant serves up excellent
Italian-Jamaican fare. Freshwater
swimming pool.

NEGRIL: Tensing Pen $$
Boutique
West End Road
Tel *876 957 0387*
W tensingpen.com
This clifftop retreat, criss-crossed
by paths, has its grounds dotted
with widely spaced cabins and
cottages fitted out to the
highest standards.

The colorful and quirky Bizot bar at Goldeneye, Oracabessa

NEGRIL: Beaches $$$
Luxury
Norman Manley Boulevard
Tel *888 232 2437*
w beaches.com
This family-focused, all-inclusive resort offers every imaginable amenity. Accommodations feature elegant plantation-style decor.

NEGRIL: The Caves $$$
Boutique
West End Road
Tel *876 957 0270*
w islandoutpost.com
Rooms here are romantic, individually designed, and stylishly furnished. There is an Aveda spa, and clifftop dining at the water's edge. Popular choice with celebrities

NEGRIL: Couples Negril $$$
Beach Resort
Norman Manley Boulevard
Tel *800 268 7537*
w couples.com/negril
A couples-only, all-inclusive resort with vibrant, well-lit rooms that feature local artwork. Spa, entertainment, and watersports.

NEGRIL: Sandals Negril Beach Resort & Spa $$$
Luxury
Norman Manley Boulevard
Tel *877 308 8204*
w sandals.com
Supremely elegant and limited to couples, this all-inclusive resort and spa offers a gamut of dining options, activities, entertainment, and watersports.

OCHO RIOS: Hibiscus Lodge $$
Boutique
83–87 Main Street
Tel *876 974 2676*
w hibiscusjamaica.com
Set amid peaceful clifftop gardens with a pool, Hibiscus Lodge has a choice of comfortable and functional rooms, some with balconies that offer lovely sea views.

DK Choice

OCHO RIOS: High Hope Estate $$
Mountain Resort
PO Box 11, St. Ann's Bay
Tel *876 972 2277*
w highhopeestate.com
A grand old house located high in the hills in beautiful graounds. The elegant rooms boast beautiful antique furniture and magnificent views. The restaurant offers delicious Jamaican seafood and meat dishes.

OCHO RIOS: Shaw Park Beach Hotel & Spa $$
Beach
Shaw Park Road
Tel *876 974 2552*
w shawparkbeachhotel.com
Located within the Shaw Park Botanical Gardens, this delightful retreat offers spacious rooms and suites with spectacular views. The Palm Room restaurant serves international gourmet food.

OCHO RIOS: Beaches Ocho Rios Resort $$$
Beach Resort
Boscobel, St. Ann
Tel *888 232 2437*
w beaches.com
Colorful and elegant, this all-inclusive resort for families has a pirate-themed waterpark, plus watersports, fun activities, and entertainment for all ages.

OCHO RIOS: Couples San Souci $$$
Luxury
Sans Souci
Tel *800 268 7537*
w couples.com/sans-souci
Exuding romance, this deluxe all-inclusive resort for couples stands over its own beach. It offers entertainment, cocktail parties, and plenty of activities.

OCHO RIOS: Couples Tower Isle $$$
Beach Resort
Tower Isle
Tel *800 268.7537*
w couples.com/tower-isle
A lovely contemporary style permeates this sophisticated couples-only resort with a choice of restaurants and a full range of activities.

OCHO RIOS: Jamaica Inn $$$
Historic
White River, Main Street
Tel *876 974 2514*
w jamaicainn.com
One of Jamaica's classiest hotels, this sedate plantation-style spot has a private beach and a croquet lawn. The accommodations exude luxury.

OCHO RIOS: The Jewels Dunn's River Beach Resort & Spa $$$
Beach Resort
Mammee Bay
Tel *876 972 7400*
w jewelresorts.com
This is a sprawling all-inclusive resort for couples. The guest rooms, in high-rise units, feature plantation decor. There is a nine-hole pitch-and-putt golf course.

OCHO RIOS: Sandals Grande Riviera Beach & Villa Golf Resort $$$
Beach Resort
Main Street
Tel *877 308 8204*
w sandals.com
A couples-only all-inclusive golf resort with classically themed public areas and Edwardian decor in the guest rooms. Choose from 15 restaurants.

OCHO RIOS: Sandals Royal Plantation $$$
Beach Resort
Main Street
Tel *888 726 3257*
w sandals.com
This intimate all-inclusive resort indulges guests with old-world elegance and 24-hour butler service. There is an excellent championship golf course, too.

ORACABESSA: Goldeneye $$$
Boutique
Main Street
Tel *876 622 9007*
w goldeneye.com
Popular with celebrities, this stylish and exclusive resort was built around the Jamaican home of author Ian Fleming *(see p148)*. Choose from individually styled villas and lagoon cottages, and enjoy activities such as yoga, watersports, and spa facilities.

DK Choice

PORT ANTONIO:
Drapers San $
B&B
Main Road, Drapers
Tel *876 993 7118*
W draperssan.com/en
Known for its hospitality, this
friendly and vibrant B&B is
owned by an Italian lady who
cooks up delicious dinners for
her guests. The colorful rooms
vary in size and facilities, and
some have shared bathrooms.

PORT ANTONIO: Mikuzi $
Boutique
Winnifred Beach, Fairy Hill
Tel *876 843 6859*
W mikuzijamaica.com/portland
Low-key rooms and cottages,
some with shared facilities.
Relax in the gardens fitted
with hammocks.

PORT ANTONIO: Goblin
Hill Villas $$
Modern
San San
Tel *876 993 7443*
W goblinhill.com
The contemporary one- and two-
bedroom villas here are staffed
by housekeepers who also cook.
Pool and tennis courts.

PORT ANTONIO: Geejam $$$
Boutique
San San
Tel *876 993 7000*
W geejamhotel.com
This luxury hotel with a state-of-
the-art recording studio draws
many international musicians.
Villas and deluxe cabins are set
in tropical beachside gardens.

PORT ANTONIO:
Mockingbird Hill $$$
Boutique
Main Road, Drapers
Tel *876 993 7134*
W hotelmockingbirdhill.com
A beautiful, eco-oriented hotel
with attentive live-in owners.
Rooms are elegantly furnished.

Chic cabin overlooking the sea at Geejam, Port Antonio

PORT ANTONIO:
Tryall Club $$$
Luxury
Tryall
Tel *876 956 5660*
W tryallclub.com
The epitome of luxury, this
hilltop resort offers sublime
comforts and a lovely view.
Fully staffed villas and a
championship golf course.

ROSE HALL: Hilton Rose Hall
Resort & Spa $$$
Luxury
Main Road
Tel *866 799 3661*
W rosehallresort.com
A white-and-chocolate color
scheme highlights the chic
modern decor at this upscale
all-inclusive resort featuring
Jamaica's largest water park.

ROSE HALL:
Hyatt Ziva Rose Hall $$$
Luxury
1 Ritz-Carlton Drive
Tel *(1) 571 529 6000 (US)*
W playaresorts.com
Sublime comfort pervades this
beach resort with lavish suites,
five restaurants, a championship
golf course, and all the world-
class amenities one can think of.

ROSE HALL: Iberostar
Grand Rose Hall $$$
Beach Resort
Main Road
Tel *876 680 0000*
W iberostargrandhotel.com
Huge five-star all-inclusive hotel
for adults only, with rooms in
three-story towers surrounding
a huge pool complex. Oversized
suites feature eclectic decor.

RUNAWAY BAY: Royal
Decameron Club Caribbean $$
Beach
Main Road
Tel *876 973 4805*
W decameron.com
A low-rise, all-inclusive place
with cottage-style rooms and
octagonal bungalows. Heaps
of activities and amenities.

RUNAWAY BAY:
Franklynn D Resort $$$
Beach Resort
Runaway Bay
Tel *876 973 4124*
W fdrholidays.com
Excellent family resort, with a wide
range of activities for youngsters
and teens. The "vacation nannies"
on duty help give the parents a
chance to relax. Spacious one-
two- and three-bedroom suites

RUNAWAY BAY: Itopia $$$
Boutique
Runaway Bay
Tel *876 965 3000*
W jakeshotel.com/stay/historic-
country-home.html
Secluded and featuring an
expansive garden, this hilltop
17th-century country house
marries old-world charm with
modern trappings. Alfresco
dining available.

TREASURE BEACH:
Mar Blue Villa Suites $$
Boutique
Old Wharf, Calabash Bay
Tel *876 965 3408*
W marblue.com
Stay in seafront villas and suites
with open design and attention
to detail. Oceanside swimming
pool and an award-winning
restaurant with a bar.

TREASURE BEACH:
Treasure Beach Hotel $$
Beach Resort
Frenchman's Bay
Tel *876 965 0110*
W jamaicatreasurebeachhotel.com
The only full-blown resort hotel
in the area, the Treasure Beach
has spacious gardens and two
swimming pools. It can feel a
bit deserted, but that just adds
to the charm.

TREASURE BEACH: Jake's $$$
Boutique
Calabash Bay
Tel *876 965 3000*
W jakeshotel.com
Jake's is a celebrity favorite, with
eclectic rooms and cottages, a
saltwater pool, great restaurants,
and a convivial bar.

WHITEHOUSE: Sandals
Whitehouse European
Village & Spa $$$
Beach Resort
Whitehouse
Tel *876 640 3000*
W sandals.com
Adjoining a wildlife reserve, this
adults-only all-inclusive resort
boasts Sandals' trademark
Edwardian styling. Facilities
include squash and scuba diving.

Where to Eat and Drink

FALMOUTH: Time 'n' Place $
Jamaican
93 Main Street
Tel *876 843 3625*
This charming, family-run hotel
has a simple open-air restaurant
and bar, which is a popular venue
for fashion shoots. Try delicious
Jamaican dishes, such as coconut
shrimp and grilled lobster.

KINGSTON: Ashanti Oasis $
Vegetarian
Pulse Complex, 38A Trafalgar Road
Tel *876 906 6465*
Delightful restaurant presided
over by a friendly owner.
The menu ranges from "stamp
and go" fritters to ratatouille
and curried ackee.

KINGSTON: Gloria's $
Seafood
Port Royal, 5 Queen Street
Tel *876 967 8066*
Tables spill onto the pavement
at this casual stop-off for fresh
seafood, such as curried shrimps
and lobster. Slow service at times,
but worth the wait.

DK Choice

**KINGSTON: Redbones
Blues Café** $$
Nouvelle Jamaican
1 Argyle Road
Tel *876 978 8262*   **Closed** *Sun*
Hip and enduringly popular
restaurant, with tables indoors
or in the garden courtyard,
where there is often live jazz or
blues. Starters might consist of
callaloo strudel with cream
cheese and chives, while main
courses range from grilled
smoked pork chops in a ginger
sauce to coconut curry shrimp.

**KINGSTON: Usain Bolt's
Tracks & Records** $$
Jamaican
67 Constant Spring Road
Tel *876 906 3903*
This huge and sophisticated
sports bar and restaurant with
a bar shaped like a running track
offers a Jamaican fusion menu.
Try the jerk-chicken quesadilla
or the curried seafood crock pot.

**KINGSTON: Norma's on
the Terrace** $$$
Nouvelle Jamaican
26 Hope Road
Tel *876 968 5488*   **Closed** *Sun*
Run by acclaimed chef Norma
Shirley, this is a classy restaurant
in Devon House. Signature
dishes include smoked pork
loin marinated in ginger.

KINGSTON: Strawberry Hill $$$
Nouvelle Jamaican
Irish Town Blue Mountains
Tel *876 944 8400*
Located in the eponymous
resort, with picturesque views
over Kingston, this classy yet
casual restaurant offers unusual
takes on jerk meats and curries.
Good Sunday brunch.

**MONTEGO BAY:
Far Out Fish Hut** $
Seafood
Greenwood
Tel *876 954 7155*
A hole-in-the-wall roadside grill
that charges by weight for fresh
catch of the day, served steamed,
grilled, or *escovitch* (marinated).

MONTEGO BAY: Mystic India $
Indian
Whittier Village, Ironshore
Tel *876 953 0659*   **Closed** *Mon*
This is the place for world-class
Indian fare, such as herb-grilled

Price Guide
Prices are based on a two-course meal
for one, including tax and service
charges and half a bottle of wine.

$	up to $15
$$	$15–40
$$$	over $40

---

shrimp with roasted garlic and
yogurt and ginger lemon dip.
Romantic ambience.

MONTEGO BAY: Pork Pit $
Jamaican
Gloucester Avenue
Tel *876 940 3008*
Long-standing local favorite for
jerk pork and chicken served with
baked yam or potatoes. Order to
go, or dine on one of the picnic
tables in the parking lot.

MONTEGO BAY: Marguerite's $$
International
Gloucester Avenue
Tel *876 952 4777*
Anchoring the Hip Strip, this lively
bar-restaurant is perfect for a
meal at sunset. The menu ranges
from seafood and steak to pastas
and nouvelle Jamaican fare.

MONTEGO BAY: The Native $$
Jamaican
29 Gloucester Ave
Tel *876 979 2769*   **Closed** *Sat & Sun*
The Native is a local favorite.
Jamaican dishes on offer includes
oxtail, ackee and saltfish, jerk
chicken, plus seafood and
vegetarian fare. Excellent service.

**MONTEGO BAY:
Houseboat Bar and Grill** $$$
Nouvelle Jamaican
Freeport Peninsula, Bogue Lagoon
Tel *876 979 8845*
On a refurbished houseboat, this
restaurant serves imaginative
food, such as mahi mahi with
caper and lime *beurre blanc*.
Divine desserts.

NEGRIL: Just Natural $
Jamaican/Italian
Hylton Avenue
Tel *876 957 0235*
Laid-back and colorful, this
roadside shack with a lovely
garden serves some of the best
Italian and vegetarian food in
Negril. Good breakfast choice.

NEGRIL: Three Dives $
Jamaican
West End Road
Tel *876 782 9990*
In a tree-filled clifftop garden
with a nightly bonfire, this
romantic restaurant specializes

Elegant alfresco dining at Stawberry Hill, Blue Mountains

Pool table and outdoor seating at the Bushbar, Port Antonio

in jerk dishes, but they also serve lobster. Check the blackboard outside for the daily specials.

NEGRIL: Kuyaba $$
Seafood
Norman Manley Boulevard
Tel *876 957 4318*
The dinner menu at this great spot in the eponymous hotel features jumbo shrimps, garlic lobster, and their signature dish: brown stew conch. Popular for breakfast, too.

NEGRIL: Rockhouse $$
Nouvelle Jamaican
West End Road
Tel *876 957 4373*
This beautifully styled restaurant is located in the Rockhouse hotel. Dishes include crab quesadillas with black bean and papaya salsa. International wine list, plus a substantial cocktail menu.

NEGRIL: The Lobster House at Sunrise Club $$$
Italian
Norman Manley Boulevard
Tel *876 957 4293*
Guests at the Sunrise Club enjoy alfresco torch-lit dining. The menu includes delicious wood-fired pizzas. End your meal with a great espresso.

OCHO RIOS: Scotchie's $
Jamaican
Main Road, Drax Hall
Tel *876 794 9457*
Get your fill of excellent traditional food – including jerk pork and chicken, sweet bread, and other local dishes – served on rough-hewn picnic tables under a tin roof.

OCHO RIOS: Coconuts on the Bay $$
International
Fisherman's Point Hotel, Turtle Beach Road
Tel *876 795 0064*
The imaginative menu of international favorites at this waterfront

restaurant includes club sandwiches and oxtail soup, as well as a scrumptious surf 'n' turf.

OCHO RIOS: Evita's $$$
Italian/Jamaican
Eden Bower Road
Tel *876 974 2333*
On the mountainside above Ocho Rios, Evita's is a local favorite for its views and delicious Italian-Jamaican fusion dishes. Arrive early and grab one of the balcony tables. Cocktails and live music.

OCHO RIOS: Le Papillon $$$
Nouvelle Jamaican
Royal Plantation, Main Street
Tel *876 974 5601* **Closed** *Mon*
The place to go for over-the-top classical elegance, formal service, and the Caribbean's only caviar-and-champagne bar. The menu fuses Caribbean ingredients and European sauces.

OCHO RIOS: The Ruins at the Falls $$$
International
17 Da Costa Drive
Tel *876 974 8888*
Enjoy alfresco dining beside a floodlit waterfall, with a menu ranging from Chinese and Jamaican dishes to surf 'n' turf. The venue alone is worth a visit.

Beautifully presented king prawn skewers at Mille Fleurs, Port Antonio

OCHO RIOS: Toscanini $$$
Italian
Main Road, Harmony Hall, Tower Isle
Tel *876 975 4785* **Closed** *Mon*
Under the verandas of a great house, Toscanini serves quality Italian food, including handmade pasta. There is a good wine list and excellent service.

PORT ANTONIO: Woody's $
Vegetarian
Draper's, Frenchman's Cove
Tel *876 436 5624*
A charming and rustic roadside grill known for its vegetarian dishes, including a scrumptious burger made with sweet plantains and peppers. Friendly service.

PORT ANTONIO: Dickie's Best-Kept Secret $$
Jamaican
Main Road, Bryan's Bay
Tel *876 809 6276*
Located in a private cliffside shack, this is an unusual venue: three-course dinners are served by advance order and may include steamed fish or garlic lobster.

PORT ANTONIO: Bushbar $$$
Nouvelle Jamaican
San San
Tel *876 561 8600*
Super-chic alfresco bar-restaurant in the Geejam Hotel. Come here for Jamaican and Asian-influenced dishes, from banana pancakes to spicy lobster pasta.

PORT ANTONIO: Mille Fleurs $$$
Nouvelle Jamaican
Mockingbird Hill, Drapers
Tel *876 993 7267*
This wonderful restaurant serves consistently delicious food. The daily menu includes specials such as jerk-spiced snapper with wafer-thin potatoes.

TREASURE BEACH: Jack Sprat Pizza and Seafood Restaurant $
International
Calabash Bay
Tel *876 965 3583*
Huge pizzas are the specialty at this quaint beachside restaurant within the boutique Jake's hotel. Also on the menu are seafood, soups, and delicious ice cream.

TREASURE BEACH: Jake's Country Cuisine $$$
Jamaican/Seafood
Calabash Bay
Tel *876 965 3000*
Laid-back gourmet restaurant with fairy-lit shade trees. The menu offers seafood, as well as nouvelle Jamaican dishes such as curried goat.

Practical Information

With its excellent tourist infrastructure, Jamaica is an easy destination to visit. The resorts are bursting with places to eat, drink, and sleep, as well as shops and currency changers, and even out-of-the-way towns and villages have a few hotels. The public transportation system is somewhat ad-hoc, being privately run outside of Kingston, but buses and minibuses are very cheap, taxis are plentiful, and car rental companies abound.

Holidaymakers climbing Dunn's River Falls near Ocho Rios

When to Go

Jamaica is at its best from mid-December to mid-April, when there is less rainfall and the heat is tempered by cooling trade winds. June through November is hurricane season, with the threat reaching its peak in September. The summer months can get uncomfortably hot.

Getting There

Jamaica is well served by direct charter and scheduled flights from Europe, the US and Canada, which land at Donald Sangster International Airport in Montego Bay, or Norman Manley International Airport in Kingston. **Air Jamaica** flies from six US cities to Kingston and Montego Bay, and **American Airlines**, **Delta**, **JetBlue**, **Spirit Airlines**, **United Airlines**, and **US Airways** also offer direct services from various US hubs. There are direct flights from Toronto with Air Jamaica and **Air Canada**. From the UK, **British Airways** and Air Jamaica fly to both Montego Bay and Kingston, as do several charter operators.

Documentation

Citizens of the European Union, US, Canada, Australia, New Zealand, Japan, and Israel have no visa requirements for a stay of less than three or six months depending on the country of origin. All visitors need a valid passport and an onward ticket. Citizens of other countries require a visa, which can often be obtained on arrival in Jamaica with production of a valid onward ticket.

Visitor Information

Jamaica Tourist Board has offices in Montego Bay, Ocho Rios, and Kingston, as well as booths at cruise ship ports and at the airports. Their website also provides detailed information.

Health and Security

Jamaica is generally safe health-wise. Water is filtered and chlorinated at most places. Visitors may bring their own prescription medicines. No vaccinations are required to enter the island unless visitors have been to an infected area.

The island is not altogether crime-free and there are incidents of drug-related violence especially in Kingston. It is best to avoid the town during any tension. Keep to the main streets and avoid lonely areas. Do not walk alone late at night in the cities or along beaches. Women travelers can expect to receive very graphic and forward comments. These tend to be directed at all women in Jamaica though such attention is generally harmless. It is best to brush off comments with humor.

Visitors are advised to avoid carrying and using drugs even if easily available. The penalties for possession are severe.

Banking and Currency

The local currency is the Jamaican dollar (J$), with notes available in the denomination of J$1,000, J$500, J$100, and J$50. Bureaux de change are widespread in the resorts, generally offering better rates than the banks. There are ATMs at all banks and also scattered around the big resorts; in the latter, some dispense US dollars rather than local currency.

Communications

Card phones proliferate throughout the island, but the popularity of cell phones has made most of them obsolete. Supermarkets and small stores sell calling cards and cheap-rate international calling cards that can be used from any landline connections. Tri-band mobiles function in Jamaica. Local pay-as-you-go SIM cards are available all over Jamaica.

Transport

In terms of public transport, with the exception of Kingston, where city buses are government-run and quite efficient, all buses (usually minibuses) are owned and run by private individuals. Routes are painted on the front or the

A police patrol car in Jamaica

side of the bus. Knutsford Express offers a regular shuttle bus service from Kingston to Montego Bay and Ocho Rios.

Route taxis running set routes are great for short trips. Taxis are freely available in all the resorts; the national association of drivers is **JUTA**.

Renting a car is the easiest way to get around, and there are rental outlets in all the resorts. **AVIS** and **Island Car Rental** are the major players.

Jamaica's tour companies range from one-man shows to huge outfits with fleets of buses that ferry visitors between the island's most popular attractions. There are plenty of outfits in the middle of these two extremes. Some of the renowned ones are **Barrett Adventures**, **Caribic Vacations**, **Sun Venture**, and **Treasure Tours**.

Shopping

Most tourist centers in Jamaica have craft markets selling souvenirs ranging from wood carvings to jewelry, straw goods and sculptures. Haggling in these markets is common unlike in stores. Jamaicans start all exchanges with a polite greeting, so it is best to greet people before asking for goods in shops. There are specialist shops that sell indigenous art, rum, cigars, and Jamaican flags. Rasta fans can also buy t-shirts, bandanas, reggae music, and red-gold-green tassels for cars in most markets. It is well worth picking up the jerk sauce and gauva jelly that are available in any supermarket. Blue Mountain coffee, sold all over the island, also makes a good souvenir.

On the north coast, there may be products made from coral and tortoiseshell. These are illegal as they are made from the endangered hawksbill turtle.

Most shops are open between Monday and Friday from around 8am to 5:30pm, and on Saturday from 8am to 5pm. Supermarkets stay open very late, even on Sunday.

Language

Jamaica's official language is English, but everyone also speaks the patois version, heavily accented and sprinkled with local slang.

Electricity

The electric current is 110 volt but some hotels may have 220 volt, 60 cycles. Plug sockets usually take two flat prongs.

Time

Jamaica runs on Eastern Standard Time, and is 5 hours behind GMT. It does not observe daylight savings.

Getting Married

To get married in Jamaica, the couple must have been on the island for at least 24 hours (not including weekends) before they can apply for a marriage license. They will need their passports, birth certificates with their father's name, Decree Absolute or death certificate if divorced or widowed, and proof of any name change. There are many companies, such as **Exclusive Tropical Weddings**, who can take care of all the formalities.

A wedding ceremony on the beach, Negril, Jamaica

A PORTRAIT OF THE DOMINICAN REPUBLIC

Spectacular beaches, lush valleys, rich flora and fauna, and the region's highest mountain are what make this a nation with extraordinary natural beauty. Historically, its capital city boasts the oldest cathedral and fortress in the New World, among other colonial treasures lining cobbled streets laid out five centuries ago

Much of the country is mountainous, particularly in the west where the Cordillera Central dominates the landscape. Rising to 10,164 ft (3,098 m), the mist-shrouded Pico Duarte is its highest peak. Carpeted with thick forests, the slopes of the Cordillera, and to the south, those of the Sierra de Neiba and Sierra de Baoruco, are the habitat of many of the republic's endemic birds. Between the two sierras, Lago Enriquillo shimmers at 131 ft (39 m) below sea level – the Caribbean's lowest point. This saline lake, lying in a broad, semiarid vale in the cactus-studded southwest, attracts more than 60 species of birds, including flamingos that gather here in large numbers at dawn and dusk. Other wildlife found here includes the American crocodile and the endangered rock iguana. In all, there are 16 national parks and other protected areas that conserve the country's rich flora and fauna.

Small stalls selling local art and craft on the beach in Bayahibe

History

The country's colorful history dates back to pre-Columbian days, when Taíno Indians adorned caverns with the area's largest galleries of rupestrian art, many of which can still be seen today. Richer still is the colonial legacy predating any in the Western Hemisphere. In 1492, Christopher Columbus landed on the island of Hispaniola (which the republic shares with Haiti today) and the Americas' first permanent

Detail of Columbus's statue, Santo Domingo

settlement was established at La Isabela a year later, marking the start of Spanish rule. In 1498, Santo Domingo, the capital, was founded. The golden age of the Spanish colony ended when the English privateer Francis Drake vandalized Santo Domingo in 1586.

The French invaded the island in the 17th century and the Treaty of Ryswyck (1697) divided Hispaniola between French Saint-Domingue to the west and Spanish Santo Domingo to the east. The French colony prospered until the late 18th century, when civil war broke out, culminating in a revolt by former slaves who drove the French out, declaring Haitian independence in 1804.

Clear blue waters and white sand at Cayo Levantado, Samaná

Continued hostilities between Santo Domingo and Haiti led to war and a 23-year occupation by the latter from 1821 to 1844, when a separate, independent Dominican Republic was created after an uprising led by Juan Pablo Duarte. Continuing unrest in the area led to a US occupation which lasted from 1916 to 1924. By 1930 Rafael Trujillo had emerged as the most brutal dictator who unleashed 30 years of authoritarian rule. He was assassinated in 1961.

The Republic Today

The Dominican Republic is a modern nation with high-rise hotels and casinos glittering on Santo Domingo's shorefront. Most other cities have a definite cosmopolitan, 21st-century buzz as well.

The republic now has a stable democratic government. Its economy is dependent on tourism and many all-inclusive luxury resorts have sprung up along Punta Cana and the Atlantic shore. The southwest coast is a favorite for eco-tourism. Inland, the Cibao region is quilted with estates producing fine coffee, sugar, and tobacco, the basis for a flourishing cigar industry.

Despite the evolved middle-class, there is no escaping the poverty – many rural families live in shacks and urban wages are often at subsistence level.

People and Culture

The culture is a mix of Taíno, African, and Spanish, which is reflected in the ethnically diverse population. Spanish is the official language. Fun-loving Dominicans swing to the fast-paced merengue and the nation's own bachata. Although a Catholic nation, many people worship spirits – a legacy of the Taíno and African heritage.

Rural landscape with green fields and thatched houses, typical of the Dominican Republic

Exploring the Dominican Republic

The scenic Dominican Republic occupies the eastern two-thirds of Hispaniola, which it shares with Haiti. Rugged mountains rise to 10,164 ft (3,097 m) atop Pico Duarte, in the western part, forming a rain shadow over much of the semiarid southwest. The land tapers east to Punta Cana, the country's major beach resort, while inland the fertile plain called the Cibao is the island's breadbasket. Almost a quarter of its 10.3 million inhabitants live in Santo Domingo, a modern metropolis with the oldest colonial city in the Americas at its core.

Locator Map

Punta Rucia
This beach is known for its cottony sands and turquoise waters. It is popular among day-trippers from Puerto Plata.

Pico Duarte
The Caribbean's highest peak is easily hiked – a three-day trek from the mountain hamlet of La Ciénaga.

Parque Nacional Sierra de Bahoruco
Around 150 species of birds live in this remote national park.

Maternity statue at the Galería de Arte Candido Bidó

For hotels and restaurants on this island see pp186–9 and pp190–91

Sights at a Glance

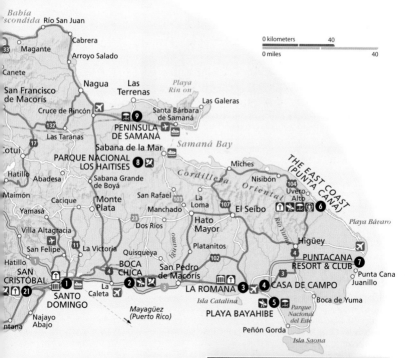

Getting Around

Santo Domingo's Zona Colonial is easily negotiated on foot, while taxis are ideally used for getting around the greater metropolis. The rest of the country is easiest explored on organized excursions, since self-drive can be a daunting experience despite the efficient road network. A 20-minute ferry ride links Samaná to Sabana de la Mar, while there are air services between Puerto Plata and Punta Cana to Santo Domingo.

The palm-lined Costa del Coco Beach on the eastern shore of the Dominican Republic

For additional map symbols *see back flap*

❶ Santo Domingo

Santo Domingo's main sites concentrate in the Zona Colonial, the historic heart of the city. This once-walled enclave of cobbled streets and leafy plazas boasts some of the oldest colonial buildings in the Western Hemisphere. Calle Las Damas echoes to the bootsteps of the first Spanish *conquistadores*, who set sail from Santo Domingo to conquer Latin America. Many colonial structures today house hotels, restaurants, and nightclubs, while the district also bustles with neighborhood life. Beyond the colonial core, the modern metropolis of three million people radiates inland in a quiltwork of districts.

Exterior of the fashionable Hotel Sofitel Nicholás de Ovando

🏛 Plaza España

N end of Calle Las Damas 🚻
Museo de las Casas Reales: Calle Damas cnr Calle Mercedes. **Tel** 809 682 4202. **Open** 9am–5pm Tue–Sun. 🅿 📷 🚻 Museo Alcázar de Colón: Plaza de España **Tel** 809 682 4750. **Open** 9am–5pm Tue–Sat, 9am–4pm Sun. 📷 Museo Mundo de Ambar: Calle Arzobispo Meriño 452. **Tel** 809 682 3309. **Open** 9am–6pm Mon–Sat, 9am–2pm Sun. 📷 📷
w amberworldmuseum.com

This broad, virtually treeless plaza is the setting for two preeminent museums. The **Museo de las Casas Reales**, in the Renaissance-style former chamber of the Royal Court, showcases colonial artifacts from antique weaponry and suits of armor to exhibits on Columbus's voyages. A massive Reloj del Sol (sundial) stands outside the entrance, which dates back to 1753.

The former home of Christopher Columbus's son Diego, a Mudejar-style two-story building dating from 1517, has been magnificently restored to house **Museo Alcázar de Colón**.

It re-creates the Columbus household with many original pieces such as carpets, silverware, and mahogany furniture, that once belonged to the family.

At night, the plaza comes alive as its numerous bars and restaurants fill up.

Located two blocks west, the impressive ruins of the Monasterio de San Francisco, dating from 1508, form a backdrop for occasional concerts. Nearby, the **Museo Mundo de Ambar** displays splendid examples of the semi-precious gem, amber.

🏨 Hostal Nicolás de Ovando

Calle Las Damas
Tel 809 685 9955. 📷 🚻
w accorhotels.com

The class act in the Zona Colonial, this hotel occupies the former home of Nicolás de Ovando, who founded the city in 1502. The stylish conversion combines contemporary sophistication with comfortable furnishings while retaining original, well-worn stone floors and walls. A superb restaurant, plus cigar lounge, swimming pool, gymnasium, and meeting rooms are other bonuses at this atmospheric hotel, a UNESCO World Heritage Site.

🏛 Calle Las Damas

Between Fortaleza Ozama and Plaza España 🚻 Panteón de la Patria: Calle Las Damas & Plazoleta de María Toledo: **Tel** 809 689 6010. **Open** 9am–5pm Tue–Sun. Museo Infantil Trampolín: Calle Las Damas: **Tel** 809 685 5551. **Open** 9am–5pm Tue–Fri, 9am–7pm Sat & Sun. 📷 📷 🚻
w trampolin.org.do

The first cobbled colonial street laid out in the New World is named for Doña María de Toledo (wife of Diego Columbus) and other ladies of the nobility. It is lined with beautifully restored historic buildings, including the **Panteón de la Patria**, completed in 1743 as a NeoClassical Jesuit church. Having been used as both a tobacco warehouse and a theatre, today it is a somber mausoleum for national heroes, guarded by a uniformed soldier. It has a stone dome and an extravagant chandelier.

Children enjoy the **Museo Infantil Trampolín**, a fun-filled educational forum covering earth sciences to social affairs.

🏛 Fortaleza Ozama

Calle Las Damas: **Tel** 809 686 0222. **Open** 9:30am–6pm Mon–Sat, 9am–3pm Sun. 📷 🚻

Overlooking the mouth of the Río Ozama, this fortress begun in 1502 is the oldest colonial military edifice in the Americas. At its heart,

Coral rock exterior of Fortaleza Ozama

For hotels and restaurants on this island see pp186–9 and pp190–91

Statue of Christopher Columbus overlooking Parque Colón

VISITORS' CHECKLIST

Practical Information
S coast of Dominican Republic.
🗺 3 million. 🛈 Plaza Colón,
Calle Isabel la Católica 103, 809
686 3858. 🏪 Mercado Modelo,
Mon–Sat. 🎭 Carnival (Feb).

Transport
✈ 🚆 🚢 🚌

the Torre del Homenaje (Tower of Homage) stands tall over a surrounding green swathe. Originally a watchtower, Fortaleza Ozama later served as a prison. Rusting cannons stand atop the riverfront wall and armaments are displayed in the esplanade, pinned by a statue of Spanish military commander, Gonzalo Fernández de Oviedo, who died in 1557.

🏛 Parque Colón
Calle El Conde & Calle Arzobispo
Meriño 🚻 Larimar Museum: Calle
Isabel la Católica 54. **Tel** 809 682 3309.
Open 9am–6pm daily. 🅿
🌐 **larimarmuseum.com**

Named after Christopher Columbus, whose larger-than-life statue dominates the square, this wide, tree-shaded plaza is a center for social life. The park is surrounded by colonial and 19th-century buildings. Looming over the southern half of Parque Colón is the grandiose Catedral Primada de América.

One block south, the **Museo de Larimar** has educational exhibits on larimar, a semi-precious blue stone, which is mined solely in the Dominican Republic. On the plaza's north-west corner, Antiguo Palacio Consistorial, built in Neo-Classical style, is the former town hall.

Nearby, Plazoleta Padre Billini is named after a 19th-century priest who founded a hospital for the poor. It is the setting for the Museo de la Familia Dominicana del Siglo XIX, which is furnished to replicate a typical middle-class 19th-century home. Visitors can also stop by at many souvenir and cigar shops, located north of the park.

🏛 Catedral Primada de América
See p171.

🏛 Parque Duarte
Calle Padre Billini & Calle Hostos.
The most intimate of Santo Domingo's colonial plazas, this small square shaded by *flamboyán* trees is a gathering spot for locals to gossip beneath the statue of the island's independence hero, Juan Pablo Duarte. On the eastern side, Iglesia y Convento de los Padres Dominicos is famous for its stone zodiac wheel in the chapel.

To the northwest of Parque Duarte, the **Museo Memorial de la Resistencia Dominicana** both honours the resistance to Tujillo's tyranny and raises awareness of human rights.

Santo Domingo

① Plaza España
② Hostal Nicolás de Ovando
③ Calle Las Damas
④ Fortaleza Ozama
⑤ Parque Colón
⑥ Catedral Primada de América
⑦ Parque Duarte
⑧ Parque Independencia

0 meters 500
0 yards 500

For keys to symbols *see back flap*

Altar de la Patria, dedicated to the island's heroes

🏛 Parque Independencia

Calle Palo Hincado & Av. Bolívar:
This bustling plaza is located
at the western end of the Zona
Colonial. The plaza has beautiful
landscaped lawns, dotted with
fountains, and is a popular
meeting place. One of its
entrances is via the 17th-century
Puerta del Conde gate where the
Dominican flag was first raised
in 1844. The Republic's three
principal heroes – Juan Pablo
Duarte, Francisco del Rosario
Sánchez, and Ramón Marias
Mella – rest within the **Altar de
la Patria**, a marble mausoleum
where an eternal flame burns
in their honor. The tomb is
guarded by a soldier in uniform.

🏛 Palacio Nacional

Calle Dr. Delgado Báez:
Tel 809 695 8000. **Open** by
appointment Mon, Wed, & Fri.
Galería de Arte Candido Bidó
Calle Dr. Báez 5. **Tel** 809 685 5310.
Open 9am–6pm Mon–Fri.
W galeriacandidobido.com
Museo Bellapart: Edificio Honda, Av.
John F. Kennedy. **Tel** 809 541 7721
(ext 296). **Open** 9am–6pm
Mon–Fri, 9am–noon Sat.
W museobellapart.com

The Palacio Nacional was
completed in 1947 as an
ostentatious palace for dictator-
president Rafael Trujillo. This
Neo-Classical structure, made
of pink roseate Samaná marble,
was designed with a domed
roof and grandiose imperial
staircases by renowned Italian
architect Guido D'Alessandro.
Prior permission is required
to view the exquisite interior
full of glistening mahogany

furniture, crystal
chandeliers, and gilt
mirrors. The Salón
de las Cariátides,
featuring walls lined
with 44 elegant
caryatids (draped
female figures), is
a highlight. The
Salón now houses
government depart-
ments. A formal
dress code (shirt
or blouse with full
sleeves) is enforced
for visitors. Shorts,
sandals, and tennis
shoes are not allowed.

A short stroll southwest of the
Palacio Nacional brings visitors
to **Galería de Arte Candido
Bidó**. This 1950s mansion is the
former studio-home of the
republic's most famous artist,
Candido Bido, who died in 2011.
His colorful artworks are on
display. Perhaps the city's most
impressive art gallery, the
Museo Bellapart exhibits a
magnificent private collection
of art by leading Dominican
artists from the mid-19th
century onwards, and includes
some stunning sculptures.

🏛 Faro a Colón

Av. Estados Unidos, Parque Mirador
del Este. **Tel** 809 591 1492.
Open 9am–5:30pm Tue–Sun.
Acuario Nacional: Av. España 75.
Tel 809 766 1709. **Open** 9:30am–
5:30pm Tue–Sun.

This massive monument in
honor of Christopher Columbus

was initiated in 1929 and
only completed in 1992, when
it was dedicated for the
quincentennial celebration
of the explorer's arrival. The
"Columbus Lighthouse" was
designed in the shape of a cross
by neophyte British architect
Joseph Lea Gleave. Soaring ten
stories high over Parque Mirador
del Este, the 680-ft (207-m) long
concrete structure is stepped
in tiered layers. Hollow within,
it houses a Gothic marble sepulcher by Spanish sculptor Pere
Carbonell i Huguet.

This contains a bronze urn,
filled, supposedly, with
Columbus's ashes, which were
transferred from the Catedral
Primada de América. A uniformed
soldier and four bronze lions
guard the explorer's remains.
On special occasions, high-power
beams are turned on to cast a
cross-shaped light in the sky.

Stretching out near the Río
Ozama, woody and pretty
Parque Mirador del Este is the
city's chief recreational area,
with various sports arenas and
centers. At its far eastern end,
Cueva Los Tres Ojos (Three Eyes
Cave) is named for three water-
filled limestone sinkholes, a
popular visiting spot for families
on weekends.

The **Acuario Nacional** or
National Aquarium overlooks
the Atlantic Ocean and has
displays of marine life such as
sharks, rays, and eels. Opposite
the aquarium, the Agua Splash,
a water-based theme park, has
pools and slides.

Neo-Classical-style façade of the stately Palacio Nacional

For hotels and restaurants on this island see pp186–9 and pp190–91

Catedral Primada de América

Diego Columbus laid the foundation stone of this cathedral in 1514. The New World's oldest cathedral was designed by architect Alonso de Rodríguez, who was inspired by the cathedral in Seville, Spain. It was revised by Luis de Moya and Rodrigo de Liendo and completed in 1541, but was added to through the 18th century. In 1920, Pope Benedict XV elevated it to the status of Basílica Menor de la Virgen de la Anunciación. Visitors should take care to avoid wearing shorts or short skirts to the cathedral.

VISITORS' CHECKLIST

Practical Information
Parque Colón, Calle Arzobispo Nouel & Arzobispo Meriño.
Open 9am–4pm daily.

Bell Tower
The cathedral combines classical, Baroque, and Gothic styles. The red-brick bell tower was added in 1625, after the original architect sailed for Mexico with the designs.

Rib-Vaulted Ceiling
Supported by 14 columns, the ceiling soars above a floor of black-and-white-checkered marble.

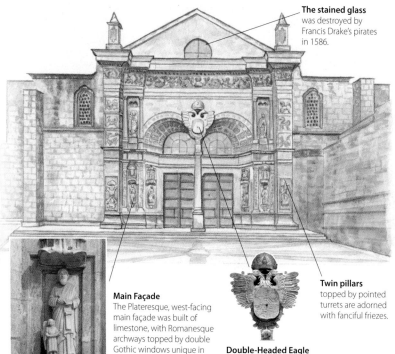

The stained glass
was destroyed by Francis Drake's pirates in 1586.

Main Façade
The Plateresque, west-facing main façade was built of limestone, with Romanesque archways topped by double Gothic windows unique in the Americas, and flanked by Renaissance pillars.

Double-Headed Eagle
The eagle bears the Spanish imperial coat of arms.

Twin pillars
topped by pointed turrets are adorned with fanciful friezes.

A busy street with bars and restaurants in Boca Chica

❷ Boca Chica

🚂 20 miles (32 km) E of Santo Domingo. 🏄 🚶 🏖 🎣 ⛵ 🚶

A darling of Santo Domingo's masses, despite a problem with prostitution, this compact beach area, a 30-minute drive from the capital, gets packed on weekends and holidays, when people spill out of the bars on to the narrow streets. The palm-fringed sands dissolve into peacock-blue shallows, good for snorkeling as it is protected by a reef. Wade out to the Isla La Mastica and Isla Los Pinos, where mangroves harbor a wealth of birdlife.

Environs
Divers are delirious about **Parque Nacional Submarino La Caleta**, where 28 dive sites include the wrecks of the *Hickory*, *El Limón*, and *Captain Alsina*.

Mamajuana

Dominicans attribute all manner of cures and medicinal qualities to their favorite home-made drink, a concoction of rum, red wine and honey steeped for weeks on end with herbs, bark, and secret ingredients. A variation is made of rum with seafood but there is no single recipe for it. This drink is considered to be an aphrodisiac and is drunk as shots in neighborhood bars.

Bottle of Mamajuana

❶ Parque Nacional Submarino La Caleta

5 miles (8 km) W of Boca Chica.
🤿 Treasure Divers, 809 523 5320.
🌐 parquemarinolacaleta.org

❸ La Romana

80 miles (129 km) E of Santo Domingo. 🚗 250,000. ✈
ℹ Av. Libertad 7, 809 550 6922.

This coastal port town is the republic's principal center for sugar production. Although modern, it retains many colonial structures centered on Parque Central, studded with wrought-iron sculptures in the shade of Iglesia Santa Rosa de Lima. El Obelisco, at the juncture of Avenida Libertad at Calle Francisco del Castillo, shows the nation's history. The main draw is Altos de Chavón, a fantastical 1970s re-creation of a Tuscan hill town complete with a "Roman amphitheater" used as a music venue by its owners, the nearby Casa de Campo resort. Its **St. Stanislaus Church** is named after Poland's patron saint, whose ashes were brought here by Pope John Paul II during his visit in 1979. It also houses the Regional Museum of Archaeology, displaying pre-Columbian Taíno artifacts.

Environs
About 5 miles (8 km) to the southwest of La Romana is Isla Catalina, a small island with great beaches. On the main road to San Pedro de Macorís is an underground cave/museum

with natural dripstone formations and over 500 pictographs, **Cueva de las Maravillas**.

🎟 **Cueva de las Maravillas**
Tel 809 951 9009. **Open** 9am–5pm Tue–Sun.

❹ Casa de Campo

🏖 81 miles (130 km) E of Santo Domingo. **Tel** 809 523 3333. 🎾 🏇
♿ 🌐 casadecampo.com.do

This exclusive resort's rooms are luxuriously furnished in plantation style by fashion designer Oscar de la Renta, as are many of the villas, favored by such guests as the Bushes, Clintons, and Hollywood stars. .

❺ Playa Bayahibe

🚂 89 miles (142 km) SE of Santo Domingo. 🏄 🚶 🏖 🎣 ⛵ 🚶

Considered one of the best places to dive in the country, the Bayahibe area has endless white-sand beaches, notably Playa Dominicus and Playa Bayahibe. The original fishing village is diminishing with the spread of all-inclusive resorts. Local tour operators offer boat excursions to Isla Saona, with its own beaches plus a lake with flamingos.

Environs
A short distance from Bayahibe is **Parque Nacional del Este**, which protects a rare stand of dry forest atop a limestone plateau pock-marked with *cenotes* (sinkholes) and caverns.

St. Stanislaus Church, La Romana

A good access point is the fishing village of Boca de Yuma. Nearby, the fortified **Casa Ponce de León**, built in 1505, is furnished in early colonial fashion. The house is kept locked but a guard will open the doors for visitors.

⚅ Parque Nacional del Este
Guaragua, 3 miles S of Bayahibe.
Tel 809 833 0022. **Open** 8am–5pm daily. 🏛

⚏ Casa Ponce de León
Calle los Jobitos, San Rafael del Yuma.
Open 9am–3pm Tue–Sun. 🏛 🛆

❻ The East Coast (Punta Cana)

🚍 150 miles (241 km) E of Santo Domingo. 🏖 🏨 🛥 🎿 🛆 🏄

This coastal zone is the setting for the majority of all-inclusive resorts. The country's most beautiful beaches, from snow white to gold, unspool along a picture-perfect coconut palm-lined coast. Resort development concentrates around Punta Cana and Playa Bávaro, but other resorts such as Uvero Alto are evolving to the north, where the virginal Playa Lavacama and Playa Los Muertos are great places to

Palm-fringed Playa Bávaro lined with resorts, Costa del Coco

escape the crowds. Jeep safaris offer excellent diversions, as do marine theme parks such as the **Manatí Park**.

Environs
A short distance inland is the regional capital city, Higüey, renowned for its Modernist cathedral, **Basílica de Nuestra Señora de la Altagracia**, designed in 1950 by French architects André Dunoyer de Segonzac and Pierre Dupré.

🐬 Manatí Park
Tel 809 221 9444. **Open** 9am–6pm daily. 🏛 🚋 🌐 **manatipark.com**

⛪ Basílica de Nuestra Señora de la Altagracia
Open 5am–7pm daily. 🛆 Note: no shorts or bare shoulders permitted.

❼ Puntacana Resort & Club

✈ 2 miles (3 km) S of Punta Cana airport. **Tel** 809 959 2262.
🚋 🏄 🎿 🛆
🌐 **puntacana.com**

Launched in 1971 as the first property in Punta Cana, the original club has metamorphosed into a deluxe resort with an all-inclusive hotel and villas with superb facilities. Its seven restaurants include two top eateries (see p190). The resort's ecological park has guided trails and organizes bird-watching tours. The resort also offers horseback riding and has two golf courses.

❽ Parque Nacional los Haitises

47 miles (75 km) NE of Santo Domingo. **Open** 8am–5pm daily.
🏛 🚋 arranged by local tour operators.

This national park protects a region of rugged limestone terrain studded with *mogotes* (ancient limestone plateau, see p83) and riddled with caverns. The dense forests are home to at least 112 bird species, including seabirds nesting on Isla de los Pájaros and swallows that swarm Cueva de las Golondrinas. The easiest access is on guided boat trips arranged by **Paraíso Caño Hondo**, an activity center with accommodations.

🚋 Paraíso Caño Hondo
7 miles (11 km) W of Sabana de la Mar.
Tel 809 248 5995.
🌐 **paraisocanohondo.com**

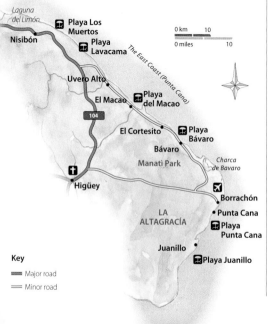

Laguna del Limón
Playa Los Muertos
Nisibón
Playa Lavacama
The East Coast (Punta Cana)
0 km   10
0 miles   10
Uvero Alto
El Macao
Playa del Macao
104
El Cortesito
Playa Bávaro
Bávaro
Charca de Bavaro
Manati Park
Higüey
LA ALTAGRACÍA
Borrachón
Punta Cana
Playa Punta Cana
Juanillo
Playa Juanillo

Key
▬▬▬ Major road
═══ Minor road

For keys to symbols *see back flap*

9 Península de Samaná

110 miles (177 km) NE of Santo Domingo. Calle Santa Barbara 4, 809 538 2332. Día de Santa Bárbara (Dec 4).

Jutting into the Atlantic Ocean, this slender peninsula is lined by white-sand beaches along its north and east shores. On the southern shore, rivers cascade down from a thickly forested mountain spine sloping down to the Bahía de Samaná, a favored wintering spot for humpback whales.

The regional capital, Santa Bárbara de Samaná, is a good base for exploring, including boat trips to **Cayo Levantado**. Just 7 miles (11 km) north of town is **El Salto de Limón** waterfall, which makes for a favorite day-trip on horseback. Nearby, at **Samana Zipline Tour** visitors can tackle a choice of ziplines and take a safari truck excursion.

The peninsula is known for its boutique hotels in the two small beach resorts: Las Terrenas on the north coast and Las Galeras in the east. While Las Terrenas is popular for its nightlife, Las Galeras is known for its gorgeous long beaches.

Samana Zipline Tour
El Valle Road. **Tel** 829 542 3005.
W **walktheplankzipline.com**

Bars and restaurants next to the beach in Cabarete

10 Cabarete

119 miles (190 km) NW of Santo Domingo. Calle Principal, 809 571 0962. Kiteboard World Cup (Jun).

With a vibrant nightlife, Cabarete is the Republic's party beach resort as well as its watersports capital. The wind-whipped beaches are among the very best in the Caribbean for kite-boarding and wind-surfing. Small hotels and colorful restaurant-bars edge up to the sands of this beach village. The watersport action centers on Kite Beach.

Environs

Just 3 miles (5 km) east of Cabarete is one entrance to the **Parque Nacional El Choco**, which has trails and a lagoon with waterfall. Another popular excursion from Cabarete is to **27 Charcos De Demajagua Natural Monument**, 2 miles (3 km) to the south. Visitors can hike along a riverbed to a series of 27 cascades and natural waterslides.

Parque Nacional El Choco
Callejón de la Loma, Cabarete.
Tel 809 472 4204. **Open** 9am–4:30pm daily.

27 Charcos De Demajagua Natural Monument
Imbert. **Open** 8am–3pm daily.
W **27charcos.com**

El Salto de Limón plunging over 131 ft (40 m) down, Península de Samaná

11 Sosúa

110 miles (175 km) NW of Santo Domingo. Calle Duarte 1, 809 571 3433. 45,000.

This clifftop beach town is laid out on either side of the long Playa Sosúa. The beach has watersports and is backed by a sandy path lined with bars, restaurants, and souvenir stores. Sosúa is divided into two areas – Los Charamicos to the west and El Batey to the east, where German and Austrian Jewish refugees settled during the 1940s. Fine wooden architecture, including the synagogue and adjoining **Museo Judío Sosúa**, can be seen here. A coral reef nearby offers fabulous scuba diving, and local dive operators offer trips that include the wreck of the *Zingara*, scuttled in 1993.

Museo Judío Sosúa
Calle Dr. Alejo Martínez. **Tel** 809 571 1386. **Open** 9am–1pm & 2–4pm Mon–Fri.

For hotels and restaurants on this island see pp186–9 and pp190–91

⑫ Puerto Plata

145 miles (233 km) NW of Santo Domingo. 147,000. Calle José del Carmen Arizo 45, 809 586 5059. Fiesta Patronal de San Felipe (May 3), Merengue Festival (Oct), International Film Festival (Nov).

Founded in 1502, this lively port town is replete with historic buildings, notably in the Zona Victoriana with its cluster of 19th-century wooden gingerbread houses inspired by the Victorian style then fashionable in Britain. At its heart lies Parque Independencia, which has the steepled Catedral San Felipe Apostól on the south side and, two blocks east, the popular **Museo del Ambar** with its amber-related exhibits in a 1919 wooden galleried mansion. Also worth visiting is the four-square **Fortaleza San Felipe**, the oldest colonial fortress of the New World, completed in 1557. The Malecón Boulevard lines Playa Long Beach, stretching for almost 2 miles (3 km) along the city shoreline.

Beyond the historic core, the modern city is an ungainly sprawl. Fine beaches extend along the coast east and west of Puerto Plata. More than a dozen all-inclusive and boutique hotels congregate on Playa Dorada, named for its palm-shaded golden sands. It has a world-class golf course and plentiful watersports. Locals gather at Playa Cofresí, a laid-back beach with few watersports but some restaurants. The 2,565-ft (781-m) **Monte Isabel De Torre**, soaring

One of Puerto Plata's many traditional houses

Insect inside amber, Museo del Ambar

Amber

Considered a semi-precious gem, amber is actually a fossilized resin of an extinct tree species, *Hymenaea protera*, and dates back as much as 40 million years. The translucent gem comes in colors ranging from gold to purple and blue, found solely in the Cordillera Septentrional, south of Puerto Plata. The Dominican Republic is renowned for amber fossils, known as "inclusions", containing insects that were trapped in the oozing sap. An export license is required to leave the Republic with rough amber with an "inclusion."

Monument at San Felipe, Puerto Plata

over Puerto Plata, lures visitors to its cool summit, where there are forest trails. A cable car accessed from Avenida Teleférico, west of town, to the summit provides stupendous views of the city.

🏛 **Museo del Ambar**
Calle Duarte 61. **Tel** 809 586 2848. **Open** 9am–6pm Mon–Sat.
W ambermuseum.com

🏰 **Fortaleza San Felipe**
Av. Gregorio Luperón. **Open** 9am–5pm daily.

⛰ **Monte Isabel De Torre**
Av. Manuel Tavárez Justo. **Tel** 809 970 0501. **Open** 8am–5pm Thu–Tue.

⑬ Ocean World Adventure Park

3 miles (5 km) W of Puerto Plata. **Tel** 809 291 1000. **Open** 9am–6pm daily. W oceanworld.net

Located in the small tourist enclave of Cofresí, this interactive marine theme park is an exciting all-day experience

for adults and children. One highlight is the option to swim with dolphins up close and personal, in addition to viewing dolphin and sea lion shows. The place also has a snorkeling reef aquarium teeming with exotic fish, sharks and stingrays, as well as tropical birds that swoop around an aviary.

⑭ Punta Rucia

20 miles (32 km) W of Puerto Plata.

Graced by cottony sands shelving gently into turquoise waters, this remote beach is a favorite of day-trippers who arrive on boat excursions from Puerto Plata. Banana boat rides and other watersports add excitement. Most excursions include a visit to Cayo Paraíso, an idyllic horseshoe-shaped cay with talcum-fine sand and crystal waters colored by a kaleidoscopic palette of fish.

Environs
A dirt track leads east from Playa Rucia to Refugio de Manatís Estero Hondo, a huge mangrove-fringed lagoon protecting manatees. Farther east is **Parque Nacional La Isabela**, which preserves the scant ruins of the first permanent settlement in the New World, established by Christopher Columbus in 1492.

⛰ **Parque Nacional La Isabela**
El Castillo. **Open** 9am–5:30pm daily.

⑮ La Vega

70 miles (113 km) NW of Santo
Domingo. 🚈 220,000.
ℹ️ Calle Mella cnr Durangé, 809 242
3231. 🎭 Carnival (Feb).
🌐 godominicanrepublic.com

Founded in 1562, La Vega is a
sprawling, chaotic city on the
banks of Río Camú in the heart
of El Cibao Valley. It is renowned
for its lively Carnival and for its
Catedral de la Concepción de
la Vega, a controversial post-
Modernist, industrial-style
design that visitors either love
or hate. The dramatic exterior,
with Gothic elements, offers a
garish counterpoint to the
sparse interior with a simple
altar. The city's other sights of
interest surround the main
square and include the Neo-
Classical Palacio Municipal
and Palacio de Justicia.

Northeast of La Vega, atop
a steep hill, lies the Santo Cerro
(Holy Hill), where an annual
pilgrimage is made every
September 24 to Iglesia Las
Mercedes. The simple church is
considered to be the site of a
miracle during the colonial days.
Nearby is the original settlement of La Concepción de la
Vega, founded in 1494 as a base
for gold-mining but destroyed
by an earthquake in 1562. The
ruins are preserved within
**Parque Nacional Arqueológico
Histórico La Vega Vieja**.

🏛 **Parque Nacional Arqueológico Histórico La Vega Vieja**
Carretera Moca, Santo Cerro. **Open**
8am–3pm Mon–Fri, 9am–4pm Sat. 🎟

⑯ Santiago de los Caballeros

88 miles (138 km) NW of Santo
Domingo. ✈️ 🚈 650,000.
ℹ️ Gobernación, Parque Duarte &
Calle del Sol; 809 582 5885.
🎭 Carnival (Feb).

Built on the banks of the
Río Yaque in the center of
El Cibao Valley, Santiago de
los Caballeros, the Republic's
second largest city, thrums with
energy and traffic. The hub of
agriculture and commerce
outside Santo Domingo, this

The colonial Catedral Santiago Apóstol,
Santiago de los Caballeros

wealthy city also boasts fine
attractions, including an easily
walked colonial core and many
monuments that recall its past
status as a tobacco boom town.
Cigar manufacture remains its
most important industry; deft
hands can be seen rolling fine
cigars at Fábrica de Cigarros La
Aurora, part of **Centro León**, a
cultural institute with a contemporary art gallery and an
anthropology museum.

Any tour should begin at
Parque Duarte, surrounded
by an eclectic assemblage of
colonial structures, including
Catedral Santiago Apóstol.
Nearby, Fortaleza San Luís has
been restored and displays
pre-Columbian artifacts.

The Monumento a los Héroes
de la Restauración, a soaring
monument capped by a 230-ft
(70-m) tall column, was erected
in 1940 by the dictator Rafael
Trujillo (1891–1961). The Museo
Folklórico Don Tomás Morel
offers an introduction to the
city's vibrant Carnival culture.

Environs
Around 45 miles (72 km) east
of Santiago, **Reserva Científica
Quita Espuela** has trails into
montane rainforest, where the
Hispaniola parrot and other
endemic birds can be spotted,
as well as various reptiles.
Another interesting place to
visit is **Casa Museo Hermanas
Mirabal**, in Salcedo, 30 miles
(48 km) east of Santiago. It is
where the sisters María Teresa,
Minerva, and Patria Mirabal,
who opposed Trujillo, grew up
in a middle-class home, now
maintained as a shrine.

🏛 **Centro León**
Av. 27 de Febrero 146. **Tel** 809 582
2315. **Open** 10am–7pm Tue–Sun.
🌐 centroleon.org.do

🗺 **Reserva Científica Quita
Espuela**
Tel 809 588 4156. **Open** 8am–5pm
Mon–Fri. 🎟 📷 Note: call to reserve
a guide and for access on Sat & Sun.
🌐 flqe.org.do

🏛 **Casa Museo Hermanas Mirabal**
Conuco Salcedo. **Tel** 809 587 8530.
Open 8:30am–5pm daily. 🎟
📷 compulsory. ♿

⑰ Jarabacoa

96 miles (154 km) NW of Santo
Domingo. 🚈 155,000. ℹ️ Plaza
Ramírez, Calle Mario Nelson Galán
between Duarte and Calle del
Carmen, 809 574 7287.

Deep in the Cordillera Central,
at a height of 1,750 ft (533 m)
and surrounded by forest, this
wealthy agricultural town draws
those escaping the heat of the
lowlands for a crisp alpine
climate. Parque Mario Nelsón
Galán, the small town square,

A rugged wooden bridge on the hike to Pico Duarte

is a good spot to watch life go by. The town nestles in the valley of the Río Yaque del Norte and is a base for whitewater rafting as well as horseback riding and for hiking, including to three local waterfalls: Salto de Baiguate, **Salto de Jimenoa**, 3 miles (5 km) southeast of Jarabacoa, and Salto de Jimenoa Alto, best reached through the **Proyecto Ecoturístico Comunitario El Gran Salto**.

Jarabacoa is also the gateway for Pico Duarte which is the tallest mountain in the Caribbean.

Salto de Jimenoa
Sabanete. **Open** 8am–5pm daily.

Proyecto Ecoturístico Comunitario El Gran Salto
El Salto de Jimenoa. **Tel** 809 541 1430. **Open** 9am–6pm.

⑱ Parques Nacionales J. Armando Bermúdez y José del Carmén Ramírez

16 miles (26 km) NW of Jarabacoa. **Tel** 809 472 4204. for a fee, Asociación de Guías de Montaña, La Ciénaga. **W** godominican republic. com

The Cordillera Central forms a rugged backbone rising to 10,164 ft (3,097 m) atop Pico Duarte, accessed from the mountain hamlet of La Ciénaga. The hulking mass is a popular, albeit challenging three-day round-trip hike to the summit, where the Dominican flag flutters over a bust of Juan Pablo Duarte (1813–73), father of the nation. This mountain terrain of razorback ridges and plunging gorges is known as the "Dominican Alps," and is enshrined within the Armando Bermúdez and José del Carmén Ramírez national parks. Rainforest smothers the lower flanks, while trails lead up through the mist-shrouded cloud forest and then pine forest above. Birding is superb here.

Bust of Juan Duarte, Pico Duarte

Fields surrounding the farming town of Constanza

⑲ Constanza

16 miles (26 km) NW of Santo Domingo. 90,000. Calle Matilda Viña 18, cnr Miguel Andrés Abreu, 809 539 2900.

With an exquisite location surrounded by mountains at 4,000 ft (1,219 m), this town is set in a broad valley that is the breadbasket of the nation. A quiltwork of fields produce much of the nation's fruit and a variety of flowers. With splendid scenery and crisp mountain air, Constanza is a good starting point for hikes, though it has been bypassed by tourism. Mountain drives by jeep guarantee great scenery. Colonia Japonesa, a hamlet on the northern outskirts of Constanza, was founded in the 1950s by Japanese farmers lured here by dictator Trujillo. Several structures here are in traditional Japanese style.

Environs
A challenging yet extremely beautiful drive south of Constanza leads to **Salto**

Aguas Blancas, a duo of waterfalls cascading 285 ft (87 m) into a chilly pool. The highest free waterfall in the Caribbean is fringed by pretty ferns and other vegetation that clings to the sheer rock faces of the canyons.

⑳ Complejo Ecoturístico Río Blanco

10 miles (17 km) SW of Banao. **Tel** 809 296 8208.

Nestled beside the Río Yamu, in the mountains west of Bonao, the Complejo Ecoturístico Río Blanco is a great location for travelers who want varied activities nearby. Organized tour options include horseback rides, guided hikes to local coffee- and cacao-growing farms, and a visit to a bamboo furniture workshop.

Nine comfortable en-suite cabins are furnished with one queen-size bed and a set of bunkbeds. Other options include a large dormitory-style room or a campground.

Faceless Dolls

The towns of El Cibao, and specifically Moca, are known for making ceramic *muñecas sin rostros* (faceless dolls) meant to symbolize the nation's multi-ethnic make-up in which no racial group is favored. The tiny, brightly painted dolls usually portray country women wearing headscarves or straw hats and holding flowers or *tinajones* (earthenware jars).

The commonly found faceless dolls in Cibao

㉑ San Cristóbal

17 miles (27 km) W of Santo Domingo.
🚂 221,000. 🚌 ℹ️ Gobernación,
Av. Constitución 25, 809 528 1844.
🎉 Fiesta Patronal (mid-Jun).

Founded in the late 16th century, San Cristóbal is steeped in historical significance. Capital of the province of the same name, this sprawling, busy city was originally named Trujillo after the dictator, Rafael Leonidas Trujillo. The name, however, was changed after he was gunned down in 1961. During his dictatorship, he built many monuments in the town to honor himself. One of them is the domed, mustard-colored **Catedral de Nuestra Señora de la Consolación**. This church also had a tomb intended for Trujillo, but he was eventually buried in Paris. The interior is decorated with murals by Spanish artist José Vela Zanetti. His work also adorns Trujillo's hilltop mansion, Castillo del Cerro, which was once embellished with gold leaf and murals. It is now a police academy and is closed to the public. Other noteworthy buildings include **Casa de la Cultura**, on the south side of Parque Colón, the main square. The Casa hosts local art exhibitions. On Parque Duarte is Iglesia Parroquial, a pretty church, built in 1946 to honor Trujillo's hometown.

Located just 2 miles (3 km) northwest of the city is Reserva Antropológica El Pomier, which protects 11 of the 54 caves adorned with pre-Columbian pictographs. More than 6,500 ancient pictographs and petroglyphs have been identified, most being spiritual symbols and animal figures. Paved paths lead through the major caverns, populated by harmless bats. There is a museum, shop, and café at the reserve.

🏛️ **Catedral de Nuestra Señora de la Consolación**
Av. Constitución & Calle Padre Brown.
Open 8am–5pm daily.

🏛️ **Casa de la Cultura**
Calle Mella. **Open** 9am–noon Mon–Fri.

The long and scenic coastline near Barahona

㉒ Barahona

120 miles (193 km) SW of Santo Domingo. 🚂 34,000. 🚌 🚕
ℹ️ Oficina de Turismo, Av. Enriquillo, 809 524 3650. 🎉 Carnival Cimarrón (Easter).

Founded in 1802 by the Haitian general, Toussaint L'Ouverture, Barahona, at the head of Bahía de Neiba, evolved as a center for sugar production in the 20th century and is today a port city. The city is the gateway to a little-visited region of enormous natural beauty. Palm-fringed beaches unfurl south along a roller-coaster road named Vía Panorámica, a scenic drive framed by the turquoise ocean.

Environs

Just 12 miles (20 km) south of the city, Playa San Rafael is a popular beach for its cool pools fed by natural spring waters. Only 25 miles (40 km) west of Barahona is Polo Magnético, an optical illusion in which the road, sloping in one direction, appears to slope the other way. Also worth visiting is **Reserva**

Científica Laguna de Cabral, 12 miles (20 km) northwest of the city. It has boardwalk trails for spotting waterfowl and wading birds.

🦩 **Reserva Científica Laguna de Cabral**
Cabral. **Tel** 809 835 3919.
Open 8am–6pm daily. 🚶 📷

㉓ Parque Nacional Jaragua

124 miles (200 km) SW of Santo Domingo. 🚕 ℹ️ Grupo Jaragua, 809 472 1036. 🚶 📷 🦩
🌐 grupojaragua.org.do

The nation's largest national park, Jaragua offers great wildlife viewing, although most of this semiarid terrain, lying in a rain shadow at the extreme southwest of the country, is off-limits. Endangered Ricord's and rhinoceros iguanas inhabit the park, accessed by trails from Fondo Paradí. Flamingos and roseate spoonbills can be seen in Laguna Oviedo, where the visitor center has a lookout

Flamingos flocking around Laguna Oviedo, Parque Nacional Jaragua

For hotels and restaurants on this island see pp186–9 and pp190–91

tower. Marine turtles nest at Bahía de las Águilas, accessible by boat or jeep.

㉔ Parque Nacional Sierra de Bahoruco

116 miles (186 km) SW of Santo Domingo. **Open** 9am–4:40pm Tue–Sun. 🛈 Grupo Jaragua, 809 472 1036.

One of the least visited in the country due to its remoteness and rugged terrain, this park is a must for bird enthusiasts. Protecting 310 sq miles (803 sq km) of forests that range from dry deciduous lowland forests to cloud forests and pines at higher altitudes, the park has 150 species of birds. White-necked crows and narrow-billed todies can be seen around Laguna La Charca and along trails from the visitor center at Hoyo Pelempito. The park's rich vegetation includes 166 orchid species. Vía Panorámica El Aceitillar, the sole access, offers magnificent scenery.

The endangered rock iguana, Isla Cabritos

㉕ Parque Nacional Lago Enriquillo y Isla Cabritos

112 miles (180 km) W of Santo Domingo. 🛈 Asociación de Guías del Lago Enriquillo, 809 816 7441. **Open** 7am–5pm daily. 🚤 boat trips 7:30am–1pm.

Encircled by mountains, super-saline Lago Enriquillo is the Caribbean's largest lake as well as its lowest point, at 131 ft (39 m) below sea level. The lake is a remnant of the Caribbean Sea left land-locked by ancient tectonic movements. About 5,000 American crocodiles inhabit the lake and are easily seen on Isla Cabritos. Flamingos tip-toe about the waters, home to more than 60 other bird species, including roseate spoonbills. Visitors will find plenty of rhinoceros iguanas around

Dry shrub on the sandy Isla Cabritos, center of Lago Enriquillo

the ranger station at La Azufrada, from where boats leave on guided tours.

Environs
Nearby **Las Caritas**, outside the hamlet of Postrer Río, has rocks etched with pre-Columbian petroglyphs showing human faces. At the western end of the lake is Jimaní, a border town abutting Haiti, known for its bustling market and brightly painted Haitian buses called *tap-taps*.

㉖ San Juan de la Maguana

140 miles (225 km) W of Santo Domingo. 🏙 130,000. 🎉 Festival de Espíritu Santo (Jun), El Día de San Juan (Jun 24).

Founded in 1508, this city is now the capital of San Juan province. Although most of the early colonial structures were destroyed during the 19th-century Haitian

invasions, it still boasts some intriguing sites, centered on Parque Central. The domed, eclectic-style Catedral San Juan Bautista, dating from 1958, features Baroque and Rococo ornamentation and an exterior spiral metal staircase. On the east side of town, Parque Duarte has the Neo-Classical Palacio Ayuntamiento and Modernist Palacio de Justicia.

Also worth visiting is the pre-Columbian site, El Corral de los Indios, just 4 miles (6 km) north of town. It has a wide stone circle used as a *bateyes* (ball courts).

Environs
Against the backdrop of the magnificent mountain range of Cordillera Central lies the **Presa de Sabana Yegua**, a popular man-made lake known for its bass and tilapia.

🐟 Presa de Sabana Yegua
15 miles (24 km) E of San Juan de la Maguana. Note: ask at the military guardpost for entry.

Ancient pre-Columbian petroglyphs in Las Caritas

Outdoor Activities and Specialized Holidays

The Dominican Republic is the Caribbean's most physically diverse nation and offers plenty of exciting activities and watersports. Cordillera Central is the only place in the Caribbean with whitewater rafting while Cabarete is considered the top spot for watersports. Diving is excellent as well, with incredible wreck-diving close to the shores. On land, the island is the region's golf capital. Other thrilling outdoor activities include jeep safaris, ATV excursions, and horse-riding, and the many national parks offer exceptional birding and hiking, especially Pico Duarte, the Caribbean's highest peak.

A kiteboarder enjoying the azure waters of the Dominican Republic

Beaches

The Dominican Republic has some of the most spectacular and varied beaches in the Caribbean, with something for every taste and interest. To escape the crowds, visitors should take their tents and camping gear and head to Bahía de las Aguilas in the southwest of the island. Choice options along the south coast include Punta Cana and Playa Bayahibe (see p172), where all-inclusive hotels line snow-white sands. The windswept Kite Beach at Cabarete on the north coast, is renowned for kiteboarding; nearby Playa Sosúa is a good base for scuba diving; and Playa Dorada, outside Puerto Plata, has a golf course amid all-inclusives. Cayo Levantado, Playa Rincón, Las Terrenas, and Cosón are the highlights of the Samaná Peninsula.

Birding and Wildlife Viewing

The Dominican Republic astounds with its wealth of birds. There are around 300 species, including 30 endemic ones. Parque Nacional Sierra de Bahoruco (see p179) and the Cordillera Central offer the largest diversity, and have well-developed trails. **Tody Tours** offers birding excursions to Sierra de Bahoruco. For those who are interested in seabirds and water-fowl, the best places to head to would be Parque Nacional Jaragua and Parque Nacional los Haitises (see p173) with **Paraíso Caño Hondo**. Flamingos color Lago Enriquillo, where crocodiles and iguanas can be easily viewed. Spotting manatees is virtually guaranteed at Refugio de Manatís Estero Hondo.

However, the crown jewel of wildlife-viewing experiences in the Dominican Republic is to see humpback whales, which can be encountered close-up in winter in Bahía de Samaná. **Whale Samana** offers trips. **Tour Samana With Terry** organizes ecotours of the Samaná Peninsula.

Diving

The Dominican Republic holds its own when it comes to diving, with some of the best wreck dives in the Caribbean. A 30-minute drive from Santo Domingo, Parque Nacional Submarino La Caleta has three wrecks; Bayahibes Bay features the wreck of the St. George, plus the underwater museum, 1724 Guadalupe Underwater Archaeological Preserve; and the world-renowned wreck Zingara can be explored off Sosúa, also known for the Airport Wall. In Samaná, divers rave about Cabo Cabrón and Islas las Ballenas. Off the far northwest, Monte Cristi is a remote spot with sensational coral and a fine wreck dive. Visitors can book through **Scubafun** in Bayahibe, **Las Terrenas Divers** in Samaná, and **Northern Coast Diving** in Puerto Plata.

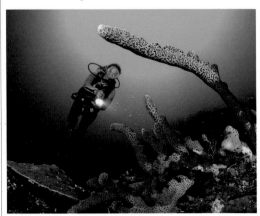

A scuba diver examining a colony of colorful sponges

Golf in the Dominican Republic

The Dominican Republic has some 40 championship golf courses – a major forte of the island – and more are being added by the leading names in golf design. All the major beach resorts have golf courses. Casa de Campo is the setting for three leading courses, and the Punta Cana-Playa Bávaro area has half a dozen, and many of them host a number of international tournaments.

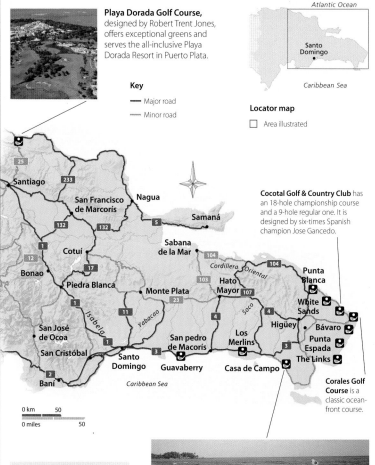

Playa Dorada Golf Course, designed by Robert Trent Jones, offers exceptional greens and serves the all-inclusive Playa Dorada Resort in Puerto Plata.

Atlantic Ocean

Santo Domingo

Caribbean Sea

Key

━━━ Major road

┄┄┄ Minor road

Locator map

☐ Area illustrated

Cocotal Golf & Country Club has an 18-hole championship course and a 9-hole regular one. It is designed by six-times Spanish champion Jose Gancedo.

Santiago

San Francisco de Marcorís — Nagua — Samaná

Cotuí — Sabana de la Mar

Bonao — *Cordillera Oriental*

Piedra Blanca — Monte Plata — Hato Mayor — Punta Blanca

White Sands

San José de Ocoa — *Yabacao* — *Soco* — Higüey — Bávaro

San Cristóbal — San pedro de Macorís — Los Merlins — Punta Espada

Santo Domingo — Guavaberry — Casa de Campo — The Links

Baní — *Caribbean Sea*

Corales Golf Course is a classic ocean-front course.

0 km 50
0 miles 50

TOP COURSES

Casa de Campo
🆆 casadecampo.com.do/golf

Corales Golf Course
🆆 puntacana.com/golf

Playa Dorada Golf Course
🆆 playadoradagolf.com

Cocotal Golf & Country Club
🆆 cocotalgolf.com

Teeth of the Dog Golf Course, rated the best course in the Caribbean, is one of the three world-renowned courses located at the Casa de Campo resort.

Windsurfer setting off from one of the beaches

Kiteboarding and Windsurfing

Cabarete is considered the Caribbean epicenter for kiteboarding, windsurfing, and dinghy sailing with perfect conditions for both novices and experts. The beaches of Cabarete face directly into the Atlantic trade winds, which whip up whitecaps good for surfing while giving lift to kiteboards. **Kite Excite** and **Laser Training Center** are two of the many places that offer tuition. For surfers, tuition and board rentals are available from **Ali's Surf Camp**. **Laurel Eastman Kiteboarding** offers kiteboarding tuition at Playa Punta Popy, at Las Terrenas.

Fishing

The Mona Passage, separating Hispaniola from Puerto Rico, teems with gamefish, as do the deep waters off the north shore. The main venues are **Casa de Campo Marina**, Punta Cana, and Puerto Plata. Typical half-day charters cost about $375 for up to four people. Leading charter companies include **Punta Cana Fishing** and Puerto Plata's **Gone Fishing**. Inland lakes offer fishing for bass and tilapia; anglers require no license.

Boat Excursions

Boat trips are a great way of viewing the coast and having fun. Catamarans and yachts depart on scheduled day and sunset excursions from every beach resort. Most of these excursions are party-hearty, with free-flowing rum cocktails. Glass-bottom boat rides reveal the fascinating beauty of the underwater world. A self-drive speedboat excursion with **Bávaro Splash** is thrilling. **Colonial Tours and Travel** offers speedboat and catamaran excursions to Punta Rucia and Cayo Paraíso, the only coral island in the Dominican Republic.

Watersports

Visitors to the main beach resorts are spoilt for choice with all manner of watersports, including Hobi Cats, banana-boat rides, Jet Skis, and speedboat safaris, which are a favorite with holiday-makers. All-inclusive resorts also do their bit in providing their guests with free use of non-motorized equipment. Enthusiasts of motorized watersports, however, have to mostly rely on the numerous private outfitters.

Rafters negotiating the rapids on a whitewater rafting trip

Whitewater Rafting

Cascading out of the Cordillera Central, the Río Yaque del Norte guarantees plenty of thrills on whitewater trips offered by **Rancho Baiguate**, in the mountain-city of Jarabacoa.

Tennis

Most resort hotels have tennis courts and most grant non-guests use of their facilities for a fee. Casa de Campo *(see p172)* has a large and modern tennis academy.

Horse-Riding

Horseback rides are available at all the beach resorts. Not to be missed is a ride to El Salto de Limón waterfall; visitors can book through **Santí Rancho**. The specialist facilities at **Casa de Campo Equestrian Center** and **Sea Horse Ranch Equestrian Center** are exceptional.

Yachts and motor boats docked at the marina of Casa de Campo

Mountain Biking

The Republic's rugged terrain is perfect for energetic cyclists. Mountain biking is offered by outfitters at most beach resorts, including **Iguana Mama** in Cabarete, with trips for beginners and hard-core cycling junkies. Rancho Cascada *(see p177)* is a great base for

Mountain bikers close to Cabarete

adventures in the Cordillera Central. Many of the major cities in the Dominican Republic have clubs for mountain biking who arrange for weekly rides.

ATV and Jeep Tours

ATV and jeep excursions are popular at many beach resort areas. Often, the "jeep" will be an open-top truck fitted to carry passengers in comfort. Some companies let visitors drive their own jeep in convoy through sugarcane fields, rainforest, and local communities. **Bavaro Runners** and **Outback Safari** have trips from Punta Cana and north coast resorts. **Tauro Tours** offers ATV tours in Las Terrenas, Samaná.

Hiking

Hiking up Pico Duarte, the Caribbean's highest peak, which stands at a height of

Hiker on the trail of Pico Duarte, the highest peak of the Caribbean

10,164 ft (3,097 m) is the ultimate challenge for hikers in these islands. Guided three-day round-trip hikes depart La Ciénaga *(see p177)*. Complejo Ecoturístico Río Blanco *(see p177)* is a good base for mountain walks. Reserva Científica Quita Espuela *(see p176)* and **Parque Nacional del Este** offer less demanding hikes.

DIRECTORY

Birding and Wildlife Viewing

Paraíso Caño Hondo
Tel 809 248 5995.
W paraisocanohondo. com

Tody Tours
Tel 809 686 0882.
W todytours.com

Tour Samana With Terry
Tel 809 538 3179.
W toursamanawith terry.com

Whale Samana
Calle Mella corner Av., La Marina, Samaná.
Tel 809 538 2494.
W whalesamana.com

Diving

Las Terrenas Divers
Playa Bonita, Las Terrenas.
Tel 809 889 2422.
W lt-divers.com

Northern Coast Diving
Tel 809 571 1028.
W northerncoast diving.com

Scubafun
Calle Principal, Bayahibe.
Tel 809 833 0003.
W scubafun.info

Kiteboarding and Windsurfing

Ali's Surf Camp
Tel 809 571 0733.
W alissurfcamp.com

Kite Excite
Kitebeach Hotel, Cabarete.
Tel 829 962 4556.
W kiteexcite.com

Laser Training Center
Calle Principal, Cabarete.
Tel 809 571 0640.
W caribwind.com

Laurel Eastman Kiteboarding
Tel 809 571 0564.
W laureleastman.com

Fishing

Casa de Campo Marina
Tel 809 523 8646.
W marinacasade campo.com.do

Gone Fishing
Plaza Tourisol, Puerto Plata. Tel 809 261 4141.

Punta Cana Fishing
Tel 809 852 8737.
W firstclassfishing.com

Boat Excursions

Bávaro Splash
Tel 809 390 7418.
W oceanadventures-puntacana.com/bavaro_splash.html

Colonial Tours & Travel
Tel 809 688 5285.
W colonialtours.com. do

Whitewater Rafting

Rancho Baiguate
Tel 809 574 6890.
W ranchobaiguate.com

Horse-Riding

Casa de Campo Equestrian Center
Tel 809 523 3333. W casadecampo.com.do

Santí Rancho
El Limón, Samaná.
Tel 829 342 9976.
W cascadalimon samana.com

Sea Horse Ranch Equestrian Center
Tel 809 571 3880.
W sea-horse-ranch. com

Mountain Biking

Iguana Mama
Tel 809 571 0908.
W iguanamama.com

ATV and Jeep Tours

Bavaro Runners
Tel 809 455 1135.
W bavarorunners.com

Outback Safari
Tel 809 320 2525.
W outbacksafari. com.do

Tauro Tours
Tel 849 658 8997.
W taurotours-excursionsamana.com

Hiking

Parque Nacional del Este
Between Bayahibe and Boca de Yuma.

Plunging waterfalls of El Salto de Limón, near Samaná ▶

Where to Stay

BARAHONA: Playazul Hotel-Restaurante $
Beach Resort
Carretera Barahona-Paraíso Km 7, Punta Prieta
Tel *809 204 8010*
A lovely, minimalist clifftop hotel over a cove with a pink-sand beach. Bright rooms are done up in pastel shades. Alfresco dining.

BARAHONA: Casa Bonita Tropical Lodge $$$
Boutique
Carretera de la Costa Km 17
Tel *809 476 5059*
W casabonitadr.com
Hanging on a mountainside, this chic eco-lodge offers designer furnishings, magnificent views, and a gourmet restaurant.

CABARETE: Agualina Kite Resort $
Beach Resort
Carretera Principal, Kite Beach
Tel *809 571 0805*
W agualina.com
A small and well-run beachside bargain favored by kiteboarders. Comfortable rooms all with lovely views. Airy restaurant, and on-site kite school.

CABARETE: Kite Beach Hotel $
Beach
Carretera Principal, Punta Goleta
Tel *809 571 0878*
W kitebeachhotel.com
Popular hotel with a thatched atrium lobby and modest one- and two-bedroom apartments, as well as penthouse suites. Excellent open-air restaurant.

CABARETE: Sereno de la Montaña $
Eco-lodge
Los Bueyes, 19 miles (30 km) S of Cabarete
Tel *809 424 7070*
W serenodelamontana.com
This rustic riverside eco-lodge in the mountains offers simple accommodations in thatched cabins with solar-heated water. Guests enjoy kayaking, hiking, and horseback-riding facilities.

CABARETE: Velero $
Beach Resort
Calle la Punta Cabarete
Tel *809 571 9727*
W velerobeach.com
Low-rise condo-hotel fronted by a small reef and shallow tidal pools. Slightly dated decor, but rooms are clean and functional.

CABARETE: Millennium Resort $$
Beach Resort
Carretera Cabarete-Sosua
Tel *809 571 0407*
W cabaretemillennium.com
A chic hotel with contemporary styling and walls of glass. Choose between rooms, suites, and three-room condos. Spa and kiteboarding school on site.

CABARETE: Natura Cabañas $$
Beach Resort
Paseo del Sol 5, Perla Marina
Tel *809 571 1507*
W naturacabana.com
This eco-sensitive resort exudes charm, with its thatched-roofed stone bungalows and rough-hewn furniture. Some rooms have kitchenettes. Spa and yoga.

CABARETE: Viva Wyndham Tangerine $$
Beach Resort
Carretera Sosua-Cabarete
Tel *809 571 0402*
W vivaresorts.com
This relaxed, family-focused, all-inclusive resort offers a Kids' Club and a paddling pool, as well as plenty of activities for adults. The guest rooms have beautiful furnishings.

JARABACOA: Hotel Gran Jimenoa $
Resort
Avenida La Confluencia
Tel *809 574 6304*
W granjimenoahotel.com
In a forest-enclosed setting beside the Río Yagua, this hotel offers no-frills rooms with simple bathrooms, as well as a riverside restaurant and horseback riding.

LA ROMANA: Casa de Campo $$$
Luxury
Casa de Campo
Tel *855 877 3643*
W casadecampo.com.do
A super-exclusive country club resort with gorgeous modern furnishings in the rooms and rental villas. Sports amenities on offer include shooting and polo.

PLAYA BAYAHIBE: Hotel Bayahibe $
Beach
Bayahibe Village, Bayahibe
Tel *809 833 0159*
W hotelbayahibe.net
A hospitable, family-run beach hotel with simple decor and a shaded open-air restaurant.

The stunning lobby at the Iberostar Hacienda Dominicus, Playa Bayahibe

PLAYA BAYAHIBE: Iberostar Hacienda Dominicus $$$
Beach Resort
Playa Dominicus, 3 miles (5 km) S of Bayahibe
Tel *809 688 3600*
W iberostar.com
All-inclusive resort with Spanish hacienda-style decor and eclectic furnishings. Kids' club, four restaurants, and diving.

PUERTO PLATA: BlueBay Villas Doradas $$$
Beach Resort
Playa Dorada
Tel *809 320 3000*
W bluebayresorts.com
At this adults-only resort, suites have minimalist furnishings and whirlpool tubs. Four restaurants. Minimum five-night stay.

PUERTO PLATA: Casa Colonial Beach & Spa $$$
Boutique
Playa Dorada
Tel *809 320 3232*
W casacolonialhotel.com
Intimate deluxe hotel resembling a coral-stone colonial mansion. Cavernous rooms, lovely rooftop spa, and pool.

PUERTO PLATA: Iberostar Costa Dorada $$$
Beach Resort
Carretera Luperón Km 4, Costa Dorada
Tel *809 320 1000*
W iberostar.com
Rooms at this all-inclusive hotel feature colorful wicker furnishings. Facilities include a vast free-form pool and a spa.

**PUNTA CANA: Four Points
by Sheraton** $
Modern
Boulevard 1ero de Noviembre
Tel *809 959 4444*
W starwoodhotels.com/fourpoints
The comfortable rooms at this
business-focused hotel near
the airport boast iPod docking
stations, and LCD TVs.

**PUNTA CANA:
Barceló Bávaro Beach** $$
Beach Resort
Playa Bávaro
Tel *800 227 2356*
W barcelo.com
An upscale adults-only resort,
with spacious rooms and stylish
decor. Casino, theater, golf,
and spa.

**PUNTA CANA:
Barceló Dominican Beach** $$
Beach Resort
Playa Cortecito
Tel *809 221 0714*
W barcelo.com
This four-star option shares
facilities with other hotels at the
huge Barceló Bávaro mega-resort,
including several restaurants.

**PUNTA CANA:
Catalonia Royal Bávaro** $$
Beach Resort
Playa Bavaro
Tel *809 412 0000*
W hoteles-catalonia.com
An adults-only all-suite resort
featuring stunning contemporary
decor and vast swimming pools,
plus private pools in most units.

**PUNTA CANA: Hotel Riu
Palace Bávaro** $$
Beach Resort
Playa de Arena Gorda
Tel *809 221 2290*
W riu.com
This mammoth all-inclusive hotel
for adults has every conceivable
facility, including a casino. Nine
room types to choose from, all
with modern furnishings.

**PUNTA CANA:
Iberostar Bávaro** $$
Beach Resort
Playa Arena Gorda
Tel *809 221 6500*
W iberostar.com
A distinguished low-rise hotel
close to the beach. Suites have
lively, tasteful decor.

PUNTA CANA: NH Real Arena $$
Beach Resort
Carretera El Cortecito, Playa Bávaro
Tel *809 285 6500*
W nh-hotels.com
A classy all-inclusive resort with
stunning stylings, state-of-the-art
amenities, and lavish rooms with
colorful furnishings. Excellent
poolside entertainment and lots
of activities for kids are available,
plus five restaurants and six bars.

**PUNTA CANA:
Paradisus Punta Cana** $$
Beach Resort
Playa Arena Gorda
Tel *809 687 9923*
W melia.com
With five pools for adults, two for
children, and colorful colonial-
style suites, this is a great family
option. There are 11 restaurants
and a 27-hole golf course, too.

DK Choice

**PUNTA CANA:
Eden Roc at Cap Cana** $$$
Luxury
Cap Cana
Tel *809 469 7469*
W edenroccapcana.com
This oceanfront resort is in a
stunning location and provides
the perfect place for rest and
relaxation. The ultra-luxurious
suites all have huge windows,
high ceilings, and private
pools. A "pillow-menu" is
available for guests to choose
from. Gourmet restaurants,
a spa, three golf courses, and
a full-service marina.

**PUNTA CANA:
Excellence Punta Cana** $$$
Luxury
Playa de Uvero Alto
Tel *809-685-9880*
W excellence-resorts.com
This deluxe resort sets a high
standard with sublime classical
colonial decor, excellent service,
and top-notch amenities:
several pools, spa, and a
relaxation center.

**PUNTA CANA: Grand Palladium
Palace Resort, Spa & Casino** $$$
Luxury
Playa Bávaro
Tel *809 221 0719*
W fiestahotelgroup.com
An elegant family-friendly resort
decorated in a Neo-Classical
style. It shares 11 restaurants
and other facilities with
neighboring sibling hotels.

**PUNTA CANA: Hard Rock
Café Hotel & Casino** $$$
Beach Resort
*Boulevard Turistico del Este,
Playa Macao*
Tel *809 687 0000*
W hardrockhotelpuntacana.com
This sprawling resort offers a
number of world-class facilities,
including 11 restaurants, a casino,
and a nightclub. Rooms feature
dramatic rock 'n' roll decor.

**PUNTA CANA: Sanctuary
Cap Cana Golf & Spa** $$$
Luxury
Cap Cana
Tel *809 562 9191*
W sanctuarycapcana.com
Located in a charming faux-
village setting, this sumptuous
all-suite hotel has a yacht marina,
a casino, several gourmet
restaurants, and a championship
golf course.

**PUNTA CANA:
Secrets Royal Beach** $$$
Luxury
Avenida Alemania, Bávaro
Tel *809 221 4646*
W secretsresorts.com
The magnificent contemporary
decor, featuring Oriental themes,
and the gourmet dining options
are the main highlights at this
chic and elegant resort.

PUNTA CANA: Tortuga Bay $$$
Luxury
Higüey
Tel *809 959 2262*
W puntacana.com
A re-creation of a plantation,
Tortuga Bay is a romantic, deluxe
all-suite villa-hotel. It is part of the
Punta Cana complex, with shared
golf and restaurant facilities.

The patio area of one of the junior suites at Tortuga Bay, Punta Cana

RIO SAN JUAN:
Bahía Principe San Juan $$
Beach Resort
5 miles (8 km) W of Río San Juan
Tel *809 226 1590*
W bahia-principe.com
This family-friendly beachfront option offers many amenities. Rooms have wicker furnishings and colorful fabrics.

RIO SAN JUAN:
Hotel La Catalina $$
Boutique
3 miles (5 km) W of Cabrera
Tel *809 589 7700*
W lacatalina.com
A handsome, breezy hillside hotel with gorgeous coastal views. Airy rooms and apartments have bougainvillea-clad balconies.

SAMANÁ PENINSULA:
Villa Eva Luna $
Boutique
Calle Marico, Las Terrenas
Tel *809 978 5611*
W villa-evaluna.com
Stay in self-catering villas with contemporary furnishings, king-sized beds, and private terraces. Yoga classes and babysitting.

SAMANÁ PENINSULA:
Albachiara Hotel $$
Beach Resort
Calle 27 de Febrero, Camino Playa de Popy
Tel *809 240 5240*
W albachiarahotel.com
This plantation-style beachfront complex has self-contained, modern apartment units. A short walk to restaurants and beach facilities.

SAMANÁ PENINSULA: Alisei
Hotel, Restaurant & Spa $$
Beach Resort
Calle Francisco Caamaño Deño, Las Terrenas
Tel *809 240 5555*
W aliseihotelspa.com
An intimate boutique hotel centered on a gorgeous pool.

Choose from several hip self-catering apartments all fitted with mahogany furniture. Gourmet restaurant.

SAMANÁ PENINSULA:
Casa Coson $$
Beach Resort
Playa Coson, Las Terrenas
Tel *809 853 8470*
W casacoson.com
This romantic French-run plantation-style inn has individually styled bungalows, plus rooms in the mansion. Spacious, palm-shaded lawns.

SAMANÁ PENINSULA: Gran
Bahía Principe Cayacoa $$
Beach Resort
Loma Puerto Escondido
Tel *809 538 3131*
W bahia-principe.com
This all-inclusive resort boasts a sensational clifftop setting and dramatic views. It is furnished in the style of an elegant Victorian plantation. Elevator to the beach.

SAMANÁ PENINSULA:
Gran Bahía Principe Cayo
Levantado $$
Beach Resort
Cayo Levantado
Tel *809 538 3232*
W bahia-principe.com
Guests are delivered by private launch to this all-inclusive hotel that commands a spectacular cay. Accommodations have luxurious fittings and sea views.

SAMANÁ PENINSULA:
Villa Serena $$
Boutique
Las Galeras
Tel *809 538 0000*
W villaserena.com
A family-run gem on a sandy cove, this plantation-themed mansion has individually designed guest rooms, some with four-poster beds. Candlelit restaurant and an emphasis on wellness, with yoga and other activities.

SAMANÁ PENINSULA:
Vista Mare $$
Beach Resort
Carretera Samana-Las Galeras Km 12
Tel *809 689 6666*
W samanavistamare.com
Choose from one-, two-, and three-room apartments, most with ocean views, at this sprawling clifftop hotel with a gorgeous setting on a beach club.

SAMANÁ PENINSULA:
The Bannister Hotel $$$
Luxury
Carretera Sánchez-Samaná Km 5
Tel *809 503 6363*
W thebannisterhotel.com
Overlooking Samaná marina, this upscale resort boasts minimalist decor, a night-lit pool, and a gourmet restaurant. The chic rooms all have private balconies.

SAMANÁ PENINSULA:
The Peninsula House $$$
Luxury
Calle Coson, Las Terrenas
Tel *809 962 7447*
W thepeninsulahouse.com
This exclusive guesthouse in a restored Victorian mansion exudes the gracious calm of an English country house. Beach restaurant and great ocean views.

SANTIAGO DE LOS
CABALLEROS: Hodelpa
Gran Almirante $$
Modern
Avenida Salvador Estrella Sadhala
Tel *809 580 1992*
W hodelpa.com
Boasting rich hardwood furniture, white linen, and cream leather furnishings, this classy hotel also has an on-site casino, cigar lounge, and nightclub.

SANTO DOMINGO:
Casa Naemie $
Boutique
Calle Isabel la Catolica 11
Tel *809 868 7556*
W casanaemie.com
Exquisite French-run bed-and-breakfast in the heart of the Zona colonial. Elegant furnishings, friendly staff, and a cozy ambience.

SANTO DOMINGO: Crowne
Plaza V Centenario Hotel $
Modern
Avenida George Washington 218
Tel *809 221 0000*
W ihg.com/crowneplaza/hotels
This oceanfront high-rise offers spacious rooms and all sorts of upscale amenities, from fine dining to extensive recreational options.

The lovely grounds and exterior of The Peninsula House, Samaná Peninsula

Key to Price Guide *see page 186*

SANTO DOMINGO:
Hotel Atarazana $
Boutique
Vicente Celestino Duarte 19
Tel *809 688 3693*
🅦 hotel-atarazana.com
This intimate hotel in a lovingly
restored mansion in the Zona
colonial has tastefully furnished
rooms. In-house spa.

SANTO DOMINGO:
Boutique Hotel Palacio $$
Historic
Calle Duarte 106
Tel *809 682 4730*
🅦 hotel-palacio.com
A handsome conversion of a
former president's home, with
stylish yet eclectic furnishings.

SANTO DOMINGO:
Hilton Santo Domingo $$
Modern
Avenida George Washington 500
Tel *809 685 0000*
🅦 hiltoncaribbean.com/
santodomingo
Shorefront high-rise with futuristic
decor and bold color schemes.
Opt for an oceanfront room for
great views. Casino and gym.

DK Choice

SANTO DOMINGO: Hostal
Nicolas de Ovando $$
Historic
Calle Las Damas
Tel *809 685 9955*
🅦 accorhotels.com
This exquisite French-run luxury
hotel, housed in three restored
early-colonial mansions, is listed
as a World Heritage Site by
UNESCO. The elegantly furnished
rooms, with sumptuous linens
and antiques, open to lovely
courtyards that are lit by candles
at night. The gourmet restaurant
is among the city's finest.

SANTO DOMINGO:
Hotel Conde de Peñalba $$
Modern
Calle El Conde and Arzobispo Meriño
Tel *809 688 7121*
🅦 condepenalba.com
Located opposite Parque Colón,
this hotel has simply appointed
colonial-style rooms and a lively
open-air restaurant.

SANTO DOMINGO:
Hotel Doña Elvira $$
Boutique
Padre Billini 207
Tel *809 221 7415*
🅦 dona-elvira.com
This thoughtfully converted
18th-century townhouse is
now a delightful B&B decorated

Breakfast is served in attractive surroundings at the Hotel El Beaterio, Santo Domingo

in tropical pastel colours. The
comfortable rooms face a
pleasant shady courtyard.

SANTO DOMINGO:
Hotel El Beaterio $$
Historic
Calle Duarte 8
Tel *809 687 8657*
🅦 elbeaterio.com
With its tasteful yet minimalist
period furnishings, this romantic
and charming former convent
recalls the colonial era. Snug
rooms are set around a pretty
inner courtyard.

SANTO DOMINGO:
Hotel Frances M Gallery $$
Historic
*Calle Las Mercedes and Arzobispo
Meriño*
Tel *866 599 6674*
🅦 mgallery.com
The red-brick walls at this French-
run boutique hotel recall its
colonial heritage. The Frances
M. Gallery is furnished in period
fashion and features an
atmospheric bar and restaurant.

SANTO DOMINGO:
Hotel Plaza Naco $$
Boutique
Presidente González 10
Tel *809 542 7782*
🅦 hotelplazanaco.com
Stay in this deluxe high-rise
with modern flair and beautiful
minimalist furnishings. Full-size
gym, plus a beauty salon.

SANTO DOMINGO:
**Renaissance Jaragua
Hotel & Casino** $$
Modern
Avenida George Washington 367
Tel *809 221 2222*
🅦 marriott.com
Soaring over the Malecón, this
convention hotel has a huge
swimming pool, a casino, fitness
center and lush gardens. The
spacious guest rooms are all
tastefully decorated.

UVERO ALTO:
Riu Palace Macao $$$
Beach Resort
Playa Arena Gorda
Tel *809 221 7575*
🅦 riupalacemacao.com
There is a mix of colonial and
contemporary decor at this
handsome, adults-only, all-
inclusive resort. Full range of
activities and entertainment.

UVERO ALTO:
Sivory Punta Cana $$$
Boutique
Playa Uvero Alto
Tel *809 330 0500*
🅦 sivorypuntacana.com
This all-suite hotel combines
minimalism and state-of-the-
art amenities with thatched
decor. There are three superb
restaurants and a world-class spa.

UVERO ALTO:
Zoëtry Agua Punta Cana $$$
Boutique
Playa Uvero Alto
Tel *809 468 0000*
🅦 zoetryresorts.com/agua
A deluxe resort hotel inspired
by traditional Taíno architecture.
Cavernous accommodations
with stylish fittings. Spa and a
chauffeured jeep for tours.

Beautiful pool area at the Sivory Punta
Cana, Uvero Alto

Where to Eat and Drink

BOCA CHICA: Restaurante Boca Marina
International $$
Calle Duarte 12A
Tel *809 688 6810*
This trendy open-air restaurant near the water serves a globe-spanning menu: from sushi and pasta to steaks and fresh seafood.

CABARETE: Blue Moon
Indian $
Moca Highway, Los Brazos
Tel *809 757 0614*
In the hills above Cabarete, Blue Moon is a great spot for family feasting while seated Indian-style on cushions. Expect spicy curries. By reservation only.

CABARETE: Kite Club Café
Café $
Calle Principal
Tel *829 644 8404*
Associated with a kite club, this cool breeze-swept beachfront café serves delicious sandwiches, burgers, wraps, and tacos, plus a range of smoothies.

CABARETE: Pomodoro Pizzeria
Italian $$
Pasillo Don Chiche
Tel *809 571 0085*
A friendly, family-run restaurant with inside and alfresco dining and simple decor. Delicious home-made pastas and gourmet pizzas. Live jazz every Thursday.

CABARETE: Bliss Restaurante
Italian/Mediterranean $$$
Callejón de la Loma
Tel *809 571 9721*   **Closed** *Sun*
This chic poolside lounge and restaurant serves scrumptious dishes. Do not miss the wonderful shrimp with passionfruit sauce.

La Yola in Punta Cana has a wonderful location on the pier

CABARETE: La Casita de Papi
Seafood $$$
Calle Principal
Tel *809 986 3750*   **Closed** *Tue*
In a former beach home, this French-owned eatery is renowned for its freshly prepared seafood, such as the must-try crayfish in coconut and anise sauce. Every dish is full of flavor. Great location.

CONSTANZA: Exquisiteces Dilenia
Dominican $$
Calle Gaston F. Feligne 7
Tel *809 539 2213*   **Closed** *Mon*
Exquisiteces Dilenia is a charming Dominican restaurant with rustic decor. The menu includes rabbit, guinea fowl, and stewed goat in red wine.

LA ROMANA: La Piazzetta
Italian $$$
Altos de Chavón
Tel *809 523 3333/5339*   **Closed** *Tue–Thu*
Amid authentic decor that replicates a Tuscan farmhouse, diners try outstanding Italian dishes, such as gnocchi stuffed with cheese and porcini mushroom risotto.

PUERTO PLATA: Hispaniola
Caribbean $
Plaza El Pueblito Playa Dorada
Tel *809 320 9612*
This simple and colorful beachside restaurant is popular with local families and renowned for its *poitín* and fresh lobster. Friendly service.

PUERTO PLATA: Sam's Bar & Grill
American $
Lóase Rosort, Playa Real 21
Tel *809 586 7267*
Favored by expatriates for its filling pancakes, steak and eggs, and Mexican scramble, this offbeat diner also serves delicious tuna salads and meat loafs.

PUERTO PLATA: Le Papillon
International $$
Villas Cofresi
Tel *809 970 7640*   **Closed** *Mon*
Flanked by aquariums, Le Papillon is a simple German-run hillside restaurant with eclectic decor. The international menu features excellent filet mignon and lobster.

> **Price Guide**
> Prices are based on a two-course meal for one, including tax and service charges and half a bottle of wine.
>
> | $ | up to $15 |
> | --- | --- |
> | $$ | $15–40 |
> | $$$ | over $40 |

PUNTA CANA: Captain Cook
Seafood $$$
Playa El Cortesito
Tel *809 552 0645*
A beachfront restaurant serving fresh, top-quality seafood prepared to order. Specialties include freshwater crabs, shrimps, calamari, and crayfish, plus paella.

PUNTA CANA: Jellyfish
Mediterranean $$$
Playa Bávaro
Tel *809 840 7684*
Choose from a Mediterranean-influenced menu heavy on seafood at this eatery with deep-cushion sofas and dramatic architecture.

PUNTA CANA: La Palapa de Eden Roc
Seafood $$$
The Caleton Beach Club, Cap Cana
Tel *809 469 7469*
This exclusive thatched beach club has a sushi bar, as well as a menu of sublime Mediterranean-influenced seafood. Do not miss the scrumptious shrimp and crab with tomato sauce and croutons.

> ### DK Choice
>
> **PUNTA CANA: La Yola** $$$
> Seafood
> *Punta Cana Marina,*
> *Punta Cana Resort & Club*
> **Tel** *809 959 2262*
> A highlight of the Punta Cana Resort & Club (*see p173*), this classy thatched restaurant on a pier offers fresh Mediterranean and Caribbean cuisine and specializes in seafood. Mouthwatering dishes include Galician style octopus, shrimp and lobster risotto, and seafood kabob. Reservations required.

PUNTA CANA: Passion
International $$$
Paradisus Palma Real Resort,
Playa de Bávaro, Avenida Alemanio
Tel *809 688 5000*
Exclusive to resort guests, Passion is the place to go for a romantic fine-dining experience. It offers an unforgettable eight-course tasting menu with wine pairings.

Tables set inside a cave at El Mesón de la Cava, Santo Domingo

SAMANÁ PENINSULA:
Bar Restaurant Spoon Beach $
International
Calle Francisco Alberto Caamaño
Tel *809 884 9971*
This is a romantic outdoor
option with lovely river and
ocean views. Choose from a
health-conscious menu that
includes excellent French-
inspired dishes. Lovely desserts
and a good cocktail menu.

SAMANÁ PENINSULA:
Paco Cabana $$
International
Calle Libertad 1, Las Terrenas
Tel *809 240 5301*
Sit on deep-cushioned Bali beds
at this elegant restaurant and
enjoy everything from burgers
to lighter dishes, such as sardines
with red peppers, or fish *carpaccio*
with passionfruit. Great cocktails,
too. Gorgeous location right
on the beach.

SAMANÁ PENINSULA:
Le Cave à Vin $$$
Tapas
Paseo de la Costanera,
Las Terrenas
Tel *829 305 8263*
A chic, contemporary wine bar
and restaurant in a shopping
plaza. There is a small yet
eclectic range of tapas and a
huge wine list. Excellent option
for lunch. Smoking permitted.

SAMANÁ PENINSULA:
Restaurante Xamana $$$
Mediterranean
Avenida La Marina, Samaná
Tel *809 538 2129*
Enjoy superb Mediterranean
dishes such as fish *carpaccio*
and seafood spaghetti at this
chic modernist restaurant.
Be sure to save room for one
of their divine desserts.

SANTIAGO DE LOS
CABALLEROS: El Pez Dorado $$
International
Calle del Sol 43
Tel *809 582 4051*
The vast menu at this bodega-
style restaurant in the heart of
town ranges from Chinese dishes
to local and international staples.
Excellent wine selection.

SANTO DOMINGO: Pastelería
La Cuchara de Madera $
Bakery
José Amado Soler 63
Tel *809 683 6544*
La Cuchara sells tempting
fresh pastries and other baked
goods, plus *empanadas*, burritos,
smoothies and gourmet coffees.

SANTO DOMINGO:
El Mesón de la Cava $$
International
Avenida Mirador del Sur 1
Tel *809 533 2818*
Approached via a rickety
staircase and occupying a
picturesque spot amid dramatic
caverns, this gourmet restaurant
has excellent seafood, steaks,
and succulent lamb chops.

SANTO DOMINGO: Falafel $$$
Mediterranean
Calle Padre Billini 352
Tel *809 688 9714*
Located on three stories of a
restored colonial building, Falafel,
true to its name, has all the Middle
Eastern and Mediterranean
staples, plus a vegan menu.

SANTO DOMINGO:
Mesón D' Bari $$$
Dominican
Calle Hostos 302
Tel *809 687 4091*
Enjoy traditional Criollo dishes
in a bohemian colonial mansion
filled with art by famous patrons.

Try the *cangrejo guisado*
(savory crab stew). Friendly staff.
Reservations are recommended.

SANTO DOMINGO: Mitre $$$
International
Avenida Lincoln & Calle Gustavo
Mejía Ricart
Tel *809 472 1787*
Mitre is a swanky modern option
that draws gourmands with fare
ranging from burgers and pasta
dishes to whitefish *carpaccio*
and Mongolian-style tenderloin.
Good wine-and-cigar lounge.

SANTO DOMINGO:
Pat'e Palo $$$
International
Calle La Atarazana 25
Tel *809 687 8089*
Located in a wonderful setting
on Plaza España, Pat'e Palo has
a menu that includes sautéed
shrimp in coconut-curry sauce
and sea bass in white wine.
The staff dress as pirates.

SANTO DOMINGO:
Sophia's Bar & Grill $$$
International
Paseo de los Locutores 9
Tel *809 620 1001*
This sophisticated retro
restaurant is favored by locals
for its eclectic menu, which
features sushi as well as a range
of Caribbean dishes. End your
meal with the warm guava
cheesecake. Cheerful music.

SANTO DOMINGO:
Vesuvio del Malecón $$$
Italian
Avenida George Washington 521
Tel *809 221 1954*
Come to this classy Italian
restaurant with alfresco seating
for fresh seafood, including garlic
crayfish and porcini mushroom
risotto in squid ink.

Practical Information

The Dominican Republic's tourist infrastructure is concentrated around Punta Cana-Bávaro, where the expansion of deluxe all-inclusives is spreading along Costa del Coco. Samaná is also rapidly growing in popularity, with new construction, but retains its laid-back ambience. Tourist offices are scattered across the island with the main offices situated in Santo Domingo, and the staff are generally helpful. Bear in mind that things often get accomplished at a slower pace here.

A sign at the Punta Cana International Airport

When to Go

The best time for visiting the Dominican Republic is November to April, the dry season, when temperatures are pleasantly moderate. Summers can be exceedingly hot, although hotels and car rental companies offer discounts. Temperatures vary with elevation; Cordillera Central is delightfully cool year-round. Cultural events occur throughout the year, but much of the country comes to a halt for Semana Santa (holy week).

Getting There

Although Santo Domingo's Las Américas International Airport (SDQ) is the main airport, most international flights serving beach resorts land at Punta Cana International Airport (PUJ), while other flights also arrive and depart from regional airports such as Aeropuerto Internacional Gregorio Luperón (POP), in Puerto Plata. **American Airlines**, **Delta**, **JetBlue**, **Spirit Airlines**, **United Airlines**, and **US Airways** offer service to the Dominican Republic, as do

many charter airlines. Several European airlines connect through Miami.

Documentation

All foreign citizens need a passport plus proof of onward travel to visit the Dominican Republic, where a tourist card ($10) valid for 30 days is issued upon arrival. Extensions for an additional 90 days cost $25 from the **Dirección General de Migración**.

Visitor Information

The Dominican Republic's **Ministry of Tourism** has offices in the US, Canada, and UK, as well as in major tourist centers in the Republic. The key local offices include one on Santo Domingo's Parque Colón, in Bávaro, and Puerto Plata. The ministry publishes a series of pocket-sized guides to the major regions. Hotel tour desks can also provide information about organized excursions, and other activities. Many tour companies and travel suppliers have websites that provide more specific information.

Health and Security

Most destinations in the Dominican Republic are safe, and endemic tropical diseases are limited to dengue, and malaria, a rare occurrence primarily along the Caribbean coast. Additional threats include sunburn, dehydration, and rip tides; check conditions with locals

before swimming. Private doctors and clinics are found in every town, and basic government-run *centros de salud* (health centers) serve most communities. **Hospiten** operates medical clinics and ambulance service in major resorts. A few safety precautions are advisable as petty theft and crime is endemic in visitor venues and remote and unlit places at night. Leave all valuables in the hotel safe when exploring on foot. Driving on isolated rural roads at night is risky due to poor lighting, so use extreme caution.

Banking and Currency

The Dominican currency is the peso (RD$), but the US dollar is accepted everywhere. Euros and pounds Sterling can be exchanged at banks, including **BanReservas**, and foreign-exchange booths. Most shops and tourist outlets accept major credit cards. Traveler's checks in US dollars are accepted in very few places. Most banks have ATMs, but they often run out of cash.

Communications

Ubiquitous public phones use prepaid phone cards, which can be purchased at stores and call centers. Calls from hotels incur a hefty surcharge. The Republic's area codes are 809 and 829. Calls within Santo Domingo require the ten-digit number including the area code, which should be preceded by 1 when dialing beyond Santo Domingo. Most hotels have Internet service; many have Wi-Fi. The main service providers are **Claro Codetel**, **Orange**, and **Tricom**. There are Internet cafés in every town and tourist center.

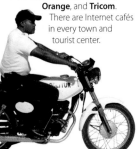

Policeman patrolling the beach in Punta Cana

Stalls selling colorful native Haitian art, Costa del Coco

Electricity

The Dominican Republic operates on 110 volts, but 220 volts is sometimes found in hotels and is usually marked as such. Outlets use US two-prong or three-prong plugs.

Visitors from Europe should bring transformers or adapters. Most large hotels have their own back-up generators to supply power during frequent outages. A surge protector or transformer is good protection against power surges.

Time

The Dominican Republic is on Atlantic Standard Time (AST), 4 hours behind Greenwich Mean Time (GMT) and 1 hour ahead of New York and Miami.

Getting Married

Getting married in the country is easily arranged. If the visitor is staying in a resort hotel, the easiest way is to have the hotel make the arrangements. Couples will need to provide passports, birth certificates, and single-status affidavits, which must be translated into Spanish and certified by a Dominican Republic Consulate.

Marriage applications are made through the local *oficialia del estado civil* (city clerk).

Transport

Taxis are the best means of getting around within cities. Tourist taxis await visitors outside most hotels. Locals rely on *carros públicos* (private unmetered cars) that operate as communal taxis, but are best avoided as drivers tend to overcharge. *Moto-conchos* (motorcycle taxis) form the main transport only for locals outside Santo Domingo and are best avoided as well. Air-conditioned buses link most destinations nationwide.

Shopping

The country is a veritable Aladdin's Cave of crafts, including amber and larimar jewelry unique to the isle. Museo del Ambar *(see p175)* and **Harrison's**

Fine Caribbean Jewelers have outlets in tourist venues. Native Haitian art is ubiquitous, but Santo Domingo also has fine galleries selling more contemporary pieces by local artists. All beaches host souvenir stalls and artisan markets spilling their art, linen blouses, and hardwood sculptures onto the sands. Most large hotels also have souvenir stores. The island is renowned for the quality of its cigars, available throughout the country.

Language

Spanish is the official language, spoken by everyone, although some locals also speak English, as do most people working in the tourism industry.

DIRECTORY

Getting There

American Airlines
Tel 800 433 7300.
w aa.com

Delta
Tel 800 221 1212.
w delta.com

JetBlue
Tel 800 538 2583.
w jetblue.com

Spirit Airlines
Tel 800 772 7117.
w spiritair.com

United Airlines
w united.com

US Airways
Tel 800 428 4322.
w usairways.com

Documentation

Dirección General de Migración
Av. George Washington, cnr of Héroes de Luperón.
Tel 809 508 2555.

Visitor Information

Ministry of Tourism
Tel 809 221 4660.
w godominican republic.com

Health and Security

Hospiten
Tel 809 541 3000
ext. 2500.
w hospiten.com/en

Police, Fire, Ambulance
Tel 911.

Banking and Currency

BanReservas
Tel 809 472 5000.
w banreservas.com

Communications

Claro Codetel
Tel 809 220 1111.
w codetel.net.do

Orange
Tel 809 859 6555.
w orange.com.do

Tricom
Tel 809 476 6000.
w tricom.net

Shopping

Harrison's Fine Caribbean Jewelers
Tel 809 586 3933.
w harrisons.com

A PORTRAIT OF PUERTO RICO

The smallest and easternmost of the Greater Antilles, Puerto Rico is as much American as Latin in flavor and mood. By far the wealthiest of the Caribbean nations, thanks to its status as a US Commonwealth, this bullet-shaped island abounds in physical beauty, offers world-class activities, and has the finest hotels and resorts.

Called Borinquén (Land of the Brave Lord) by the native Taínos, Puerto Rico lies between Hispaniola, to the west and the Virgin Islands, to the east. It is exceedingly mountainous inland of the coastal plain and dense forests cover a rugged backbone sweeping down to the Atlantic and Caribbean shores, edged with pristine blues and greens. The sea is lined with coral reefs and beaded with beach-fringed cays, plus Vieques and Culebra – the Spanish Virgin Islands – floating off the north-east shore of the mainland. Home to two-thirds of Puertorriqueños, San Juan is the political and cultural capital. It is a contemporary city with a well-preserved colonial core.

History

The Taínos had evolved a modestly advanced culture when Christopher Columbus arrived here on November 19, 1493. As elsewhere in the Caribbean, the indigenous people were rapidly decimated by the Spaniards. The first settlement was founded in 1508 by the conquistador Juan Ponce de León, the island's first governor, who christened the isle Puerto Rico (Rich Port). In 1521, San Juan was founded and became the capital, with a flask-shaped harbor well protected by forts. However, under the Earl of Cumberland, the English invaded and seized San Juan. In 1598, an epidemic swiftly forced the occupation

Cobbled street lined with restored buildings, Old San Juan

People in colorful costumes at the Three Kings festival celebrations, Ponce

army to flee. The Spanish finally reoccupied the island after a brief invasion by the Dutch in 1625. The 18th century witnessed a coffee boom, and many of the island's towns date from this period. Although Spain granted autonomy to Puerto Rico in 1897, the island was captured by US troops during the Spanish-American War in 1898 and it became a US Protectorate.

Government and Politics

The Commonwealth of Puerto Rico is a self-governing US territory – a controversial status dating back to 1898. Ever since, the islanders have been torn between a minority who long for independence, some who hope to become a US state, and a majority happy with the current status as a "Free Associated State," granted in 1952. Puerto Ricans were given US citizenship in 1917, prompting mass migration to the US mainland. Currently, more people of Puerto Rican ancestry live in the US than on the island itself. However, the island is not represented in the US Congress, and Puerto Ricans may not vote during the US presidential election; however, they can vote in the primaries.

Economy

Puerto Rico is the Caribbean's most industrialized island, and its citizens are by far the region's wealthiest. Today, less than 3 percent work in agriculture. The pharmaceutical industry is well developed as is the tourism industry. More than 5 million visitors arrive here annually and the opening of the Caribbean's largest convention center in 2007 has further boosted the island's stature.

Lifestyle and Culture

Puerto Rico's 3.9 million Spanish-speaking people are proud of their rich cultural heritage – a mixture of Hispanic, African, and Taíno. Following more than a century of US domination, the lifestyle and culture today lie on the cusp between cultures: part Hispanic and part American. The march of modernity has been so thorough, however, that the *jíbaro* (mountain-dwelling peasant) now belongs to the distant past, and folkloric music has faded in favor of merengue and salsa.

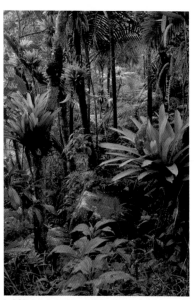

Lush foliage, including bromeliads flourishing in the rainforests of Puerto Rico

Exploring Puerto Rico

Oblong-shaped Puerto Rico is a mountainous, beach-fringed depiction of virtually everything the Caribbean offers. Old San Juan's colonial treasures gleam after restoration, while the modern capital city hops to a hip *vida loca* beat. The rugged interior is at its best along the mountain-crest Ruta Panorámica, linking historic towns. Beaches range from cottony whites to black and are most glorious on Vieques and Culebra. Rincón offers excellent surfing while Playa Dorado has top-end golfing.

Locator Map

Getting Around

The easiest way of discovering the island is to hire a rental car or to stitch together a series of island excursions. These can be taxi tours, day trips offered by tour companies, plus hiking and caving outings, and even sailing trips. Domestic flights connect San Juan to Vieques and Culebra – the Spanish Virgins – but the most pleasant way to visit these out-lying islands is by ferry from Fajardo, which takes about an hour. Crowded minivans provide public transportation between towns. Driving in Puerto Rico has its own challenges and traffic jams are ubiquitous in urban centers.

Souvenirs on display near Parque Ceremonial Indígena Caguana

For hotels and restaurants on this island see pp214–16 and pp217–19

Key

══ Highway
▬ Major road
═ Minor road
--- Ferry route

View from Mirador on Route 143, La Ruta Panorámica

Vieques
One of the Spanish Virgin Islands, Vieques's chief appeals are its boutique hotels, gorgeous white-sand beaches, and its phosphorescent bay.

El Yunque National Forest
The Caribbean National Forest protects the only tropical rainforest in the US National Park System.

0 kilometers   20
0 miles   20

Sights at a Glance

① San Juan pp198–201
② Dorado
③ Arecibo Observatory
④ Parque Las Cavernas del Río Camuy
⑤ Parque Ceremonial Indígena Caguana
⑥ Playa Jobos
⑦ Rincón
⑨ Mayagüez

⑩ Boquerón
⑪ San Germán
⑫ La Ruta Panorámica pp204–5
⑬ Ponce
⑭ Centro Ceremonial Indígena de Tibes
⑮ Hacienda Buena Vista
⑰ Playa Piñones
⑱ Luquill

⑲ El Yunque National Forest
⑳ Fajardo
㉒ Vieques
㉓ Culebra

Featured Hotels and Resorts

⑧ Horned Dorset Primavera
⑯ Copamarina Beach Resort
㉑ El Conquistador Resort

For keys to symbols see back flap

❶ San Juan

Founded in 1521, San Juan was laid out in a grid on a headland protecting a large, flask-shaped bay. Known as San Juan Viejo ("old"), this historic core has been restored, with beautiful 17th- and 18th-century buildings painted in tropical fruit pastels lining the narrow, cobblestoned streets. Some of the houses have been converted into charming boutique hotels. Two castles guard the colonial city, a port-of-call for cruise ships which dock alongside the ancient harbor. Inland, modern San Juan has an altogether different feel (see p201).

Interior courtyard of Museo de San Juan

🏛 Plaza del Quinto Centenario

Calle Norzagaray and Calle del Cristo. 🚹 Museo de las Américas: Calle del Morro. **Tel** 787 724 5052. **Open** 9am–noon, 1–4pm Tue–Sat; noon–5pm Sun. 🌐 **museolasamericas.org** Casa Blanca: Calle San Sebastián 1. **Tel** 787 725 1454. **Open** 8am–4:30pm Wed–Sun. 🐾

This triple-tiered plaza, laid out in 1992 for the 500th anniversary of Columbus's arrival, is pinned by Totem Telúrico, a granite totem representing the island's peoples. The plaza is surrounded by the Ballajá barracks, now housing **Museo de las Américas**, with exhibits on New World culture, and the 16th-century Convento de los

Dominicos. Nearby is Parque de Beneficencia, a peaceful setting for the Neo-Classical Instituto de la Cultural Puertorriqueña, displaying historical artifacts from art to religious icons. Built in 1521, **Casa Blanca** now serves as a museum depicting early colonial life.

🏛 Plaza de San José

Calle del Cristo and Calle San Sebastián. 🚹 Museo de Pablo Casals: Calle San Sebastián 101. Tel 787 723 9185. **Open** 9:30am–4:30pm Tue–Sat. 📷 🚹

The most intimate of San Juan's colonial plazas has at its heart a bronze statue of the conquistador Ponce de León (1474–1521), the island's first governor. Along Calle San Sebastián, quaint colonial mansions come alive at night as lively bars and trendy restaurants. Step inside Iglesia San José to view the magnificent muraled ceiling, then browse through **Museo de Pablo Casals**, celebrating the life of Spanish-born cellist Pablo Casals (1876–1973), who lived his last two decades in San Juan. Also worth stopping by is the **Museo de San Juan** on Calle Norzagaray

which has an excellent art collection and displays on local history.

☎ El Convento

Calle del Cristo 100. **Tel** 787 723 9020. 🅿 🚹 🌐 **elconvento.com**

This charming boutique hotel (see p215) was once a convent, built in 1651. It has gracious period furnishings, an excellent restaurant and a tapas bar. The upstairs terrace looks over the cathedral.

🏛 Calle del Cristo

Between Calle Norzagaray and Calle Tetuán. 🚹

Sloping downhill from Plaza de San José, the Calle del Cristo is paved with blue-tiled cobblestones and to each side, charming two-story townhouses graced by wooden balustrades double as art galleries, boutiques, and cafés. A good time to explore is on a Tuesday

Stained glass at Catedral de San Juan Bautista

night, during Noche de Galerías, when the galleries remain open late. The Neo-Classical Catedral de San Juan Bautista was completed in 1852 atop the site of the city's first cathedral. Admire the trompe-l'oeil ceiling and the marble mausoleum containing the remains of Ponce de León. The street ends at the tiny Capilla del Cristo (Christ Chapel), adjoining the Parque de las Palomas named after the pigeons that flock here.

🏛 Plaza de Armas

Calle San José and Calle San Francisco. 🚹

San Juan Viejo's central plaza originated as a 16th-century parade ground and later became the administrative center. Open and airy, it has lost much of its early charm to fast-food outlets. Still, the Alcaldía (City Hall), dating from 1789, impresses, as do the Neo-Classical Diputación (Provincial Delegation) and Intendencia, now the State Department offices.

Displays in Museo de San Juan

For hotels and restaurants on this island see pp214–16 and pp217–19

Headquarters of Puerto Rico Tourism Company

🖼 Paseo de la Princesa

Between Calle La Marina and El Morro headland. 🛈 Puerto Rico Tourism Company, 800 866 7827.
♿ 🚢 Sat & Sun.

This waterfront promenade begins at the dock-front and leads west, tracing the course of the towering city walls and ending beneath Fortaleza San Felipe del Morro, at the tip of the headland. The 1.5-mile (2.4-km) long walkway of the Princess esplanade is lined with wrought-iron street lamps. Tree-shaded Plaza del Inmigrante hosts several fascinating buildings and soaring over the north side, the Art Deco Banco Popular. Walking west, visitors will pass the former La Princesa prison, now the **Puerto Rico Tourism Company**'s headquarters.

🖼 Plazuela de la Rogativa

Caleta de las Monjas and Calle Recinto del Oeste. ♿

The tiny Plaza of the Divine Intervention features a monument celebrating the delivery of San Juan from a British siege in 1797. The Modernist bronze statue shows a bishop leading a torch-lit procession that fooled the invaders into believing that the civilian torch-bearers were a large garrison of Spanish troops.

To the south, the plaza offers fine views of La Fortaleza, the governor's mansion built in 1533, as well as the Puerta de San Juan, at the end of Paseo de la Princesa, which was the main entrance to the walled city in colonial days and still bears its heavy wooden gates.

VISITORS' CHECKLIST

Practical Information
N coast of Puerto Rico.
🗺 435,000. 🛈 La Casita,
500 Calle Tanca, 800 866 7827.
🎭 Casals Fest (Feb–Mar);
Heineken Jazzfest (May).
🌐 seepuertorico.com

Transport
✈ 🚗 🚢 San Juan-Cataño.

🏰 Fortaleza San Felipe del Morro

Calle del Morro. **Tel** 787 729 6960.
Open 9am–6pm daily. 🐾 📷 ♿ 🚢
🏠 🌐 nps.gov/saju

Initiated in 1539 to guard the harbor entrance, the headland fortress was completed in 1786. A lighthouse offers fine perspectives of the castle and the green swathe toward the Campo del Morro.

The Main Battery looking south, Fortaleza San Felipe del Morro

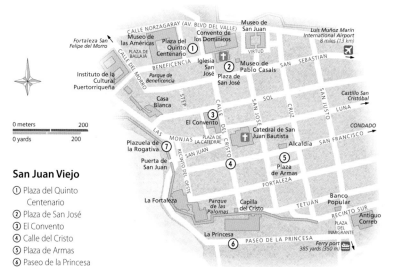

San Juan Viejo

① Plaza del Quinto Centenario
② Plaza de San José
③ El Convento
④ Calle del Cristo
⑤ Plaza de Armas
⑥ Paseo de la Princesa
⑦ Plazuela de la Rogativa

For keys to symbols *see back flap*

Castillo San Cristóbal

Commanding the Atlantic clifftop at San Juan Viejo's eastern entrance, Castillo San Cristóbal was initiated in 1634 and completed in 1783. It was designed by military engineers Tornis O'Daly and Juan Mestre to prevent a land assault. It last saw action in 1898 during an artillery exchange with US warships but the US military occupied the fortress until 1961. Now a UNESCO World Heritage Site, it is administered by the US National Parks Service.

VISITORS' CHECKLIST

Practical Information
Calle Norzagaray.
Tel 787 729 6960. ℹ San Juan National Historic Site, 787 729 6777. **Open** 9am–6pm daily. ♿ 10am & 2pm (in English). ⓦ nps.gov/saju

Devil's Sentry Box
A lonely lookout post, this is the oldest surviving element of San Cristóbal. Sentries regularly shouted "Alerta!" to keep themselves awake during the long night watch.

Ordóñez Cannon
This is the north-facing battery which fired the first shots of the Spanish-American War in Puerto Rico on May 12, 1898.

The Great Moat, a wide-open space, was designed to trap enemy troops in a cross-fire.

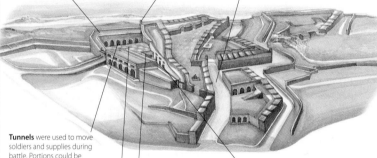

Tunnels were used to move soldiers and supplies during battle. Portions could be destroyed by gunpowder to block an enemy's advance.

The Chapel has an image of St. Barbara, patron saint of artillery men to whom gunners prayed before battle.

Plaza de Armas, the main parade ground, overlays massive cisterns.

The imposing walls of Castillo San Cristóbal

Barracks
The barracks have eight vaulted rooms on two levels, with the one on Plaza de Armas furnished as it was 200 years ago.

Modern San Juan

The modern metropolis evolved around San Juan Viejo, the original colonial city. The area comprising Condado, Ocean Park, and Isla Verde is an upscale residential district teeming with Art Deco and Modernist structures. Southward, separated by the Marin Peña channel, lies the commercial zones of Santurce and Hato Rey, with the university and many of the city's cultural venues. Beyond, traffic-jammed thoroughfares fan out to the sprawling residential suburbs and industrial zones of Carolina, Trujillo Alto, Guaynabo, Cataño, and Bayamón, setting for the Bacardí rum company headquarters.

Works by local artists, Museo de Arte de Puerto Rico

Condado

Puerto Rico's first resort built in 1950s, Condado became popular with the tourists only after the 1980s. Lined with towering high-rise condominiums and hotels, this upscale district occupies a slender isthmus wedged between the Atlantic Ocean and Laguna Condado.

The main thoroughfare, Avenida Ashford, is a favored shopping district among the locals and visitors. Only 2 miles (3 km) from Avenida Ashford, Condado Beach, a talcum-white beach lining the seashore, draws sun-seeking locals on weekends. The place is also well-known for its great nightlife with plenty of bars and restaurants that come to life after sunset.

Connecting Condado eastward is the trendy residential neighborhood of Ocean Park, favored by beach-going youth and a great place to enjoy parasailing and other watersports. The good beaches extend east to Isla Verde, the setting of some of the city's finest hotels *(see pp214–16)*.

Santurce

Museo de Arte de Puerto Rico: Av. De Diego 229. Tel 787 977 6277. **Open** 10am–5pm Tue & Thu–Sat, 10am–8pm Wed, 11am–6pm Sun. **mapr.org**

Fundación Luis Muñoz Marín: Carretera 877 Km0.4. Tel 787 755 4506. **Open** 10am–2pm Mon–Fri, 10:30am–1pm Sat–Sun. **flmm.org**

The heart of metropolitan San Juan lies inland of Condado, centered around Ponce de León. This formerly posh region had declined in recent decades, but has seen a rebound with the opening of Centro de Bellas Artes, the city's main performing arts venue; and **Museo de Arte de Puerto Rico**, boasting a superb collection by Puerto Rican artists spanning three centuries. The Plaza del Mercado de Santurce, a traditional market, is housed in a Renaissance-style structure erected in 1909. Santurce merges west into Miramar, the most desirable residential address in the city. The nation's premier university, Universidad de Puerto Rico, is located in Hato Rey district, southwest to Santurce, and hosts Museo História Antropología y Arte, displaying Puerto Rico's foremost collection of pre-Columbian exhibits. Nearby, **Fundación Luis Muñoz Marin** honors the legendary politician considered "father" of modern Puerto Rico.

Bacardi Rum Distillery

Carretera 888 Km2.6, Cataño. **Tel** 787 788 8400. **Open** 9am–6pm Mon–Sat, 10am–5pm Sun. compulsory. **casabacardi.org**

Luis A Ferré Science Park: Carretera 167, Plaza del Sol Bayamón. **Tel** 787 740 6868. **Open** 9am–4pm Wed–Fri, 10am–6pm Sat–Sun.

Spanning 127 acres (51 ha) of landscaped grounds, the world's largest rum distillery, Bacardi, produces more than 100,000 gallons (378,540 liters) daily. Visitors are given a tour that traces the history of the company and of rum manufacture. Guests are offered a free tasting in the bar and can visit the nearby **Luis A Ferré Science Park**, which has an excellent zoo. The park is also home to a planetarium and an aerospace museum.

The world-famous Bacardi Rum Distillery

View of Arecibo Observatory, the world's largest radio telescope

❷ Dorado

15 miles (24 km) W of San Juan.
⛰ 35,000. 🚃

Named for the golden sands stretching along the palm-shaded Atlantic shore, Dorado provides a gateway to the beaches for San Juan families and deluxe hotels command the best beachside turf. It became a fashionable sunspot in the 1950s, with the Dorado Beach Hotel attracting celebrities such as the Kennedys. The best public beaches include Cerro Gordo and Playa Sardinera. The town has a main square, Plaza de Recreo, and local history exhibits can be seen at **Museo La Casa del Rey**, built as a parador in 1823 and later a Spanish garrison.

Environs
West of Dorado, **Guajataca Forest Reserve** protects a vast tropical forest. Nearby is the Lago Guajataca which has picnic and fishing facilities.

🏛 **Museo La Casa del Rey**
Calle Méndez Vigo 292. **Tel** 787 796 1030. **Open** 8am–4:30pm Mon–Fri. 🚿

❸ Arecibo Observatory

55 miles (88 km) W of San Juan.
Tel 787 878 2612. 🚃 **Open** 9am–4pm daily. 🚿 🌐 **naic.edu**

The world's largest single-dish radio telescope is a bowl suspended between towering *mogotes* in the Gaurionex Mountains. It opened in 1963 under the Department of Defense to study the upper atmosphere and outer space using radio frequency transmission. Officially known as the National Astronomy and Ionosphere Center, and operated by Cornell University and National Science Foundation, it is the headquarters of the Search for Extraterrestrial Intelligence. The observatory's Angel Ramos Foundation Visitor Center has excellent informational exhibits.

❹ Parque Las Cavernas del Río Camuy

57 miles (92 km) SW of San Juan. **Tel** 787 898 3100. 🚃 **Open** 8:30am–5pm Wed–Sun. 🚿 🍴 🚿 ⛰ for a fee.
🌐 **parquesnacionalespr.com**

Puerto Rico's largest cave system is also the world's third largest, with more than 220 caverns, of which only 16 can be visited on guided tours. These begin with a steep downhill trolley ride to the Cueva Clara de Enpalma, followed by an hour-long walk on concrete pathways that snake through the cool cavern, which soars 170-ft (52-m) high. Key dripstone formations are spot-lit. Bats flit about overhead and a blind endemic fish species swims in the black underground river. This is followed by a ride in the tram to Tres Pueblos Sinkhole, plunging 400 ft (122 m). In its depths, an underground river can be seen emerging from a cavern and entering another.

❺ Parque Ceremonial Indígena Caguana

65 miles (105 km) W of San Juan. **Tel** 787 894 7325. 🚃 **Open** 9am–4:30pm daily. 🚿 ♿ Note: trails can be muddy during the rains.

Surrounded by lush montane forests, Parque Ceremonial Indígena Caguana provides an excellent overview of ancient Taíno culture. The archaeological site – excavated in 1915 – was once used for ceremonial and recreational purposes. It features 10 ceremonial *bateyes* (ball courts) surrounded by monolithic granite slabs that are etched with petroglyphs of human figures, most notably the Mujer de Caguana, a fertility figure showing a woman in childbirth. A small museum displays ancient artifacts, and a gift shop sells *zemis* (worshipped figures).

Stalactites in the spectacular caves of Cavernas del Río Camuy

❻ Playa Jobos

82 miles (132 km) W of San Juan.

Surfers ride the Atlantic breakers that wash ashore at this long beach which shines like silver lamé. The sands here have been pushed into dunes by the winds. Beach bars, restaurants, and hotels line twin beaches separated by a craggy headland of ironshore (limestone-coral formation). El Pozo de Jacinto (Jacinto's Well) is a small natural blowhole that attracts many visitors.

Environs
Punta Borinquen, southwest of Playa Jobos, has some spectacular beaches, including Playa Crash Boat, which offers great diving just offshore, and is popular with surfers. The point served as a former US air force base. Visitors can enjoy a round on the old Base Ramey golf course. Columbus first set foot on the island near the town of Aguadilla, where the Caribbean's largest aquatic theme park, **Parque Acuático Las Cascadas,** is located.

Parque Acuático Las Cascadas
Carretera 126 Km2, Aguadilla.
Tel 787 819 0950. **Open** Mar–Sep, May–Jul 10am–5pm.

❼ Rincón

Carretera 115, 88 miles (140 km) W of San Juan. 17,000. Aguadilla Airport, 5 miles (8 km). Whale Festival (Mar).

Considered the premier surfing spot in Puerto Rico, this beach resort midway down the west side of the island combines rugged beauty, a laid-back social scene, and a lively nightlife. A network of roads link several beaches and rustic communities, including Rincón, spread across the pointy Punta Higuero peninsula. Tide-pooling here is fun, while snorkeling is great in the

Breakfast on the beach at the Horned Dorset Primavera

protection of the scattered reefs, and open waters offer superb diving. Winds whip up waves that can reach as high as 40 ft (12 m), drawing surfing aficionados in search of the ultimate ride. Sunsets are a blaze of sensational color and humpback whales are often sighted from shore as they migrate through the Mona Passage during winter.

Ocean Front Restaurant, Playa Jobos

Environs
Rincón faces the Mona Passage, studded by **Isla Mona,** a rocky, uninhabited outcrop populated by bird species, iguanas, and marine turtles. This wildlife refuge requires a permit from Departamento de Recursos Naturales (see p212) to visit. **Moca,** inland of Rincón, produces *mundillo* (lace) and hosts the Mundillo Festival each June.

❽ Horned Dorset Primavera

Carretera 429 Km3, Rincon.
Tel 787 823 4030.
open to public 7–9:30pm.
W horneddorset.com

Named after a breed of English sheep, the Horned Dorset Primavera is a Spanish hacienda-style hotel which sits right atop its own tiny beach, where kayaks are available for free use. A splendid experience awaits the visitors who choose to stay here. The restaurant (see p214) is acclaimed for its gourmet cuisine and draws diners from as far afield as San Juan. There is also a good bar. The hotel's spacious suites are decorated in a regal fashion with gorgeous plantation antiques. A dress code is applicable in the evenings. Horned Dorset Primavera welcomes children and is a pet-friendly establishment.

Karst Country
Karst topography is remarkable for its dramatic limestone landscapes studded with sinkholes, caverns, canyons, and isolated cone-shaped hillocks known as *mogotes*. The features are remnants of a limestone plateau that rose from the sea about 160 million years ago, after which underground rivers and rain gradually dissolved the limestone, to form caverns that finally collapsed, leaving freestanding hummocks.

Impressive topography, northern Puerto Rico's karst region

❾ Mayagüez

100 miles (150 km) SW of San Juan.
🏛 105,000. ✈ 🚢 Carnival (May);
Festival de la Cocolia (Jul).

Puerto Rico's third largest city, Mayagüez, was founded in 1760. But it shows little sign of its early past following a series of devastating fires. Nonetheless, its spacious main square – Plaza Colón – is adorned with fine buildings,

View of the Plaza Colón and the façade of the Town Hall, Mayagüez

most notably the Neo-Classical Town Hall and behind it, the Teatro Yagüez. Also notable are the square's 16 bronze statues, and that of Christopher Columbus. Locals gather here to play dominoes beneath jacaranda trees.

Children love to visit the nation's main zoo, **Parque Zoológico Dr. Juan A. Rivero**, which has an excellent collection of animals from around the world, including gorillas, elephants, lions, and Bengal tigers.

Mayagüez is home to an important tuna-processing industry and is also a departure point for sportfishing.

🦁 **Parque Zoológico Dr. Juan A. Rivero**
Carretera 108, Barrio Miradero.
Tel 787 834 8110. **Open** 8:30am–5pm Wed–Sun (also Tue in summer). 🦽 ▢ 🏠

A clapboard house, Boquerón

❿ Boquerón

15 miles (24 km) S of Mayagüez.

Locals flock to this slightly rough-around-the-edges beach town, with a lovely beach hidden behind old clapboard houses and a string of restaurants and bars. A special treat is to buy freshly caught oysters from street stands. Bosque Estatal de Boquerón protects a dry tropical and mangrove forest and offers tremendous birding, as does nearby **Refugio de Aves de Boquerón**, which has

---

⓬ La Ruta Panorámica

The panoramic route, officially known as La Ruta Panorámica, runs along the island's mountainous backbone from Yabucoa to Mayagüez. About 40 separate highways make up the clearly-marked, well-paved route. It passes Cerro de Punta, the island's highest peak, as well as a variety of dense montane forests. The route is best traversed with at least an overnight stay at a parador.

0 kilometer   15
0 miles   15

PUERTO RICO

Caribbean Sea

Locator Map
☐ *Area Illustrated*

Anasco — Lares — Las Marias — Utado
Mayagues ✈ — 105 ❾ — Adjun
Hormigueros — La Ruta Panorámica
San German — 2
Yauco

⑧ Cerro de Punta
A thread-thin spur road switchbacks to the summit of Puerto Rico's highest peak, at 4,390 ft (1,338 m).

⑦ Jayuya
In the center of Puerto Rico lies this town with its Museo El Cemi, a fine museum of indigenous culture. It is designed like a giant *cemi*, an earthly representation of Taíno divinities.

⑨ Maricao
This town is a center of coffee production. From here, the road descends to Mayagüez.

blinds for close-up viewing of various waterfowl and manatees.

Environs
South of town lies the **Cabo Rojo Peninsula**, where a semi-derelict lighthouse pins a dramatic headland named for its red-hued rocks. Nearby, simple accommodations at **Playa El Combate** cater to island families who gather to sun, flirt, and party on this narrow beach. An hour's drive east of Boquerón, the south coast community of **La Parguera** is one of Puerto Rico's liveliest coastal resorts. The mangrove-fringed bay is despoiled by buzzing Jet Skis and excessive construction, including wharfs touting boat trips to Isla Magueyes and **Phosphorescent Bay**.

Refugio de Aves de Boquerón
Carretera 301 Km 5.1. **Tel** 787 851 4795. **Open** 7:30am–4pm daily.

⓫ San Germán

30 miles (48 km)
SE of Mayagüez. 38,000.
Fiesta Patronal (Jul 31).

This quaint hillside town was founded in 1573 and is home to the most intact colonial core outside San Juan Viejo. Colorful reminders of the wealth generated by the 19th-century coffee boom adorn its leafy plazas: 249 buildings are listed on the National Register of Historic Places. The Iglesia Porta Coeli, dating from 1606, exhibits religious statuary and *santos* in the Museo de Arte Religioso. The church stands over Plaza Santo Domingo, which is note-worthy for the 19th-century gingerbread Casa Morales. A short walk west leads to the Plaza Francisco Mariano Quiñones, graced by the Neo-Classical Iglesia de San Germán de Auxerre, which was rebuilt in 1737 after an earthquake.

Historic buildings in the center of San Germán

① **Carite Forest Reserve**
Sierra palms and bamboo are among the lush flora lining the road here.

② **Aibonito**
The island's highest town enjoys a scenic mountain setting and spring-like climate year-round.

Tips for Drivers

Starting point: Yabucoa.
Length: 166 miles (266 km).
Stop-off points: Roadside lechonerías at Guavate, for roast pork on the spit. For lodging: Hacienda Gripiñas.

③ **Barranquitas**
The town has a pretty church and former homes of father-son politicians Luis Muñoz Rivera and Luis Muñoz Marin (exterior detail of their house above).

④ **Orocovis**
This town is known for producing *santos* figurines.

⑥ **Hacienda Gripiñas**
This historic parador is a perfect place to rest your head (*see p214*).

⑤ **Toro Negro Forest Reserve**
Sodden with rains, this 11 sq mile (28 sq km) reserve has spectacular waterfalls.

Key

▬▬ Driving route
═══ Other road

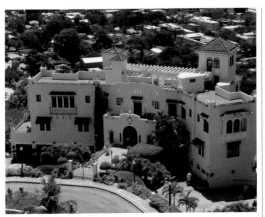
Impressive façade of the Castillo Serallés, Ponce

⓭ Ponce

78 miles (125 km) S of San Juan.
🚏 187,000. ✈ 🚌 🚢 ℹ Plaza las
Delicias, 787 841 8044. 🎭 Carnival
(Jan). 🌐 **visitponce.com**

Founded in 1692, Ponce still
remains an important port
city and abounds in cultural
institutions reflecting its
historical preeminence as a
center for artists and political
thinkers. Architecturally distinct
from San Juan, its downtown
area reminds many visitors of
New Orleans, notably so during
its renowned Carnival, when
dancers parade through the
streets in extravagant *vejigante*
(horned) masks. The city was a
major slave-trading port during
the early colonial days and
African heritage is firmly rooted
in local culture.

The city witnessed a steady
decline in the 20th century.
Fortunately, the "Ponce en
marcha" restoration project
was initiated in the mid-1980s,
and most of the city's notable
historic buildings are once
again gleaming. Tourist trolleys
have made exploring the
colonial center convenient.

At the heart of Ponce, the
spacious Plaza Las Delicias
goes by various other names
including Plaza Central. It
actually comprises two squares
– Plaza Luis Muñoz Rivera and
Plaza Federico Degetau, to the
north and south, respectively, of
the Catedral Nuestra Señora de
la Guadalupe and the famous,

black-and-red striped **Parque
de Bombas**. This whimsical fire
station has an antique fire truck
and vintage cars on display. The
twin squares have several statues,
and the Lion's Fountain, bought
at the 1939 World's Fair in New
York, which looks splendid when
floodlit at night. The buildings
around the square are a medley
of architectural styles spanning
three centuries and ranging
from Spanish colonial to Neo-
Classical and Art Deco. The most
commanding building is the
Neo-Classical Teatro La Perla,
which has served as a performing
arts center since 1941. The surrounding streets, notably Calle
Cristina, are graced by pretty
homes fronted by wrought-iron
grills. Adjoining the theater, the
Museo de la Historia de Ponce
is the nation's foremost history

Vintage car displayed at Parque de Bombas
fire station, Ponce

museum. One block east, Casa
Serallés is an exemplar of Art
Nouveau styling. Today it
houses the **Museo de la Música
Puertorriqueña**, which traces the
evolution of music on the island.

Towards the north, the city
is flanked by Loma Vigía
(Watchman's Hill), which is
dominated by La Cruceta de
Vigía, a huge cement cross
consisting of a hollow tower
with a horizontal sky bridge.
At its base, **Castillo Serallés**, a
Spanish Revival mansion built in
1926 for the rum magnate Don
Juan Serallés, is furnished with
a few splendid colonial pieces
and also serves as a Museum
of Sugar & Rum. The gardens
in its complex are exquisite.
The **Museo de Arte de Ponce**,
a Modernist structure designed
by Edward Durrell Stone, has
works of artists such as
Gainsborough, Diego Rivera,
and Delacroix, as well as some
avant-garde Puerto Rican artists.

Parque de Bombas
Plaza Las Delicias. **Tel** 787 284 3338.
Open 9am–5:30pm Wed–Mon.

🏛 **Museo de la Historia de Ponce**
Calle Isabel 53. **Tel** 787 844 7071.
Open 8am–4pm Tue–Sun. 🈵 ♿

🏛 **Museo de la Música
Puertorriqueña**
Calle Isabel 45. **Tel** 787 848 7016.
Open 8:30am–4:30pm Tue–Sun. ♿

Castillo Serallés
Cruzeta El Vigía 17. **Tel** 787 259 1774.
Open 9:30am–6:30pm Tue–Sun. 🈵
🚋 Note: free tram from Plaza Las
Delicias. 🌐 castilloserralles.org

🏛 **Museo de Arte de Ponce**
Av. Las Américas 2325. **Tel** 787 840
1510. **Open** 10am–6pm Wed–Mon.
Closed pub hols. 🈵 🏛
🌐 museoarteponce.org

⓮ Centro Ceremonial Indígena de Tibes

2 miles (3 km) N of Ponce. **Tel** 787 840
2255. **Open** 8am–4:30pm Tue–Sun.
🈵 📷 obligatory. ♿ 🖥 🏛

Discovered after Hurricane
Eloise in 1975, Centro
Ceremonial Indígena de Tibes
is a pre-Columbian site which
is still being excavated. Today,

it covers 5 acres (2 ha), and includes nine *bateyes (see p202)* plus burial grounds, all hemmed by granite boulders etched with petroglyphs. The site is unusual as it displays signs of two cultures: the Igneris, who settled on the island around AD 300, and the Taíno, who overran the Igneris around AD 1000. A small museum displays remarkable exhibits including pottery, axe-heads, and *cemi (see p204)* excavated at this site, along with an adult skeleton curled up in a fetal position. A reconstruction of a traditional Taíno village helps educate visitors on the lifestyle of the indigenous people. Visits are by guided tour only and it is advisable to make reservations in advance.

Souvenir mask

⑮ Hacienda Buena Vista

7 miles (11 km) N of Ponce. **Tel** 787 722 5882. **Open** two-hour guided tours Fri–Sun at 8:30am, 10:30am, 1:30pm (English only) and 3:30pm; reservations required.

Deep in the mountains north of Ponce, this beautiful plantation can be traced to 1833. Although a primary producer of coffee, it also grew rice and maize. Original mill machinery shows how the maize was

The great house of the plantation Hacienda Buena Vista

milled and the still working water-turbine can be seen alongside other hacienda memorabilia, the elegant two-story great house, warehouses, and slave quarters. It is administered by the Conservation Trust of Puerto Rico, which has resurrected the farm as a working coffee estate. The place is also used for educational purposes.

⑯ Copamarina Beach Resort

20 miles (32 km) SW of Ponce. **Tel** 787 821 0505. **w** copamarina.com

This lovely low-rise hotel opens onto palm-shaded lawns fringing a coral-colored beach with Bali beds for shaded lounging. All guest rooms and suites have an ocean view. The resort has plenty of options for watersports, such as parasailing and scuba diving, and other activities including tennis. A spa offers massages and beauty treatments, and day visitors can also use the airy restaurant *(see p217)* and bar.

Environs

North of Copamarina Beach Resort is a great base for hikes in **Bosque Estatal de Guánica**, a dry forest reserve studded with cactus. Visitors on a day trip from Guánica can also enjoy picnicking on **Gilligan's Island**, a small cay fringed with talcum sands and turquoise waters, while divers will thrill to the exceptional coral formations along **The Wall** *(see p211)*, which is the island's foremost dive site stretching for 20 miles (32 km) parallel to the south coast.

Sprawling gardens and sandy beach, Copamarina Beach Resort

Cyclist on the Paseo Piñones Recreational Trail

⓱ Playa Piñones

🚗 19 miles (30 km) E of San Juan.
👫 🏊

This golden beach located on
Carretera 187 is favored by the
locals on weekends, when
families set up picnics beneath
the palms. Weekend traffic jams
the roads, so it is ideal to visit
the beach on weekdays.
Roadside restaurants sell fried
seafoods. **Paseo Piñones
Recreational Trail** runs along
the shore, providing a scenic
thoroughfare for cyclists,
joggers, and strollers.

Environs
The beach extends east to **Playa
Vacia Talega**, known for its
"cemented" sand dunes. **Bosque
Estatal Piñones**, inland of the
beaches, protects a prize
wetland habitat for waterfowl
and wading birds. Occupying
the coastal flatlands east of
Playa Vacia Talega, the small,
relatively impoverished town
of **Loíza Aldea** is a center for
African culture. Every year in late
July it plays host to the week-
long Fiesta de Santo Apóstol,
Puerto Rico's premier carnival.

⓲ Luquillo

🚗 45 miles (72 km) E of San Juan.
👫 🏖 🏊 ⛱

A string of golden-white
beaches decorates the northeast shore between the towns
of Río Grande and Luquillo.
The beauty is enhanced by the
brooding Sierra Luquillo in the
backdrop. The sands meld into
warm, reef-protected waters

of peacock blues
and greens.
Snorkeling and
tide-pooling is
great in these
shallows. Playa
Luquillo is lined
by a number of
upscale resorts.
To the west, Playa
Río Mar is a rela-
tively uncrowded
setting for the
mammoth Río Mar
Beach Resort & Spa
(see p215) and Rio Mar Country
Club. East of Playa Luquillo are
the wind-whipped Playa Azul
and Playa La Selva, where
breakers bring surfers ashore.

⓳ El Yunque National Forest

25 miles (40 km) SE of San Juan.
Tel 787 888 1880. **Open** 7:30am–6pm
daily. 🚗 for El Portal Visitor Center
only. 🕐 hourly 9am–5pm Sat–Mon.
♿ El Portal Visitor Center & some
trails. 📷 🌐 **fs.usda.gov/elyunque**

The 44 sq-mile (114 sq-km)
El Yunque National Forest, formerly the Caribbean National
Forest, is the only tropical
rainforest within the US National
Park system. Ranging from an
elevation of 30 ft (9 m) at its
base to 3,533 ft (1,077 m) at
the top of Cerro El Toro, the

rain-sodden park – named
for a flat-topped mountain,
"the anvil" – features various
ecosystems, including high
mountain cloud forest and
dwarf forest atop the highest
slopes. El Portal Rain Forest
Center, the main visitors' center,
offers splendid exhibits on
local geology, geography,
and ecosystems. The park
has a number of hiking trails
(see p213) from easy to
strenuous amidst plunging
waterfalls and steep ravines.
This region offers hikers some
of the best birding and wildlife
viewing on the island.

⓴ Fajardo

36 miles (58 km) SE of San Juan.
🏔 40,000. 🛥 🚢
🎉 Fiesta Patronal (Jul).

The sprawling coastal town
of Fajardo is a major maritime
center for sportfishing and
sailing charters, available at
Marina Puerto Real and Puerto
del Rey Marina. Scheduled
ferries also depart here for
Vieques and Culebra.

Environs
The 316-acre (128-ha) **Las
Cabezas de San Juan Nature
Reserve**, immediately north of
Fajardo, protects a mangrove
forest where manatees paddle

Hikers on one of the trails in El Yunque National Forest

Municipal building in Isabel Segunda, Vieques

about in freshwater lagoons and dozens of waterfowl can be seen on the boardwalk trail. The El Faro lighthouse, built in 1882, is beautifully preserved. Nearby **Playa Seven Seas** offers good snorkeling in reef-protected shallows.

Las Cabezas de San Juan Nature Reserve

Carretera 987. **Tel** 787 722 5882.
included in entrance fee; 8:30am, 9:30am, 10am, 10:30am and 2pm Wed–Sun (in English). Note: reservation required.

㉑ El Conquistador Resort

1000 Conquistador Av., Fajardo. **Tel** 787 863 1000.
w elconresort.com

Puerto Rico's largest resort enjoys a sensational hilltop position overlooking Vieques Sound. The mega-resort includes a championship golf course and a children's water-park, plus a casino, a full-service spa, and more than 20 restaurants *(see p217)*, bars, and lounges. Nine types of rooms and villas offer cosmopolitan contemporary decor and the latest amenities.

The resort has an exclusive lease on Isla Palomìnos, a beautiful cay wrapped in a cottony beach, in the calm waters off Fajardo. Various watersports are on offer to guests who are transported from the resort by funicular to a marina from where there is a boat shuttle.

㉒ Vieques

20 miles (32 km) SE of Fajardo.
9,500. Festival de Cultura (Apr).

Largest of the 24 isles of the Spanish Virgin archipelago surrounding Puerto Rico, Vieques moves at a far more lackadaisical pace than Puerto Rico. Most of the inhabitants live in Isabel Segunda, a little town that remains charmingly old world, with little traffic. During World War II the US Navy began using the isle for gunnery practice – a deterrent to development during the next five decades. The bombardment ceased in 2003, when the navy pulled out. Today, Vieques is a chic spot for tourists seeking off-the-beaten-track charm to see deer, manatee, and four species of marine turtles at Vieques Wildlife Refuge. The isle is fringed by the sugary sands of Playa Sombé, Playa Media Luna, Green Beach, and Blue Beach. Hotels are small-scale and

trendy, and found mostly around Esperanza, a sleepy village overlooking a gorgeous bay. Nearby Phosphorescent Bay literally comes alive at night, when bioluminescent micro-organisms glow when disturbed: a kayak trip lets visitors slip into the waters to spark their own halo. Manatees also frequent the coastal lagoons. In addition, Vieques is a major nesting site for marine turtles. The **Vieques Art and History Museum**, in the 19th-century Fort Conde Mirasol, has exhibits on island history.

Vieques Art and History Museum

Fuerte Conde de Mirasol, Rt. 989, Isabel II. **Tel** 787 741 8850. **Open** 11am–4pm Tue–Sun.

㉓ Culebra

27 miles (43 km) E of Fajardo.
2,000.
Fiesta Patronal (Jul).

Vieques' even more somnolent smaller sister is renowned for its scintillating beaches, including undisputably Puerto Rico's finest, Playa Flamenco, a broad, long scimitar of pure white sand and gorgeous ocean waters drawing day-trippers from Puerto Rico on weekends. Nearby Playa Carlos Rosario has a coral reef within a short distance of the shore, while Playas Resaca, Brava, and Flamenco are protected as marine turtle nesting sites within Culebra National Wildlife Refuge.

Powdery white sands of Playa Flamenco on the island of Culebra

Outdoor Activities and Specialized Holidays

Hiking is a great way to discover Puerto Rico's amazing diversity of terrains and ecosystems, including tropical lowland dry forest, montane rainforest, and mangrove wetlands. There are plenty of opportunities for scuba diving and snorkeling, as well as for surfing and numerous other watersports including sportfishing, windsurfing, parasailing, and kayaking. Cavers are spoilt for choice, and golfers will find some of the Caribbean's best courses here on this island.

Watersport enthusiast on the Ocean Park Beach

Beaches

Visitors don't have to leave San Juan to enjoy Puerto Rico's gorgeous beaches. Playa Condado, Ocean Park, and Isla Verde line the shore of those eponymous districts and offer parasailing and a youthful social scene. On weekends many *sanjuaneros* escape the madding crowd (but add to a traffic melee) and head east to Playa Piñones and Playa Luquillo.

Surfers prefer Playa Jobos and Playa Crashboat, near Aguadillas, in the northwest, although their most preferred destination is Rincón, with its dozen or so wave-washed beaches such as Playa Barrero and Sandy Beach.

The south coast has a relative paucity of nice beaches. Notable exceptions are Playa El Combate and Playa Caña Gorda. The lion's share of white-sand beaches lies off the east shore of mainland Puerto Rico. One such is Isla Palominos, just one hour from Fajardo. The most beautiful beaches are found in the Spanish Virgin Islands. Visitors are spoilt for choice on Vieques where Playa Sombé, Playa Media Luna, Playa Navío, Green Beach, Red Beach, and Blue Beach are prize-winning beaches. Culebra claims Playa Flamenco, by far the most spectacular beach of all.

Birding and Wildlife Viewing

The varied ecosystems of Puerto Rico are habitats for a veritable ark of colorful creatures, including 270 species of birds. Seeing them is easy along trails that wind through various forests. El Yunque National Forest *(see p208)* is acclaimed for sighting the Puerto Rican parrot. Waders and waterfowl are easily seen in Bosque Estatal de Boquerón and Las Cabezas de San Juan Nature Reserve, both with boardwalks and blinds, while the open deciduous woodlands of Bosque Estatal de Guánica make viewing the endemic species such as Puerto Rican whippoorwills, easy.

To view marine turtles laying eggs, head to Vieques Wildlife Refuge and Culebra National Wildlife Refuge. Manatees can also be seen here, and in Reserva Natural Laguna Tortuguero. In winter, head to Rincón for whale-watching trips in the Mona Passage. The El Faro Lighthouse Park has a whale-viewing vantage point, and **Taino Divers** offers excursions. **Adven Tours** also organizes birding trips to various Puerto Rico areas.

Caving

Puerto Rico is riddled with caves, although spelunking is for experienced cavers only and is best done with an organized group. The preeminent cave system is Parque Las Cavernas del Río Camuy. Rappelling and caving in the Angels Sinkhole is offered through **Aventuras Tierra Adentro**.

Surfing

Puerto Rico offers some of the finest surfing in the Caribbean, centered on Rincón, where **Rincón Surf School** offers classes and **El Rincón Surf Shop** rents and sells boards. Other prime surfing sites include Boca de Cangrejos, off San Juan; Playa Jobos and Playa Crashboat, in the northwest; and La Pared, at Luquillo.

Diving

The island is a paradise for divers, with fabulous coral reefs ringing almost three-quarters of the isle.

Enjoy a whale-watching tour

Divers exploring the magnificent underwater world of sponges

The water temperatures range from 70° F (20° C) in winter to mid-80° F (25° C) in the summer. In winter it is best to head to the south shore, as north coast diving is subject to rough seas and full wet suits are a must. The almost 300 species of fish include major pelagics, such as grouper, sharks, and large rays, and marine turtles are also common. The Isla Desecho dive site, off Aguada, has a wreck of a World War II PT boat to explore. The Wall, which parallels the south coast for 20 miles (32 km), is easily accessed from Copamarina Beach Resort *(see p207)* and Guánicà. The waters off Fajardo are placid and good for beginners, as are the fringing reefs off Vieques and Culebra, where wreck sites include a tugboat. **Sea Ventures Dive Centers** has three outlets, in Fajardo, Humacao, and Guánica. In the Spanish Virgin Islands, **Culebra Divers** take visitors to the best diving sites.

Fishing

Puerto Rico offers splendid deep-sea fishing out of San Juan, Mayagüez, and most resort towns, including Fajardo. The north shore is known as Blue Marlin Alley. Sailfish, tuna, and wahoo are other game fish that give a prize fight, while anglers can cast for tarpon and bonefish in inshore waters and flats. Many world records have been set here, and the numerous fishing tournaments are highlighted by the **San Juan International Billfish Tournament** in August/

September. Winter is the best season for gamefishing, although blue marlin are more numerous in summer. Recommended outfitters for fishing include **Puerto Rico Angling**, **Puerto Rico Fishing Charters**, and **Magic Tarpon**. Mountain lakes are good for peacock bass and tilapia. Among the best inland freshwater sites is Lago Guajataca. Visitors need to contact the **Departamento de Recursos Naturales** for information and a license.

Boat Excursions

Few activities induce a sense of romance as the experience of a sunset cruise under sail. Several companies offer day and evening excursions by yacht or by catamaran, with most craft setting sail from Fajardo to the archipelago of tiny cays known as La Cordillera. Most cruises feature stops for snorkeling. Key options include **Erin Go Bragh Charters**, which uses a 50-ft (15-m) cutter, the **Spread Eagle II** catamaran, and **Ventajero Sailing Charters**. **Katarina Sail Excursions** in Rincón offers sunset cruises.

Hiking

With more than a dozen forest reserves, Puerto Rico is a nirvana for

hikers. The diverse habitats provide plenty of contrasts, too, so that on one day visitors can hike the El Yunque *(see p213)* cloud forests while on the next they can follow the coastal trails of Bosque Estatal de Guánica. For more scenic drama, Bosque Estatal de Cambalache and Bosque Estatal de Guajataca have a number of trails that slide between towering *mogotes* *(see p203)*. There are many more mountain reserves to choose from here, while on the island of Vieques, the easy trails of Refugio de Vida Silvestre de Vieques combine spectacular ocean views with the possibility of plentiful animal and bird sightings.

For detailed information on hiking within the individual reserves, visitors have to contact the **Departamento de Recreación y Deportes**. For organized hikes, visitors can also try the company Aventuras Tierra Adentro.

A few precautions need to be taken by visitors before heading for any hike. It is essential to carry plenty of water since none will be available along the route. It is also advisable to use an insect repellent.

Hiking on the Big Tree Trail, El Yunque

Kayaking at the Copamarina Beach Resort, Rincón

Watersports

The beach resorts have all manner of watersports, from windsurfing and parasailing to Jet Skis. Waterskiing is offered where the waters are placid. Large hotels usually offer free use of non-motorized equipment, while commercial concessionaires offering motorized sports have outlets on the most popular beaches. A good option is kayaking, which is available at

Rincón, Copamarina Beach Resort, and Playa Jobos, and at Vieques' Phosphorescent Bay, where **Island Adventures Biobay Eco-tours** will take visitors out at night to swim in the bioluminescent waters. **Kayaking Puerto Rico** arranges guided excursions.

Golf

Few Caribbean islands can outdo Puerto Rico, which has some 20 championship courses designed by renowned architects. Top clubs include the Río Mar Beach Resort & Country Club *(see p215)* and El Conquistador Resort *(see p209)*. At the northwest tip of the island, the **Punta Borinquen Golf Club** occupies the former US Air Force Ramey Base. Visitors can call **Puerto Rico Golf Association** for information about tournaments.

Tennis

Most major resort hotels have their own courts. For those looking for some fun workout on the courts it is best to head to the Río Mar Beach Resort & Country Club, which has 14 courts, or the El Conquistador Resort, with seven courts. **Puerto Rico Tennis Association** provides information on local tennis clubs and facilities.

The well-kept tennis courts at El Conquistador Resort

DIRECTORY

Birding and Wildlife Viewing

Adven Tours
Main Office, 1102 Uroyan, Alturas de Mayagüez.
Tel 787 530 8311.
W adventourspr.com

Taino Divers
Black Eagle Marina, Rincón.
Tel 787 823 6429.
W tainodivers.com

Caving

Aventuras Tierra Adentro
Av. Jesús Piñero 7268A, San Juan.
Tel 787 766 0470.
W aventuraspr.com

Surfing

El Rincón Surf Shop
PO Box 250171, Aguadilla.
Tel 787 890 3108.
W elrinconsurfshop.com

Rincón Surf School
PO Box 1333.
Tel 787 823 0610.
W rinconsurfschool.com

Diving

Culebra Divers
Tel 787 742 0803.
W culebradivers.com

Sea Ventures Dive Centers
Tel 787 863 3483.
W divepuertorico.com

Fishing

Departamento de Recursos Naturales
Tel 787 999 2200.
W drna.gobierno.pr

Magic Tarpon
Tel 787 644 1444.
W magictarpon.com

Puerto Rico Angling
Tel 787 724 2079. W puertoricofishing.com

Puerto Rico Fishing Charters
Tel 787 382 4698.
W puertoricofishing charters.com

San Juan International Billfish Tournament
Club Nautico de San Juan, 482 Fernández Juncos Av., San Juan. **Tel** 787 722 0177. W sanjuaninter national.com

Boat Excursions

Erin Go Bragh Charters
Tel 787 860 4401.
W egbc.net

Katarina Sail Excursions
Tel 787 823 7245.
W sailrinconpuertorico. com

Spread Eagle II
Villa Marina, Fajardo.
Tel 787 887 8821.
W snorkelpr.com

Ventajero Sailing Charters
Marina Puerto del Rey, Ceiba.
Tel 787 863 1871.
W sailpuertorico.com

Hiking

Departamento de Recreación y Deportes
Tel 787 721 2800.
W drd.gobierno.pr

Watersports

Island Adventures Biobay Eco-tours
Road 996, Puerto Real Sector, Vieques.
Tel 787 741 0720.
W biobay.com

Kayaking Puerto Rico
HC-4, Río Grande.
Tel 787 435 1665.
W kayakingpuertorico. com

Golf

Puerto Rico Golf Association
264 Matadero St., Suite 11, San Juan.
Tel 787 793 3444.
W prga.org

Punta Borinquen Golf Club
Golf St., Ramey, Aguadilla.
Tel 787 890 2987.
W puntaborinqu engolf.com

Tennis

Puerto Rico Tennis Association
Tel 787 726 8782.
W caribbean.usta.com

Hiking in Puerto Rico

Puerto Rico's numerous forest reserves and its mountainous terrain provide ample trekking and climbing opportunities. Most visitors who choose to hike in Puerto Rico make El Yunque National Forest *(see p208)* their prime focus. This reserve alone has 23 trails that weave through the varied habitats. The Toro Negro Forest Reserve, Maricao State Forest, and Bosque Estatal de Guánica are among other areas that have several marked trails for hikers. Most are short and uni-directional, but intersect with other trails to make for easy loops. Some trails are strenuous and slippery. Waterproof clothing and footwear are essential.

El Yunque Trails
El Yunque National Forest is the most popular trekking spot in Puerto Rico with 36 miles (60 km) of trails. Among them are the El Yunque Trail, Baño de Oro Trail, Los Picachos Trail, El Toro (Tradewinds) Trail which leads through four different habitats, and the moderately difficult Big Tree Trail, which is one of the best maintained.

La Mina Trail is a moderately difficult 1-hour downhill hike that follows Río Mina and ends at La Mina Falls.

Mount Britton Trail leads to a mountaintop observatory; passing through sierra palms of the rainforest and dwarf cloud forests.

The Puerto Rican parrot is among the 50 species of birds found in the national forest. Apart from birds, a number of lizards and crabs can also be spotted.

Trails in other Reserves

Puerto Rico has 14 forest reserves besides El Yunque. Some of the best ones for hiking are the arid Bosque Estatal de Guánica, the Toro Negro Forest Reserve, and the Bosque Estatal de Maricao.

Bosque Estatal de Maricao is located near Maricao on La Ruta Panorámica *(see pp204–5)*. Trails pass through beautiful cloud forests, plantations, and up large hills.

Bosque Estatal de Guánica is home to the endangered bufo lemur toad, birds, and 700 plant species. The dry forest has marked trails.

Toro Negro Forest Reserve, along La Ruta Panorámica, has five trails. One leads to an observation tower that provides great views. Lago El Guineo, Lago de Matrullas, and the headwaters of several main rivers are located in the park.

Where to Stay

CEIBA: Ceiba Country Inn $
B&B
Route 977 Km1.2
Tel *787 885 0471*
W ceibacountryinn.com
Mountainside bed-and-breakfast
good for hikers and birdwatchers.
Bright, comfortable rooms have
splendid ocean views.

CULEBRA: Casa Ensenada
Waterfront Guesthouse $$
Boutique
Calle Escudero 142
Tel *787 241 4441*
W casaensenada.com
Friendly live-in owners attend
to guests at this pet-friendly
waterfront B&B, which has just
three simply yet brightly
furnished units.

CULEBRA: Club Seabourne $$
Resort
Fulladoza Bay
Tel *787 742 3169*
W clubseabourne.com
Peaceful hillside hotel set in
lush gardens. Rooms, cottages,
and villas have colonial-style
reproduction furnishings. Library-
lounge, sundeck, and kayaks.

FAJARDO: El Conquistador
Resort $$
Beach Resort
1000 Conquistador Avenue, Fajardo
Tel *787 863 1000*
W elconresort.com
Puerto Rico's largest resort enjoys
a sensational hilltop position, a
championship golf course, a
children's waterpark, and more
than 20 excellent restaurants.

GUANICA: Copamarina
Beach Resort $$
Beach Resort
20 miles (32 km) SW of Ponce
Tel *787 821 0505*
W copamarina.com
Lovely low-rise hotel set amid
palm-shaded lawns. Elegantly
furnished rooms with ocean
views. Watersports include
parasailing and scuba diving.

JAYUYA: Hacienda
Gripiñas $$
Historic
Route 527 Km2.5
Tel *787 828 1718*
W haciendagripinas.tripod.com
Old-world charm pervades this
19th-century coffee estate in
the mountains. Simply furnished
rooms. A good base for hikers.

PATILLAS: Caribe Playa
Sea Beach Resort $
Beach Resort
Route 3 Km112.1
Tel *787 839 6339*
W caribeplaya.com
This 1960s-era resort has a
lovely palm-shaded setting and
studio rooms, some have air-
conditioning and king-sized
beds. Cozy restaurant.

PONCE: Hotel Bélgica $
Historic
122 Calle Villa
Tel *787 844 3255*
W hotelbelgica.com
In the historic town center,
this 19th-century Neo-Classical
style hotel has simple but
tastefully furnished rooms.
Breakfast only.

> **Price Guide**
> Prices are based on one night's stay in
> high season for a standard double room,
> inclusive of service charges and taxes.
>
> | | |
> |---|---|
> | $ | up to $100 |
> | $$ | $100–300 |
> | $$$ | over $300 |

PONCE: Hilton Ponce Golf
and Casino Resort $$
Modern
1150 Av. Caribe
Tel *787 259 7676*
W hiltoncaribbean.com
Massive resort on a gray-sand
beach. Guest rooms have ocean
views and crisp contemporary
decor. Facilities include tennis,
a casino, and a spa.

PONCE: Hotel Meliá $$
Historic
Plaza Degetau y Calle Cristina
Tel *787 842 0260*
W hotelmeliapr.com
Family-run 19th-century Art Deco
hotel. Clean rooms with period
details. Lovely wood-paneled
lounge and a rooftop terrace.

RINCÓN: Lazy Parrot $
Beach Resort
Route 413 Km4.1
Tel *787 823 5654*
W lazyparrot.com
Basic hillside hotel offering good
value, with functional and cozy
rooms. Alfresco restaurant.

RINCÓN: Rincón Beach Resort $$
Beach Resort
Route 115 Km5.8, Añasco
Tel *787 589 9000*
W rinconbeach.com
Refurbished Spanish colonial
hotel boasting a chic, modern
style. The two-bedroom villas are
a good option for families. Infinity
pool and flat-screen TVs.

> **DK Choice**
>
> **RINCÓN: Horned Dorset**
> **Primavera** $$$
> Boutique
> *Carretera 429 Km3*
> **Tel** *787 823 4030*
> W horneddorset.com
> Named for a breed of
> English sheep, the Horned
> Dorset Primavera is a Spanish
> hacienda-style boutique hotel
> that sits atop its own tiny
> beach. The spacious and regal
> suites are decorated with
> gorgeous plantation antiques
> and the gourmet restaurant is
> acclaimed. A dress code is
> applicable in the evenings.

The exterior of the Horned Dorset Primavera, Rincón

The historic facade of El Convento, San Juan

RIO BLANCO:
Casa Cubuy Ecolodge　　$$
Ecolodge
Río Blanco
Tel *787 874 6221*
Ⓦ casacubuy.com
This is a simple mountain lodge adjoining the Caribbean National Forest, with its own trails. Spacious, sparsely furnished rooms. Breakfast only.

RIO GRANDE: Gran Meliá
Puerto Rico Golf Resort　　$$
Luxury
200 Coco Beach Blvd., Highway 955-I
Tel *787 809 1770*
Ⓦ melia.com
A sophisticated all-suite resort with a golf course, a huge lagoon-style pool, and whirlpool tubs. Rooms are located in two-level bungalows.

RIO GRANDE: Río Mar Beach
Resort & Spa　　$$
Beach Resort
6000 Río Mar Boulevard
Tel *787 888 6000*
Ⓦ wyndhamriomar.com
This huge beachfront golf resort is sprawled across a former coconut plantation and has 11 restaurants. The bright rooms all have wonderful views.

RIO GRANDE: The St. Regis
Bahia Beach Resort　　$$$
Luxury
Route 187 Km4.2
Tel *787 809 8000*
Ⓦ starwoodhotels.com
Ultra-deluxe beach resort with lavishly appointed rooms featuring high-tech amenities. Championship golf course.

SAN JUAN: Hotel Milano　　$
Boutique
307 Fortaleza Street
Tel *787 729 9050*
Ⓦ hotelmilanopr.com
Located in the heart of Old San Juan, this renovated 19th-century warehouse features modern decor in its spacious rooms. Enjoy lovely views of the water from the top-floor restaurant. Good breakfast.

SAN JUAN: Acacia
Boutique Hotel　　$$
Boutique
Taft Street 8, Condado
Tel *877 725 0668*
Ⓦ acaciaboutiquehotel.com
This lovingly restored 1920s Spanish mansion houses romantic guest rooms with terra-cotta floors, as well as a chic bar and restaurant. No pool, but has a huge Jacuzzi.

SAN JUAN:
At Wind Chimes Inn　　$$
Boutique
1750 McLeary Avenue, Condado
Tel *787 727 4153*
Ⓦ atwindchimesinn.com
A lovely guesthouse in a restored Spanish manor, At Wind Chimes has beautiful rooms with high ceilings. Great outdoor pool. Gay friendly.

SAN JUAN: Canario
Boutique Hotel　　$$
B&B
Ashord Avenue 1317
Tel *787 722 3861*
Ⓦ canarioboutiquehotel.com
Homey bed-and-breakfast with contemporary furnishings plus rattan pieces on creaky wooden floors. Well located, one block from the beach.

SAN JUAN: Caribe Hilton　　$$
Beach Resort
Calle Los Rosales, Condado
Tel *787 721 0303*
Ⓦ hiltoncaribbean.com
Set on its own private beach, this mammoth 1950s hotel has accommodations ranging from studio rooms to deluxe villas, all well decorated and with state-of-the-art amenities.

SAN JUAN: CasaBlanca Hotel　$$
Boutique
Calle Fortaleza 316
Tel *787 725 3436*
Ⓦ hotelcasablancapr.com
Exuding a lovely North African vibe, this art-filled boutique hotel is steps away from great restaurants. Rooftop lounge.

SAN JUAN: Cervantes　　$$
Boutique
Calle Recinto Sur 329, Old San Juan
Tel *787 724 7722*
Ⓦ cervantespr.com
Occupying a converted three-story townhouse, this art-filled boutique hotel oozes good taste and comfort. Continental breakfast and free Wi-Fi.

SAN JUAN: Conrad Condado
Plaza Hotel and Casino　　$$
Beach Resort
999 Ashford Avenue, Condado
Tel *787 721 1000*
Ⓦ condadoplaza.com
Trendy high-rise hotel decorated in minimalist style, with its own beach and tennis courts. There is a 24-hour casino on site.

SAN JUAN: Da House Hotel　$$
Boutique
312 San Francisco Street
Tel *787 977 1180*
Ⓦ dahousehotel.com
In a converted townhouse above a famed nightclub, this artsy boutique hotel mixes elegant yesteryear and modern decor.

SAN JUAN: El Canario by
the Lagoon　　$$
Beach
Clemenceau Street 4, Condado
Tel *787 722 5058*
Ⓦ canariohotels.com/lagoon.htm
Clean, no-frills city hotel in a five-story structure two blocks from the beach. Perfect for budget travelers.

SAN JUAN: El Convento　　$$
Boutique
Calle del Cristo 100
Tel *787 723 9020*
Ⓦ elconvento.com
This charming hotel was once a convent, built in 1651. Rooms are equipped with period furnishings, and there is a great restaurant and a tapas bar.

SAN JUAN: Gallery Inn　　$$
Boutique
204 Calle Norzagaray
Tel *787 722 1808*
Ⓦ thegalleryinn.com
Delightful, quirky townhouse run by eccentric live-in owners. Perfect place to socialize with other travelers.

Large pool with lovely sea views at the Hacienda Tamarindo, Vieques

SAN JUAN: La Terraza $$
Boutique
Calle del Sol 262
Tel *787 722 2014*
W laterrazahotelsanjuan.com
An intimate option for urban sophisticates, with individually styled rooms. Breakfasts and evening tapas.

SAN JUAN: Numero Uno Guest House $$
Beach Resort
Calle Santa Ana 1, Ocean Park
Tel *787 726 5010*
W numero1guesthouse.com
Numero Uno is a two-story pet-friendly spot overlooking the beach. It has a plunge pool, a bar, and a good restaurant.

SAN JUAN: Renaissance La Concha Resort $$
Luxury
Ashford Avenue 1077
Tel *787 721 7500*
W laconcharesort.com
This hotel's stunning architecture and furnishings appeal to trendy young people. Also has a casino and lively lounge bar.

SAN JUAN: Verdanza $$
Luxury
Tartak Street 8020, Isla Verde
Tel *800 625 0312*
W verdanzahotel.com
Sophisticated and stylish hotel with an unassuming exterior, dramatic spiral staircase, and exquisitely appointed rooms. The pool includes a spray park.

SAN JUAN: El San Juan Hotel and Casino $$$
Luxury
6063 Isla Verde
Tel *787 791 1000*
W elsanjuanhotel.com
Signature beachfront hotel, with an opulent lobby, three swimming pools, a casino, a spa, and nine restaurants. Rooms have a lily-white modern styling.

SAN JUAN: Intercontinental San Juan Resort $$$
Luxury
Isla Verde Avenue 5961, Isla Verde
Tel *787 791 6100*
W icsanjuanresort.com
Retro decor is the highlight of this deluxe hotel. There are also gourmet restaurants and 24-hour room service. Spa and casino.

SAN JUAN: Olive Boutique Hotel $$$
Boutique
Aguadilla Street 55, Condado
Tel *787 705 9994*
W oliveboutiquehotel.com
The beautiful one-of-a-kind decor in this chic hotel includes sleigh beds and glass-walled en-suite showers. Good rooftop lounge bar.

SAN JUAN: Ritz-Carlton, San Juan Hotel, Spa & Casino $$$
Luxury
6961 Av. Los Gobernadores, Isla Verde
Tel *787 253 1700*
W ritzcarlton.com
San Juan's premier hotel, the Ritz-Carlton offers sumptuous accommodations with every facility imaginable. Has an impressive casino and spa.

SAN JUAN: The Water Beach Club Hotel $$$
Boutique
2 Tartak Street, Isla Verde
Tel *787 728 3666*
W waterbeachhotel.com
Trendy, luxurious boutique hotel with minimalist ambience. Walls of glass offer spectacular ocean views. Choose from two gourmet restaurants and a hip bar.

The casual bar area at the Casa Grande Mountain Retreat, Utuado

UTUADO: Casa Grande Mountain Retreat $$
Ecolodge
Route 612
Tel *787 894 3939*
W hotelcasagrande.com
On a former coffee plantation surrounded by forest. The simply furnished wooden cabins rise over a lush garden.

VIEQUES: Bananas Guesthouse $
Beach Resort
Calle Flamboyan 142, Esperanza
Tel *787 741 8700*
W bananasguesthouse.com
Unpretentious option with small, spartan rooms that have ceiling fans and louvered windows. Popular open-air restaurant.

VIEQUES: Bravo Beach Hotel $
Boutique
North Shore Road 1
Tel *787 741 1128*
W bravobeachhotel.com
Gleaming white rooms with top-notch linens, iPod docking stations, and private patios or balconies. Two-bedroom villas for families available.

VIEQUES: Blue Horizon Boutique Resort $$
Boutique
Route 996 Km4.2, Esperanza
Tel *787 741 3318*
W bluehorizonboutiqueresort.com
Spectacular hillside setting and ocean vistas. The intimate Mediterranean-themed villas are without phones or TVs.

VIEQUES: Hacienda Tamarindo $$
Beach Resort
Route 996 Km4.5, Esperanza
Tel *787 741 8525*
W haciendatamarindo.com
Lovely Spanish-style, family-run plantation home. The airy and well-lit rooms sport chic Caribbean-style furnishings.

VIEQUES: Hix Island House $$$
Boutique
Route 995 Km1.6
Tel *787 741 2302*
W hixislandhouse.com
Eco-friendly hotel with dramatic postmodernist architecture. Spacious loft apartments. Yoga and spa treatments available.

VIEQUES: W Retreat and Spa $$$
Luxury
Route 200 Km3.2
Tel *787 741 4100*
W wvieques.com
Beachfront hotel blending modern aesthetics with luxurious Spanish-style villa decor. Deluxe spa.

Where to Eat and Drink

CANA GORDA: Alexandra $$$
International
Carretera 333 Km6.5
Tel *787 821 0505*
Located in the Copamarina
Beach Resort, Alexandra is
known for its seafood, steaks, and
creative comfort dishes, such
as grilled pork chops with
pineapple chutney.

CULEBRA: Homeless Dog Café $
Puerto Rican
Calle Feliciano 26
Tel *939 452 9563* **Closed** *Tue*
Island dishes including roast
pork, plus breaded fish, corn
bread, and slaw are on offer at
this Puerto Rican eatery. Choose
from superb desserts such as
chocolate peanut butter cake.

CULEBRA: Susie's Restaurant $$
Puerto Rican
Sardinas 2, Dewey
Tel *787 340 7058* **Closed** *Mon*
Amid simple surrounds, owner
Susie fuses lobster, mahi mahi,
and other local ingredients for a
thoroughly enjoyable meal.

DORADO: El Ladrillo $$
Surf 'n' Turf
Calle Mendez Vigo 334
Tel *787 796 2120*
Charming brick-lined restaurant
known for its surf 'n' turf,
including prime American
Angus beef and filet mignon.
Fresh seafood includes lobster.

DORADO: Grappa $$
Italian
Calle Mendez Vigo 247
Tel *787 796 2674* **Closed** *Mon & Tue*
Grappa is a small, cozy family-run
affair producing superb risottos
and home-made pastas, breads,
and ice creams.

FAJARDO: Blossoms $$$
Asian
1000 Conquistador Avenue
Tel *787 863 1000*
This menu at this upscale Asian
restaurant in the El Conquistador
Resort has dishes ranging from
Hunan to Szechuan specialties.

FAJARDO: La Piccola Fontana $$$
Italian
1000 Conquistador Avenue
Tel *787 863 1000*
Elegant contemporary restaurant
at the El Conquistador Resort
with a romantic alfresco terrace.
Reservations required.

HUMACAO: Chez Daniel $$$
French
Marina Palmas del Mar, Km86.4
Tel *787 850 3838* **Closed** *Tue*
Casual alfresco waterfront dining.
Dishes on the menu include
bouillabaisse, escargots, onion
soup, and *coq au vin*.

LUQUILLO: Brass Cactus $$
TexMex
*Carretera 3, Complejo Turístico
Condominio*
Tel *787 889 5735*
Appeals to North Americans with
its familiar menu of burgers and
spicy ribs. There is a sports bar
and jukebox, and live bands are
often hosted.

PONCE: Chez Mademoiselle Coco $$
Mediterranean
Calle 6, Barrio Singapur, Juana Diaz
Tel *787 604 9791* **Closed** *Mon–Fri*
This casual oceanfront restaurant
surprises with gourmet French
fare, including frog's legs, *foie
gras*, and *crème brûlée*.

PONCE: La Terraza $$
International
1150 Av. Caribe
Tel *787 259 7676*
Casual atrium restaurant in the
Hilton Ponce Golf and Casino
Resort. Range of international
and local dishes, plus an all-you-
can-eat buffet.

PONCE: La Cava $$$
Nouvelle Continental
1150 Av. Caribe
Tel *787 259 7676* **Closed** *Mon*
Sleek restaurant in the Hilton
Ponce Golf and Casino Resort.

The seasonal menu highlights
nouvelle Continental dishes.
There is also an excellent
wine list.

RINCÓN: La Copa Llena $$
Eclectic
*Black Eagle Marina, Barrio
Ensenada*
Tel *787 823 0896*
Casual, relaxed restaurant
with gorgeous sunset views.
The menu features everything
from Puerto Rican to French
fare, made with fresh, local
ingredients. Try the duck confit.

RINCÓN: Lazy Parrot $$
International
*Carretera 413 Km4.1,
Barrio Puntas*
Tel *787 823 5654*
Hotel-restaurant with an open-
air pavilion and tropical garden
seating. Serves such favorites
as seared mahi mahi and grilled
rib-eye steak.

RINCÓN: The English Rose $$
Eclectic
Carretera Interior 413, Km2.0
Tel *787 823 4032* **Closed** *Mon*
This hotel-restaurant serves an
excellent English breakfast, plus
huevo rancheros, eggs Benedict,
and more on an oceanview
terrrace. A children's menu is
also available.

Beautiful artwork adorns the walls at El Ladrillo, Dorado

DK Choice

RINCÓN: Horned Dorset Primavera $$$
International
Carretera 429 Km3
Tel *787 823 4030*
Drawing gourmands from as far as San Juan, the oceanfront restaurant at this hotel has the island's strictest dress code, requiring men to wear jackets. Chandeliers reflect on the black-and-white marble floors. The owner-chef serves a five-course daily menu and a nine-course tasting menu of fusion dishes, making for an unmissable culinary experience.

SAN JUAN: Al Dente $$
Italian
Calle Recinto Sur 309
Tel *787 723 7303* **Closed** *Sun*
Warm, inviting Italian-owned restaurant serving staples such as *osso buco*, and calamari with polenta. Known for its top-notch bilingual service.

SAN JUAN: Ali Baba $$
Turkish
1214 Ashford Avenue, Condado
Tel *787 722 1176* **Closed** *Mon*
Ali Baba offers delicious *baba ghanoush*, kabobs, vegetarian casseroles, and more. Turkish-owned, with good service and Middle Eastern decor.

SAN JUAN: Amadeus $$
Nouvelle Puerto Rican
Av. Chardon 350, Hato Rey
Tel *787 641 7450* **Closed** *Sun*
Fashionable contemporary restaurant with banquet seating. The menu features delicious appetizers such as spicy tuna tartare. Lots of entrées, including the delicious coconut shrimp.

Elegant dining area of the Trois Cents Onze, San Juan

Customers dining at the popular Aguaviva restaurant, San Juan

SAN JUAN: Cafetería Mallorca $$
Diner
Calle San Francisco 300
Tel *787 724 4607*
Retro diner known for *mallorca* pastries sprinkled with powdered sugar. Another house specialty is the *mallorca con jamon y queso* with *salsa criolla*. Open for breakfast and lunch, this place is usually packed with locals.

SAN JUAN: Che's $$
Argentinian
Calle Coaba 35, Punta Las Marías
Tel *787 726 7202*
Traditional Argentine steak house with simple decor and good service. Succulent *churrasco* meat dishes, as well as seafood.

SAN JUAN: Dragonfly $$
Asian/Fusion
Calle Fortaleza 364
Tel *787 977 3886*
Blood-red Asian-inspired decor makes Dragonfly seem like part-bordello, part-opium den. Chef Roberto Trevino's Latin and Asian fusion dishes come in portions meant for sharing.

SAN JUAN: La Casita Blanca $$
Puerto Rican
351 Calle Tapia, Villa Palmeras
Tel *787 726 5501*
Locals queue for country-style Creole cuisine served by friendly staff. Standouts are rabbit stew and *bacalao* with *seviche* sauce.

SAN JUAN: Pamela's Caribbean Cuisine $$
Caribbean
Calle Santa Ana 1, Ocean Park
Tel *787 726 5010*
Housed in the beachfront Numero Uno Guest House, Pamela's Caribbean fusion menu features daily specials, as well as tapas. Try the calamari with spicy alioli.

SAN JUAN: Panza $$
Puerto Rican/Fusion
Recinto Sur 329
Tel *787 724 7722* **Closed** *Mon*
Chic restaurant in the Cervantes Hotel. Creative dishes on the menu include lobster bisque with coconut, and roasted boar chop with white-bean chili.

SAN JUAN: Parrot Club $$
Nouvelle Puerto Rican
Calle Fortaleza 363
Tel *787 725 7370*
Vivacious nightspot with bare walls, strong cocktails, and loud music. The Nuevo crab cakes and pan-seared tuna with rum sauce are justly famous.

SAN JUAN: St. Germain Bistro & Café $$
Bistro
Calle Sol 156
Tel *787 725 5830* **Closed** *Mon*
Tiny French-run bistro in the Colonial core of the city. The health-conscious menu includes fresh salads and sandwiches, as well as vegetarian dishes.

SAN JUAN: 1919 $$$
Puerto Rican/Fusion
1055 Ashford Avenue
Tel *787 724 1919* **Closed** *Sun & Mon*
This trendy restaurant uses the freshest organic, sustainable ingredients to craft its food. Try the venison with pumpkin, roasted pasta, bacon, and chestnut.

SAN JUAN: 311 Trois Cents Onze $$$
French
Calle Fortaleza 311
Tel *787 725 7959* **Closed** *Mon*
Elegant restaurant in the heart of Old San Juan serving artfully presented cuisine. Has special food-and-wine-pairing nights. Huge wine list.

SAN JUAN: Aguaviva $$$
Seafood
Calle Fortaleza 364
Tel *787 722 0665*
Ultra-hip restaurant serving delicious Latin nouvelle seafood. Signature dish is the *torre del mar* seafood tower, piled with oysters, shrimp, and more.

SAN JUAN: Il Nuovo Perugino $$$
Italian
Calle Cristo 105
Tel *787 722 5481* **Closed** *Mon*
Exuding old-world elegance, this lovely Italian restaurant is known for its ravioli stuffed with chicken liver, spinach, and black truffles, as well as the delicious veal entrecôte with mushrooms.

The striking exterior of the Lemongrass restaurant, San Juan

SAN JUAN: Lemongrass $$$
Asian/Fusion
Caribe Hilton, Calle Los Rosales
Tel *787 721 0303*
Lemongrass provides the perfect sleek, airy, postmodernist venue for enjoying Pan-Asian Latino fusion cuisine, such as spare ribs in hoi sin tamarind sauce. Sushi bar.

SAN JUAN: Marmalade $$$
Caribbean/Fusion
317 Calle Fortaleza
Tel *787 724 3969*
Inventive food served in a stunning minimalist space. The menu includes the must-try Colorado lamb shank with pomegranate and minted yogurt.

SAN JUAN: Palio $$$
Italian
Calle Brumbaugh 100
Tel *787 289 1944*
Tuscan chophouse with lovely views of the San Juan harbor. Excellent lasagne and veal chops, as well as the specialty, filet mignon with rum peppercorn glaze.

SAN JUAN: Perla $$$
Seafood
La Concha Renaissance San Juan Resort, Ashford Avenue 1077
Tel *787 977 3285*
Savor gourmet seafood amid spectacular architecture at this signature hotel restaurant. The many fusion delights on the menu include black truffle soup.

SAN JUAN: Pikayo $$$
Puerto Rican/Fusion
San Juan Condado Plaza Hotel and Casino, Ashford Avenue 999
Tel *787 721 1000*
Starkly minimalist restaurant serving artful Cajun-inspired fusion dishes. Try the *mofongo* (fried plantain-based dish) topped with saffron shrimp.

SAN JUAN: Rosalia International Cuisine $$$
International
Calle Loiza 2324, Punta Las Maria
Tel *787 268 7328*   **Closed** *Mon*
This stylish lounge bar-restaurant serves a creative globe-spanning menu. Try the delicious seared scallops purée of pumpkin, and red snapper *en papillote*.

SAN JUAN: Santaella $$$
Puerto Rican/Fusion
Calle Canals 219, Santurce
Tel *787 725 1611*   **Closed** *Sun & Mon*
Airy contemporary restaurant with an interior garden. Serves delicious tapas along with inspired dishes such as goat-cheese quesadilla with arugula.

SAN JUAN: Zest $$$
Puerto Rican/Fusion
Calle Tartak 2, Isla Verde
Tel *787 728 3666*
A chic contemporary restaurant with a wall cascade. Zest uses sustainably sourced ingredients to prepare its scrumptious experimental fusion dishes.

VIEQUES: Bananas Bar & Grill $
American
Calle Flamboyan 142, Esperanza
Tel *787 741 8700*
Unpretentious waterfront bar-restaurant with concrete tables. The menu features delicious baby-back ribs and burgers along with local favorites.

VIEQUES: Chez Shack $
Puerto Rican
Carretera 995 Km1.8
Tel *787 741 2175*   **Closed** *Sat & Sun*
Bohemian off-beat shack serving wholesome dishes such as fish filets, baked crab, chicken, and steaks. Live reggae on Mondays.

VIEQUES: Isla Nena Café $
Puerto Rican
Vieques Airport Terminal
Tel *787 435 6331*
Cozy café in the airport terminal serving local favorites such as conch fritters, pulled pork sandwiches, and vegetable black-bean mango wraps.

VIEQUES: Carambola $$
Asian/Fusion
Route 996 Km4.2, Esperanza
Tel *787 741 3318*   **Closed** *Mon*
Located in the Inn on the Blue Horizon, Carambola offers an Asian-Mediterranean fusion menu along with tapas. Gorgeous ocean views.

VIEQUES: Next Course $$
International
Route 201
Tel *787 741 1028*   **Closed** *Thu*
Choose from a globe-spanning menu at Next Course, amid colorful Asian decor. The tuna tartare on fried avocado, and sesame-crusted yellowfin tuna with seaweed salad are must-tries.

The charming dining room at the Carambola restaurant, Vieques

Practical Information

Puerto Rico is a modern and sophisticated society with a top-notch infrastructure. Much of it, such as the postal service, is shared with the US mainland. Tourist hotels are highly concentrated at specific beaches, and large sections of coastline, as well as the Cordillera Central, have few options. The densely populated island has horrendous traffic congestion in most towns, and many of the beach resorts popular with locals can get crowded and terribly littered.

When to Go

As in most of the Caribbean, the best weather here is from December to April. The other months get more rain and are hotter, although breezes help keep things cool year-round. Parts of the southwest are in a rain shadow and also receive few breezes. Accommodation rates are generally lower during summer months, but cultural events are spread through the year.

Getting There

Most scheduled flights arrive at San Juan's Luis Muñoz Marin International Airport (SJU), with flights from more than 20 US cities. Some flights arrive at regional airports in Ponce, Mayagüez, and San Juan's Isla Grande Airport (SIG). **American Airlines**, **Delta**, **JetBlue**, **Spirit Airlines**, **United Airlines**, and **US Airways** offer services to Puerto Rico, as do **Air Canada** and numerous charter airlines. Several European airlines such as **British Airways** connect through Miami, while **Iberia** has direct flights.

The regional partner of American Airlines, American Eagle connects the provincial airports within Puerto Rico, including Vieques and Culebra, which can also be reached by ferry from Fajardo.

A small plane used for internal flights, Vieques airport

Documentation

All visitors, except US citizens, must show a passport when visiting Puerto Rico. Visitors from Europe may enter the country for 90 days without a visa, but must register with **ESTA**, the US government's web portal. This can take up to 72 hours for approval and there is a charge. Travel requirements may change – check before travel. All visitors must have a ticket for onward travel.

Visitor Information

The **Puerto Rico Tourism Company** has offices in the US, Canada, Germany, Spain, and the UK that provide brochures. Within Puerto Rico, it has offices on Paseo de la Princesa and by the cruise port in San Juan. Hotel tour desks also have details of organized tours and activities.

Health and Security

Puerto Rico is safe and there are no endemic tropical diseases. Violent crime against visitors is rare, but carjackings and opportunistic snatch-and-grab theft are not uncommon in San Juan. Avoid wearing jewelry in public and keep valuables in a hotel safe. Puerto Rican drivers have little regard for traffic rules, so drive cautiously. Check with locals about tidal conditions before swimming. Private medical clinics, such as **Clínica Las Américas**, are ubiquitous and all major towns have hospitals. Hotels can arrange for a doctor in any emergency.

Banking and Currency

The US dollar is the official and sole currency of Puerto Rico, although locals still use the term "peso" or "billetes" for the dollar. Traveler's checks in US dollars are accepted in many hotels, restaurants, and stores, although credit cards are always preferable. There are banks with ATMs in almost every town.

An ATM machine at the town center in Fajardo

Communications

Puerto Rico has a highly efficient telephone system currently operated by Mexico's América Móvil company under their international **Claro** brand. Public phones are present islandwide and prepaid phone cards can be purchased at many stores. Calls from hotels incur a hefty surcharge.

Puerto Rico's area code is 787. To call the island from North America, dial 1, then 787 and the local number; from the UK, dial 00 for international access, then 1 787 and the local number. Calls within Puerto Rico require 787 and the seven-digit number. Most hotels offer Internet access; many have Wi-Fi. There are Internet cafés on all the islands.

Taxis at the Plaza de Armas, Old San Juan

Transport

The island has an extensive road system, but traffic congestion is severe, and a frightening disregard for traffic regulations makes driving in Puerto Rico quite risky. Most major international car rental companies, such as **AVIS**, **Hertz**, and **Budget**, are represented. Renting a scooter is a good option for exploring Vieques and Culebra, but be sure to wear a helmet.

Taxis offer efficient service within San Juan. The hotel concierge or front desk can call for a taxi waiting outside most tourist hotels. Locals rely on *públicos* (private minivans) that operate communal taxi services for town-to-town travel. Puerto Rico Tourism Company can provide information on taxi companies.

Shopping

San Juan's historic center has many stores selling local crafts, including the island's trademark *santos* (saint figurines) as well as cigars, rum, and clothing items. Most tourist hotels also sell crafts, and have upscale boutiques, as does Avenue Ashford in San Juan's Condado district and Plaza Las Américas mall. Puerto Rican coffee and lace items make great souvenirs, as do hand-made crafts, such as *vejigante* masks, *santos*, and other wooden carvings that can be bought at source in studios around Orocovis and Utuado. There is no sales tax, and no duty is payable upon return to the US mainland.

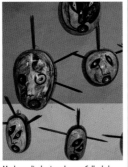
Masks on display in a shop on Calle de la Fortaleza, San Juan

Language

Spanish is Puerto Rico's official language, spoken by everyone, although many locals also speak English, as do most Puerto Ricans working in tourism.

Electricity

Puerto Rico operates on 110 volts. Outlets use US two- or three-prong plugs. Visitors from Europe should bring transformers or adapters.

Time

Puerto Rico is on Eastern Standard Time (EST), 5 hours behind Greenwich Mean Time (GMT), like New York and Miami. Daylight saving is not observed in Puerto Rico, which is therefore one hour behind EST from the last Sunday of March through the last Sunday of October.

Getting Married

At least two months' forward planning is needed to get married in Puerto Rico. Both parties' passport or identification card, plus original birth certificate, and divorce and spouse's death decrees, if applicable, are required. Blood tests within two weeks and a medical examination within 10 days of the wedding are also needed. Any couple wanting to go it alone will need to visit the Marriage License Bureau of the **Registro Demográfico**, or make arrangements through **Wed Affair**.

DIRECTORY

Airlines

Air Canada
🔳 aircanada.com

American Airlines
🔳 aa.com

British Airways
🔳 ba.com

Delta
🔳 delta.com

Iberia
🔳 iberia.com

JetBlue
🔳 jetblue.com

Spirit Airlines
🔳 spiritair.com

United Airlines
🔳 united.com

US Airways
🔳 usairways.com

Documentation

ESTA
🔳 cbp.gov/esta

Visitor Information

Puerto Rico Tourism Company
Tel 787 721 2400.
🔳 seepuertorico.com

Health and Security

Emergencies
Tel 911.

Clínica Las Américas
Tel 787 765 1919.
🔳 clinicalasamericas. com

Communications

Claro
Tel 787 775 0000.
🔳 claropr.com

Transport

AVIS
Tel 787 253 5926.
🔳 avis.com

Budget
Tel 787 791 0600.
🔳 budget.com

Hertz
Tel 787 791 0840.
🔳 hertz.com

Getting Married

Registro Demográfico
171 Calle Quisqueya,
Hato Rey,
San Juan.
Tel 787 767 9120.

Wed Affair
🔳 wedaffair.com

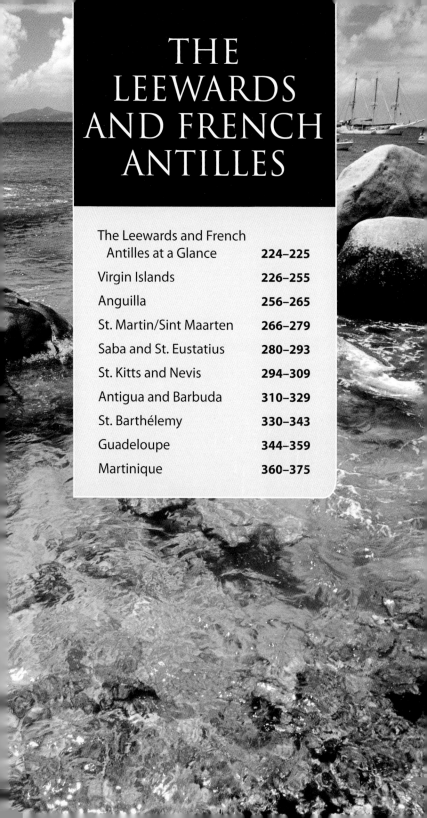

THE LEEWARDS AND FRENCH ANTILLES

The Leewards and French Antilles at a Glance

The Leeward Islands, comprising the Virgin Islands, Anguilla, Antigua and Barbuda, Saba and St. Eustatius, and St. Kitts and Nevis, are a paradise for tourists in search of adventure. From renowned sailing regattas in Antigua to strenuous hiking in Saba, all the islands offer exciting outdoor activities. On the other hand, the French Antilles, St. Martin/ Sint Maarten, St. Barthélemy, Guadeloupe, and Martinique, have fantastic beaches, world-class hotels and restaurants, and great shopping.

Locator Map

Charlotte Amalie ○ Road Town

ANGUILLA
(See pp256–65)

○ The Valley

VIRGIN ISLANDS
(See pp226–55)

ST. MARTIN/ SINT MAARTEN
(See pp266–79)

ST. BARTHÉL
(See pp332–4.

○ Christiansted

SABA AND ST. EUSTATIUS
(See pp280–93)

Basseterre

ST. KITT AND NEV
(See pp294–3

The Virgin Islands, with their spectacular beaches, emerald waters, stunning coral reefs, and amazing flora, leave most visitors breathless. The islands are popular among adventure tourists who come for snorkeling, hiking, and sailing.

St. Martin/Sint Maarten is almost divided equally between France and The Netherlands. Sint Maarten is more tourist oriented, while St. Martin is quieter and peaceful.

Saba, with its volcanic peak, rises steeply out of the sea. It presents to visitors an experience of peace and tranquility with its ecolodges, unspoilt hiking trails, serene beaches, and dive sites, making it different from any other Caribbean island.

◀ Snorkeler at The Baths, British Virgin Islands

Antigua and Barbuda has long winding coastlines, azure waters, and a generally laid-back feel perfect for relaxation. Antigua offers plenty of activities including diving, sailing, and snorkeling to old ship-wrecks and some of the best coral reefs anywhere. The small island of Barbuda, on the other hand, is a haven for birdwatchers and eco-tourists.

ANTIGUA AND BARBUDA
(See pp310–29)

St. John's

MONTSERRAT
(See pp322–25)

Guadeloupe, a small archipelago and part of the French Republic, is highly urbanized. However, it is also known for its rugged mountains, waterfalls, thick rainforests, and great hiking trails. It is home to La Soufrière, an active volcano.

Pointe-à-Pitre

GUADELOUPE
(See pp344–59)

Basse-Terre

0 kilometers	50
0 miles	50

DOMINICA
(The Windwards, see pp380–93)

MARTINIQUE
(See pp360–75)

Fort-de-France

Martinique's landscape is dotted with sugarcane fields – the island's major crop. Its dense and lush green forests cover over one-third of the island.

Exploring the Virgin Islands

Except for the flag flying overhead, the US and British Virgin Islands share many similarities. Visitors come for swimming, snorkeling, and sailing as well as hiking, shopping, and relaxing. St. Croix (USVI) to the south is larger and flatter than most islands in the north; except for Anegada, the BVI are peaks jutting out of the clear waters. Anegada, far to the east of the BVI chain, is a coral atoll fringed with powdery white sands.

Locator Map

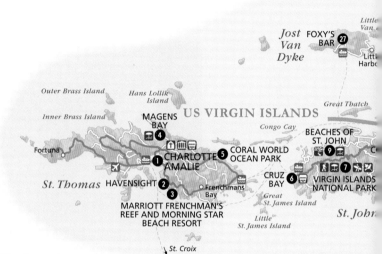

Getting Around

If not flying in to the airports on St. Thomas, St. Croix, Tortola, or Virgin Gorda, visitors can hop on a ferry to get around among the islands. Seaplanes, small aircraft, and a ferry connect St. Thomas and St. Croix. St. John and St. Thomas are also linked by ferry service. To Tortola, a ferry is available at Charlotte Amalie or Cruz Bay. Virgin Gorda is reached by ferry from St. Thomas, St. John, and Tortola. Ferries also go from Tortola to Jost Van Dyke and Anegada.

Key

━━━ Major road

═══ Minor road

------ Ferry route

▬▬▬ International border

△ Peak

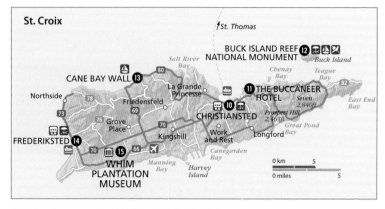

For hotels and restaurants on these islands see pp248–51 and pp252–3

Anegada

Cow Wreck Bay
Windlass Bight
Jack Bay
Loblolly Bay
Flamingo Pond
Table Bay
✈
The Settlement
Caribbean Sea
Lower Bay
White Bay
Tortola ↓

0 km   3
0 miles   3

Necker Island
Mosquito Island
Prickly Pear Island
Saba Rock
George Dog
Great Camanoe
West Dog
Great Dog
Savannah Bay
25 🚶 🚠
GORDA PEAK NATIONAL PARK
Guana Island
Scrub Island
🚲 MARINA CAY **21**
DRIVING TOUR OF VIRGIN GORDA **24**
Spanish Town
Virgin Gorda
CANE RDEN BAY
JR O'NEAL BOTANICAL GARDENS NATIONAL PARK
THE VALLEY
22
Coppermine National Park
20
🚲 **17**
16 ROAD TOWN
Tortola
23 THE BATHS
Fallen Jerusalem
RTH ORE
18 SAGE MOUNTAIN NATIONAL PARK
Ginger Island
Round Rock
BRITISH VIRGIN ISLANDS
26 🚲
Salt Island
Cooper Island
🛥 RMS RHONE MARINE PARK
Peter Island
Pelican Island
CARIBBEAN SEA
Norman Island

0 kilometers   5
0 miles   5

Sights at a Glance

The lush greenery of the JR O'Neal Botanical Gardens National Park

For additional map symbols *see back flap*

St. Thomas

While visitors can be as laid-back as they like on St. Thomas, the island offers plenty of watersports, good shopping, excellent restaurants, and some nightlife. The scenery is stunning, with lush mountains reaching skyward from turquoise bays fringed by white sandy crescents. St. Thomas, together with St. John and St. Croix, was under Danish control for centuries, a heritage clearly reflected in the busy town of Charlotte Amalie with its red roofs and many streets still carrying a Danish name.

❶ Charlotte Amalie

SW coast of St. Thomas. ⊞ 19,000.
✈ 🚢 🚉 🚤 Carnival (Apr).

While there are ample stores filled with everything from T-shirts to crafts to luxury items that beckon, Charlotte Amalie, long the center of commerce, offers more than just shopping opportunities. The island's history reveals itself in stores that formerly served as ware-houses or merchants' homes centuries ago. A short walk takes visitors to **Fort Christian**, a military construction begun in 1672 by the Danish, who controlled the island at the time. Today it has been con-verted into a museum that displays exhibits on the island's

The magnificent façade of Fort Christian, Charlotte Amalie

history and culture. Just across the Veterans Drive from Fort Christian, the big green building that now serves as home to the local **Legislature** was the site for the March 31, 1917, transfer of power from Denmark to the US of all three islands.

The purchase cost the US government $25 million. Every year on the same day, residents observe the transfer anniversary in the Legislature's garden.

History aside, Charlotte Amalie presents excellent shopping opportunities with the **Vendor's Plaza** offering great bargains. Various art galleries are scattered around the **Shopping District**.

Two streets inland from the Shopping District's Main Street, **St. Thomas Synagogue** has served as the spiritual home to the island's Jewish population since 1833. Other historic churches are scattered around Charlotte Amalie. The Neo-Classical white building, just uphill from the Shopping District, is the seat of the local government's administrative branch and is where the governor has his office.

Lunch can be enjoyed at any of the numerous restaurants that range from simple sandwich eateries to more formal ones, sitting along Main Street and on the streets and alleys that connect Main Street to the waterfront and the streets inland.

Charlotte Amalie

① Fort Christian
② Legislature
③ Vendor's Plaza
④ Shopping District
⑤ St. Thomas Synagogue

0 meters   200
0 yards   200

Airport
2.5 miles
(4 km) ✈

St. John Island
11 miles (18 km)

Shoppers scanning through the displays, Havensight Mall

❷ Havensight

2 miles (3 km) SE of Charlotte Amalie. 🏨 🚉 ℹ Havensight Mall, 340 774 1780. Dept. of Tourism, 340 777 5313. 🌐 wico-vi.com

Home to the island's largest cruise ship dock, Havensight bustles with activity. Those who arrive on a cruise ship can join their sailing, scuba, or exploring excursions at the dock. Many prefer a short stroll to the vast Havensight shopping area. It stretches from **Havensight Mall** to Port of Sale Mall and around the corner past Wendy's fast food restaurant to Yacht Haven Grande Mall. Several downtown Charlotte Amalie stores have branches here, but there are dozens of others as well. Many visitors buy liquor here, it is available at much better prices than anywhere else.

The area is home to many restaurants, so cruise ship passengers not eating on board will not go hungry.

❸ Marriott Frenchman's Reef and Morning Star Beach Resort

🚗 Rt 315, 5 Estate Bakkeroe. **Tel** 340 776 8500. 🚉 🏊 🍴 ♿ 🌐 marriott.com

The vast Marriott Frenchman's Reef and Morning Star Beach Resort is the kind of place where guests can settle for more than a few days, but day visitors are also welcome.

The resort is easily reached by taxi, car or the Reefer, a small boat that ferries visitors to the resort from the Charlotte Amalie waterfront.

The beach, a white sandy confection, is one of the most popular on the island. Sailing and snorkeling trips depart from the dock, Jet Skis are available and the hotel's restaurants make a great spot for lunch or dinner.

Visitors can also make an appointment at the hotel's spa – the LAZULE Sea Spa and Salon – for a massage, manicure, or a fitness session.

❹ Magens Bay

🚗 Rt 35. **Tel** 340 777 6300. 🚉 🏊 ⚠ 🍴 🏊 🌐 magensbayauthority.com

Ever popular Magens Bay beach stretches along a U-shaped bay. This beach has a snack bar, snorkel gear and small sailboat rentals, a beachwear shop, showers, and bathrooms.

On cruise ship days the beach can get crowded. Locals like to party on weekends and holidays when music gets very loud and the atmosphere more than lively. For some solitude, it is best to stroll down to either end of the beach.

Inland from the beach is the Magens Bay Arboretum, a botanical garden with native and imported plants.

❺ Coral World Ocean Park

4 miles (6 km) NE of Charlotte Amalie. **Tel** 340 775 1555. 🕐 **Open** 9am–4pm daily. 🏊 🏊 🏊 🏊 🏊 🌐 coralworldvi.com

A popular spot with families, Coral World Ocean Park appeals to anyone who is interested in marine life. The undersea observatory is reached by a bridge that takes visitors 100 ft (30 m) offshore and down 15 ft (5 m) to the briny depths in the middle of a coral reef. The round structure features huge windows for extensive views of colorful fish swimming by. Included in the admission price is a walk along a nature trail, a view of the 21 aquariums that feature a variety of sea life, and a chance to feed stingrays.

The 5-acre (2-ha) park offers various other guided attractions including an in-pool swim with sea lions, a swim with sharks and turtles, and Sea Trek, a scuba-like adventure. These activities have an extra charge.

Undersea observatory, Coral World Ocean Park

For hotels and restaurants in this region see pp248–51 and pp252–3

St. John

St. John is a jewel with the Virgin Islands National Park at its center. The island offers varied accommodations that lure visitors bent on sampling the park's white sandy beaches, hiking trails heading up verdant hillsides, and a variety of restaurants and shops. Most of the island remains untouched thanks to the park, but the eastern and western fringes serve as centers of commerce, the bustling town of Cruz Bay is the main point of entry.

Families wandering around in Cruz Bay Park

❻ Cruz Bay

W coast of St. John. 🔼 2,750. 🚌 🚢
ℹ️ Henry Samuel Street, 340 776
6450. 🇼 visitusvi.com

Most vacationers pass through Cruz Bay, St. John's main town: ferries from St. Thomas and the British Virgin Islands pull into the port, it has the widest choice of restaurants and shops, and many watersports excursions depart from here. Near the ferry dock, in Cruz Bay Park, taxi drivers wait to pick up visitors and people relax on the benches scattered around the park. Shops and restaurants are anchored by Wharfside Village shopping center, sitting beachfront near the ferry dock, and the Mongoose Junction shopping center is located where the North Shore Road starts uphill and out of Cruz Bay.

The town is home to a few historical sites. The red-roofed Battery, on the north side of the harbor, dates back to 1825 and is currently the seat of the territorial government. Farther afield, at Tamarind Court, is the Elaine Ione Sprauve Library located in a restored 1757 plantation house.

❼ Virgin Islands National Park

4 miles (6 km) E of Cruz Bay.
🇹 ℹ️ Cruz Bay Visitors' Center,
Cruz Bay, 340 776 6201. **Open** 24
hours a day. 🎣 🛥️ 🚻 🥾
🇼 nps.gov/viis

Covering nearly two-thirds of St. John, Virgin Islands National Park encompasses 11 sq miles (29 sq km) above ground and 9 sq miles (23 sq km) of marine sanctuary. It was established in 1956, thanks to land donations by philanthropist Laurance S. Rockefeller. The Visitors' Center in Cruz Bay has exhibits, books for sale, and rangers on duty to answer questions and distribute brochures about various beach, watersports, and hiking opportunities. The park offers guided programs including beach walks and birding trips.

❽ Coral Bay

6 miles (10 km) E of Cruz Bay. 🇹

About 200 years ago, Coral Bay was the only large settlement on St. John. Today, it is home to a handful of shops and restaurants along the main road. It is anchored by the Skinny Legs Bar and Grill complex *(see p252)* and the Cocoloba shopping center to the south. The Emmaus Moravian Church is an important historical site. The congregation dates to 1756, but the church was rebuilt after the 1916 hurricane.

The Visitors' Center of Virgin Islands National Park, near Cruz Bay

For hotels and restaurants on these islands see pp248–51 and pp252–3

View of the blue waters and white sand, Trunk Bay

❾ Beaches of St. John

For those who want to venture beyond their hotel beach, St. John has a wealth of luscious sands to explore, with or without facilities. Many are on the north coast, easily accessible by car via the North Shore Road, but it is also worth heading down to the south coast where beachlife can be combined with a hike.

Northeast of Cruz Bay, in front of the upscale Caneel Bay Resort, is Caneel Bay, the only one of the resort's beaches that welcomes non-guests; it has a snorkeling point at the east end. Hawksnest Bay, a short distance away from Caneel Bay, is a local favorite with good snorkeling above the reef patches dotted around the bay. The smallish Jumbie Bay, farther north from

Hawksnest, has excellent snorkeling and is also popular with the locals. Jumbie is a common word for ghost and this beach has plenty of ghost stories. It is accessed via some stairs down from the road.

The ever popular **Trunk Bay** can be crowded with cruise ship visitors, but its far fringes offer some solitude. Alternatively, visitors could come early or late in the day to snorkel around the underwater trail, where the features are marked with explanatory signs. Trunk Bay has a snack bar, snorkel gear rentals, a gift shop, and picnic pavilions.

Cinnamon Bay, farther along North Shore Road, is a good bet for a day out although the white sandy beach can be windy in winter. There are restrooms and a small convenience store. A watersports center rents snorkel gear and kayaks. The Cinnamon

Nature Trail, across the road from the beach, takes visitors through interesting plantation-era ruins. The gorgeous Maho Bay is just a short drive away. However, there are no restroom facilities on the beach.

The south shore also has some excellent beaches. Salt Pond Bay is a scimitar of white sand with great snorkeling opportunities. It is also the starting point for hiking trails including the Drunk Bay Trail and the hike up to Ram's Head. A 15-minute drive down a mostly-paved road leads to the remote Lameshur Bay's small white sandy beach, which has good snorkeling along the east edge, a nice walk to Yawzi Point, and a restroom.

Kayaking in the warm waters of Cinnamon Bay

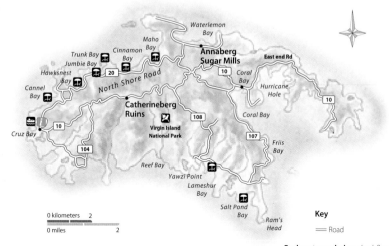

Key

═══ Road

For keys to symbols *see back flap*

St. Croix

St. Croix is an island of many facets. Plantation ruins sit side-by-side with suburban developments and a large oil refinery. The main town of Christiansted is filled with shops and restaurants, and reminders of the era when St. Croix, St. John, and St. Thomas were Danish. Frederiksted is a quiet place, occasionally a stop on the cruise ship route. Pretty beaches fringe the coasts, with small resorts and modest hotels in the two main towns.

⑩ Christiansted

N coast of St. Croix. 🚼 3,000. ✈️
🚢 🛈 ℹ️ Government House, King Street, 340 773 1404.
🌐 **visitusvi.com**

Home to Christiansted National Historic Site and its massive waterfront Fort Christiansvaern,

The old Danish customs house in Christiansted

this charming town is also the jumping-off point for trips to Buck Island Reef National Monument. Rangers at the fort offer information on the site's highlights. Christiansted was erected in the 18th century and most of the buildings date back to then. They have been restored, most now housing shops and restaurants. The Tourism Department office, in the 18th-century Government House, has maps and brochures about St. Croix.

Tours of this historic structure, built as a home for a Danish merchant in 1747, are available.

Visitors can stroll on the Christiansted Boardwalk that passes along the harbor past Fort Christiansvaern. Benches are strategically placed for prime harbor viewing. The town is also home to a handful of small hotels, but the closest beach is at the Hotel on the Cay (see p248), located in the midst of the Christiansted Harbor.

⑪ The Buccaneer Hotel

🚗 Rt 82, Shoys.
Tel 340 712 2100. 🛏️ 〰️ 🎾 ♿
🌐 **thebuccaneer.com**

With a historic sugar mill as a centerpiece, The Buccaneer is one of the oldest St. Croix hotels. There has been a building at this site since 1653, but what is now the hotel grounds served as a cattle ranch earlier. The hotel has welcomed the rich, famous, and just plain folks since 1947. An array of activities and sports are available.

⑮ Whim Plantation Museum

This historical landmark is one of the oldest plantations on St. Croix. Its history dates back to 1743, when it started as a cotton plantation with slaves brought here from West Africa. After cotton, sugarcane was grown until 1952. The museum includes the restored great house, sugar factory ruins and mills, plots of sugarcane, and gardens.

Windmill
The plantation's windmill was built in the late 1700s and used until the 1880s. Cane grown in the surrounding fields was turned into juice when slaves fed it into rollers powered by the mill's wind-driven sails.

Animal Mill
These mills, pulled by draft animals, were used in the sugar factory to process the cane.

For hotels and restaurants on these islands see pp248–51 and pp252–3

⑫ Buck Island Reef National Monument

1 miles (1.6 km) NE of Christiansted. **Tel** 340 773 1460. 🚢 **Open** daylight. 🅿 Ⓦ **nps.gov/buis**

Day-sail and power boats leave from Christiansted waterfront and Green Cay Marina to this 176-acre (70-ha) national park. The colorful reefs that make up the underwater trail at the eastern side of the monument offer some good snorkeling. After the snorkel stop, most boats head around to anchor off a gorgeous white sandy beach at the western end. Visitors can also hike uphill to the island's highest point, at 328 ft (99 m) above sea level.

⑬ Cane Bay Wall

7 miles (12 km) W of Christiansted. Ⓣ

Stretching along St. Croix's north side, the famous Cane Bay Wall attracts divers from around the world. Most prefer to go out on a boat with dive operators, but the wall is accessible from Cane Bay Beach and other locations along the island's north shore. It sits just 100 ft (30 m) to 200 ft (60 m) offshore. Canyons plummet over 2,000–3,000 ft (610–920 m) down, giving novice and experienced divers a view of colorful corals (including the rare black coral), sponges, and fish as well as the occasional shark.

Fort Frederik in Frederiksted

⑭ Frederiksted

12 miles (19 km) SW of Christiansted. 👥 3,800. 🚢 Ⓣ 🛈 Strand Street, 340 772 0357.

St. Croix's second town is a sleepy place. However, it is the site of the territory's most historic event. On July 3, 1848, about 8,000 slaves marched from nearby Estate LaGrange to Fort Frederik to demand their freedom. Standing in a carriage parked in front of the fort, Danish Governor-General Peter von Scholten announced that freedom was theirs. The Danish government recalled von Scholten home, while the former slaves continued to work the plantations. Frederiksted was later the scene of other labor uprisings by discontented workers.

The town does not have many shops and only a few restaurants and a small hotel in the downtown area, but when cruise ships pull in, this is where they arrive. A lovely white sandy beach stretches north from Fort Frederik.

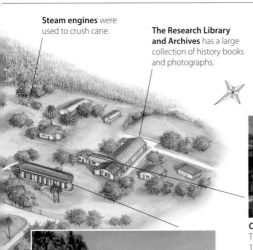

Steam engines were used to crush cane.

The Research Library and Archives has a large collection of history books and photographs.

Cookhouse
The original cookhouse dates to around 1766. Its raised hearth helped keep the room cooler.

Great House
The oval great house is filled with antiques to show how planters lived a long time ago. It is a site for musical concerts in winter.

Outdoor Activities and Specialized Holidays

Activities in the US Virgin Islands mainly focus on the outdoors. Most involve the water in some form or other such as lounging at the pristine beaches, snorkeling, scuba diving, sailing excursions, fishing, and kayaking. However, some visitors come just to hike in the hills of Virgin Islands National Park or to play golf at one of the magnificent courses on St. Thomas and St. Croix. Vacationers will find plenty of outfitters ready to rent equipment and plan tours.

Pool and beach of Ritz-Carlton hotel, St. Thomas

Beaches

Nearly everyone makes it to the beach at one time or the other during their vacation to the US Virgin Islands. Many hotels have their own beaches, just steps away from their rooms, while others have to rely on nearby public beaches. Whatever the case, since the islands are small, a good strip of sand is never more than a short drive away. Some beaches have numerous amenities while others just feature lovely white sand and clear blue sea. For safety's sake, it is best to stick to the more visited beaches on St. Thomas and St. Croix.

On St. John, the best beaches are strung out along the North Shore, but visitors will find a few in other locations. Trunk Bay *(see p231)*, the most popular, is equipped with all facilities.

St. Thomas' best beach is Magens Bay *(see p229)*, which gets lots of traffic and has the most amenities of any beach in the US Virgin Islands.

Brewer's Bay is popular with the locals. It sits right along Route 30 near the University of the Virgin Islands. Visitors might find vans selling sandwiches and the like parked along the road. Most of the other top beaches in St. Thomas are located mainly at the hotels.

On St. Croix, visitors will find lovely beaches north and south of Frederiksted. There are no safety issues at the beaches near the several restaurants tucked in between Frederiksted and Sprat Hall or near Sandcastle on the Beach, south of Frederiksted.

Diving and Snorkeling

It is possible to get up close and personal with the island's rich undersea life on either a snorkeling or diving tour. All gear, including a mask, snorkel, and fins, can be rented at the watersports shops located in most hotels or any of the others scattered across the territory. Among the established operators are **Aqua Action**, **Coki Beach Dive Club**, and **Cruz Bay Watersports**.

Diving is slightly more complicated but visitors can learn the ropes through a diving introductory course at most watersports shops. The instructor will go over the ins and outs of the equipment, show beginners how to dive, and supervise

Snorkeling in the crystal-clear waters of the US Virgin Islands

Golfers at the luxurious Mahogany Run Golf Course, St. Thomas

closely. Visitors can get a certification card at their hometown dive shop. Some watersports centers such as **Cane Bay Dive Shop**, **St. Croix Ultimate Bluewater Adventures**, **Low Key Watersports** and **Dive Experience**, rent gear and take divers out to the top sites, if they already hold a certification card.

Day Sails

With the wind in your face and the good company of other sailors, set sail on any one of the charter boats that leave from various locations around the islands. After a few hours of sailing, the captain will drop the anchor for a snorkeling session and lunch, prepared by the crew and eaten under a canopy.

On St. John, day sail boats leave from Cruz Bay and the hotels for trips to offshore cays or one of the island's bays. More information can be provided by **St. John Concierge Service**. In St. Thomas, sail boats depart from the hotels, Red Hook, or Charlotte Amalie for trips to Buck Island Reef National Monument (see p233), a small cay south of St. Thomas, and other offshore cays on St. John. **The Charter Boat Center** can be contacted for day sails.

St. Croix day sail boats leave from Christiansted or Green Cay for Buck Island Reef National Monument. Tour operators here include **Big Beard's Adventure Tours** and **Buck Island Charters**.

Golf

The **Mahogany Run Golf Course** on St. Thomas is designed by acclaimed golf course designers, George and Tom Fazio. It is home to the Devil's Triangle, a wicked trio of holes that sits right above the ocean.

On St. Croix, **The Buccaneer Golf Course** vies for attention with **Carambola Golf Club**, which are both 18-hole gems. **The Reef Golf Course** is a 9-hole course and is definitely worth a try.

St. John only has an 18-hole mini-golf course at Pastory, especially popular with families looking for an hour of fun after dinner.

Hiking

St. John offers some good hiking. While the Reef Bay Trail (see p237) gets the most visitors, Virgin Islands National Park (see p230) has plenty of other trails. In the Cruz Bay area, follow the Lind Point Trail for about 1 mile (2 km) to Lind Point for great views of Cruz Bay. A taxi can be hired to the start of Cinnamon Bay Trail, which is a good hike down hill to Cinnamon Bay Campground. The Johnny Horn Trail is nearly 2 miles (3 km), stretching from Emmaus Moravian Church in Coral Bay to the secluded Brown Bay. A few trails such as Ram's Head Trail and Salt Pond Trail begin from the southern shore. It is possible to enjoy walks through estate ruins such as the Annaberg Plantation.

Hikers on the Reef Bay Trail, St. John

American yacht harbor at Red Hook, St. Thomas

Kayaking

There is kayaking off many beaches across the Virgin Islands, but Salt River in St. Croix is the prime destination. It is possible to kayak among mangroves and over reefs all the way to the ocean. Operators here are **Caribbean Adventure Tours** and **Virgin Kayak Tours**. On St. John, kayakers can head for any of the small cays that sit offshore. **Arawak Expeditions** and **Crabby's Watersports** are good operators here. In St. Thomas it is best to paddle along the fringes of various bays to view birds and other coastal inhabitants. **V.I. Ecotours** operates tours here.

Fishing

Most fishing boats head out to the sea from Red Hook, St. Thomas and Christiansted, St. Croix. Visitors can either fish on half-day or day-long excursions. The main operators are **Capt. Byron Oliver**, **Caribbean Sea Adventures**, **Gone Ketchin**, **Abigail III**, and **Marlin Prince**.

DIRECTORY

Diving and Snorkeling

Aqua Action
Secret Harbor Beach Resort, Off Rt 332, St. Thomas.
Tel 340 775 6285.
W aadivers.com

Cane Bay Dive Shop
Rt 80, Cane Bay, St. Croix.
Tel 340 718 9913.
W canebayscuba.com

Coki Beach Dive Club
Coki Beach, Rt 388, St. Thomas.
Tel 340 775 4220.
W cokidive.com

Cruz Bay Watersports
Lumberyard Shopping complex, Cruz Bay and the Westin Resort and Villas, St. John.
Tel 340 776 6234.
W divestjohn.com

Dive Experience
1111 Strand Street, Christiansted, St. Croix.
Tel 340 773 3307.
W divexp.com

Low Key Watersports
Cruz Bay, St. John.
Tel 340 693 8999.
W divelowkey.com

St. Croix Ultimate Bluewater Adventures
1104 Strand Street, Christiansted, St. Croix.
Tel 340 773 5994.
W stcroixscuba.com

Day Sails

Big Beard's Adventure Tours
Christiansted Waterfront, St. Croix.
Tel 340 773 4482.
W bigbeards.com

Buck Island Charters
Green Cay Marina, St. Croix.
Tel 340 773 3161.

The Charter Boat Center
Red Hook, Rt 38, St. Thomas. **Tel** 340 775 7990. W charterboat.vi

St. John Concierge Service
Cruz Bay, St. John.
Tel 340 514 5262.
W stjohnconcierge service.com

Golf

The Buccaneer Golf Course
Rt 82, Shoys, St. Croix.
Tel 340 712 2144.
W thebuccaneer.com

Carambola Golf Club
Rt 80, Davis Bay, St. Croix.
Tel 340 778 5638.
W golfcarambola.com

Mahogany Run Golf Course
Rt 42, Mahogany Run, St. Thomas.
Tel 340 777 6250.
W mahogany rungolf.com

The Reef Golf Course
Teague Bay, St. Croix.
Tel 340 773 8844.

Fishing

Abigail III
Sapphire Beach Marina, Rt 38, St. Thomas.
Tel 340 775 6024.
W visportfish.com

Capt. Byron Oliver
St. John.
Tel 340 693 8339.

Caribbean Sea Adventures
59 Kings Wharf, Christiansted, St. Croix.
Tel 340 773 2628.
W caribbeansea adventures.com

Gone Ketchin
St. Croix.
Tel 340 713 1175.
W goneketchin.com

Marlin Prince
6100 Red Hook Quarters 2, St. Thomas.
Tel 340 693 5929.
W marlinprince.com

Kayaking

Arawak Expeditions
Wharfside Village, Cruz Bay, St. John.
Tel 340 693 8312.
W arawakexp.com

Caribbean Adventure Tours
Rt 80, Salt River Marina, St. Croix.
Tel 340 778 1522.
W stcroixkayak.com

Crabby's Watersports
Rt 107, South Coral Bay, St. John. **Tel** 340 714 2415. W crabbys watersports.com

V.I. Ecotours
Mangrove Lagoon, Rt 32, St. Thomas. **Tel** 340 779 2155. W viecotours.com

Virgin Kayak Tours
Rt 80, Cane Bay, St. Croix.
Tel 340 514 0062 or 340 626 7775.
W virginkayaktours.com

Hiking in St. John

St. John is the US Virgin Islands' premier hiking destination and appeals to both the experienced hiker and the casual stroller. The Reef Bay guided hike is the most popular, with trips departing from the Virgin Islands National Park's Cruz Bay Visitors' Center several times a week. The island also has other trails including the historic walk through the Annaberg Plantation and the Ram's Head Trail along the southern shore. A brochure available at the Visitors' Center describes nearly two dozen hikes ranging in length and difficulty.

Reef Bay Trail

The 2-miles (3-km) long Reef Bay Trail begins on Centerline Road, from where it heads downhill to a sandy beach. A boat picks up hikers for the return trip to Cruz Bay.

Reef Bay great house, now in ruins, is a remnant of bygone days when plantations dotted St. John.

The Reef Bay sugar factory ruins and beach mark the end of the Reef Bay Trail. The old mill has been partially restored. The grave of former owner Will Marsh is tucked back in the bushes.

Ancient petroglyphs, possibly carved by Taínos, are found along the edges of rock pools.

Shorter Hikes

St. John has several fairly easy hiking trails that cut across flat terrain. Many of these, including the Salt Pond Trail and Francis Bay Trail, are no more than 1 mile (2 km) long.

The Annaberg Plantation path leads visitors through a 518-acre (209-ha) sugar plantation. Now in ruins, the plantation's sugar mill, factory, and kitchen date back to the 18th century.

Ram's Head Trail, beginning at Salt Pond Bay, stretches across a rocky beach with a short climb uphill to an overlook with fantastic views of the Caribbean Sea.

Salt Pond Trail offers pleasant hiking through arid vegetation to the pretty Salt Pond Bay Beach. This easy hike takes less than 20 minutes to complete.

Tortola

Tortola is a study in contrasts. Road Town, its main hub, is busy with travelers shopping and office workers heading to and from work, but a drive just five minutes out of the town brings visitors to the island's rural roots. On the north side this is even more evident – here it is common to have to wait a few minutes for a herd of goats or sheep to cross the road. A drive along the south coast offers views of sailboats bobbing in the breeze as they head up Drake's Passage.

A cruise liner at the port in Road Town

⓰ Road Town

SE coast of Tortola. 🚌 12,600.
✈ 🚢 🛈 ℹ AKARA Building,
de Castro Street, 284 494 3134.
📅 August Festival (Aug).
W bvitourism.com

Road Town bustles on days when cruise ships tie up, but even on days when no cruise ships are in port, the British territory's main town is active. It is the seat of BVI commerce and home to a large offshore banking industry, government offices, shops, and restaurants. Ferries from Virgin Gorda and St. Thomas in the US Virgin Islands tie up at the Road Town ferry dock, further adding to the town's traffic. It is a working town rather than just a tourist destination, visible in the even mix of locals and visitors having lunch in the many restaurants. Road Town sprawls along the Waterfront Highway. The very heart of the town runs from the waterfront inland one block to the narrow Main Street.

East of here, restaurants, shops, and banks overflow on Wickham's Cay I, that is also home to marinas. Farther east sits Wickham's Cay II, base of the huge Moorings charter operations, but with only a few shops and restaurants.

⓱ JR O'Neal Botanical Gardens National Park

Road Town, off Main Street. **Tel** 284 494 2069. **Open** 9am–5pm Mon–Sat.
📷 W bvinpt.org

Road Town's Botanical Gardens provide a pleasant respite from the commotion. Visitors can walk here from the heart of town, but on a hot day a taxi is a better bet. Once here, the gardens offer plenty of shade and benches for resting. The 3-acre (1-ha) gardens feature collections that represent the different plant habitats, exotic species, and a vast collection of palms. Orchids bloom in the gazebo, lilies float in the pond, and cacti grow in the tropical sun.

⓲ Sage Mountain National Park

3 miles (5 km) SW of Road Town.
Tel 284 494 2069. 📷 W bvinpt.org

Established in 1964, the Sage Mountain National Park is BVI's first national park, founded through a donation from philanthropist Laurance S. Rockefeller. Stretching over 86 acres (35 ha), the park reaches a lofty 1,716 ft (523 m) and is the highest point on the entire Virgin Islands. It sits so high that Sage Mountain creates rain; as warm moist air rises from the east and south, it cools as it crosses the mountain, falling as rain on the park's northern side.

The park offers lovely panoramic views to hikers willing to spend some time walking its trails. It is home to many native and introduced species of trees and plants, including mahogany, white cedar, and mamey trees. Hikers on its dozen trails, including the popular Mahogany Forest Trail and the Rainforest Trail, might glimpse mountain doves and thrushes flitting among the trees. Much of the vegetation is second growth owing to clearing activity that was carried out by farmers for agricultural purposes, before the establishment of the park.

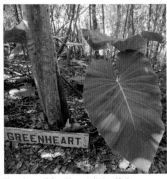
Plant along trail, Sage Mountain National Park

Handicrafts on display at Apple Bay, North Shore

⑲ North Shore

Visitors can enjoy spending part of their day in Tortola driving the North Coast Road for some glorious ocean views and a glimpse into the island's local life.

The drive can be challenging in spots, with lots of twists, turns, and steep hills on the narrow roads. Those driving should remember to keep to the left and watch out for wandering livestock. The intersection of Zion Hill Road and North Coast Road, where Sebastian's on the Beach (see p250) is located, is a good place to start the drive. The road west from here leads to Long Bay Beach Club (see p251) where local dishes are served for lunch. Past the hotel a bumpy road snakes down to the lovely Smuggler's Cove Beach. The beach has no amenities, so it is best to carry snacks, water, sunblock, and other essentials.

Heading east, back to Sebastian's, visitors can make a stop at its beachfront restaurant (see p253) or spend some time on the lovely white sands of **Apple Bay**. Here, just down the road, there is a gaggle of thrown-together boards that makes up Bomba's Shack, the site of legendary full moon parties and other similar events. Another particularly popular

Apple Bay Beach is the one in front of the Sugar Mill Hotel (see p251). Farther ahead, visitors will reach the village of Carrot Bay, home to small restaurants and some more beaches. The trip ends in Cane Garden Bay.

⑳ Cane Garden Bay

4 miles (6 km) NW of Road Town. 🚕
🎵 BVI Music Fest (May). 🏖

Stretching along part of the North Coast Road, Cane Garden Bay is the destination of choice for many vacationers who wish to relax in a laid-back rural

atmosphere and walk barefoot to the beach, restaurants, and bars. Accommodations available here largely consist of small hotels and apartments. The bay provides the perfect opportunity for a swim at the white sandy beach and the casual restaurants that line the gorgeous beach make a good stop for lunch or drinks.

It is also a popular anchorage for the many boaters on week-long sails through the British Virgin Islands (see pp244–5).

The beach, especially in front of the popular hotel Myett's (see p251), can get very busy on cruise ship days, but once the passengers leave after a drink or two at the bar, the beach returns to its normal quiet self. In May, the annual BVI Music Fest brings out thousands of people for a weekend of fun.

㉑ Marina Cay

Off Tortola's NE coast. 🚤
Tel 284 494 2174.

Home to Pusser's Marina Cay Hotel and a popular boating anchorage, the 8-acre (3-ha) Marina Cay makes an interesting day trip from Tortola. American newly-weds Robb and Rodie White set up house on the island in 1937 and lived here for three years. In his 1985 book, Two on the Isle, Robb White tells the story of their adventures.

What is left of their home serves as part of the hotel, and guests can wander the grounds, take a dip in the ocean from the sandy beach, and enjoy the salty ambience of the bar and restaurant. Activities include strolling the nicely planted grounds and snorkeling colorful reefs sitting just off the island's white sandy beach. Those with a thirst for a bit more adventure can enjoy scuba diving from the beach or a boat.

Yachts lining the harbor at Marina Cay

Virgin Gorda and Outer Islands

With luscious white sandy beaches, Virgin Gorda and the outer islands beckon visitors who want to relax with a good book and a frosty drink in hand. Virgin Gorda has a handful of restaurants, a bit of nightlife, and some modest shopping, but the real draw is the beach and the chance to do nothing but gaze at the glorious sunrises and sunsets. It is the same with the outer islands, some of them home to just one resort and excellent sailing anchorages.

Wooden beach villas framed by palm trees, The Valley

㉒ The Valley

SW coast of Virgin Gorda. 🏝 2,000. ✈ 🚢 🚕 ℹ Virgin Gorda Yacht Harbour, 284 495 5181. W bvitourism.com

Also called Spanish Town, The Valley on Virgin Gorda is the heart of the island's activity. Most of it is centered at Virgin Gorda Yacht Harbour, a smallish marina and the shopping area. A few restaurants are sprinkled along the main road of what is not much more than a village. The Yacht Harbour is home to Buck's Grocery where visitors can pick up essentials.

The tourist office is in the same building and has maps and brochures. Ferries land at the jetty a short walk away, where visitors from the US Virgin Islands go through the routine customs checks.

㉓ The Baths

S point of Virgin Gorda. **Tel** 284 494 2069. 🚕 🐾 W bvinpt.org

The Baths National Park, a collection of massive granite boulders that form lovely pools, is on the must-do list for nearly every visitor to

Virgin Gorda as well as parties of charter boat sailors plying these waters. Some of the boulders are 40 ft (12 m) in diameter. They were formed when molten rock seeped into existing volcanic rock layers. Erosion exposed them and they are weathered around the corners. Similar rocks are found in other areas near the Baths.

It is a bit of a walk down from the parking area but, in addition to the boulders, there are white sandy beaches and excellent snorkeling opportunities. Two restaurants and a few shops near the parking area provide lunch, drinks, and the obligatory T-shirt, as well as other souvenir items.

㉔ Driving Tour of Virgin Gorda

Visitors to Virgin Gorda should rent a car for at least a day to get out and about. The 8-sq mile (21-sq km) island has one road running about 6 miles (10 km) from the Baths at the southwest end to North Sound at the northeast and a handful of side roads, so it is just about impossible to really get lost. Maps can be picked up at the tourism office at Virgin Gorda Yacht Harbour.

Farther west on Lee Road from The Valley, a side road heads off to the left to Coppermine Point, a ruin of a mine which was originally built in the 1800s by Cornish miners. Back on Lee Road, vacationers

Huge boulders dotting the crystal-clear waters of The Baths

For hotels and restaurants on these islands see pp248–51 and pp252–3

Ruins of an old copper mine in Coppermine Point, Virgin Gorda

can drive on to the Baths, the island's premier attraction. Spring Bay National Park, sitting seaside just before the Baths, sees far fewer people and is an ideal spot to relax for a few hours after snorkeling at the Baths. A short drive east from The Valley, an unpaved road leads to gorgeous Savannah Bay, which is great for sunbathing and swimming. Back on the main road, Gorda Peak National Park makes a good spot to stop for a hike. Lovely views abound in this hilltop area, and the BVI government has installed several viewing platforms. The drive can end at Gunn Creek, which is the jumping-off point for ferry trips to North Sound, and has a few small restaurants serving local cuisine.

㉙ Gorda Peak National Park

North Sound Road, Virgin Gorda.
Tel 284 494 2069. **W** bvinpt.org

The Gorda Peak National Park covers 260 acres (105 ha) of land and is one of the last remaining examples of the Caribbean dry forest in the region. It is home to a couple of endangered and threatened plant species, as well as the world's smallest lizard – the Virgin Gorda gecko. Two trails lead up to the Gorda Peak, Virgin Gorda's highest point at 1,370 ft (417 m), where a lookout tower offers panoramic views of the BVI. On a clear day, it is possible to see Anegada

to the northeast. A picnic table is placed under the shade of a mango tree where the two trails meet, and provides a pleasant place for lunch or snacks. During the hike uphill, the forest gets moister with increasing altitude and the vegetation changes from species that survive only in dry scrubby areas to those that thrive in slightly damp soil.

㉖ RMS Rhone Marine Park

Off Salt Island. **Tel** 284 494 3904.
W bvinpt.org

The Royal Mail Steamer *Rhone* went down in an 1867 hurricane. Today, it is the main dive destination in the British Virgin Islands. The 310-ft (95-m) vessel sits in two parts at depths

Signage, National Park Trust, BVI

ranging from 20 to 80 ft (6m to 25m). Much of the ship is intact, with parts such as the propeller, boilers, and more still identifiable. The *Rhone* is encrusted with marine growth and serves as a home to many types of fish and marine life. Dive trips depart from Tortola and other British Virgin Islands as well as St. Thomas and St. John in the US Virgin Islands. Those who wish to dive the site need a permit from the National Parks Trust.

㉗ Foxy's Bar

Great Bay, Jost Van Dyke **Tel** 284 495 9258. **W** foxysbar.com

The legendary Foxy Callwood entertains at his eponymous Foxy's Bar, the number one draw on Jost Van Dyke. Day-sail and power boats as well as ferries from West End on Tortola also stop here, making it easy to reach. Visitors on a day trip can enjoy lunch and Foxy's own style of Caribbean music during the afternoon, plus a swim in the warm waters of Great Bay. The last ferry to West End leaves in the early evening, so visitors will have to sleep over or anchor in the harbor if they want to stay for dinner during the week and for barbecues on Friday and Saturday evenings.

A diver swimming through the wreck of the RMS Rhone

Outdoor Activities and Specialized Holidays

The sea is the star when it comes to activities in the British Virgin Islands. Visitors can spend time sunning at the beach, but most guests come here because they want to practise their sailing in small boats off the beach or set sail either for a day, a week, or more through the chain of small islands that make up the British Virgin Islands. At most anchorages, snorkeling over colorful reefs and wrecks beckons. Hiking in the national parks is also popular.

Boat rental sign in Cane Garden Bay, Tortola

One of the many beach bars on Tortola

Beaches

The beaches in British Virgin Islands come in all shapes and sizes, from tiny pockets of soft sand at some small cay to the gorgeous stretch of white sand at Savannah Bay on Virgin Gorda. Many of the beaches have few facilities right on the sand and none are patrolled by lifeguards. Some do have restaurants and beach bars while others offer nothing but perfect sand and sea. If visitors prefer more amenities, a beachfront hotel is a good idea.

Every island has its share of beaches, but flat Anegada gets the prize for its talcum-powder beaches that nearly fringe the entire island.

Virgin Gorda does not lack when it comes to beaches either. In addition to Savannah Bay, the beaches in the area around the Baths offer good snorkeling spots. The island's resorts also have their share of white sandy strands.

Jost Van Dyke's beachy attitude lures folks who want to amble up to a local watering hole after having spent some time lounging at the beach.

Tortola's best beach treasures stretch along the north coast and include the ever popular Cane Garden Bay (see p239), but rough water can be a problem, particularly during the winter months when storms in the north stir up the water. When that is the case, it is a good idea to head to Beef Island, located off Tortola's eastern edge and home to the airport and the gorgeous Long Bay. The BVI Tourism website provides details (see p255).

Sailing

With numerous small islands and rocky outcrops that serve as anchorages and sit close to Tortola and Virgin Gorda, day-sails are easily accomplished. However, for those not keen on a boat with sails,

plenty of motorized boats are also available to make the same trips.

Tortola in particular has plenty of sail and power boats ready to depart from Road Town, West End, Nanny Cay, and other locations. If leaving from Virgin Gorda, a day trip aboard a motor boat can get people as far away as Anegada.

Some vocabulary to help pick the right sailboat – monohulls have one hull, catamarans have two, and trimarans have three. Boats with more than one hull tend to provide a more stable sail. Power boats may provide a smoother trip.

Most day-sail and motor-boat trips provide lunch, snorkeling gear, and instructions on how to use it when the boat drops anchor one or more times during the day. The most popular tour operators offering day-sails are **Aristocat Charters** and **White Squall II**. For more information on boat rentals, visitors can contact **King Charters**.

Apart from day-sails, there are also week-long charters that take people on a longer tour around the islands. Some of the reputable charters are **BVI Yacht Charters**, **The Moorings**,

Catamaran setting out on a cruise

Surfer at Apple Bay in Tortola

Regency Yacht Vacations, **Sunsail**, **Catamaran Charters**, and **Voyages**.

Other Activities

When the weather is good, the islands offers myriad watersports activities. It is possible to rent masks, snorkel and fins from hotels and watersports shops. For diving, if visitors are not certified to dive by one of the national agencies like NAUI or PADI, dive operators offer a learn-to-dive course. For a great diving experience in the islands, it is best to sign on with a charter to the wreck of the *Rhone*, near Salt Island. Main dive and snorkel operators are **Blue Water Divers**, **Jost Van Dyke Scuba**, **Dive BVI** and **Sunchaser Scuba**. Fishing boats leave from various spots around Tortola, Virgin Gorda, and Anegada. **Caribbean Fly Fishing Outfitters** offer guided fishing trips that include all equipment. Brisk winds blow across the islands, with Trellis Bay in Tortola a hotbed of windsurfing activity. Boards can be rented, while lessons are offered by the handful of watersports shops at Trellis Bay

and other locations around the islands. The main operators include **Boardsailing BVI**, **HiHo**, and **Bitter End Yacht Club**.

Head inland for an easy hike at Sage Mountain National Park (*see p238*) on Tortola or Gorda Peak National Park (*see p241*) on Virgin Gorda. However, these parks do not have rangers leading guided tours. The island of Prickly Pear, in Virgin Gorda's North Sound, has a hiking trail but it takes a boat ride to get to the island. In Road Town, Tortola, the JR O'Neal Botanical Gardens National Park (*see p238*) is a relaxing place for a walk.

Hiking trail visible from Gorda Peak, Virgin Gorda

DIRECTORY

Sailing

Aristocat Charters
Soper's Hole, Tortola.
Tel 284 499 1249.
W aristocat charters. com

BVI Yacht Charters
Road Town, Tortola.
Tel 284 494 4289.
W bviyachtcharters. com

Catamaran Charters
Village Cay Marina, Tortola. Tel 284 494 6661.
W catamarans.com

King Charters
Nanny Cay Marina, Tortola. Tel 284 494 5820.
W king charters.com

The Moorings
Wickham's Cay II, Tortola.
Tel 284 494 2322.
W moorings.com

Regency Yacht Vacations
Wickham's Cay I, Tortola.
Tel 284 495 1970.
W regency vacations. com

Sunsail
Wickham's Cay II, Tortola.
Tel 284 495 4740.
W sunsail.co.uk

Voyages
Tel 284 494 0740.
W voyage charters. com

White Squall II
Village Cay Marina, Tortola. Tel 284 494 2564.
W whitesquall2.com

Other Activities

Bitter End Yacht Club
North Sound, Virgin Gorda.
Tel 284 494 2746.
W beyc.com

Blue Water Divers
Nanny Cay and Soper's Hole, Tortola.
Tel 284 494 2847.
W bluewater diversbvi. com

Boardsailing BVI
Trellis Bay, Tortola.
Tel 284 495 2447.
W windsurfing.vi

Caribbean Fly Fishing Outfitters
Nanny Cay, Tortola.
Tel 284 494 4797.
W caribflyfishing.com

Dive BVI
Virgin Gorda Yacht Harbor and Leverick Bay Resort and Marina, Virgin Gorda; Scrub Island, Little Dix Bay.
Tel 284 495 5513.
W divebvi.com

Hiho
Trellis Bay, Tortola.
Tel 284 494 0337.
W go-hiho.com

Jost Van Dyke Scuba
Great Harbour, Jost Van Dyke.
Tel 284 495 0271.
W jostvandyke scuba. com

Sunchaser Scuba
North Sound, Virgin Gorda.
Tel 284 495 9638.
W sunchaser scuba. com

Sailing the British Virgin Islands

The British Virgin Islands is one of the premier destinations for sailing. Anchorages are just an easy sail apart, and range from deserted cays with not a single boat to busy bays known for their salty conviviality. Numerous charter companies rent bare boats, where visitors can serve as captain, or charter boats that come complete with captain and crew. Most boats are rented in Tortola, but charters to the British Virgin Islands also set sail from St. Thomas and St. John in the US Virgin Islands. Both St. Thomas and Tortola have large grocery stores with everything that sailors will need to provision their boats.

Boats at Wickhams Cay, Tortola

Cane Garden Bay is a good anchorage on the north side of Tortola. The bay is a party spot with more than a handful of bars and restaurants perfect for whiling away a few hours and escaping from galley duties. Supplies are available at a couple of small markets situated along the main North Coast Road.

Jost Van Dyke has several anchorages. It is mandatory to clear customs check at Great Harbour if coming from the US Virgin Islands. Vacationers can relax with a beer at Foxy's, pull up anchor, and motor around to White Bay for some peace and quiet.

West End in Tortola is a busy marina during the day when ferries come and go. Sailors will have to clear customs here if they are coming from the US Virgin Islands and have not done so already. Travelers can take their dinghy ashore on the opposite side of the harbor for a browse around the shops.

For keys to symbols see back flap

Marina Cay is home to Pusser's Bar and Restaurant, and the infamous painkiller rum drinks that lure sailors from far and wide. A small shop sells books, souvenirs, and more.

North Sound has excellent sailing conditions given its location and facilities. The few restaurants, bars, and resorts cater primarily to sailors. Watersports outlets offer an entire gamut of activities.

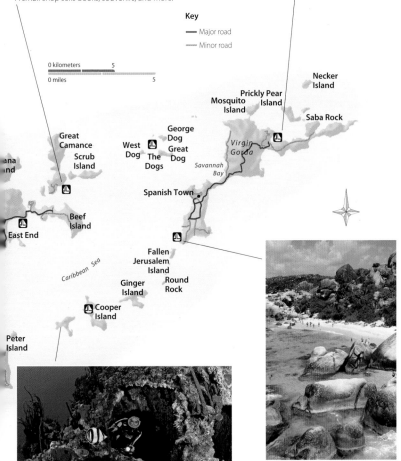

Key

— Major road

— Minor road

0 kilometers 5

0 miles 5

Necker Island

Prickly Pear Island

Mosquito Island

Saba Rock

Great Camanoe

Scrub Island

West Dog

George Dog

Great Dog

The Dogs

Virgin Gorda

Savannah Bay

ana nd

Spanish Town

Beef Island

East End

Fallen Jerusalem Island

Round Rock

Caribbean Sea

Ginger Island

Cooper Island

Peter Island

Salt Island has great diving opportunities, such as the RMS *Rhone* nearby. Cooper Island is an ideal stop for lunch for those sailing down the string of small islands that lie south of Tortola. Peter Island offers some fine dining, while Norman Island is home to several caves perfect for snorkeling.

The Baths in Virgin Gorda is where nearly everyone stops to snorkel among the giant boulders. Visitors can also hike up the path to a small shopping area and have lunch at Top of the Baths, replenish the larder at Buck's Food Market, and buy souvenirs at a gift shop.

The Baths at Virgin Gorda, British Virgin Isles ▶

Where to Stay

US Virgin Islands

ST. CROIX: Carringtons Inn $
B&B
4001 Estate Hermon Hill
Tel *877 658 0508 or 340 713 0508*
W carringtonsinn.com
Attractive rooms centered around a pool, nice views, and a friendly host make this adults-only inn a good base for exploring St. Croix. Delicious breakfasts, too.

ST. CROIX: Chenay Bay Beach Resort $
Modern
Route 82, Green Cay
Tel *866 357 2970 or 340 718 2918*
W defenderresorts.com/chenaybay
A stay at this small resort is great for families who want to enjoy a long vacation in simple but attractive cottages with kitchens.

ST. CROIX: Hotel Caravelle $
Modern
Queen Cross Street, Christiansted
Tel *800 524 0410 or 340 773 06874*
W hotelcaravelle.com
In addition to modest rooms with sea views, the Caravelle provides a restaurant, parking, and proximity to shopping, other restaurants, and historic sites.

ST. CROIX: Hotel on the Cay $
Beach Resort
Protestant Cay, Christiansted Harbor
Tel *855 654 0301 or 340 773 2035*
W hotelonthecay.com
A short ferry ride takes guests from Christiansted boardwalk to this small island resort. The beach provides sunning and swimming opportunities; shops and restaurants are nearby.

ST. CROIX: Sandcastle on the Beach $
Beach Resort
Route 71, Frederiksted
Tel *800 524 2018*
W sandcastleonthebeach.com
With a variety of room styles that include studios, suites, and villas, this resort provides plenty of options for its mainly gay and lesbian guests. The neighborhood isn't the greatest, but the beach is superlative.

ST. CROIX: Villa Margarita $
Waterfront
Off Route 80, Salt River
Tel *340 713 1930*
W villamargarita.com
With an oceanfront location in a residential neighborhood, this small inn provides comfortable accommodations with kitchens for independent travelers. A sandy swimming beach is only a short walk away.

ST. CROIX: Waves at Cane Bay $
Waterfront
Route 80, Cane Bay
Tel *340 718 1815*
W canebaystcroix.com
Enjoy the lovely sea views at this small hotel located right at the water's edge. Swimming is just down the road at sandy Cane Bay Beach. Pleasant, comfortable rooms, and free Wi-Fi.

ST. CROIX: Divi Carina Bay Resort $$
Beach Resort
Route 60, Turner Hole
Tel *877 773 9700 or 340 773 9700*
W divicarina.com
This attractive resort offers chic, well-appointed rooms with lovely views. With a casino, mini-golf, tennis courts, a watersports center, and an all-inclusive dining plan, a stay at this hotel is a good fit for active vacationers.

ST. CROIX: Hibiscus Beach Resort $$
Beach Resort
Off Route 752, La Grande Princess
Tel *800 442 0121 or 340 718 4042*
W hibiscusbeachresort.com
Step out the door and onto the sand at this modestly appointed resort with an on-site beachfront restaurant. Comfortable rooms feature a tropical decor, but the beach is the star attraction.

Grand entrance to the Divi Carina Bay Resort, St. Croix

ST. CROIX: Renaissance St. Croix Carambola Beach Resort $$
Beach Resort
Route 80, Davis Bay
Tel *888 503 8760 or 340 778 3800*
W marriott.com
It is a bit of a drive to Christiansted and Frederiksted, but this resort provides gracious rooms with an equally nice beach, plenty of activities, and a relaxing atmosphere that make it worth the trip.

ST. CROIX: Sugar Beach $$
Beach Resort
Route 752, Golden Rock
Tel *800 524 2049 or 340 718 5345*
W sugarbeachstcroix.com
With full kitchens, ocean views, and a beach, this condo complex is a great setting for the perfect tropical vacation. Furnishings vary since the apartments are individually owned.

DK Choice

ST. CROIX: The Buccaneer Hotel $$
Beach Resort
Route 82, Shoys
Tel *800 255 3881 or 340 712 2100*
W thebuccaneer.com
A member of the Historic Hotels of America, The Buccaneer sits beachfront but close to Christiansted's shopping, restaurants, and historic sites. There is a variety of lovely rooms in many price ranges, as well as a beach house. The resort's golf course, extensive watersports, tennis, fine dining, and other activities keep guests busy, but it is just as easy to spend the vacation relaxing with a good book.

ST. CROIX: The Palms at Pelican Cove $$
Beach Resort
Off Route 752, La Grande Princess
Tel *800 548 4460 or 340 718 8920*
W palmsatpelicancove.com
A small resort with a restaurant and an attractive beach, The Palms at Pelican Cove has nice rooms in a tropical style. It is 10 minutes away from the shops and restaurants in Christiansted.

ST. CROIX: Villa Madeleine $$
Resort
Off Route 82, Teague Bay
Tel *877 788 0361 or 340 718 0361*
W villamadeleine-stcroix.com
Each condominium here comes with a full kitchen and a private pool. There are tennis courts on site, and grocery shops are a 10-minute drive away. Superb views.

ST. JOHN:
Cinnamon Bay Camp $
Beach Resort
Route 20, Cinnamon Bay
Tel *800 539 9998 or 340 776 6330*
W cinnamonbay.com
A choice of cottage, tent, or bare site gives campers several options here. A great place for social vacationers on a budget who enjoy the beach and watersports.

ST. JOHN: Coconut
Coast Villas $$
Waterfront
Near Frank Bay, Cruz Bay
Tel *800 858 7989 or 340 693 9100*
W coconutcoast.com
Located in a quiet, residential neighborhood, these villas are an easy walk away from Cruz Bay's shops and restaurants. All the units have kitchens.

DK Choice

ST. JOHN: Concordia
Eco-Resort $$
Eco-Resort
Off Route 107, Concordia
Tel *800 392 9004 or 340 693 5855*
W concordiaeco-resort.com
With a choice of condos with kitchens or kitchenettes and tents with solar showers and composting toilets, this eco-concious option attracts back-to-nature types who want some comforts. Souvenir shop on site.

ST. JOHN: Estate Lindholm $$
B&B
Route 20, Cruz Bay
Tel *800 322 6335 or 340 776 6121*
W estatelindholm.com
Featuring gorgeous landscaping, this inn has 14 crisp rooms with white accents. Be aware: if you walk into town, it's a steep hike back. Stunning views of Cruz Bay.

ST. JOHN: Estate Zootenvaal $$
Waterfront
Route 10, Zootenvaal
Tel *340 776 6321*
W estatezootenvaal.com
A good spot for exploring St. John, this estate offers pleasant rooms with kitchens and a beach. Grocery shopping in Coral Bay is 5 minutes away.

Stunning mountain view from the attractive pool area at the Westin Resort and Villas, St. John

ST. JOHN: Garden by the Sea $$
B&B
Near Small Pond, Cruz Bay
Tel *340 779 4731*
W gardenbythesea.com
With delicious breakfasts and a location within walking distance of Cruz Bay's shops and restaurants, this B&B is a great home away from home.

ST. JOHN: St. John Inn $$
Inn
Off Route 104, Cruz Bay
Tel *800 666 7688 or 340 693 8688*
W stjohninn.com
It is an easy walk to shops and restaurants from this sociable inn. Rooms are on the basic side but more than comfortable.

ST. JOHN: Westin Resort
and Villas $$
Beach Resort
Route 104, Great Cruz Bay
Tel *866 716 8108*
W westinresortstjohn.com
Plenty of watersports, a spacious beach, a pool, and several dining options make this resort a good bet for families who want all amenities close at hand. Both rooms and villas are available.

ST. JOHN: Caneel Bay Resort $$$
Beach Resort
Route 20, Caneel Bay
Tel *855 226 3358 or 340 776 6111*
W caneelbay.com
This place offers comfort rather than glitz. With seven beaches, restaurants, watersports, tennis, and activities for children, Caneel Bay is ideal for families.

ST. JOHN: Gallows
Point Resort $$$
Waterfront
Bay Road, Cruz Bay
Tel *800 323 7229 or 340 776 6434*
W gallowspointresort.com
Charming units with kitchens, just five minutes from Cruz Bay's

restaurants and shops. There is an oceanfront Jacuzzi and a small snorkeling beach. Lovely views.

ST. JOHN:
Grande Bay Resort $$$
Waterfront
Bay Street, Cruz Bay
Tel *340 693 4668*
W grandebayresort.com
Nice harbor views, spiffy condo-style units, pool, spa, and parking can all be had at this complex. It is close to Cruz Bay's restaurants, nightlife, and shopping.

ST. JOHN: Sea Shore Allure $$$
Waterfront
Pond Mouth Road, Cruz Bay
Tel *855 779 2800 or 340 779 2800*
W seashoreallure.com
The condos at Sea Shore Allure center around a spacious pool. Rooms feature top-of-the-line amenities that will please vacationers who like some glitz. It is an easy walk to Cruz Bay.

ST. THOMAS: Crystal Palace $
B&B
Crystal Gade, Charlotte Amalie
Tel *866 502 2277 or 340 777 2277*
W crystalpalaceusvi.com
Rooms at the Crystal Palace are furnished with beautiful period antiques and come with history lessons, since the owner is a noted amateur historian. A stay here is a gracious step back in time.

ST. THOMAS: Best Western
Emerald Beach Resort $$
Beach Resort
Route 30, Lindbergh Bay
Tel *800 233 4936 or 340 777 8800*
W emeraldbeach.com
A soft sandy beach is right on the doorstep of this small motel-style resort near the airport. A restaurant, bar, and watersports are available. A spa, a salon, and free Wi-Fi round out the facilities.

DK Choice

ST. THOMAS: Bolongo Bay $$
Beach Resort
Route 30, Bolongo
Tel *800 524 4746 or 340 775 1800*
W bolongobay.com
This resort offers spacious rooms strung out along a luscious white-sand beach that fronts a gorgeous turquoise bay. The focus is on watersports, with day sails, scuba, snorkeling, and a personal watercraft right at the beach. Iggie's Beach Bar and Grill is a local hot spot.

ST. THOMAS: Frenchman's Reef & Morning Star Marriott Beach Resort $$
Beach Resort
Route 315, Bakkeroe
Tel *800 524 2000 or 340 776 8500*
W marriott.com
Luxurious rooms come in a range of sizes and styles. There are also several restaurants, a handful of beaches, and watersports galore.

ST. THOMAS: Pavilions and Pools $$
Beach Resort
Off Route 38, Smith Bay
Tel *800 524 2001 or 340 775 6110*
W pavilionsandpools.com
An all-villa property with lovely water and mountain views and comfortable accommodations. Each unit comes with its own private pool and a full kitchen.

ST. THOMAS: Sapphire Beach Resort $$
Beach Resort
Off Route 32, Smith Bay
Tel *800 524 2025*
W antillesresorts.com
A fabulous white-sand beach, simple but comfortable units, and gorgeous views lure vacationers to this condominium complex.

ST. THOMAS: Secret Harbour $$
Beach Resort
Off Route 322, Nazareth
Tel *800 524 2250*
W secretharbourvi.com
A choice of beachfront or beach-view condo-style rooms, with a sandy beach just a few steps away. Nice, simple rooms.

ST. THOMAS: Sugar Bay Resort and Spa $$$
Beach Resort
Route 38, Smith Bay
Tel *800 927 7100 or 877 894 4461*
W sugarbayresortandspa.com
This all-inclusive resort has lovely rooms with splendid sea views, a great beach, and enough activities to keep anyone busy.

Luxurious junior suite at the Peter Island Resort & Spa, Peter Island

British Virgin Islands

ANEGADA: Neptune's Treasure $
Waterfront
Anegada
Tel *284 495 9439*
W neptunestreasure.com
This family-run hotel offers simple rooms in a divine setting, right on a gorgeous beach. At the on-site restaurant, fresh lobster is the dish *du jour*.

COOPER ISLAND: Cooper Island Beach Club $$
Island Resort
Cooper Island
Tel *800 542 4624 or 284 495 9084*
W cooperislandbeachclub.com
Pleasant rooms with views, a great restaurant, a range of watersports, and a convivial atmosphere await at this resort. Arrival is by launch.

DK Choice

GUANA ISLAND: Guana Island Resort $$$
Island Resort
Guana Island
Tel *800 544 8262 or 212 482 6247*
W guana.com
Simple but comfortable rooms, superb beaches, fabulous meals including wine, and a good selection of watersport activities are what make the Guana Island Resort special. It is the only resort on this small, privately owned island. Arrival is by private launch from the airport on Beef Island or by water taxi from St. Thomas.

JOST VAN DYKE: Sandcastle Hotel $$
Beach Resort
Jost Van Dyke
Tel *284 495 9888*
W soggydollar.com
The beach is a massive draw, but many guests head to this small resort for its Soggy Dollar Bar. There are no TVs or telephones in the simple but adequate rooms. Choice of cottages – garden or beachfront – as well as rooms.

PETER ISLAND: Peter Island Resort & Spa $$$
Island Resort
Peter Island
Tel *800 346 4451 or 284 495 2000*
W peterisland.com
Beautiful rooms, elegant food, lovely beaches, a fabulous spa, and plenty of watersports. A ferry picks guests up from Tortola.

TORTOLA: Fort Burt Hotel $
Historic
Waterfront Drive, Road Town
Tel *284 494 2587*
W fortburt.com
A variety of room styles with sea views. The hotel is conveniently located for Road Town's shops and restaurants. Parking is tight.

TORTOLA: Maria's by the Sea Hotel $
Modern
Waterfront Drive, Road Town
Tel *284 494 2595*
W mariasbythesea.com
The rooms are basic but clean and cheerful, and the hotel has a parking lot. Shops, restaurants, nightlife, and day sails are nearby.

TORTOLA: Sebastian's on the Beach $
Beach Resort
Long Bay Road, Apple Bay
Tel *800 336 4870 or 284 495 4212*
W sebastiansbvi.com
This small beachfront resort is located within walking distance to several bars and restaurants.

TORTOLA: Fort Recovery Beachfront Villas and Suites Hotel $$
Beach Resort
Waterfront Drive, Pockwood Pond
Tel *855 349 3355*
W fortrecovery.com
Offering spacious suites that come with kitchens, this small resort is a good place to spend a week or two. The beach is small, but the views are lovely.

TORTOLA: Frenchman's $$
Beach Resort
Off Sir Francis Drake Hwy, Soper's Hole
Tel *284 494 8811*
W frenchmansbvi.com
Each unit here includes a kitchen, lovely views, and fabulous decor done by a local designer. Beach, tennis, and a restaurant on site.

TORTOLA: Long Bay
Beach Club $$
Beach Resort
Long Bay Road, Long Bay
Tel *866 237 3491 or 305 444 4033*
W longbay.com
This resort offers beaches, a pool, watersports, tennis, shops, and restaurants, as well as attractive rooms in multiple categories.

TORTOLA: Myett's $$
Beach Resort
Cane Garden Bay
Tel *284 495 9649*
W myetts.com
The rooms may be simple, but Cane Bay's bars and restaurants are just an easy stroll away from this eco-friendly beachfront hotel.

TORTOLA: Pusser's
Marina Cay Resort $$
Island Resort
Marina Cay
Tel *284 494 2174 or 284 340 5678 (reservations)*
W pussers.com
This tiny resort, with simple rooms and villas, plus the fabled Pusser's Bar, is a favorite with boaters. A launch leaves from Trellis Bay.

TORTOLA: Sugar Mill Hotel $$
Beach Resort
North Coast Road, Apple Bay
Tel *800 462 8834 or 284 495 4355*
W sugarmillhotel.com
Lovely rooms dot the hillside, with the Sugar Mill Restaurant at the center of the complex. There is a small beach across the road.

TORTOLA: The Mariner
Inn Hotel $$
Modern
Wickham's Cay II, Road Town
Tel *800 535 7289 or 284 494 2333*
W bvimarinerinnhotel.com
A hot spot for vacationers leaving on a week's charter boat holiday. Landlubbers like it for the buzz of activity and the spacious rooms.

TORTOLA: Scrub Island $$$
Island Resort
Scrub Island
Tel *877 890 7444 or 284 394 3440*
W scrubisland.com
Posh rooms, a great pool, several restaurants, lots of activities, and a lovely remote beach are the highlights of Scrub Island.

DK Choice

TORTOLA: Surfsong Villa
Resort 579 $$$
Luxury
Off Beef Island Road, Beef Island
Tel *284 495 1864*
W surfsong.net
Seven beautiful villas in various sizes sit beachfront in a serene compound. Guests enjoy plenty of relaxation – at the small beach, the tree-shaded courtyard, or in tucked-away locations. A short drive from the main road that connects the airport with the rest of Tortola.

VIRGIN GORDA:
Fischer's Cove Beach Hotel $
Beach Resort
Lee Road, The Valley
Tel *284 495 5252*
W fischerscove.com
Rooms are a little pedestrian, but the hotel has a good beachside setting and is close to Spanish Town. Good restaurant on site.

VIRGIN GORDA: Leverick Bay $
Waterfront
Leverick Bay Road, Leverick Bay
Tel *800 848 7081 or 284 495 7421*
W leverickbay.com
Adjacent to a busy marina, with a small beach and pool, this apartment complex provides basic rooms with kitchens. It also has tennis and watersports.

VIRGIN GORDA:
Guavaberry Spring Bay $$
Beach Resort
Tower Road, Spring Bay
Tel *284 495 5227*
W guavaberryspringbay.com
Units with kitchens sit on both sides of the road to the Baths. With kitchens and access to a lovely beach, they are great for families.

Comfortable cabanas by the pool at Biras
Creek Resort, Virgin Gorda

VIRGIN GORDA:
Mango Bay Resort $$
Beach Resort
Nail Bay Road, Mahoe Bay
Tel *284 495 5672*
W mangobayresort.com
A lovely beach is just steps away from both the beachfront and garden villas at this resort. The units aren't posh, but all have kitchens and are perfect for a relaxed beach vacation.

VIRGIN GORDA:
Nail Bay Resort 280 $$
Beach Resort
Off Nail Bay Road, Nail Bay
Tel *800 871 3551 or 284 494 8000*
W nailbay.com
With everything from studios to deluxe villas, all equipped with cooking facilities, this resort sits hillside above the beach. Plenty of activities, plus a swim-up bar.

DK Choice

VIRGIN GORDA:
Biras Creek Resort $$$
Luxury
North Sound
Tel *877 883 0756 or 284 394 3555*
W biras.com
Reachable by launch, this luxurious resort has suites set on expansive, lush grounds. With a private white-sand beach, pool, tennis courts, watersports, and a Relais & Châteaux-rated restaurant, guests are happy to spend their vacation right on the property. However, for a diversion, a launch will drop guests at other resorts scattered around the bay.

VIRGIN GORDA: Bitter End
Yacht Club $$$
Beach Resort
North Sound
Tel *800 872 2392 or 284 494 2746*
W beyc.com
Sailing and other watersports are the focus here, but the narrow beaches also beckon. Rooms vary in size and decor, but all are attractive. Access is by hotel launch.

VIRGIN GORDA:
Rosewood Little Dix Bay $$$
Beach Resort
Off North Sound Road, The Valley
Tel *284 495 5555*
W littledixbay.com
Understated luxury and lush landscaping are the hallmarks of this upscale resort. It comes complete with lovely beaches, good restaurants, plenty of watersports activities, tennis, and a top-notch spa.

Where to Eat and Drink

US Virgin Islands

ST. CROIX: Avocado Pitt $
Café
Christiansted Boardwalk
Tel *340 773 9843* **Closed** *Dinner*
Eat alfresco or at the counter at
this downtown spot. The home-
made oatmeal is a good choice
for breakfast; for lunch, try the
fresh tuna on a crispy roll.

ST. CROIX: Turtles Deli $
Deli
*38 Strand Street at Prince Street,
Frederiksted*
Tel *340 772 3676* **Closed** *Sun*
The sandwiches here come piled
sky-high with meats like roast
turkey and beef. The chef adds
flavorful cheeses, veggies, and
more for extra bursts of flavor.

ST. CROIX: Blue Moon $$
International
7 Strand Street, Frederiksted
Tel *340 772 2222* **Closed** *Mon*
The style of food at Blue
Moon ranges from Cajun and
Caribbean to whatever else
may take the chef's fancy.
Occasional live music.

DK Choice

ST. CROIX: Eat @ Cane Bay $$
International
Route 80, Cane Bay
Tel *340 718 0360* **Closed** *Tue*
Located across the road from
busy Cane Bay Beach, this open-
air spot dishes up some of the
best food on the island. There
is a build-it-yourself burger,
along with a blackboard filled
with fine-dining options that
include steak and lobster. The
rum cake is absolutely divine.

ST. CROIX: Rum Runners $$$
International
*Christiansted Boardwalk,
Christiansted*
Tel *340 773 6585*
With everything from ribs to
lobster on the menu, this alfresco
eatery is always busy. It is also a
great spot for people-watching.

ST. JOHN: Sam and Jack's Deli $
International
*Marketplace Shopping Center,
Route 104, Cruz Bay*
Tel *340 714 3354* **Closed** *Sun*
With only a few tables scattered
outside, take-out is often the
better option at this deli. Foodies
line up for favorites like frozen

wild mushroom and truffle
ravioli, which can be cooked
up in a couple of minutes.

ST. JOHN: Skinny Legs Bar and Restaurant $
International
Route 10, Coral Bay
Tel *340 779 4982*
Locals mingle with vacationers
at this popular bar and eatery.
Burgers and chips are served all
day, and the big-screen TV shows
the sporting event of the day.

ST. JOHN: Vie's Snack Shack $
Caribbean
Route 10, Hansen Bay
Tel *340 693 5033* **Closed** *Sun & Mon*
Fluffy conch fritters and Vie's own
garlic chicken star at this outdoor
roadside stand, close to a lovely
white-sand beach. Delicious
home-made pies as well.

ST. JOHN: Lime Inn $$
Seafood
Lemon Tree Mall, King Street, Cruz Bay
Tel *340 776 6425* **Closed** *Sun*
The Wednesday all-you-can-eat
shrimp at the Lime Inn is an
island institution, but if you miss
it, the rest of the menu has
something for everyone. Seafood,
chicken, and beef dishes reign at
this alfresco restaurant.

ST. JOHN: Sun Dog Café $$
Café
*Mongoose Junction Shopping
Center, Cruz Bay*
Tel *340 693 8340*
Light bites and more substantial
meals are on tap for lunch and
dinner. The spinach quesadilla
and jerk chicken sandwich are
great lunch choices.

Outside seating at the Sweet Plantains,
St. John

Price Guide

Prices are based on a two-course meal
for one, including tax and service
charges, and half a bottle of wine.

$	up to $30
$$	$30–55
$$$	over $55

ST. JOHN: Asolare $$$
Asian
Route 20, Lind Point, Cruz Bay
Tel *340 779 4747*
Asolare's seasonal menus always
have an Asian twist. Pork chops
come with a spicy General Tso's
sauce, while the lobster tails are
served with a mango butter sauce.

ST. JOHN: Fish Trap Restaurant $$$
Seafood
Bay and Strand streets, Cruz Bay
Tel *340 693 9994* **Closed** *Mon*
Seafood is the star at this alfresco
spot. The chef does lobster
several ways, as well as scallops,
mahi mahi, and grouper. Try a
bowl of chowder for a snack.

DK Choice

ST. JOHN: Sweet Plantains $$$
Caribbean
Route 107, Coral Bay
Tel *340 777 4653* **Closed** *Tue*
This place takes Caribbean
classics to a new level, with
dishes like grouper filet served
with a coconut and tomato
sauce flavored with allspice. The
rum tasting menu offers the best
Caribbean rums. Dine outdoors
under umbrellas for a view of
the sea just across the street.

ST. THOMAS: Bill's Texas Pitt BBQ $
American
Red Hook Plaza, Route 32, Red Hook
Tel *340 776 9579* **Closed** *Sun*
With locations on the waterfront,
near the hospital, and in Subba,
the taste of tangy barbecue is
never far away. Ribs, brisket, and
chicken come with potato salad,
rice, or coleslaw. Take-out only.

ST. THOMAS: Greenhouse Restaurant and Bar $$
International
Waterfront Drive, Charlotte Amalie
Tel *340 774 7998*
Popular with vacationers as well
as locals, Greenhouse offers pasta
dishes, burgers, wrap sandwiches,
seafood, and steaks. Several
nights a week, it becomes one
of the island's hot night spots.

ST. THOMAS:
Randy's Bistro $$
International
Al Cohen Plaza, Route 38, Raphune
Tel *340 775 5001* **Closed** *Sat & Sun*
The turkey Reuben at this local favorite comes piled high with coleslaw, but the pasta of the day or a juicy steak are great for dinner. Good early-bird specials.

ST. THOMAS: Virgilio's $$$
Italian
Off Main Street, Charlotte Amalie
Tel *340 776 4920* **Closed** *Sun*
Rub shoulders with the island's movers and shakers while dining on fine Italian fare. Great homemade pasta with delectable sauces, *osso buco*, and tiramisu.

British Virgin Islands

DK Choice

JOST VAN DYKE: Foxy's Tamarind Restaurant $$
International
Great Harbour
Tel *284 495 9258*
Foxy's is famous thanks to Foxy Callwood's ad-lib prowess with the guitar. Charterboaters and folks who hop the ferry for a day trip crowd this open-air bar and restaurant. Weekends feature an all-you-can-eat barbecue and plenty of partying.

TORTOLA: Capriccio di Mare $
Italian
Waterfront Drive, Road Town
Tel *284 494 5369* **Closed** *Sun*
Stop by for a light lunch or an afternoon snack at this alfresco spot. Try a crispy pizza or a basil and mozzarella salad, and end your meal with a perfect espresso.

TORTOLA: Myett's Garden and Grille $$
International
Cane Garden Bay
Tel *284 495 9649*
Vacationers flock here for sandwiches, as well as seafood, pasta dishes, and steaks. Conch chowder and fritters are the house specialties.

TORTOLA: Pusser's Landing $$
International
Frenchman's Cay Road, Soper's Hole
Tel *284 495 4554*
Start your meal with a Pusser's rum drink. Lunch (downstairs) runs to snacks and pizzas, while entrées for dinner (upstairs) include fish and steak.

Colorful entrance to the Top of the Baths eatery, Virgin Gorda

TORTOLA: Sebastian's Seaside Grille $$
International
Long Bay Road, Apple Bay
Tel *284 495 4212*
Almost on the beach, this eatery has a menu of seafood, as well as pasta, chicken, and beef. Try the *roti*, a burrito filled with chicken, conch, or vegetables.

TORTOLA: Sugar Mill Restaurant $$
Fine Dining
North Coast Road, Apple Bay
Tel *284 495 4355*
A centuries-old sugar mill sets the stage for a lovely dinner. Try the fish of the day baked in banana leaves, the lobster bisque, or shrimp and vegetable skewers over pineapple salsa.

TORTOLA: The Dove $$
International
67 Main Street, Road Town
Tel *284 494 0313* **Closed** *Sun & Mon*
The food here features creative takes on standards like nori-wrapped tuna or shrimp with a ginger glaze. Finish with soursop *crème brûlée*.

TORTOLA: Brandywine Estate $$$
French
Off Blackburn Hwy, Brandywine Bay
Tel *284 495 2301* **Closed** *Tue*
Enjoy terrific food and sea views here. Lunch can be a goat cheese salad or steak tartare. For dinner, try fish dishes like salmon and mahi mahi served with a tarragon sauce, potatoes, and vegetables.

VIRGIN GORDA: Bath and Turtle $$
International
Yacht Harbour, Spanish Town
Tel *284 495 5329*
Popular with locals, this is also a hot spot for boaters who dock at the adjacent marina. Pizzas, burgers, chicken, and seafood.

VIRGIN GORDA: Fischer's Cove Restaurant $$
Caribbean
Fischer's Cove Hotel, Tower Road, The Valley
Tel *284 495 5252*
A lovely spot with a porch overlooking the beach. Salads and sandwiches are available at lunch; at dinner, local seafood like snapper is the highlight.

VIRGIN GORDA: Top of the Baths $$
International
Tower Road, The Valley
Tel *284 495 5497*
Come here for sandwiches, steaks, burgers, and seafood. The Sunday barbecue is popular. Located near the island's premier sightseeing spot, with fabulous views.

VIRGIN GORDA: Chez Bamboo $$$
Fine dining
Lee Road, Spanish Town
Tel *284 495 5752*
The menu here always features lobster in some form – try the pasta Alfredo, with lobster and lemongrass. Good tapas menu.

VIRGIN GORDA: Sugarcane $$$
Fine Dining
Nail Bay Resort, Nail Bay Road, Nail Bay
Tel *284 852 6107*
From burgers and sandwiches to Puerto Rican *churrasco* steak, this place serves delicious food. Try the Key lime pie. There is a swim-up bar near the poolside tables.

VIRGIN GORDA: The Rock Café $$$
Café
Tower Road, The Valley
Tel *284 495 5482*
Sitting among big boulders, The Rock Café offers seafood as well as Italian fare that includes gnocchi with garlic and basil, and olive-crusted salmon.

Practical Information

The tourist infrastructure across the US and British Virgin Islands works fairly well. The islands are quite small, and traveling from one end to the other on St. Croix, the largest island, takes under an hour. That said, other than a highway on St. Croix, roads are narrow and winding. Drivers often stop to chat with passersby and so one needs to be patient while driving. Inter-island ferries and planes connect the islands.

When to Go

The Virgin Islands generally have good weather throughout the year. The hurricane season runs from June to November, reaching its peak in September. Rates tend to be low during this season, but some hotels may be closed in August and September.

Getting There

Vistors can fly directly from the US mainland to St. Croix and St. Thomas, but will have to change planes in San Juan, Puerto Rico, for Tortola and Virgin Gorda destinations. Flights are offered by **American Airlines**, **Delta**, **JetBlue**, **Spirit Airlines**, **United Airlines**, **US Airways**, **Air Sunshine**, **LIAT**, and **Seaborne Airlines**. It is also possible to reach St. John, St. Thomas, Jost Van Dyke, Anegada, Tortola, and Virgin Gorda by ferry.

Documentation

Citizens of USA do not need a passport to visit the US Virgin Islands, though one is required for all visitors to the British Virgin Islands. More details regarding visa and passport regulations can be obtained from **US Department of State** and the tourism websites.

Visitor information

Visitors' centers provide information, brochures, and maps. Opening hours are usually 9am–5pm. More information on where to stay, restaurants, activities, and more can be obtained from the various **USVI Tourism** and **BVI Tourism** offices or their websites.

Health and Security

Hospitals are located on the bigger islands including **Juan F. Luis Hospital**, **Myrah Keating Smith Community Health Center**, **Peebles Hospital**, **Roy L. Schneider Hospital**, **Virgin Gorda Government Health Clinic**. The British Virgin Islands outer islands have their own health clinics.

Use normal precautions to ensure your safety. Avoid dark alleys and deserted beaches.

Banking and Currency

Both the US and British Virgin Islands use American currency. Banks are located on St. John, St. Thomas, St. Croix, Tortola, and Virgin Gorda. All banks have ATMs, while independent ATMs are found in bars and restaurants. Most hotels, restaurants, and other tourist facilities accept credit cards.

Communications

From the US Virgin Islands to the US mainland, calls are inexpensive, but calling the US mainland from the British Virgin Islands is considered an international call. The US-based carrier **AT&T** has the most cell coverage across the US Virgin Islands. In the British Virgin Islands, it can be accessed from the southeast coast of Tortola and near the ferry dock on Virgin Gorda. Phone cards are available at pharmacies and stores. Some hotels offer Internet access and major towns have cybercafés.

Local phone booth in Tortola

Transport

Renting a car is the best way to get around on the Virgin Islands. Car rental agencies have booths at airports and at ferry terminals. Driving is on the left. There are a number of global rental agencies such as **AVIS** and **Hertz** as well as local companies that operate in St. Croix, St. Thomas, Tortola, and Virgin Gorda. A valid driver's license is needed to rent a car on the Virgin Islands. It is advisable to make prior reservations during the high season. Rates are high, particularly on the smaller islands. Fuel is also more expensive than on the US mainland.

Taxis meet arriving planes and ferries and are stationed at major hotels. There is a bus service on the main US Virgin Islands, but none on the British Virgin Islands.

The Great Harbour ferry terminal and docks, Jost Van Dyke

Shopping

Duty-free shops in Charlotte Amalie in St. Thomas sell jewelry, spices, and local crafts. British Virgin Islands also has a few stores selling a variety of goods. Store timings are typically 9am–5pm, but shops tend to open till late when cruise ships are in port.

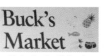

Market sign, Spanish Town in Virgin Gorda

Language

English is the official language spoken on the Virgin Islands.

Electricity

The electrical system operates on 110 volts and 120 volts in the British Virgin Islands and US Virgin Islands respectively.

Time

The Virgin Islands are on Atlantic Standard Time, 1 hour ahead of the Eastern Standard Time in the US and 4 hours behind Greenwich Mean Time. The islands do not observe daylight savings.

Getting Married

In the British Virgin Islands, couples must apply for a marriage license in person at the **Attorney General's Office**. Once ready, it also needs to be collected in person. In the US Virgin Islands, apply for a license at the **Superior Court** offices on St. Thomas and St. Croix. Here, applications need not be made in person, but the people concerned need to pick the license up themseves. Wedding planners such as **Anne Marie Weddings** or **Weddings the Island Way** help couples through the legalities, and organize the ceremony.

Villas

Many people visiting the Virgin Islands stay in vacation villas. The villas range from small one-bedroom places to houses that are quite impressive. St. John alone has at least 400 villas available through **Catered To Vacation Homes**, **Vacation Vistas**, **Caribbean Villas**, and **Island Getaways** to name a few.

Other reputable rental agencies are **Villa Dawn**, **Smith's Gore**, **McLaughlin Anderson**, **Vacation St. Croix**, **Areana Villas**, and **Virgin Gorda Villa Rentals**.

DIRECTORY

Getting There

Air Sunshine
w airsunshine.com

American Airlines
w aa.com

Delta
w delta.com

JetBlue
w jetblue.com

LIAT
w liatairline.com

Seaborne Airlines
w seaborne airlines. com

Spirit Airlines
w spiritair.com

United Airlines
w united.com

US Airways
w usairways.com

Documentation

US Department of State
w travel.state.gov

Visitor Information

BVI Tourism
w bvitourism.com

USVI Tourism
w visitusvi.com

Health and Security

Juan F. Luis Hospital
St. Croix.
Tel 340 778 6311.

Myrah Keating Smith Community Health Center
St. John.
Tel 340 693 8900.

Peebles Hospital
Tortola.
Tel 284 494 3497.

Police and Fire
US Virgin Islands.
Tel 911.
British Virgin Islands.
Tel 999.

Roy L. Schneider Hospital
St. Thomas.
Tel 340 776 8311.

Virgin Gorda Government Health Clinic
Virgin Gorda.
Tel 284 495 5337.

Communications

AT&T
w att.com

Transport

AVIS
w avis.com

Hertz
w hertz.com

Getting Married

Anne Marie Weddings
w stjohn weddings.com

Attorney General's Office
Road Town, Tortola.
Tel 284 468 3701.

Superior Court
w visuperiorcourt.org

Weddings the Island Way
w weddingstheisland way.com

Villas

Areana Villas
w areanavillas.com

Caribbean Villas
w caribbeanvilla.com

Catered To Vacation Homes
w cateredto.com

Island Getaways
w island-getaways.net

McLaughlin Anderson
w mclaughlin anderson.com

Smith's Gore
w smithsgore.com

Vacation St. Croix
w vacationstcroix.com

Vacation Vistas
w vacationvistas.com

Villa Dawn
w villadawn.com

Virgin Gorda Villa Rentals
w virgingordabvi.com

Exploring Anguilla

A small but beguiling British Overseas Territory, Anguilla is fairly flat and covered in dry vegetation. Its coral base, however, gives the island superb bright white sand and truly spectacular blue sea dotted with coral reefs and tiny cays. The island is overwhelmingly modern in its appearance and has luxurious accommodations with some of the most impressive villas and resorts in the Caribbean, second only to St. Barthélemy.

Locator Map

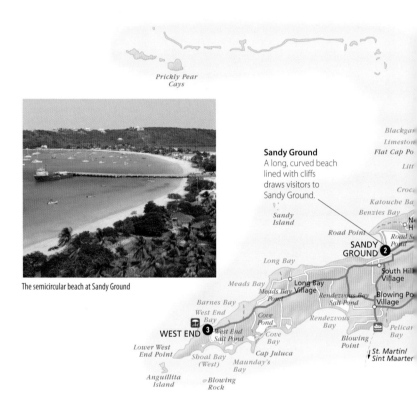

The semicircular beach at Sandy Ground

Sandy Ground
A long, curved beach lined with cliffs draws visitors to Sandy Ground.

Sights at a Glance

1 The Valley
2 Sandy Ground
3 West End
4 Island Harbor and the East End

0 kilometers 3
0 miles 3

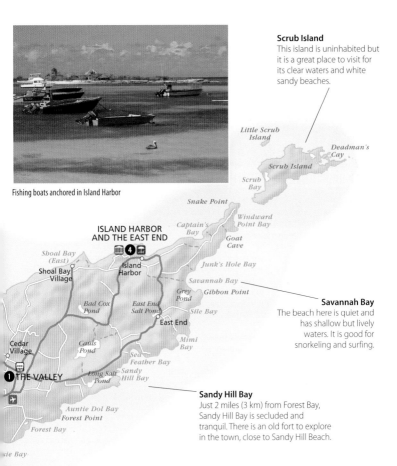

Fishing boats anchored in Island Harbor

Scrub Island
This island is uninhabited but it is a great place to visit for its clear waters and white sandy beaches.

Little Scrub Island

Deadman's Cay

Scrub Island

Scrub Bay

Snake Point

Windward Point Bay

Captain's Bay

ISLAND HARBOR AND THE EAST END

Goat Cave

Island Harbor

Junk's Hole Bay

Shoal Bay (East)

Shoal Bay Village

Savannah Bay

Grey Pond

Gibbon Point

Savannah Bay
The beach here is quiet and has shallow but lively waters. It is good for snorkeling and surfing.

Bad Cox Pond

East End Salt Pond

Sile Bay

East End

Mimi Bay

Cedar Village

Cauls Pond

Sea Feather Bay

①THE VALLEY

Long Salt Pond

Sandy Hill Bay

Sandy Hill Bay
Just 2 miles (3 km) from Forest Bay, Sandy Hill Bay is secluded and tranquil. There is an old fort to explore in the town, close to Sandy Hill Beach.

Auntie Dol Bay
Forest Point

Forest Bay

sie Bay

Key

▬▬ Major road
═══ Minor road
– – Tracks
- - - Ferry route

Getting Around

Close to the island's capital, The Valley, is the small airport. There is no public transport in Anguilla and so the easiest way to get around the island is by taxi or a hired car. These can be ordered through the hotel front desk. Island tours are also possible and take just a couple of hours.

St. Gerard's Roman Catholic Church, The Valley

For keys to symbols *see back flap*

Wallblake House, one of the oldest buildings on the island

❶ The Valley

Center of Anguilla. 🗻 2,035. ✈ 🚉
ℹ Anguilla Tourist Board, Coronation
Av., 8am–5pm Mon–Sat, 264 497
2759. 🛒 People's Market (Mon–Sat).
🎭 Anguilla Summer Festival (Aug).
W ivisitanguilla.com

The capital of Anguilla, The
Valley is so small it barely seems
like a town. Along the broad
Queen Elizabeth Avenue, there
are a few civic buildings,
including the government
offices, the post office, the
telecommunications office,
and a couple of shopping malls.
At the foot of the street is the
open-sided People's Market,
where fruit and vegetables
are sold.

The oldest section of the
town is Coronation Avenue,
which runs north past the
Anguilla Tourist Board and up
the hill towards Crocus Bay.
A gentle climb up the hill has
a handful of the town's original
stone buildings, including the
Warden's Place, a former sugar
plantation greathouse, which
has an excellent bakery.

Along Queen Elizabeth
Avenue, towards the airport,
is the brightly decorated St.
Gerard's Catholic Church with
its three pebble-dashed arches.
The adjoining building,
Wallblake House, is one of
the oldest buildings in Anguilla.
Built in 1787, this old plantation
house has been restored.
It has a stone foundation and
a clapboard upper set behind
a picket fence. The kitchens,
stables, and workers' quarters
are all intact. The house was
donated to a Catholic church
in 1959 but proved too small
to hold services.

Wallblake House
Wallblake **Road**. **Tel** 264 497 6613.
📷 📷 10am–2pm Mon, Wed, Fri.
W wallblake.ai/history.html

❷ Sandy Ground

2 miles (3 km) W of The Valley. 🚉

Road Bay is Anguilla's deep-
water port, but the sand still
is as good as some of the best
beaches on the other islands.
Set in a cliff-bound bay, the
west-facing harbor and its small
settlement, Sandy Ground, are
well protected. The long stretch
of sand is magnificent, backed
by beachfront restaurants and
bars, houses, and the pier.

Offshore, fishing and pleasure
boats can be seen anchored in
the bay. This is the home of
Anguilla sailing. Around the
lagoon, which was once used
for the cultivation of salt by
evaporation, the low mud
walls that sectioned the solar
pans can still be seen. Salt was
once a thriving Anguillan
industry and a major export
until the 1980s. The **Anguilla
National Trust** conducts a
Heritage Tour (by appointment)
to many heritage sites
and places of natural importance. Tours take between 20
minutes and 4 hours and are
entirely customized.

Anguilla National Trust
The Valley. **Tel** 264 497 5297. 📷 by
appointment, 8am–4pm Mon–Fri.
W axanationaltrust.org

❸ West End

8 miles (13 km) W of The Valley. 🚉

All of Anguilla is rimmed with
excellent sand, but the West
End has the greatest concentration of beaches, and consequently hotels. The West End is
fed by a central road along the
spine of the island, lined with
shops, some art galleries, and
mini-markets. An interesting
place to stop by on the main
road in West End is **Cheddie's
Carving Studio**, where Cheddie,
a local artist, sculpts works of art
from driftwood. On the north
side, Meads Bay and Barnes Bay
are two fantastic beaches.

While Anguilla has little visible
architectural tradition of its own,

The beautiful sea and sand of the West End, one of the Caribbean's most alluring spots

The modern-looking Covecastles resort on the beach at Shoal Bay, West End

in the past 20 years, the island has seen some extraordinary buildings in some of its villas and hotels. The most original and modern Covecastles on Shoal Bay (West), near the western tip of the island. Designed by architect Myron Goldfinger, these villas resemble storm-swept white faces buried to their necks in the sand, staring southwards to St. Martin.

Next door at Altamer, Goldfinger has developed his distinctive white concrete design further, with triangular roofs that reflect the sails of Anguillian yachts. Meanwhile, the Villas at Long Bay Estate have a stylish, almost geometrical theme, with clean-lined columns, cubes and crow-stepped walls, also in white concrete. Lastly, Cap Juluca (see p262) features 18 villas standing in a line on the stupendous Maunday's Bay, a compendium of Moorish arches and domes all dressed in white, standing stark

against the spectacular blues of the sea and sky. The villas are the most alluring place to stay – more than anywhere else in the Caribbean.

Cheddie's Carving Studio
The Cove. **Tel** 264 497 6027.
Open 10am–6pm, Mon–Sat.
W **cheddie.ai**

❹ Island Harbor and the East End

6 miles (10 km) E of The Valley. 🅣

The East End of the island has a slightly stronger Anguillian feel than the West End, with local houses, churches, and schools scattered in small settlements.

Two roads encircle the East End, starting at The Valley and meeting again at the only other town of any size, Island Harbor. The north road leads via Shoal Bay (East), the liveliest beach on the island and one which is ideal for independent travelers.

The south road passes through occasional settlements and comes to East End. Here, opposite the East End Lagoon, seasonal home to some of Anguilla's birds, visitors will find the **Heritage Collection Museum**. The museum has an excellent, if eccentric, collection of artifacts illustrating Anguillian natural life and history through geology, Amerindian, and colonial times to recent days. Displays also include pottery, coins, old gramophone players, and plenty of photographs. A little farther ahead is Island Harbor, a fishing community, where brightly colored boats bob at anchor out in the bay. The Anguilla National Trust (see p261) arranges hikes to some of the island's few archaeological sites in this area. Beyond the settlement, towards the end of the island, are some remote beaches, including Captain's Bay and Savannah Bay.

🏛 **Heritage Collection Museum**
Liberty Road, East End.
Tel 264 497 4092.
Open 10am–5pm Mon–Sat. 📷 ♿

An aerial view of Shoal Bay (West)

The History of Anguilla

Anguilla's early history is mostly clouded in mystery and legend. It is mainly a story of tenuous settlements and piracy. Originally called Malliouhana, which supposedly means sea serpent, it later took its current name from Spanish colonists, perhaps after its long, thin shape (Anguilla means "eel" in Spanish). It was never a successful plantation island and the slaves were encouraged to look after themselves by growing their own crops. Eventually the islanders took to traveling and trading, and as a result their descendants are scattered around the Caribbean. There is a large community of Anguillians in the Dominican Republic, some of whom have returned because of the island's recent development.

Brightly painted boats anchored in the bay at Island Harbor

Outdoor Activities and Specialized Holidays

Most of the activities in Anguilla are centered around the sea and its superb beaches, and the island promotes various watersports, including snorkeling, scuba diving, and sailing. There are relatively fewer activities on land, but hiking, biking, and horse-riding are popular pastimes. There are golf courses, while many of the hotels have spas and tennis courts.

Villa overlooking the stunning blue waters of the Atlantic Ocean, Shoal Bay

Beaches

With powder-soft, bright, fluorescent white sand that sparkles at night in some places, the beaches in Anguilla are some of the finest in the Caribbean. There are lots of undeveloped stretches but not much natural shade, though hotels and beach bars have parasols and covered bars.

The most popular beach is Shoal Bay (East) which is liveliest on Sundays. It has several beach bars, an excellent snorkeling reef, and watersports operators. Sandy Ground, too, comes alive on Sundays with its string of bars and activities. Other beaches with great sand and easy access include Meads Bay, Barnes Bay, and Cove Bay. Among more secluded beaches are Little Bay, Captain's Bay, and the offshore Sandy Island and Prickly Pear Cays.

Anguilla's beach bars are among its finest features. They vary from classic West Indian shacks to sophisticated restaurants on the sand, and make an ideal base for the day (or a day trip to the offshore islands). Shoal Bay (East) is home to well-known bars and

restaurants such as Uncle Ernie's, Madeariman Reef, Elodia's, and Gwen's Reggae Grill. Sandy Ground is the setting for the popular bar, Johnno's.

Elsewhere, classic West Indian bars are set on endless stretches of sand. Smokey's is another favorite on Cove Bay. The Dune Preserve located on Rendezvous Bay is an institution in itself. The classy Trattoria Tramonto on Shoal Bay (West) offers great Italian cuisine and Scilly Cay in Island Harbor serves the freshest seafood in Caribbean style.

Johnno's brightly colored shack, Sandy Ground

Sailing

A sailing trip often promises to be the most memorable day of a Caribbean holiday and Anguilla has something unique to offer in this respect. Sailboats and motorboats sail regularly to the offshore islands, Sandy Island and Prickly Pear Cays, which are not much more than sandbars with a few palm trees and an excellent beach. Lunch, typically lobster and salad, is included in the trip, which can be arranged through the concerned hotel or through concessionaires such as **Shoal Bay Scuba**, **Sandy Island Enterprises**, or the independent catamaran, **Chocolat Sail**. For others who do not wish to spend a full day sailing, an interesting variation is the popular **Gorgeous Scilly Cay**, set on a tiny island just offshore in Island Harbor. Operators also organize glass-bottom boat trips. St. Martin/Sint Maarten (*see pp266–79*), which is popular for shopping, is just a 20-minutes ferry ride south of Blowing Point. The island, part French and part Dutch, is ideal for a day trip from Anguilla. The last ferry returns to Anguilla at 7pm, but water taxis are also available.

Deep-Sea Fishing

Deep-sea fishing is a popular activity off Anguilla. Boats head off to the deep water beyond the smaller islands to the north and northeast. Here they trawl for wahoo, sailfish, and tuna among others. **Gotcha Sea Tours** is among the known fishing charters on the island. Deep-sea fishing is also available through Shoal Bay Scuba and Sandy Island Enterprises.

Watersports

Anguilla offers reasonable opportunities for great watersports off some of its alluring beaches. Crocus Bay is well protected and ideal for watersports. Many of the hotels have some equipment including snorkeling gear, kayaks, surf boards, and small sailing boats.

Visitors who wish to set out on their own have the option of hiring equipment at Shoal Bay, either at Shoal Bay Scuba or at **Anguillan Divers**.

Scuba Diving

The clear water and excellent reefs make scuba diving in Anguilla worthwhile. With little freshwater run-off, the island has good corals, reef fish, and the occasional larger fish. But the main draws are the five wrecks that were intentionally sunk to provide remarkable dive sites, some of which are penetrable. Diving trips are arranged by operators such as Anguillian Divers and Shoal Bay Scuba.

Snorkeling

The word "shoal" means reef and considering that there are two Shoal Bays on the island, it might be expected that snorkeling in Anguilla would be good. The best reefs are in Shoal Bay (East), where there is a marked snorkeling trail, and Little Bay, a small cove backed by cliffs on the north shore, near The Valley. Road Bay, Maunday's Bay, and Barnes Bay also have excellent snorkeling. Equipment is available on most of the popular beaches.

Hiking

There are some unexpectedly remote areas around Anguilla's eastern end, which can be explored on foot. The **Anguilla National Trust** organizes a walk around Island Harbor that includes archaeological sites.

Horse-riding and Biking

Horseback rides through the countryside and on the res-plendent beaches are available through **Seaside Stables**. The land is relatively flat and therefore mountain biking is another great way to get acquainted with Anguilla's interior. Biking equipment can be hired from outlets such as **Exotic Plus**.

Golfer playing at the sprawling golf course, CuisinArt Golf Club

Golf

The 18-hole, par 72 CuisinArt Golf Club was designed by famous golf course designer Greg Norman. The first golf course to be built in Anguilla, it was opened in Merrywing in 2006. Stretching for 4 miles (6 km), it has lush green gardens, flowing streams and sweeping views of the Caribbean Sea and nearby St. Martin/Sint Maarten.

Spas

There are two excellent purpose-built spas attached to the Malliouhana Hotel and the Cuisinart Resort and Spa *(see p262)*. The Malliouhana Spa stands just above Meads Bay and has three treatment rooms, including a "his and hers" suite, and a gym. The Venus Spa at Cuisinart Resort has been redeveloped to include a hydrotherapy room and a well-equipped gym.

Divers set to explore the thriving marine life off Sandy Ground

Where to Stay

EAST END: Milly's Inn $
Modern
Shoal Bay East
Tel *264 581 5398 or 264 497 4274*
w millysinn.ai
A small hillside inn, Milly's offers one-bedroom units with full kitchens, sleeper sofas, and patios. The property overlooks beautiful Shoal Bay Beach.

EAST END: Serenity Cottages $$
Modern
Shoal Bay East
Tel *264 497 3328*
w serenity.ai
Secluded beachside cottages house beautifully furnished one- and two-bedroom suites with TVs and full kitchens. There are also studios with mini-fridges.

MEADS BAY: Patsy's Seaside Villas $
Beach
Blowing Point Beach
Tel *264 476 7419*
w patsy-seaside-villa.com
These one- and two-bedroom villas with kitchens are excellent value, especially for families looking for low-cost alternatives right on the beach. Great views.

MEADS BAY: Anacaona Boutique Hotel $$
Beach Resort
Meads Bay
Tel *877 647 4736*
w anacaonahotel.com
Built in a Mediterranean style, this hotel is a comfortable, stylish alternative to more expensive hotels nearby. The beach is a short stroll away.

MEADS BAY: Yacht Club Villas at Callaloo $$
Beach
Cul de Sac, Blowing Point
Tel *264 498 8600*
w callalooclub.com
Air-conditioned villas and apartments with between two and 15 bedrooms. Most villas have pools and views to the sea. Wi-Fi available.

MEADS BAY: Carimar Beach Club $$$
Beach Resort
Meads Bay
Tel *264 497 6881*
w carimar.com
Stay right on Meads Bay Beach in home-like comfort. Carimar's one- and two-bedroom units offer full kitchens, plus dining and living rooms. Free Wi-Fi.

Wonderful ocean views from the golf course at the Cuisinart Golf Resort & Spa, Meads Bay

DK Choice

MEADS BAY: Cuisinart Golf Resort & Spa $$$
Beach Resort
Rendezvous Bay
Tel *264 498 2000*
w cuisinartresort.com
Many feel that the debate about which is the best hotel on the island was settled when this resort acquired the gorgeous Greg Norman-designed 18-hole golf course. Rooms are spacious and well appointed, and the five outstanding restaurants benefit from the resort's own hydroponic farm.

SANDY GROUND: Sydans Apartments $
Beach
Sandy Ground
Tel *264 497 3180*
w inns.ai/sydans
A group of simply furnished apartments, all with kitchens, opposite Sandy Ground Beach.

SANDY GROUND: Ambia Boutique Hotel $$
B&B
South Hill
Tel *264 461 8686*
w anguillabnb.com
These charming Asian-style suites with private terraces overlook Sandy Ground. A complimentary full breakfast can be had in the room. Swimming pool and Wi-Fi.

SANDY GROUND: Villa Nirvana $$$
Modern
Shannon Hill, Sandy Ground
Tel *264 235 7096*
w gobeach.com/anguilla/nirvana.htm
This dramatic four-bedroom villa sitting high above the coast has

luxurious Indonesian furnishings and many extras. Guests also enjoy the panoramic views.

THE VALLEY: Lloyd's Bed & Breakfast $
Historic
Crocus Bay, The Valley
Tel *264 497 2351*
w lloyds.ai
A small inn where each of the rooms has its own name, plus unique decor and artworks. Rooms have air-conditioning, ceiling fans, and TVs.

THE VALLEY: Las EsQuinas Boutique Bed & Breakfast $$
B&B
Little Harbour
Tel *264 476 3351*
w lasesquinas.com
A villa converted into an intimate beachside inn, with suites done in Mexican, Mediterranean, Balinese, and Moroccan decor.

WEST END: West End Bay Holiday Suites $$
Modern
Shoal Bay West
Tel *264 498 2525*
w westendbay.com
These self-contained one- and two-bedroom units with kitchens are just steps away from Shoal Bay West Beach, restaurants, shops, and entertainment. Free Wi-Fi.

WEST END: Cap Juluca $$$
Beach Resort
Maunday's Bay
Tel *264 497 6666*
w capjuluca.com
The island's most luxurious hotel, Cap Juluca is set on a crescent-shaped white-sand beach. All rooms face the ocean. Great amenities, plus activities such as tennis, watersports, and volleyball.

WEST END: Caribella Beach Resort $$$
Luxury
Meads Bay
Tel *978 369 2546*
w lambertventures.com
These spacious beachfront villas and apartments with patios have a Spanish feel. The apartments have two bedrooms with kitchens.

Where to Eat and Drink

**EAST END: On Da Rocks
Seafood Grill & Bar** $$
Caribbean
Island Harbour
Tel *264 772 3017* **Closed** *Mon*
A waterfront restaurant offering amazing and great-value crayfish at weekends. Fresh seafood entrées prepared on the grill, plus soups, wraps, and burgers.

**EAST END:
Serenity Restaurant** $$$
Continental
Shoal Bay East
Tel *264 497 3328*
This beachfront eatery and beach bar offers gorgeous views and a varied menu, including pastas, grilled meats, and seafood.

**LONG BAY:
Blanchards Beach Shack** $$
American
Meads Bay
Tel *264 498 6100* **Closed** *Sun*
Reasonably priced high-quality burgers, sandwiches, wraps, and salads. The eclectic menu also features tacos and rice bowls.

**LONG BAY: Fire Fly
Restaurant & Bar** $$$
Caribbean
Meads Bay
Tel *264 497 6827*
Caribbean cuisine with a twist. There is a fixed-price Chinese menu on Tuesday nights, plus Anguillan Culture Night (Thu) and Latin Night (Fri).

**LONG BAY:
Oliver's Seaside Grill** $$$
Continental
Long Bay
Tel *264 497 8780*
The best in grilled fresh seafood, plus meat and pasta. The house specialty is Rock Oven Baked Whole Chicken. Reserve ahead.

SANDY GROUND: A' Burger $
American
Lower South Hill
Tel *264 497 3535* **Closed** *Sun*
A classic burger joint in an outdoor setting, with Black Angus beef, fish, and veggie burgers. Great fries, too.

**SANDY GROUND:
Roy's Bayside Grill** $$
Continental
Sandy Ground Village
Tel *264 497 2470*
The best fish 'n' chips on the island, plus grilled meats and fish, as well as appetizers and desserts.

**SANDY GROUND: Dolce Vita
Italian Beach Restaurant** $$$
Italian
Sandy Ground Village
Tel *264 497 8668* **Closed** *Sat lunch; Sun*
Dolce Vita is the place to go for good-quality Italian food with the occasional Anguillan twist. Open-air beachfront location with sunset views. Reserve ahead.

**SANDY GROUND: E's Oven
Restaurant & Bar** $$$
Continental
South Hill
Tel *264 498 8258* **Closed** *Tue*
Eclectic mix of Caribbean favorites, including grilled fish and meat entrées, from one of the Caribbean's most famous chefs.

DK Choice

**SANDY GROUND:
Veya Restaurant** $$$
International
Sandy Ground
Tel *264 498 8392* **Closed** *Sun*
Offering "cuisine of the sun," with flavors from the Moroccan, Vietnamese, Indian, and Chinese traditions among others, this restaurant produces what many guests call the best food not just in Anguilla, but in the whole Caribbean. Artistic presentations in a dreamy garden setting with a koi pond and waterfalls.

**THE VALLEY: Fat Cat
Gourmet to Go** $
Deli
Stoney Ground
Tel *264 497 2307* **Closed** *Sun*
Surprising array of meals to go, including lasagna, quiches, beef burgundy, and curried goat, as well as delicious baked entrées, salads, and desserts.

Price Guide

Prices are based on a two-course meal for one, including tax and service charges, and half a bottle of wine.

$	up to $30
$$	$30–60
$$$	over $60

**THE VALLEY:
Da'Vida Restaurant** $$$
Caribbean/Asian
Crocus Bay
Tel *264 498 5433*
Seafood takes center stage at Da'Vida, with lobster, crayfish, and scallop entrées, all beautifully seasoned with Asian or island spices. There is a delicious tapas menu, too.

**WEST END:
Picante Restaurant** $$
Mexican
West End
Tel *264 498 1616* **Closed** *Tue*
Choose from a solid selection of Mexican favorites (plus a long list of margaritas), all served in a casual open-air setting.

**WEST END: Smokey's
at the Cove** $$
Caribbean
Cove Bay
Tel *264 497 6582*
Laid-back but upscale, this beach bar has a varied menu that includes seafood, salads, wraps, and ribs, plus specialties like Creole lobster cakes and fish carpaccio.

**WEST END: Mango's
Seaside Grill** $$$
Seafood
Barnes Bay
Tel *264 497 6479* **Closed** *Tue*
Mango's specializes in local fish and lobster, either on the grill or pan-seared. Delicious homemade desserts. Great sunsets.

Simple decor at E's Oven Restaurant & Bar, Sandy Ground

Practical Information

Anguilla is one of the most exclusive and expensive destinations in the region. The island has seen an extraordinary building boom over recent years, but has retained its laid-back character and high standards in tourism. Its hotels and villas are top-notch and restaurants offer a world-class dining experience. A good time to visit Anguilla is during the island's festivals, generally held during July and August.

Ferry boat leaving from the Blowing Point terminal

When to Go

Anguilla's average annual temperature is around 80° F (27° C), with the hottest weather during the hurricane season that runs from July to October. The lightest rainfall occurs from February to April, and the heaviest from August to November. The island has mild weather from December to April.

Getting There

No carriers fly directly from North America into Anguilla, so access is easiest via neighboring St. Martin/Sint Maarten or Puerto Rico, where visitors can transfer to **American Eagle** or a private charter. There are many carriers into St. Martin from where the crossing to Anguilla can be made by ferry or private water taxi which includes the **Link**, or by the local airline **Winair**. Europe is linked to St. Martin from France and Holland. Most UK visitors travel via Antigua, from where Caribbean flights (**LIAT** and Winair) run up the island chain to Anguilla.

Documentation

Visitors to Anguilla require a valid passport with at least six months' validity remaining, as well as a return or onward ticket. Visas are not needed by US citizens, Canadians, or EU travelers, but citizens of some other countries do require them.

If in doubt, visitors should check with the closest British High Commission for details regarding entry visas. A departure tax and an airport security charge needs to be paid when leaving the island.

Visitor Information

The **Anguilla Tourist Board** has its main office in The Valley. International offices of the board are located in the UK and the US. There is also an information booth at the Wallblake airport. Visitors can pick up maps, brochures, and magazines at the airport.

Health and Security

Anguilla is a very safe island. There are hardly any problems concerning personal security and theft is extremely rare. However, it is advisable not to leave any valuables unattended. Sunburn is the main health hazard. Mosquitoes can be a problem after it rains. No vaccinations are necessary unless visitors are coming from a yellow-fever infected area. There is an accident and emergency department at **Princess Alexandra Hospital**.

Banking and Currency

The currency of Anguilla is the Eastern Caribbean dollar (EC$), which is shared with current and former British territories as far south as Grenada. The US dollar is also widely accepted. Banks follow regular business hours, Monday to Thursday 8am to 3pm, and to 5pm on Fridays. Credit cards are accepted in almost all establishments except in the smallest shops. There are ATMs attached to several banks, and also free-standing in some malls. They give a choice of Eastern Caribbean and US dollars.

Communications

The international dialling code for Anguilla is 1 264, followed by a seven digit island number. When calling out of Anguilla, dial 011 and the international code. When calling locally, all seven digits need to be dialled. The island has complete cell coverage

Anguilla Tourist Board office, The Valley

and visitors can use their personal phones, if on roaming. Handsets and SIM cards with local numbers are available at the **Digicel** and **Cable & Wireless** offices on the island. Almost all the hotels and villas have Wi-Fi, which is available to their guests.

Transport

Car hire companies are not officially permitted to deliver to the airport or ferry port, and will first take visitors to their office to complete formalities. However, they do drop passengers to hotels and villas. Driving is on the left side of the road, and a temporary Anguilla driver's license, in addition to a valid driving license, is mandatory. This can be purchased at any of the car-rental agencies such as **AVIS**, **Island Car Rentals**, and **Carib Rent A Car**. The airport and ferry terminals have taxi stands and usually the rate is fixed for two passengers and two pieces of luggage. There are no public buses in Anguilla. Hitch-hiking works sometimes, but as is the case anywhere, there is no guarantee of a ride.

Shopping

While Anguilla is not really known for its shopping, the island has a number of art galleries, which offer handicrafts, paintings, and sculptures by resident artists alongside imported works. The **Loblolly Art Gallery** and the **Savannah Gallery** in The Valley exhibit Caribbean art, while the **Devonish Art Gallery** displays the clay, stone, and wood creations of internationally known potter and sculptor Courtney Devonish. Similarly, **La Petite Art Gallery** showcases paintings by Susan Graff. **Albert's Market Place** is the largest supermarket in The Valley. **Irie Life** is a good place to shop for colorful beachwear and accessories.

Language

The language of Anguilla is English, which the Anguillians speak with a slightly Irish-sounding lilt.

Electricity

The usual electricity supply in Anguilla is 110 volts AC (60 cycles). Most hotels have two-pin sockets in US style.

Savannah Gallery, displaying contemporary Caribbean art

Time

Anguilla is on Atlantic Standard Time (AST), 4 hours behind Greenwich Mean Time (GMT) and 1 hour ahead of Eastern Time in the US.

Getting Married

A marriage license can be obtained once both parties have been on the island for 48 hours. Documents required include proof of identity, decree nisi if divorced, and spouse's death certificate if widowed. Visitors can contact any of the many hotels and tour companies, including **Malliouhana Travel and Tours**, which organize weddings.

DIRECTORY

Getting There

American Eagle
W aa.com

LIAT
W liatairline.com

Link
W link.ai

Winair
W fly-winair.com

Visitor Information

Anguilla Tourist Board
Tel 264 497 2759 (The Valley), 914 287 2400 (USA), 207 736 6030 (UK), Toll free 866 348 7447 (Canada).
W ivisitanguilla.com

Health and Security

Police, Fire and Ambulance
Tel 911.

Princess Alexandra Hospital
Stoney Ground.
Tel 264 497 2551.

Communications

Cable & Wireless
The Valley.
Tel 1800 804 2994.
W time4lime.com

Digicel
Babrow Building,
The Valley.
Tel 264 498 7500.
W digicelanguilla. com

Transport

AVIS
The Quarter, The Valley.
Tel 264 497 2642.

Carib Rent a Car
Meads Bay.
Tel 264 497 6020.

Island Car Rentals
Airport Road,
The Valley.
Tel 264 497 2723.
W islandcar.ai

Shopping

Albert's Market Place
Stoney Ground Road,
The Valley.
Tel 264 497 2240.

Devonish Art Gallery
Tel 264 497 2949.

Irie Life
Back Street, South Hill.
Tel 264 497 6526.
W irielife.com

La Petite Art Gallery
Tel 264 497 6068.

Loblolly Art Gallery
Tel 264 497 6006.
W loblollygallery.com

Savannah Gallery
Tel 264 497 2263.
W savannahgallery. com

Getting Married

Malliouhana Travel and Tours
Tel 264 497 2431.

Exploring St. Martin/Sint Maarten

St. Martin/Sint Maarten occupies the smallest land mass governed by two nations. This 37-sq m (96-sq km) island is divided almost equally between France and the Netherlands, making it one of the most diverse vacation destinations in the Caribbean. The Dutch side, Sint Maarten, is known for casinos, high-rise luxury resorts, and non-stop activity. St. Martin, the French side, is less developed but popular for its gourmet bistros, naturist beaches, chic boutiques, and hotels. Each side of the island is distinct in many ways and vacationers can sample the best of both, since there is no real border or document control between the two.

Locator Map

Marigot
St. Martin's charming capital is filled with Creole homes, boutiques, and tiny bistros surrounding a lively marina.

0 kilometers   2

0 miles   2

Simpson Bay
The Simpson Bay area, with many shops, restaurants, and resorts, is the center for tourists on the Dutch side.

Getting Around

A rental car is the best way to get around St. Martin/Sint Maarten. A two-lane highway encircles the coast and the secondary roads are in good condition. Public transport is limited to small daily buses between Philipsburg, Marigot, and Grand Case. Taxis are easily accessible at the airport, ship docks, and main towns. Rates are set by the government and posted in each cab. Commercial jets arrive at the international airport, located on the Dutch side. Small aircraft fly to nearby islands from L'Esperance Airport on the French side. Island-hopping is possible by high-speed ferry to St. Barts and by catamaran to Anguilla and Saba.

Anguilla

Saba

FALAISE DES OISEAUX
④

Baie aux Prunes

Terres Basses

Baie Rouge

Baie Nettlé
Sandy Ground

Baie Longue

Cupecoy Bay

Simpson Bay Lagoon

MARIGO

Mullet Bay

Maho Bay

Burgeaux Bay

SIMPSON BAY AND AROUND
③

Pelican Key

Ba

Koo

Cruise ship off the coast of Philipsburg, Sint Maarten

For hotels and restaurants on this island see p276 and p277

Sights at a Glance

1. Philipsburg
2. Sint Maarten Park and Zoo
3. Simpson Bay and Around
4. Falaise des Oiseaux
5. Marigot
6. Colombier
7. Pic du Paradis
8. Grand Case
9. Butterfly Farm
10. Old House
11. Baie Orientale
12. Îlet Pinel and Île Tintamarre

Grand Case

Grand Case has earned the title "gastronomic capital of the Caribbean" due to the many cafés lining the main road.

Vintage car parked on a street lined with shops, Philipsburg

Philipsburg

The Dutch capital, Philipsburg, curves around the Great Bay. It is a major stop for cruise ships.

Key

━━ Major road

═══ Minor road

--- Ferry route

▬▬▬ International border

△ Peak

For additional map symbols *see back flap*

① Philipsburg

S coast of Sint Maarten. 🚠 18,000.
✈ 🚌 🚕 ℹ️ Vineyard Office Park,
WG Buncamper Rd. 🎭 Carnival
(Apr–May). 🌐 **st-maarten.com**

The capital city of Dutch Sint
Maarten stretches a mile (2 km)
across a narrow strip of land
that separates the sea from a
marshy inland pond. Of the
four roads that run from one
end of the town to the other,
the popular Front Street brims
with waterfront cafés, flashy
casinos, and duty-free shops.
Town beautification projects
have replaced aging brick
pavements and outfitted new
sidewalks with palm trees and
decorative lampposts. Sand,
dredged from the bottom of
the sea, was spread on Great
Bay Beach, which flaunts an
impressive new boardwalk.

Cyrus Wathey Square on Front
Street, across from Captain
Hodge Pier, has a striking white
courthouse built in 1792 by
the Dutch commander Willem
Hendrik Rink. The square is an
excellent starting point for a
walking tour as it has a tourist
information booth and is at
the beginning of the shopping
district. Old Street and Sea
Street are pedestrian-only
walkways lined with flowers,
potted palms, and shops.

The **Guavaberry Emporium**
occupies a late 18th-century
cedar town house, once home
to a former governor. Flavored
liqueurs from the local
guavaberry fruit are the shop's
chief product alongside other
island-made goods. Set in a
restored 19th-century two-story
house, the **Sint Maarten
Museum** displays local historic
artifacts such as the replica of a
typical Arawak *pirogue* (canoe),
which stands at the entrance, a
photo exhibit of daily island life
in the early 1900s, and rescued
articles from HMS *Proselyte*, a
frigate that sank off Fort
Amsterdam in 1801.

At the far east end of town,
locally known as the Head of
Town, Bobby's Marina and
Great Bay Marina have car
rental agencies, a dive shop,
and a marine supply store.

🎵 **Guavaberry Emporium**
8–10 Front Street. **Tel** 721 542 2965.
Open 10am–6pm daily.
🌐 **guavaberry.com**

🏛 **Sint Maarten Museum**
7 Front Street. **Tel** 721 542 4917.
Open 10am–4pm Mon–Fri. 🖼 📷

② Sint Maarten Park and Zoo

0.5 mile (1 km) N of Philipsburg,
Sint Maarten. **Tel** 721 543 2030. Ⓣ
Open 9am–5pm daily. 🖼 📷 🖼

Animal lovers and children
are fascinated by the 200 or
more species at the 3-acre
(1-ha) Sint Maarten Park and
Zoo, located in the residential
area of Madame Estate. More
than one hundred parrots
perch on trees above
numerous turtles and iguanas.
An interesting sight is the

Golden lion tamarin monkeys at the Sint
Maarten Park and Zoo

rare golden lion tamarin, a
monkey with a long tail and
a lion-like mane. The grounds
also have lovely tropical plants.

③ Simpson Bay and Around

2 miles (3 km) W of Philipsburg,
Sint Maarten. 🚌

The Simpson Bay area includes
the bay and beach abutting
Princess Juliana International
Airport on the island's south
coast, and the Simpson Bay
Lagoon, which at 11 sq miles
(29 sq km) is the largest lagoon
in the eastern Caribbean.
A narrow strip of land circles
it, separating it from the sea,
and several of the most
popular resorts, restaurants,
and activities are located here.
The invisible Dutch-French
border runs through the
lagoon, so everything on
the south shore including

View of Philipsburg, with Great and Little Bay beaches

For hotels and restaurants on this island see p276 and p277

the Maho Bay, Mullet Bay, and Cupecoy Bay areas with their great beaches, is Dutch. Marigot touches the lagoon on the north (French) side at the trendy Port La Royale.

❹ Falaise des Oiseaux

7 miles (11 km) W of Philipsburg, St. Martin.

The high ridge of cliffs which lies along the Simpson Bay Lagoon, overlooking the Caribbean Sea on the western edge of Terres Basses (Lowlands), is called Falaise des Oiseaux (Cliff of the Birds). Many indigenous and migrating bird species nest in the cliff's caves and bird-watchers gather here to observe great blue herons, ospreys, yellow warblers, and bullfinches. Pretty homes and villas are scattered along the *falaise* between Baie Rouge (Red Bay) and Baie aux Prunes (Plum Bay).

❺ Marigot

10 miles (16 km) NW from Philipsburg, St. Martin. 12,700. Route de Sandy Ground, 590 875 721. Carnival (Feb–Mar).
st-martin.org

Marigot, the capital of French St. Martin, is a charming town built along the sandy curve of a yacht-filled bay. Contemporary boutiques have moved into colonial buildings and Creole-style houses, and the new blends pleasantly with the old in the center of town. A quaint public square near the harbor is the site of a daily market that offers fresh produce and several locally-made products. The largest markets are open on Wednesdays and Saturdays, and mornings are the best time to visit.

Nearby, Fort Saint-Louis overlooks the sea. Built between 1767 and 1789 by the French, the fort was captured and held for two years by the British from 1794 until 1796. The hilltop fortress offers a panoramic view of Marigot and the island's western shore. **Sur les Traces des Arawaks** (On the Trail of the Arawaks) is a history and archaeology museum with exhibits such as tools, pottery, and jewelry crafted by the native tribes who lived on the island as early as 1800 BC. Experts, by comparing the design of these pieces, trace the history of the Arawaks to South American natives and follow their migration from the Orinoco River basin in Venezuela.

On the waterfront of Simpson Bay Lagoon, Port La Royale marina complex is lined with boutiques and small restaurants reminiscent of those on the French Riviera. During high season, carnival-like entertainment takes place on several evenings each week.

Sur les Traces des Arawaks
7 Rue Fichot. **Tel** 690 567 892.
Open 9am–5pm Mon–Fri.
Closed pub hols.

Oyster Pond, meeting point of French and Dutch

The Great Divide

Between 1648, when the French and the Dutch signed the Treaty of Concordia, and 1817, when the borders of the island were officially set, St. Martin/Sint Maarten changed government 16 times. Legend says that the Dutch and French settlers decided to partition it by staging a march. A Frenchman began walking south from the north coast, while a Dutchman headed north from the south coast. The French and Dutch citizens cheered their representatives on by offering them cups of wine and shots of gin, respectively. While the drowsy Dutchman stopped for a nap, the Frenchman trudged on. When the two met near Oyster Pond, the French had claimed a larger portion by 4 sq miles (10 sq km).

Cattle grazing in the lush meadows, Colombier

❻ Colombier

3 miles (5 km) E of Marigot, St. Martin.

Just inland from Baie de Friar, this fertile hilly area at the foot of Pic du Paradis (Paradise Peak, *see p270*) provides the vegetables and fruit sold at the public market in Marigot. At one time, residents produced large crops of sugarcane, mangoes, and coffee. The big plantations no longer exist, and goats now graze along the road that runs past scattered Creole houses.

Colorful displays at the market place, Boulevard de France, Marigot

A child taking the Fly Zone tour at Loterie Farm, Pic du Paradis

❼ Pic du Paradis

4 miles (6 km) E of Marigot, St. Martin.
ℹ Loterie Farm, 590 878 616.
Open 9am–3:30pm Tue–Sun. 🐾 🌿
✏ 🏕 **W** loteriefarm.net

The island's highest point at 1,391 ft (424 m) offers great views of Baie Orientale and neighboring islands, and is well worth the trouble of getting to the top. A steep, rutted secondary road, off the coastal highway to Colombier, leads inland up the west side of the mountain to within 1 mile (2 km) of the peak, but only a 4-wheel-drive vehicle can manage the drive.

Tours leave from trails beginning at Loterie Farm, 3 miles (5 km) east from Marigot. The farm is a private nature park covering more than 150 acres (61 ha) at the base of Pic du Paradis. Trails lead into the tropical forest, which is home to hundreds of species of plants that shelter a variety of birds and animals. Guides take individuals and small groups on nature walks and moderate to difficult hikes, including a 1-hour trek up Pic du Paradis. A popular attraction is the **Fly Zone** tour, where participants are strapped to a safety harness that is attached to sturdy cables, and zip along through the tree tops. Rope ladders and suspended swing bridges add to the excitement. The farm's Hidden Forest Café is a destination in itself. Its dining room is set in a reconstructed section of an 18th-century sugar mill. The menu has dishes made from produce grown in the farm's organic garden.

❽ Grand Case

4 miles (6 km) N of Marigot, St. Martin.
🚹 2,500. 🚌 📅 Harmony Nights Street Fest (Jan–Apr).
W grandcase.com

Called the Gastronomic Capital of the Caribbean, the tiny town of Grand Case has one main road, a fine beach, and many excellent restaurants run by European-trained chefs. The gourmet restaurants are housed in quaint Creole-style houses that sit side by side, allowing prospective diners the opportunity to stroll from one to another comparing menus that are posted outside. In addition, local cooks serve island specialties from open-air lo-los (locally owned – locally operated) set up along the same street. Here, local cooks grill fresh seafood and meats over oil-drum barbecue pits, and patrons sit at picnic tables. Although the town is known for fine dining rather than swimming, the 1-mile (2-km) long sandy beach with gentle waters is perfect for swimming and has some great snorkeling spots. The bay also offers a spectacular view of neighboring Anguilla and Creole Rock.

On Tuesday nights in the winter the town hosts Harmony Nights Street Festival. Local bands play music on everything from home-made drums to fine brass instruments. Residents also sell traditional art and crafts, and cooks prepare favorite dishes that are local to the island.

❾ Butterfly Farm

5 miles (8 km) NE of Marigot, St. Martin. **Tel** 590 873 121.
Open 9am–3:30pm daily. 🐾
🌿 9am–3pm. ♿ 🖥 🏕
W thebutterflyfarm.com

Hundreds of butterflies from all parts of the world swirl about in this mesh-enclosed garden, which features fish ponds and waterfalls. More than 40 species of butterflies are found in the farm. The best time to visit is early morning, when the butterflies are born. Displays here show the progression from egg to caterpillar to pupae.

A butterfly in the Butterfly Farm

The gift shop sells unusual butterfly art, books, and jewelry. Admission fees include return visits, so visitors can drop in several times during the vacation.

The beach at Grand Case, ideal for snorkeling

The beach at Baie Orientale, with different types of watersports available

❿ Old House

5 miles (8 km) NE of Marigot,
St. Martin. **Tel** 590 873 267.
Open 10am–4pm Tue–Sun.

Once the main house of a
thriving plantation, this renovated Creole-style building has
an interesting selection of
antique tools and machines
once used in cultivating sugarcane and producing rum. The
manor house sits at the top
of a hill overlooking the Spring
Estate, which is still held by
the Beauperthuy family, the
original owners. The living
room and master bedroom
of the authentically restored
home hold treasures collected
by the family over six generations and include photographs, rare lithographs and
ancient maps arranged among
the period furniture as they
might have been during the
1700s, when sugar and rum
production drove the island's
economy. There is a rum and
coffee museum on-site.

⓫ Baie Orientale

4 miles (6 km) NE of Marigot,
St. Martin.

Watersports operators, bars,
and restaurants line the
popular 4-mile (6-km) beach
that spreads along this highly
developed bay. Calm water
and a protective reef make
this an ideal spot for swimming
and snorkeling, and motorized
and wind-powered watercraft
add to the fun.

Environs

Nearby, **Plantation Mont
Vernon** is a park and interactive
museum on more than 5 acres
(2 ha) of landscaped land on a
mountainside overlooking Baie
Orientale. Walking paths and
an audio handset guide visitors
past labeled tropical plants,
historical buildings, coffee
museum, and a sugar and
rum museum.

Plantation Mont Vernon
Route d'Orient Baie. **Tel** 590 295 062.
Open 9am–5pm daily.
(includes rum and coffee tasting).

⓬ Îlet Pinel and Île Tintamarre

Îlet Pinel: 0.5 miles (1 km) N of Baie
Orientale, St. Martin. French Cul
de Sac (N of Baie Orientale).
Île Tintamarre: 1 mile (2 km) NE of Îlet
Pinel, St. Martin. day-sails to
Tintamarre from Grand Case.
one-day excursions.

These two undeveloped offshore
islands are within the protected
waters of the nature reserve,
and their beaches are usually
deserted. Both islands are difficult
to reach when the wind is strong,
but in fine weather each makes
an ideal day trip. Pinel is easier
to reach by boat, and more likely
to have visitors, but the north
side is isolated and its shore is
battered by crashing surf. Water
taxis regularly shuttle passengers
from the beach at French Cul de
Sac, just north of Baie Orientale,
to Îlet Pinel. The south coast
beaches face St. Martin and
have gentle waves, snack
shacks, and equipment rentals
for watersports.

Tintamarre is less visited, but
day-sail excursions often make
this a snorkeling stop, as underwater life is amazing. White-sand
beaches ring the 200-acre (81-ha)
island, nicknamed Flat Island.
Mud from the beaches is said to
have healing powers and visitors
often slather it over their bodies.

Pretty houses overlooking Baie Orientale Beach

Outdoor Activities and Specialized Holidays

While many vacationers plan to just relax on a beach during their visit to St. Martin/Sint Maarten, there are also plenty of options for those seeking a bit of excitement. Watersports are the prime focus and range from snorkeling to kiteboarding. On land, activities offered include bird-watching and mountain biking. Several companies act as a one-stop outlet for both land and sea adventures, and there are also operators who specialize in specific activities.

Visitors basking in the sun on Dawn Beach, Sint Maarten

Beaches

St. Martin/Sint Maarten has 36 named beaches, most with powdery white sands. Many of the best are highly developed, making them lively, crowded, and fun. However, it is still possible to find secluded stretches, usually on the French side. The Atlantic coast beaches have bigger waves, more wind, stronger currents, and are preferred by watersports enthusiasts. The Caribbean side is calmer and favored by swimmers, snorkelers, and families with children. All beaches are public, but resorts may reserve sands for registered guests.

Great Bay in Philipsburg has an amazing beach with white sand that was dredged up from the sea floor to deepen the harbor for large cruise ships. It tends to get crowded, especially when passengers disembark from the ships, but this adds to the festive ambience. West of town, gorgeous beaches lie along a narrow strip of land that separates the Caribbean Sea from Simpson Bay Lagoon. At Maho Bay Beach, a sign warns of low-flying aircrafts, but it is

always crowded and beach-goers cheer and snap pictures as jumbo jets drop close to the sand on final approach. The hotels, casinos, and restaurants at Maho are among the most popular on the island.

Cupecoy Bay Beach, western-most on the Dutch side, is small and dramatic, with a clothing-optional end. It is backed by towering cliffs and the sand is constantly reshaped by the surf, so the place rarely looks the same from one day to the next. The drop-off between the beach and sea is sharp, and waves often top 2 ft (0.6 m).

Game fishing boat at Marigot in St. Martin

The French side of the west coast has a section called Terres Basses lined with an almost continuous stretch of white sand. Baie Longue is quiet with calm turquoise waters and Baie aux Prunes is popular with surfers when the waves are high. Baie Rouge has a few snack shacks and huts that rent umbrellas and chairs. Grand Case (see p270) has a popular beach for jogging, sunbathing, swimming, and snorkeling, with calm waters that lap onto nicely-packed white sand.

On the east coast, Baie Orientale (see p271) is home to Club Orient, a well-known naturist resort. This stunning 2-mile (3-km) long bay has five connecting beaches. The entire bay is dotted with open-air boutiques, bars, restaurants, massage huts, watersport shops, and live music.

Back on Dutch soil, Dawn Beach is popular with early risers who like to watch the sun rising on this east coast beach. A large, shallow reef protects it from crashing waves and provides excellent snorkeling and surfing.

Fishing

The sea around St. Martin/Sint Maarten teems with fish such as marlin, wahoo, tuna, and snapper. International tournaments include the Blue Marlin Tournament in June and the Anglers Big Fishing Tournament in March.

Visitors can charter boats at full- or half-day rates throughout the year, and captains structure the trips to meet the skills and interests of each group. Bait, gear, and refreshments are included in the rates. One of the best areas for wahoo and tuna is the drop-off at Baie Longue, where the fish feed at depths of 200 ft (60 m).

The Proselyte Reef off Great Bay is excellent for all types of reef fish that feed in depths of 8–12 ft (2.4–3.6 m). **Lee's Deep Sea Fishing**, **Taylor Made Charters and Deep Sea Fishing**, and **Rudy's Deep Sea Fishing** are popular operators.

Casinos on Sint Maarten

Dutch Sint Maarten has more than a dozen casinos, most in or near Philipsburg, where shoppers and cruise ship passengers come to enjoy refreshments and play their favorite slots and table games. Outside the capital, Casino Royal in Maho Bay, Princess Casino at Port de Plaisance, and Atlantis World in Cupecoy are the largest and offer the most entertainment and glamour. Smaller casinos are more basic and draw a relaxed crowd looking just for slot machines and icy rum punch. The mid-range casinos offer a good selection of games, live music or big-screen TVs tuned to sports events, and a variety of bar food.

Westin Dawn Beach Resort Casino is a Vegas-style casino that has several games from blackjack dealer to hit-the-slots.

Casino Royale has well-dressed guests who come to see glamorous productions at the Showroom Royale, dance to music in the Q-Club, and win or lose at 200 slot machines and great games.

The croupier spins the wheel and sends the ball rolling along the track in opposite directions.

Roulette is an extremely popular game in most of the casinos.

Diamond Casino is popular and features an outstanding selection of table and card games, such as Caribbean stud poker, roulette, blackjack, and baccarat, as well as nickel to $5 slots.

Princess Casino
The largest casino on the island, Princess Casino at Port de Plaisance is a glitzy, two-level venue for gaming tables including roulette, slots, private high-dollar salons, and nightly entertainment.

CASINOS

Casino Royale
W playmaho.com

Diamond Casino
W diamondcasinosxm.com

Jump Up Casino
W jumpupcasino.com

Princess Casino
W princessportdeplaisance.com/casino

Westin Dawn Beach Resort Casino
W westinstmaarten.com

Jump Up Casino has daily, dazzling parades in bright and colorful costumes and traditional Caribbean music reliving the carnival spirit of Sint Maarten.

Children SNUBA diving in the waters of Sint Maarten

Diving and Snorkeling

Much of the water surrounding the island is protected by environmental agencies, such as the Dutch Nature Foundation and the French Réserve Naturelle, so coral reefs and sea creatures are thriving in most areas or recovering in others. Interesting marine life along the reefs include banded coral shrimps, blue crabs, queen conch, and fireworms. Green moray eels, yellow goatfish, stoplight parrotfish, barracuda, and nurse sharks are among the local fish found here. Visibility is typically clear for 100 ft (30 m), and often up to 150 ft (45 m). Shore diving and snorkeling are good at Dawn Beach, where the reef runs parallel to the shore directly out from the center of the beach, and Baie de Friar, where coral grows on rocks and a shallow reef runs out from the shore for about 100 ft (30 m). The best sites are off Îlet Pinel, Île Tintamarre, Caye Verte, and Anse Marcel. Most resorts and marinas are affiliated with dive shops, such as **Scuba Fun**, **The Scuba Shop**, and **Dive Safaris** that rent and sell equipment, provide discovery and certification classes, and run scheduled scuba trips for certified divers.

Blue Bubbles outlets offer SNUBA, a tank-free system that allows divers, including children and uncertified adults, to dive and stay underwater while breathing through a long hose that reaches the air at the surface.

Boating and Sailing

Many international regattas are held annually, the largest being the 3-day Heineken Regatta, drawing more than 200 boats from two dozen countries to compete in 20 categories. The **Sint Maarten 12-Metre Challenge** is a mini-race between 40-ft (12-m) yachts and tourists can also participate. This activity takes place daily, and all passengers are seen as working crew members and allowed to learn or display sailing skills. For those who prefer motorboats, trips are organized through agencies based at marinas throughout the island. Charter companies, such as **The Moorings**, **Captain Alan's Boat Charters**, and **Captain Morgan**, arrange crewed and bareboat rentals for sailing vacations, and full- or half-day outings are offered through booking agencies while watersport kiosks on the beaches and resorts rent small boats. **Atlantis Submarines** offers the Seaworld Explorer, a 49-ft (15-m)

semi-submarine, that leaves Grand Case daily for an underwater exploration of reefs and marine life around Creole Rock.

Watersports

There are several watersports operators, such as **Aqua Mania** and **Tropical Wave and Chez Pat**, and resorts usually offer guests complimentary use of non-motorized equipment. Colorful Hobie Cats, Jet Skis, banana boats, kayaks, and parasail-toting speedboats fill the waters at Baie Orientale, Great Bay, and Simpson Bay Lagoon. Kiteboarding and windsurfing are popular at Le Galion Beach, and wakeboarding on Simpson Bay Lagoon, Nettle Bay, and Grand Case Bay. Boardsurfing is excellent from November through March on the island's north and west coasts, and from July through October, along the east coast.

Hiking

Trails on Pic du Paradis (see p270), are popular with hikers as it is cool here and the views are exceptional. **Loterie Farm**, at the base of the mountain, offers guided and self-guided hikes, but trails are accessible from back roads between Baie de Friar and the west side of Pic du Paradis. **National Heritage Foundation** organizes hikes geared to various fitness levels through other scenic parts of the island. **Tri-Sport** in Simpson Bay and **Authentic French Tours** in Marigot arrange group and private hikes with local guides.

Windsurfers off Le Galion Beach, St. Martin

Cyclist riding through the coastal region, Mullet Bay, St. Martin

Biking

Mountain and biking off the road is a great way to explore the countryside and isolated coastal areas. Many biking routes are along hiking trails, others are little-used back roads in less populated areas. Tri-Sport and Authentic French Tours rent bikes and arrange guided rides for all skill levels.

Horse-Riding

Professional equestrian guides lead rides for all ages and skill levels through the countryside, along beaches, and into the surf. **Lucky Stables** takes riders through the Cape Bay area while **Bayside Riding Club** has a Pony Club for kids and offers vacation horse rentals.

Golf

The 18-hole **Mullet Bay Golf Course** is still popular among golfers, even though Mullet Bay Resort and the golf club remain closed since Hurricane Luis in 1995. Players may rent a cart or walk the course, and all fees, including club rental, are based on games of either 9 or 18 holes.

Tennis

Many of the large resorts like **Sonesta Maho Beach Resort**, **Pelican Resort**, and Divi Little Bay Beach Resort *(see p276)* have tennis courts and allow non-guests to play by reservation, and for a fee. The **American Tennis Academy** gives lessons to adults and children. Courts may be reserved for private play 24 hours in advance.

DIRECTORY

Fishing

Lee's Deep Sea Fishing
84 Welfare Road, Cole Bay, Sint Maarten. **Tel** 721 544 4233. W leesfish.com

Rudy's Deep Sea Fishing
Airport Road, Simpson Bay, Sint Maarten. **Tel** 721 545 2177. W rudysdeep seafishing.com

Taylor Made Charters and Deep Sea Fishing
Simpson Bay Lagoon, Sint Maarten. **Tel** 721 552 7539. W taylormade-charters.com

Diving and Snorkeling

Blue Bubbles
153 Front Street, Philipsburg, Sint Maarten. **Tel** 721 556 8484. W bluebubblessxm. com

Dive Safaris
Simpson Bay, Sint Maarten. **Tel** 721 545 2401. W divestmaarten.com

Scuba Fun
Great Bay Marina, Philipsburg, Sint Maarten. **Tel** 721 542 3966. W scubafundivecenter. com

The Scuba Shop
Tel 590 874 801 (Oyster Pond, St. Martin), 721 545 3213 (Simpson Bay, Sint Maarten). W thescubashop.net

Boating and Sailing

Atlantis Submarines
15 Walter Nisbeth Road, Philipsburg, Sint Maarten. Tel 599 542 4078. W atlantissubmarines. com/stmaarten

Captain Alan's Boat Charters
Oyster Pond, Sint Maarten. Tel 721 524 1386. W captainalan.com

Captain Morgan
Great Bay Marina, Philipsburg, Sint Maarten. Tel 721 866 627. W captainmorgan-daycharters.com

The Moorings
Captain Oliver's Marina, Oyster Pond, St. Martin. Tel 590 873 255. W moorings.com

Sint Maarten 12-Metre Challenge
Bobby's Marina, Philipsburg, Sint Maarten. **Tel** 721 542 0045. W 12metre.com

Watersports

Aqua Mania
Pelican Marina, Simpson Bay. **Tel** 721 544 2640. W stmaarten-activities.com

Tropical Wave and Chez Pat
Le Galion Beach, St. Martin. **Tel** 590 873 725. W sxm-orientbeach. com/chezpat

Hiking

Authentic French Tours
Rue de Hollande, Marigot, St. Martin. **Tel** 590 870 511.

Loterie Farm
Route Pic du Paradis, St. Martin. **Tel** 590 878 616. W loteriefarm.net

National Heritage Foundation
Sint Maarten Museum, 7 Front Street, Philipsburg, Sint Maarten. **Tel** 721 542 4917. W speetjens.com

Tri-Sport
14B Airport Boulevard, Simpson Bay, Sint Maarten. **Tel** 721 545 4384. W trisport sxm.com

Horse-Riding

Bayside Riding Club
Le Galion Beach, St. Martin. **Tel** 590 873 664.

Lucky Stables
2 Traybay Drive, Cay Bay, Sint Maarten. **Tel** 721 544 5255.

Golf

Mullet Bay Golf Course
Mullet Bay, Sint Maarten. **Tel** 721 545 2801.

Tennis

American Tennis Academy
Cul de Sac, St. Martin. **Tel** 590 690 382217. W americantennis academy.net

Simpson Bay Resort
Simpson Bay, Sint Maarten. **Tel** 954 736 5807. W simpsonbayresort. com

Sonesta Maho Beach Resort
Maho Bay, Sint Maarten. **Tel** 721 545 2115. W sonesta.com/ MahoBeach

Where to Stay

St. Martin

DK Choice

ANSE MARCEL: Radisson Blu Resort, Marina & Spa $$$
Beach Resort
Anse Marcel
Tel *590 876 700*
🅦 radissonblu.com
This luxury hotel is set in its own little hamlet, away from the bustling crowds. Contemporary Euro-Caribbean furnishings, extensive Le Spa offerings, a private beach, and a large infinity pool surrounded by cabanas set the tone for a relaxing, pampered stay.

**GRAND CASE:
Hotel L'Esplanade** $$$
Luxury
Grand Case
Tel *590 870 655*
🅦 lesplanade.com
This European-style hotel on a hill above town has loft units with dark wood paneling. It is an easy walk to restaurants and shops.

**GRAND CASE/ANSE MARCEL:
The Dove's Nest** $
Beach
Petit Plage, Grand Case
Tel *590 874 946*
🅦 st-martin-vacation.com
This small retreat above Petit Plage Beach gives easy access to great restaurants and shopping. All units have kitchens.

**GRAND CASE/ANSE MARCEL:
Le Domaine de Lonvilliers** $$$
Luxury
Anse Marcel
Tel *590 523 535*
🅦 hotel-le-domaine.com
An elegant, secluded resort that has a private beach with cabanas

and lounges. There are also a restaurant, a beach bar, and a thalassotherapy spa.

MARIGOT: Fantastic Guest House $
Guesthouse
40 Lowtown, St. James
Tel *590 877 109*
🅦 thefantasticguesthouse.com
Centrally located guesthouse with a pool and terrace overlooking Simpson Bay Lagoon.

MARIGOT: Hotel Beach Plaza $$
Beach Resort
Marigot
Tel *590 878 700*
🅦 hotelbeachplazasxm.com
The Beach Plaza is a modern hotel just outside the city, set on a beach popular with snorkelers.

MARIGOT: La Samanna $$$
Luxury
Baie Longue
Tel *590 876 400*
🅦 lasamanna.com
Regarded as one of the best luxury hotels in the Caribbean, La Samanna has private villas, lavish suites, and a spacious spa.

ORIENT BAY: Club Orient $$
Beach Resort
Orient Bay
Tel *590 873 385*
🅦 cluborient.com
The only naturist (nudist) resort on the island, Club Orient has direct beach access and its own restaurant and wellness center.

ORIENT BAY: L'Hoste Hotel $$
Beach Resort
Orient Bay
Tel *590 874 208*
🅦 hostehotel.com
Situated on a popular beach, this hotel has one-bedroom suites. Guests have charge privileges at the five beach restaurants. Complimentary Wi-Fi.

Price Guide
Prices are based on one night's stay in high season for a standard double room, inclusive of service charges and taxes.

$	up to $200
$$	$200–400
$$$	over $400

**OYSTER POND:
Colombus Hotel** $$
Modern
30 Rue de l'Escale, Oyster Pond
Tel *590 874 252*
🅦 colombus-hotel.com
All rooms at this small gem near Dawn Beach have kitchens, as well as sitting and dining areas.

**OYSTER POND:
Coral Beach Club** $$
Beach Resort
Dawn Beach
Tel *721 543 6306*
🅦 coralbeach-club.com
Well-appointed villas, townhouses, and apartments with kitchens in a dramatic beachfront setting.

Sint Maarten

PHILIPSBURG: L'Esperance $
Modern
4 Tiger Road, Cay Hill
Tel *721 542 5355*
🅦 lesperancehotel.com
This small inland hotel has one- and two-bedroom suites with full kitchens. Free Wi-Fi.

PHILIPSBURG: Divi Little Bay $$
Beach Resort
Little Bay
Tel *721 542 2333*
🅦 divilittlebay.com
This self-contained large resort is located on a peninsula between two bays. The best rooms are the luxurious Casita Suites.

**SIMPSON BAY:
Turquoise Shell Inn** $
Beach
34 Simpson Bay Road
Tel *721 545 2875*
🅦 tshellinn.com
An intimate hotel adjacent to several beaches. Only one-bedroom suites are available.

**SIMPSON BAY:
Royal Palm Beach Resort** $$$
Beach Resort
115 Welfare Road, Cole Bay
Tel *721 544 3737*
🅦 royalpalmbeachresort.com
This resort offers one-, two-, and three-bedroom suites – all with ocean views.

Stylish lounge area in one of the luxurious villas at La Samanna, Marigot

Where to Eat and Drink

St. Martin

ANSE MARCEL:
Le Ti' Bouchon $$$
French
110 Route de Cul de Sac
Tel *690 648 464* **Closed** *Sun*
An authentic *bouchon* (intimate
French café) in a refurbished
Creole cottage. The imaginative
menu changes frequently to take
advantage of available products.
Warm, personal service.

BAIE ORIENTALE: Le Piment $
Italian/French
Village de la Baie Orientale
Tel *590 524 312* **Closed** *Mon*
Pizzas, pasta dishes, and salads in
a colorful village setting. There
is live music and theme nights
on Wednesdays, Fridays, and
Sundays. Very good value.

GRAND CASE:
La Villa Restaurant $$$
French
93 Boulevard de Grand Case
Tel *590 523 659*
Popular, quaint restaurant
offering traditional entrées with
some Caribbean twists. A three-
course fixed price menu and a
kids' menu are also available.
Wide selection of French wines.

GRAND CASE: Le Pressoir $$$
French
32 Boulevard de Grand Case
Tel *590 877 662* **Closed** *Sun in
low season*
Set on the beach, this long-time
favorite is housed in a Creole
home dating from 1871. The
menu has classic French cuisine
with Caribbean influences, and
an extensive wine list.

GRAND CASE: Spiga $$$
Italian
4 L'Esperance Road
Tel *590 524 783* **Closed** *Sun;
May–Dec*
Offering "creative Italian cuisine,"
this favorite serves pastas and
regional favorites in a setting
away from the crowds in Grand
Case. Good wine list.

MARIGOT: Le Marrakech $$$
Moroccan
169 Rue de Hollande
Tel *590 275 448* **Closed** *Sun*
This restaurant gets high marks
for its authentic presentation
of North African food, such as
couscous and tagines, as well
as interesting desserts. Try the
meze platter. Generous portions.

MARIGOT: Mario's Bistro $$$
French
Rue de Sandy Ground
Tel *590 870 636* **Closed** *Sun;
Aug–Sep*
This popular place offers
traditional cuisine accented with
interesting Caribbean, Spanish,
Italian, and Asian spices and
ingredients. Reservations are
a must. Pleasant water views.

Sint Maarten

**DAWN BEACH: Daniel's
by the Sea** $$
Continental
Dawn Beach
Tel *721 543 6828*
Favorites such as veal *piccata*,
shrimp scampi, and filet mignon
are served in a pleasant seaside
setting that doubles as Mr.
Busby's Beach Bar during the day.

**DAWN BEACH: Canoa at
Oyster Bay** $$$
Caribbean
Emerald Merit #14, Oyster Pond
Tel *721 543 6442*
This place is named for its
signature beef dish, which is
served in a plantain "canoe".
Also on the menu are favorites
such as Caribbean gumbo and
conch St. Martin, along with
meat, poultry, and pastas.

PHILIPSBURG: Hard Rock Café $
American
65 Front Street, Boardwalk
Tel *721 542 7014*
Consistent with other HRCs
around the world: sandwiches,
smoked meats, salads, and entrées
served in air-conditioned comfort
with lots of memorabilia.

**PHILIPSBURG: Chesterfield's
Waterfront Restaurant & Bar** $$
International
Great Bay Marina
Tel *721 542 3484*
A waterfront restaurant with a
view to Philipsburg, Chesterfield's
has lots of seafood entrées on
the menu, plus steaks and pasta
dishes. It gets really busy at lunch
when cruise ships are in.

SIMPSON BAY: Crave $
Mediterranean
101 Welfare Road
Tel *721 586 0467*
Crave's varied menu of entrées
with Persian spices and accents
receives excellent reviews.
Kebabs, stews, and burgers.

Bright, colorful exterior of Le Pressoir,
Grand Case

SIMPSON BAY: FIG Restaurant $$
Continental
130 Rhine Road, Cupecoy Bay
Tel *721 545 1041*
Grilled meats, fish, and seafood
at reasonable prices and with a
range of sauces – chimichurri,
satay, and pesto among them.

**SIMPSON BAY: Jimbo's Rock
& Blues Café** $$
Tex-Mex
Simpson Bay Marina
Tel *721 544 3600*
Enjoy colorful drinks and made-
to-order Mexican entrées,
burgers, and combination plates
in a relaxed atmosphere. There is
also a pool for swimming.

DK Choice

SIMPSON BAY:
Temptation $$$
Caribbean/Fusion
Cupecoy Beach, Atlantis Casino
Tel *721 545 2254* **Closed** *Sun*
Part of the Simpson Bay Resort,
Temptation and its sister
restaurant Rare serve up trendy
new cuisine merging various
influences in hip, stylish dining
rooms. Entrées include artfully
presented tempura fish, sashimi
tuna, chicken pad thai, osso
buco, and certified Angus beef
steak and rib. Desserts range
from simple to delightfully
creative and complex.

Practical Information

Both the French and Dutch sides of the island are tourist oriented and well set up to meet the needs and demands of international vacationers. The range of accommodations, dining venues, and leisure activities is wide, but focused on the upmarket. Government Tourist Boards have offices in Philipsburg and Marigot, as well as in Europe, the US, and Canada. Their websites have links to a number of businesses that cater to travelers. Maps and brochures are available from car rental agencies, hotels, and activity-booking agencies.

Visitors strolling down the esplanade, Philipsburg

When to Go

While the island of St. Martin and Sint Maarten enjoys sun-shine all year round, the best time to visit is during the high season – December through to April. During this time, Carnival, a two-week fiesta, takes place. Humidity starts to build up in May and does not dissipate until late November. Tropical storms blow through and hurricanes can strike between June to November.

Getting There

The island has frequent flights to and from North America and Europe, as well as other Caribbean islands. All inter-national flights land at Princess (Queen) Juliana Airport (SXM) on the Dutch side. Regional carriers land at both the Dutch airport and the French airport, Aeroport de l'Esperance (SFG). Major carriers flying in include **Delta**, **United Airlines**, **US Airways**, **American Airlines**, **Air Canada**, **KLM**, **Air France**, **Air Caraïbes**, **Air Antilles**, **Winair**, and **LIAT**.

Documentation

Citizens of the European Union may enter St. Martin and Sint Maarten by presenting a national ID or valid passport. Citizens of all other countries must show a valid passport.

All visitors must possess an onward or return ticket off the island. No visa is required for stays of up to three months. More information can be obtained from the **Embassy of France** in Washington DC, **Passport Canada**, and **UK Passport Services**.

Passengers boarding a Winair flight at Princess (Queen) Juliana Airport

Visitor Information

Visitor information kiosks are located at the airports, main marinas, and cruise ship docks. **Sint Maarten Tourist Bureau** has its office in Philipsburg and **Office du Tourisme de Saint-Martin** has a branch in Marigot. Local weekly and monthly publications listing current events and activities are available free of cost throughout the island.

Health and Security

Theft is a problem on the island, further complicated by the fact that the Dutch and French police do not readily exchange information. Rental cars are a prime target, as are the valuables left in them. Isolated beaches and hiking trails are other areas where theft is rampant. Report all crimes to the police, and get a report of the incident.

Banking and currency

Banks and ATMs are located at many locations throughout the island, with the majority in the capital cities, larger towns, and big resort areas. Most hotels, resorts, restaurants and shops accept major credit cards. The US dollar is widely accepted on both sides of the island, but officially the currency on the French side is the euro and on the Dutch side, in Sint Maarten and Curacao, is the Caribbean guilder.

Communications

To use a personal cell phone on the island, travelers must check with their service provider for instructions before leaving home. Hotel reception desks offer information regarding short-term cell phone rental outlets. Phone cards are available at major post offices. On St. Martin/Sint Maarten, the area code for the Dutch side is 721 and the area code for the French side is 590; calls between the two are considered inter-national. Many resorts have wireless Internet service, and Wi-Fi hotspots are scattered around the island.

Transport

Most large international agencies such as **AVIS** and **Hertz** rent cars on the island, and many local companies such as **Paradise** meet or beat their rates. Book well ahead during the high season. Several agencies have booths at the airports and large resorts usually have rental cars on-site. Taxis are abundant and charges are government regulated. Rates increase in the evening, and drivers may charge extra for more than three passengers and any excess luggage.

Shopping

Philipsburg is second only to Charlotte Amalie in the Virgin Islands for excellent duty-free bargains. Shops in Marigot are stocked with French merchandise at lower prices than those found in North America and some parts of Europe.

Visitors should check government duty-free exemptions before they leave home to determine the amount of goods they may bring back to their home country without paying a customs tax. Caribbean-specialist travel agencies and government websites provide further information.

Most shops on the Dutch side are open Monday to Saturday, from 9am to 6pm. On the French side, stores are open on the same days from 8:30am to 12:30pm and from 2pm to 7pm. Many shops on both sides keep longer hours when cruise ships are docked on the island.

Shop signages, Philipsburg

Best buys include loose gemstones, local art and crafts, porcelain figurines, china and crystal, watches and island-made liqueurs and Caribbean rum.

Language

The official language is Dutch on the Dutch side and French on the French side, but those who work in the tourism business can speak some English and maybe some Spanish. Among themselves, some locals speak in Papiamento (a Creole form of Spanish) or in a French patois.

Electricity

On the French side, electricity is 220 volts, and plugs must fit French outlets. On the Dutch side, electricity is 110 volts and appliances made for use in North America do not need a converter or plug adapter, however the ones made for use in Europe would require a converter and adapter.

Time

Both sides of the island are on Atlantic Standard Time (AST), 4 hours behind Greenwich Mean Time (GMT). Neither the French nor the Dutch side observes daylight savings.

Getting Married

To get married in Sint Maarten allow at least two months to make plans and process documents. **Tropical Wedding and Honeymoon** help to save time and avoid confusion. To marry in St. Martin, requirements are far more complicated. It is possible to have the official ceremony on the Dutch side and have the reception on the French side. Many resorts make special arrangements for newlyweds as well.

DIRECTORY

Getting There

Air Antilles
🔲 airantilles.com

Air Canada
🔲 aircanada.com

Air Caraïbes
🔲 aircaraibes.com

Air France
🔲 airfrance.com

American Airlines
🔲 aa.com

Delta
🔲 delta.com

KLM
🔲 klm.com

LIAT
🔲 liat.com

United Airlines
🔲 united.com

US Airways
🔲 usair.com

Winair
🔲 fly-winair.com

Documentation

Passport Canada
Tel 800 567 6868.
🔲 pptc.gc.ca

UK Passport Services
Tel 0300 222 0000.
🔲 ukps.gov.uk

Embassy of France, Washington DC
Tel 120 294 46000 (USA).
🔲 ambafrance-us.org

Visitor Information

Office du Tourisme de Saint-Martin
Tel 590 875 721.
🔲 st-martin.org

Sint Maarten Tourist Bureau
Tel 721 542 2337.
🔲 st-maarten.com

Health and Security

Dutch Fire, Police, and Medical Assistance
Tel 911.

French Fire and Police
Tel 17.

French Medical Assistance
Tel 112.

Transport

AVIS
Tel 721 545 2847.
🔲 avis.com

Hertz
Tel 721 545 4541.
🔲 sxmrentacar.com

Paradise
Tel 721 545 3737.
🔲 paradiseca rrentalsxm.com

Getting Married

Tropical Wedding and Honeymoon
Tel 721 520 7986.
🔲 sintmaarten-wedding.com

Exploring Saba and St. Eustatius

Many people have not even heard of these two small volcanic islands. Saba, only 5 sq miles (13 sq km) in size, has a rough coastline with few natural harbors. The interior is hilly, dominated by Mount Scenery, the extinct volcano now clad in tropical vegetation. St. Eustatius, or Statia, is more spread out and has The Quill – an extinct volcano with a deep crater that is home to a dense rainforest. The islanders have made an effort to preserve their history, making these two gems a must for those looking beyond all the glitz and glamour of the Caribbean.

Locator Map

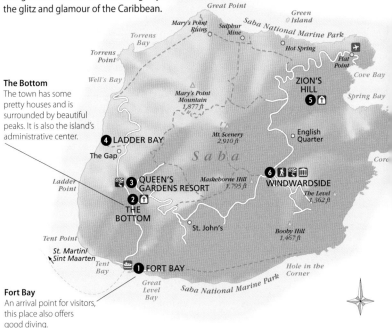

The Bottom
The town has some pretty houses and is surrounded by beautiful peaks. It is also the island's administrative center.

Fort Bay
An arrival point for visitors, this place also offers good diving.

0 kilometers 1
0 miles 1

Sights at a Glance

① Fort Bay
② The Bottom
④ Ladder Bay
⑤ Zion's Hill
⑥ Windwardside
⑦ Oranjested
⑨ National Park Visitors' Center
⑩ Lynch Plantation Museum
⑪ Miriam Schmidt Botanical
   Gardens

Featured Hotels and Resorts

③ Queen's Gardens Resort
⑧ The Old Gin House

For hotels and restaurants on these islands see p290 and p291

Scuba divers exploring the colorful reefs off Saba's coast

The small town of The Bottom, nestling beneath an extinct volcanic peak, Saba

Key

═══ Minor road

‒ ‒ Track

‑‑‑ Ferry route

△ Peak

Getting Around

The only way that Saba and St. Eustatius can be reached is by traveling through Sint Maarten. There are several flights each day from the Princess (Queen) Juliana Airport (SXM) to the islands, and between them. In addition, there are ferry services to Saba from St. Martin/ Sint Maarten. Once on the islands, the best way to get around is by taxi or rental car. It is easy to find your way as there is only one main road on Saba, and a limited amount of roads in St. Eustatius. Sometimes taxis can be scarce, so it is best to contact the tourism offices and make arrangements ahead of time.

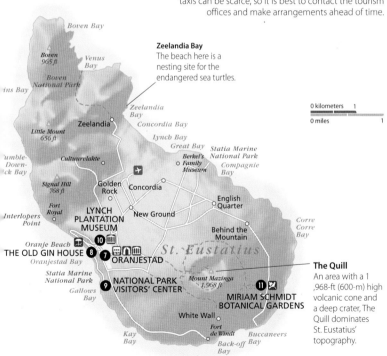

Zeelandia Bay
The beach here is a nesting site for the endangered sea turtles.

0 kilometers 1
0 miles 1

The Quill
An area with a 1 ,968-ft (600-m) high volcanic cone and a deep crater, The Quill dominates St. Eustatius' topography.

For additional map symbols *see back flap*

❶ Fort Bay

SW coast of Saba.

Saba's main port, Fort Bay is also the starting point for diving excursions. With a harsh coastline and no sandy beaches or real harbors for boat docking, the island was hard to access. In 1972, the Dutch government built a 277-ft (84-m) deep-water pier at Fort Bay, making it easier for landing cargo and for ferry services. The only gas station on the island is located here, along with the office of Saba Deep Divers and the Saba Marine Park Visitor's Center and Hyperbaric Facility *(see pp284–5)*.

Lacework at Saba Foundation

The adjacent In Two Deep café and Pop's Place are two relaxing places to enjoy a cool drink and their famous sandwiches with fantastic views of the sea.

❷ The Bottom

1 mile (1.6 km) N of Fort Bay, Saba.
600. Summer Festival

On the winding road up from Fort Bay, the first town is The Bottom – the largest on the island and the seat of

Heleen Cornet's mural at Sacred Heart Church

government. Before The Road was built, the main mode for transporting goods from the sea was walking up 200 steps from Fort Bay or 800 steps from Ladder Bay, and then onto 900 more steps into Windwardside.

Most buildings are in the typical Saban style with white clapboard houses with red roofs and trimmed lawns, all neatly kept with pride. Among the town's highlights are **Sacred Heart Church**'s sacristy adorned with original paintings done by local artist Heleen Cornet, and the **Saba Artisan Foundation** where Saban lace and other handwork are sold. Both are within walking distance from the center of the town. Other notable buildings here include the grand governor's house, and Saba University School of Medicine.

Saba Artisan Foundation
The Bottom. **Tel** 599 416 3260.
Open 8am–noon & 2:30–5pm Mon–Fri.

❸ Queen's Gardens Resort

Troy Hill, Drive 1, Saba. **Tel** 599 416 3494. **queensaba.com**

High on the hill above The Bottom sits the Queen in all her splendor. Set amidst the hill's flora overlooking the Caribbean Sea, with 100-year-old mango trees and other tropical plants, this luxury hotel is cut off from the hustle-bustle of the town. The hotel features spacious one- and two-bedroom suites with full kitchens, dining and living areas, and private outdoor Jacuzzis facing the ocean. There is also a three-bedroom villa, which is perfect for those wishing for complete privacy. On the main deck below the rooms is a restaurant, a patio bar, and the largest swimming pool on Saba, with spectacular views of the sea. The Bottom is only a short walk down the pretty hill.

The luxurious Queen's Gardens Resort situated on Troy Hill

❹ Ladder Bay

1 mile (1.6 km) NW of The Bottom, Saba. **Open** dawn–dusk daily.
hiking fee. Saba Conservation Foundation. **sabapark.org**

Saba's first port, Ladder Bay served the island before the pier was constructed at Fort Bay in 1972. More than 800 steps leading from Ladder Bay up to The Bottom were the major mode of transportation for people and goods until as late as the 1970s.

Today, visitors can climb down to Ladder Bay through the Ladder Trail, which begins near The Bottom. The only route to reach the bay, this trail continues down a steep road through a residential area where the steps veer off to the left. Views from the steps to the ocean are impressive, but the hike is strenuous and takes about 40 minutes each way. Although the trail can be done without a guide, it is advisable not to stray off the track as it crosses private land. The highlight of this route is the remains of the old Customs House.

The bay has several areas ideal for diving, including Ladder Bay Deep, a sloping reef that resembles a pinnacle, dropping to a maximum depth of 110 ft (33 m). This is a great place to see nurse sharks and schools of barracuda.

For hotels and restaurants on these islands see p290 and p291

❺ Zion's Hill

2 miles (3 km) NE of The Bottom, Saba.
🏘 100. ➤ ⓣ

Perched on the little Zion's
Hill, Hell's Gate is a small town,
closest to Juancho E Yrausquin
Airport and can be reached
only by The Road, a winding
one-lane thoroughfare which
rises up to 2,000 ft (609 m).
Since many residents did
not appreciate the negative
name, the town is also known
as Zion's Hill.

One of the main highlights
in this town is the Holy Rosary
Church. Made to resemble a
structure from the medieval
period, it was in fact built in
1962. Behind the church is
Saba Lace Boutique, where
some of the best lacemakers on
the island exhibit and sell their
delicate pieces of art. The town
is also well-known for its locally
produced and very potent
spice rum called Saba Rum.

Zion's Hill is the closest to
the Saba National Marine Park
(see p285) and the now-closed
old sulphur mines.

🏠 Saba Lace Boutique
Zion's Hill. **Open** 9am–noon & 2:30–
5pm Mon–Fri.

❻ Windwardside

1 mile (1.6 km) E of The Bottom, Saba.
🏘 600. ⓣ ℹ Tourism Office,
599 416 2231. ✉ 🅦 sabatourism.
com

Beyond Zion's Hill, The Road
passes through thick forests
offering fantastic views of
the island before reaching
the charming town of

Artist JoBean in her Hot Glass Studio,
Windwardside

The Road that could not be Built

Before the 1930s, Saba did not have a road, which made everyday
activities, such as shopping, quite difficult. Goods arriving by sea
had to be transported up steep steps to the towns. When the
Sabans asked the Dutch government to build a road in the 1930s,
both Dutch and Swiss engineers believed it was impossible for
a road to be built because of the island's steep hills and valleys.
Undaunted, a Saban named Josephus Lambert Hassell took up
the challenge. He enrolled in a correspondence course in civil
engineering, and convinced a crew of locals to start building a
road in 1938. After five years the first section, from Fort Bay to
The Bottom, was completed. The first motor vehicle arrived here
in 1947. It took until 1951 to finish the section to Windwardside
and St. Johns, and finally in 1958 the entire road to the airport,
north of Zion's Hill, was constructed. It is aptly and simply called
"The Road".

The long and winding Road of Saba

Windwardside. A sleepy little
place, this town is a step
back in time, with its quaint
shopping area and several
restaurants. However, the
real interest is the
residential area
that encircles
the town center,
with outstanding
examples of typical
Saban cottages, many
historical in nature.

At the far end of the village,
The Trail Shop offers a map
that shows the name, location,
and construction dates of
these lovely houses.

Windwardside is also known
as the base for hiking trips and
beyond the Trail Shop begins
the hike to Mount Scenery
(see p284). Other highlights
are the **Harry L. Johnson
Museum**, a sea captain's
160-year-old cottage now
used as a museum. The original
furnishings of the Victorian
era have been left as they were.

*Glass artifact at
JoBean's Studio*

In addition, a collection
of Amerindian artifacts is
displayed. Another
interesting place to
visit is **JoBean's Hot
Glass Studio** at the
southern end of
town going toward
Booby Hill. Visitors
can learn to make
glass beads or even
watch Jo Bean at work.

Other opportunities for
shopping are at El Momo Folk
Art, which has interesting
tapestries called Molas, and
The Peanut Gallery *(see p293)*,
for local arts and crafts.

🏛 **Harry L. Johnson Museum**
Windwardside. **Tel** 599 416 2231.
Open 10am–noon & 2–4pm Mon–Fri.
🅦 sabatourism.com/
museums.html

JoBean's Hot Glass Studio
Windwardside. **Tel** 599 416 2490.
Open 10am–5pm Mon–Sat,
10am–3pm Sun.
🅦 jobeanglassart.com

Outdoor Activities and Specialized Holidays

The combination of a hilly topography and volcanic origins makes Saba a prime choice for those who love hiking and diving. Through natural evolution and the lack of large-scale tourism, the island remains an eco-escape where visitors can explore rare elfin forests, winding trails robed in tropical plants, underwater pinnacles and chasms, and a host of other features.

Hiker on a trail on the extinct volcano, Mount Scenery

Hiking

Saba is quite simply a hiker's paradise with its many steep hills and deep valleys. The trails that crisscross the island were once the only means of travel and are still maintained in excellent condition.

Dominating the island's skyline is Mount Scenery, an extinct volcano. The Mount Scenery Trail begins from Windwardside (see p283). It has 1,064 steps and takes up to two hours each way. At the lowest levels, cactus, red-woods, mountain fuchsia, and fruit trees can be found. The flora changes to palms, tree ferns, elephant ears, and wild plantain trees as the trail rises. At the top, climbers can view the elfin rainforest full of ferns, bromeliads, orchids, and mountain mahogany. Hikers are rewarded with sightings of Saba's rich bird species, totaling about 60.

Among other trails the Crispeen Track is the most accessible and least demanding trail, affording great views, and transporting hikers from Windwardside to The Bottom. The Sandy Cruz Trail through the valley between Mount Scenery and Mary's Point is not too demanding either. The Ladder Trail offers fantastic views of Ladder Bay (see p282), while those looking for a longer hike with spectacular scenery will have to find a guide to take them along the North Coast Trail, running from Lower Zion's Hill to Wells Bay.

Another trail is the Sulphur Mine Track, which starts at Zion's Hill and winds through forests, before opening up to a meadow leading down to the sea. At the ocean's bluff, hikers descend to the mine, which can be explored through flashlights. One of the best ways to ply the trails is with guide James "Crocodile" Johnson, who knows every trail. **Saba Conservation Foundation Trail Shop** can book tours with him. All hikers have to pay a fee.

Diving and Snorkeling

Saba is rapidly earning a reputation as a premier dive destination in the Caribbean. Because the influx of tourists has been low, the dive sites have not been heavily explored. No dive boats, except the licensed Saban dive operators, are allowed to moor at the dive sites in the marine park. This ensures that the reefs are protected and all diving is done in a safe environment. **Saba Deep Dive Center**, **Saba Divers**, and **Sea Saba** offer an upgrade to Nitrox air for free. Divers need to pay a park fee at the **Saba Marine Park Visitors' Center** or through their dive operators. Another important resource is the Hyperbaric Facility run by the Saba Conservation Foundation. This four-person decompression chamber at Fort Bay is designated to serve divers in the area from Puerto Rico to Barbados. Travelers can also visit Saba University Medical School that offers a program in hyperbaric medicine.

Sea and Learn, an annual month-long celebration in October, offers one of the best introductions of Saba to marine explorers. It includes workshops, lectures, and field projects relating to environmental awareness.

(see p282), (see p283)

DIRECTORY

Hiking

Saba Conservation Foundation Trail Shop
Windwardside, Saba.
Tel 599 416 2630.
ⓦ sabapark.org

Diving and Snorkeling

Saba Deep Dive Center
Fort Bay, Saba.
Tel 599 416 3347,
toll free USA: 1 866 416 3347.
ⓦ sabadeep.com

Saba Divers
Scout's Place Hotel,
Windwardside, Saba.
Tel 599 416 2740.
ⓦ sabadivers.com

Saba Marine Park Visitors' Center
Fort Bay, Saba.
Tel 599 416 3295.
ⓦ sabapark.org

Sea and Learn
Tel 599 416 2246.
ⓦ seaandlearn.org

Sea Saba
Windwardside, Saba.
Tel 599 416 2246.
ⓦ seasaba.com

Divers setting out on a dive off Saba

Saba National Marine Park and Saba Bank

Just offshore from this tiny volcanic island is a dramatic underwater world of deep chasms, sheer walls, 99-ft (30-m) pinnacles, and teeming coral reefs. This environment is protected by the Saba Conservation Foundation. They have designated the area from the high-water mark to a depth of 197 ft (60 m) all around the island as the Saba National Marine Park since 1987. In addition, 3 miles (5 km) southwest of the island lies a large submerged atoll known as the Saba Bank, a biodiversity hotspot which environmentalists are trying to protect from supertankers.

Well's Bay

SABA

Caribbean Sea

Locator map

- Yacht moorings
- Fishing and diving
- Recreational diving
- All-purpose area

Colorful corals in great abundance are protected by the marine park.

Pinnacles are suitable only for experienced divers.

Saba Bank offers some of the most diverse marine life in the Caribbean. An expedition in 2006 located 200 species of fish, including two previously unidentified species.

The Pinnacles of Saba rise from the deep-sea floor allowing for a "bottomless" dive, making it a popular diving site.

Dive sites, totaling 29 in the marine park, offer a range of depths for divers of all experience levels. Most of the sites are along the Caribbean Sea on the western side of the island where the waters are not as rough as on the Atlantic side.

The underwater Marine Park is flush with numerous varieties of tropical fish as well as eels, sharks, and the occasional humpback whale or whale shark.

Visitors at the ruins of Honem Dalem Synagogue, Oranjestad

❼ Oranjestad

South coast of St. Eustatius. 🏛 2,000.
✈ 🛈 in Fort Orange, 599 318 2433.
🎭 Statia-America Day (Nov 16).
🌐 **statiatourism.com**

The island of St. Eustatius, or Statia, was known during the colonial period as the Golden Rock, because of its importance as a center for international trade. The population during the peak trading years jumped to over 20,000, and the main town of Oranjestad was a thriving, cosmopolitan place. Since 2000, a concerted effort has been made by the St. Eustatius Historical Foundation to restore much of the town area. Now, a stroll through the Upper Town is like stepping back in time, with graceful 17th- and 18th-century wood and stone structures lining the cobblestone streets.

Detail, salute pillar, Fort Oranje

Shops and restaurants are just steps away down the streets lined with traditional wooden cottages. The town offers the second largest collection of standing wooden 18th-century buildings in the Americas, exceeded only by Colonial Williamsburg in the US. The **St. Eustatius Historical Foundation** is housed in the 18th-century home of merchant Simon Doncker. On the main level are period rooms filled with authentic furnishings and many household goods from the 18th century. The museum staff coordinates guided walking tours of the town. The Government Guest House is an old stone structure that has been restored and is now in use as an office building. It first served as barracks for the troops at **Fort Oranje** which sits on a bluff overlooking Lower Town and Gallows Bay. Originally built by the French in 1629, the fort has been fully restored, with the Tourist Office occupying one of the buildings. One of the noted landmarks is the flagstaff, flying the flags of St. Eustatius and the US. Just to the south of the fort are the ruins of the **Dutch Reformed Church**, built in the 1750s, and the adjacent cemetery. The outer structure of the main church is occasionally used for weddings. The tower gives an overall view of the town. Another historic site is **Honem Dalem Synagogue**, one of the oldest synagogues in the Americas. Now in ruins, plans for its restoration are underway with support from St. Eustatius Center for Archeological Research (SECAR). Built in 1739, the structure and grounds include a cemetery, dating back to the same period, and a *mikvah*, a ritual bath, that was discovered during one of the SECAR excavations.

🏛 **St. Eustatius Historical Foundation**
Wilhelminaweg 3. **Tel** 599 318 2288.
Open 9am–5pm Mon–Fri.
🌐 **steustatiushistory.org**

🏰 **Fort Oranje**
Kerkweg. 🛈 599 318 2433.
Open sunrise–sunset. 📷
🌐 **statiatourism.com**

⛪ **Dutch Reformed Church**
Kerkweg. **Open** sunrise–sunset. 📷
🌐 **steustatiushistory.org**

🕍 **Honem Dalem Synagogue**
Breedeweg. **Open** sunrise–sunset. 📷

❽ The Old Gin House

📍 Lower Town, Oranjestad, St. Eustatius. **Tel** 599 318 2319.
🚻 ✍ 🌐 **oldginhouse.com**

Formerly a cotton processing unit, this historic structure has now been turned into the island's only luxury inn *(see p290)*. The main building houses the lobby, the bar, the restaurant, and the rooms; furnished with colonial repro-duction furniture these face the manicured garden and pool behind it. Across the street, the hotel has a patio café overlooking the sea and serving breakfast and lunch. The hotel also houses a small but good bar. Oranje Beach and the National Park Visitors' Center are only a short distance down the road. A walkway, with steps leading up to Oranjestad's Upper Town, is adjacent to the property.

❾ National Park Visitors' Center

Gallows Bay, below Oranjestad, St. Eustatius. **Tel** 599 318 2884. **Open** 8am–5pm Mon–Thu, 8am–4pm Fri.
📷 🍴 🏠 🌐 **statiapark.org**

The St. Eustatius National Park Foundation (STENAPA) oversees its many programs from the Visitors' Center in Gallows Bay. It offers exhibits, a small souvenir shop, an Internet

The interiors of the bar in the Old Gin House

Volunteers at work at Miriam Schmidt Botanical Gardens

café, showers, public bathrooms, and a picnic area. Visitors can book tours, make taxi reservations, pay fees for park usage or diving, and even purchase plants from the botanical gardens.

⑩ Lynch Plantation Museum

1 mile (1.6 km) N of Oranjestad, St. Eustatius. **Tel** 599 318 2338. **Open** on request.

This small domestic museum was constructed by the Berkel family on their homestead. The exhibition house, which was built by the family in 1916, is a replica of the original house and displays furniture, artifacts, and tools from the plantation. A private school also shares the plantation grounds, which are well maintained with fruit trees as well as the natural flora of the island. An area on the side with a bower is used for weddings and receptions.

Berkel Museum on the sprawling grounds of the Lynch Plantation

⑪ Miriam Schmidt Botanical Gardens

3 miles (5 km) E of Oranjestad, St. Eustatius. **Tel** 599 318 2884. **Open** sunrise–sunset. **w statiapark.org**

As one of the national parks under the direction of STENAPA, this developing site serves to educate locals and visitors about the varied plant life of the island, thus helping to protect and preserve the island's native and endangered flora. Development of the gardens began in 1998, and volunteers work daily on improving various areas. Already completed are the Sensory Garden, Palm Garden, Shade House, Lookout Garden (with views of St. Kitts and humpback whales), and the Jean Gemmill Bird Observation Trail. Guided tours are arranged by the National Park Visitors' Center in Gallows Bay.

Statia in American History

November 16, 1776, was a day like any other in colonial St. Eustatius, when the American Brig-of-War *Andrew Doria* came sailing into Gallows Bay. The ship fired off a 13-gun salute, commemorating America's new independence from England. The troops at Fort Oranje fired back an 11-gun salute, thereby making St. Eustatius the first foreign nation to officially recognize the new nation of the United States of America. The event was not overlooked by the British fleet in the Caribbean, which expended its wrath on Statia. Franklin D. Roosevelt, during his term as US President, presented the island with a plaque in commemoration of its support of the US in those early times. In return, the Statians named their airport after him. Each year, the island celebrates the American connection with the Statia-America Day, held on November 16. Usually, the week before the big day is filled with musical events and a carnival-like atmosphere. On the big day itself there is a flag-raising ceremony at Fort Oranje.

Cannon pointing out to sea at Fort Oranje in St. Eustatius

Outdoor Activities and Specialized Holidays

Just like Saba, the natural beauty of St. Eustatius attracts those looking for unspoiled forests and reefs to explore. But unlike Saba, St. Eustatius has a few beaches to add to the attractions, although their use is limited. The volcanic origin of the island makes for a variety of hikes and the dense concentration of colonial period artifacts offers a unique opportunity for excavating.

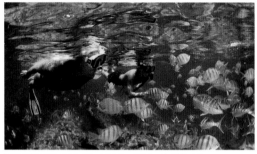

Snorkeling amidst a school of sergeant majors, off the coast of St. Eustatius

Beaches

Most Caribbean islands are blessed with multitudes of beautiful beaches, but St. Eustatius is not one of them. While swimming is an option on some, Statia, as it is popularly known, has three beaches best used for sunbathing, playing in the sand, and flying kites.

Oranjestad Bay is the most accessible and swimmer-friendly beach on the Caribbean Sea side. Located in Oranjestad, it has patches of tan and black sand interrupted by rocks jutting into the sea. The water is shallow and calm. The renowned inn, The Old Gin House (see p286) is just down the road.

Lynch Bay is a stretch of brown sand midway down the island's Atlantic Coast. The water is shallow near the beach, but develops an undertow farther out so swimmers have to be careful. Visitors need to bring essentials since there are no amenities here.

Zeelandia Bay is a 2-mile (3-km) long Atlantic strand that looks inviting, but activities should be restricted to sunbathing and sand castle building. The water has a heavy undertow, so swimmers are warned to stay out of it.

Hiking

St. Eustatius offers hikers a variety of hiking trails in the national park that encompasses the Boven and The Quill peaks. The STENAPA was founded in 1988 to manage these two areas plus the marine park and botanical gardens. It maintains the hiking trails, posts signs, monitors animal and plant life, and conducts guided hikes. All hikers must pay a fee at the STENAPA Visitors' Center (see p286).

The Boven National Park area consists of five hills on the northern point of the island. Most of the trails are not maintained at this point because of unresolved property disputes. However, visitors can still follow four trails, including Boven, Venus Bay, Gilboa Hill, and Bergje. All trails start at the end of road in Zeelandia, and range in length from 60 to 120 minutes to complete.

Diving, Snorkeling, and Kayaking

Diving is the reason why most visitors come to St. Eustatius. The Statia National Marine Park is considered one of the top five dive sites in the Caribbean. The park extends from the shore to a 99-ft (30-m) depth and around the entire coast. The park authority maintains 42 mooring sites.

Diving is allowed only through the three local dive operators, and divers must pay either annually or for each dive at the Gallows Bay Visitors' Center.

St. Eustatius has nearly 200 ship wrecks and other underwater structures such as coral reefs on volcanic substrates, including lava flows shaped like fingers and a spur and groove zone. These can be seen at Hangover, Five Fingers North and South, and the Ledges dive sites.

Among the 36 dive sites are historical areas such as Double and Triple Wreck, Stingray City, and Anchor Reef. Deep dive sites including Grand Canyon/ Off the Wall, Coral Gardens, and Doobie's Crack range from 85–99 ft (26–30 m). **Golden Rock Dive Center** rents out underwater cameras and organizes guided dives. The prime sites for snorkeling in Oranjestad Bay have an entire range of submerged sea walls, warehouses and old piers, which are accessible from Oranje Beach or the Golden Era hotel pier. An interesting way to snorkel is using the Sea-Doo underwater scooters that **Dive Statia** rents out. **Scubaqua** and Golden Rock Dive Center also offer snorkeling trips.

Some of the bays are inaccessible by road but can be reached by kayaks. Dive Statia has Malibu Two XI ocean kayaks for hire.

Signages at the Quill Trail

Hiking The Quill

In Dutch, a "kuil" is a pit, and this is how the high mountain crater called The Quill got its name. This volcanic cone's topography ranges from rough slopes leading up to the edge of the crater to the broad inner floor, surrounded by a national park. Throughout The Quill National Park the vegetation zones vary from thorny woodland on the outer slopes of The Quill, to lush evergreen seasonal forest in the crater and a rare elfin forest on the rim at the highest point, called Mount Mazinga. Ten hiking trails surround The Quill.

Caribbean Sea

ST. EUSTATIUS

Locator map

☐ *Area illustrated*

Oranjestad

Mount Mazinga
1,968 ft

Fort de Windt

Birds of various kinds can be found in the area. The Bird Trail has posted signs indicating the species that can be seen at certain points.

| 0 kilometers | 1 |
| 0 miles | 1 |

Key

— Around the Mountain Trail
— Bird Trail
— Botanical Garden Trail
⋯ Couchar Mountain Trail
— Crater Trail
Mazinga Trail
⋯ Panoramic Point Trail
— Quill Trail
— Rosemary Lane Trail
— Tompi Hill Trail

The Quill Trail leads to the rim of the crater. It is rated as one of the moderate hikes. The view from the rim shows the vast and varied vegetation zones.

Hikers can choose from the easy Bird Trail to the difficult Crater Trail, and from the longest Around the Mountain Trail to the relatively short and steep Panoramic Point Trail.

Excavating

Called "The Pompeii of the New World" by archaeologists, St. Eustatius has over 600 documented archaeology sites with artifacts dating from the slavery era. The **St. Eustatius Center for Archaeological Research** hosts digs where students and volunteers help uncover the remnants of household goods and tools from the ruins of slave houses, warehouses, and domestic buildings that existed during that time.

DIRECTORY

Diving, Snorkeling, and Kayaking

Dive Statia
Lower Town, Oranjestad.
Tel 599 318 2435.
Ⓦ divestatia.com

Golden Rock Dive Center
Lower Town, Oranjestad.
Tel 599 318 2964.
Ⓦ goldenrockdive.com

Scubaqua
Lower Town, Oranjestad.
Ⓦ scubaqua.com

Excavating

St. Eustatius Center For Archaeological Research
Lampeweg, Oranjestad.
Tel 599 524 6770.
Ⓦ secar.org

Where to Stay

Queen's Garden Resort surrounded by rainforest, Troy Hill, Saba

Saba

**BOOBY HILL: Saba on
the Rocks** $$
Modern
Booby Hill
Tel *410 610 7780*
W sabaontherocks.com
This spacious villa located 1,400
feet (426 m) above sea level has
two bedrooms, plus a lower-level
apartment. There is also a unique
stone grotto dipping pool.

**BOOBY HILL:
Shearwater Resort** $$
Boutique
Booby Hill
Tel *599 416 2498*
W shearwater-resort.com
Formerly Willard's of Saba,
this luxury hotel is perched
dramatically on the side of the
hill, offering spectacular views.

DK Choice

**TROY HILL: Queen's
Garden Resort** $$
Boutique
Drive 1
Tel *599 416 3494*
W queensaba.com
A hillside hotel with antiques
and artworks in all the suites,
each of which occupies an
entire floor of the building.
Most also have open-air private
Jacuzzis and views over The
Bottom and to the sea. Good
restaurant, lounge, and pool.

TROY HILL: Haiku House $$$
Luxury
Drive 1
Tel *599 416 3494*
W sabavillas.com
Based on the design of a 16th-
century Japanese villa, this large
house is the ultimate retreat.
Private pool and a Jacuzzi.

**WINDWARDSIDE: Ecolodge
Rendez-Vous** $
Ecolodge
Crispean Track
Tel *599 416 3348*
W ecolodge-saba.com
For those willing to "rough it,"
this small hotel offers basic
accommodations in rustic
lodges with eco-amenities.

**WINDWARDSIDE:
Catseye Cottage** $$
Historic
Windwardside
Tel *800 883 7222*
W catseye-saba.com
A restored 1879 cottage with one
bedroom, plus kitchen, living
room, and decks. Panoramic
views of the town and the ocean.

**WINDWARDSIDE:
Cottage Club Hotel** $$
Modern
Windwardside
Tel *599 416 2386*
W cottage-club.com
A collection of one-bedroom
cottages with balconies facing
the sea and all the conveniences
of a hotel.

WINDWARDSIDE: Juliana's $$
Modern
Windwardside
Tel *599 416 2269*
W julianas-hotel.com
One of the island's few real
hotels, with rooms available in
the main building, as well as in
two cottages and an apartment.

**WINDWARDSIDE: Selera
Dunia Boutique Hotel** $$
Boutique
The Level
Tel *599 416 5443*
W seleradunia.com
High on a hill, this hotel has a
range of suites with individual
decor, such as Dutch or from
the Iban culture of Borneo.

**WINDWARDSIDE:
Hummingbird Villa** $$$
Modern
Windwardside
Tel *619 567 6965*
W sabahomesforrent.com
A two-bedroom private villa
with a poolside guesthouse and
incredible views of the sea. There
is also a large outdoor deck.

**WINDWARDSIDE:
Villa Fairview** $$$
Luxury
Windwardside
W villasaba.nl
This villa, high up on a hill, has
a large deck with a pool and a
gazebo overlooking the sea.

St. Eustatius

CONCORDIA: Country Inn $
Inn
Concordia
Tel *599 318 2484*
W statiatourism.com/country_inn_
page.htm
This small hotel has simple and
comfortable rooms with views
to Zeelandia Bay.

**ORANJESTAD:
Golden Era Hotel** $$
Historic
Oranjestad
Tel *599 318 2345*
W goldenerahotel.com
A restored 18th-century
warehouse, this beachside hotel is
perched on the edge of the sea.

ORANJESTAD: Old Gin House $$
Historic
Oranjestad
Tel *599 318 2319*
W oldginhouse.com
The best luxury hotel on the
island is housed in a former
gin factory. Atmospheric bar.

WHITE WALL: Statia Lodge $$
Boutique
White Wall
Tel *599 318 1900*
W statialodge.com
Ideal for families, these wooden
bungalows have sea views, one
or two bedrooms, full kitchens,
and terraces.

Where to Eat and Drink

Saba

BOOBY HILL: Bistro del Mare $$$
Seafood
Shearwater Resort
Tel *599 416 2498*   **Closed** *Sun*
Savor some of the finest fresh
fish and seafood here. Monday
night is Thai night. Good
international wine selection.

FORT BAY: Deep End Bar & Grill $
Saban
Fort Bay Harbour
Tel *599 416 3347*   **Closed** *dinner*
This eatery at Saba Deep Dive
Center offers soups, sandwiches,
and fresh fish. Harbor views.

FORT BAY: Pop's Place $
South American
Fort Bay Harbour
Tel *599 416 3640*   **Closed** *Mon*
Owned and managed by
Colombians, Pop's Place serves
a daily changing menu of
empanadas, sandwiches, and
other Colombian delicacies.

THE BOTTOM:
Saba Coffee House $
Café
The Bottom
Tel *599 416 3636*   **Closed** *Sat*
This coffeehouse features locally
produced Café Luna Roastery
coffee, plus pastries and bistro-
style lunches, as well as frozen
coffee drinks and smoothies.

WINDWARDSIDE:
Chinese Restaurant $
Chinese
Windwardside
Tel *599 416 2353*   **Closed** *Mon*
Classic Cantonese dishes, plus
steaks and salad, are served up
in a hillside setting with town
views. Carry out or eat in.

WINDWARDSIDE: Brigadoon $$
International
Flat Point
Tel *599 416 2380*   **Closed** *Tue*
Known for its welcoming service,
great food, and cozy setting.
Prime rib on Thursdays and sushi
on Saturdays. Reserve ahead.

WINDWARDSIDE:
Swinging Doors $$
American
Windwardside
Tel *599 416 2506*
Basic, hearty food from the grill,
with steak on Sunday nights, and
BBQ nights on Tuesdays and
Fridays. There is also a popular
and colorful bar. Cash only.

DK Choice

WINDWARDSIDE:
Rainforest Restaurant $$$
Caribbean/Indonesian
Ecolodge Rendez-Vous
Tel *599 416 7012 or 599 416 7032*
Closed *Wed*
Getting to Rainforest Restaurant
is a bit of a hike, but the dishes
– jerk and curry flavors, served
in a beautiful tropical setting –
make the trip worth it. Specials
change daily, depending on
what is available from the
garden and the sea. Enjoy
home-made ice cream and
pies for dessert. Candlelit
dinners on Wednesdays.

WINDWARDSIDE:
Restaurant Eden $$$
Continental
Lambee's Place
Tel *599 416 2539*   **Closed** *Tue*
Fresh seafood, steaks, and duck
entrées are prepared from locally
sourced produce and served in
an idyllic garden gazebo, with an
open kitchen and outdoor patio.

St. Eustatius

CHERRY TREE:
Papaya Restaurant $$
Mediterrenean
18 William Plantz Road
Tel *599 318 0044*   **Closed** *Fri dinner,*
Sat lunch
Salads, soups, pastas, and entrées
including local fish are served in a
warm atmosphere. The emphasis
is on fresh ingredients and spices.

GALLOWS BAY: Smoke Alley
Bar & Grill $
American
Lower Town
Tel *599 318 2002*   **Closed** *Sun*
Enjoy Smoke Alley's basic menu
of burgers and ribs while

admiring the sea views. There are
"Two for Tuesday" specials and
live entertainment every Friday.

ORANJESTAD: Chinese Bar
& Restaurant $
Chinese
H.M. Queen Beatrixstraat
Tel *599 318 2389*
Expect standard Chinese fare, as
well as some Indonesian dishes
and good vegetarian options.
Take out or eat in. No credit cards.

ORANJESTAD:
Ocean View Terrace $
Caribbean
Government Guest House
Tel *599 318 2934*   **Closed** *Sun*
Ocean View Terrace is located on
the terrace of a historic building
overlooking Fort Oranje. On the
menu are local specialties and
fresh seafood.

ORANJESTAD:
Old Towne Pizzeria $
Italian
Van Tonnengenweg
Tel *599 318 3131*   **Closed** *Fri*
Head to Old Towne for a delicious
selection of fresh pizzas, Italian
entrées, and sandwiches. Hungry
diners should order the excellent
whole-baked chicken.

ORANJESTAD:
Golden Era Hotel $$
West Indian/Creole
Harbourside
Tel *599 318 2455*
Eat in the pleasant indoor dining
room or poolside. On the menu
are West Indian specialties and,
of course, freshly caught lobsters
and seafood.

This Saban house, built in the 1800s, is now home to Brigaddon, Windwardside, Saba

Practical Information

These charming little islands have been closely affiliated to the Netherlands, so the general appearance, hospitality, and culture are European. The people, who are very proud of their islands, are warm and welcoming to visitors. If lost, visitors just need to stop and ask the locals for directions. A taxi is the best way to get around since the islands are small. Saban lacework makes an especially pretty souvenir.

Office of the Saba Tourist Bureau at Windwardside

When to Go

The climate on both islands is pleasant year round, and nights can be cool. The summer months are hotter and more humid, and the peak hurricane season is from June through to October. Many people go to Saba in July for the Summer Festival, or in October for the Sea and Learn workshops. In St. Eustatius the special days include Carnival in mid-July, and November 16, the designated Statia-America Day.

Getting There

Winair operates several flights daily from Princess Juliana International Airport (SXM) in St. Martin to Juancho E. Yrausquin Airport (SAB) in Saba. It also has daily flights between St. Eustatius and Saba. Ferries, including the **Dawn II** and **The Edge**, operate on a weekly schedule between Saba and St. Martin.

St. Eustatius can be reached via air transport on Winair, with several daily flights from St. Martin to Franklin D. Roosevelt Airport (EUX), daily flights from Saba, and a weekly flight from Golden Rock Airport (SKB), St. Kitts. There is no ferry service at present, but private boats can be chartered in St. Martin.

Documentation

For both islands, travelers need a valid passport and onward/return ticket. Residents of certain countries are required to obtain a visa to enter the Dutch Caribbean islands; for a list of these countries, it is advisable to consult the website of the tourism bureau. There is a departure fee to be paid just before getting on the plane to return home. The two islands have different departure fees and one can expect a lower fee if the final destination shown on the onward ticket is another Caribbean island.

Visitor Information

Information on Saba can be obtained from the office of the **Saba Tourist Bureau** located in Windwardside and on St. Eustatius at the **St. Eustatius Tourism Office** in Fort Oranje. Both have their own tourist websites. There are tourist desks at the airports providing maps and brochures, as well as assistance with transportation.

Health and Security

Saba and St. Eustatius, being small islands, are relatively crime-free. For health-related emergencies, there are hospitals such as

A M Edwards Medical Center and **Queen Beatrix Hospital** on both islands which are staffed by local physicians. Both islands have hyperbaric chambers.

Banking and Currency

The official currency in both Saba and St. Eustatius is the US dollar. There are no limitations on the import and export of currency. Credit cards and traveler's checks are widely accepted. ATM machines are available at the banks in Windwardside and The Bottom in Saba, and in Oranjestad in St. Eustatius.

Communications

In Saba, hotels have direct dialing worldwide, and Landsradio has phone booths in Windwardside and The Bottom for international calls. The **St. Eustatius Telephone Company NV (EUTEL)** provides international phone services, and visitors can buy calling cards. Internet connections are available at most of the hotels, as well as at **Island Communication Services**. Internet access is available at the **Public Library** and **Computers and More**.

Transport

Taxis are the favored way to get around both islands, since there is no public transport. Tourist desks at the airports can connect you with available drivers, and the drivers in their turn give customers their cell phone number so that they

Plane landing at Juancho E. Yrausquin Airport, Saba

can be contacted whenever transport is needed. Saba has only one car rental agency, **Caja's Car Rental**, while in St. Eustatius, there are several, including **ARC Car Rental**, **Brown's Car Rental**, **Schmidt Car Rental**, and **Trep Car Rental**, providing small cars capable of navigating the narrow roads.

Shopping

While both islands are duty-free ports, there is not a great deal of shopping, unlike on other Caribbean islands. In Saba, there is a collection of shops in Windwardside that include a gallery, **The Peanut Gallery**, and a gift boutique. Also, there are several sites where Saban lace can be purchased. In St. Eustatius, there are only two small shops – the **Mazinga Gift Shop** and the **Historical Society Museum Shop**.

Language

Dutch is the official language on both islands but English is spoken everywhere.

Electricity

Electricity on both islands is 110 volts. For 220-volt appliances a converter is needed.

Time

Both islands are in the Atlantic Time Zone, 5 hours behind GMT. When the US is on daylight saving time, the islands follow the time on the US East Coast.

Getting Married

To marry in Saba, a couple must apply for a wedding date a month in advance by writing to the Lieutenant Governor at the **Census Office**, along with the necessary documents. If getting married at a location other than the Court Room at the Government Building, approval for the venue is also required. For St. Eustatius, the couple needs to submit the documents at least a week in advance but then must wait for the government to approve all documents. Details can be obtained from the websites of Saba Tourist Bureau and St. Eustatius Tourism.

Interior of a gift boutique in Saba

DIRECTORY

Getting There

Dawn II
Fort Bay, Saba.
Tel 599 416 2299.
W sabactransport.com

The Edge
St. Maarten.
Tel 721 544 2640.

Winair
Tel 599 416 2255 (Saba);
599 318 2381
(St. Eustatius).
W fly-winair.com

Visitor Information

Saba Tourist Bureau
Windwardside, Saba.
W sabatourism.com

St. Eustatius Tourism Office
Fort Oranje, Oranjestad.
W statiatourism.com

Health and Security

A M Edwards Medical Center
The Bottom, Saba.
Tel 599 416 3289/88.

Queen Beatrix Hospital
Oranjestad, St. Eustatius.
Tel 599 318 2211.

Communications

Computers and More
Oranjestad.
Tel 599 318 2596.

Island Communication Services
Windwardside, Saba.
Tel 599 416 2881.
W icssaba.com

Public Library
Fort Oranje, Oranjestad.
Tel 599 318 2222.

St. Eustatius Telephone Company NV (EUTEL)
Oranjestad, St. Eustatius.
Tel 599 318 2210.

Transport

ARC Car Rental
St. Eustatius.
Tel 599 318 2595.

Brown's Car Rental
St. Eustatius.
Tel 599 318 2266.

Caja's Car Rental
Saba.
Tel 599 416 2388.

Schmidt Car Rental
St. Eustatius.
Tel 599 318 2788.

Trep Car Rental
St. Eustatius.
Tel 599 318 2626.

Shopping

Historical Society Museum Shop
Oranjestad, St. Eustatius.
Tel 599 318 2856.

Mazinga Gift Shop
Oranjestad, St. Eustatius.
Tel 599 318 3345.

The Peanut Gallery
Windwardside, Saba.
Tel 599 416 2509.

Getting Married

Census Office
The Bottom, Saba.
Tel 599 416 3497/3311/3312. **W** statia government.com

Exploring St. Kitts and Nevis

St. Kitts divides fairly naturally into two halves. While the north is mountainous with pretty villages and delightful former plantations such as Romney Manor Plantation, the south of the island is more active due to the beach-based tourism. Luxury hotels and hotel chains here are scattered in Frigate Bay. Nevis is a smaller island and is also divided in a similar way but here the beach activities dominate in the north while former plantations, now converted into charming inns, sit higher on the mountainside in the south. A good way to discover Nevis is to go for a drive around the base of Nevis Peak, stopping off at the plantations for lunch or afternoon tea.

Locator Map

ANGUILLA
ST. MARTIN/ SINT MAARTEN
VIRGIN ISLANDS
ST. BARTHÉLEMY
ANTIGUA AND BARBUDA
SABA AND ST. EUSTATIUS
ST. KITTS
NEVIS
GUADELOUPE
Caribbean Sea
MARTINIQUE

Dieppe Bay Town
Willet's Bay
Convent Bay
St. Paul's
Parson's Ground
Sadle
San
Be
Newton Ground
Belle Tete
North West Range
Mount Liamuiga 3,792 ft
Pump Bay
Sandy Point Town
BRIMSTONE HILL FORTRESS ④ 🏛🌿
Middle Island
Half Way Tree
ARA CAR
OLD ROAD ③
ROMNEY MANOR PLANTATION
Challenge
Palmete

0 kilometers 5

0 miles 5

View of St. Kitts and St. Eustatius from the Brimstone Hill Fortress

Sights at a Glance

❶ Basseterre
❷ Romney Manor Plantation
❸ Old Road
❹ *Brimstone Hill Fortress pp296–7*
❺ Arawak Carvings
❻ Frigate Bay Resorts
❼ Southeastern Peninsula
❽ Oualie Beach
❾ Charlestown
❿ Fig Tree Church
⓫ Botanical Garden of Nevis
⓬ Nevis Plantation Inns

Key

— Major road
⋯⋯ Minor road
– – Track
⋯⋯ Ferry route
△ Peak

For hotels and restaurants on these islands see p306 and p307

A beach at Frigate Bay South, St. Kitts

Ottley's
Ottley's Plantation Inn above Ottley's is unique and surrounded by tropical gardens.

Getting Around

Both islands have airports – Robert L. Bradshaw International Airport (St. Kitts) and Vance W. Amory International Airport (Nevis). The ferry is the most commonly used transport between the islands. There are car ferries between Major's Bay in the south of St. Kitts and Cades Bay in Nevis. The trip between Basseterre and Charlestown takes 45 minutes and there are about eight or ten crossings each day. For day visits, the car hire rental agency may allow (with advanced warning) visitors to drop the rented car at the ferry terminal and then pick up another car on arrival in the other island. Buses leave from the two main towns and run in both directions around the islands. There is no schedule, instead buses leave when they are full or on the decision of the driver. There are no bus services to Frigate Bay or the Southeastern Peninsula on St. Kitts.

Frigate Bay
This is the most crowded bay with a few well-known resorts and hotel chains.

Nevis Plantation Inns
Nevis has some of the loveliest plantation inns in the Caribbean including Hermitage, Old Manor, Golden Rock, and Nisbet Plantation.

Berkeley Memorial clock at The Circus, Basseterre

For additional map symbols see back flap

❶ Basseterre

S coast of St. Kitts. 🗻 13,000. ✈ 🚌
🚢 ℹ Pelican Mall, Bay Road.
📅 Annual Music Festival (Jun).
🌐 **stkittstourism.kn**

Basseterre sits on the Caribbean, or leeward, coast of St. Kitts – *basse-terre* is French for the sailing term leeward. It is a pretty West Indian town, where many of the original Georgian buildings are still intact.

A century ago all visitors to the island would arrive by sea, passing through the arch of the old colonial Treasury Building, with its rich volcanic stonework, white frames, and a dome. The Treasury Building houses the **National Museum of St. Kitts**, which displays artifacts from the Amerindian era, including pottery and axe-heads, and colonial military and domestic items such as muskets and irons, as well as maps and prints of plantation life. Nowadays visitors are more likely to arrive via Port Zante, the cruise ship dock with a few duty-free shops such as the Amina Craft Market and the Pelican Mall.

West from the port, and beyond the Treasury Building, is the Nevis ferry dock, the bus station, and the main market building. The waterfront here is a busy area of the town. Inland from the Treasury Building is The Circus. At its center stands the quaint Victorian Berkeley Memorial Clocktower, which dates from 1883. There is a café with a balcony upstairs with a view of the bustle below. Southeast of here is **Independence Square**, a grassy park surrounded by a white picket fence overlooked by stone and wooden buildings. Originally the commercial center of Basseterre, it once held the slave market. At the eastern end of the square is the catholic Co-Cathedral of the Immaculate Conception, which has a barrel-vaulted nave and a distinctive rose window. Next to it is the Court House and, in a

Basseterre's grand Independence Square

❹ Brimstone Hill Fortress

This massive fortress is a vast network of defensive structures. Built in stages between 1690 and 1790, when the wars for a British Empire were at their fiercest, Brimstone Hill stands at 800 ft (243 m) and commands an exceptional view of the islands. Its name is indicative of the hellish smell of sulphur, or brimstone, the result of St. Kitts' volcanic geology.

The remnants of the Infantry Officers' Quarters

The Magazine Bastion was constructed with a paved water catchment.

Prince of Wales Bastion
The first building to be fully restored, this bastion housed the Brigade Office and the main Guard Barracks.

The Orillon Bastion
Once the location of the bomb-proof Ordnance Store and a hospital, the Orillon is also the site of a cemetery, with tombstones still intact.

For hotels and restaurants on these islands see p306 and p307
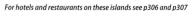

pretty wooden Creole building on the north side, the Spencer Cameron Gallery, which exhibits work by Caribbean artists.

Located on Cayon Street is the Anglican St. George's, the main church built by the British in 1706. Fortlands District, on the western edge of the town, has luxurious homes and one hotel, Ocean Terrace Inn *(see p306)*, which hosts a lively streetside grill on Friday nights. The northern outskirts of the town has modern buildings, with supermarkets and light industry. Warner Park, the national stadium, lies on Wellington Road, which runs towards the airport. Built for the Cricket World Cup in 2007, it now hosts cricket matches and the annual music festival.

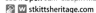

National Museum of St. Kitts
Old Treasury Building. **Tel** 869 465 5584. **Open** 9am–5:30pm Mon–Fri.
stkittsheritage.com

Manicured gardens of Romney Manor Plantation

❷ Romney Manor Plantation

4 miles (6 km) NW of Basseterre, St. Kitts. **Tel** 869 465 6253.
Open 9am–5pm Mon–Fri.

Set in extensive and attractive gardens, Romney Manor is a restored former plantation estate house. It was originally owned by an ancestor of Thomas Jefferson, third President of the US. The house

was then renamed Romney Manor after its acquistion by Earl of Romney in the 17th century. This plantation was the first in St. Kitts to free its slaves in 1834.

❸ Old Road

6 miles (9 km) NW of Basseterre, St. Kitts.

Situated at the foot of the concave slopes of the main St. Kitts mountain range, Old Road is a simple town of clapboard and stone buildings. Settled in 1624 by Thomas Warner, Old Road was the capital of the English part of St. Kitts when the island was known as the "Mother Colony of the West Indies". It was so called as it was the first permanent intrusion by French and English nationals into the Spanish domain.

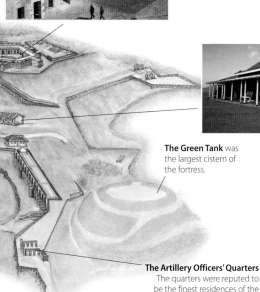

The Citadel
Called Fort George, it is the central defensive structure, a fortress within a fortress.

The Green Tank was the largest cistern of the fortress.

The Artillery Officers' Quarters
The quarters were reputed to be the finest residences of the Fortress with good views.

VISITORS' CHECKLIST

Practical Information
10 miles (16 km) NW of Basseterre, St. Kitts. **Tel** 869 465 2609. **Open** 9:30am–5:30pm daily.
brimstonehillfortress.org

Transport

Visitors' Center
Located in the reconstructed Commissariat Building, the visitors' center has displays of the history of the fort and a gift shop.

Royal St. Kitts Golf Course, Frigate Bay resort area

❺ Arawak Carvings

6 miles (9 km) NW of Basseterre, St. Kitts. 🚌

Before the arrival of the Europeans, St. Kitts, then called Liamuiga, meaning fertile land, was inhabited by the Arawak and subsequently Carib Indians. Inland from Old Road town, in an unassuming setting on a lawn behind a white picket fence, is a small but touching reminder of their life and art. These Arawak carvings, also known as petroglyphs, are depictions of a man and a woman (or possibly male or female gods of fertility), carved in a graphical design into boulders of black volcanic rock. They have been painted white to emphasize their square bodies, waving arms, and antennae.

❻ Frigate Bay Resorts

3 miles (5 km) S of Basseterre, St. Kitts. 🏖 🛈 🖉 🖵 🏠
Ⓦ stkittstourism.kn

Frigate Bay is the heartland of tourism in St. Kitts and it has a very different atmosphere from the north of the island. From the top of the hills, there is a panoramic view of Frigate Bay, a low-lying sliver of land between the Atlantic Ocean and Caribbean Sea.

On the Atlantic side is Frigate Bay North where the sandy beach is lined with condominiums and large resort hotels offering an array of entertainment and activities. This is the location of the Marriott hotel *(see p306)* with its casino and several restaurants

and bars. Just inland lie the fairways and bunkers of the Royal St. Kitts Golf Course *(see p305)*. The golf course stretches right up to the coast and the onshore ocean winds can have a considerable effect on play.

On the Caribbean side, Frigate Bay South, also known as "The Strip", has calmer seas, but a livelier atmosphere. Instead of hotels, a string of beach bars and watersports operators stand shoulder to shoulder, giving the beach a partylike, easy-going vibe. It is particularly lively at sundown on Thursday and Friday evenings, when there is a bonfire and live music at some of the bars, and at weekends, when the locals come to spend the day on the beach.

❼ Southeastern Peninsula

St. Kitts. 🛈 🖵 🏠

While the north of St. Kitts is characterized by Kittitian villages dotting the flanks of volcanic, rainforested mountains, the lower-lying hills of the southern part of the island are much less populated and drier. The area is worth visiting because the island's prettiest beaches are situated here, and there are some excellent beach bars as well. Unlike the more developed

Southeastern Peninsula overlooking the turquoise Caribbean Sea

For hotels and restaurants on these islands see p306 and p307

A beach and bar restaurant in Oualie Beach, Nevis

Frigate Bay to the north, the Southeastern Peninsula is only now being built-up. The road along the peninsula leads up and out of Frigate Bay from where, switch-backing several times, it descends to Friar's Bay. The beach at **South Friar's Bay** is probably the best strip of sand on the island. Although it was projected for development, nothing has happened so far. Instead, the beach bars that line the beach continue their laid-back trade as travelers come to spend the day. The road climbs and falls, sashaying over the hills until it reaches the southern tip of the island. En route, visitors are likely to spot green velvet monkeys on the way to White House Bay. East of Great Salt Pond, but on the Atlantic Coast, is the quiet **Sand Bank Bay**.

On the southern coast, there are several beaches with lovely views across the 2-mile (3-km) The Narrows to Nevis. The liveliest are **Turtle Beach**, which tends to get a bit crowded due to cruise ship passengers, and Cockleshell Beach. Both have restaurants, bars, and some watersports and offer stunning views of Nevis. This whole area is under construction with plans to build a number of hotels and a marina here. Farther south, at **Major's Bay**, a roll-on-roll-off car ferry leaves for Cades Bay in Nevis. Offshore, the tiny Booby Island (accessible by boat) has spectacular marine life and is popular with snorkelers and divers.

❽ Oualie Beach

North coast of Nevis. 🚌 🛥 🖉

Oualie was the original name for Nevis. Pronounced as "oo-wah-lee", meaning beautiful waters, it referred to the freshwater springs on Nevis. Oualie Beach is quite lively with pale yellow sands backed by palms and a great view of St. Kitts across The Narrows. Oualie Bay, formerly known as Mosquito Bay, is well protected, so swimming and other watersports are good here. There is a watersports and mountain biking shop, and a scuba diving outfit. Scuba Safaris Ltd. *(see p305)* offers diving and snorkeling lessons for both novice and experienced divers. Children aged 8 and over are accomodated for, and those who want to join the scuba safari but stay aboard the boat, affectionately named "bubble watchers", are also welcome.

The bay has a small dock, where visitors from St. Kitts can be dropped off by water taxis. The pretty Oualie Beach Resort *(see p306)* is located on this beach as well. The family who runs this resort has been on the island for nearly 350 years.

The Annual Nevis Sport Fishing Tournament takes place each year on Oualie Beach, with participants traveling from all over the Caribbean to take part.

Environs
Towards the north, the road swings around Nevis Peak before reaching Nisbet Beach. Facing the Atlantic, Nisbet is a pretty beach dotted with coconut trees strung with hammocks which makes it a pleasant place to relax.

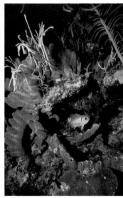

Marine life in the waters of Oualie Bay, Nevis

Horatio Nelson and Fanny Nisbet

As a young captain in the 1780s, Horatio Nelson was based in Antigua on HMS *Boreas*. He had the unpopular job of enforcing the Navigation Laws, which prevented the lucrative trade between the British Leeward Islands and the newly independent United States of America. Horatio visited Nevis frequently and eventually married a native widow, Fanny Nisbet, at Montpelier. At the wedding, she was "given away" by Prince William Henry, later King William IV, who was also based in Antigua at the time. The marriage did not last and when he returned to England Nelson took up with Emma Hamilton, who was the wife of the ambassador to Naples.

Portrait of Horatio Nelson

Charlestown's Alexander Hamilton House, now the Museum of Nevis History

❾ Charlestown

4 miles (6.5 km) S of Oualie Beach,
Nevis. 🏙 1,500. ⛴ 🚌 🚕 ℹ Nevis
Tourism Authority, Main Street, 869
469 7550 🛍 Tue & Sat.

Charlestown is a classic, pretty
West Indian waterfront town,
set on the protected Caribbean
coast of Nevis. As the small
capital of a quiet island, it is
never really that busy or
crowded, but it is a lovely place
to spend an hour wandering
around. A small network of
streets with attractive stone
and wooden buildings sits
behind the main esplanade,
where many of the buildings
have been restored.

The ferry port is located at the
southern end of the esplanade,
a good place to start any
exploration of the small town.
Inland from here is the Cotton
Ginnery, which now houses
local craft vendors. The
Charlestown Market has local
fruit and vegetables on sale in
stalls under a pitched tin roof.

The heart of the town, Main
Street, has banks, businesses,
and a tourist information office
at the Nevis Tourism Authority.
Heading south, Main Street cuts
diagonally inland, creating two
"squares" that are actually
triangular and surrounded by
some of the town's most
attractive wooden and stone
buildings. In the smaller of the
two squares, D.R. Walwyn Plaza,
is the tiny Nevis Sports Museum
which has exhibits on famous
Nevisian athletes, cricketers, and

other sportsmen and women.
Next is the Memorial Square,
a small war memorial and a
clocktower. The island buses
leave from these two squares.

To the north, standing
between the esplanade and
Main Street, is a pretty stone
building called Alexander
Hamilton House. Alexander
Hamilton, father of the United
States' constitution and portrayed
on the US$10 bill, was born here
in 1757. Known as the "Little
Lion", Hamilton was killed in a
duel in 1884. Alexander Hamilton
House is home to both the Nevis
Assembly, the five-member
Nevisian Parliament that sits just
four or five times a year, and the
Museum of Nevis History. The
museum has displays of Nevis
through the ages, with artifacts
including Amerindian pottery

and colonial porcelain. North
of here, the road out of town
leads to the palm-fringed
Pinney's Beach. The most
manicured parts of this beach
belong to the Four Seasons
Resort (see p306) but there are
access tracks to the rest.

On the southern outskirts
of town the road runs on to
the Bath Hotel. This large stone
building was one of the glories
of the island in the late 1700s
and one of the first hotels in
the Caribbean. Many European
visitors came here to treat
ailments using the volcanic hot
springs nearby. Now the building is used by the Nevis government. Close to Bath Hotel is the
Horatio Nelson Museum.
Dedicated to the British admiral
(see p299), it has an excellent
series of displays, with maps
and models of 18th-century
ships, and the largest collection
of Nelson memorabilia in the
world, including portraits, clay
pipes, and statuettes. Some of
the porcelain from Nelson and
Fanny Nisbet's marriage feast
can be seen here.

🏛 **Museum of Nevis History**
Alexander Hamilton House.
Tel 869 469 5786. **Open** 9am–4pm
Mon–Fri, 9am–noon Sat. 🅿 ♿ 📷
ⓦ **nevis-nhcs.org**

🏛 **Horatio Nelson Museum**
Belle Vue. **Tel** 869 469 5786.
Open 9am–4pm Mon–Fri, 9am–noon
Sat. 🅿 📷 ⓦ **nevis-nhcs.org/
nelsonmuseum.html**

Charlestown Architecture

The lovely old houses of this small town are outstanding
examples of 18th- and 19th-century colonial architecture.
Several streets in Charlestown (Nevis) and many in Basseterre
(St. Kitts) still have traditional houses
embellished with fret-cut woodwork
called "gingerbread trim". Most of
the structures here are made of the
distinct dark volcanic stone found
locally. These buildings tend to have
massive foundations and walls, often
over 4 ft (1.2 m) thick, with a rubble-
filled interior space. Also common, the
"skirt and blouse" design consists of a
stone first floor and a light, wooden
second floor. This enables the houses
to withstand high winds and
earthquakes, common to
the region.

Typical "gingerbread trim"
building, Charlestown

❿ Fig Tree Church

2 miles (3 km) E of Charlestown, Nevis.

The round-island road that climbs inland from the town of Charlestown passes Fig Tree Church, where Horatio Nelson and Fanny Nisbet were married in 1787 (see p299). The original church was built in the 1680s, but the current building actually dates from 1838. It is a stone structure with a bell tower and a red tin roof. Inside, it is possible to see a copy of the marriage certificate that the Nelsons signed at their marriage. Their wedding celebration took place at Montpelier Plantation, where it is commemorated on a plaque on the gates.

⓫ Botanical Garden of Nevis

3 miles (5 km) SE of Charlestown, Nevis. **Tel** 869 469 3509.
Open 9am–4pm Mon–Sat.
Closed pub hols.
W botanicalgarden nevis.com

The Botanical Garden of Nevis is spread over 7 acres (3 ha). The attractive gardens display plants from across the tropical world. They are laid out in several areas covering different environments, including the Tropical Vine Garden, the Orchid Terrace, the Rose Garden, and a Rainforest

The grand old Hermitage Plantation Inn, Nevis

Conservatory. The conservatory has re-created Mayan temple ruins and a few waterfalls. Other delights include fruit trees, cacti, and several flowering shrubs and trees. A café and a gift shop are set in an attractive Creole building.

⓬ Nevis Plantation Inns

Nevis has some of the loveliest plantation inns in the Caribbean. While they are excellent places to stay, it is also possible to just visit for lunch, afternoon tea, or dinner to get a sense of a long bygone era. Dating from the late 1600s, the main house at the **Hermitage Plantation Inn** (see p306) is one of the finest wooden buildings

in the Caribbean. It has attractive "gingerbread" woodwork, shingle walls and a red tin roof. Montpelier Plantation Inn was restored in the 1960s and is well worth a stop for lunch or dinner. Other plantation inns include **Old Manor**, in Gingerland, whose old chimney and sugar-crushing gear are on view, and farther ahead, above the Atlantic Coast, the Golden Rock has a spectacular view over the coastline. The only plantation inn with the advantage of being on the beach is in Nisbet Plantation, which has a magnificent view from its great house through tall and slender palms to the sea.

🏚 Old Manor
Gingerland. **Tel** 869 469 3445. Fax: 869 469 3388. **W** oldmanornevis.com

Well-tended flower beds in the Botanical Garden, with Nevis Peak in the background, Nevis

Outdoor Activities and Specialized Holidays

St. Kitts and Nevis have great beaches and visitors can expect to spend much time swimming, snorkeling, sailing, or deep-sea fishing. Both islands also have excellent golf and very good hiking into the rainforested mountains. For a small island, Nevis offers outstanding sport and first-class mountain-biking. Between them, the two islands have an interesting and visible history to explore on organized tours of attractive Creole buildings, plantation houses, inns, and ruins.

Horse-riding along Half Moon Bay, St. Kitts

Hiking

The islands of St. Kitts and Nevis are small but full of stunning scenery, run through by trails of varying difficulties. On Nevis in particular, there are many historic plantation ruins to explore, some set amongst lush rainforest greenery. There are several companies offering guided walks to various places of historical and natural interest on Nevis, two of the most popular being **Sunrise Tours** and **Earla's Eco Tours**. Hikes tailored to different abilities explore the wilder side of the island, ranging from nature walks along old island paths through the rainforest, birdwatching tours, and visits to local villages and plantation ruins, to the challenging climb to the top of Nevis Peak at 3,232 ft (985 m).

St. Kitts also has a number of guided tours. Earl Vanlow of **The Duke of Earl Adventures** leads hikes through old cane-fields, past plantation ruins and into the rainforest, often above Romney Manor Plantation (see p297). Other trips head for the top of Mount Liamuiga. Tours, by both vehicle and on foot, are also available with **Greg's Safaris**, located in Basseterre.

Mountain Biking

Windsurf 'N' Mountainbike Nevis offers tours to mountain bikers of all levels, from simple road excursions through local villages to hard-core single tracks. Owner and operator Winston Crooke takes bikers on rides such as the historic Upper Round Road, which once linked the higher sugar estates. He also offers triathlon training and stages an annual triathlon, which is usually held in March, out of Charlestown.

Horse-Riding

Trinity Stables in St. Kitts offer trips along the narrow trails in the rainforest on the flanks of the central mountain range and down to the windswept beaches on the Atlantic Coast. Guides explain local history and the medicinal properties of plants along the way. **Nevis Equestrian Centre** provides both leisurely beach rides on Pinney's Beach and more difficult trail rides in the hills, as well as riding lessons from the owners Erika and John.

Shipwreck Beach Bar sign

Beaches

Although particularly beautiful, the volcanic nature of St. Kitts and Nevis means that their beaches vary in color between white and jet black, often a mid-brown. There are plenty of good strips of sand though, with classic beach bars and watersports, that are frequented by the islanders. The busiest beach in St. Kitts is Frigate Bay South, which teems with bars such as Jam Rock Real Jerk (see p307), as well as sports operators. The excellent Reggae Beach bar is located on Cockleshell Bay.

Beaches in the north of the island tend to have dark sand, but along the Southeastern Peninsula (see pp298–9), the sand improves and the bays are also less developed. There are some inviting strips of sand where visitors may enjoy a near Robinson Crusoe experience for a day. Such isolated stretches include South Friar's Bay, which has some facilities now such as the Shipwreck Beach Bar & Grill. Major's Bay and Sand Bank Bay are some other remote bays.

By contrast, the beaches in Nevis range from brownish sand to light colored sand. Oualie Beach (see p299), which overlooks St. Kitts, is the most active with several watersports opportunities. The 3.5 miles (6 km) of golden sand on Pinney's Beach is gorgeous with Nevis Peak rising in the background, and is perfect for swimming. It has hotels and bars such as Sunshine's and Chevy's. Lover's Beach, at the northern tip of the island, though hard to get to and sometimes windy, is a lovely remote stretch of light-colored sand.

Hiking on St. Kitts and Nevis

St. Kitts and Nevis have exceptionally good hiking. In addition to the unspoilt landscape, there is an extraordinary variety of fauna and flora, as well as evocative plantation ruins to explore along the trails. The dormant volcano of Mount Liamuiga is, with its height of 3,792 ft (1,156 m), one of the toughest mountains to climb in the Caribbean. This tour can start with a horseback-ride from the Belmont plantation, followed by a rigorous hike to the top. Nevis Peak also offers a challenging trek, and both hikes should be attempted only with an experienced guide. Hotels also recommend guides and operators who take visitors for volcanic hikes.

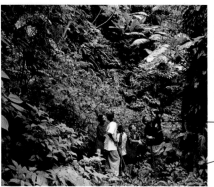

Nature Hikes

Both St. Kitts and Nevis have a considerable diversity of environment. The dry littoral forests rise from the coasts through immensely fertile, cultivable slopes. But it is the rainforest, where ancient paths criss-cross the gullies and slopes, that is the most captivating.

Informative guides usually relate fascinating botanical and historical facts.

Many plants found in the forest have practical or medicinal uses. Some are even used in *obeah* or black magic.

Volcano hikes are popular on both islands. On Nevis a steep climb necessitates a scramble near the top. The dormant Mount Liamuiga in St. Kitts has a crater into which hikers descend.

Bird-watching hikes are rewarding and a variety of birds can be found in the different habitats on the islands, including wading birds in the remote lagoons of St. Kitts' Southeastern Peninsula.

Hikes to the Past

At the height of the sugar era, St. Kitts and Nevis were cultivated up to a height of around 1,000 ft (305 m). The plantation ruins, now shrouded in overgrowth, are atmospheric and interesting to explore with a well-informed guide.

Plantation ruins can include remains of boiling houses, storage areas, stables, dormitories, workshops, and even hospitals, most of which were built in the 18th century.

Conical shells of old sugar mills dot the landscapes of St. Kitts and Nevis. Many mills still have their old crushing gear, massive metal rollers between which the cane was crushed to a dry pulp, and are a poignant reminder of those who lived here under harsh conditions.

Yacht anchored just off Pinney's Beach, Nevis

Sailing

The Narrows, which is the stretch of water separating St. Kitts and Nevis, is very scenic and spending a day aboard a sailing boat is a delightful way of exploring the area. Day sails, leaving from both islands, tend to steer to the isolated bays of the Southeastern Peninsula in St. Kitts, where there is a stop for snorkeling before a sail across The Narrows. Drinks and lunch, often a barbecue on the beach, are included in the rate. Companies that provide day sails include **Leeward Island Charters**, which picks up passengers in both islands, **Blue Water Safaris** in St. Kitts and **Nevis Yacht Charters**.

Scuba Diving

While St. Kitts and Nevis might not be known as scuba destinations, there are some spectacular dives that make a worthwhile addition to a holiday on the islands. Dive sites tend to be in The Narrows, and along St. Kitts' Southeastern Peninsula (easily reached by boat from Nevis or from Basseterre), so it actually does not matter which island visitors are based on. Divers can expect to see good reefs, pinnacles, drop-offs, as well as reef fish and occasional pelagic fish. There are also some interesting wrecks and

reefs farther northwest along the Caribbean Coast of St. Kitts. **Pro Divers St. Kitts**, based in Nevis, and **Kenneth's Dive Centre** in St. Kitts are among the popular diving operators on the islands.

Snorkeling

Besides scuba diving, St. Kitts and Nevis also offer some outstanding snorkeling opportunities. Reefs can be reached from many of the beach hotels, but some of the best reefs are along the undeveloped bays of the Southeastern Peninsula of St. Kitts – to which the day sailing trips head for a snorkeling stop as a part of their itineraries. On Nevis, **Scuba Safaris Ltd.** offers various diving and snorkeling excursions throughout the year, including

a whale and dolphin snorkel safari. Lessons are led by a Dive Master and are followed by onboard refreshments.

Watersports

Visitors will find many opportunities for different watersports on the two islands. On St. Kitts, the best bet is to head for Frigate Bay South, where operators, such as **Mr X's Watersports**, hire out equipment for all sorts of watersport activities. These usually include kayaks, windsurfers, small catamarans, and Jet Skis.

On Nevis, outlets including Windsurf 'N' Mountainbike Nevis rent out equipment. The large hotels, such as The Four Seasons Resort in Nevis (see p306), offer water-based activities.

A watersports center on Oualie Beach, Nevis

Deep-Sea Fishing

Deep-sea fishing is readily available through a handful of captains with their own fishing boats that can be chartered by the day or half-day. Barracuda, mahimahi, and marlin are found in the waters off St. Kitts and Nevis. **Tropical Tours** in St. Kitts organizes daily deep-sea fishing trips. Refreshments are included in the rates. **Speedy 4 Charters** are popular fishing outfitters and offer special packages.

The fabulous Royal St. Kitts Golf Course, Frigate Bay

Golf

Both islands have good 18-hole golf courses, and golfers have been known to fly from St. Barthélemy to play at the 6,766 yards (6,186 m) par 71 Four Seasons Golf Course (see p306), designed by famous golf course architect, Robert Trent Jones II. It is set on the Caribbean Coast and climbs into the hills, providing some challenging holes, with fantastic views over The Narrows and out to the sea. The 6,900 yards (6,310 m) par 71 **Royal St. Kitts Golf Course** is in Frigate Bay and also has some spectacular holes along the Atlantic coastline. More golf courses are slated for development on St. Kitts, the Southeastern Peninsula, and in the north of the island.

Island Tours

An interesting way to explore St. Kitts is on the **St. Kitts Scenic Railway Tour**. The old narrow-gauge railway that formerly brought the cut sugar cane to the main factory near the airport is now used as a tour train. The carriages have large glass windows to enable breathtaking views of the island during this leisurely ride along the Atlantic coast. Tours by minibus are popular and tend to head around the north of the island and take in the major sights such as Brimstone Hill Fortress (see pp296–7), with a stop in Basseterre.

In Nevis, tours are generally offered by taxi drivers. For visitors who prefer setting out on foot, there are also ample hiking tours (see p303).

DIRECTORY

Hiking

The Duke of Earl Adventures
St. Kitts.
Tel 869 663 0994.

Earla's Eco Tours
Tel 869 469 2833.

Greg's Safaris
Basseterre, St. Kitts.
Tel 869 465 4121.
W gregsafaris.com

Sunrise Tours
Gingerland, Nevis.
Tel 869 469 2758.
W nevisnaturetours.com

Mountain Biking

Windsurf 'N' Mountainbike Nevis
Oualie Beach. **Tel** 869 664 2843. W bikenevis.com

Horse-Riding

Nevis Equestrian Centre
Pinney's Beach, Nevis.
Tel 869 662 9118.
W nevishoreback.com

Trinity Stables
Basseterre, St. Kitts. **Tel** 869 465 3226. W trinityinnapartments.com

Sailing

Blue Water Safaris
Basseterre, St. Kitts. **Tel** 869 466 4933. W bluewatersafaris.com

Leeward Island Charters
St. Kitts. **Tel** 869 465 7474.
W leewardislandscharters.com

Nevis Yacht Charters
Oualie Beach, Nevis.
Tel 869 664 9171.
W sailnevis.com

Scuba Diving

Kenneth's Dive Centre
Basseterre, St.Kitts.
Tel 869 465 2670.
W kennethdivecenter.com

Pro Divers St. Kitts
Basseterre, St. Kitts.
Tel 869 660 3483.
W prodiversstkitts.com

Snorkeling

Scuba Safaris Ltd.
Oualie Beach, Nevis.
Tel 869 469 9518.
W scubanevis.com

Watersports

Mr X's Watersports
St. Kitts.
Tel 869 762 3983.
W mrxshiggidyshack.com

Deep-Sea Fishing

Speedy 4 Charters
Frigate Bay, Nevis.
Tel 869 662 3453.
W speedy4charters.com

Tropical Tours
Basseterre, St. Kitts.
Tel 869 465 4167.

Golf

Royal St. Kitts Golf Course
Frigate Bay, St. Kitts.
Tel 866 785 4653.
W royalstkittsgolfclub.com

Island Tours

St. Kitts Scenic Railway Tour
Basseterre, St. Kitts.
Tel 869 465 7263.
W stkittsscenicrailway.com

Where to Stay

St. Kitts

BASSETERRE:
Ocean Terrace Inn $$
Resort
Wigley Avenue, Fortlands
Tel *869 465 2754*
W oceanterraceinn.com
This small hotel located on
the edge of the city features a
man-made lagoon meandering
through its lush gardens.

FRIGATE BAY:
Timothy Beach Resort $
Beach Resort
1 South Frigate Bay Beach
Tel *869 465 8597*
W timothybeach.com
Timothy Beach Resort boasts
beachfront units (initially
designed as timeshares) nestled
into the hillside overlooking a
golf course. Rooms are well
equipped and comfortable.

FRIGATE BAY: Half Moon Villa $$
Villa
Half Moon Bay
Tel *801 915 6349*
W halfmoonvilla.com
A three-bedroom villa situated
high on a hill overlooking the bay.
It can be rented as a one- or two-
bedroom unit.

FRIGATE BAY: St. Kitts Marriott
Resort & Royal Beach Casino $$
Beach Resort
858 Frigate Bay Road
Tel *869 466 1200*
W marriott.com
This large self-contained resort
offers a five-story hotel and villas,
plus several restaurants on a
lovely beach at the edge of the
golf course.

FRIGATE BAY: Sealofts $$
Beach Resort
Frigate Bay North
Tel *888 876 0926*
W sealoft.com
Sealofts consist of three-level
condo units with two bedrooms.
Each unit is individually owned,
so amenities vary.

NORTH END: Mule House $
Guesthouse
Brighton Plantation, Cayon
Tel *869 466 8086*
W homeaway.co.uk
Surrounded by pretty gardens,
this small guesthouse offers
self-contained two-bedroom
apartments on a historic
plantation. Communal laundry
facilities are available.

Attractive exterior and lovely grounds at
Ottley's Plantation Inn, North End, St. Kitts

NORTH END:
Ottley's Plantation Inn $$
Boutique
Ottley's Village
Tel *869 465 7234*
W ottleys.com
This small, family-owned gem,
originally a sugar plantation, has
rooms as well as cottages – some
with private pools and Jacuzzis.

SOUTHEAST PENINSULA:
Turtle Beach House $$$
Luxury
Turtle Beach
Tel *159 064 1147*
W turtlebeachhousestkitts.
shutterfly.com
An elegant, family-friendly villa
perched on a hill just across the
beach, with three air-conditioned
bedrooms and an infinity pool.

Nevis

DK Choice

GINGERLAND:
Hermitage Plantation Inn $$
Historic
Hermitage Road
Tel *869 469 3477*
W hermitagenevis.com
Step back in time at this inn
on the edge of a rainforest.
Accommodation is in quaint
cottages scattered throughout
the grounds and furnished
with a mix of antiques and
comfortable furniture. The
restaurant is said to be one of
the best on the island. There is
also a complimentary breakfast.

NORTH END: Ocean
View Guesthouse $
B&B
Shaws Road, Newcastle
Tel *869 469 9580*
W oceanviewnevis.com
The charming owners of this
simple, comfortable guesthouse
go out of their way to satisfy the
needs of their guests.

NORTH END:
Oualie Beach Resort $$
Beach Resort
Oualie Bay, Newcastle
Tel *869 469 9735*
W oualiebeach.com
A serene resort with cottages just
steps from a white-sand beach. It
offers a range of watersports and
a mountain-biking center nearby.

NORTH END: Nisbet
Plantation Beach Club $$$
Luxury
St. James Parish
Tel *869 469 9325*
W nisbetplantation.com
One of the few plantation inns
on the beach, Nisbet has cottages
lining a long, grassy promenade.

PINNEYS BEACH:
Four Seasons Resort $$$
Luxury
Pinneys Beach
Tel *869 469 1111*
W fourseasons.com
Large self-contained five-star
resort with a Robert Trent Jones-
designed golf course. Choose
from rooms, suites, or villas.

SOUTH END: Banyan Tree
Bed & Breakfast $
B&B
Morningstar Village
Tel *869 469 3449*
W banyantreebandb.com
This delightful, small place set on
acres of farmland offers rooms
in the main house or a cottage.

SOUTH END: Golden Rock Inn $$
Historic
Charlestown
Tel *869 469 3346*
W goldenrocknevis.com
Cozy cottages combine with 19th-
century buildings in lush gardens;
the Sugar Mill suite is the most
romantic. Views to the sea.

Where to Eat and Drink

St. Kitts

BASSETERRE: El Fredo's Restaurant & Bar $
Caribbean
Sandown & Bay roads
Tel *869 466 8871*   **Closed** *Sun*
This family-run neighborhood restaurant has good local cuisine, including curried meats, *rotis*, and stews. Local fruit drinks and delicious desserts are also available.

DK Choice

BASSETERRE: Nirvana Restaurant $$
Creole/Fusion
Boyds, Fairview Great House
Tel *869 465 3021*
On the grounds of a restored plantation house, Nirvana creates haute cuisine using local herbs and produce. Also on offer are an elegant lunch, a West Indian afternoon tea, and the Island Flavours cooking class, where guests learn about local culture and food while executive chef Janice Ryan prepares dinner in front of them.

BASSETERRE: Sprat Net Bar & Grill $$
Caribbean
Main Road, Old Road Bay
Tel *869 466 7535*   **Closed** *Mon & Tue*
A beach-shack atmosphere and fare such as grilled fish, ribs, chicken, lobster, and pizza in a relaxed outdoor setting. Live music on Wednesdays.

BASSETERRE: Serendipity Restaurant & Lounge Bar $$$
International
3 Wigley Avenue, Fortsland
Tel *869 465 9999*   **Closed** *Mon; lunch Sat & Sun*
Come here for grilled steaks and seafood prepared with an array of seasonings, and luscious home-made desserts. Choose to dine indoors or on the terrace overlooking the harbor.

FRIGATE BAY: Cathy's Ocean View Bar & Grill $
Caribbean
Timothy Beach
Tel *869 665 0561*
Considered the best place for lobster, Cathy's also boasts excellent jerk pork and ribs. Good rum punch, too. Lovely beach setting.

FRIGATE BAY: Rituals Sushi $
Japanese
Frigate Bay Road
Tel *869 466 7874*
Rituals, the only dedicated sushi bar on the island, offers the usual rolls, fresh sushi, and sashimi.

FRIGATE BAY: Bombay Blues Restaurant $$
Indian
858 Zenway Boulevard, Sugar Club
Tel *869 662 7599*   **Closed** *Mon*
The menu here will please vegetarians and meat-lovers alike. Go for the Sunday buffet.

FRIGATE BAY: Jam Rock Real Jerk $$
Caribbean
South Frigate Bay
Tel *869 662 5150*
A relaxed beach bar specializing in Jamaican jerk grilled foods, plus burgers, sandwiches, and pasta dishes. Good for families.

FRIGATE BAY: Marshall's $$$
Continental
Horizons Villa Resort
Tel *869 466 8245*
In a poolside setting, Marshall's serves classic grilled or roasted seafood, meat, and poultry, as well as some Caribbean favorites.

SOUTHEAST PENINSULA: Lion Rock Beach Bar & Grill $
Caribbean
Cockleshell Beach
Tel *869 663 8711*
Enjoy grilled entrées accompanied by a cold beer or the famous Lion rum punch at this beach bar.

SOUTHEAST PENINSULA: Spice Mill Restaurant $$
International
Cockleshell Beach
Tel *869 662 6706*
Situated on the beach with views to Nevis. Entrées include jerk and curries made using spices from around the world. There are also firewood baked pizzas.

Nevis

NORTH END: Indian Summer $$
Indian
Nelson Spring Beach Villas, Cades Bay
Tel *869 469 5410*   **Closed** *Mon*
The authentic cuisine gets high marks from visitors, although the decor is a bit spartan. All the usual favorites feature on the menu. Try the butter chicken.

PINNEY'S BEACH: Coconut Grove $$$
French/Caribbean
Main Island Road, Clifton's Estate
Tel *869 469 1020*
Reputed to be one of the best eateries on the island, with a beautiful beach setting, a good wine cellar, and delicious entrées.

SOUTH END: Oasis in the Gardens $$
Thai
Botanical Gardens, Montpelier Estate
Tel *869 469 2875*   **Closed** *Sun*
Try Asian specialties prepared with spices grown in the Botanical Gardens. Oasis boasts a beautiful setting within the park. Occasional wine tastings.

SOUTH END: Bananas Restaurant $$$
International
Upper Hamilton Estates
Tel *869 469 1891*
Set in a building reminiscent of an old chattel house and tucked away in the rainforest, Bananas has a varied range of dishes, as well as tasting and *prix-fixe* menus. Good vegetarian options, too.

Enchanting decor at the Bananas Restaurant, South End, Nevis

Practical Information

St. Kitts and Nevis are relatively undeveloped in terms of tourism but since there is little else to bring in foreign exchange, their economies are directed towards the tourism industry and there is considerable development on the drawing board for both islands. But today, Nevis in particular still has a low-key approach, with charm rather than speed characterizing services. When it comes to banking and communications, the islands are fully in the 21st century, with credit cards widely acceptable and local SIM cards and Internet access easily available.

Inter-island carrier, St. Kitts airport

When to Go

The best time to go to St. Kitts and Nevis is between mid-December and mid-April, when the weather is cooler although this is also the most expensive time to visit. It is humid during August and September.

Getting There

St. Kitts has direct flights from the US on **American Airlines**, **Delta**, and **US Airways**. From the UK, there is a weekly direct flight on **British Airways**. On other days, the best alternative is to fly via Antigua, which is linked by **LIAT**. Another hub is St. Martin/Sint Maarten, which is served by **Winair**.

Getting to Nevis is not easy. Traveling via St. Kitts is one alternative, from where it is possible to cross via ferry from Basseterre to Charlestown or to take a flight (although these are not frequent). If arrival is too late in the day, a water taxi can make the crossing. From within the Caribbean, there are daily flights from San Juan with American Airlines. From Antigua there is a hopper service that is supposed to

meet the North American and European flights that land in the mid–late afternoon.

Documentation

All visitors to St. Kitts and Nevis should travel on a valid passport with a valid onward ticket. Citizens of most European countries and the US do not need a visa. Guests have to pay a departure tax when leaving the island.

Visitor Information

The **St. Kitts Tourism Authority** has offices in the US, Canada, and the UK. On the island, its main office is in Basseterre. The **Nevis Tourism Authority** has its head office and information office in Charlestown.

Health and Security

The main hospitals are **Joseph N France General Hospital** in Basseterre and **Alexandra Hospital** in Charlestown. Vaccinations are necessary if you are coming from a yellow-fever infected area. St. Kitts and particularly Nevis are safe

islands. There are few problems with personal security (virtually none in Nevis) and theft is very rare, though it is advisable not to leave valuables visible in a car or unattended on the beach.

Banking and Currency

Credit cards are accepted in almost all establishments that are accustomed to dealing with tourists in both islands. There are ATMs in Basseterre and Charlestown. The currency of St. Kitts and Nevis is the Eastern Caribbean Dollar. Banks follow regular business hours, 8am–2pm Mon–Thu, 8am–4pm Fri.

Communications

The international direct dialing code for St. Kitts and Nevis is +1 869, followed by a seven-digit island number. On the islands dial the seven digits. Handsets and SIM-cards with local numbers for rental are available through **Cable and Wireless** and **Digicel**. When phoning out of the islands, dial 011 and the international code. Most of the hotels and some villas have wireless Internet available. There are cyber cafés as well.

Transport

Car hire companies will deliver to the airport, ferry terminals, hotels, and villas. They will also issue the obligatory local driving license. Car rental companies include **TDC Thrifty** (both islands), **AVIS**, and **Delisle Walwyn** (St. Kitts) and **Nevis Car Rental** at the airport in Nevis.

Small Internet café in Basseterre, St. Kitts

Taxis are available at all hotels and at the airport and ferry terminals. Taxi stands include **Circus Taxi Stand** in Basseterre and **Charlestown Taxi Stand** in Nevis. Bus services are good on both islands, but as they are designed for local people, no buses run to Frigate Bay. They emanate from the main towns, on the waterfront in Basseterre and the two squares in Charlestown.

Shopping

As a cruise ship destination, St. Kitts has extensive shopping, around the dock, Port Zante and in Basseterre. There are several duty-free shops and Caribbean chains, including **Driftwood Duty Free**, **Ashbury's**, and **Brinley Gold** for local spice rums. The **Spencer Cameron Art Gallery**, set in a pretty building in Independence Square, is well worth a visit, as is **Caribelle**

Batik display at Caribelle Batik in Romney Manor, St. Kitts

Batik, which sells batik clothing. **Island Fever** in Charlestown is good for beach wear. The Museum of Nevis History *(see p300)* has some great historical material, including maps, for sale.

Language

The language of the islands is English, which is spoken with a Caribbean lilt.

Electricity

There is a mix of three square-pin sockets in UK style and two-pin sockets in US style. The hotel front desk will often have an adapter.

Time

Both islands are 4 hours behind Greenwich Mean Time and an hour ahead of Eastern Standard Time. The islands do not observe daylight savings.

Getting Married

Couples may obtain a license once they have been resident in the island f or 48 hours. The license then takes 24 hours to produce. Couples must show a photo ID and a birth certificate, with a decree nisi if divorced and the spouse's death certificate if widowed. Many hotels also arrange weddings.

DIRECTORY

Getting There

American Airlines
Tel 869 465 2273.
w aa.com

British Airways
w ba.com

Delta
w delta.com

LIAT
w liatairline.com

US Airways
Tel 1800 622 1015.
w usairways.com

Winair
Tel 869 469 5302.
w fly-winair.com

Visitor Information

Nevis Tourism Authority
Main Street, Charlestown, Nevis. Tel 869 469 7550 (Nevis), 0808 234 2064 (UK), 1-407 287 5204 (US), 1-403 770 6697 (Canada).
w nevisisland.com

St. Kitts Tourism Authority

Pelican Mall, Bay Road, Basseterre, St. Kitts.
Tel 914 949 2164, 1-800 582 6208 (NY), 020 7376 0881 (UK).
w stkittstourism.kn

Health and Security

Alexandra Hospital
Charlestown, Nevis.
Tel 869 465 5473.

Joseph N France General Hospital
Basseterre, St. Kitts.
Tel 869 465 2551.

Communications

Cable and Wireless
PO Box 86, Basseterre, St. Kitts.
Tel 869 465 1000.
w time4lime.com

Digicel
Cable Building, Basseterre, St. Kitts.
Tel 869 466 3400.
w digicelstkitts andnevis.com

Transport

1st Choice Car Rental
Shaws Road, Newcastle, Nevis.
Tel 869 469 1131.
w neviscarrental.com

AVIS
Basseterre, St. Kitts.
Tel 869 465 6507.
w avisstkitts.com

Charlestown Taxi Stand
Nevis.
Tel 869 469 5621.

Circus Taxi Stand
Basseterre, St. Kitts.
Tel 869 466 6999/869 465 9053.

Delisle Walwyn
Liverpool Row, Basseterre.
Tel 869 465 2631.
w delislewalwyn.com

TDC Thrifty
Tel 869 465 2511 (St. Kitts), 869 469 1005 (Nevis).
w tdclimited.com

Shopping

Ashbury's
Pelican Mall, St. Kitts.
Tel 869 465 8175.

Brinley Gold
Port Zante, St. Kitts.
w brinleygoldrum.com

Caribelle Batik
Romney Manor, St. Kitts.
Tel 869 465 6253.
w caribellebatikstkitts. com

Driftwood Duty Free
Port Zante, St. Kitts.
Tel 869 466 2432.
w driftwooddutyfree. net

Island Fever
Henville's Plaza, Charlestown, Nevis.
Tel 869 762 8799.

Spencer Cameron Art Gallery
Basseterre, St. Kitts.
Tel 869 465 1617.
w spencercameron. com

Exploring Antigua and Barbuda

Antigua and sister island Barbuda lure cruise ship passengers, yachtsmen, and casual travelers with world-class service and entertainment, gorgeous beaches, luxury resorts, and plenty of historic sights. Antigua is internationally renowned for its sailing festivals, while Barbuda's rare frigate birds colony is a bird-watcher's paradise. A British overseas territory, the neighboring volcanic island of Montserrat offers a true eco-experience.

Locator Map

Boats moored at the busy marina at Nelson's Dockyard, Antigua

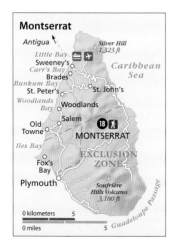

Montserrat

0 kilometers 5
0 miles 5

Key

— Major road
═ Minor road
--- Ferry route
△ Peak

Getting Around

V.C. Bird International Airport in Antigua is a major regional airline hub, while the port of St. John's welcomes large cruise ships on a regular schedule. Antigua and Barbuda are connected by air and sea, with daily flights and ferry service. Antigua has three protected harbors with marinas and immigration checkpoints for yachts wanting to tour the coastline and visit Barbuda. Daily flights from Antigua land at Gerald's Airport in Montserrat. Taxis are readily available on all three islands, while cars can also be hired on Antigua and Montserrat.

For hotels and restaurants on these islands see p326 and p327

Limestone formation, Two Foot Bay National Park, Barbuda

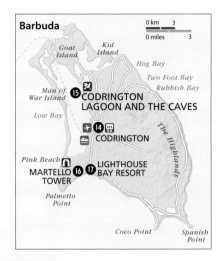

Barbuda

0 km   3
0 miles   3

Goat Island
Kid Island
Hog Bay
Two Foot Bay
Rubbish Bay
Man of War Island
 15 **CODRINGTON LAGOON AND THE CAVES**
Low Bay
14 **CODRINGTON**
The Highlands
Pink Beach
MARTELLO TOWER **16** **17** **LIGHTHOUSE BAY RESORT**
Palmetto Point
Coco Point
Spanish Point

nan's
Long Island
al Point
2 3 **JUMBY BAY, A ROSEWOOD RESORT**
b Point
dge
Maiden Island
Great Bird Island
Barnacle Point
Rabbit Island
Blackmans Point
Crabs Peninsula
Guiana Island

Guiana Bay
Crump Island
Parham
Mercer's Creek Bay
Pelican Island
Long Bay
Indian Town Point
Seatons
5 **LONG BAY**
6 **DEVIL'S BRIDGE**
Pares
Willikies
Flat Point
eemans
BETTY'S HOPE **4**
Glanvilles
Nonsuch Bay
Hughes Point
Green Island
7 **HARMONY HALL**
Potworks Dam Reservoir
Newfield
Freetown
Great Deep Bay
York Island
Friars Head
ta
Bethesda
Christian Point
St. Philips
Christian Hill
Willoughby Bay
8 **HALF MOON BAY**
outh
Cobbs Cross
Hudson Point
English Harbour
Isaac Point
Mamora Bay
outh
bour
9 **10** **SHIRLEY HEIGHTS**
ISH HARBOUR
& NELSON'S
OCKYARD

Long Bay Beach with resorts in the background, Antigua

Sights at a Glance

0 kilometers   3
0 miles   3

For additional map symbols *see back flap*

Twin towers of St. John's Anglican Cathedral

❶ St. John's

W coast, Antigua. ✈ 39,000. ✈ ⛴
🚢 ℹ Goverment Complex, Queen
Elizabeth Highway, 268 462 0480. 🛍
🍴 Fri–Sat. 🎭 Carnival (early Aug).
🌐 antigua-barbuda.org

This bustling, historic port city
is the governmental and commercial hub of Antigua. At the
center is the cruise ship dock at
Heritage Quay, lined with upscale
duty-free shops and restaurants.
Next to this area is the Vendors
Mart where visitors can purchase
local souvenirs, and Redcliffe
Quay, a more quaint shopping
and dining area. Other points
of interest include the twin-
steepled **St. John's Anglican
Cathedral**. A wooden church
was first built here in 1681 but
after a series of earthquakes,
the present cathedral was built
in 1847. Church services are
held on Sunday mornings and
evenings. Also worth seeing is
the **Museum of Antigua and
Barbuda**, and the Public Market
Complex on Market Street, where
local farmers sell their produce.
Parking is difficult to find, so it is
recommended that visitors use
taxis or buses to come in for a
day of shopping or touring.

Environs
On the eastern outskirts of St.
John's is the legendary **Antigua
Recreation Ground**, which has
seen many cricket matches and
records since it opened in 1978.
A new stadium was built farther
east for the 2007 World Cup, and

named after local
hero Sir Vivian
Richards, a former
West Indies cricket
team captain.
   At the far end
of Fort Bay is **Fort
James**, built in the
early 1700s. It was
the primary fortifi-
cation to protect the
harbor of St. John's.
Among the artillery
were ten cannons
that formed part of
the ramparts. When
most of the other
forts on the island
were disassembled,
these cannons were left intact.
Adjacent to the fort is Russell's,
a full-service restaurant installed
in a historic building.

🏛 **St. John's Anglican
Cathedral**
Newgate Street. **Tel** 268 462 0820.
Open vary.

🏛 **Museum of Antigua and
Barbuda**
Long Street. **Tel** 268 462 1469.
Open 8:30am–4pm Mon–Fri,
10am–2pm Sat. 🛍 📷

❷ Sandals Grande Antigua

🏖 Dickenson Bay, Antigua.
Tel 268 462 0267. 🏊 🚫 🛂
🌐 sandals.com

This sprawling extravagant
complex on one of the best
beaches on the island was
expanded in 2007 with the
addition of the Mediterranean
Village, a resort within the
resort with its own huge pool,

restaurants and bars, as well
as an all-suite layout. The
original Caribbean Village is
extensive, with 5 restaurants,
5 pools, a fitness center, and
the Red Lane Spa.
   Honeymooners love
the rondavels, small round
buildings near the beach
housing one-bedroom suites
with private plunge pools.
One of the exclusive Sandals'
features is a personal butler
service, available for the
rondavels as well as for the
Mediterranean penthouse
suites. If the entertainment
in the all-inclusive resort
is not enough, the Rush
Entertainment complex,
with Madison's Casino and
Conors Sports Bar is just down
the road in Runaway Bay.

❸ Jumby Bay, A Rosewood Resort

🚤 Long Island. **Tel** 268 462 6000.
🏊 🚫 🛥 🌐 rosewoodhotels.
com/en/jumby-bay-antigua

One of the premiere luxury
resorts of the world, this elegant
all-inclusive gem is located
on its own island off the north
coast of Antigua. It has been
popular with celebrities, such
as Oprah Winfrey and Paul
McCartney, as a place to get
away from everything in
surroundings that are uniquely
British colonial.
   In addition to the hotel
suites, pool, restaurants, bars,
and great beach, the island
also offers large luxury villas
for rent, many with their own
beach and plunge pools.

One of the luxurious pools at Sandals Grande Antigua, Dickenson Bay

For hotels and restaurants on these islands see p326 and p327

A section of the popular Long Bay Beach, Antigua

❹ Betty's Hope

5 miles (7 km) E of St. John's, Antigua.
Tel 268 462 1469. 🚌 ℹ️ Betty's Hope
Visitors' Center, 268 462 1469.
Open 10am–4pm Tue–Sat. 🎨 📷
🌐 antiguamuseums.org

Remains of 17th- and
18th-century sugar plan-
tations are everywhere
throughout the Caribbean,
but it is unusual to find an
actual working windmill
of the type used to
grind sugarcane on
those plantations.
Betty's Hope offers
that rare find, in one
working and one
non-working mill
surrounded by
ruins of a plantation
that was a major
agricultural contributor to
the economy of the island
from about 1650 to the 1920s.
Exhibits of the island's
plantation era are displayed
in the visitors' center. An eco-
tourism enhancement project
aims to continue the
conservation of the site.

**An old plantation windmill,
Betty's Hope**

❺ Long Bay

10 miles (16 km) E of St. John's,
Antigua. 🚌

The highlights of Long Bay, on
the northeast coast (Atlantic
side), are the 1,600-ft (488-m)
crescent of white sand and
the good snorkeling sites
on the barrier reef close to
shore. The bay accommodates

guests from **Grand Pineapple
Resort**, as well as local families
with children.
    The luxurious Grand Pineapple
Resort has pools, restaurants,
tennis courts, spa, and watersports. Rooms are brightly done
in white wicker and floral textiles, most with gorgeous ocean
views out to the
Atlantic. Those that are
high up on the hill and
the ones down on the
beach offer the most
spectacular vistas.
Visitors on the Long
Bay Beach can get
lunch from the Beach
House restaurant,
which also serves
dinner and puts on
evening barbeques.
Colorful trinkets and
souvenirs are on sale from the
beach vendors.

🏨 Grand Pineapple Resort
Long Bay. **Tel** 268 463 2006. 🛏️ 📶 🍴
🌐 grandpineapple.com

❻ Devil's Bridge

11 miles (17 km) E of St. John's
Antigua. 🚌 📷 Kite Festival
(Mar–Apr).

This natural formation on
the Atlantic Coast draws
visitors who want to see the
dramatic coastline. The bridge
itself is a stone arch over the
sea; during high tide the area
below becomes a pool with
the waves cresting over the
top of the bridge. It is said
that anyone falling from the
bridge is bound to drown,
and legend has it that many
slaves chose this fate by
throwing themselves off the
bridge into the sea. The area,
designated a national park,
is also the site of the annual
Kite Festival, because the
very strong winds off the
ocean are perfect for aerial
kite maneuvers.

Environs
Adjacent to Devil's Bridge
National Park and sprawling
over 30 acres (12 ha) is the
grand eco-friendly **Verandah
Resort & Spa**. This pretty
hotel features two spectacular
protected beaches, a spa
and fitness center, children's
center, tennis court, and three
restaurants. The rooms are
spacious and easily accommodate small families. Some
can be interconnected for
larger families. All rooms have
air-conditioning, flat-screen
satellite TVs, and small kitchens.

🏨 Verandah Resort & Spa
Long Bay. **Tel** 268 562 6848. 🛏️ 📶 🍴
🌐 verandahresortandspa.com

Devil's Bridge rock formation at the eastern end of Antigua

Interior of the art gallery in Harmony Hall

❼ Harmony Hall

8 miles (13 km) SE of St. John's, Antigua. **Tel** 268 460 4120. Ⓣ **Open** 10am–6pm Tue–Sun. ∅ Ⓦ **harmonyhallantigua.com**

Located on the southeastern coast of Antigua, near Freetown village, Harmony Hall is a charming art gallery in Brown's Bay Mill. Fine paintings, sculptures, jewelry, photographs, and pottery by local artists are on display here. Harmony Hall also holds regular exhibitions from November to April. The complex has a restaurant on a terrace that overlooks Brown's Bay and offers delicious Italian cuisine.

❽ Half Moon Bay

🚊 14 miles (22 km) SE of St. John's, Antigua. 🏨 🏖

One of the most beautiful beaches on Antigua, Half Moon Bay's crescent-shaped strand offers two completely different beach experiences – the rough surf on the Atlantic side and calm, clear waters at the far eastern end.

Snorkeling is a favorite activity along the reef that forms the bay's breakwater, but there are no watersports operators so visitors need to bring their own equipment. There is a small bar at the entrance with limited food service, and bringing a picnic basket and cooler is recommended.

❾ English Harbour and Nelson's Dockyard

On the southern coast of Antigua sits its historic gem: the 15-sq-mile (38-sq-km) Nelson's Dockyard National Park and English Harbour. Some of the main buildings here can be traced to the late 18th century when the British ruled the island. The dockyard park has a museum, restaurants, and an inn *(see p326)*. English Harbour, along with the adjacent Falmouth Harbour, is known as an international yachting center and hosts several regattas and races.

VISITORS' CHECKLIST

Practical Information
11 miles (18 km) S of St. John's.
Tel 268 481 5028. **Open** 8am–5pm daily. 🅿 ∅
Ⓦ **nationalparksantigua.com**

Transport
🚌

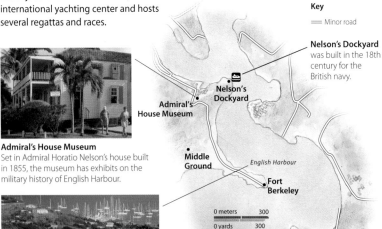

Key
═══ Minor road

Nelson's Dockyard
was built in the 18th century for the British navy.

Nelson's Dockyard

Admiral's House Museum

Middle Ground

Fort Berkeley

English Harbour

Fort Shirley

Admiral's House Museum
Set in Admiral Horatio Nelson's house built in 1855, the museum has exhibits on the military history of English Harbour.

0 meters 300
0 yards 300

English Harbour
This protected harbor was a haven for pirates and military fleet alike. It now plays host to the world-renowned Antigua Sailing Week *(see p319)*.

❿ Shirley Heights

12 miles (19 km) S of St. John's, Antigua. **Tel** 268 728 0636/764 0389. 🕐 🚲 ⏰ 9am–10pm Tue–Sun, 9am–sunset Mon. 🅦 shirleyheightslookout.com

High on the hill above English Harbour sits this renovated historical site, overlooking the sea. It is famous for its panoramic views and on clear days, visitors can see as far as Guadeloupe and Montserrat. It is popular for its Sunday evenings when the place hosts the biggest party on the island, including steel band and soca band entertainment. The complex also has a restaurant and a band plays on Thursday evenings.

⓫ Fig Tree Drive

8 miles (13 km) SE of St. John's, Antigua. 🕐 ⏰ 🏛

Heading south from the village of Swetes, the winding road passes through the most thickly forested area on the island – Fig Tree Hill. Ironically there are no fig trees here but banana and mango trees line the road. A lovely stop on the way is the Fig Tree Culture Shop where visitors can buy fresh fruits, juices, jams, and locally-made food products. A favorite stopover is Wallings Dam, a historic park with a picnic area, hiking trails, and canopy tours (see p321). In the heart of the rainforest is also the Fig Tree Studio Art Gallery,

Peaceful Turner's Beach, on Antigua's southwestern coast

that features the art of local artist Sallie Harker as well as crafts from island's artists. Most of the tour operators and taxi drivers offer tours of the area.

Located along Fig Tree Drive at Old Road Village, **Curtain Bluff Resort** is an elegant all-inclusive resort. Owned by Howard and Michelle Hulford, the resort has 72 rooms and suites, pool, spa, 2 beaches, 2 restaurants, and a beautiful garden setting.

🏨 **Curtain Bluff Resort**
Morris Bay. **Tel** 268 462 8400. 🚐 ⏰ 🐾 ♿ 🅦 curtainbluff.com

⓬ Turner's and Darkwood Beaches

🚐 3 miles (5 km) SW of St. John's, Antigua. 🍴 🏊

Along Antigua's southwestern coast lie these two wide, golden-sand beaches. Both offer good restaurants and beach bars with lounge chair rentals, and are perfect for those not

staying at the beach resorts. The snorkeling off Turner's Beach is good, but visitors need to bring their own equipment. Cruising yachts often anchor just offshore so passengers can enjoy the beach. Darkwood Beach has a lovely stretch of sand and is a great spot to swim.

Yachts lined up at the Jolly Harbour marina

⓭ Jolly Harbour

2 miles (3 km) SW to St. John's, Antigua. **Tel** 268 462 6042. 🚏 🚤 ⛵ Sailing Week (Apr–May). 🅦 jolly-harbour-marina.com

North of Darkwood Beach, this marina complex has a little of everything: a great beach, shopping center, elegant casino and nightclub building, an 18-hole golf course, and tennis courts, as well as a number of restaurants and bars. It also offers a world-class marina for visiting yachts and is one of the harbors for the annual Sailing Week. Spreading out alongside the beautiful beach is Jolly Beach Resort (see p326), one of the largest all-inclusives on the island.

Driving through the forested Fig Tree Drive

For hotels and restaurants on these islands see p326 and p327

⑭ Codrington

Eastern edge of the Lagoon, Barbuda.
🏔 1,800. ✈ 🚌 🚐 🛥 Caribana
Festival (May). 🌐 **barbudaful.net**

The small town of Codrington is Barbuda's capital and the commercial and government center. Many of the original buildings from the 19th century still exist, and have been enlisted for other uses: the former Ginnery now houses offices and the stables of the Government House have been converted into a school. The town also has several

Wa Omoni's popular local restaurant, Codrington

supermarkets, grocery stores, bars, bakeries, and restaurants; lobster lunches featuring the spiny lobster caught off

Barbuda's shores, are a favorite with visitors. On the outskirts of Codrington is an Internet café, a pharmacy, an ice-cream parlor, a souvenir shop, and the Art Café, home of local artist Claire Frank. Here, visitors can browse through her collection of hand-painted silks.

The town has many small guesthouses which provide economical overnight lodging.

⑮ Codrington Lagoon and the Caves

A sheltered waterway separated from the ocean by a narrow spit of land, Codrington Lagoon is home to 170 species of birds. It serves as a major habitat for the frigate birds, of which 5,000 make their home here. The caves nestled into the sea bluffs on the northeastern side of the island are rich in history from the days when Arawak Indians and later runaway slaves sought the protection of these underground grottos.

Frigate Birds Colony
One of the largest colonies in the world, this is home to the frigate birds. The birds can be seen nesting in the mangrove swamps around the lagoon.

Darby Cave
This 180-ft (55-m) deep sinkhole leads to a broad cavern that ends in five freshwater pools.

Two Foot Bay is dotted with caves which feature Amerindian rock carvings. It is best to go with a guide since there are no marked trails.

Key
═══ Road

Two Foot Bay

Man of War Island

The Highlands

Rubbish Bay

Codrington Lagoon

Codrington

Barbuda

Codrington Lagoon
Separated from the Caribbean Sea by a narrow piece of land, this lagoon occupies a large part of this small island.

VISITORS' CHECKLIST

Practical Information
West of Codrington, Barbuda.
🌐 **barbudaful.net**

Transport
🚕 Note: taxi drivers can arrange boat tours of the lagoon.

Martello Tower, rising to 32 ft (10 m), served as an observation post.

0 km   2
0 miles   2

For keys to symbols *see back flap*

The luxury Lighthouse Bay Resort on the 11 Mile Beach

⑯ Martello Tower

3 miles (5 km) S of Codrington, Barbuda. ⬛ **Open** 6am–8pm daily. ⬛ ⬛ ⬛ **barbudaful.net**

Early attempts at settling upon Barbuda by the English were resisted by the fierce Carib Indians. Barbuda was eventually colonized by John and Christopher Codrington, who came over from Antigua in 1685 to establish a provisioning station and, legend has it, a slave-breeding home for their plantations in Antigua, under a 99-year lease from Queen Anne of England.

Between 1750 and 1800, the British built a fort at a point called River, which included the 52-ft (17-m) high observation tower now known as Martello. It was modeled after a tower built on Cape Mortella in Corsica during the Napoleonic Wars. The fort

was equipped with three guns. Apart from defense purposes, the fort was also used as a high vantage point to spot shipwrecks on the reefs surrounding the island.

At the beach's edge adjacent to the Martello Tower is the laidback **Pink Sand Beach Bar**, the only beach bar on Barbuda. This locally-owned restaurant prepares a variety of seafood including fish and lobster dishes, served with traditional Barbudan vegetables, such as squash, beans, pumpkin, and peppers, as well as cool drinks. With some spectacular ocean views, the bar is a favorite venue for beach parties.

Pink Sand Beach Bar
River Beach.
Open 10am–midnight daily.

⑰ Lighthouse Bay Resort

⬛ Low Bay, Barbuda. **Tel** 888 214 8552 or 877 766 6718 (reservations). ⬛ ⬛ ⬛ ⬛ **lighthousebay resort.com**

This small luxury resort, sits on a strip of land at the southeastern edge of Codrington Lagoon, on the spectacular pink-sand 11 Mile Beach. The sense of being out at the end of the world is pervasive, since there are no other resorts or facilities nearby. The property includes the Lighthouse Bay Bar. The hotel concierge can arrange activities such as deep-sea fishing, tours of the Frigate Bird Sanctuary, water-skiing, cave exploring, and diving.

The Spiny Lobster

In the Caribbean, when a menu says "lobster" it generally means the spiny lobster, endemic to the warm tropical waters. Unlike the New England-type lobsters that have the fat frontal claws, these creatures have long, straight spikes coming off the head, great for defense, but not very edible. However, the lobster meat is delectable. Fishermen in the waters around Barbuda bring in large quantities of the catch, and visitors can buy them right off the docks, still alive. Those lucky enough to be traveling the islands' waters by boat often buy them fresh, fuel up the grill, cut the lobsters in half and brush with a little butter, then throw them on the heat – a quick and easy meal fit for a king. Land-based visitors can find them already grilled at many of the roadside food vendors' stands, and of course, at all the better restaurants.

The robust exterior of the Martello Tower

Grilled spiny lobster

For hotels and restaurants on these islands see p326 and p327

Outdoor Activities and Specialized Holidays

Antigua's most outstanding natural resource is its coastline – its numerous coves and bays provide an array of opportunities for water-based activities. Offshore, the island is ringed by reefs providing diving and snorkeling sites, as well as by small islands perfect for day explorations. Antigua is also an island of rolling hills, broad valleys, and in the southernmost area, a rainforest. Hiking or biking through the hill areas, touring off-road and overland, riding a zip line through the rainforest, or golfing are all available to active tourists.

The busy beach at Dickenson Bay

Beaches

Each beach on Antigua features different types of wave action, wind, sand, and vegetation depending on its location. The Atlantic Coast has rougher surf and sand, while the tame beaches of the Caribbean side offer powdery sand and clear seas.

All beaches are open to the public. Some resorts offer day passes which allow use of their facilities or all-inclusive passes which also include food and drink. On beaches without resorts, bars and restaurants offer beach chair rentals and facilities, and some have water-sports equipment for hire.

Among the best Atlantic beaches are Long Bay *(see p313)*, Green Island, and Half Moon Bay *(see p314)*. Popular ones on the west coast are Dickenson, Runaway, Deep, Hawksbill, and Lignum Vitae Bays. Turner's and Darkwood Beaches *(see p315)* are top spots on the southwest coast, as well as Cades and Rende-zvous Bays.

In Barbuda, Pink Beach is well known for its rose-hued sands.

Sailing and Kayaking

One of the best ways to explore Antigua is by sea, in a sailboat or catamaran. Depending on the tour operator, these tours can take on a party atmosphere or be an educational trip where passengers learn about ecolo-gical efforts to preserve marine life. **Pirates of Antigua** even offers pirate cruises on a beautifully restored schooner. **Adventure Antigua** is run by Eli Fuller, a local who competed in the 1988 Olympics as part of

A sailboat arriving at Nelson's Dockyard

a sailing crew. He and his staff offer eco-tours on traditional yachts. Boat trips may include a stop at **Stingray City Antigua**, an offshore habitat where visitors can swim with the friendly stingrays *(see also ATV/4X4 Tours, p320)*.

Day and cruise ship charters are available at **Adventure Caribbean Yacht Charters** and bareboat and crewed charters can be hired from **Antigua Yacht Charters Ltd.** and **Nicholson Yacht Charters**.

Kayak tours are offered by **Paddles Kayak & Snorkel Eco-Adventures**. Passengers climb into individual crafts and are guided through interesting sections of coastline or waterways. Other operators include **Sailing Antigua** and **Wadadli Cats**.

Diving and Snorkeling

The sheltered western and southern coasts are the islands' primary diving areas. Among the best sites are Cades Reef, the Pinnacles of Hercules, Big John's Reef, and Ffryes Shoal.

Most dive operators are PADI certified, own custom-designed dive boats, have equipment and packages, and conduct classes on all levels. Some also have underwater cameras for rent, so divers can return with unique souvenirs of their dives. Tour operators include **Extreme Marine Scuba**, **Dive Antigua**, **Jolly Dive**, and **Indigo Divers**.

Kitesurfing and Windsurfing

The north coast of Antigua is blessed with perfect conditions for kitesurfing. The wind is constantly high and side-on, the water has enough swells for good bump and jump conditions. Equipment rentals have everything a beginner or advanced surfer may need. Operators include **Kitesurf Antigua**.

Windsurfing equipment and lessons are available at Windsurf Antigua on the north coast of Dutchman Bay.

Sailing in Antigua

An almost circular island with a raggedy coastline of deep bays and harbors sitting between the wild and windy Atlantic Ocean and the more serene Caribbean Sea, Antigua is a yachter's paradise. Among the many offerings of the island are international yachting events, bareboat or crewed charters, and learn-to-sail schools. Colorful marinas capable of servicing everything from small monohulls and catamarans to super yachts are located at English Harbour, Falmouth Harbour, and Jolly Harbour. Services at these locations include marine engineering, electronics, and rigging, making this a one-stop destination for the yachting industry.

Regattas and Races

For yachtsmen around the world, Antigua is the place to be in the spring. Among the international yacht racing events held here are the Classic Yacht Regatta in early April, and then the Stanford Sailing Week in late April. Yachts of all sizes can be seen participating in the various races.

Stanford Sailing Week includes several classes ranging from large yachts and monohulls to gunboats. The week is filled with beach parties at locations around the island where locals join in the fun.

Ondeck Ocean Racing offers a chance for individuals to become a member of the crew for a day on a Beneteau 40.7 or a Farr 40 or 60 yacht. An ocean race is set up so that participants get a genuine racing experience.

Other Events and Activities

Antigua has four yacht clubs and hosts an annual inter-club race in January. English Harbour and Jolly Harbour, with their lively clubs, restaurants, and shops, serve as yachting centers that attract gatherings of yachtsmen year round.

Learn-to-sail programs are offered at many resorts and sailing clubs. Private tuition as well as dinghy sailing classes are available for beginners at Nonsuch Bay *(see p326)*. Refresher classes and advanced clinics are also on offer.

Charters are available all around Antigua. Several companies offer crewed and bareboat charters on yachts and will provision and set the itinerary according to individual preferences.

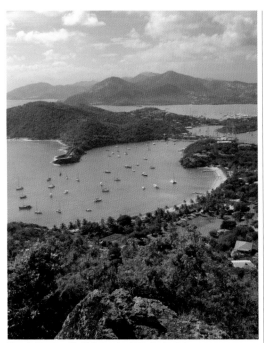

A breathtaking view of English Harbour from Shirley Heights, Antigua

Hiking

Many of the trails in Antigua are not fully developed, but lead to interesting historic sights or natural wonders. Trails in the English Harbour area *(see p314)* lead from Nelson's Dockyard to Fort Barrington and up to Shirley Heights. A trail starting in the Half Moon Bay National Park leads to a promontory looking out to the neighboring butterfly-shaped island of Guadeloupe. Trails through the beautiful rainforest area start at Wallings Dam and head up Boggy Peak, the highest point on the island, and out to Rendezvous Bay, which is not accessible by road. The **Environmental Awareness Group** and the **Antigua Historical and Archeological Society** occasionally sponsor hikes in these areas.

Bikes and Scooters

For fresh-air touring, there is nothing like the immediacy of a bicycle or scooter. Most of the roads are flat or on rolling hills, making this form of transportation ideal. **Bikes Plus** in St. John's offers mountain bike rentals and they also have a stock of spare parts and equipment. **Paradise Boat Sales** in Jolly Harbour also rents out mountain bikes with special children's seats, by the day. **Barbuda Bike Tours** on Barbuda provides guided mountain-biking trips and also rents bikes and cycling gear to independent bikers.

For motorized fun, **Cheke's Scooter Rentals**, located in St. John's, has scooters ranging from 50–150cc, for rent by the day. This is inclusive of two helmets, maps, as well as instructions.

Rainforest Zip Line Tours

Soaring high above the rainforest canopy is an exhilarating experience. At **Antigua Rainforest Canopy Tour**, the guides, well trained in safety, attach state-of-the-art harnesses and helmets to ensure that everyone arrives in great shape at the end of one of the four available tours. After zooming through the high-altitude lines, participants then end at the "Leap of Faith" (similar to bungee-jumping but safer), and then on to the Challenge Course. The last physical test is then the 400-step climb back to the top. Children can participate, if taller than 5 ft (1.52 m). It is advisable to make reservations.

ATV/4x4 Tours

The interior of Antigua is hilly, dotted with historical ruins and small villages.

Several tour operators offer trips overland into these oft-unexplored parts of the island. Tour agencies such as **Tropical Adventures** combine inland safaris in open jeeps with kayaking or a visit to Stingray City Antigua. **Estate Safari Jeep Tours** takes visitors around in air-conditioned comfort. Lunch in Parhamtown is included. Some tour operators also offer quad bikes (or ATVs). Adventure Antigua offers a Quad Off-Road Tour that involves only adventure trails and no streets.

A jeep safari at Betty's Hope, Antigua

The sprawling Jolly Harbour Golf Club on the ground of Jolly Beach Resort, Antigua

Golf

There are two picturesque 18-hole courses on the island, taking advantage of the rolling hills, tropical landscapes and sea views.

Cedar Valley Golf Club, in the northern part of the island, is a par 70, 6,157 yard course for all skill levels, and also offers a 300-yard (274-m) driving range and a resident pro. The place offers panoramic views of the Caribbean coastline. **Jolly Harbour Golf Club**, a par 71, 5,587 yard (5,108 m) course, was designed by well-known golf course architect Karl Litton, and is set next to the Jolly Harbour marina. Its clubhouse has a pro shop, snack bar, showers, and locker rooms. Both are open to the public, and many hotels can arrange for guests to use the courses.

DIRECTORY

Sailing and Kayaking

Adventure Antigua
Tel 268 726 6355.
W adventureantigua.com

Adventure Caribbean Yacht Charters
Tel 268 764 0595.
W adventurecaribbean.com

Antigua Yacht Charters Ltd.
Tel 268 463 7101.
W antiguayachtcharters.com

Nicholson Yacht Charters
Tel 268 460 1530.
W nicholson-charters.com

Paddles Kayak and Snorkel Eco Adventures
Tel 268 720 4322.
W antiguapaddles.com

Pirates of Antigua
Tel 268 562 7946.
W piratesofantigua.com

Sailing Antigua
Tel 268 726 6355.
W sailing-antigua.com

Stingray City Antigua
Tel 268 562 7297.
W stingraycityantigua.com

Wadadli Cats
Tel 268 462 4792.
W wadadlicats.com

Diving and Snorkeling

Dive Antigua
Tel 268 464 3483.
W diveantigua.com

Extreme Marine Scuba
Tel 268 725 7777.

Indigo Divers
Jolly Harbour, Antigua.
Tel 268 562 3483.
W indigo-divers.com

Jolly Dive
Jolly Harbour, Antigua.
Tel 268 462 8305.
W jollydive.com

Kitesurfing and Windsurfing

Kitesurf Antigua
Jabberwock Beach, Antigua.
Tel 268 720 5483.
W kitesurfantigua.com

Hiking

Antigua Historical and Archeological Society
Tel 268 462 1469.
W antiguamuseum.org

Environmental Awareness Group
Tel 268 462 6236.

Bikes and Scooters

Barbuda Bike Tours
Barbuda.
Tel 268 773 9599.

Bikes Plus
Independence Drive,
St. John's, Antigua.
Tel 268 462 2453.

Cheke's Scooter Rentals
St. John's,
Antigua.
Tel 268 562 4646.
W antigua-barbuda.org

Paradise Boat Sales
Jolly Harbour,
Antigua.
Tel 268 463 7125.
W paradiseboats.com

Rainforest Zip Line Tours

Antigua Rainforest Canopy Tour
Fig Tree Drive,
Antigua.
Tel 268 562 6363.
W antiguarainforest.com

ATV/ 4X4 Tours

Estate Safari Jeep Tours
Tel 268 463 2061.

Tropical Adventures
St. John's, Antigua.
Tel 268 480 1225.
W tropicalad.com

Golf

Cedar Valley Golf Club
St. John's,
Antigua.
Tel 268 462 0161.
W cedarvalleygolf.ag

Jolly Harbour Golf Club
Jolly Harbour,
Antigua.
Tel 268 462 7771.
W jollyharbourgolfclub.com

⑱ Montserrat

During the 1990s, the Soufrière Hills Volcano repeatedly roared to life with activity that buried the main town of Plymouth and a significant portion of the southern half of Montserrat in ash. In the years since the tragedy, the island has developed a new role, offering "volcano tourism," with people coming just to see the devastation and the cloud-shrouded mount. A hardened dome covers the active core of hot lava, quieting the major threat, but there is still significant seismic activity as well as gas and steam venting. The island is divided into the Exclusion Zone, covering the southern half, and the northern hills where the locals have rebuilt their governmental center and cultural core at Brades.

Red phone box almost buried in volcanic ash, Plymouth

Lava covering what was once the Golf Club

The Exclusion Zone

Southern part of Montserrat. **Open** daylight hours. Avalon's Taxi-Tours: Brades. Tel 664 491 3432 or 664 492 1565. Clifford "Shaw-Duck" Ryan: Brades. Tel 664 492 1849. Grant Tours: Brades. Tel 664 491 9654. 'JIG' Tours: Brades. Tel 664 491 2752, 664 492 2752 or 664 496 2752.

In 1995, the Soufrière Hills Volcano erupted, spewed ash that covered the main town of Plymouth and darkened the sun for 15 minutes. A year later, the town was abandoned, buried under layers of ash and mud deposited by pyroclastic activity. Houses on the hills around the center of the island, as well as the W.H. Bramble Airport on the eastern side of the island, were similarly buried and now stand as a modern-day Pompeii for all to observe. If volcanic activity is at a minimum, people are allowed to go briefly into some areas of the Exclusion Zone to observe the devastation from a closer vantage point. But nobody can enter the zone without a

qualified guide, and must follow the restrictions and safety measures. Since no one is allowed near the town of Plymouth, the best place to view it is from Richmond and Garibaldi Hills, where many of the homes remain half-buried in ash. To arrange a tour, contact the Montserrat Tourist Board or one of the tour operators.

Another interesting way to view the effects of the volcano is on a boat tour starting from Little Bay. From this vantage point, the town of Plymouth and the paths of the volcanic flows are visible.

On the eastern side of the island, the remains of Bramble Airport and the lava dome can

be viewed from the lookout at Jack Boy Hill. From this point, the airport as well as the severely damaged Indian burial grounds and villages can be seen. The specially constructed building offers a viewing platform, a telescope to see the volcanic dome (if the clouds have lifted), and picnic areas.

Montserrat Volcano Observatory

Flemmings, Montserrat. **Tel** 664 491 5647. **Open** 10:15am–3:15pm Mon–Thu. 🚫 🖥 🅿 🚹 🌐 mvo.ms

The Montserrat Volcano Observatory, which is responsible for monitoring the volcano and issuing status alerts, has its own headquarters at Flemmings, built in 2003. At the Interpretation Center, posters provide an explanation of the techniques used in monitoring volcanic activities and video shows give

View of Montserrat's former airport from Jack Boy Hill

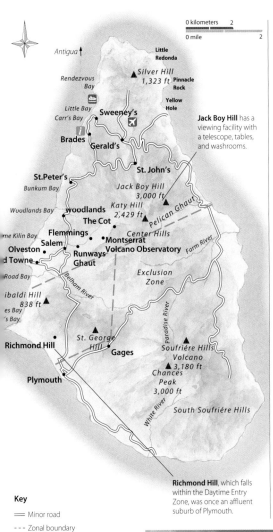

0 kilometers 2
0 mile 2

Antigua

Little
Redonda

▲ *Silver Hill*
1,323 ft Pinnacle
Rock

*Rendezvous
Bay*

Yellow
Hole

Little Bay
Carr's Bay

Sweeney's

Jack Boy Hill has a
viewing facility with
a telescope, tables,
and washrooms.

ℹ
Brades

Gerald's

St.John's

St.Peter's
Bunkum Bay

Jack Boy Hill
3,000 ft ▲

Woodlands Bay

Woodlands

Katy Hill
2,429 ft ▲

Pelican Ghaut

me Kilin Bay

The Cot

Flemmings

Salem

Center Hills

Olveston

**Montserrat
Volcano Observatory**

Farm River

Runways

d Towne

Ghaut

Road Bay

Belham River

*Exclusion
Zone*

Paradise River

ibaldi Hill
838 ft ▲
es Bay
's Bay

▲
*St. George
Hill*

Richmond Hill

Gages

*Soufriére Hills
Volcano* ▲
▲ 3,180 ft
*Chances
Peak*
3,000 ft

Plymouth

White River

South Soufriére Hills

Richmond Hill, which falls
within the Daytime Entry
Zone, was once an affluent
suburb of Plymouth.

Key

═══ Minor road

--- Zonal boundary

a synopsis and examples of the
volcano's recent activity, along
with a touch screen and displays
of rocks, ash, and artifacts.
Scientists are available to answer
questions at sessions held on
Tuesdays and Thursdays.

The website gives the most
up-to-date information about the
volcano through weekly status
reports. Those planning to visit
the island should check this site
before traveling. Also of interest is
the photo gallery that is updated
weekly and has an archive of
photographs taken during the
periods when the dome was still
growing. For those interested in
learning more about volcanos,
the site also offers extensive
information on volcano-specific
events and their monitoring
methods. A CD as well as a
sample set to aid teaching
geology, geography, and science
for children aged 11 to 18 are
also available.

Visitor Safety

Visitors can pick up a brochure
titled Guide to Volcanic Hazards
at the tourist board office or at
the observatory. This gives a brief
history of the volcano and the
current risk assessments. It out-
lines the Exclusion Zone, the
criteria for entering it, and the
safety rules to be observed while
traveling through it (such as
carrying ash masks and drinking
water). It also lists emergency
numbers and what to do if the
early-warning sirens go off.

View of the volcano from the Montserrat Volcano Observatory

For additional map symbols *see back flap*

Outdoor Activities and Specialized Holidays

In contrast to the southern part of Montserrat, which resembles a moonscape and is largely inaccessible, the northern area reminds both locals and visitors of what the island used to be. The hills are covered by lush greenery, sparkling creeks in deep ravines *(ghauts)* trickle down to the sea, and winding roads lead to charming villas and guesthouses. It is an ideal place for rest and relaxation. The prime activities here, apart from volcano watching, are sunning on the beaches, hiking through the many trails of the Center Hills rainforest, as well as snorkeling and diving through the offshore reefs.

The black-sand beach of Bunkum Bay, Montserrat

Beaches

The island is ringed by many beaches, with some dramatically changed by the pyroclastic flows. Rendezvous Bay, accessible only by boat or hiking, is at the northwestern tip of the island. The most popular is Little Bay Beach, a little farther south near the main town of Brades, at the port area. It has some facilities such as a good restaurant and diving operations. Farther down the Caribbean coast are Bunkum Bay and Woodlands Bay, both featuring volcanic black sand. Bunkum is good for snorkeling, and also has a beach bar. Woodlands offers a covered picnic area on a bluff overlooking the sea, but the surf is a little rougher here. Just north of the Exclusion Zone is Old Road Bay, which was extended so far out in the sea by the flows, so that now Jumping Jack's Beach

Bar is a considerable distance away from the beach. During heightened volcanic activity, this beach is often included in the Exclusion Zone.

Hiking and Bird-Watching

The center of the northern area is filled with a lush rainforest around the Center Hills, noted for its biological diversity. This includes 132 tree species, 13 mammal species, and 117 species of birds including the native Montserrat oriole. The galliwasp lizard and the endangered mountain chicken, a large frog that is a local delicacy, are also found here. The area is host to the Center Hills Project, a British Darwin Initiative-funded project that does ecological assessments and informs the government and public about activities that may have an impact on the protected species here.

The trails leading up into the hills are somewhat challenging in places, so they are not for the casual walker. The Blackwood Allen Trail, for example, offers steep climbs and deep valleys, with a viewing platform to look out over the northern villages and the sea. Bird-watching is a favorite activity on the Oriole Walkway, deceptively named because it too has some steep areas. Among the birds seen on this trail are the rare forest thrush, the bridled quail dove, the mangrove cuckoo, the trembler, and the purple-throated carib. Other popular trails include the one running from Little Bay to Rendezvous

Legend of the Runaway Ghaut

The deep ravines, or ghauts as they are called in Montserrat, are marked by sparkling clear streams carrying fresh water from the

Sign of the Runaway Ghaut

hills down to the sea. Visitors are invited to taste the water, which is of astonishingly high quality, at an unassuming little tap at the side of the road near Runaway Ghaut. The legend goes that if you drink from this tap you will be drawn back to Montserrat time and again. Since it is not clearly marked, visitors should ask their guide to include it in their tour. Adjacent to the tap is a trail that provides a pleasant and easy walk into a lush picnic and strolling area.

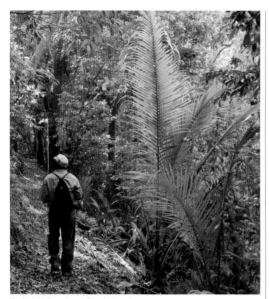
The Oriole Walkway, known for its bird-watching opportunities

Bay, because of its access to the island's only white-sand beach as well as some excellent snorkeling areas. The trail to The Cot winds through an old banana plantation up to an elevation of 1,000 ft (305 m) with commanding views of the sea and parts of the Exclusion Zone.

Another favorite activity is turtle-watching, since several species of sea turtles – including the green turtle, the hawksbill, and the loggerhead – can be found on the black-sand beaches. The **Montserrat National Trust** sponsors guided turtle treks during the peak months of August and September.

The trust has published detailed road and trail maps, which are available in the Oriole Complex on the Salem Main Road. They can also arrange guided hikes.

Diving and Snorkeling

Montserrat has always been known as a good diving area, with reefs teeming with coral, sponges, and tropical fish. However, many experts

believe that after the volcano calms down and the reefs off the southern shores are accessible, the diving opportunities will be spectacular because of the changes in the landscape from the volcanic activity. Right now, the main dive areas are in the northern part of the island, off the western coast and include Carr's Bay, Lime Kiln Bay, Woodlands Bay, Rendezvous Bay, and Bunkum Bay. Other diving spots, such as Little Redonda, the Pinnacles, and Yellow Hole, are on the northeastern side, but high

Montserrat's famous oriole

seas sometimes prohibit diving altogether. Dive operators include the **Green Monkey Inn and Dive Shop**, which provides simple accommodations, a beach bar, the full array of lessons and dives, sea scooters, and sea kayaks. They also organize deep-sea excursions and boat tours that allow visitors to get expansive views of the volcano-affected areas.

The other dive operator in Montserrat is **Scuba Montserrat**, located in Little Bay, which offers professional instruction and introductory lessons for beginners and children, and rental equipment. It also organizes fishing trips and boat tours to Plymouth.

Diving through underwater passages, off Montserrat

Where to Stay

Antigua

**DICKENSON BAY:
Anchorage Inn** $
Beach
Anchorage Road
Tel *268 462 4065*
🅦 antiguaanchorageinn.com
Located across the salt pond
from the beach, this small hotel
is a short walk to restaurants.

**DICKENSON BAY: The Villas
at Sunset Lane** $$
Villas
Sunset Lane, McKinnons
Tel *268 562 7791*
🅦 villasatsunsetlane.com
This hillside adults-only retreat
has views to Dickenson Bay.
Accommodations range from
regular and poolside suites to
two-bedroom villas.

**DICKENSON BAY:
Sandals Grande Antigua
Resort & Spa** $$$
Luxury
St. John's
Tel *268 484 0100*
🅦 sandals.com
All-inclusive resort on a stunning
beach. Accommodations range
from butler suites in the high-rise
to rondavels on the beach.

**ENGLISH HARBOUR:
The Admiral's Inn** $
Historic
Nelson's Dockyard
Tel *268 460 1027*
🅦 admiralsantigua.com
Beautiful restored inn adjacent to
the sail pillars, in a historic park.
Small but comfortable rooms.

**ENGLISH HARBOUR:
Curtain Bluff Resort & Spa** $$$
Luxury
Old Road, St. Mary's
Tel *888 289 9898*
🅦 curtainbluff.com
This all-inclusive resort is located
on a peninsula reaching out
into the sea, with beaches on
both sides. All rooms boast
spectacular sea views.

**ENGLISH HARBOUR:
Keyonna Beach** $$$
Beach Resort
Johnson's Point
Tel *268 562 2020*
🅦 keyonnabeach.com
A couples-only all-inclusive
hotel, Keyonna Beach is set on a
gorgeous white-sand beach. Four-
poster king beds and open-air
showers. Bali beds on the beach.

**ENGLISH HARBOUR: The Inn
at English Harbour** $$$
Beach Resort
Freeman's Bay
Tel *268 460 1014*
🅦 theinnantigua.com
Built in British colonial style, this
resort offers options ranging
from hillside rooms to rooms
with beachfront views.

**JOLLY HARBOUR:
Jolly Beach Resort & Spa** $
Beach Resort
Bolans Village
Tel *268 462 0061*
🅦 jollybeachresort.com
A large resort with a range of
activities for families and a choice
of all-inclusive or no-meal plans.

**JOLLY HARBOUR:
Cocobay Resort** $$
Beach Resort
Valley Church
Tel *268 562 2400*
🅦 cocobayresort.com
All-inclusive resort with a relaxed,
romantic atmosphere. Stay in a
cottage or a plantation home.

**JOLLY HARBOUR:
Hermitage Bay Resort** $$$
Luxury
Hermitage Bay
Tel *268 582 5500*
🅦 hermitagebay.com
An elegant all-inclusive resort
that has individual cottages with
verandas facing the sea. Some
cottages are right on the beach.

DK Choice

**LONG BAY: Nonsuch
Bay Resort** $$
Beach Resort
Hughes Point, St. Phillips
Tel *268 562 8000*
🅦 nonsuchbayresort.com
This resort is a great choice
for those who love sailing.
Accommodations are dotted
around the bay, where breezes
are ideal for learning to sail or
taking part in local regattas.
The Bay Restaurant offers a
romantic evening in a setting
overlooking the water. There is
also a good Kids' Club program.

**LONG BAY: Verandah Resort
& Spa** $$$
Beach Resort
Indian Town Road, St. Phillips
Tel *800 858 4618*
🅦 verandahresortandspa.com
This self-contained, eco-friendly,
all-inclusive resort on the

Sandals tower and pool at the Sandals Grande
Antigua Resort & Spa, Dickenson Bay, Antigua

northeast coast is adjacent to
Devil's Bridge. The Kids' Club
features a splash pool.

Barbuda

**CODRINGTON: Lighthouse
Bay Resort Hotel** $$$
Luxury
Codrington
Tel *888 214 8552 or 877 766 6718*
🅦 lighthousebayresort.com
A small, luxurious resort wedged
between the Codrington Lagoon
and the Caribbean. Amazing
beach and gorgeous suites.

Montserrat

ST. PETERS: Gingerbread Hill $
Mountain Retreat
St. Peters
Tel *664 491 5812*
🅦 volcano-island.com
A relaxed, family-run complex
of villas and rooms with an
emphasis on planning eco-
adventures for guests.

**SWEENEY'S: Tropical
Mansion Suites** $
Boutique
Sweeney's
Tel *664 491 8767*
🅦 tropicalmansion.com
This is the only hotel currently
operating on the island, in the
main town area. Its amenities
include a pleasant pool.

Where to Eat and Drink

Antigua

DK Choice

EAST END: The Bay at Nonsuch $$$
Caribbean
Hughes Point, Freetown
Tel *268 562 8000*
Amazing cuisine from the award-winning chef Mitchell Husbands, with Asian and island accents. The menu features excellent seafood, including soft-shelled crab, conch, and lobster, as well as steak, pork, and chicken entrées. Open-air setting overlooking the water.

ENGLISH HARBOUR: Cloggy's Café $$
International
Antigua Yacht Club Marina
Tel *268 460 6910* **Closed** *Mon*
Popular eatery, with views of yachts, Cloggy's serves pasta, burgers, skewers, and seafood. Wednesday is BBQ and dance day.

ENGLISH HARBOUR: OJ's Beach Bar & Restaurant $$
Caribbean
Crabbe Hill Beach
Tel *268 460 0184*
Beach restaurant offering seafood, as well as burgers, ribs, and steaks. Try the amazing fresh red snapper and lobster salad.

ENGLISH HARBOUR: Ristorante Paparazzi $$
Italian
The Slipway
Tel *268 562 8136* **Closed** *Mon*
Pasta and wood-oven pizzas, plus Angus tenderloin and grilled lobster, all served in a waterside setting. Delivery also available.

JOLLY HARBOUR: Al Porto Italian Restaurant $$
Italian
Super Yacht Terminal
Tel *268 562 7848*
Open-deck dining on the water, with a good selection of pastas and pizzas. Tuesday is two-for-one pizza night and Thursday is all-you-can-eat pasta.

JOLLY HARBOUR: Carmichael's $$$
Caribbean/Fusion
Sugar Ridge Resort
Tel *268 562 7700* **Closed** *Sun*
Elegant restaurant with scenic views to the Caribbean and an infinity pool from next to the bar. Delicious lobster, steaks, lamb, and seafood. Fixed-price menu.

JOLLY HARBOUR: Sheer Rocks $$$
Mediterranean
Cocobay Resort, St. Mary's
Tel *268 464 5283* **Closed** *Tue & Sun*
Open-air restaurant sitting on a bluff overlooking the sea, with unique entrées featuring unusual combinations. There is also a plunge pool with daybeds for sunset watching.

NORTH END: Le Bistro $$$
French
Hodges Bay
Tel *268 462 3881* **Closed** *Mon*
A long-time favorite because of the excellent service and food, with the lobster dishes especially popular. Good range of French wines and champagnes.

NORTH END: The Tides Restaurant $$$
Caribbean/Fusion
Dutchman's Bay, Coolidge
Tel *268 462 8433*
This seaside restaurant offers a mix of Caribbean, Mediterranean, and Asian flavors. Pool area with a grill; Wine Night on Fridays and buffet lunch on Sundays.

ST. JOHN'S: Big Banana Pizzas in Paradise $
American
Redcliffe Quay
Tel *268 480 6985* **Closed** *Sun*
Enjoy pizzas, burgers, and more at this casual eatery in the Redcliffe Quay. Eat inside or out, under a tree. Also has a café at the airport.

ST. JOHN'S: Hemingway's Caribbean Café $$
Caribbean
Lower St. Mary's Street
Tel *268 462 2763*
A longtime downtown favorite, with a terrace on the second story overlooking Heritage Quay. Great seafood, salads, and lighter fare, plus Caribbean entrées.

Price Guide
Prices are for a two-course meal for one, including tax and service charges and half a bottle of wine.

$	up to $40
$$	$40–60
$$$	over $60

Barbuda

BARBUDA: Uncle Roddy's Beach Bar & Grill $$
West Indian
Ocean Drive, Coral Group Bay
Tel *268 785 3268* **Closed** *Sun*
This relaxed beach bar serves hearty grilled entrées with typical Caribbean side dishes in a great beach setting. Lunch and dinner. By reservation only.

Montserrat

MONTSERRAT: Olveston House $$
English/Caribbean
Olveston
Tel *664 491 5210*
Considered one of the best eateries on the island, Olveston House serves basic hearty food. BBQ buffet on Wednesday, pub nights on Fridays, and a roast every Sunday.

MONTSERRAT: Ziggy's Restaurant $$
Caribbean
Mahogany Lane, Woodlands
Tel *664 491 8282*
Fine dining in a remote setting carved out of the rainforest. Seafood, steaks, and more feature on a daily changing menu. Dinner only, and reservations are required.

Relaxing outdoor seating area at The Bay at Nonsuch, East End, Antigua

Practical Information

Antigua, Barbuda, and Montserrat, at the farthest eastern edge of the Leeward Islands, offer visitors the perfect tropical vacation with a British accent. Antigua is the most cosmopolitan, with the major transportation hub of V.C. Bird International Airport, and the shopping and historic delights of St. John's. Barbuda is ideal for getting away from the world, and visitors will find that there are few services other than tours of the island. Apart from the ruined city, Plymouth, the island of Montserrat also has a busy commercial center on the non-volcanic side of the island, with new shops and attractions being added continuously.

Visitors alighting at V.C. Bird International Airport, Antigua

When to Go

While Antigua, Barbuda, and Montserrat are basically warm year round, the heat can get sticky from June to October, which is also the hurricane season. Peak times for visitors to Antigua other than the winter holidays are late April (Sailing Week), August (Carnival), and November (Independence Day); March (St. Patrick's Day – the only one on the islands) in Barbuda; May (Caribana); and July (Calabash) in Montserrat.

Getting There

V.C. Bird International Airport (ANU) in Antigua is served by major airlines such as **British Airways**, **Air Canada**, **Delta**, **United Airlines**, **US Airways**, **American Eagle**, and **Virgin Atlantic** as well as regional airlines such as **LIAT** and **Caribbean Airlines**. The smaller regional airlines, **Winair** and **Montserrat Airways**, have flights from Antigua to Barbuda and Montserrat.

Barbuda and Antigua are also linked by a **Barbuda Express Ltd.** daily ferry. **Caribbean Helicopters** operates from Antigua to Montserrat.

Documentation

Travelers are required to have a valid passport to enter Antigua, Barbuda, and Montserrat. Visitors also need to have return tickets and confirmed accommodations. Visas are not required for US, some European, and certain other countries. Check with the embassies for details.

Visitor Information

For Antigua and Barbuda, visitors can contact the tourism offices located in the US, Canada, and the UK. The **Antigua and Barbuda Ministry of Tourism** also operates an information kiosk at Heritage Quay in downtown St. John's and has information available at the V.C. Bird International Airport. The Montserrat Tourist Board *(see p323)* has its main office at Farara Plaza in Brades, as well as offices in London. Useful information for visitors is also available at the island's Gerald's Airport.

Health and Security

The primary health facility for Antigua and Barbuda is **Holberton Hospital**, located in St. John's. In Montserrat, **Glendon Hospital** offers emergency services to both locals as well as visitors.

While not idyllically crime-free, these islands are relatively safe for visitors. However, it is advisable to take the normal precautions of keeping valuables guarded, sticking to well-populated areas, and not roaming around alone at night.

Banking and Currency

The currency for all three islands is the East Caribbean (EC) dollar. Antigua has a number of banks and cash can be obtained (as EC dollars) at most ATMs. Credit cards are accepted in Antigua and many vendors also accept US dollars (but not euros or British pounds). In Barbuda and Montserrat, credit cards are not as commonly accepted and vendors prefer EC dollars.

Communications

In Antigua and Barbuda, **Cable & Wireless** and **Digicel** offer inexpensive phones with prepaid minutes and local SIM cards. Cable & Wireless also provides cell services in Montserrat. Some US cell phone services such as Cingular work on Antigua. Montserrat and Antigua have Internet cafés and most hotels in Antigua offer high-speed Internet connections.

Transport

Car rentals on Antigua and Montserrat are plentiful and easy to arrange either in advance or at the airport but in Barbuda,

Entrance of a bank building in Brades, Montserrat

there are no cars for hire. **AVIS** and **Hertz Rent-A-Car** in Antigua, and **Neville Bradshaw Agencies** and **Equipment & Supplies Ltd.** in Montserrat are popular car rental agencies. In Antigua, vans and minibuses are available. The public bus system runs on an unscheduled basis. In Barbuda, a popular way to get around this flat island is by bike and rentals can be arranged. Taxi drivers on the islands double as tour guides. In Montserrat, drivers can also arrange for a guided trip into the Exclusion Zone if the volcano is not threatening.

Shopping

Downtown St. John's in Antigua is a shoppers' delight. Activity centers around the dock area, specifically Heritage Quay and Redcliffe Quay duty-free areas and the adjacent Vendor's Mall. There are also clothing boutiques, bookstores, and shoe stores on St. Mary's Street. For authentic Antiguan food, try the Farmer's Market complex on Market Street. Other supermarkets include the Epicurean in Woods

Popular shopping area of Heritage Quay in St. John's, Antigua

Mall and Jolly Harbour. Barbuda does not have much by way of shopping. Montserrat has a few stores in the Brades area. For souvenirs, visit the Oriole Gift Shop in the Montserrat National Trust complex or the Montserrat Arts and Crafts Association shop in Brades.

Language

English is the official language spoken on Antigua, Barbuda, and Montserrat.

Electricity

The electricity is mainly 220 volts though some hotels have 110 volts as well.

Time

The islands are on Atlantic Standard Time, 1 hour ahead of US Eastern Standard Time.

Getting Married

Antigua has emerged as a major destination for couples looking to tie the knot, with several incredibly romantic settings and no residency requirement. The couple need to apply for a license at the **Ministry of Legal Affairs**, show their passports and other appropriate documents (divorce papers or death certificate of spouse), and pay the fees. Many of the hotels also offer wedding coordinators who can assist in getting the necessary documents. In Montserrat, the residency requirement is 3 days. The couple can apply for a marriage license at the **Department of Administration** in Brades.

DIRECTORY

Getting There

Air Canada
W aircanada.com

American Eagle
W aa.com

Barbuda Express Ltd.
Tel 268 560 7989.
W antiguaferries.com

British Airways
W ba.com

Caribbean Airlines
Tel 268 480 2900.
W caribbean-airlines.com

Caribbean Helicopters
Tel 268 460 5900.
W caribbeanhelicopters.com

Delta
W delta.com

LIAT
W liatairline.com

Montserrat Airways
Tel 664 491 3434.
W flymontserrat.com

United Airlines
W united.com

US Airways
W usairways.com

Virgin Atlantic
W virgin-atlantic.com

Winair
W fly-winair.com

Visitor Information

Antigua and Barbuda Ministry of Tourism
Tel 268 462 0480 (Antigua), 305 381 6762 (USA), 01245 707 471 (UK), 416 961 3085 (Canada). W antigua-barbuda.org

Health and Security

Glendon Hospital
St. John's, Montserrat.
Tel 664 491 2552.

Holberton Hospital
Queen Elizabeth Highway, St. John's, Antigua.
Tel 268 462 0251.

Communications

Cable & Wireless
W time4lime.com

Digicel
Tel 268 480 2050.
W digicelantiguaandbarbuda.com

Transport

AVIS
V.C. Bird International Airport, St. John's, Antigua.
Tel 268 462 2840.
W avisantigua.com

Equipment & Supplies Ltd.

Olveston, Montserrat.
Tel 664 491 2402.

Hertz Rent-A-Car
Airport Road, St. John's, Antigua.
Tel 268 481 4455.

Neville Bradshaw Agencies
Olveston, Montserrat
Tel 664 491 5270.

Getting Married

Department of Administration
Brades, Montserrat.
Tel 664 491 2365.

Ministry of Legal Affairs
Queen Elizabeth Highway, St. John's, Antigua.

A PORTRAIT OF THE FRENCH ANTILLES

St. Barthélemy, Guadeloupe, and Martinique stand out from other Caribbean isles due to their unapologetic Frenchness. While history and geography have left their marks, France influences everything from language to politics and culture. Citizens carry French passports, buy French goods, and enjoy a French lifestyle.

St. Barthélemy (often called St. Barths or St. Bart) was an elite playground for the rich, and although facilities and services are first-class, the prices are still shockingly high. Guadeloupe, 155 miles (250 km) south, though comparatively larger in area is significantly different, while Martinique, about 100 miles (160 km) to the south of Guadeloupe, is just as sophisticated, yet less opulent than St. Barths.

History

In the 15th century, when Columbus and the early explorers encountered the South American Arawak inhabitants, they thought that these islands were inhospitable and of little commercial value. This way of thinking changed, however, when they recognized the favourable agricultural conditions here. Over the next decades,

as economic growth soared, several colonial powers fought with each other to establish control of the islands, and African slaves were imported to work the fields. France gained, lost and regained control of St. Barths, Guadeloupe, and Martinique as the Netherlands, England, and Sweden battled for dominance. Pirates and government-sponsored privateers contributed by attacking merchant ships. By 1794, as a result of the French Revolution, slavery was declared illegal, and many wealthy land owners were guillotined. Six years later, Napoléon Bonaparte reversed the law, but his decision was opposed by abolitionists and defeated by the French parliament in 1848 due to the influence of leaders such as Victor Schoelcher. In 1946, Guadeloupe, Martinique, St. Martin, and St. Barths became French overseas departments.

Hiking through the rainforest at the base of La Soufrière volcano, Guadeloupe

Musée Schoelcher, Guadeloupe, dedicated to the Parisian instrumental in abolition of slavery

the population speaks French, many English-speaking visitors have difficulty communicating, especially in small towns.

Lifestyle and Culture

In the French Antilles, there is no occasion that does not call for good food, rum, music, and dance. Music and dance are as important as cooking, and all these pleasures feature during Carnival. Parades, fireworks, concerts, and non-stop street parties run continuously. Zouk is the current rhythm of choice, but locals are just as adroit with the waltz, mazurka, and beguine. Zouk, French Creole for party, was started in the 1980s by Jacob Desvarieux and Pierre Eduard Decimus from Guadeloupe who founded the band Kassav', featuring well-known singer Jocelyn Beroard.

The French Antilles have also produced many world-class writers such as the Martinique-born author and politician Aimé Césaire (1913–2008), the Guadeloupe-born Nobel Laureate, Lexis Léger, known as Saint-John Perse (1887–1975), and the novelist Maryse Condé (b.1934).

Economy

Tourism is the mainstay of St. Barths' healthy economy and a majority of the population speaks English as well as other languages. Guadeloupe's economy is still based on agriculture, with about 25 percent of land under cultivation. The chief exports include sugar, rum, bananas, coffee, andcocoa. About 75 percent of the tradeis with France, which is one of the reasons why most residents speak only French or French Créole. However, since the 1980s, Guade-loupe has seen a decline in revenue from the export of agricultural products and depends on France for financial aid. Marti-nique is also dependent on France for economic shortfalls from exports, which include refined petroleum products, rum, sugarcane, and bananas. About 6 percent of the GDP comes from agriculture. Tourism is gaining importance here, however, since

Men playing drums on the streets at the Carnival held during Lent in Martinique

Exploring St. Barthélemy

With a distinct French flavor, St. Barths is one of the most sophisticated and expensive of the Caribbean islands. For a dry outcrop, it has a surprisingly dramatic and attractive terrain, ranging from rocky peaks to picturesque coves and excellent white-sand beaches. Trendy upscale boutiques line the streets of Gustavia, the main harbor town, while the most luxurious resorts and villas are scattered around the island. The adventurous can hike down to the beaches to escape from the crowds. With French chefs and a good supply of produce via St. Martin, the island is also known for its great cuisine.

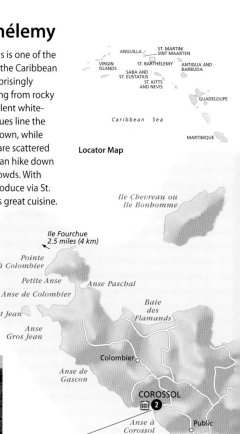

Locator Map

Key

═══ Minor road

- - - Ferry route

△ Peak

Spectacular view from the hike to Anse de Colombier

Corossol
This small town is perhaps the last remaining traditional Barthian village. Its brown sand beaches are shaded by latanier palms.

Gustavia
The capital of the island, Gustavia is the most developed town and has some excellent Swedish-style architecture.

Sights at a Glance

❶ Gustavia

❷ Corossol

❸ St-Jean

❹ East End

❺ Beaches of St. Barthélemy

0 kilometers 1

0 miles 1

The little village of Flamands overlooking the Baie des Flamands

Eden Rock Hotel
This hotel was St. Barths' first hotel and has fabulous views and lovely cottages.

4 EAST END

Anse de Grande Saline
This area is known for its large salt pond, which is harvested for salt. The beach here is one of the best in the Caribbean.

Getting Around

The only airport on this island, Aeroport Gustave III, also has the second shortest runway in the world, after Saba. Only small aircraft can land here. There are infrequent ferries from Gustavia to St. Martin, only 15 miles (24 km) to the northeast, but the sea can be a bit rough. Most of the hotels in St. Barths offer a pick-up and drop service on arrival and departure. Although hiring a car can be quite expensive, most visitors opt for this as St. Barths has few taxis and no buses or other public transport.

For additional map symbols see back flap

Red-roofed buildings overlooking Gustavia's harbor

● Gustavia

W coast of St. Barthélemy.
▨ 3,500. ⬚ ⬚ ⬚ Quai General
de Gaulle, 590 278 727. ⬚
⬚ St. Barths Music Festival (Jan).
w stbarthsmusicfestival.org

Gustavia is one of the prettiest
harbor towns in the Caribbean.
Its steep bay walls tumble to a
rectangular waterfront, with
attractive red-roofed buildings
overlooking the harbor from
three sides. Much of the waterfront itself is a boardwalk, where
tenders moor at the restaurants
and bars, which gives the bay a
very pleasant ambience. At
Christmas and New Year,
Gustavia harbor is one of the
most fashionable places in the
world. Luxury yachts anchor
shoulder to shoulder, sterns to
the boardwalk, hosting parties
for celebrities.

Onshore, the streets are steep
and narrow but full of character.
There is often a lively buzz around
the many bars and shops, particularly on the boardwalk. The
streetfronts are lined with serious
names in the world of fashion,
Armani, Dolce & Gabbana, and
Bulgari *(see pp338–9)*. On the
waterfront at the head of the
bay is the Anglican church and
behind it the Catholic church.
Above them, the Swedish clock
tower can be seen from several
points around the harbor. It
can be recognized by its small
triangular roof.

At the far point of the bay's
outer arm, beneath the fort, are
two notable buildings. The Mairie
de St. Barth (town hall) is a
modern version of the mayoral
buildings that are seen all over
France and its dominions.
Adjacent to it and housed in the
Wall House, an old stone Swedish
warehouse, is the **Wall House
Museum**. This displays an eclectic
series of artifacts, photographs,
and paintings illuminating
island's history, including the
Swedish period. The exhibits
include models of traditional St.
Barthian houses (low buildings
that face away from the prevail-
ing wind), household items, and
articles woven from the local
latanier palm.

The diminutive Swedish clock tower with its
distinct red roof, Gustavia

Just a few elements of Swedish
heritage remain in the small
town, which took its name from
King Gustav III, the Swedish
ruler at the time the island
became Swedish. Only a
handful of the pretty stone
buildings date from this era,
as sadly most were destroyed in
a devastating hurricane and fire
in 1850. However, several streets
carry Swedish names, including
Prinsgatan and Kungsgatan.

🏛 **Wall House Museum**
La Pointe, Gustavia Harbor. **Tel** 590
297 155. **Open** 8:30am–noon & 2:30–
6pm Mon–Fri, 9–11am & 2:30–6pm
Sat. 🅿 **w** st-barths.com/museum

Swedish Heritage
in St. Barths

The island of St. Barths
was Swedish for a century.
In the late 1700s, King
Gustav III of Sweden decided
to capitalize on the growing
global seaborne trade and
looked for an outpost in the
Caribbean. A deal was struck
with France and the island
was loaned to Sweden in
return for a French presence
in Gothenburg and trading
rights in the Baltics. For a
while, as a free port (open to ships of any nationality without tax),
St. Barths became a very successful entrepôt and the population
rocketed. In the mid-1800s, the trade tailed off and the island
gradually went into a decline. Eventually, in 1878 King Oskar II of
Sweden put nationality to a referendum and the islanders voted
to return to France. There is not a lot of evidence of Swedish
interest left in St. Barths, beyond the name of the capital, several
street names, and some buildings.

❷ Corossol

1 mile (2 km) N of Gustavia.

The pretty village of Corossol, situated on a protected bay to the north of Gustavia, is one of the distinctly local areas of St. Barths. Corossol is home to many "Barthéleminois" families and has a slightly more local character. It is an excellent destination for those who wish to experience some of the traditional culture of St. Barths, from fishermen mending their nets on the beach to villagers weaving intricate straw baskets. On special occasions, the local women don traditional costumes and bonnets. At sunset, head to Corossol Beach, just off the main road, to take a few atmospheric pictures.

❸ St-Jean

1 mile (2 km) E of Gustavia.
 500.

The second and only other sizable town in St. Barths, St-Jean sits on the island's north shore on Baie de St-Jean, just over the hill from Gustavia, overlooking a spectacular blue bay. The small airport is set at one end, on the aptly named Plaine de la Tourmente (Plain of Torment), a very difficult runway to land on, and there are several hotels and bars along the beach, the most fashionable on the island. At the center of the beach stands the iconic Eden Rock Hotel *(see p340)*, set on its own promontory. Behind the beach is the small town, which has two rows of shops and several restaurants and bars. Roads lead inland past a couple of hotels to many of St. Barths' numerous villas.

❹ East End

2 miles (3 km) E of Gustavia.

The East End is the least developed area of St. Barths. Beyond St-Jean, the settlements of Lorient, Grand Cul-de-Sac, and Petit Cul-de-Sac along the north coast are home to several

luxurious resorts. The south of the island, however, is largely untouched by progress. Here, a few of the remaining traditional St. Barthian houses, often a series of *cases* or small square buildings with tin roofs, can still be seen.

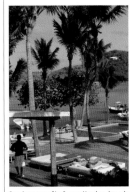

Beach terrace of Le Sereno Hotel on Anse de Grand Cul-de-Sac

❺ Beaches of St. Barthélemy

Cut into the extremely rough and steep land along the south coast are two of St. Barths' remote beachs. The first is the unrivalled Anse de Grande

Saline, considered one of the best on the island. Just inland, behind the beach is a large salt pond, which was earlier used for salt harvesting. Stilts and other waterbirds can be found at the pond.

Next beach in line, accessed only by a very steep road, is the Anse du Gouverneur, another superb stretch of sand hemmed in by high cliffs. Like Anse de Grande Saline, it is undeveloped and has a good view of other islands to the south.

While most beaches on St. Barths are easily accessible, the white-sand **Anse de Colombier** in the northwest can only be approached by sea or by a steep hiking path overland. This remote strip of sand is a favorite getaway for St. Barthians on holidays and special occasions. The view from Colombier stretches to the northwest, towards the offshore island of Ile Fourchue, which has a good beach in a protected cove. Both these beaches can be reached on a day-sail with one of the watersports companies *(see p337)*. In true St. Barths' style, it is even possible to arrange a gourmet picnic, with foie gras, and chilled champagne on the sand.

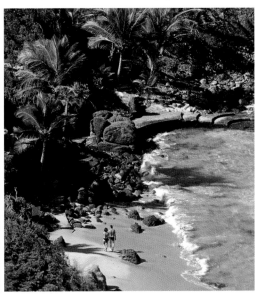

Secluded coves of the scenic Anse de Colombier

Outdoor Activities and Specialized Holidays

For a small island, St. Barths boasts a surprising array of day activities. In keeping with the style of the island, there are even lunchtime fashion shows here. Beaches are great, with good snorkeling and diving spots, and a range of watersports are on offer. Several companies organize top-notch sailing trips. On land there are fewer activities, but some hotels have tennis courts and horse-riding is exhilarating on the rough terrain. Two spas cater to visitors who want to unwind here.

The remote and less-crowded Anse du Gouverneur

Beaches

Set in extremely attractive, often steep-sided bays, the beaches on St. Barths have bright white and soft sand that descends gently into shallow, often startlingly blue water. Some beaches have activities such as watersports, while others are remote and undeveloped, offering a quiet escape. Going topless is the norm on St. Barths beaches, and on the south coast, Anse de Grande Saline and Anse du Gouverneur also have areas for naturists.

St-Jean is the most popular beach. There are a handful of hotels and beach bars such as the famous Nikki Beach (see p341) with its wispy white drapes and bamboo furniture. At Eden Rock, the Sand Bar at Eden Rock Hotel (see p340) is stylish too. La Plage in Tom Beach Hotel is less ostentatious, but often lively.

Anse de Grand Cul-de-Sac is set on a shallow lagoon, making it popular with families and the islanders at the weekends. It is also a favorite spot for watersports with excellent wind and kite-surfing. Cocoloba here has a sweeping view over the lagoon. There is passable sand at Shell Beach outside Gustavia, which has a good beach bar, Do Brasil, a classic Caribbean feel with great music and a fantastic sunset view.

Less-crowded beaches can be found at Flamands, a great stretch of sand with a couple of hotels, and the quieter Lorient. The Le Manapany hotel (see p340) at Flamands has a very attractive setting and offers beachfront rooms and suites.

Three of the best beaches on St. Barths have little in the way of amenities, making them ideal for beach-goers in search of complete peace and quiet.

Of these, Anse de Grande Saline and Anse du Gouverneur are relatively secluded and have no facilities, though there are restaurants within walking distance of Salines. The third, Anse de Colombier, a lovely stretch of sand on the northwestern coast, can only be reached by boat or on foot.

Deep-Sea Fishing

The Atlantic waters to the east of St. Barths offer fairly good fishing. Fish that ply the deep include wahoo, tuna, marlin, and kingfish. Day- and half-day trips can be arranged through watersports companies such as **Ocean Must Marina** and **Nautica FWI**.

Boat Trips

St. Barths offers a good variety of offshore day trips by motor yacht and sailing yacht, and these are often the highlights of a holiday here. Trips take visitors to the remoter beaches, particularly Anse de Colombier in the northwest, where there is good snorkeling, but they also head to the smaller islands between St. Barths and St. Martin/Sint Maarten. The closest is Ile Fourchue, which has a protected beach without facilities, but there are also two small islands just off St. Martin/Sint Maarten itself – Pinel and Tintamarre, both with excellent beaches and snorkeling. Some trips also go to Anguilla, 20 miles (32 km) to the northeast. These trips are generally arranged by the watersports agencies based in Gustavia,

The grand Eden Rock Hotel on the shore of Baie de St-Jean

Yachts anchored in Gustavia harbor

including **Jicky Marine Service** and **Master Ski Pilou**, both of whom also offer Jet Ski rides and waterskiing trips.

Hiking

There are hiking paths in the northwest of St. Barths, leading down to Anse de Colombier, and around Toiny in the far east of the island, from where the views are spectacular. There are some (self-guided) hikes around Gustavia. Leaflets are available at the tourist office on the waterfront.

Visitors hiking to Anse de Colombier

Horse-Riding

Galop des Iles is based at Ranch des Flamands, high above the coast between Anse des Cayes and Flamands in northwestern St. Barths. The stable offers rides through the rough and rocky terrain in this area and along the sand and waves of Anse des Flamands Beach.

Scuba Diving and Snorkeling

There are many underwater reefs in several of the bays, but the best area is in the northwest of St. Barths, in Petite Anse and Colombier. Scuba dive companies such as **Plongée Caraibes**, **St. Barth's Plongee**, **Carib Waterplay**, **Splash**, and **Coté Mer** offer equipment and trips. There are several diving areas; most sites are in the west, protected from Atlantic waves, and off the islands towards St. Martin/Sint Maarten. There is also a marine reserve with sections in the west off Gustavia and in the east toward the Atlantic.

Spas

For an island as luxurious as St. Barths, there are surprisingly few spas. Hotel Guanahani and Spa *(see p340)* has six treatment rooms. In Flamands, Hotel Saint-Barth Isle de France has two treatment rooms. Both spas offer massages and beauty treatments and are also open to non-guests. There are many independent practitioners in the island's main towns that can be contacted through the tourism office in Gustavia.

Kitesurfing at Anse de Grand Cul-de-Sac

Watersports

Hotels generally have watersports equipment to offer their guests but visitors staying in villas depend on outside operators for equipment. These are on beaches such as St-Jean and Grand Cul-de-Sac, which is known for its windsurfing and kitesurfing. The main operators are **Wind Wave Power**, **Hookipa Surf Shop**, **Totem Surf Shop**, and **Kitesurf**.

DIRECTORY

Deep-Sea Fishing

Nautica FWI
Gustavia.
Tel 590 275 650.

Ocean Must Marina
Gustavia.
Tel 590 276 225.

Boat Trips

Jicky Marine Service
Gustavia.
Tel 590 277 034.

Master Ski Pilou
Tel 690 613 707.

Horse-Riding

Galop des Iles
Ranch des Flamands.
Tel 690 398 701.

Scuba Diving and Snorkeling

Carib Waterplay
St-Jean. **Tel** 690 618 081.

Coté Mer
Tel 690 565 671.

Plongée Caraibes
Gustavia.
Tel 590 277 034/ 690 546 614.

Splash
Tel 690 569 024.

St. Barth's Plongee
Gustavia.
Tel 690 419 666.

Watersports

Hookipa Surf Shop
Tel 590 277 131.

Kitesurf
Grand Cul-de-Sac.
Tel 690 692 690.

Totem Surf Shop
Tel 590 277 798.

Wind Wave Power
St-Jean Beach.
Tel 590 278 257.

Shopping in St. Barthélemy

The best place in the Caribbean for luxury tax-free shopping, St. Barths has plenty of options and caters to the whims of the island's wealthy and elegant clientele. It boasts the crème de la crème of international designer labels, with designer clothes well represented, as well as jewelry, watches, and other luxury items, including cigars and excellent wines. The main shopping areas are in Gustavia, on Rue de la République and Rue du Bord de Mer, and St-Jean.

Designer boutiques on Rue de la République, Gustavia

Clothes and Accessories

Many major luxury fashion outlets can be found in St. Barths, selling prêt-à-porter clothing, shoes, lingerie, jewelry, perfumes, and leather goods. Labels include Cartier, Hermès, Armani, La Perla, Versace, Ralph Lauren, and even Petit Bateau for children.

Haute-couture shops are clear indicators of the passion for fashion in Gustavia. There is even a shop called Vintage that sells imported contemporary as well as vintage clothing.

Le Carré d'Or, a shopping mall on Rue de la République, has outlets of several leading fashion brands. It is also a good place to linger as there is a restaurant, Caviar Island, serving tapas-sized portions of caviar and foie gras.

Pati de St. Barth, a French designer, artist, and resident of St. Barths since the 1980s, has two boutiques here and her own line of tropical clothing for men, women, and children.

Leatherware, by international labels such as Louis Vuitton and Hermès, includes bags and shoes. Local St. Barth collections, including Kokon and Elysées Caraïbes, are also available.

Watchmakers and jewelry shops, which carry some of the leading brands in the world, are mainly located in Gustavia, close to the waterfront.

Designer jewelry can be found at Cartier, Chopard, and Donna del Sol in the Carré d'Or or at Bulgari and Louis Vuitton in Gustavia's Cour Vendôme mall.

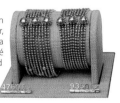

Other Luxury Products

In addition to haute couture and jewelry, St. Barths is a treasure trove for furniture, antiques, and other luxury goods that are sought after by the island's wealthy villa-owners and visitors on holiday. Patisseries and delicatessens offer a marvelous range of the finest food, including foie gras and French cheese and wine.

Le Cellier du Gouverneur Gustavia is a leading liquor shop selling alcohol and wine from all over the world. Wines are imported young so they suffer less damage on the ocean crossing.

Ligne de St. Barth, based in Lorient and Gustavia, makes its own line of perfumes as well as face and body care products. Most of the leading brands are also available at this and the other cosmetics outlets on the island.

Cigars from Central America and around the Caribbean, including the world-renowned ones from Cuba, are on sale in St. Barths.

Balinese Furniture is much in demand among wealthy house-owners. Gustavia's Tek and The House, where many famous French designers have worked, specializes in Oriental tropical furniture.

Local Shopping

Many artists and some skilled craftsmen are based here, and their creations can make for great souvenirs. These can be found in the numerous art galleries and studios around the island and include locally-made jewelry, paintings, and traditional woven straw work.

T-shirts with the popular "St. Barth French West Indies" logo designed by Pati de St. Barth are available at Villa Créole, a small shopping mall in the village of St-Jean.

Art galleries such as the Galerie Bagdad and Pipiri Fine Art Gallery in Gustavia showcase the paintings and sculptures of the island's several talented artists.

Straw work made by the islanders can be found in Corossol. The straw of the latanier palm is used to weave hats and bags. Some artisans also make jewelry from shells and corals; however, St. Barths does not have as many handicrafts on sale as the other Caribbean islands.

Hat

Purse

Basket

Where to Stay

FLAMANDS: Auberge de Terre-Neuve $
Modern
Route de Flamands, 97133
Tel *590 27 75 32*
Ⓦ auberge-de-terre-neuve.com
A small family-run inn offering cottages with sea or garden views. Rental car included in rate.

FLAMANDS: Hotel Baie des Anges $$
Beach Resort
Flamands, 97098
Tel *590 27 63 61*
Ⓦ hotel-baie-des-anges.com
This relaxed resort comprising two-bedroom beachfront rooms as well as sea-view rooms in the main house. Excellent restaurant.

FLAMANDS: Le Manapany $$$
Beach Resort
Anse des Cayes, 97098
Tel *590 27 66 55*
Ⓦ lemanapany.com
Chic decor and great service are the highlights of this luxe resort. Rooms and suites on the beach and along the hillside.

FLAMANDS: Taiwana Hotel $$$
Beach Resort
Baie des Flamands, 97133
Tel *590 29 80 08*
Ⓦ hoteltaiwana.com
This exclusive, stylish beach resort offers one-, two-, and three-bedroom suites. Some come with private pools, while others have gardens and great views.

GRAND CUL-DE-SAC: Hostellerie de Trois Forces $$
Inn
Vitet, 97133
Tel *590 27 61 25*
Ⓦ 3forces.net
High above Cul-de-Sac is this welcoming inn, with unique cottages named for the different signs of the zodiac.

GRAND CUL-DE-SAC: Hotel Guanahani & Spa $$$
Beach Resort
Grand Cul-de-Sac, 97133
Tel *590 27 66 60*
Ⓦ leguanahani.com
Relaxed West Indian luxury on the Atlantic side, with a good beach along the lagoon. Has an excellent Clarins Spa.

GRAND CUL-DE-SAC: Hotel Les Ondines $$$
Beach Resort
Grand Cul-de-Sac, 97133
Tel *590 27 69 64*
Ⓦ stbarth-lesondineshotel.com
Charming small hotel on a great beach, with one- and two-room suites including kitchenettes and patios. Also offers a hillside villa.

DK Choice

GRAND CUL-DE-SAC: Hotel Le Toiny $$$
Luxury
Anse de Toiny, 97133
Tel *590 27 88 88*
Ⓦ letoiny.com
High on a bluff overlooking the Caribbean sits this elegant small hotel, prized by celebrities seeking privacy. The beach below is noted for snorkeling and surfing. Bungalows house luxurious suites, with private pools, gardens, and gorgeous views. The on-site restaurant Le Gaïac is one of the finest on the island.

GUSTAVIA: Sunset Hotel $
Boutique
Rue de la Republique, 97133
Tel *590 27 77 21*
Ⓦ st-barths.com/sunset-hotel
Simple accommodations in the heart of Gustavia, good for business travelers. Rooms on the inside are quieter, while the outer ones have good views.

GUSTAVIA: Hotel Carl Gustaf $$$
Luxury
Rue des Normands, 97099
Tel *590 29 79 00*
Ⓦ hotelcarlgustaf.com
A sophisticated luxury hotel and spa overlooking the harbor. All suites have private plunge pools.

LORIENT: Hotel Les Mouettes $$
Boutique
Quartier Lorient, 97133
Tel *590 27 77 91*
Ⓦ lesmouetteshotel.com
Charming cottages set right on the beach or on the hill, with kitchenettes and patios facing the sea.

POINTE MILOU: Christopher Hotel $$$
Boutique
Pointe Milou, 97133
Tel *590 27 63 63*
Ⓦ hotelchristopher.com
Graceful contemporary hotel with many refurbished rooms. The Panoramic Ocean Suites have living rooms with two sofa beds – a great choice for families.

ST-JEAN: Hotel Le Village St. Barth $$
Boutique
Colline de St Jean, 97133
Tel *590 27 61 39*
Ⓦ villagestjeanhotel.com
On the hill above the village, this four-star hotel offers rooms, suites, family cottages, and two villas, all well equipped.

ST-JEAN: Les P'tits Julie $$
Modern
St-Jean, 97133
Tel *590 61 20 02*
Ⓦ vrbo.com/197691
This small place has only two one-bedroom cottages near St. Jean beach, with the choice of mountain or sea views. Simply furnished and well maintained.

ST-JEAN: Eden Rock Hotel $$$
Luxury
Baie de St Jean, 97133
Tel *0590 29 79 99*
Ⓦ edenrockhotel.com
Eden Rock is a legendary hotel with themed rooms, as well as beach rooms, garden cottages, and rental villas.

The iconic Eden Rock Hotel is situated right by the sea, St-Jean

Where to Eat and Drink

Soft lighting adds to the ambience at Bonito, Gustavia

FLAMANDS: Chez Rolande $$
Caribbean
Flamands, 97133
Tel *590 27 51 42* **Closed** *Sun dinner; Mon*
A relaxed neighborhood gem, with West Indian stews, entrées with Creole flavors, plus burgers, paninis, and baguette sandwiches. Play area for kids.

FLAMANDS: Le Taiwana (days)/ Casa Flamands (nights) $$$
Mediterranean
Taiwana Hotel, 97133
Tel *590 29 80 08*
Le Taiwana emphasizes freshness, originality, and simplicity, with a variety of salads and fish and meat dishes. By night, Casa Flamands is all about elegance and romance, with diners enjoying delicious dishes by candlelight. The location is stunning.

GRAND CUL-DE-SAC: La Gloriette $$
French/Creole
Grand Cul-de-Sac, 97133
Tel *590 29 85 71* **Closed** *Wed*
Beachside café with a menu of tasty French and Creole appetizers and entrées. There are also several *prix-fixe* options, and excellent pizza for dinner. Great desserts, too.

GRAND CUL-DE-SAC: Restaurant Le Gaiac $$$
French
Hotel Toiny, 97133
Tel *590 27 88 88*
With Relais & Châteaux branding, this is one of the higher-end restaurants on the island. Serves imaginative French cuisine prepared with produce from their organic greenhouse.

GUSTAVIA: La Creperie $$
American/French
Rue du Roi Oscar II, 97133
Tel *590 27 84 07*
At the heart of Gustavia, this crêperie offers a casual menu of savory and dessert crêpes along with burgers, paninis, and more. Very reasonably priced.

GUSTAVIA: Le Bête à Z'Ailes $$$
Sushi
Gustavia Harbor, 97133
Tel *590 29 74 09* **Closed** *Sun*
Also known as the Baz Bar, this open-air sushi bar is located along the waterfront. The menu includes sushi, sashimi, *maki*, and their own unique combinations.

DK Choice

GUSTAVIA: Bonito $$$
French/Latin
Rue Lubin Brin, 97133
Tel *590 27 96 96*
Bonito is a chic beach house-style restaurant overlooking the harbor, serving cuisine they describe as "Latin gastronomic compass with a French trend." The unusual *seviche* bar, with tartars and *tiraditos* (Peruvian raw fish in a spicy sauce), forms the hub of the restaurant. The terrace offers comfortable seating, live music, specialty cocktails, and lovely sunset views.

GUSTAVIA: L'Isola Ristorante $$$
Italian
Rue Roi Oscar II, 97133
Tel *590 51 00 05*
Elegant, minimalist setting with Italian classics done well. Considered by many as some of the best Italian food on the island.

LORIENT: Koya Sushi Place $$
Sushi
Proche du Ccial L'Oasis, 97133
Tel *590 52 96 17* **Closed** *Wed*
Koya has a lovely tropical garden setting and serves traditional sushi and sashimi perfectly prepared by a master chef. Takeout available all night.

LORIENT: La Table de Jules $$
French
Proche du Ccial L'Oasis, 97133
Tel *590 29 76 78* **Closed** *Wed*
Cozy bistro in a tropical garden, with authentic French cuisine that can be sampled through their excellent three-course fixed-price menu.

SALINE: Le Grain de Sel $$
Creole
Route de Saline, 97133
Tel *590 52 46 05*
The dinner menu here is devoted to Creole and Caribbean flavors featured in a multitude of seafood entrées. Open-air seating on the edge of the salt flats.

SALINE: Restaurant Le Santa Fe $$$
French
Rue de Lurin, 97133
Tel *590 27 61 04* **Closed** *Wed*
Beautiful open-air restaurant perched atop a hill, with views of other islands. The chef cooks delectable French cuisine with Mediterranean accents.

ST-JEAN: Kiki-e Mo $$
Italian/Deli
St-Jean, 97133
Tel *590 27 90 65*
A good option for takeout dinners or light meals on the terrace. Serves fresh salads, sandwiches, pizzas, and pastas at affordable price.

ST-JEAN: Nikki Beach $$$
French/Sushi
St-Jean Beach, 97133
Tel *590 27 64 64*
Stylish beach restaurant with a selection of sushi, salads, seafood, and slow-roasted meats. Enjoy the delicious food on sunbeds on the beach. Cabaret night on Wednesdays and Beach BBQ every Thursday.

Practical Information

Politically, St. Barthélemy is part of France and many of its regulations and services are the same as in metropolitan France and most of the European Union. The standards of service are generally good. In terms of tourism, the facilities on the island are top-notch though often quite informal. Once the initial challenge of getting to St. Barthélemy is dealt with, visitors will find that the island provides excellent amenities and has some of the best, albeit quite expensive, food and shopping *(see pp338–9)* options in the Caribbean.

Revelers at the Mardi Gras Festival, St. Barthélemy

When to Go

The weather in St. Barths is generally good year round. The dry season lasts from December through May, while heavier rains are expected between June and November during the hurricane season. Most visitors arrange a trip during the winter season from January to April, when there are also a handful of cultural and sporting events.

Getting There

There are no direct flights to St. Barths and a change of planes will be necessary. From neighboring St. Martin/ Sint Maarten, there are island-hopping flights into Aéroport Gustave III on St. Barths itself. Scheduled flights are offered by **WinAir** and **St Barth Commuter**, and **Air Caraïbes**. **Tradewind Aviation** flies from San Juan, Puerto Rico. Visitors can also charter a plane through these companies. Travelers from Britain may choose to

fly via Antigua, from where chartered planes to the island are available.

It is also possible to make the link from St. Martin/Sint Maarten by boat. Daily ferries are also available. However, taking one of these might entail an overnight stay on St. Martin. The **Voyager** offers daily ferry service between St. Martin, Saba, and St. Barths. Though expensive, boats are available for private charter from agencies such as **Jicky Marine Service**.

Documentation

Entry regulations are the same as in France and the European Union. EU travelers are permitted entry without a visa. US and Canadian citizens can also enter on a passport without a visa. Other nationalities should check with their local French embassy. An onward or return ticket is needed.

Visitor Information

There is an efficient tourist office, the **Office du Tourisme**, on the waterfront in Gustavia. Abroad, the publicity for

St. Barths is handled through the various **Maisons de France** around the world. Many publications on St. Barths offer useful information on facilities and activities available here.

Health and Security

No vaccinations are needed to enter St. Barths. For medical emergencies there is an Accident and Emergency department at the **Hôpital de Bruyn** in Gustavia. However, it does not have enough facilities to handle complicated procedures and patients are transferred either to St. Martin or farther afield to Puerto Rico. There is little likelihood of a security problem on St. Barths.

Banking and Currency

The official currency of St. Barths is the euro. Banks are located in Gustavia and St-Jean, while ATMs are found around the island. Some American cards may not work in the local ATMs so visitors must check with their bank beforehand. Credit cards are accepted at all establishments connected with tourism, and some restaurants may offer a choice of either paying in euros or US dollars.

Communications

The telephone system in St. Barths is overseen by France Telecom and other providers such as **Orange Caraïbe**, which offer good mobile coverage and Internet in addition to landlines. Mobile phones can be hired through a handful of shops.

Aircraft taking off from the short runway of Aéroport Gustave III, St-Jean

St. Barths' International Direct Dialing code is 590. This is followed by a nine-digit number that begins with 590 for landlines and 690 for cell phones. Local calls can be made by dialing 0 before the nine-digit number. Gustavia has the main post office.

Transport

Hiring a car is the best option in St. Barths. Vehicles can be delivered to the respective hotels and returned at the airport on departure. Most car rental companies such as **Gumbs Car Rental**, **Europcar**, and **Top Loc Car Rental** are at the airport. A local driving license is not required here.

Taxis are not readily available, particularly after dark, and during high season they may have to be booked days in advance. However, many hotels have their own cars that pick up guests arriving at the airport or the ferry dock. There are taxi stands at the airport and at the municipal parking in Gustavia.

Language

The language of St. Barths is French. However, most islanders involved with tourism also speak good English.

The post office in Gustavia, part of the French postal system

Electricity

The St. Barths' electrical system delivers 220 volts at 60 cycles through standard French sockets. British and American appliances will need an adapter and perhaps a transformer as well.

Time

St. Barths is on Atlantic Standard Time, 4 hours behind Greenwich Mean Time and 1 hour ahead of US Eastern Time during the winter. The island does not observe daylight saving, so when the Northern Hemisphere changes its clocks between March and end of October, the island is the same as Eastern Time.

Getting Married

Getting married on St. Barths is quite complicated. One party needs to be a resident for a month before the wedding. A number of documents need to be provided, including proof of identity and marital status. **Premium IV St Barts** and **Destination Management Services** provide assistance.

Hired cars lined up at a lookout, Anse de Grande Saline

DIRECTORY

Getting There

Air Caraïbes
Tel 0820 835 835.
🅦 aircaraibes.com

Jicky Marine Service
Tel 590 277 034.
🅦 boatrentalstbarth.com

St Barth Commuter
Tel 590 275 454.
🅦 stbarthcommuter.com

Tradewind Aviation
🅦 tradewindaviation.com

Voyager
Tel 590 871 068.
🅦 voy12.com

WinAir
Tel 590 276 101.
🅦 fly-winair.com

Visitor Information

Maisons de France
Tel 020 7399 3545 (UK).
Tel 1 212 838 7800 (US).
🅦 franceguide.com

Office du Tourisme
1 Quai Général de Gaulle, Gustavia.
Tel 590 278 727.

Health and Security

Hôpital de Bruyn
Rue Jean-Bart, Gustavia.
Tel 590 276 035.

Police, Fire, and Ambulance
Tel 18.

Communications

Orange Caraïbe
Espace Neptune, St-Jean.
🅦 orangecaraibe.com

Transport

Europcar
Aéroport Gustave III, St-Jean.
Tel 590 277 434.

Gumbs Car Rental
Aéroport Gustave III, St-Jean.
Tel 590 277 532.

Top Loc Car Rental
Aéroport Gustave III, St-Jean.
Tel 590 290 202.

Getting Married

Destination Management Services
Rue de la Colline, Gustavia.
Tel 590 298 454.

Premium IV St Barts
Les Galeries du Commerce, St-Jean.
Tel 690 882 212.
🅦 premiumiv.com

Exploring Guadeloupe

Guadeloupe is two islands hinged together like an open oyster shell. Smaller outer islands float nearby like spilled pearls in a turquoise sea. Grande-Terre, the eastern half, is a flat field of sugarcane dotted with colorful towns. Basse-Terre, the western half, is a mountainous forest marked by waterfalls and rivers. The two are joined by bridges over the Rivière-Salée (Salt River). Of the outer islands, Marie-Galante is the most developed. Les Saintes are a cluster of eight islands with Terre-de-Bas the most developed. La Désirade has a minimum of tourist facilities but great natural appeal.

Locator Map

Key

 Major road

 Minor road

– – Track

- - - Ferry route

△ Peak

Getting Around

Guadeloupe has a well-maintained network of highways and secondary roads that connect every part of the main island and a rental car is the best way to travel from one point to another. Taxis are easy to find at the airport and boat docks, but rates are high, especially at night and on holidays. Buses run throughout the island. The outer islands, connected to the main islands via ferry, can be navigated on foot or by bicycle. Marie-Galante has a minivan service between towns, but most visitors take group tours or rent a car.

Route de la Traversée
This road cuts across Basse-Terre passing through mountains and rainforest.

Île à Fajou

Grande Anse

Sainte-Rose

Deshaies

Sofaïa

Le Lamentin

Baie Mahault

Gran Cul-de-Mari

Basse-Terre

Baille-Argent

Pointe-Noire

Acomat

Versailles

Petit-Bourg

JACQUES COUSTEAU UNDERWATER RESERVE ⑧

ROUTE DE LA TRAVERSÉE ⑥

Îlets Pigeon
Pigeon
Malendure

Bouillante

Les Mamelles 2,519 ft

Cascade aux Ecrevisses

Vernou

Pitons de Bouillante 3,569 ft

PARC NATIONAL DE LA GUADELOUPE ⑦

Goy

Marigot

Matéliane 4,258 ft

Sainte-

Vieux-Habitants

Chutes du Carbet

PLANTATIONS ⑨

La Soufrière 4,813 ft

Capes Bell

Baillif

Saint-Sauveur

Saint-Claude

Basse-Terre

Monts Caraïbes 2,254 ft

Banani

Trois-Rivières

Vieux-Fort

TERRE-DI HAU

Grande Anse

Terre-de-Bas

La Coche

Les Saintes

The Cascade aux Ecrevisses on Route de la Traversée, Basse-Terre

For hotels and restaurants on these islands see p356 and p357

Sights at a Glance

1 Pointe-à-Pitre
2 Gosier
3 South Coast Beaches
4 Morne-à-l'Eau
5 Porte d'Enfer and Pointe
  de la Grande Vigie
6 Route de la Traversée

7 Parc National de la Guadeloupe
8 Jacques Cousteau
  Underwater Reserve
9 Plantations
10 Terre-de-Haut
11 Marie-Galante
12 La Désirade

0 kilometers   10
0 miles   10

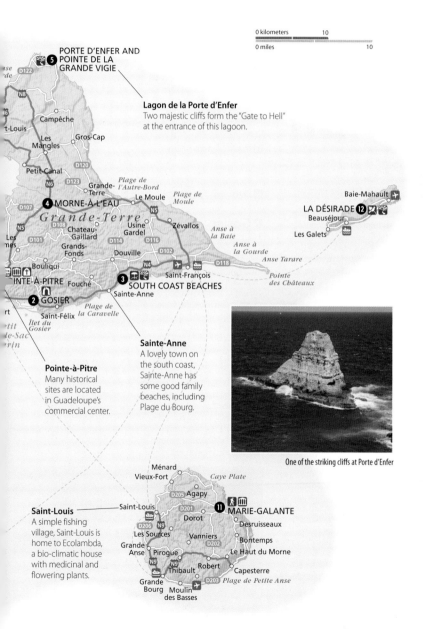

PORTE D'ENFER AND POINTE DE LA GRANDE VIGIE

Lagon de la Porte d'Enfer
Two majestic cliffs form the "Gate to Hell" at the entrance of this lagoon.

Campêche · Gros-Cap · Les Mangles · Petit-Canal · Grande-Terre · Le Moule · *Plage de l'Autre-Bord* · *Plage de Moule* · Baie-Mahault

MORNE-À-L'EAU · *Grande-Terre* · Zévallos · Usine Gardel · **LA DÉSIRADE** · Beauséjour · Les Galets

Chateau-Gaillard · Grands-Fonds · Douville · *Anse à la Baie* · *Anse à la Gourde* · *Anse Tarare*

Bouliqui · **INTE-À-PITRE** · Fouché · Saint-François · *Pointe des Châteaux*

GOSIER · Sainte-Anne · **SOUTH COAST BEACHES**

Saint-Félix · *Plage de la Caravelle* · *Îlet du Gosier*

Sainte-Anne
A lovely town on the south coast, Sainte-Anne has some good family beaches, including Plage du Bourg.

Pointe-à-Pitre
Many historical sites are located in Guadeloupe's commercial center.

One of the striking cliffs at Porte d'Enfer

Saint-Louis
A simple fishing village, Saint-Louis is home to Ecolambda, a bio-climatic house with medicinal and flowering plants.

Ménard · Vieux-Fort · Saint-Louis · *Caye Plate* · Agapy · Dorot · **MARIE-GALANTE** · Desruisseaux · Les Sources · Vanniers · Bontemps · Grande Anse · Pirogue · Le Haut du Morne · Thibault · Robert · Capesterre · Grande Bourg · Moulin des Basses · *Plage de Petite Anse*

Musée Saint-John-Perse, Pointe-à-Pitre

❶ Pointe-à-Pitre

W coast of Grande-Terre. 🗺 25,000.
✈ 🚌 🚢 ℹ Office
Départemental du Tourisme de la
Guadeloupe, 5 Square de la Banque,
590 820 930.

Guadeloupe's commercial
center, and the main town on
Grande-Terre, Pointe-à-Pitre
sits on the eastern shore of
Petit Cul-de-Sac Marin, at the
southern end of Rivière Galée,
the waterway that separates
Grande-Terre from Basse-Terre.
   Though battered by fires and
hurricanes over the years, Pointe-
à-Pitre boasts many interesting
historical sites. One such highlight
is Place de la Victoire (Victory
Square), an atmospheric site
surrounded by colonial buildings.
It once held the guillotine used
to behead aristocrats who were
opposed to a revolutionary
French government. Now, ferry
boats ply from Quai de La Darse
at one end of this square, while
street vendors sell fresh produce,
fragrant spices, and colorful
dresses. Place Gourbeyre is
dominated by the Neo-Classical
L'Eglise Saint-Pierre et Saint-Paul.
The spacious interior of this
church is a fine example of the
hurricane- and earthquake-
resistant metal-frame construction made popular by
Gustave Eiffel. Across the square
is the Art Deco courthouse
known as Palais de Justice.
A couple of streets south, **Musée
Victor Schoelcher** has a collection
of art and memorabilia related
to the rich Parisian, who was
instrumental in the abolition of
slavery in the French
West Indies. Located
near the museum is
the Sougues-Pagès
House, a lovely
example of French
Caribbean architec-
ture popular during
the 1800s. It houses
the **Musée Saint-
John-Perse**, which
honors the island's
Nobel Laureate
(1960), Alexis de
Saint-Léger, better
known as the poet
Saint-John Perse.

🏛 **Musée Victor Schoelcher**
24 Rue Peynier. **Tel** 590 820 804.
Open 9am–5pm Mon–Fri. 🚢

🏛 **Musée Saint-John-Perse**
9 Rue Nozières. **Tel** 590 900 192.
Open 9am–5pm Mon–Fri,
8:30am–12:30pm Sat. 🚢 🎫
🌐 sjperse.org

❷ Gosier

4 miles (6 km) SE of Pointe-à-Pitre,
Grande-Terre. 🗺 25,360. 🚌

Historically, Gosier was an
important defense point for
the island. The ruins of Fort Louis
still sit atop a hill at the entrance
of the waterway that divides the
eastern and western parts of
Guadeloupe. Built in 1695, the
fort was renamed Fort l'Union
during the French Revolution.
Another citadel, Fort Fleur
d'Épée, was built by the English
in 1756. Below the ruins, **Musée
Fort Fleur d'Épée** is located
in the trendy Bas-du-Fort area.
It displays a fine repertoire of
objects from the 18th-century
war between France and
England. For marine life
enthusiasts there is **L'Aquarium
de la Guadeloupe**, which
showcases sea life, corals,
and mangroves of the
French Caribbean region.
   The town's beach is lined with
outlets offering trips to the offshore islands, deep-sea fishing,
sailing, diving, and watersports. Vendors sell
colorful clothes, spicy aromas
waft from waterfront cafés,
and there are all-budget hotels
closeby. The best strip of sand
is along Pointe de la Verdure,
west of town. Shops, hotels,
and nightclubs fill the area.

🏛 **Musée Fort Fleur d'Épée**
Bas-du-Fort. **Tel** 590 909 461. **Open**
10am–5pm Mon, 9am–5pm Tue–Sun.

🐠 **L'Aquarium de la Guadeloupe**
Place Creole, Bas-du-Fort Marina.
Tel 590 909 238. **Open** 9am–6:30pm
daily. 🚢 🎫 ♿ 🚢 🚢
🌐 aquariumdelaguadeloupe.com

❸ South Coast Beaches

Gosier marks the western edge
of a string of sandy beaches that
run along the south coast of
Grande-Terre to Saint-François
and the narrow peninsula of
Pointe des Châteaux, together
forming Guadeloupe's most
popular tourist area. Busy hotels,
restaurants, and snack bars are
set on the sand. Dive shops
and watersport centers offer
equipment and guided trips.
The beach at Anse-Dumant in
Saint-Félix is often deserted,
while Plage du Bourg in Sainte-
Anne is an active family beach.
Plage de la Caravelle, and Plage

A sunny beach lined with deck chairs, Gosier

Trademark checkerboard styled tomb, Morne-à-l'Eau

de Bois Jolan are two gorgeous beaches to the east. Between Sainte-Anne and Saint-François, the coast road leads through a rural area dotted with isolated coves. The hills above, known as Les Grands-Fonds, offer a splendid view of the coast. At the end of the main road, Avenue de l'Europe, two beaches called Plage des Hotels provide a wide ribbon of soft sand for some upscale resorts.

The D118 coast road leading to Pointe des Châteaux is flanked by excellent small unnamed beaches, reached by cutting through wild vegetation that grows between the road and the water. On the Atlantic side, Anse à la Gourde is a beach popular with locals while Anse Tarare is a sheltered cove with crystal-clear waters favored by naturists, and good snorkeling. Pointe des Châteaux is a narrow peninsula that juts into the ocean, ending in a line of huge freestanding boulders.

❹ Morne-à-l'Eau

11 miles (18 km) N of Pointe-à-Pitre, Grande-Terre. 🚗 7,800. 🚆 📵 Town Hall, Place de la Mairie, 590 242 709. 📅 The Day of Crabs (Easter weekend); All Saints' Day (Nov 1).

This fishing and agricultural village was once a major sugar-producing town. Today, the only reason to visit is to see the famous cemetery which sits on a hillside above the intersection of highways N5 and N6.

This unique above-ground graveyard has elaborate shrines dedicated to deceased islanders. Originally, the monuments were constructed of black-and-white tiles set in a checkerboard pattern, but other colors and materials have also been added. On All Saints' Day, people come here to honor the dead and thousands of candles illuminate the site.

❺ Porte d'Enfer and Pointe de la Grande Vigie

13 miles (21 km) N of Pointe-à-Pitre, Grande-Terre. 🚆

Two of Guadeloupe's dramatic natural sites lie on the north coast of Grande-Terre. At land's end, Pointe de la Grande Vigie provides great views. The northern end of Grande-Terre

is a series of craggy headlands that soar over the sea. Cliffs along this shoreline tower more than 250 ft (76 m) above the rocky coast. Two extraordinary lookouts reached by driving south down the east coast are Pointe du Piton, a signed viewpoint, and Porte d'Enfer, a sheltered lagoon guarded by two majestic cliffs that form "The Gate of Hell". Nearby is Trou de Madame Coco, a spot where legend says Madame Coco, a lady whose identity is not known, disappeared. Chemin de la Grande Falaise is a 7-mile (11-km) path that runs south along the coastal ridge to Pointe Petit-Nègre and takes a 2-hour hike to complete.

The striking shoreline at Pointe de la Grande Vigie

Victor Schoelcher

Statues honoring Victor Schoelcher stand in several public plazas throughout the French Antilles. Born in 1804, he began publishing anti-slavery articles in 1833, founded an abolition society in 1834, and led the commission that emancipated slaves in all French colonies in 1848. Guadeloupe and Martinique credit him with beginning the republican political movement on the islands after the abolition of slavery. He served as their representative to the French National Assembly between 1848 and 1851, when he was forced into exile for opposing the coup d'état of Louis Napoléon Bonaparte. He returned in 1871 and was declared senator for life in 1875. He died in 1893, on Christmas night.

Bust of Schoelcher, Musée Victor Schoelcher

Parc Zoologique et Botanique des Mamelles

❻ Route de la Traversée

1 mile (2 km) W of Versailles, eastern Basse-Terre. 🅘 La Maison de la Forêt, Route de la Traversée, 10am–5pm daily.

The cross-island roadway D23, known as Route de la Traversée, cuts east-west across Basse-Terre through the mountains and rainforest of the Parc National de la Guadeloupe. While the drive itself is a pleasant shortcut from one coast to the other, the stops along the way are the true appeal. Beginning at the eastern end, the Route leaves Highway N1 near the commune of Versailles. After traveling for approximately 7 miles (11 km), a turn south on a small road leads to the settlement of Vernou and Sault de la Lézarde (Lizard's Leap), a magnificent 45-ft (14-m) waterfall that cascades into a rocky pool which is safe for swimming. Visitors are advised to wear shoes with good traction, and carry a swimsuit for a dip in the waterfall's pool. From the parking lot on the outskirts of Vernou, the hike leads through resplendent green fields and forest for 20 minutes along a groomed, but steep, trail to the falls. West of Vernou, after about 5 miles (8 km), the Route leads to Cascade aux Ecrevisses (Crayfish Waterfall), which is one of the most popular attractions on

Basse-Terre, as well as the easiest to reach. The walk from the parking lot takes less than 15 minutes, which explains why visitors flock here. Two paths lead up to the top of the falls, and the one on the left is used as a 20-ft (6-m) slide into the Corossol River. Visitors may stop at the visitors' center – **La Maison de la Forêt** (Forest House), to pick up information and explore the three interpretive trails, then continue along Route de la Traversée through the Col des Deux Mamelles (Pass of Two Breasts), which sits between two lofty peaks, Mamelle de Petit-Bourg at 2,349 ft (716 m) and Mamelle de Pigeon at 2,519 ft (768 m), before sloping back towards sea level.

The final stop is at the **Parc Zoologique et Botanique des Mamelles** (Zoo and Botanical Gardens). Besides the interesting flora and fauna, the park also features an elevated rope bridge and zip line through the tree tops.

🛈 Parc Zoologique et Botanique des Mamelles

Route de la Traversée, D23. **Tel** 590 988 352. **Open** 9am–6pm daily. 🚻 🖥 📷 🌐 **parcdesmamelles.com**

❼ Parc National de la Guadeloupe

3 miles (5 km) S of Vernou. 🅘 Habitation Beausoleil, Montéran, 97120 Saint-Claude, 590 808 600. 📷 🔇 🌐 **guadeloupe-parcnational.com**

La Soufrière, a 4,813-ft (1,467-m) high active volcano, towers over the tropical forest at the southern end of Basse-Terre that makes up Guadeloupe's national park. In 1992, UNESCO designated 74,100 acres (30,000 ha) around the volcano as a biosphere reserve because of its importance as a diverse habitat for more than 300 species of trees and bushes.

Most days, the top of the volcano, the highest peak in the Lesser Antilles *(see p354)*, is hidden by clouds and rain, but several maintained hiking trails lead to the summit and other viewpoints. Parc National operates an office in the town of Saint-Claude, which is the base for many guided and independent tours of the park. Visitors can pick up maps, guide recommendations, brochures, and other information from here before heading into the park.

The biosphere reserve extends outside the park to include 9,200 acres (3,723 ha) of coral reefs, mangrove forests, freshwater swamps, and sea-grass beds in and around Grand Cul-de-Sac Marin, the northern lagoon that separates Grande-Terre and Basse-Terre. This sensitive area has turtles, giant sponges, soft corals, sea urchins,

Picnic area at Parc National de la Guadeloupe

Glass-bottom boat exploring Jacques Cousteau Underwater Reserve

and many fish species. The mangrove forest also shelters kingfishers, terns, pelicans, herons, and other migratory and native birds.

❽ Jacques Cousteau Underwater Reserve

West coast of Basse-Terre. **Tel** 590 988 172. **ℹ** Office du Tourisme, Plage de Malendure, 590 988 687. 🖰 **W** cip-guadeloupe.com

The dark-sand beaches of Malendure and Pigeon, just north of Bouillante, are the gateway to the Jacques Cousteau Underwater Reserve, a protected sea park that pays homage to the legendary "Man-Fish", recognized as the father of underwater exploration. The reserve, which extends from the steep-sided coast to nearby Îlets Pigeon, teems with marine life and shelters two sunken ships that provide excellent conditions for scuba divers. Also available are glass-bottom boats, which skim the water, enabling non-divers to view the tropical fish living along the park's pristine coral reef. In January 2004, the town of Bouillante honored Jacques-Yves Cousteau, who died in

1997, by commissioning a bust of the underwater pioneer and submerging it 39-ft (12-m) deep in Coral Garden off Îlets Pigeon. Cousteau developed the first scuba and declared the west coast of Guadeloupe as one of the world's ten best dive sites.

❾ Plantations

West coast of Basse-Terre. **W** ca.rendezvousenfrance.com

Plantations played a major role in Guadeloupe's development, but today only a few remain as eco-museums, inns, or rest-aurants. Coffee lovers will want to visit **Musée du Café** and **Maison du Café**, both in Vieux-Habitants, where coffee, cocoa, and vanilla became important crops as early as the mid-1700s. The Musée du Café presents a historical tour of coffee production, while the House of Coffee, set in a working plantation, has guided tours, a shop, a museum, and restaurant. Farther up the western coast in Pointe-Noire, **Caféière Beauséjour** is a coffee plantation with a carefully restored, splendid 1764 planter's house. It sits 1,000 ft (305 m) above the Caribbean with marvelous views of the surrounding valley. Chocolate lovers will find bliss at **La Bonifierie**, an old sugar plantation and coffee estate in the hills of Saint-Claude, where a small Créole-style house has been converted into a gourmet chocolate factory with an adjoining tasting room.

🏛 Musée du Café
Le Bouchu, 97119 Vieux-Habitants. **Tel** 590 985 496. **Open** 9am–5pm daily. 🖰 **W** cafe-chaulet.com

🏛 Maison du Café
Vallée de Grand'Rivière, 97119 Vieux-Habitants. **Tel** 590 986 306. **Open** 9am–5pm daily. **Closed** Sep–mid-Oct. 🖰 🖰 🖰 🖰

🍴 La Bonifierie
Morin, 97120 Saint-Claude. **Tel** 590 800 605. **Open** 9am–4:30pm, Tue–Sun. 🖰 🖰 🖰 🖰

🏛 Caféière Beauséjour
Acomat, 97116. **Tel** 590 981 009. **Open** 10am–5pm, Tue–Sun. 🖰 🖰 🖰 🖰 **W** cafeierebeausejour.com

Musée du Café, housed in former plantation buildings

Typical houses at the base of a hillock, Terre-de-Haut

⑩ Terre-de-Haut

9 miles (15 km) SW off Basse-Terre's coast. 👥 1,750. ✈ 🛥 🚌 ℹ Tourist Office, 39 Rue Jean Calot, Terre-de-Haut, 590 995 860. 🎭 Carnival (last week of Feb).

Of the eight islands that make up Les Saintes, only Terre-de-Haut and Terre-de-Bas are populated. Terre-de-Haut attracts more visitors given its harbor, natural beauty, picturesque fort, and easy access. The flat outer island is only 3 miles (5 km) long and 2 miles (3 km) wide, making it ideal for exploring on foot, but, if you prefer to take a ride, group tours by minibus are offered from the harbor.

The main town is Le Bourg, which sits in the curve of a striking bay midway along the western coast and a 5-minute walk from the airstrip. Brightly-painted houses, restaurants, and boutiques line the narrow streets. An old cemetery with graves of the island's first French settlers is located in the center of the town. The fortified summit of Morne du Chameau, at the east end of town, is the island's highest point at 1,014 ft (309 m), and offers stunning views of the sea and nearby islands. A hike up and back takes about 3 hours.

Fort Napoléon, which sits 374 ft (114 m) above La Baie des Saintes, is the biggest tourist attraction on the island and offers spectacular views in all directions. Though Fort Napoléon was

never fired upon or called on to defend the region, a section of the fort houses a museum featuring pictures, maps, drawings, and artifacts attesting to the violent period of Caribbean history during the 17th and 18th centuries. Other parts of the fort have been renovated as a modern art museum exhibiting more than 250 paintings, none with a military theme. A cactus garden surrounds the fort and boasts some of the most exotic and best maintained species in the Caribbean. Directly across the bay, at the top of Îlet à Cabrit, sit the ruins of Fort Joséphine, named in honor of Emperor Napoleon's wife.

Most visitors spend their time on the island's splendid beaches or explore underwater with one of several dive operators (see p355). In town, Baie du Bourg is a UNESCO World Heritage Site and listed as one of the world's most beautiful bays. Plage de

Entrance of the Fort Napoléon, Terre-de-Haut

Pompierre is a popular, palm-shaded beach that curves around yet another bay on the northeast shore and is connected by a 2.4-mile (4-km) hiking trail called Trace des Crêtes to Grande Anse, a beautiful but unsafe-for-swimming beach midway down the east coast, a trip that takes over an hour one way. Anse Crawen, near the southern tip of the west coast, allows topless sunbathing and swimming. However, snorkelers prefer the nearby Plage Figuier. Watersports equipment, including Hobie Cats and kayaks, can be rented at Plage de Marigot.

🏛 **Fort Napoléon**
Le Chameau. **Tel** 690 610 151.
Open 9am–4pm daily. **Closed** pub hols. 🗺 in French only.

⑪ Marie-Galante

27 miles (44 km) S off the coast of Grande-Terre. 👥 13,000. ✈ 🛥 🚌 🚕 ℹ Office du Tourisme de Marie-Galante, Rue du Fort, 590 975 651. 🎭 🎵 Terre de Blues (May). 🌐 ot-mariegalante.com

Marie-Galante is called The Island of a Hundred Windmills, though only 72 of the 19th-century stone structures remain, giving the flat isle a nostalgic ambience. Ox-drawn carts, once the chief means of transportation, are not an uncommon sight. On weekends from June through February, islanders and visitors from Guadeloupe turn out for oxen tug-of-war competitions. Sugar production remains an important part of the economy, but tourism is gaining ground due to the island's superb beaches and old-fashioned appeal.

Among the most interesting sights, **Murat Plantation** stands out. Once a huge sugar plantation requiring the labor of more than 200 slaves, its Neo-Classical mansion has been restored to its original state and is now an eco-museum featuring colonial memorabilia. The grounds include a garden, windmill, and sugar refinery. The reconstructed **Moulin de**

Bézard (Bézard Windmill), on the southeast coast, is another top attraction. Built in 1814, it was restored in 1994 and is now in working condition. A shop set up in an adjacent former slave cabin offers locally-made products. Three rum distilleries offer tours and tastings. Of these, **Distillerie Bielle** is the largest producer and turns out well-known rums in various flavors, such as the gold-medal winning Shrubb, which tastes of oranges. Close to the simple fishing village of Saint-Louis, the **Ecolambda** is a bio-climatic house with medicinal and flowering plants. The adjacent shop sells Z'Oliv Rum, made on-site. Several hiking trails are maintained by the Office National des Forêts. There are a dozen lovely beaches along the west coast. The best for swimming are the southern reef-protected waters at Plage du Grand-Bourg and Plage de la Feuillère at Capesterre.

🏛 Murat Plantation
Section Murat 97112, Grand-Bourg.
Tel 590 979 441. **Open** 9am–noon & 2:30pm–5:30pm Mon–Fri. 🌀

🏚 Moulin de Bézard
Section Bezard 97140, Capesterre.
Tel 590 974 495. **Open** 10am–1pm daily. 🌀 🌀 🌀

🏭 Distillerie Bielle
Section Bielle 97112, Grand-Bourg.
Tel 590 979 362. **Open** 9:30am–1pm Mon–Sat, 10am–noon Sun. 🌀

🏛 Ecolambda
Section Saragot 97134, Saint- Louis.
Tel 590 973 180. **Open** by reservation. 🌀 🌀

Moulin de Bézard, restored to former glory, Marie-Galante

Day Trips to the Outer Islands

A day trip to one of the outer islands is an opportunity to explore a less populated area, scuba or snorkel unspoiled reefs, and enjoy a solitary picnic or dine with the locals. Overnight accommodations are basic, but charming. The islands are accessible from Guadeloupe by air and by sea. Organized guided tours *(see p355)* are the best way to see the islands on a day trip. Independent travelers can arrange transportation and plan activities through the various tourist board offices.

Visitors arriving at the main harbor, Marie-Galante

🕐 La Désirade

6 miles (10 km) off Grande-Terre's east coast. 🏔 1,700. ✈ 🚢 🛈 Tourist Board of La Désirade, Capitainerie, 590 850 086.

La Désirade is the most off-the-beaten-track island of Les Saintes. Most visitors consider the 7-mile (11-km) long and 1-mile (2-km) wide isle perfect for a day trip, but there are also many places to stay overnight. Only the south coast is populated and a single road links Beauséjour, the principal town, with smaller settlements that dot the reef-sheltered shore. A bike or motor scooter is ideal for exploring the white-sand beaches, protected by a long strand of pristine coral reefs. The island is home to an astonishing variety of plants and rare animals. Development is catching up as more visitors discover the untouched beauty of the beaches and hiking trails.

The picture-perfect Plage du Souffleur, La Désirade

The main town features a public square, seamen's cemetery, and a small hilltop chapel with splendid views. Plage de Beauséjour or Grande-Anse, at the town's edge, is a popular beach. Inland trails run across the central plateau and hikers are rewarded at the end of a steep climb with panoramic views from the 895-ft (273-m) Grande Montagne. Fine beaches lie off the road, the most beautiful at Souffleur and Petite Rivière near Baie-Mahault, a former lepers' colony. Visitors can see the remains of the colony, explore the ruins of a cotton factory, and stop at the cemetery dedicated to sailors and run by Soeurs de la Charité (Sisters of Charity), before strolling on to the lighthouse.

Outdoor Activities and Specialized Holidays

Guadeloupe and its nearby outer islands offer an immense choice of outdoor activities, varying from trekking the lush rainforests with gushing waterfalls to diving a marine reserve, which has coral reefs teeming with rainbow-colored fish. For first-time visitors, perhaps the best starting point may be an orientation trip and day sailing around the islands. The islands of Grande-Terre and Basse-Terre offer a wide range of specialized holidays, while the outer islands are less developed. To sample a completely different aspect of Guadeloupe, a tour of a rum distillery is a great choice.

tour companies run full-day, half-day, and evening cruises that include a variety of activities, typically coastal sightseeing, swimming, snorkeling or diving, with lunch on board or in a secluded cove. Most often, day cruises depart around 8am on a large, modern catamaran that accommodates up to 20 passengers. Trips to the nearby outer islands are also popular. A tour to the Jacques Cousteau Underwater Reserve by the glass-bottom boat, **Le Nautilus**, leaves the beach at Malendure daily and gives passengers a panoramic view of the sea life at a depth of 5 ft (1.5 m) in the Caribbean Sea.

The best way to explore the mangroves is by canoe or kayak, and sea-kayaking is the rage in the Reserve and around the Îlets Pigeon. **Caraibe Kayak**, **Ti-Evasion**, and **Rando Passion** offer kayaking trips.

Palm-lined sands of Plage de Pompierre, Terre-de-Haut

Beaches

The most popular beaches lie along the south coast of Grande-Terre *(see pp346–7)*. Elsewhere on Grande-Terre, surfers flock to Plage du Moule, where waves break on the reefs and reach heights of up to 8 ft (2.5 m). Beginners do best on the northwest coast, around Port-Louis, where the swells roll in low and soft. On Basse-Terre, Grande Anse on the north coast is a beautiful beach. Palm-shaded, golden sands slope steeply to gentle surf, and there are snack bars, watersport huts, and shops nearby. Farther south, Anse Caraïbe is a small, less crowded strip of sand. Divers congregate on the beaches that border Jacques Cousteau Underwater Reserve *(see p349)*. A day trip to Marie-Galante invariably leads to time spent on the beaches near Capesterre – Plage de Petite Anse, and Plage de la Feuillière, one of the most stunning beaches in the Caribbean. It has a long stretch of sand and a coral reef that tempers the surf, making

the water ideal for swimming. On Terre-de-Haut, Plage de Pompierre is a crescent-shaped golden strand situated northeast of Le Bourg. Petite Rivière and Souffleur are two gorgeous white-sand beaches on the southern shore of La Désirade.

Boating and Sailing

Internationally known as a prime destination for sailors, Guadeloupe has even amateurs sailing from the marinas of Saint-François, Malendure, Pointe-à-Pitre, and Gourbeyre. **Corail Caraibes**, **Antilles-Sail**, and **Privilege Croisières** rent motor and sail boats, and local

Surfing

Both amateur and experienced surfers find excellent wave action off the Atlantic Coast near Le Moule, especially during October, November, February, and March. Trade winds blow most of the year causing waves to break over the reefs and the different tide levels vary surfing conditions throughout the day. Skilled surfers enjoy tackling the extraordinary swells during hurricane season from late summer through October. Other areas of the island offer good surfing, and local surfers have identified more than 30 spots with fine waves. **No Comply Surf School** offers lessons. **Karukera Surf Club**, **POYO Surf Club**, and **Arawak Surf Club** are among the popular surfing clubs.

Sea-kayaking on the clear blue waters of the Atlantic Ocean, Grande-Terre

Distillery Tours in Guadeloupe

More than just a drink, rum is an essential part of Guadeloupe's history, economy, and culture. Jean-Baptiste Labat, a French Catholic priest stationed here as a missionary in the late 17th century, is credited with scientifically improving the local method of producing crude spirits from sugarcane. Said to have been miraculously cured of an illness by a bitter, foul-smelling tonic called *taffia*, a fermented and distilled by-product of sugarcane, he then designed copper stills to produce an agreeable-tasting liquor from the juice. Guadeloupe now produces four types of *rhum agricole* (agricultural rum) at small family-owned distilleries. A visit to rum distilleries such as Rhum du Père Labat, Distillerie Bielle *(see p351)*, and Rhum Damoiseau provides an insight into 300 years of tradition.

Distillerie Reimonenq, Musée du Rhum, in north Basse-Terre, displays farming artifacts, distillery machinery, a sugar mill, and a barrel-making workshop.

The Making of Rum

Sugarcane juice and molasses are fermented and distilled. The resultant clear liquid is aged with the help of yeast in barrels for different periods of time to produce either light or dark varieties of rum.

Sugarcane Fields cover up to 25 percent of Guadeloupe's landscape. Cane is still cut by hand with machetes.

Final Products include a 59-proof agricultural rum that is regarded as one of the best in the world, due to its unique taste and fragrance acquired from high-quality cane.

Distillery Machines in Rhumeries Agricoles de Bellevue grind and press up to nearly 22 lb (10 kg) of cane to obtain 2 pints (1 liter) of rum.

MAIN DISTILLERIES

Distillerie Reimonenq
W musee-du-rhum.fr

Domaine de Séverin
W severinrhum.com

Rhum Damoiseau
W damoiseau.fr

Rhum du Père Labat
W rhumbielle.com

Rhumeries Agricoles de Bellevue
Tel 590 972 650

Domaine de Séverin arranges a train tour that traverses the property of the rum distillery, which includes a fishing pond, sugarcane field, plantation home, and spice and rum factories. Rum and punch tasting follows the tour.

Diving and Snorkeling

With an impressive underwater environment, snorkelers and divers can explore the amazing sea life and thriving reefs in shallow water off most beaches. Dive shops, including **Tropical Sub**, **La Dive Bouteille Plongées des Saintes**, **Pisquettes Club de Plongée des Saintes**, and **Ti'bulles**, provide rental equipment, guided dives, and instruction leading to certification. Some large resorts offer introductory classes in their pools and follow up with guided diving or snorkeling excursions through approved dive shops. In addition, most half- and full-day cruises offer snorkeling stops, and have scuba equipment for certified divers.

Watersports

Watersport equipment is available for rent, and introductory lessons are offered at watersport huts on many beaches. **Club Nautique Sportif de Basse-Terre** has a full menu of activities for all skill levels. **Club UCPA**, **Jet l'Eponge**, and **Caraibes Evasion** rent jet skis, Hobie Cats, and kayaks. The larger hotels usually have watersport shops open to the public, and small independent operators set up huts at the beaches along the south coast of Grande-Terre and the west coast of Basse-Terre.

Sportfishing

The waters off Guadeloupe and the outer islands lure anglers

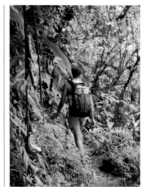
Hiker in a forest near Soufrière volcano

with the promise of grand adventure, gorgeous scenery, and a bounty of bonefish, tarpon, snook, and other indigenous Caribbean species. Several outlets offer instruction, guided saltwater fly fishing, light tackle spin fishing, and day-long deep sea excursions. Tuna and bonito are in season from December until May, and barracuda and kingfish are in season from January through May. Most hotels arrange for private charters and book space on scheduled trips. Outfitters include **Ekwatafly**, **Michel Peche au Gros**, and **Les Hauts de Deshaies**.

Hiking

More than 186 miles (300 km) of marked trails wind through the mountainous rainforest on Basse-Terre and the steep cliffs on Grande-Terre. Maps and information are available from the La Maison de la Forêt (see p348), and professional guides may be contacted through Organisation des Guides de Montagne de la Caraibe in Basse-Terre. Several companies lead hikes or make hiking part of a larger eco-tour, including **Vert Intense**. The most popular hiking routes are on Basse-Terre, including the trek up La Soufrière. The trails leading up the slope of the volcano begin gently, but the difficulty increases with elevation and only avid hikers are able to reach the steaming, sulfurous summit. Easier trails nearby lead to La Citerne, a water-filled crater surrounded by dense vegetation, and Cascade Vauchelet, a waterfall. The most popular hiking routes in Grande-Terre are along the precipices at Pointe des Châteaux and Porte d'Enfer.

On La Désirade, Coulée du Grand Nord runs across the island's central plateau offering some spectacular views. Ardent hikers cannot resist the hour-long trek to the summit of Morne du Chameau (see p350), on Terre-de-Haut. An easier trip along the popular Sentier des Crêtes is a 40-minute hike though the lush countryside.

Marie-Galante is easily explored on foot. Guelle Grand Gouffre offers incredible views of Grande-Terre and the *gouffre* itself is a deep chasm with a rock arch that allows the sea to rush in and spew skyward. The path continues along low cliffs to Caye Plate and Anse du Coq, about 1 mile (2 km) farther along the shore.

Cycling

Each August, Guadeloupe hosts a ten-day international bike race, Tour de la Guadeloupe, a mini version of the Tour de France with nine strenuous routes. The smooth, flat roads on Grande-Terre are ideal for casual riders, but given the lack of designated bike lanes, most vacationers prefer to pedal the less-traveled back roads through small villages. **Eli Sport** rents equipment and offers cycling excursions around the island.

A watersports center, Plage de la Verdure

Horse-Riding

A vigorous horseback ride in the surf or a leisurely canter in the forest are great ways to spend an afternoon in Guadeluope. Stables including **Le Haras de Saint-François**, **Ranch des Deux Îlets Ferne Equestre**, and **La Bellencroupe** offer lessons and guided rides to both skilled and novice riders and even children can participate. The best locations are along the secluded waterfront between Saint-François and Pointe des Châteaux on Grande-Terre, the dirt roads, creek-side paths, and deep forest on Basse-Terre, and anywhere on Marie-Galante.

The spectacular Golf International de Saint-François, Grande-Terre

Golf

The **Golf International de Saint-François** is a lovely 18-hole golf course, designed by well-known golf course architect Robert Trent Jones II. Golfers enjoy stunning views of the ocean and Grande-Terre from every hole and tee. The par 71 course sprawls across 6,670 acres (2,700 ha) and includes a restaurant, club house, and pro shop. Most of the staff speaks English, equipment rentals are available, and lessons may be arranged.

Tennis

Most large hotels have at least one tennis court, and many are lighted for night play. Tennis clubs such as the **Marina Tennis Club** welcome non-members when courts are not booked for league play.

DIRECTORY

Boating and Sailing

Antilles-Sail
Grande-Terre.
Tel 590 901 681.
w antilles-sail.com

Caraibe Kayak
Basse-Terre.
Tel 690 743 912.

Corail Caraibes
Grande-Terre.
Tel (33) 05 45 61 07 00.
w corail-caraibes.com

Le Nautilus
Basse-Terre.
Tel 590 988 908.
w lesnautilus.com

Privilege Croisières
Grande-Terre.
Tel 590 846 636.
w tip-top-one.com

Rando Passion
Basse-Terre.
Tel 590 289 873.
w randopassion.fr

Ti-Evasion
Grande-Terre.
Tel 590 828 706.
w ti-evasion.com

Surfing

Arawak Surf Club
Grande-Terre.
Tel 590 236 068.
w arawak-surf.gp

Karukera Surf Club
Grande-Terre. Tel 590 236 615. w lovestef.free.fr

No Comply Surf School
Grande-Terre.
Tel 690 579 747.

POYO Surf Club
Basse-Terre.
Tel 690 764 607.
w poyosurfclub.com

Diving and Snorkeling

La Dive Bouteille Plongées des Saintes
Plage de la Colline, Terre-de-Haut.
Tel 590 995 425.
w dive-bouteille.com

Pisquettes Club de Plongée des Saintes
Le Mouillage, Terre-de-Haut. Tel 590 998 880.
w pisquettes.com

Ti'bulles
Grand Bourg, Marie-Galante. Tel 0690 677 060.
w tibulles-plongee.com

Tropical Sub
Basse-Terre.
Tel 590 285 267.
w tropicalsub-guadeloupe.com

Watersports

Caraibes Evasion
Basse-Terre.
Tel 590 953 362.

Club Nautique Sportif de Basse Terre
Basse-Terre.
Tel 590 813 996.

Club UCPA
Baie de Marigot, Terre-de-Haut. Tel 590 995 494.

Jet l'Eponge
Grande-Terre.
Tel 690 325 018.
w jetlepongenew.net

Sportfishing

Ekwatafly
Grande-Terre.
Tel 590 218 685.

Les Hauts de Deshaies
Deshaies, Basse-Terre.
Tel 690 728 404.

Michel Peche au Gros
Basse-Terre.
Tel 590 991 918.
w michelpecheaugros.com

Hiking

Organisation des Guides de Montagne de la Caraibe
Tel 0690 516 608.
w ogmc-guadeloupe.org

Vert Intense
Basse-Terre.
Tel 690 554 047.
w vert-intense.com

Cycling

Eli Sport
Grande-Terre.
Tel 590 903 750.

Horse-Riding

La Bellencroupe
Centre de Tourism Équestre, Saint-Louis, Marie-Galante.
Tel 590 971 869.

Le Haras de Saint-François
Grande-Terre.
Tel 690 589 992.

Ranch des Deux Îlets Ferne Equestre
Basse-Terre.
Tel 590 285 193.
w ranch-2-ilets.ffe.com

Golf

Golf International de Saint-François
Grande-Terre.
Tel 590 884 187.

Tennis

Marina Tennis Club
Grande-Terre.
Tel 590 908 408.

Where to Stay

DESHAIES: Fleur des Iles $
Beach Resort
Plage Grande-Anse
Tel *590 285 444*
ⓦ fleursdesiles.com
Small resort on Grand Anse
beach offering comfortable
bungalows with kitchenettes.

**DESHAIES: Langley Resort
Hotel Fort Royal** $
Beach Resort
Petit Bas Vent
Tel *590 687 670*
ⓦ fortroyal.eu
A large resort for families, with a
beach, tennis courts, and pool.
Delightful beach and garden
bungalows for couples.

**DESHAIES: Rochers Caraibes
Eco-Village** $
Modern
9 Route de Rochers, Pointe Noire
Tel *590 943 383*
ⓦ rocherscaraibes.com
A collection of colorful, eco-
friendly cottages including a
three-bedroom villa with a
private pool.

DESHAIES: Caraib'Bay Hotel $$
Eco Lodge
Allee du Coeur
Tel *590 284 171*
ⓦ caraib-bay-hotel.com
Duplexes and villas set in a lush
tropical garden, with an emphasis
on ecotourism. Breakfast included.

**GOSIER: La Creole Beach
Hotel & Spa** $$
Beach Resort
BP 61
Tel *590 904 646*
ⓦ creolebeach.com
Large hotel, self-contained with
four restaurants, pools, a spa, and
a good beach with watersports.

GOSIER: Le Relais de l'Ilet $$
Beach Resort
Rue Alexandre Lemercier
Tel *590 836 712*
ⓦ lesrelaisdelilet.com
This oceanfront inn in the
heart of Gosier has two apart-
ments, each with a full kitchen.
Views toward Gosier Island
and the sea.

DK Choice

**GOSIER: MGallery Auberge
de la Vieille Tours** $$$
Beach Resort
Montauban
Tel *590 842 323*
ⓦ mgallery.com
Built around an 18th-century
windmill, this picturesque,
elegantly decorated resort has
terraces overlooking a garden
that cascades down to the
sea. Good restaurant, pool,
and tennis court. Try their
Memorable Moment, a
featured rum tasting.

LES SAINTES: Lo Bleu Hotel $
Waterfront
Fond de Cure, Terre-de-Haute
Tel *590 924 000*
ⓦ lobleuhotel.com
This serene, intimate inn sits right
on the beach in town. As such,
it is a good base for exploring
Les Saintes.

**LES SAINTES: Chambres
d'Hotes Amarelao** $$$
Luxury
Rue de l'Anse Figuier, Terre-de-Haute
Tel *590 991 958*
ⓦ amarelao.fr
A spacious villa with two
beautifully appointed rooms,
and a pool on-site. Short walk
to three beaches.

Price Guide
Prices are based on one night's stay in
high season for a standard double room,
inclusive of service charges and taxes.

$	up to $200
$$	$200–400
$$$	over $400

**MARIE GALANTE: Coco Beach
Resort** $
Beach Resort
Les Basses, Grand Bourg
Tel *590 971 046*
ⓦ cocobeachmariegalante.com
A modern, small resort with a
beach and pool. Basic rooms and
suites with kitchenettes available.

**MARIE GALANTE: La Rose
du Bresil** $
Modern
Route du Littoral, Capesterre
Tel *590 974 739*
ⓦ manmandlo.fr
This charming hotel is close to
two beaches. Studios, suites,
bungalows, and a villa with
hammocks and barbecue grills.

**SAINT ANNE: Club Med La
Caravelle** $$$
Beach Resort
Quart Carvelle
Tel *888 932 2582*
ⓦ clubmed.com
Sprawling beachfront resort with
all-inclusive accommodations. Lots
of activities and a kids' program.

**SAINT FRANÇOIS: Hostellerie
des Chateaux** $
Beach Resort
Pointe des Chateaux
Tel *590 855 408*
ⓦ hostellerie-des-chateaux.com
Located on a hill overlooking the
sea, offering comfortable rooms
around a swimming pool.

**SAINT FRANÇOIS: Hotel
Amaudo** $$
Beach Resort
Anse a la Barque
Tel *590 888 700*
ⓦ amaudo.fr
An intimate hotel on a bluff over
Saint François, with stunning
views. All rooms have terraces and
ocean views. Breakfast available.

**SAINT FRANÇOIS: Hotel La
Cocoteraie** $$$
Luxury
Avenue de l'Europe
Tel *590 887 981*
ⓦ lacocoteraie.com
Set on Champagne Beach in a gar-
den this hotel has beautiful rooms.
Access to the 18-hole golf course.

Wonderful sea views from the pool area at the Coco Beach Resort, Marie Galante

Where to Eat and Drink

BOUILLANTE:
L'Eddy Papillon $$$
Creole
40 Abel Racon, Le Bourg
Tel *590 998 010*
Delightful open-air restaurant
featuring Cajun and Creole
seafood and meat entrées, plus
a large selection of pizzas. Fixed-
price menus for holidays.

DK Choice

BOUILLANTE:
La Touna $$$
Caribbean
Pigeon-Galets
Tel *590 987 010* **Closed** *Mon*
Seaside restaurant offering
seafood, steaks, tapas, and other
delights, including a conch
burger – the house specialty.
Fresh lobster from the tanks is
either grilled, simmered in court
bouillon or done in a Creole
fricassee, and grilled crayfish is
also available. Lovely views to
Pigeon Island.

DESHAIES: Kote Lagon $
Creole
Plage de Grand Anse
Tel *590 717 575*
A pleasant beachside café
offering local delicacies including
lots of seafood in a relaxed and
welcoming atmosphere. Live
entertainment on Saturdays.

DESHAIES: Pizzeria Peppine $
Pizzeria
Chemin Forban
Tel *590 834 337*
Highly rated stone-oven pizzeria
offering traditional as well as
imaginative toppings. The paella,
served on Friday nights, is a
specialty. Eat in or take out.

GOSIER: A Petit Creux $
Bistro
11 Rue Nicolas Baller Bourg
Tel *590 844 919* **Closed** *Sun*
A charming little bistro offering
a long list of sandwiches, pizzas,
crostinis, and crêpes. Excellent
desserts as well.

GOSIER: Restaurant Hong $$
Vietnamese
10-4 Lot Bas du Fort
Tel *590 909 510* **Closed** *Sun*
Vietnamese and Antillean cuisine
in a lovely atmosphere, with
a range of meats and seafood
choices plus noodles and rice.
Takeout menu offers three-
course meals.

Lush vegetation surrounds the entrance to
the Iguane Café, Saint François

GOSIER: Vapor e Vous $$
International
51 Rue Becquerel, Baie Mahault
Tel *590 867 292* **Closed** *Sat & Sun*
The menu at this intimate
restaurant changes every week,
depending on what strikes the
chef's fancy. Seafood features
regularly. Cash only.

LES SAINTES:
Au Bon Vivre $$$
French/Caribbean
31 Rue Jean Calot, Terre-de-Haut
Tel *590 941 984* **Closed** *Wed lunch &
Sat lunch*
The chef here offers French
cuisine with Caribbean influences,
including curries and brochettes,
plus incredible home-made
desserts such as crème brûlée.

LES SAINTES: Ti Kaz'La $$$
French/Seafood
10 Rue Benoit Cassin, Terre-de-Haut
Tel *590 995 763* **Closed** *Wed*
A French brasserie on the water
overlooking the harbor, with
emphasis on amazingly fresh
seafood. Two fixed-price menus
plus a children's menu available.

MARIE GALANTE: Le Reflet
de l'Ile $
Caribbean
3 Rue Marine, Capsterre
Tel *590 974 130* **Closed** *Mon*
A welcoming restaurant serving
Caribbean and Creole cuisine
including grilled lobster, fish
brochettes, sausages, fritters,
and more. Coconut blancmange
and passion fruit crème brûlée are
favorites among dessert lovers.

MARIE GALANTE: Manman'dlo
La Sirene $$$
International
La Rose du Bresil Hotel, Capsterre
Tel *590 975 743*
This hotel-restaurant is one of
the best on the island, with a
range of entrées focusing on
organic products. Pleasant
poolside seating.

SAINT FRANÇOIS: Café
Wango $$$
International
St. François Marina
Tel *590 835 041*
While many international dishes
feature on the menu at Café
Wango, selecting from the
Asian choices is a good bet–
including sushi, wok, and
Japanese entrées. Also on offer
are tartares, carpaccio, pastas,
brochettes, and salads.

SAINT FRANÇOIS: I, Pates $$$
Italian
5 Rue de la Republique
Tel *590 741 341*
I, Pates is an Italian grocery
that has branched into serving
food. It boasts excellent home-
made pastas and authentic
desserts like tiramisu, pannacotta,
and sorbets. Lunch available only
on Saturdays and Sundays.

SAINT FRANÇOIS:
Iguane Café $$$
Caribbean
Route de la Pointe des Chateaux
Tel *590 892 340*
Offering a unique combination
of Indian and Asian spices
combined with bright African
colors, the dishes at Iguane are
full of unusual flavors. There is
also a tasting menu and a pirate
menu with lobster.

SAINT FRANÇOIS:
Restaurant L'O $$$
French
12 Rue de la Republique
Tel *590 831 621* **Closed** *Mon*
This waterfront open-air
restaurant offers the best of
French cuisine either à la carte or
in three-course fixed-price menus.
Specialties include grilled lobster,
and there is a wide selection of
Caribbean rums to choose from.

Practical Information

As an overseas department of France, Guadeloupe is a tropical destination with a truly French touch when it comes to infrastructure, cuisine, culture and, of course, language (although most people in contact with tourists speak some English). Visitors fly into the international airport near the main city of Pointe-à-Pitre. Once there, getting around is easy by car, taxi, and ferry, and tourist offices are plentiful. Shopping here is rewarding with lots of local crafts and rum on offer.

A pharmacy at the town center in Le Moule, Guadeloupe

When to Go

While air temperature varies little from one month to another, February through June is the driest period, with rain and humidity picking up in July and lingering through early January. Carnival begins the Friday after Epiphany Sunday and ends on Mardi Gras (Fat Tuesday). Following the French tradition, businesses close for several weeks during August and September.

Getting There

Guadeloupe has only one international airport, Guadeloupe Pôle Caraïbes in Pointe-à-Pitre, and seven regional airstrips, including Marie-Galante Grand-Bourg, Terre-de-Haut Airport and La Désirade Airport. The outer islands of the archipelago may be reached by ferry service. Both air and sea service change seasonally, but **Air Canada**, **American Airlines**, and **Delta** offer flights from North America, at least weekly during high season. **Air France** provides non-stop service from Paris, and **Air Caraïbes** and **LIAT** connect the islands within the Antilles. The ferry companies between these islands are **L'Express des Iles**, **Comatrile**, and **Jean's Ferry Service**.

Documentation

Other than the French, the citizens from all countries within the EU must present a valid passport to enter the island. Citizens of France may show a passport, an official identity card, or a valid French residence permit. Immigration officials may ask to see an onward or return ticket, proof of sufficient funds for the planned stay and an address where visitors will be staying.

Visitor Information

Tourist information kiosks are located at the arrival area of the airports and other tourist-oriented sites on all islands. **Comité du Tourisme des Îles de la Guadeloupe** maintains tourism offices on each of the Guadeloupen islands.

Health and Security

Crime is rare in Guadeloupe and the outer islands, but take simple precautions and do not leave valuables in rental cars. Bottled water is sold every-where, but tap water in main towns is drinkable. There are several modern medical facilities located throughout the islands, including the **Centre Hôpitalier Universitaire de Pointe-à-Pitre** with a 24-hour emergency room.

Banking and Currency

Most major credit cards are accepted, but may not be welcome at small cafés, especially on the outer islands. The legal currency is the euro, and other currencies can be exchanged at 24-hour ATMs and banks, which are open in all the main towns from 8am–4pm Mon–Fri. Some US cards may not work in the local ATMs.

Communications

The country code for Guadeloupe is 590 followed by the 6-digit local number. Within Guadeloupe, including the outer islands, dial only the 6-digit local number, which begins 690 for mobiles. From France or other French islands, dial 0 plus the 9-digit local number. Calling cards are needed for local phone booths. Cell phones can be purchased from Orange Caraïbe offices. Hotels may offer Internet service, and Wi-Fi hotspots are scattered around the island. Cybercafés are located in larger towns. Post offices may have terminals for public use, but the keyboards are French.

Transport

Most large international agencies rent cars on the island. Book well ahead during high season. Large hotels may have rental cars on site for daily or weekly rental. Several agencies such as **AVIS**, **EuropCar**, **Quickly**, **Budget**, and **Voitures des Îles** have booths at the airport. Taxis are abundant at the airports, ferry docks, and cruise-ship termi-nals. They have meters and legally add a hefty

A tourist office in Pointe-à-Pitre

surcharge to fares between 9pm and 7am and on Sundays and holidays. The operators for taxis are **Taxi Art**, **Tele-Taxi**, **C.D.L Taxi**, **Taxi Les Saintes Travel**, **Elie Castanet**, **Etienne Leveille**, and **Taxi: La Désirade**. There are frequent bus services throughout the island but it is best to know some French to communicate with the drivers.

Shopping

The markets in Pointe-à-Pitre and Basse-Terre town have great souvenirs, locally-made foods, and Caribbean art. This is the place to find Colombo seasoning (a local type of curry powder), fruit punch spiked with island rum, and Madras fabric (the bright check material seen in Creole festive dress). Most markets are open daily, except Sundays, from early morning to noon. In Pointe-à-Pitre, there is Marché de la Darse and Marché Artisanal, and a smaller market in Basse-Terre on Boulevard du Général de Gaulle. For gifts and souvenirs, **Tee Shirt Adventure** is ideal. The largest shopping center on the island is **Centre Commercial Destreland**, with more than 170 stores. **Centre Commercial Milenis** is another big center. Along the south coast of Grande-Terre, stop at **Village Artisanal** to visit shops with unique items, and **Artisan d'Art Aquaverre** to see the hand-painted glass objects.

Language

The official language is French, but Creole is widely spoken, and recognized as a language.

Electricity

Gaudeloupe uses 220 volts AC, 50 cycles and most places have French-style outlets so adaptors might be necessary.

Time

Guadeloupe is on Atlantic Standard Time (AST), 4 hours behind Greenwich Mean Time (GMT), and does not observe daylight savings time.

Getting Married

Getting married in the archipelago is quite complicated for non-French citizens; the same rules apply as for Martinique (*see p375*). Check the website of Comité du Tourisme des Îles de la Guadeloupe for more details regarding the legalities.

DIRECTORY

Getting There

Air Canada
Tel 590 211 277.
Ⓦ aircanada.ca

Air Caraïbes
Tel 0820 835 835.
Ⓦ aircaraibes.com

Air France
Tel 0820 820 820.
Ⓦ airfrance.gp

American Airlines
Tel 590 211 180.
Ⓦ aa.com

Comatrile
Saint-Francois,
Grande-Terre.
Tel 590 222 631.

Delta
Tel 0800 225 630.
Ⓦ delta.com

Jean's Ferry Service
Gare Maritime Bergevin,
Pointe-à-Pitre.
Tel 825 010 125.
Ⓦ jeansforfreedom.
com

L'Express des Iles
Gare Maritime de
Bergevin, Grande-Terre.
Tel 0825 359 000.
Ⓦ express-des-iles.
com

LIAT
Tel 590 211 393.
Ⓦ liatairline.com

Visitor Information

Comité du Tourisme des Îles de la Guadeloupe
Pointe-a-Pitre. **Tel** 590 820 930 (Grande-Terre), 590 325 101 (Basse-Terre), 590 975 651 (Marie-Galante), 590 995 860 (Terre-de-Haut) 590 850 086 (La Désirade).
Ⓦ lesilesde
guadeloupe.com

Health and Security

Centre Hôpitalier Universitaire de Pointe-à-Pitre
Pointe-à-Pitre,
Grande-Terre.
Tel 590 891 010.

Fire
Tel 18.

Medical
Tel 15.

Police
Tel 17.

Transport

AVIS
Tel 590 842 227.
Ⓦ avis.com

Budget
Tel 590 214 657.
Ⓦ budget-antilles.com

C.D.L Taxi
Grande-Terre.
Tel 590 207 474.

Elie Castanet
Marie-Galante.
Tel 590 973 334.

Etienne Leveille
Marie-Galante.
Tel 590 978 783.

EuropCar
Tel 590 387 388.
Ⓦ europcar-gpe.com

Quickly
Tel 590 211 360.
Ⓦ quickly.fr

Taxi Art
Pointe-à-Pitre, Grande-Terre. **Tel** 590 822 626.

Taxi: La Désirade
La Désirade.
Tel 690 385 408.

Taxi Les Saintes Travel
Terre-de-Haut, Les Saintes.
Tel 590 995 677.

Tele-Taxi
Guadeloupe.
Tel 590 943 340.

Voitures des Iles
Tel 590 892 210.
Ⓦ voituresdesiles.com

Shopping

Artisan d'Art Aquaverre
Saint-François,
Grande-Terre.
Tel 590 886 844.

Centre Commercial Destreland
N1, Baie-Mahault,
Basse-Terre.
Tel 590 385 385.
Ⓦ destreland.com

Centre Commercial Milenis
N1, Les Abymes,
Grand-Terre.

L'Abeille Creole
Route de la Chapelle,
Gosier, Grande-Terre.
Tel 690 487 856.

Tee Shirt Adventure
4 Quai Ferdinand de
Lesseps, Pointe-à-Pitre.
Tel 590 212 101.

Village Artisanal
N4, west to Sainte-Anne,
Grande-Terre.

Exploring Martinique

With tropical flowers carpeting the countryside, which inspired French artist Paul Gauguin's famous landscapes, Martinique is breathtakingly beautiful all year round. The dormant volcano Mont Pelée and the Pitons du Carbet dominate the island, and Fort-de-France, the capital, lies in proximity of a lush rainforest. The primary tourist area, along the south coast, extends west into the sea forming a beach-lined peninsula. A scenic route cuts through the island's northern forest preserve to the Atlantic Coast, with some of the most spectacular bays in the Antilles.

Locator Map

Craft shop in Village de la Poterie, Trois Ilets

Getting Around

A rental car is the best way to get around the island. Regular ferry service runs between Fort-de-France and the resort areas on the Trois-Islets peninsula, and many visitors use these vedettes to go back and forth across the bay that curves deep into the west coast between the capital and the hotel district. Taxis are easy to find and some drivers give private tours. Collective taxis leave from Pointe Simon, near the cruise-ship terminal in Fort-de-France, and travel to most towns on the island but these minivans are often full, and do not follow a reliable schedule.

Le Carbet
French painter Paul Gauguin came here in 1887 to find a tropical paradise and paint in his characteristic Impressionist style.

Sights at a Glance

0 kilometers 5
0 miles 5

Key

━━━ Major road
═══ Minor road
– – Track
---- Ferry route
△ Peak

Allée Pécoul, leading to Distillerie Depaz in Saint-Pierre

Sainte-Marie
Renowned for its blossoms, this town is officially designated as the Flower Town.

Château Dubuc
Once disguised as a sugar plantation, this estate was infamous as a hideout for selling slaves and treasures from looted ships.

Le François
According to local lore, Napoleon's wife, Empress Josephine, is said to have bathed here in the shallow basins called les fonds blancs.

For additional map symbols *see back flap*

❶ Fort-de-France

West coast of Martinique. 🏙 *150,000.*
✈ 🚢 ℹ *Office du Tourisme de
Fort-de-France, 76, Rue Lazare Carnot
97200, 596 602 773.* 🏛 *Indoor market
6am–4pm Mon–Sat.* 🎭 *Carnival (Jan/
Feb); Cultural Festival (Jul).*
🌐 **tourismefdf.com**

The capital of Martinique is
a lively city with French flair
wrapped in tropical colors.
Next to the harbor in Baie des
Flamands, the lovely, green
Place de la Savane, full of palm
trees and flowers, is an ideal
starting point for a walking tour.

Fort Saint-Louis occupies a
peninsula on the east side of
Place de la Savane. The fortress
was built in 1638 during the rule
of Louis XIII. Part of the fort is still
used by the military, so it is not
open to the public, except on
special occasions such as
Heritage Day in September. East
of Fort Saint-Louis is Fort Desaix,
which was built from 1768 to
1771, and is now the military
headquarters.

On the west side of the
park, the two-story **Musée
d'Archéologie et de Préhistoire**
is set up in a historic building
with well-organized relics and
exhibits of the island's pre-
Columbian inhabitants and
its early European colonists.
Among the impressive artifacts
are the ceramics and stone

The busy indoor market in Fort-de-France

tools used in pre-Columbian
times. The museum also has
an interesting display of clay
figureheads used by the
Arawaks to decorate their vases.
Just a short distance from
Musée d'Archéologie et de
Prehistorie is the **Cathédrale
Saint-Louis**. Built in the late
1800s on the site of six
earlier churches (the first
constructed in 1671) and
renovated in 1978,
this cathedral is the
masterpiece of Henri
Picq, a renowned
French architect. Many
of the island's former
governors are buried
beneath the church's
choir gallery, and an
enormous pipe organ
dominates the interior. The
church has a 187-ft (57-m) high
steeple and lovely stained-glass
windows. The larg-
est market in town
is located
just north of the
cathedral on Rue
Antoine Siger. Each
morning farmers lay
out their produce
under the building's
metal roof as the
city wakes up. Main
products on offer
are spices, vanilla,
peppers, flavored
rums, and a vast
variety of vegeta-
bles and fruits.
The most out-
standing building
in Fort-de-France,
also designed by
Henri Picq, is the
**Bibliothèque
Schoelcher** *(see p63),*

which pays homage to the
French abolitionist writer
Victor Schoelcher. The domed
coral-and-white library, a mix
of architectural styles, was
constructed in Paris for the
1889 World Exposition, then
dismantled and shipped here,
and reassembled in 1893. Today
it houses more than 130,000
books, many of which were
donated by Schoelcher
himself. The collection
here ranges from old
texts to crime novels.
North of La Savane is
**Musée Régional d'Histoire
et d'Ethnographie**.
Housed in a Neo-Classical
villa, the museum is
elegantly decorated
with mahogany
furniture and fine latticework.
The prime attraction here are
the dolls dressed in lace and
gold jewelry.

Statue of Schoelcher

🏛 **Musée d'Archéologie et
de Préhistoire**
9 Rue de la Liberté. **Tel** 596 715 705.
Open 1–5pm Mon, 8am–5pm Tue–
Fri, 9am–noon Sat. 🔲 🔲

⛪ **Cathédrale Saint-Louis**
Corner of Rue Victor Schoelcher and
Rue Antoine Siger. **Tel** 596 735 978.
Open 6:30–11:30am daily, 2:30–5pm
Tue–Thu.

📖 **Bibliothèque Schoelcher**
1 Rue de la Liberté. **Tel** 596 556 830.
Open 1–5pm Mon, 8:30am–5:30pm
Tue–Thu, 8:30am–5pm Fri, 8:30am–
noon Sat.

🏛 **Musée Régional d'Histoire
et d'Ethnographie**
10 Boulevard Général de Gaulle.
Tel 596 728 187. **Open** 8:30am–5pm
Mon, Wed–Fri, 2–5pm Tue,
8:30am–12:30pm Sat. 🔲
🌐 **cr-martinique.fr**

Interior of Cathédrale Saint-Louis

For hotels and restaurants on this island see p372 and p373

❷ Trois-Ilets and Around Pointe du Bout

18 miles (28 km) S of Fort-de-France. 🚢 ℹ Office du Tourisme des Trois-Ilets, Place Gabriel Hayot, 596 684 763; Marina de la Pointe du Bout, Trois-Ilets, 596 634 879. 🌐 **trois-ilets.com**

Located on a peninsula that forms the southern curve of the Baie de Fort-de-France, Martinique's prime tourist district lies just across the water from the capital. Frequent ferries connect Fort-de-France to the marina at Pointe du Bout, on the peninsula's north shore. It is possible to drive between the capital city and the peninsula along the curve of the bay, but traffic on the national highway is usually heavy.

In addition to the large marina and picturesque beaches offering a range of watersports, the district has a golf course, luxury resorts, upscale restaurants, and cafés.

In Trois-Ilets, **L'Eglise Notre Dame de la Bonne Délivrance** (Our Lady of Good Deliverance) dominates the square. This church was where the parents of Empress Josephine, Napoleon's wife, were married in 1761, where the future empress was baptized in 1763, and the site of her mother's funeral in 1807. Now designated a historic monument, the lovely white church is open to visitors who wish to see the baptismal font.

On the outskirts of Trois-Ilets lies **Le Village de la Poterie**, home to potters and other craftspeople

House where Empress Josephine was born, Musée de la Pagerie

who sell their wares here. Nearby, **Domaine Château-Gailliard** is a complex of studios and shops producing and selling primarily pottery, as well as an assortment of art, spices, handmade soaps and candles, and various food products. The shopping complex also houses **Le Musée du Café & Cacao**, which showcases information about the farming and production of coffee and chocolate on the island. Domaine Château-Gailliard also offers helicopter tours of Martinique. Farther west is **La Maison de la Canne**, part of an 18th-century plantation that includes the old Vatable rum distillery.

Located to the east of Trois-Ilets, in La Pagerie, is **Musée de la Pagerie**, which is filled with mementos of Empress Josephine, who was born here in 1763.

Heading south, the drive from Trois-Ilets to the town of Le Diamant on Highway D7 is one of the most picturesque areas

on Martinique. Le Diamant is a charming hamlet of pretty houses with colorful façades. It is also the starting point of the 3-hour hike to Morne Larcher 1,570 ft (478 m), which is the island's highest point. From its base, visitors can get marvelous views of Rocher du Diamant, a 600-ft (183-m) chunk of rock that sits about 2 miles (3 km) offshore. In 1804, during the Napoleonic wars, the British Navy fortified it with cannons and more than 100 sailors, and registered it as the warship HMS *Diamond Rock*. From this unsinkable ship, the English managed to blockade Martinique for 17 months, before the French floated barrels of rum to the rock, got the sailors drunk, and captured the stronghold.

🏠 L'Eglise Notre Dame de la Bonne Délivrance
Place Centrale de la Commune, Trois-Ilets. **Open** 9:15–11:45am daily.

Domaine Château-Gailliard
Route des Trois-Ilets. **Tel** 596 681 568. **Open** 9am–6pm daily. 🖥 📷

📷 Le Musée du Café & Cacao
Route des Trois-Ilets, Domaine Château-Gaillard. **Tel** 596 482 440. **Open** 9am–5:30pm daily.

La Maison de la Canne
Point Vatable. **Tel** 596 683 204. **Open** 8:30am–5:30pm Tue–Thu, 8:30am–5pm Fri–Sat, 9am–5pm Sun.

📷 Musée de la Pagerie
La Pagerie, D7, Trois-Ilets. **Tel** 596 683 834. **Open** 9am–4:30pm Tue–Fri, 9:30am–2:30pm Sat–Sun, 9:30am–12:30pm public hols. 🖼 🖼

Pottery studio at Le Village de la Poterie, outskirts of Trois-Ilets

❸ Caravelle Peninsula

17 miles (27 km) NE of Fort-de-France.
i Office de Tourisme de Trinité, Centre Commercial le Galion, 596 586 998. **w** ot-trinitemartinique.fr

Jutting 7 miles (11 km) into the Atlantic Ocean off the east coast of Martinique, Caravelle Peninsula, a sheer strip of steep cliffs descending to picturesque beaches, almost looks like an independent islet. The tip of this ragged peninsula is protected within the **Réserve Naturelle de la Caravelle**, which is intersected by several hiking trails. The lighthouse here, rising over Galleon Bay, is the island's oldest working one and has great views over Tartane, a popular beachfront village.

The ruins of **Château Dubuc** lie within the reserve and visitors can explore its grounds and stone relics. Built in about 1770 by the legendary Dubuc de Rivery family, the estate, in the guise of a sugar plantation, was allegedly used for smuggling operations and acquired great wealth from selling slaves and valuables from looted ships. A nature trail begins just outside the château grounds and winds through a mangrove forest.

🏞 **Réserve Naturelle de la Caravelle**
Tel 596 644 259.

🏠 **Château Dubuc**
Caravelle Peninsula. **Tel** 596 644 259.
Open 8:30am–5pm daily. 🎫 📷

Remnants of the Château Dubuc on the Caravelle Peninsula

❹ Route de la Trace

A scenic drive through the interior rainforest, Route de la Trace or N3 climbs from Fort-de-France, on the Caribbean coast, to Le Morne Rouge, the highest village on the island at 1,500 ft (457 m). Flanked by lush vegetation, the route follows an old path laid by Jesuit priests in the 1700s. Visitors now drive on the well-paved road winding through the mountain range and professional guides lead 4WD excursions off-road and through rugged terrain. However, some areas can only be navigated on foot. A popular hiking trail is the Trace des Jésuites, which runs along a ridge above the Route de la Trace and offers sweeping views of Mont Pelée.

④ **Plateau Boucher**
The route passes a gorge cut by the Rivière Blanché and trailheads at Plateau Boucher, where a network of paths lead up the five *pitons* (peaks).

③ **Jardin de Balata**
The Garden of Balata is laid out around an old Creole house and features a collection of labeled trees, plants, and tropical flowers. The garden's flora was introduced from around the world by horticulturist Jean-Philippe Thoze.

Bellefont

N2

Case-Pilote

Fond Lahaye · Terrev

Schoelcher ·

Ba

② **Eglise de Balata**
This Balata church was built along the lines of Basilica of Sacré-Coeur (Blessed Heart Basilica) in Montmartre, Paris.

① ② Fort-de-France

① **Fort-de-France**
The capital *(see p362)* has many historic sites, ideal for exploration.

⑤ Pitons du Carbet
The Carbet Mountains or the Pitons du Carbet comprise five peaks, the tallest, Piton Lacroix reaching up to 3,925 ft (1,200 m).

Tips for Drivers

Starting point: Fort-de-France.
Length: 24 miles (39 km).
Driving the Route: Take N3 north from Fort-de-France toward Balata. The main road is paved and well maintained. Various tour operators offer guided excursions (see p371) to the more rugged areas of the national park and rainforest.

Key

▲ Peak
▬▬ Route
═ Other road
--- Trace des Jésuites

⑥ Fonds-Saint-Denis
From Deux-Choux, a detour on the D1 leads to Fonds-Saint-Denis, a pretty village with abundant flowers, and a church and square named after Jules Pain, the village's former mayor.

⑦ Observatoire du Morne des Cadets
West of Fonds-Saint-Denis, the Observatoire du Morne des Cadets offers exceptional views of Mont Pelée and the Pitons.

⑧ Le Morne Rouge
This village stretches along the slope of the volcanic Mont Pelée and was destroyed on August 30, 1902, by an eruption. Annually, on the anniversary of the devastation in which 1,500 people were killed, islanders gather in Morne Rouge to pay homage to the Virgin Mary while kneeling before her beautiful statue, that was carved in Normandy, France.

Some of the items on display in Musée du Rhum, Sainte-Marie

❺ Sainte-Marie

21 miles (34 km) NE of Fort-de-France. 🏙 20,290. 🛈 Office Samaritain du Tourisme, Town Hall, Coast Road, 596 691 383. 🎉 Fête du Rhum (Dec). 🌐 **saintemarie-martinique.fr**

The town of Sainte-Marie, an officially-designated Ville Fleurs (Flower Town), is the largest urban area on the Atlantic side of the island, and Martinique's fourth largest city. Most of the daily activity takes place along the lovely waterfront, which faces Ilet de Sainte-Marie, a scrap of land 1,320 ft (400 m) offshore. This is accessible by foot via a *tombolo* (sandbar) when the tide is low, usually from January to April. The island's hiking club organizes guided walks along the *tombolo* via the town's tourism office, when sea and weather conditions permit. The sandbar is also a popular destination for cyclists and ATV riders. While the geological formation is rare and worth seeing and a major highlight of the town, strong ocean currents usually make swimming dangerous in the coves carved into the sediment strip, and hiking on the Ilet can be extremely arduous.

The **Musée du Rhum** is located on the edge of town at Distillerie Saint-James. Tours of the museum feature an overview of rum production in Martinique. Set in a beautiful colonial house on the former Sainte-Marie Sugar Plantation, the museum holds a fine collection of antique machinery, photographs, documents, and a tasting bar.

The **Habitation Fond Saint-Jacques**, 1 mile (1.6 km) north of town, is one of the best preserved estates on Martinique. Self-guided tours include a visit to the renovated chapel, warehouses, kitchen, and ruins of other buildings where Père Jean-Baptiste Labat developed a rum still and oversaw the profitable production of the liquor by Dominican priests in the late 1600s.

🏛 Musée du Rhum
Distillerie Saint-James, Le Bourg-Sainte-Marie. **Tel** 596 693 002. **Open** 9am–5pm Mon–Sat. 🃏 ♿ ✏ 📷

🏚 Habitation Fond Saint-Jacques
194 Rue du Pavé, 97230. **Tel** 596 691 012. **Open** 9:30am–4:30pm Mon–Fri. 🗓 Sun by appointment. 🌐 **fondsaintjacques.com**

❻ Le Prêcheur

40 km (25 miles) NW of Fort-de-France. 🏙 2,100. 🛈 Le Syndicat d'Initiative du Prêcheur, Le Bourg, Espace Samboura, Le Prêcheur, 596 529 145.

The Caribbean coast at the base of Mont Pelée was the first area of the island to be settled during the 17th century, and the villages of Le Prêcheur and Saint-Pierre became the center of Martinique's thriving sugar and cocoa industries.

Once home to an elite society that included French aristocrats, Le Prêcheur is now a simple fishing village. Just south of town, the coastal road passes steep cliffs known as Tombeau des Caraïbes, where, according to legend, a band of native Caribs jumped to their death to avoid being captured or shamefully defeated by French settlers in the 1600s.

Distillerie Neisson is one of the last producers to grow its own sugarcane, and connoisseurs claim the rum made from this cane is one of the best in the world.

Distillerie Neisson
Domaine Thieubert. **Tel** 596 780 370. **Open** 9am–5pm Mon–Fri, 8am–noon Sat. 🌐 **neisson.fr**

Lithograph of the Mont Pelée eruption by Clement A. Andrieux (1902)

Mont Pelée Eruption 1902

A few days before the 1902 eruption, Mont Pelée emitted large clouds of volcanic ash. Although Saint-Pierre's residents had experienced many natural disasters, including two volcanic explosions, in 1792 and 1851, and frequent earthquakes, they ignored these signs of imminent danger. At 8am on May 8, 1902, Mont Pelée erupted, spewing molten ash over Saint-Pierre city. All but one of the 30,000 residents were killed, the largest number of casualties from a volcanic eruption in the 20th century. The sole survivor, an inmate of the local jail, was rescued 3 days later by French sailors.

➐ Saint-Pierre

Founded in 1635 as the island's first capital, Saint-Pierre was the economic hub of Martinique and a thriving cosmopolitan city when it was devastated by the eruption of Mont Pelée in 1902. The town was rebuilt, and today is a prosperous urban area with modern buildings, shops, and restaurants, all constructed around and into the ruins left by the volcano's fury. The best way to get an overview of the present-day city and the overgrown volcanic remains is to take the Cyparis Express, a mini-train that travels through the narrow, one-way streets, with stops at interesting sites.

VISITORS' CHECKLIST

Practical Information
12 miles (20 km) NW of Fort-de-France. 🛈 Office Municipal de St. Pierre, Rue Victor-Hugo, 596 783 405. **Open** 9am–1pm & 2–5pm Mon–Fri. 🚋 Cyparis Express **Tel** 596 555 092; Sat & Sun by appointment, other days according to demand. 📷 💻 📷 Musée Vulcanologique: Rue Victor Hugo. **Tel** 596 781 516. **Open** 9am–5pm daily.

Transport
🚌

Eglise du Fort
On the morning of the eruption, the fort was filled with residents celebrating Ascension Day and all in attendance died. Overgrown with vegetation, the church's stone remains are still a haunting reminder of that fateful day.

0 meters 50
0 yards 50

Eglise du Fort

Cachot de Cyparis
Built in 1660, these thick prison walls saved inmate Auguste Cyparis, the sole survivor of the catastrophe. The prison was named after him.

Musée Vulcanologique
Created by American geologist Franck Perret in the 1930s, the museum displays relics from the disaster – deformed clocks that stopped at 8am, a melted bell, and photographs from when the city was known as the Little Paris of the West Indies.

Ancien Théatre
The staircases leading to the lobby of the Ancien Théatre still stand as a symbol of the grandeur of the city's 800-seat theater that was built in 1786 to resemble the performance hall in Bordeaux in France.

Outdoor Activities and Specialized Holidays

With more than 100 miles (161 km) of marked trails, hiking is a major highlight on Martinique. Other activities include touring the countryside on horseback or in an all-terrain-vehicle, engaging in watersports, diving along coral reefs or into caves or wrecked ships, and lounging on soft sand in a sheltered cove. Many first-time visitors sign up for a tour of the coast by sail or motorboat, hire a guide for a private land tour, or rent a car for independent exploring. The main tourist areas south of Fort-de-France, between Trois-Ilets and Le Diamant, offer a vast number of options for tours and watersports.

The palm-fringed Anse d'Arlet Beach, western coast of Trois-Ilets

Beaches

Grande Anse du Diamant, across from Rocher du Diamant on the south shore, is the longest beach on the island with 3 miles (5 km) of soft white sand. Grand Anse d'Arlet, on the western coast of the Trois-Ilets peninsula, is ideal for families. Colorful fishing boats line up on the sand at Anse Noire and Anse Dufour. Grand Anse des Salines, between Sainte-Anne and Pointe d'Enfer on the southern cape, is called the pearl of the Antilles. Wave action picks up at the southern tip of the promontory, where the Atlantic meets the Caribbean, but surfers favor Anse Trabaud and Baie des Anglais, two excellent little beaches. The golden sand at Anse Macabou is almost always deserted, except by land crabs. Among the west coast black-sand beaches, Anse Turin is popular in the Le Carbet area, and Anse Couleuvre, north of Le Prêcheur, offers snorkeling.

Diving and Snorkeling

The graveyard of sunken ships off Saint-Pierre interests many experienced divers but Martinique also has caves and tunnels to discover off Rocher du Diamant, and splendid coral gardens near Cap Enragé. Novice divers enjoy shallow-water exploration of coral reefs that are inhabited by an enormous variety of fish. Visitors interested in scuba can take a course given in a hotel pool, then dive with an instructor in the waters near the shore. Among the dive operators that offer bilingual staff, **Espace Plongée** is easily recognized by the orange and blue boat at the marina of Pointe du Bout. Also in the Trois-Ilets tourist area, Laurent and Sophie run **Aliotis Plongée** near Anse Mitan. Diving around Diamond Rock is done best with **Antilles Sub Diamond** or **Okeanos Club**, and Lionel and Françoise Lafont at **Tropicasub** are the people to contact for wreck diving in the bay off Saint-Pierre.

Boating and Sailing

One of the largest annual events on Martinique is the Tour des Yoles Rondes, a regatta for traditional canoe-like yawls made of wood and powered by two sails. Locals and visitors turn out to watch the racers maneuver the brilliantly-painted boats around the island from the starting point in Le François.

Charters, both crewed and bareboat, are available from **Autremer Concept** and **Sparkling Charter** at the marina in Le Marin. Full-day, half-day, and multi-day excursions by **A Fleur d'Eau** leave from the marina at Pointe du Bout, across the harbor from Fort-de-France, and include cruises around the coast of Martinique and day trips to St. Lucia. Self-drive motorboat rentals are available at Pointe du Bout from **Turquoise Yachting**.

Watersports

Many hotels have watersports gear available for registered guests and sports shacks on the beaches rent a variety of equipment. The most popular activities are sea kayaking, Jet Skiing, and windsurfing. Wind conditions are best for surfing of all types on the Atlantic coast and around the southern cape. Kayaking through the lagoons and mangroves is a great eco-adventure, and several outfitters on the Trois-Ilets peninsula offer guided trips. Operators are **Madinina Surf Club**, **Lagon Evasion**, **Fun Caraïbes**, **Club Nautique du Robert – Windforce**, **Windsurf Club**, **Alize Fun Dilon**, **Kayak Nature Evasion**, and **Zagayaks**.

Surfing in the waters of Martinique

Wreck-Diving off Saint-Pierre

The sea bottom off Saint-Pierre is a graveyard of sunken ships. When Mont Pelée erupted in 1902, at least a dozen ships were in the port and each sank fast to the floor of the deep-water harbor. Only one ship survived the catastrophic incident. Today, diving to these wrecks is a popular pastime. The wrecks are underwater treasure troves for divers to explore the varieties of colorful fish and corals. There are several tour operators who take visitors to explore these sites.

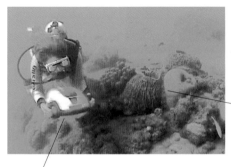

Popular wrecks

There are at least 10 wrecks resting at varying depths just off the shore. Among these, the ones that attract the most divers are Roraima, Teresa Lo Vico, and Raisinier.

Sea sponges and corals cover the wrecks of sunken ships.

Water scooters are normally used to explore the underwater world. They are available on daily rental basis.

The Main Hull of Raisinier, a Canadian barge, was overturned by strong oceanic currents. Due to its shallow depth, the 131-ft (40-m) shipwreck is the best dive site for beginners.

Corals thrive around the wreck of the *Raisinier*, which has become an ideal habitat for a wide variety of sea flora.

Tiles and rope remain stacked on the wrecked *Teresa Lo Vico*, lying 100 ft (30 m) below the surface. Built in 1874, the wooden vessel was carrying building supplies at the time of eruption. Only three crew members survived.

Roraima became the best-known shipwreck after it was filmed for television by underwater explorer Jacques Costeau in 1977.

The engine room of Roraima is still intact after many years. Of its 50 passengers, 35 died when the ship sank with all its cargo.

Well-marked trails, common in the parks of Martinique

Sportfishing

The deep waters surrounding Martinique are a fisherman's paradise. The easiest way to book a fishing trip is through major hotels. Also, the marina offices in Pointe du Bout and Le Marin can suggest operators for fishing charters. Visitors can contact Yves Pélisson at **Centre de Pêche**. Other operators include **Association Coup de Senne**, **Somatras Marina**, **Little Queeny and Maverick Too**, and **Le Marin Pêcheur**.

Hiking and Biking

There are more than 100 miles (161 km) of marked trails laid out across the island and an unlimited number of well-worn paths and back roads. Serious hikers welcome the challenge of reaching the Mont Pelée summit or making it through the thick foliage of the rainforest along the north coast. Casual trekkers enjoy shorter walks along nature trails. Visitors can bike or hike the trails that cut through the **Parc Naturel**.

Official park guides conduct organized outings. Bike rentals are offered at **V.T. Tilt** and at **Aventures Tropicales**.

Canyoning

Guides from the **Bureau de la Randonnée et du Canyoning** and the regional Parc Naturel conduct tours of Martinique's rivers and canyons which include rafting, swimming, and climbing. Itineraries vary from 3-hour excursions to 12-hour technical climbs. One of the most popular circuits is the Gorges de la Falaise, a picturesque gully in the center of the rainforest surrounding Mont Pelée that leads to a waterfall. In the Carbet region, Rivière Mitan and Absalon Falls are favored for their beautiful terrain.

Canopy Tours

An exhilarating adventure, canopy tours allow thrill seekers to soar through the treetops, secure in a harness attached to a zip line, and walk high-wire lines while protected by safety ropes. The main operator is **Mangofil**.

Jeep and ATV Tours

Four-wheel-drive vehicles allow visitors to get off the road to explore the island's wildest areas. **Kata Mambo** combines 4WD excursions with catamaran sea adventures. **Evasion Tropicale** has jeep tours of either the southern or northern sections of the island, and **Martinique Quad Explorer** does outback tours by self-drive all-terrain vehicles.

Water Parks

Many locals and visitors to Martinique enjoy a day at **Aqwaland**, a water park for people from all age groups. Set in 10 acres (4 ha) of lush tropical vegetation, the French-designed park features water slides and a wave pool. A small-scale version of Aqwaland is set up for kids at **Maya Beach Club**. Activities here include large trampolines and waterslide toboggans.

Golf

Designed by Robert Trent Jones Sr and opened in 1976, the **Martinique Golf and Country Club** is a superb course with good landscaping and more than 155 acres (63 ha) of prime land. English-speaking pros offer lessons through the David Leadbetter Golf Academy, and provide assistance with tee times and equipment rental. They have a well-stocked shop as well.

Well-manicured grounds of Martinique Golf and Country Club, Trois-Ilets

Horse-Riding

Horse-riding along the beach is spectacular, and there is no easier way to see the rainforest. **Black Horse Ranch** offers guided tours and up to 5-day vacation packages. Try a moonlight ride along the ocean with the guides at **Ranch des Caps** on the south coast. Pony rides are suggested for young children without experience.

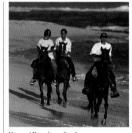

Horse-riding along the shore, Martinique

Tennis

Hotels that have at least two tennis courts include Hôtel Carayou and MGallery Bakoua *(see p372)*. The Martinique Golf and Country Club and the **Tennis Club Sainte-Marie** have lighted courts. **La Ligue Régionale de Tennis** and the tourist office in Fort-de-France can also recommend available courts on the island.

DIRECTORY

Diving and Snorkeling

Antilles Sub Diamond
Pointe de la Cherry, Le Diamant. **Tel** 596 761 065. **w** plongee martinique.fr

Aliotis Plongée
Anse Marette. **Tel** 696 904 025. **w** aliotis.plongee. free.fr/diving_center_ martinique.htm

Espace Plongée
Marina Pointe du Bout, Les Trois Ilets. **Tel** 596 660 179. **w** espace.plongee. free.fr

Okeanos Club
Village Pierre & Vacances, Saint-Luce.
Tel 596 625 236.
w okeanos-club.com

Tropicasub
Madi Créoles Resort, Le Carbet. **Tel** 696 242 430.
w tropicasub.com

Boating and Sailing

A Fleur d'Eau
Marina de la Pointe du Bout, Trois-Ilets. **Tel** 596 660 217. **w** afleurdeau.fr

Autremer Concept
Tel 596 747 911. **w** autre merconcept.com

Sparkling Charter
Tel 596 746 639.
w sparkling-charter. com

Turquoise Yachting
Blvd Allègre, Le Marin.
Tel 596 747 003.
w turquoise-yachting. com

Watersports

Alize Fun Dillon
Route de Pérou, Le Marin. **Tel** 596 747 158.
w alizefun.com

Club Nautique du Robert – Windforce
Pointe-Fort, Le Robert.
Tel 596 655 970.

Fun Caraïbes
Tel 596 548 834.
w funcaraibes.com

Kayak Nature Evasion
Trois-Ilets. **Tel** 596 682 710. **w** kayak-nature-evasion.com

Lagon Evasion
Anse Michel, Saint-Anne.
Tel 696 909 574.
w lagon-evasion.com

Madinina Surf Club
Tartane. **Tel** 596 580 236.
w madininasurfclub. jimdo.com

Windsurf Club
Pointe-du-Bout, Trois-Ilets. **Tel** 596 661 906.

Zagayaks
Plage de l'Autre-Bord, Caravelle Peninsula, La Trinité. **Tel** 596 483 890.

Sportfishing

Association Coup de Senne
Bellefontaine.
Tel 596 551 388.

Centre de Pêche
Port de Plaisance, Le Marin. **Tel** 596 762 420.

Le Marin Pêcheur
Port de Plaisance, Le Marin. **Tel** 596 746 754.

Little Queeny and Maverick Too
Le Diamant.
Tel 596 762 420.

Somatras Marina
Pointe du Bout.
Tel 596 660 774.
w marina3ilets.com

Hiking and Biking

Aventures Tropicales
14 Chemin Bois Thibault-Didier, Fort-de-France.
Tel 596 645 849.

Parc Naturel
Maison du Tourisme Vert, 9 Boulevard du Général-de-Gaulle, Fort-de-France
Tel 596 552 800.

V.T. Tilt
Pointe du Bout, Trois-Ilets.
Tel 596 660 101.

Canyoning

Bureau de la Randonnée et du Canyoning
Quartier Jolimont, Morne-Vert.
Tel 596 550 479.
w bureau-rando-martinique.com

Canopy Tours

Mangofil
Forêt Rateau, Trois-Ilets.
Tel 596 680 808.

Jeep and ATV Tours

Evasion Tropicale
Mapou, Trois-Rivières, Sainte-Luce.
Tel 696 227 358.

Kata Mambo
Marina Pointe du Bout.
Tel 596 661 183.

Martinique Quad Explorer
Distillerie Trois-Rivières, Sainte-Luce.
Tel 696 293 344.
w martinique-quad-explorer.blogspot.com

Water Parks

Aqwaland
Route des Pitons, Carbet.
Tel 596 784 000.
w aqwaland.fr

Maya Beach Club
Plage de l'Hôtel, Anse Caritan, Sainte-Anne.
Tel 596 762 653.

Golf

Martinique Golf and Country Club
Quartier Esperance, Trois-Ilets. **Tel** 596 683 281.

Horse-Riding

Black Horse Ranch
La Pagerie, Trois-Ilets.
Tel 596 683 780.

Ranch des Caps
Cap-Macré, Le Marin.
Tel 696 231 818.
w ranchdescaps.com

Tennis

La Ligue Régionale de Tennis
Petit Manoir, Lamentin.
Tel 596 510 800.

Tennis Club Sainte-Marie
Sainte-Marie.
Tel 596 692 363.

Where to Stay

DK Choice

LA TRINITÉ: Le Domaine St. Aubin $
Boutique
Petite Rivière Salee, 97220
Tel *596 693 477*
W ledomainesaintaubin.com
Housed in a Creole mansion, this guesthouse is filled with antiques and surrounded by gardens. Accommodations range from manor and lodge rooms to cottages and apartments, some facing the ocean. Excellent restaurant.

LA TRINITÉ: Residence Oceane Hotel $
Boutique
Rue du Surf, Anse Bonneville, 97220
Tel *596 587 373*
W residenceoceane.com
Clean, comfortable bungalows with kitchenettes and sea views. Breakfast is available on site.

LA TRINITÉ: Villa Ilet $$
Villas
Islet Chancel, Robert Bay
W martinicaonline.it
A Creole cottage on a private islet where there are only a few houses. Private pier and a motorboat. Kitchen opens onto a terrace.

LE DIAMANT: Casa Creole $$$
Modern
Rue de la Muscade, Quartier O'Mullane, 97223
Tel *596 335 022*
W casacreole.fr
A contemporary villa close to the beach, with a pool and views to Diamond Rock. Full kitchen, mini library, and an office with Wi-Fi.

LE FRANÇOIS: Hotel Fregate Bleue $
Boutique
Fregate Est 4, 97240
Tel *596 545 466*
W fregatebleue.com
A charming hotel with rooms, suites, and an apartment. Some rooms have kitchenettes, and there is a small restaurant on site.

LE FRANÇOIS: Les Bungalows de la Prairie $$
Apartments
Pointe Madeleine, Cap Est, 97240
Tel *596 549 416*
W bungalowsdelaprairie.com
Two-story sea-facing bungalows set in a park, with a pier. All units have kitchenettes.

LE FRANÇOIS: Cap Est Lagoon Resort & Spa $$$
Beach Resort
La Prairie, 97240
Tel *596 548 080*
W capest.com
This luxury resort offers elegant suites, many with private plunge pools. White-sand beach, tennis court, and spa.

SAINTE-ANNE: Residence Orcea $
Apartments
51 Domaine de Belfond, 97227
Tel *596 443 385*
W location-orcea.com
Apartments with full kitchens are housed in charming bungalows surrounded by lush gardens.

SAINTE-ANNE: Club Med Buccaneer's Creek $$$
Beach Resort
Pointe Marin, 97227
Tel *596 767 272*
W clubmed.us
Beautiful, all-inclusive Creole-style resort set on a gorgeous beach. Tennis school, wakeboard and water-ski school, and spa.

SAINTE-LUCE: Hotel Corail Residence $
Boutique
Anse Mabouya, 97228
Tel *596 621 101*
W hotelcorail.com
This small hotel overlooks Anse Mabouya and Diamond Rock. All rooms have sea views.

SAINTE-LUCE: Pierre & Vacance Sainte-Luce Holiday Village $$
Beach Resort
Ponite Philippeau, 97228
Tel *596 621 662*
W pierreetvacances.com
A large beach resort with two beaches, pools, an aquatic center, and plenty of activities. Lodgings include studios and apartments.

Price Guide
Prices are based on one night's stay in high season for a standard double room, inclusive of service charges and taxes.

$	up to $200
$$	$200–400
$$$	over $400

TARTANE: Karibea Residence La Goelette $
Boutique
Presquile de la Caravelle, 97220
Tel *596 586 530*
W karibea.com
A small hillside hotel overlooking the fishing town of Tartane. Choose between standard rooms and suites with kitchenettes.

TROIS-ILETS: Hotel La Pagerie $$
Modern
La Pointe Dubout, 97229
Tel *596 660 530*
W hotel-lapagerie.com
Rooms at this hotel are primarily singles with extra beds. Some have kitchenettes, too. Tropical pool with swim-up bar.

TROIS-ILETS: La Suite Villa $$
Boutique
Route du Fort d'Alet, Anse Mitan, 97729
Tel *596 598 800*
W la-suite-villa.com
In the hills overlooking Anse Milan and the Caribbean is this gem with suites and villas. On-site facilities include a pool, a sun deck, and a restaurant.

TROIS-ILETS: MGallery Bakoua $$$
Beach Resort
La Pointe du Bout, 97229
Tel *596 660 202*
W mgallery.com
A stunning luxury resort built on the ruins of a colonial residence. Tennis courts and a beach, plus two restaurants.

The beautifully designed interiors at La Suite Villa are packed with modern art, Trois-Ilets

Where to Eat and Drink

FORT-DE-FRANCE:
Nuevo Mejico $
Mexican
108 Rue Ernest Desproges, 97200
Tel *596 606 021*
A long list of Mexican favorites, as well as daily international specials, served in generous portions at reasonable prices. Good location.

FORT-DE-FRANCE:
Entre Nous $$
Cajun/Creole
Bois Neuf, Saint-Joseph, 97212
Tel *596 225 144* **Closed** *Sun–Tue*
Entre Nous boasts a relaxed setting in a Creole house with the choice of indoor, patio, or poolside seating. The daily changing menu features varied entrées made with Creole and Caribbean spices.

FORT-DE-FRANCE:
Restaurant 1643 $$$
International
Anse Latouche, Le Carbet, 97200
Tel *596 781 781* **Closed** *Sun & Mon*
Located in an old Creole house, this restaurant offers an ever-changing menu of meat and seafood entrées with a range of spices and flavors.

FORT-DE-FRANCE:
Torii Sushi $$$
Japanese
Route de Didier, 97200
Tel *596 582 903* **Closed** *Sun*
This traditional Japanese restaurant serves sushi, sashimi, tempura, and *yakitori* selections in a cool, modern setting. They also offer a Sushi School and have a second location in Jambette-Lamentin.

LE DIAMANT: Pizzbook $
Pizzeria
24 Route Arawak, 97223
Tel *596 387 223* **Closed** *Sun*
Pizzbook is a gourmet pizzeria with a choice of unusual combinations as well as several traditional ones. Try the white pizza or one of the dessert pizzas. Outdoor seating is adjacent to the beach.

LE FRANÇOIS: Le Toucan $
French
Pointe Faula, Le Vauclin, 97280
Tel *596 742 588* **Closed** *Sat*
This small family-run open-air restaurant offers fresh, flavorful food in the French-Creole style. The owners are warm and friendly. Open for lunch only.

Elegant dining area at the Plein Soleil, Le François

LE FRANÇOIS: Le Belem $$$
French
Cap Est Lagoon Resort & Spa, 97240
Tel *596 548 080*
The poolside restaurant at the luxury Cap Est resort offers à la carte gourmet dining. The size of the entrées can be somewhat small, but there is no denying the quality of the food.

LE FRANÇOIS: Plein Soleil $$$
French
Hotel Plein Soleil, Pointe Thalemont, 97240
Tel *596 380 777* **Closed** *Sun dinner*
Enjoy stellar seafood and meat entrées in a serene setting decorated in tones of white and beige, with a nearby koi pond. Finish your meal with one of the several fine home-made desserts. Attentive staff.

SAINTE-ANNE:
Chez Nadiege et Serge $
Beach Café
Anse des Salines, 97227
Tel *596 769 583* **Closed** *Mon*
An upscale Caribbean beach shack offering grilled ribs, chicken, lobster, and seafood plates, as well as good fish fritters. Cash only.

SAINTE-ANNE:
Al Casanova $$
Italian
Avenue Nelson Mandela, 97227
Tel *696 208 111* **Closed** *Thu*
A pleasant open-air restaurant just a short walk from the town, Al Casanova offers fresh pasta dishes and various other Italian specialties, plus home-made tiramisu and panna cotta. The chef is very friendly and enjoys chatting with patrons.

Price Guide
Prices are based on a two-course meal for one, including tax and service charges, and half a bottle of wine.

$	up to $40
$$	$40–60
$$$	over $60

DK Choice

SAINTE-LUCE:
Restaurant L'Hibiscus $$
Caribbean
23 Lotissement Panoramique, Trois-Rivières, 97228
Tel *596 625 569* **Closed** *Tue & Wed*
This serene restaurant receives consistently high marks for its food. Caribbean flavors and ingredients are used with French flair, producing intriguing and unusual entrées with beautiful presentations. Try the tuna tartare with ginger and lemon. Excellent desserts, a daily fixed price "discovery menu", and views to the sea.

SAINTE-LUCE: Pura Vida
Restaurant $$$
French/Caribbean
Villa B14, Gros Raisin, 97228
Tel *596 538 935* **Closed** *Mon*
Classic French dishes are given a Caribbean twist with the use of spices and local produce. Children's menu and play area.

TROIS-ILETS: O' Coup d'Coeur $
Bakery
Village de la Poterie, 97229
Tel *596 697 032* **Closed** *Sun*
A pleasant bakery/tea room in an old Creole house at the edge of the pottery village. On the menu are excellent freshly made pastries, as well as focaccia sandwiches and salads.

TROIS-ILETS: Le VERT'ical $$
Belgian
Rue des Amandiers, Anse Mitan, 97229
Tel *596 731 944* **Closed** *Mon*
Belgian, French, and Creole specialties are the stars here, along with great home-made ice cream and whimsical desserts. Good selection of Belgian beers and three fixed-price menus.

TROIS-ILETS: L'Essentiel $$$
International
Village de la Poterie, 97229
Tel *596 481 325* **Closed** *Sun & Mon*
This lovely place, set in a Creole house, offers a truly international range of tastes: from sashimi and seared tuna to rack of lamb and beef filets. Daily changing menu.

Practical Information

Pleasant most of the year, visitors flock to this beautiful island during summer. Carnival time is busy, so all bookings must be made well in advance if visiting during the festive season. As an overseas province of France, Martinique has excellent infrastructure at par with mainland France and most of the European Union. The standards of service are decent and the island is well-connected with public transport and its friendly people are always eager to help. Shopping is superlative here and it is also a good wedding destination.

Drummers in their regalia at the Carnival parade

When to Go

Temperatures vary little from one month to another, but February through June is the driest period, with rain and humidity picking up in July and lingering through to the end of the year. The annual Carnival often begins in January and runs non-stop into late March. Budget travelers and students prefer the summer months, when prices are lower and crowds are lighter, but tropical storms regularly pass over the region and sometimes develop into hurricanes. Following the French tradition, some businesses close for several weeks during August and September.

Getting There

Martinique has a modern international airport, Airport Aimé Césaire in Lamentin. Air services change seasonally, but airline companies including **Delta**, **Air Canada**, and **American Eagle**, offer flights from North America at least weekly during high season. **Air France** has direct flights from Paris and **Air Caraïbes** connects Martinique with several nearby islands. There are no direct flights to Martinique from the

UK. The largest ferry companies, with frequent service between Martinique and Guadeloupe, Les Saintes and Marie-Galante, are **Express des Iles** and **Compaignie Maritime West Indies**. Martinique's main port is in Fort-de-France and there is a cruise ship terminal within walking distance of the capital.

Documentation

Citizens of countries other than France must present a valid passport to enter Martinique. Citizens of France may show a passport, an official identity card, or a valid French residence permit. In addition, immigration officials may ask to see a return ticket, proof of sufficient funds for the planned stay, and an address where visitors will be staying on the island.

Visitor Information

Tourist information kiosks with maps and brochures are found at the airports and near the ferry docks. The **Office de Tourisme** in Fort-de-France and the **Martinique Tourism Authority** offices provide valuable information. Tourism offices are also found in the US,

Canada, and UK. Websites run by the official tourism offices have photographs, maps, details about vacation planning, and links to a large number of tourist-oriented businesses. Much of the information is in French.

Health and Security

Crime is relatively rare on Martinique, with crimes against tourists even more uncommon. However, visitors are advised to take precautions, especially against theft from rental cars. Report any crime to the police and request a written report. While tap water in the main towns is potable, avoid drinking tap water in rural areas, and note that the words *eau non potable* mean the water is not drinkable. Medical facilities are modern and conveniently located throughout the island. The main hospital is **Hospital Pierre Zobda Quikman**.

Banking and Currency

Most major credit cards are widely accepted, but may not be welcome at small cafés and shops, especially in rural areas. The legal currency is the euro, and other currencies are exchanged at banks in the main towns. Bank hours are Monday to Friday, 8am–4pm. Most major towns have ATMs.

Communications

The country code is 596. When calling from abroad, dial the access code plus 596 followed by the 9-digit local number. On the island, dial the 9-digit local number, which begins with 596

Aircraft on the runway of the Airport Aimé Césaire, Lamentin

for landlines and 690 for cell phones. Phone cards, sold at post offices and retail stores, or a major credit card must be inserted into the phones in most public booths to initiate a call. **Orange Caraïbe** provides mobile network on the island. Some hotels have wireless Internet, most large towns have Internet cafés, and Wi-Fi hotspots are scattered around the island.

Transport

Most large international agencies and many local companies including **AVIS**, **Europcar**, and **Budget Rent-a-Car** rent cars on Martinique. Book well ahead during the high season when rates are higher. Large hotels may have rental cars on site. Agencies either have booths or deliver to the airport. It is advisable to have insurance that covers rentals, especially for theft and damage. Check the vehicle for preexisting damage.

Taxis are abundant at the airports, cruise ship terminals, and ferry docks. Hotels also arrange taxis for guests. Taxis are equipped with meters and legally add a hefty surcharge to fares 8pm–6am and on Sundays and holidays. If the taxi does not have a working meter, a rate and surcharges should be agreed upon beforehand.

Souvenir dolls displayed in a street market, Fort-de-France

Shopping

Several street markets located in Fort-de-France offer souvenirs, spices, locally-made food, and Caribbean crafts. The largest market covers a block on Rue Isambert. Shops on Rue Victor Hugo stock French items. Most shops are open Monday to Saturday from 8:30am to 5:30pm. Large shopping malls are on the outskirts of town. **Centre Commercial Le Phare** and **Centre Commercial La Galleria** are popular malls.

Each town has small boutiques filled with island-made goods and imports from France, but do not expect bargains here.

Language

French is the official language of Martinique but Creole is also widely spoken. Most residents who work in tourist-related jobs speak many languages, including English.

Electricity

Martinique uses 220 volts AC, 50 cycles. Most places only have French-style outlets.

Time

Martinique is on Atlantic Standard Time, 4 hours behind Greenwich Mean Time.

Getting Married

Getting married in Martinique is complicated for visitors who are not French citizens. Birth certificates, blood test, certificates of good legal status, and proof of single status are needed to obtain a marriage license, which takes about a month. Medical certificates and residency cards need to be presented. All documents must be in French. Having the official rites beforehand, followed by a *faux* ceremony and/or the reception on the island is easier. Contact the Martinique Tourism Authority for details.

DIRECTORY

Getting There

Air Canada
W aircanada.com

Air Caraïbes
W aircaraibes.com

Air France
W airfrance.com

American Eagle
W aa.com

Compaignie Maritime West Indies
Tel 596 749 338.

Delta
W delta.com

Express des Iles
Tel 596 420 405.
W express-des-iles.com

Visitor Information

Martinique Tourism Authority
Pointe de Jaham,
Schoelcher.
Tel 596 616 177.
W martinique.org

Office de Tourisme
Fort-de-France.
Tel 596 602 773.
W tourismefdf.com

Health and Security

Ambulance
Tel 15.

Fire
Tel 18.

Hospital Pierre Zobda Quikman
Fort de France.
Tel 596 552 000.

Police
Tel 17.

Communications

Orange Caraïbe
W orangecaraibe.com

Transport

AVIS
W avis.com

Budget Rent-a-Car
W budget-antilles.com

Europcar
W europcar.com

Shopping

Centre Commercial La Galleria
Lamentin.
W galleria.mq

Centre Commercial Le Phare
Fort-de-France.

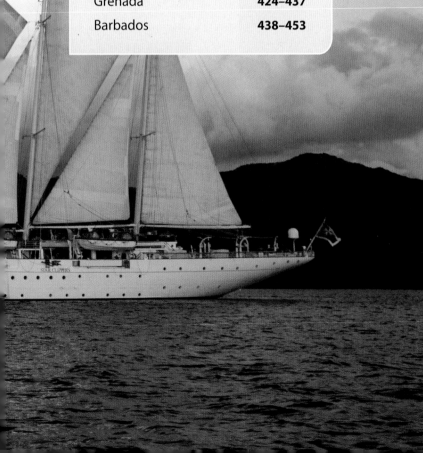

THE WINDWARDS AND BARBADOS

The Windwards and Barbados at a Glance

The Windward Islands comprises Dominica, St. Lucia, St. Vincent and the Grenadines, and Grenada. This configuration of islands once included Barbados and Tobago, both of which were detached in the 1800s. Except for the Grenadines, the islands are part of a long volcanic arc rising from the eastern edge of the Caribbean Sea, as evidenced by St. Lucia's steaming sulphurous vents. With rainforest-covered mountains, tumbling waterfalls, endless green fields, and a rich diversity of flora and fauna, all are great choices for eco-tourists and adventure seekers.

DOMINI
(See pp380
Roseau

Dominica is popularly known as the nature island. This eco-paradise is covered by tropical forests and abounds in lakes, streams, and waterfalls. Its national parks ensure it remains a great place to explore nature, be it diving or hiking.

St. Vincent and the Grenadines, 32 islands and cays steeped in old world charm, attract a lot of famous visitors as well as dedicated yachters. The islands' rare flora and fauna are protected by numerous wildlife agencies.

Grenada's capital St. George's is one of the most beautiful cities of the Caribbean. The tranquil island with verdant rainforest is well known for its rum and aromatic spices.

GREN.
(See pp4

St. George's

◀ A Star Clippers sailing cruise ship in the waters off Dominica

Locator Map

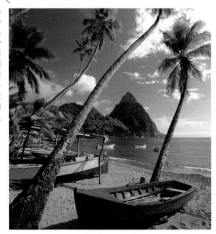

Barbados boasts a bevy of amazing white sand beaches. The most cosmopolitan of the English islands with a thriving nightlife, this long-time favorite has offerings to fit all budgets as well as natural wonders such as the remarkable Harrison's Cave.

MARTINIQUE
(The French Antilles, see pp360–75)

Castries

ST. LUCIA
(See pp394–409)

Soufriére

town

VINCENT AND E GRENADINES
(See pp410–23)

Speightstown

BARBADOS
(See pp438–53)

Bridgetown   Oistins

St. Lucia's most famous landmarks, the Pitons, leave no doubt of the island's volcanic origins. Lushly forested, it is also blessed with unspoilt beaches and seas teeming with tropical fish, along with top-of-the-line resorts, great cuisine, and a renowned jazz festival.

0 kilometers   50

0 miles   50

Exploring Dominica

Dominica is a treasure island of nature which has remained largely undisturbed for thousands of years. Most of the 72,000 islanders live in and around the capital, Roseau, which leaves much of the rest of the island unpopulated and an eco-paradise. Tropical forests, such as Morne Trois Pitons National Park, cover two-thirds of the island's spectacular mountain interior and contain more than 1,200 species of plants and 160 species of birds. There are great unspoilt beaches and reefs, and a growing number of national parks to ensure that Dominica's reputation as the nature island of the Caribbean is protected for future generations.

DOMINICA

ST. LUCIA

BARBADOS

ST. VINCENT AND THE GRENADINES

GRENADA

Locator Map

Emerald Pool

Sights at a Glance
1 Roseau
2 Trafalgar Falls
3 Petite Soufrière
4 *Morne Trois Pitons National Park p383*
5 Massacre Village
6 Emerald Pool
7 Carib Territory
8 Morne Diablotin National Park
9 Cabrits National Park

0 kilometers _____ 5
0 miles _____ 5

Getting Around

Getting around Dominica is fun and hiring a car allows visitors to fully explore the island. Most of the roads are paved and much of the island is now accessible by car even if the last leg of the journey may have to be made on foot – to the start of a hiking trail or to a deserted beach. Heavy rains can cause sudden landslides so watch out for potholes. If lost, it is best to ask one of the locals for directions. Buses are also available everywhere and ply dawn to dusk.

Key
━━ Major road
══ Minor road
△ Peak

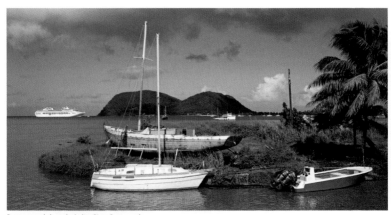

Boats moored along the Indian River, Portsmouth

For hotels and restaurants on this island see p390 and p391

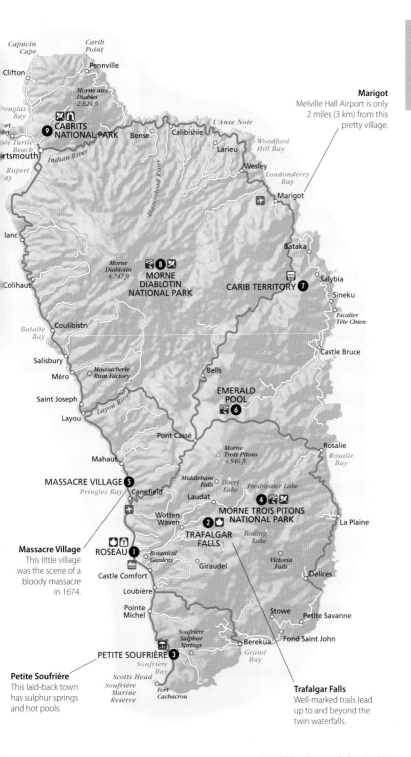

Capucin Cape

Carib Point

Clifton

Pennville

Morne aux Diables 2,824 ft

ouglas Bay

ey

ort

le Turtle Beach

CABRITS NATIONAL PARK **9**

Bense

Calibishie

L'Anse Noir

Woodford Hill Bay

Larieu

Wesley

tsmouth

Indian River

Rupert ay

Hampstead River

Londonderry Bay

Marigot

lanc

Bataka

olihaut

Morne Diablotin 4,747 ft

8 MORNE DIABLOTIN NATIONAL PARK

CARIB TERRITORY **7**

Salybia

Sineku

Escalier Tête Chien

Coulibistri

Batalie Bay

Salisbury

Méro

Macoucherie Rum Factory

Bells

Castle Bruce

Saint Joseph

Layou River

Layou

Pont Cassé

EMERALD POOL **6**

Mahaut

Morne Trois Pitons 4,546 ft

Rosalie

Rosalie Bay

MASSACRE VILLAGE **5**

Pringles Bay

Canefield

Middleham Falls

Boeri Lake

Laudat

Freshwater Lake

4 MORNE TROIS PITONS NATIONAL PARK

Wotten Waven

2 TRAFALGAR FALLS

Boiling Lake

La Plaine

ROSEAU **1**

Botanical Gardens

Giraudel

Victoria Falls

Delices

Castle Comfort

Loubière

Pointe Michel

Stowe

Petite Savanne

Soufrière Sulphur Springs

Berekua

Fond Saint John

PETITE SOUFRIÈRE **3**

Soufrière Bay

Grand Bay

Scotts Head

Soufrière Marine Reserve

Fort Cachacrou

Marigot
Melville Hall Airport is only 2 miles (3 km) from this pretty village.

Massacre Village
This little village was the scene of a bloody massacre in 1674.

Petite Soufrière
This laid-back town has sulphur springs and hot pools.

Trafalgar Falls
Well-marked trails lead up to and beyond the twin waterfalls.

For additional map symbols *see back flap*

Colorful souvenir dolls in Old Market Square, Roseau

❶ Roseau

36 miles (58 km) SW of Melville Hall Airport. 🗺 15,000. 🚌 ⛴ 🚕
ℹ️ First Floor, Financial Center, 767 448 2045. ⛴ daily. 🎭 Carnival (Feb/Mar) and Independence Day (Nov 3).

The capital, Roseau, is a busy, bustling, colorful, and noisy town during the day and very quiet at night. The town is small enough to be easily explored on foot.

The oldest part of town is around Old Market Square, formerly the original slave market, and has several interesting old buildings and many specialty craft stores. Also near the Old Market Square is the Dominica Museum which has a small collection of artifacts tracing the island's history. The newer part, along the southern banks of the Roseau River, has offices, shops, and bazaars where goods of all kinds spill out onto the sidewalks. The New Market on Bay Front is best visited early in the morning when it is at its busiest and liveliest.

Also worth visiting is the **Roman Catholic Cathedral of Our Lady of Fair Haven**, built of volcanic stones gathered from the banks of the river. Its construction started in 1841 but the building was not completed until 1916 when the west steeple was added. The cathedral has been undergoing renovation work but is expected to open to visitors once again sometime during 2014. The **Botanic Gardens**, on the site of an old sugar plantation, cover 40 acres (16 ha), and comprise the largest open space in the city.

🏛️ Roman Catholic Cathedral of Our Lady of Fair Haven
Virgin Lane. **Open** dawn to dusk.

🌿 Botanic Gardens
Bath Road, Morne Bruce.
Open 7am–7pm daily. 🏷️
🌐 **da-academy.org/dagardens.html**

❷ Trafalgar Falls

5 miles (8 km) E of Roseau. 🚌 🏛️
Open daily. 🏷️ 📷 ♿

Trafalgar Falls are the easiest to reach of the island's many waterfalls. They are a short drive from Roseau through the Roseau Valley to the start of the trail and then a gentle 15-minute walk along a well-marked trail, although the rocks can sometimes be slippery. There are two falls cascading down a gorge into pools

littered with huge black rocks and surrounded by lush vegetation. The larger of the falls, on the left, is known as "father" and the other as "mother". If visitors scramble up the rocks to the left of "father", there is a hot pool to relax in. Close to the falls is the **Papillote Wilderness Retreat and Nature Sanctuary**. The small eco-resort *(see p390)* is set in magnificent tropical gardens with many rare orchids and has its own mineral pools, natural hot springs, and waterfalls. There are long stretches of beautiful hiking trails and at the end of the day visitors can dine on the terrace of the retreat's delightful restaurant.

🌺 Papillote Wilderness Retreat and Nature Sanctuary
Papillote Wilderness Retreat, Roseau.
Tel 767 448 2287. **Open** daily. 🏷️ 🖥️
📷 🌐 **papillote.dm**

❸ Petite Soufrière

7 miles (11 km) S of Roseau.
🗺 1,500. 🚌

Petite Soufrière is a small village noted for its palm-fringed beach, fishing boats, and waterside church with its murals of village life. It was named by early French settlers after the sulphur which belches out from the ground nearby. Visitors can walk up to the sulphur springs and hot pools along the Soufrière river valley through huge stands of towering bamboo.

Trafalgar Falls amid lush vegetation

❹ Morne Trois Pitons National Park

This national park dominates the southern half of the island and can be accessed by several roads from the coast. The park is named after the mountain with three peaks, the highest being at 4,546 ft (1,385 m). In 1975, this 17,000 acre (6,800 ha) park was the first to be designated a nature reserve in the Caribbean and it contains many of Dominica's most spectacular attractions including the Titou Gorge, Boeri and Freshwater Lakes, Boiling Lake, and the Middleham Falls just to the northeast of Laudat.

Boeri Lake is the highest crater lake in Dominica at 2,850 ft (869 m).

Boiling Lake sits inside a deep basin, always covered in steam, with its center emitting hot gases.

Morne Trois Pitons Peak
A UNESCO-designated World Heritage site and Dominica's second highest mountain, it affords great views of the island.

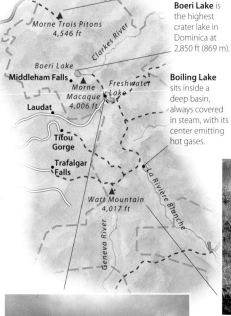

Morne Trois Pitons 4,546 ft

Clarkes River

Boeri Lake

Middleham Falls

Morne Macaque 4,006 ft

Freshwater Lake

Laudat

Titou Gorge

Trafalgar Falls

La Riviere Blanche

Watt Mountain 4,017 ft

Geneva River

Valley of Desolation
Hot springs and bubbling mud pools are features of the volcanic landscape in this valley. Vegetation is sparse because of the sulphur-laden gas from more than 50 vents.

Freshwater Lake
The largest lake in Dominica is located 2,500 ft 762 m) above sea level and supports a wealth of wildlife. According to legend, a giant serpent lurks under its surface.

0 km   2
0 miles   2

Key
▲ Peak
━━ Major road
═══ Minor road
- - - Trail
- - - Park boundary

❺ Massacre Village

4 miles (6 km) N of Roseau.

Just north of the Canefield Airport lies Massacre Village. The little village was the scene of one of the bloodiest massacres in the country's history and hence has a special place in island lore. Sir Thomas Warner, governor of St. Kitts, had a son from a Carib woman and another son, Philip, with his English wife. When the governor died, the Carib son had no one to protect him so he fled to Dominica and became a powerful chief.

In 1674 Philip was chosen by the new governor to lead a military force to Dominica to quell the Caribs who were trying to keep Dominica for themselves. According to legend, the two half-brothers met for a feast that Philip had arranged on board his ship. But Philip stabbed his half-brother to death and his troops then massacred the remaining Caribs. Shortly after, the French gave the village its name – presumably to embarrass the English. Later, Jean Rhys set part of her famous novel *Wild Sargasso Sea* (1965) in this small village.

Indigenous souvenirs made by the Caribs on display, Carib Territory

❻ Emerald Pool

8 miles (14 km) NE of Roseau.

Located mid-way between Canefield and Castle Bruce, Emerald Pool is one of the most visited sites on the island. It is a 5- to 10-minute walk through montane rainforest from the road about 3 miles (5 km) northeast from Pont Cassé. The pool is a grotto with its own waterfall and surrounded by tropical plants, flowers, and ferns. Notable are the gommier trees and the mont blanc trees along the trail with their buttress roots, the many varieties of orchid, giant epiphytes, and anthuriums. The thick canopy does not allow too many ground-hugging plants to flourish. The rich birdlife includes hummingbirds, jaco parrots, and the elusive mountain warbler. A short section of the trail is paved with slabs of rocks laid by the Caribs centuries ago. The pool does get crowded at times and a morning visit is best.

❼ Carib Territory

20 miles (32 km) NE of Roseau.
guides from Kalinago Barana Aute.

Carib Territory occupies 3,700 acres (1,480 ha) with an extensive coastline and agricultural land behind. The land was given back by Queen Victoria of England to the descendants of the island's original inhabitants in 1903. Today, the Caribs engage in mostly agriculture and fishing, still making their canoes by hand. They are also expert potters and weavers – traditions that have been passed down for centuries – and their baskets are so tightly woven they are watertight. Traditional music, dance, and herbal medicine are still practiced here. There are more than 16 arts and crafts shops in the territory selling various handicrafts made by the locals. Exper-ience the heritage of the Kalinago people at the Carib cultural village – **Kalinago Barana Aute**. It has traditional buildings by Crayfish River.

Visitors enjoying themselves at the Emerald Pool

For hotels and restaurants on this island see p390 and p391

❽ Morne Diablotin National Park

14 miles (23 km) N of Roseau.

The Morne Diablotin National Park is home to the "Little Devil" Mountain, Dominica's highest peak at 4,747 ft (1,447 m) and covers 34 sq miles (88 sq km) of oceanic rainforest, including the area known as Syndicate, which is home to the Jaco and rare sisserou parrot. Morne Diablotin is not named for the devil but for the devilish call of the black-capped petrel that used to breed on the higher slopes of the mountain. The park is part of the vast Northern Forest Reserve and teems with birdlife and hundreds of species of towering trees, plants, and exotic flowers.

Visitors need to allow themselves six to seven hours to climb the mountain, have a picnic lunch at the top and descend after that. The trail starts at a height of about 1,700 ft (518 m) and gets progressively steeper and can be wet in places. The Syndicate Nature Trail, on the edge of the park, is much easier and ideal for the less adventurous. It takes about 30 minutes but it is best to allow for more time in order to fully enjoy everything there is to see along the way.

A short distance away, the trail runs through a section of forest that contains most of the avian species to be found on the island. There are three lookout points along the trail.

Fort Shirley's cannons looking out toward the sea, Cabrits National Park

❾ Cabrits National Park

20 miles (32 km) N of Roseau.

Cabrits National Park covers 1,313 acres (525 ha) of upland and 1,053 acres (421 ha) of the surrounding underwater park, Cabrits Marine Reserve. The site contains the ruins of the 18th-century **Fort Shirley**, the volcanic peaks of East and West Cabrits, tropical forest, the largest swamp on the island, sandy beaches, and coral reefs just offshore to the north. *Cabri* is a French word for young goat. The place got its name from the practice of French sailors to leave goats on the peninsula so that they would have fresh meat when they returned.

Fort Shirley and the garrison was largely built by the British but the French added to it during their years of occupation. Altogether there were more than 50 major buildings although many of them were covered by vegetation after the fort had been abandoned. At its height, the fort had seven gun batteries. Today, cruise ships dock at the pier in Prince Rupert's Bay to visit the park. There are fabulous views from Fort Shirley across the bay and inland to the mountains.

Signage, Cabrits National Park

Basket weaver at work in Carib Territory

Caribs and Maroons on Dominica

The Caribs were warlike Indians who migrated north from South America in about AD 1000 and settled the islands, ousting the peaceful Arawaks (Amerindians) who had arrived 1,000 years earlier. Their war canoes, holding more than 100 men, were fast enough to catch a sailing ship. The Caribs built villages and cleared land to farm. They were skilled potters too. About 3,000 Caribs, direct descendants of those early settlers, still live on the island which they call Waitukubuli, which means "tall is her body". In the late 18th century, Dominica became the home for large numbers of slaves who had managed to escape from surrounding islands. They took refuge in the heavily forested, mountainous terrain and were known as Maroons. They developed a system of inland trails that allowed them to travel quickly – many are still used today. They raided settlements, encouraged slaves on the island to join them and fought a running guerrilla war against the British troops until 1814 when they were finally defeated and their leaders executed. After Emancipation in 1848, however, the island again became a refuge for slaves escaping from the surrounding French islands where slavery was still practiced. They were allowed to stay and farm small plots of land and fish.

Outdoor Activities and Specialized Holidays

Dominica, with its fabulous beaches and vast and unexplored wilderness, has everything a visitor could dream of in a tropical island. The beaches are fringed with gently swaying palms overlooking the warm and calm turquoise seas. Many beaches consist of fine volcanic sand which varies from black to grey, while there are golden sand beaches on the northeast coast beyond Melville Hall. The island's flora and fauna is best viewed on guided boat or rainforest tours. Many tour operators take visitors to see the fascinating marine life on the island.

Purple Turtle Beach near Portsmouth – a typically beautiful spot for relaxing

Beaches

The best beaches for swimming are on the sheltered western coast, although there are many fine, unspoilt beaches to be discovered on the north coast. Some pretty beaches to visit are located around Portsmouth, especially Purple Turtle Beach, and near Calibishie, L'Anse Noir and Woodford Hill Bay in the north and northeast of Dominica. On the east coast, beaches are long but usually have choppier seas, making them great places for surfing and windsurfing.

Indian River Boat Trips

A trip up the Indian River is memorable in more ways than one. It allows visitors to see many different island habitats and view the flora and fauna up close. There is a standard price for a trip from the jetty in Portsmouth or by the bridge at the north of the estuary. Visitors travel on a row boat; outboard motors are not allowed on the river, because the noise scares the wildlife. (Visitors must also purchase an ecotourism site pass to visit the Indian River, as well as other protected sites.) The journey takes visitors through swamps and reed beds teeming with fish, crabs, and birdlife. Look out for iguanas basking under the sun on the branch of a tree.

The boatman-guides give running and often very humorous commentaries as the boat meanders upriver. The boats stop at a ramshackle river bar, where they serve a very good coconut punch, before the return trip. If time permits, it is also worth going for a short walk inland through fields of banana, plantain, and pumpkin to the edge of a large marsh which is home to thousands of birds.

Rainforest Tours

Dominica is rich in forest life: trees, plants, and rivers, bats, birds, and myriad animals. Rainforest tours are a great way to experience the splendor of the island's natural beauty, with trips to waterfalls, sulphur springs, the Carib Territory, and adventures that include river-tubing and turtle-watching. Tour operators include **Antours**, **Hibiscus Eco-Tours**, and, for a different way to experience the natural beauty of the island, **Rainforest Riding**, which offers tours on horseback.

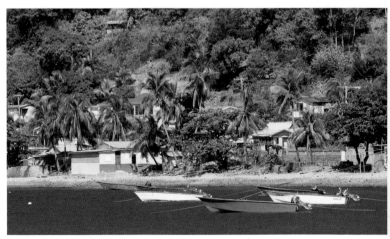

Boats moored at Scotts Head, where the Atlantic meets the Caribbean

Diving and Watersports

Dominica offers great diving with its warm, clear waters and reefs teeming with marine life. Best dive areas are around Cabrits National Park and Cabrits Marine Reserve (see p385), Douglas Bay on the northwest coast, and around Scott's Head in the Soufrière Marine Reserve on the southwestern tip of the island. All dive sites have permanent moorings.

A great variety of watersports ranging from yachting, parasailing, and snorkeling to windsurfing are on offer in Dominica. A day's cruise can be arranged around the island or a yacht can be hired with a crew to spend several days touring the islands.

Most dive operators cater not only to divers but also offer other watersports. The main ones are **Anchorage Whale Watch and Dive Center**, which includes whale-watching, **Cabrits Dive Center**, and **Dive Dominica**. **Nature Island Dive** also organizes adventure activities. **Al Dive and Watersports** has interesting packages that include dives and personal guides for surfing tours.

Apart from these activities, every year Dominica holds Dive Fest in July. It is an annual scuba diving event hosted by the Dominica Watersports Association, to educate the islanders and visitors about the need to protect the marine environment.

Whale-Watching

Dominica is often called the whale-watching capital of the Caribbean because so many species of whale can be seen year round, although the peak season is between November and June. The west coast is the best place to spot them and most whales and dolphins congregate in the warm waters offshore to feed and breed during the peak season. The most commonly encountered ones are sperm whales; during winter, migrating humpback whales also make an appearance. Visitors can spot pilot,

Visitors going out for a dive with the help of a guide

pygmy, false-killer, and melon-headed whales as well as Atlantic spinner dolphin and spotted dolphin. Altogether 22 species have been recorded. **Anchorage Whale Watch and Dive Center** and **Dive Dominica** run boat tours for whale-watching.

Deep-Sea Fishing

Fishing is an island pursuit and Dominicans will fish for hours from harbor walls or jetties. Operators such as **Island Style Fishing** and other operators organize deep-sea and game fishing, which is mostly for blue marlin and tuna that can weigh up to 1,000 lbs (450 kg), wahoo, and the fighting sailfish. Snapper, grouper, bonito, dorado, and barracuda can all be caught closer to the shore.

Surfer enjoying the waves of a Dominica beach

Hiking in Dominica

The best way to see Dominica is on foot, along one of the many hiking trails. In fact, hiking is the only way to reach some of the island's hidden treasures – emerald pools, cascading waterfalls, and bubbling lakes. The island's best hiking trails are found in the magnificent Morne Trois Pitons National Park *(see p383)*. The hikes run from the less-strenuous ones to the spectacular Trafalgar Falls to the more arduous climbs to Boiling Lake. Some trails require an experienced guide's assistance and a local guide will ensure that hikers get much more out of their trip.

The views from Morne Anglais hike

Easy Level

Many of the hiking trails are designated easy, which means they are of short duration and can be tackled by most people. Trails to Emerald Pool and Trafalgar Falls can be very busy on days when cruise ships are in port. The earlier visitors set out on a hike, the greater are their chances of spotting wildlife.

Emerald Pool is a well signposted, family-friendly 10-minute hike which allows visitors to explore the lush vegetation of the tropical rainforest and wildlife on the way to the pool. Those who bring swimwear can also take a dip in the very cool water.

Trafalgar Falls is one of Dominica's most popular natural attractions. The twin falls are only a short hike from the visitors' center just outside Trafalgar. Hikers can swim in the pool below the smaller waterfall to cool off.

Location of Trails

① Cabrits
② Syndicate
③ Morne Diablotin
④ Emerald Pool
⑤ Morne Trois Pitons
⑥ Boeri Lake
⑦ Glassy
⑧ Sari Sari Falls
⑨ Freshwater Lake
⑩ Middleham Falls
⑪ Titou Gorge
⑫ Trafalgar Falls
⑬ Boiling Lake
⑭ Victoria Falls
⑮ Morne Anglais
⑯ Scotts Head
⑰ Waitukubuli National Trail

Titou Gorge can be reached by a short hike and the trail passes through a series of pools, surrounded by solidified lava formations and a canopy of trees. A hot spring, just outside the entrance of the gorge, is ideal for swimming.

TOUR COMPANIES

Antours
Tel 767 440 5390. W antours.dm

Bumpiing Tours
Tel 767 265 9128.
W bumpiingtours.com

Hibiscus Eco-Tours
Tel 767 445 8195.
W hibiscusvalley.com

Wacky Rollers
W wackyrollers.com

Waitukubuli National Trail
Tel 767 266 3593.
W waitukubulitrail.com

Moderate Level

Moderate level walks take longer to hike and involve more difficult terrain that may require some scrambling. It is best to begin the Middleham Falls hike from Laudat. The initial hike is a little steep but the path levels out before descending to the falls.

Middleham Falls is one of Dominica's highest waterfalls, it takes about an hour to hike through the beautiful, pristine rainforest to reach these high-altitude falls. The forest is home to numerous bird species.

Difficult Level

There are strenuous but exhilarating hikes for experienced hikers. It takes at least 6 hours for the roundtrip to Boiling Lake and the Valley of Desolation, and about the same time to scramble up to the summit of Morne Diablotin and back.

Sisserou Parrot is found only on the island. Dominica's national bird is a large, shy creature that can be spotted in the dense rainforests, especially at higher elevations.

Boiling Lake is the world's second-largest actively boiling lake and is enveloped in a vaporous cloud. The lake seems to disappear as gases fill the center of the crater.

Syndicate starts at the Syndicate Visitors' Center and the walk passes through spectacular scenery. It takes about 2 hours and follows the gorge of the Picard River, which runs into the sea at Portsmouth. Hikers can arrange a pick-up, if they do not want to hike back.

Where to Stay

Tastefuly decorated room at Crescent Moon Cabins

BATALIE BAY: Sunset Bay Club and Seaside Dive Resort $$$
Beach Resort
Batalie Beach
Tel *767 446 6522*
W sunsetbayclub.com
Located on the west coast, this cozy resort is ideal for exploring the island. Features its own dive center, as well as a sauna.

CALABISHIE: Calabishie Lodges $$
Modern
Main Road
Tel *767 445 8537*
W calibishie-lodges.com
Lodges and apartments built in typical Caribbean style, all of them offering gorgeous sea views and surrounded by a working plantation.

CARIB TERRITORY: Carib Territory Guest House $
Guesthouse
Crayfish River
Tel *767 445 7256*
W avirtualdominica.com/ctgh.htm
Small and friendly place that offers excellent guided tours to the nearby forest reserves and National Park. Run by a hospitable, helpful couple.

CASTLE BRUCE: Beau Rive $$
Modern
between Castle Bruce and Sineku
Tel *768 445 8992*
W beaurive.com
Beau Rive offers rooms with ocean views set amid large tropical gardens with nearly 200 fruit and flowering trees. Children under 16 not allowed.

CASTLE COMFORT: Castle Comfort Lodge $
Waterfront
main road, 1 mile south of Roseau
Tel *767 448 2188*
W castlecomfortdivelodge.com
Family-owned and run diving lodge that offers great-value packages and tours. Guests can dive straight off the lodge's private dock.

MARIGOT: Hibiscus Valley Inn $
Guesthouse
Concord #6
Tel *767 445 8195*
W hibiscusvalley.com
Three nature bungalows as well as two semi-deluxe guestrooms with verandas, air-conditioning, and cable TV. The on-site restaurant serves local cuisine.

MARIGOT: Silks $$$
Boutique
Hatton Garden
Tel *767 445 8846*
W silkshotel.com
Relaxing luxury hotel built in the style of a 17th-century mansion. The beautiful rooms are furnished, with wooden floors and four-poster king-size beds. Alfresco fine-dining restaurant.

PORTSMOUTH: Secret Bay $$$
Luxury
Tibay
Tel *767 445 4444*
W secretbay.dm
Small, exclusive resort with plush villas and bungalows hidden atop a cliff overlooking the Caribbean Sea. Serves fresh, organic, local cuisine.

RIVIERE LA CROIX: Crescent Moon Cabins $$
Eco Lodge
River La Croix
Tel *767 449 3449*
W crescentmooncabins.com
Comfortable cabins in the foothills of the National Park, making it the perfect spot for hiking and exploring enthusiasts. Has a spring-water-fed plunge pool, as well as a heated hot tub.

ROSALIE: 3 Rivers Rosalie Forest Eco Lodge $
Eco Lodge
Newfoundland Estate
Tel *767 446 1886*
W rosalieforest.com
Bamboo tree houses, natural Carib forest cabins, isolated jungle cabins, and dormitories, all secluded in the rainforest are offered at the 3 Rivers.

ROSEAU: Cocoa Cottages and Gallery $$
Eco Lodge
Roseau
Tel *767 448 0412*
W cocoacottages.com
Cocoa Cottages is tucked away in tropical gardens and rainforest, offering a variety of adventure tours, including canyoneering.

ROSEAU: Fort Young Hotel $$
Modern
Victoria Street
Tel *767 448 5000*
W fortyounghotel.com
All rooms and suites at this waterfront property have private balconies, most offering fabulous ocean views.

ROSEAU: Garraway Hotel $$
Modern
1 Dame Mary Eugenia Charles Blvd.
Tel *767 449 8800*
W garrawayhotel.com
Located on Roseau's bayfront, this excellent business and leisure hotel is run by descendants of James Garraway, a Scottish planter who settled in Dominica in the 1800s. All rooms have either ocean or mountain views.

STOWE: Zandoli Inn $$
Eco Lodge
Roche Cassée
Tel *767 446 3161*
W zandoli.com
A small, secluded hideaway offering pleasantrooms, ocean views, and several forest trails. No TVs, radios, or phones.

DK Choice

TRAFALGAR FALLS: Papillote Wilderness Retreat $$
Eco Lodge
Trafalgar Falls Road
Tel *767 448 2287*
W papillote.dm
Dominica's first eco-resort, Papillote is a small, secluded inn set in a tropical garden, offering comfortable rooms. Waterfalls, hot pools, and exotic plant species make for an absolutely idyllic haven and a perfect holiday spot for honeymooners and families alike.

Where to Eat and Drink

BATALIE: Four Seasons $$$
Caribbean/European
*Sunset Bay Club & Dive Center,
Batalie Beach*
Tel *767 446 6522*
Friendly, laid-back restaurant with
great views of the beach and sea.
Good choice for lunch, dinner, or
snacks, with delicious fresh fish
and seafood on offer.

**CASTLE BRUCE: Islet View
Restaurant and Bar** $$
Caribbean
Castle Bruce
Tel *767 446 0370*
Choose from a menu of
Caribbean favorites along with
an interesting selection of
infused rums at this lovely
garden restaurant. Stunning
views of the bay.

**CASTLE BRUCE: Sea Surge
Restaurant** $$$
Caribbean/French
Evergreen Hotel, Loubiere Road
Tel *767 448 3288*
Come to Sea Surge to sample
delicious local cuisine with a
French touch. Set in a tropical
garden overlooking the sea,
with Roseau in the distance.
Seasonal menu.

LA PLAINE: Riverside Café $$
Caribbean
Citrus Creek Plantation
Tel *767 446 1234*
Located on the east coast, this is
a great place to stop for a good
meal while touring the island.
Offers lunch and snacks made
using the freshest local produce.
Dinner only by prior reservation.

**PORTSMOUTH:
The Champs** $$$
Caribbean/International
Blanca Heights, Picard
Tel *767 445 4455*
The Champs offers fine dining
on Friday and Saturday evenings
and casual meals the rest of the
week. With amazing views of the
Caribbean Sea and the Cabrits
National Park. Offers a range of
signature cocktails at the bar.

ROSEAU: Cocorico Restaurant $
French/Caribbean
corner of Bayfront and Kennedy Ave.
Tel *767 449 8686* **Closed** *Sun*
Cocorico is a relaxing seaside
eatery featuring artwork on the
walls. The emphasis is on fresh
local cuisine with French-Creole
infusions, with a range of sand-
wiches, salads, crêpes, and pastas.

ROSEAU: Cartwheel Café $$
Caribbean
Roseau
Tel *767 448 5353* **Closed** *Sun*
Small café in a historic stone
building. Good option for local
food, with excellent breakfasts
and lunches.

ROSEAU: Pearl's Cuisine $$
Caribbean/Seafood
Sutton Place Hotel, 25 Old Street
Tel *767 448 8707* **Closed** *Sun*
Pearl's is an institution, known
for its authentic home-made
Dominican cuisine, accompanied
by delicious fresh fruit juices.

**ROSEAU: Restaurant
Le Bistro** $$
European
19 Castle Street
Tel *767 440 8117* **Closed** *Sat & Sun*
This French-style bistro features
an upstairs patio and beautiful
sea views. The menu changes
regularly but is always good.

DK Choice

**ROSEAU: TAO Restaurant
& Lounge Bar** $$
International
11 Victoria Street
Tel *767 316 6666* **Closed** *Tue–
Thu; Sun*
This elegant yet relaxed
restaurant has a wonderful
ambience, with outdoor seating
on a balcony overlooking the
Caribbean Sea. The diverse
menu features cuisines from
around the world, including
Peruvian, Spanish, and
Japanese, as well as great
vegetarian options. There is also
an art gallery on the premises.

ROSEAU: Waterfront Café $$
Caribbean/International
Fort Young Hotel, Victoria Street
Tel *767 448 5000*
Waterfront Café offers a romantic
atmosphere, with views of the
Caribbean Sea. Dine on the

veranda or in the air-conditioned
interior. Everything from Creole
classics to international specialties.

ROSEAU: Zam Zam Café $$
Mexican
Citronier
Tel *767 612 7471* **Closed** *Mon & Tue*
Zam Zam sits on the beach
looking out to the most
magnificent sunsets. The menu
is international with an emphasis
on Mexican cuisine. Good burritos.

**TRAFALGAR FALLS: Papillote
Rainforest Restaurant** $$$
Caribbean/Seafood
*Papillote Wilderness Retreat,
Trafalgar Falls Road*
Tel *767 448 2287*
In a beautiful garden setting near
a natural mineral hot pool, this
restaurant is part of a rainforest
eco-resort. The focus is on
organic, healthy Caribbean food,
with vegetarian options.

**WESLEY: Randy's Restaurant
and Bar** $$
Caribbean/International
Hunt Road
Tel *767 315 7474*
Randy's is known for its local
Creole cuisine and international
favorites, as well as its popular
reggae parties every Wednesday.
Don't miss the chicken curry,
mahi-mahi, or the rum punch.

**WOTTEN WAVEN:
Le Petit Paradis** $$
Caribbean/International
Wotten Waven
Tel *767 440 4352*
Eco-conscious restaurant set amid
lush gardens. Delicious meals are
served on the terrace. Reservations must be made in advance.

Stunning sea views from the dining area at The Champs, Portsmouth

Practical Information

Dominica is one of the few countries in the world that does not have an international airport in a deliberate effort to preserve the unspoilt beauty of the island. The Dominicans do not want massive jets roaring in and out of their island, upsetting their own very special brand of eco-tourism. However, this is no great inconvenience for visitors as there are still plenty of options for flying in and it is a relatively small price to pay if it preserves Dominica, as it is, for generations to come.

Duty-free shopping center in Dominica's capital, Roseau

When to Go

The best time to visit the island is between January and June when it is generally dry. The rainy season is between August and October, when hurricanes can occur.

Getting There

There are no direct international flights from North America or Europe to Dominica. Airlines fly into Puerto Rico, Antigua, St. Martin, Barbados, Martinique, and Guadeloupe. From these islands there are connecting flights on **LIAT** and **Seaborne Airlines** to the Melville Hall airport. While Canefield is 15 minutes from Roseau, Melville Hall is a 90-minute drive from the capital.

There is a high-speed catamaran ferry service between Dominica and St. Lucia, Guadeloupe, and Martinique, and cruise ships regularly dock at the island. The main ferry operator is **L'Express des Îles**. It is ideal to check the timetables before traveling.

Documentation

Visitors are required to show a valid passport on arrival in Dominica to immigration officials. They need to show a return ticket and have to pay a departure tax when leaving Dominica. Visitors from North America and Europe do not require a visa. Customs officers may ask visitors to open their luggage for a quick inspection. It is a good idea to carry a copy of proof of ownership such as receipts for expensive items.

Visitor Information

Discover Dominica Authority in Roseau helps visitors find their way around the island. It guides them on where to stay, activities, and more. There are overseas offices in the USA, UK, Germany, and France.

Health and Security

Dominica has three major hospitals, **Portsmouth Hospital** and **Princess Margaret Hospital** in Roseau, with the latter having an intensive care unit, and the smaller **Marigot Hospital**. Princess Margaret Hospital has the island's only hyperbaric chamber. Visitors should have adequate personal insurance and medical cover. Most big hotels also have a doctor on call in case of minor medical emergencies. Dominica has a low crime rate but it is better not to wear expensive jewelry or carry large sums of money. It is also sensible not to leave valuables unattended on the beach or in view in parked rental cars. In case of an emergency, contact the police.

Banking and Currency

The local currency is the East Caribbean dollar. However, most places on the island accept US dollars. All major credit cards are widely accepted although some restaurants take only cash so check in advance. Banks are open from 8am to 2pm from Monday to Thursday and 8am to 4pm on Fridays.

One of the many cruise ships arriving at the Roseau cruise ship terminal

Indigenous crafts from the Carib region on display

Communications

The island's area code is 767. To call from and to the US dial 1 and then the number. For calls to the UK dial 011 44 and then the number (omitting the first 0). For phone services, contact **LIME Dominica**.

Transport

The best way to explore the island is to hire a car and there are several rental agencies such as **Valley Car Rental** and **Best Deal Rent-a-Car**. Most rentals are based in the capital, Roseau. Visitors need to buy a month's valid license and have to be over 25. Public buses can be flagged down on the road. Taxis are also available from the airports and Roseau but are usually expensive.

Shopping

Most of the stores are usually open from 8am to 4pm from Monday to Friday and from 9am to 1pm on Saturdays. There are lots of arts and crafts stalls all around the island, perfect for getting souvenirs for friends and family. In Roseau, there are several stalls in the Old Market Square offering a wide range of coconut, straw, and Carib craft specialty products.

Time

The island is on Atlantic Standard Time, 4 hours behind Greenwich Mean Time. Dominica does not observe daylight saving time.

Language

English is the official language although many people speak Kweyol, a dialect that is based on French.

Electricity

Dominica operates on 220–240 volts and US visitors need to carry adaptors and transformers for their appliances.

Getting Married

At least one member of the couple must be in Dominica for at least two days before the wedding. The stamp in the passport will be considered proof.

A completed marriage application form (which can be downloaded from the **Discover Dominica Authority** website) must be signed by both parties and witnessed by a magistrate, a justice of the peace, notary public, commissioner of oaths, or registrar. The couple will also need birth certificates and legal proof that any previous marriage is over. Each of them must then sign a completed declaration form before a commissioner of oaths and attach a stamp to both these forms and a marital status form. All these forms should be returned to the ministry which will then issue a marriage license. This is presented to the registrar before the wedding ceremony.

Many hotels, such as **Jungle Bay Resort and Spa** and **Fort Young Hotel**, offer wedding and honeymoon packages. There are also several marriage consultants such as **JTAS Weddings** who can make all the arrangements.

DIRECTORY

Getting There

L'Express des Îles
W express-des-iles.com

LIAT
Tel 767 445 7242.
W liat.com

Seaborne Airlines
Tel 866 359 8784.
W seaborneairlines.com

Visitor Information

Discover Dominica Authority
1st Floor, Financial Ctr., Kennedy Ave., Roseau. Tel 767 448 2045.
W discoverdominica.com

Health and Security

Ambulance, Police, and Fire
Tel 999.

Marigot Hospital
Marigot. Tel 767 445 7091.

Portsmouth Hospital
Portsmouth. Tel 767 445 5237.

Princess Margaret Hospital
Roseau. Tel 767 448 2231.

Communications

LIME Dominica
W time4lime.com

Transport

Best Deal Rent-a-Car
15 Hanover Street, Roseau.
Tel 767 449 9204.

Valley Car Rental
Melville Hall Airport.
Tel 767 275 1310.

Getting Married

Discover Dominica Authority
See Visitor Information.

Fort Young Hotel
Victoria Street. Tel 767 448 5000.
W fortyounghotel.com

Jungle Bay Resort and Spa
Pointe Mulatre. Tel 767 446 1789.
W junglebaydominica.com

JTAS Weddings
PO Box 1528, Roseau.
Tel 767 440 5827.
W experiencescaribbean.com

Exploring St. Lucia

St. Lucia lies in the eastern Caribbean about 21 miles (34 km) south of Martinique and 26 miles (42 km) northeast of St. Vincent – both of which can be seen on clear days. The island has had a turbulent history and for centuries was fought over because of its strategic position, changing hands 14 times between the English and French. Today, there are few reminders of this troubled past and St. Lucia offers unspoiled beaches such as Marigot Bay and Choc Bay, and turquoise seas teeming with tropical fish, a wealth of watersports and land-based activities, breathtaking scenery with tropical rainforests and a drive-in volcanic area, world-class resorts, and great food.

Locator Map

The well-maintained Derek Walcott Square, in Castries

Getting Around

Hiring a car is the best option here but taxis are cheap and plentiful, and drivers attend special courses so they make excellent guides. Taxis can be hired for a trip, by the hour or by the day, but always negotiate a price first. Privately owned minibuses are the island's chief means of transport and ply along the main routes. There are frequent services between Castries and Gros Islet and less frequent services to Soufrière and Vieux Fort. The southern-bound buses do not run late in the evening. There are boat services between Castries and Soufrière.

Sights at a Glance

① Castries
③ Fond Doux Holiday Plantation
④ Soufrière
⑤ The Pitons
⑥ Vieux Fort and East Coast
⑦ Choc Bay
⑧ Rodney Bay

⑨ Gros Islet
⑩ *Pigeon Island National Landmark p399*

Featured Hotels and Resorts

② Discovery at Marigot Bay

The Pitons
A World Heritage Site, the Gros Piton and the Petit Piton lure the adventurous with excellent hiking opportunities.

For hotels and restaurants on this island see p406 and p407

**GEON ISLAND
ATIONAL
ANDMARK**
10
9 GROS ISLET
8 RODNEY BAY

Cap
Estate Cas-en-Bas

Marisule
Estate

7 CHOC BAY
Grande
Rivière

Union
Nature
Trail
Bonneau

Paix
Bouche

Grande
Anse

Desbarras

Marquis Bay

Espérance River

Choc River

Gros Islet
This lively
fishing village
transforms into
a carnival every
Friday night
with reggae
music concerts
and dancing in
the streets.

The fishing harbor at Choiseul, south of Soufrière

0 kilometers   5
0 miles   5

Dennery
A quiet fishing village,
Dennery has a few lovely
beaches and some excel-
lent seafood restaurants.

Key

━━ Major road
══ Minor road
--- Ferry route
△ Peak

Grande
Rivière

La
Belle Vie

Mount
La Combe
1,442 ft

Errard
Plantation

Dennery
Dennery
Island
Dennery Bay

Dennery River

Mamiku River

Praslin
Mamiku

Praslin Bay

Mamiku
Gardens

Mon Repos
Anse
Patience

Patience

Malgrétoute

Fond
Bay

Troumassee River

Micoud

Desruisseaux

Anse Ger

Grace

**Mankote Mangrove
Swamps**
The largest mangrove
swamp on the island,
about 98 acres (40 ha),
is home to many
different bird species.

Savannes
Bay

Mankote
Mangrove Swamps

Coconut
Bay
Pointe Sable

6
VIEUX FORT
D EAST COAST

Maria Islands
Anse des Sables

Cape Moule
à Chique Lighthouse

Swaying palms at the popular Marigot Bay

For additional map symbols *see back flap*

The Roman Catholic Cathedral, Castries

❶ Castries

NW coast of St. Lucia. 🏙 66,000. ✈
🚌 🚢 ℹ Pointe Seraphine, 758 452
3036. 🎷 St. Lucia Jazz Festival (May).

Castries is a bustling little city
of gingerbread houses that hug
the hillsides surrounding the
shops and busy harbor. It has
suffered four major fires over
the last 200 years, but the last
one enabled the planners to
rebuild the city on a grid,
making it very easy to explore.
The colorful market on Peynier
Street has interesting local produce, such as straw items,
spices, and herbs. A market
guide, available for a small tip
at the entrance, explains the
use of these goods.

Built in 1899, the **Roman
Catholic Cathedral of the
Immaculate Conception**
contains many paintings with
biblical scenes in which all
the characters are black. The
cathedral is located on the
eastern side of Derek Walcott
Square, named after the island's
1992 Nobel laureate in literature,
Derek Walcott. The large samaan
tree in the square is thought to
be at least 400 years old.

Environs
A short walk north of town,
Pointe Seraphine offers world-
class duty-free shopping next
to the cruise ship terminal.
The main tourist information

center is located here
as well as several good
restaurants, cafés,
and bars.

A hill to the south
of town, The Morne
offers a superb aerial
view of Castries. Given
its strategic position,
the French built **Fort
Charlotte** near its
summit in the late
18th century, which
was later added to by
the British. The area is
now a protected historic
sight and has many
restored military build-
ings. However, it is the
panoramic views from
The Morne that are
undoubtedly the
most breathtaking.

🏛 **Roman Catholic Cathedral
of the Immaculate Conception**
Laborie Street. **Tel** 758 452 2416.
Open 8am–4pm daily.

🏚 **Fort Charlotte**
The Morne. **Open** dawn to dusk daily.

❷ Discovery at Marigot Bay

🏖 Marigot Bay.
Tel 758 458 5300. 🏨 ✏ 🏊
🌐 **discoverystlucia.com**

A short drive from the main
road leading to the water's
edge, Marigot Bay is about
7 miles (11 km) south of
Castries. Surrounded by lush
foliage-covered hills, the bay
is considered among the

most beautiful anchorages
in the Caribbean and has
been the setting for several
films, including the original
Dr. Dolittle (1967) and
Firepower (1979). The busy
marina here is full of local
craftsmen at work.

Discovery at Marigot
Bay is a luxury resort with
accommodations nestled in
the hillside overlooking the
Marigot Bay. Some of the suites
have private plunge pools
and most units offer fabulous
views of the palm-fringed
bay. The restaurant *(see p407)*
features everything from the
finest haute cuisine to casual
tropical tastes, and excellent
drinks are mixed at the bar.
The Lapli Spa provides a wide
range of beauty treatments.
The hotel's restaurants and spa
are open to non-guests too.

❸ Fond Doux Holiday Plantation

Soufrière. **Tel** 758 459 7545.
Open 9am–3pm daily.

The Fond Doux Holiday
Plantation is one of the oldest
working plantations in the
Caribbean. It was granted to the
Devaux brothers by Louis XIV
in 1713 and produced coffee,
cocoa, and, later, sugarcane.
It is now a heritage site offering
luxury accommodations. The
135-acre plantation produces
more than 30 types of trees
and food crops and is a model
of organic agriculture.

View of Marigot Bay from the lookout point above

For hotels and restaurants on this island see p406 and p407

❹ Soufrière

15 miles (24 km) S of Castries.
7,500.

St. Lucia's first settled town and former capital during French rule, Soufrière is now a picturesque fishing town. During the French Revolution, the Revolutionary Council ordered that all French names must be changed, so Soufrière became La Convention and a guillotine was built in the town square. While most Royalist plantation owners fled, some were executed. The town, which has a beach fringed with coconut palms, is divided into two by the Soufrière River. Most of the shops, craft centers, restaurants, and guesthouses are located in the few streets inland from the jetty. Traditional Creole homes with their ornate filigree friezes and elaborate balconies stand out, and the market is decorated with colorful murals.

Malmaison, situated on the outskirts of town, is where Napoleon Bonaparte's wife Josephine (see p398) spent her childhood.

Environs
Other estates in the area that can be explored include the **Diamond Estate**, famous for its therapeutic mineral baths and gardens. Visitors can see coconuts, copra, and cocoa being processed at the Morne Coubaril Estate (see p401).

The **Soufrière Volcanic Area** is located just south of town. There is a giant crater, formed during an eruption 40,000 years ago that blew the mountain apart. There are 24 cauldrons of bubbling mud that boil at around 340° F (171° C) within the 7-acre (3-ha) site. It is advisable to keep to the marked paths. Guides can be hired at the entrance.

❺ The Pitons

20 miles (32 km) S of Castries.

The island's most famous and most photographed landmark, the volcanic Pitons dominate the landscape as one drives

View of Soufrière with the Pitons rising up in the background

south from Soufrière. Rising like two sugar loafs out of the sea, Petit Piton (the northernmost) is 2,437 ft (743 m) high while Gros Piton reaches 2,529 ft (771 m). The latter is the easier to climb although it is steep towards the summit. It would take about 5 hours to climb and descend either peak. Gros Piton Tours (see p403) offer guided hikes.

❻ Vieux Fort and East Coast

25 miles (40 km) S of Castries.
16,500.

Vieux Fort is close to the southern tip of the island and commands fine views across to St. Vincent. Once the island's capital and main harbor, and named after a fort built here in the 17th century, Vieux Fort is now the island's windsurfing center. On its outskirts, the **Mankote Mangrove Swamps** is a favorite spot with bird-watchers.

Farther north along the eastern coast is **Savannes Bay**, famous for its bird reserve. While the west coast is sheltered, the rocky east coast is often battered by Atlantic breakers, making it popular with surfers. Farther ahead from Micoud are the **Latille Gardens**, which present a blaze of tropical color, exotic fruits, and waterfalls.

Dennery, farther north, is one of the island's most beautiful villages and has a long tradition of fishing and boatbuilding. Some of the boats are still constructed by hand from trees felled in the rainforest.

Mankote Mangrove Swamps
Tel 758 452 5005. **Open** dawn to dusk daily. Note: there are short trails and a wooden viewing tower overlooking the swamp.

Savannes Bay
Open dawn to dusk.

Latille Gardens
Tel 758 489 6271.

Derek Walcott

Born in Castries in 1930, Derek Walcott is one of the island's most famous poets. Both his grandfathers were white while his grandmothers were apparently of slave descent. His father, an artist, died when Derek was young and his mother ran the town's Methodist school. All this influenced his works, which are a blend of Caribbean, English, and African traditions. His first poems were published at the age of 18 and he has produced many widely acclaimed volumes of poetry and plays since. Awarded the Nobel Prize for Literature in 1992, he continues to write and teach in the Caribbean and the United States.

Portrait of playwright and poet Derek Walcott

The sweeping Choc Bay on the northwest coast of St. Lucia

❼ Choc Bay

3 miles (5 km) N of Castries.

Choc Bay boasts a tree-lined stretch of sand, with gentle waves lapping the shore. A popular tourist area, it is well developed with several classy hotels and all-inclusive resorts, restaurants, and galleries.

Inland from the bay, Union Trail is a short self-guided nature walk. It starts at the Union Agricultural Center's Interpretive Center on Babonneau Road. The herb garden here was used for traditional medicinal practice. The trail is an easy looped walk through the rainforest. The rare multi-hued St. Lucia parrot can be spotted here.

Nearby, **Fond Latisab Creole Park**, in the Fond Assau community, is part of St. Lucia's Heritage Tourism Program. It provides a glimpse of the Creole traditions of preparing cassava bread, cooking on macambou leaves, catching freshwater crayfish, and log sawing to the rhythms of a traditional *chak chak* (musical instrument) band.

Fond Latisab Creole Park
Babonneau. **Tel** 758 450 5461.
Open 9am–4pm daily.

❽ Rodney Bay

6 miles (10 km) N of Castries.

One of the most popular yachting destinations in the Caribbean, Rodney Bay has a beautifully landscaped marina with restaurants, bars, shops, and galleries. It is also one of the leading charter centers in the Caribbean and many charter companies are based here. The bay is worth visiting during the day to browse through the shops and enjoy a waterside

Yacht moored in Rodney Bay marina

lunch, and at night when it becomes lively thanks to its many nightlife venues.

❾ Gros Islet

8 miles (13 km) N of Castries.
19,000.

Across Rodney Bay is Gros Islet, a small fishing village and home to the famous Friday night "Jump Up". This huge open-air party fills the streets and lasts until the early hours of the morning. Tables and chairs are placed in the narrow streets and loud music booms from huge speakers, as revelers move from one bar to the next, drinking beer and dancing the night away. It is also a great place to try local food specialties from the scores of street vendors.

Empress Josephine

Empress Josephine was born as Marie-Joseph-Rose de Tascher de la Pagerie on June 23, 1763, at Morne Paix Bouche, in the north of St. Lucia. In 1779, Rose, as she was known, accompanied her father to France and married the wealthy landowner Alexandre Vicomte de Beauharnais. During the Reign of Terror in 1794, both she and her husband were imprisoned. While he was guillotined in Paris, she was freed. She met Napoleon Bonaparte in 1795, when he was still a general in the army, and they married in March 1796. Called Josephine by Bonaparte, who did not like the name Rose, she was crowned empress in 1804. She died on May 29, 1814.

Portrait of Empress Josephine

⑩ Pigeon Island National Landmark

Jutting out into the sea, the Pigeon Island National Landmark is connected to the mainland by a causeway. Covering an area of 44 acres (18 ha), it was first fortified by the French in 1778, who were ousted the following year by a huge British naval force. It was from here that English Admiral Rodney attacked the French fleet in 1782. The ensuing Battle of Saintes ended French domination in the Caribbean. Pigeon Island remained one of the most formidable forts for decades but was eventually abandoned in 1861. Since then it has been a whaling station and served as a US Naval Air Station during World War II.

VISITORS' CHECKLIST

Practical Information
8 miles (13 km) N of Castries.
Tel 758 452 5005. ℹ️ Interpretive Center, near the entrance gate.
Open 9am–6pm daily. 🗺️ 📷 ✏️
📱 📷

Transport
🚌 🚌

Interpretive Center
The former officers' quarters hosts the Interpretive Center and museum, which displays items of local historical interest, such as this bust of Admiral Rodney.

Key

- - - Walking path

Pigeon Island entrance gate

Signal Peaks
Pigeon Island is dominated by two small peaks which made excellent observation posts.

Officer's Kitchen

0 metres 100
0 yards 100

Gros Islet 2.5 miles (4km)

Bakery

US Signal Station

Cemetery

Lookout

Barrack Ruins
Remnants of military barracks and encampments are scattered about on the eastern side of the island.

Fort Rodney
Once a British stronghold, Fort Rodney is in ruins today. The top of the fort offers sweeping views of Rodney Bay.

Pigeon Island Beaches
A number of excellent, white-sand beaches around the island provide good swimming opportunities.

Outdoor Activities and Specialized Holidays

St. Lucia is an outdoors wonderland with a wealth of land and water activity opportunities. Visitors can hike, go in search of rare and elusive wildlife in the rainforest, ride on horseback along the sand or scuba dive over pristine reefs in warm, crystal-clear water. Farther out to sea, there is deep-sea fishing and year-round whale- and dolphin-watching. Back on land, there is tennis, golf, rock climbing, and cycling.

The all-inclusive Sandals Grande resort at Rodney Bay

Beaches

The beaches in St. Lucia are fabulous for sunbathing, swimming, and snorkeling. All are open to the public even if some hotels and resorts make it difficult to access them. There will be a public path down to the beach although visitors may have to search a little to find it.

The southwest coast of the island is relatively sheltered and safer for swimming. Anse des Pitons is a fabulous crescent-shaped beach overlooked by the Pitons.

Anse Chastanet, located just north of Soufrière, is a picture postcard beach with 1 mile (1.6 km) of soft, white sand fringed by gently swaying palms and lapped by warm, crystal-clear blue water. Soufrière itself has a stretch of dark sandy beach to the north of town which is a favorite spot with the local residents.

On the northwest coast, the popular Marigot Bay *(see p396)* is home to another spectacular beach. The bay itself is surrounded on three sides by forested hills and vacationers

can find a number of restaurants, bars, cafés, and shops nearby. For those looking for some peace and quiet, there is an inlet close by with a couple of secluded, sandy coves.

Choc Bay *(see p398)* is a sweeping, sandy bay near Castries. The calm waters make it a good place for families with children and palm trees provide shade during the hottest parts of the day. Farther north, Labrelotte Bay is a small, sandy beach with

Diving preparation at Anse Chastanet, near Soufrière

sparkling blue water, located close to Windjammer Landing.

Reduit Bay and Rodney Bay *(see p398)*, St. Lucia's main beach area, has several bars and watersport activities but can get a bit crowded, especially during the weekends.Pigeon Island *(see p399)* is both a historic landmark and a very popular recreation area, with several small but attractive beaches.

Anse des Sables, on the south coast, is an accessible, sandy but windy beach looking out to the Maria Islands. It is popular with surfers and windsurfers and also a great beach for sunning.

Information about the various beaches and beach activities is available at hotel desks and tourist centers including Pointe Seraphine in Castries *(see p396)*.

Resort-based Activities

The different resorts around the island provide the widest range of land and water activities, including canoeing and kayaking, windsurfing, sailing, waterskiing, hydro biking, kneeboarding, snorkeling, and scuba diving – all usually included in the price of the stay or day pass. Land activities include table tennis, shuffleboards, croquet, fitness routines, golf, tennis, beach volleyball, and billiards.

It is also possible to get pampered with a wide range of treatments at the resort spa. Many spas offer special side-by-side treatment programs for couples and will accept reservations from non-guests.

Visitors not staying at luxury all-inclusive resorts can still enjoy the facilities they offer through half-day or one-day passes. Sandals, which has three fabulous all-inclusive resorts – the Grande, Halcyon, and Regency St. Lucia – offers a day pass. The price includes food, drinks, and watersports, and visitors can also spend the day in the landscaped pool and beach areas. Those who do not want a day pass can use the resort's beach chairs and umbrellas for a small fee.

Plantations of St. Lucia

Plantations are the living history of St. Lucia. They were worked by African slaves whose descendants now populate the island. Several plantations are still working estates with their great houses and the original heavy machinery, imported from Europe to process sugarcane, cotton, and tobacco, intact. Many estates still bear their French names, often given in anticipation of great things to come, such as L'Espérance (Hope) and Tranquilité (Peace). There are many tours available to working plantations which try to show what life was like for both the owners and the slaves in olden days.

Soufrière Estate, home to the oldest watermill still operating in the Caribbean, shows how local crops are grown and processed.

Fond Latisab Creole Park *(see p398)* demonstrates ancient Creole farming practices and traditional cooking methods.

Marquis Estate offers tours and has displays of old agricultural equipment.

Morne Coubaril Estate, a fully working plantation, allows visitors to experience traditional agricultural activities such as the making of copra (dried coconut kernel), cocoa, and cassava.

Fond Doux Holiday Plantation *(see p396)*, an 18th century working estate with spectacular views, uses historic cocoa-drying sheds to process cocoa. Visitors can also walk the estate trails.

Cap Estate
Gros Islet
Grande Rivière
Castries
Paix Bouche
Babonneau
Marquis Bay
Anse la Raye
Dennery
Mount La Combe 1,442 ft
Fond d'Or Estate
Barre de l'Isle Ridge
Errard Estate
Soufrière
Morne Gimie 3,118 ft
Soufrière Bay
Mount Grand Magazin 2,022 ft
Gros Piton 2,529 ft
Micoud
Choiseul
Laborie
Vieux Fort

0 km   5
0 miles   5

Plantations

Balenbouche Estate
Tel 758 455 1244.
w balenbouche.com

Fond Doux Holiday Plantation
Tel 758 459 7545.
w fonddouxestate.com

Morne Coubaril Estate
Tel 758 459 7340.

Soufrière Estate
Tel 758 459 7565.

Key

♣ Estate
▲ Peak
— Major road
— Minor road

Balenbouche Estate, a 19th-century estate, is surrounded by a charming garden. Nearby are the remains of an impressive 18th-century sugar factory.

View of Gros Piton from a hiking trail

Hiking

Hiking is one of the best ways to explore the quieter side of St. Lucia, especially with a guide, who has a good knowledge of the local terrain and wildlife.

Hikers should wear sturdy, non-slip footwear and carry a hat, insect repellent, and drinking water. It is a good idea to pack a pair of binoculars for wildlife spotting; 8x40 are ideal.

St. Lucia's interior is covered in mountainous rainforests rising to almost 1,800 ft (548 m) and there are 29 miles (47 km) of trails. On these, visitors can see rare birds and exotic plants. Walks include the Union Nature Trail, an easy loop walk through lush vegetation rich in wildlife that ends at a mini-zoo, which is home to many local species, such as the rare St. Lucia parrot and the St. Lucia iguana.

Barre de l'Isle Trail, off the highway between Castries and Dennery, is an easy walk through a forest reserve. It gets its name because it divides the eastern and western halves of the island. It takes about an hour to walk this 1-mile (1.6-km) trail and another hour to climb up to the Mount La Combe ridge, but it is worth it for the panoramic views.

The Edmund Forest Reserve Trail starts at the entrance to the reserve. A strenuous walk, it takes about 4 hours to complete and ends at the Des Cartiers Rainforest Trail. Various species of orchids grow along the trail. A side trail leads to Morne Gimie, which at 3,118 ft (950 m) is the highest point on the island.

The trails can only be accessed with the permission of the **Forest and Lands Department**. A list of walks can be obtained from the tourist offices as well as well-known tour operators, such as **Heritage Tours** and **GrosPiton Tours**.

Canopy Tours

An aerial tram journey into and over the tropical rainforest offers a bird's-eye view of the forest and its flora and fauna. Gondolas are suspended from cables and guides provide a running commentary during the tour. For more information and guides, contact **Rainforest Aerial Trams**.

Diving and Snorkeling

The clear, warm waters off St. Lucia are ideal for scuba divers of all levels and the reefs teem with an amazing variety of plant and marine life. It is possible to swim among nurse sharks, turtles, and shoals of tropical fish. Some of the more spectacular dive sites include Key Hole Pinnacles and Superman's Flight, a drift drive along a wall that drops to 1,600 ft (488 m), situated just off Petit Piton. Just down the coast, off Gros Piton, are the spectacular Coral Gardens, rising from a depth of 15 to 50 ft (5 to 15 m). Well-known operators include **Sunsail**, **Tornado Kite and Surf**, **Scuba Steve's Diving**, **Sailing Let's Go**, and **Mako Watersports**. For diving trips, popular agencies to contact are **Island Divers** and **Dive Fair Helen**.

Stunning coral reef in the waters off St. Lucia

Horse-Riding

The **International Riding Stables** and **Trims National Riding Academy** offer an assortment of trail rides to suit all levels of experience, from riding through the forest to a splashing gallop along the water's edge.

Golf

Visitors can enjoy a round of golf in the most stunning of settings. There are 9- and 18-hole courses that test the most skilled golfer and views are breathtaking. Guests are welcome at the private clubs. The **Sandals Regency Golf Resort and Spa** and **St. Lucia Golf & Country Club** have 18 holes while Jalousie Plantation has 9 holes.

Tennis

There are lots of courts but only a few are floodlit. It is better to play early before the sun becomes too hot. Most hotels allow visitors to use their tennis courts for a fee.

Cycling

Cycling is a great way to get around trails, especially in Anse Mamin, a historic plantation. The island is hilly so fit and experienced cyclists can make the most of it.

Sailing

A major yachting center, St. Lucia is home to many yachting and charter agencies such as **Destination St. Lucia, Escape to Paradise, Tradewind Yachts,** and **Moorings St. Lucia**. It is possible to charter yachts for a day sail or to tour the islands.

Fishing

World-class charter and deep-sea fishing boats are available for whole and half-day excursions. Reputed fishing concessionaires include Mako Watersports.

Whale-Watching

Over 20 whale species, such as sperm, humpback, and pilot whales, can be spotted off St. Lucia's coast year round.

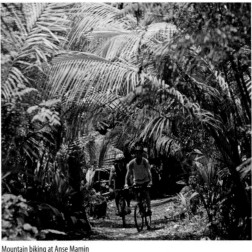

Mountain biking at Anse Mamin

DIRECTORY

Hiking

Forest and Lands Department
Tel 758 468 5645.

Gros Piton Tours
Soufrière.
Tel 758 489 0136.

Heritage Tours
La Clery, Castries.
Tel 758 458 1454.
w heritagetoursstlucia.org

Canopy Tours

Rainforest Aerial Trams
Near Fond Asseau.
Tel 758 458 5151.

Diving and Snorkeling

Dive Fair Helen
Castries. Tel 758 451 7716.
w divefairhelen.com

Island Divers
Ti Kaye Village, Anse Cochon. Tel 758 456 8110. w islanddivers stlucia.com

Mako Watersports
Tel 758 452 0412.

Sailing Let's Go
Rodney Bay.
Tel 758 452 8234.

Scuba Steve's Diving
Tel 758 450 9433.
w scubastevesdiving.com

Sunsail
Rodney Bay Marina.
Tel 758 452 8648.

Tornado Kite and Surf
Tel 758 713 2110.
w tornado-surf.com

Horse-Riding

International Riding Stables
Tel 758 452 8139.

Trims National Riding Academy
Gros Islet.
Tel 758 450 8273.

Golf

Sandals Regency Golf Resort and Spa
Tel 758 452 3081.
w sandals.com

St. Lucia Golf & Country Club
Cap Estate, Rodney Bay.
Tel 758 450 8523.
w stluciagolf.com

Sailing

Destination St. Lucia
Rodney Bay.
Tel 758 452 8531.
w dsl-yachting.com

Escape to Paradise
Tel 758 452 0344.

Moorings St. Lucia
Marigot Bay.
Tel 758 451 4357.
w moorings.com

Tradewind Yachts
Rodney Bay.
Tel 758 452 8424.

Where to Stay

Beautiful bedroom at the Windjammer Landing, Labrelotte Bay

Price Guide
Prices are based on one night's stay in high season for a standard double room, inclusive of service charges and taxes.
$ up to $100
$$ $100–300
$$$ over $300

DK Choice

ANSE CHASTANET:
Anse Chastanet   **$$$**
Beach Resort
Old French Road
Tel *758 453 2073*
W ansechastanet.com
A resort in tune with its natural habitat, Anse Chastanet offers the choice of hillside or beachside villas on an expansive estate. Phones and TVs are replaced by breathtaking vistas of the Pitons, making this the perfect choice for a long-awaited, secluded, and peaceful retreat.

CASTRIES:
Auberge Seraphine   **$$**
Modern
Vielle Bay, Pointe Seraphine
Tel *758 453 2073*
W aubergeseraphine.com
An intimate getaway with spacious rooms overlooking Vigie Cove and the marina. Renowned for its creative restaurant.

CASTRIES: Bel Jou Hotel   **$$**
Modern
La Pansee
Tel *758 456 1810*
Set on a hill overlooking Castries Harbour, and close to deep-sea fishing, sunset sailing cruises, volcano tours, and the market. Chic rooms.

COCONUT BAY: Coconut Bay
Resort and Spa   **$$$**
Luxury
Vieux Fort
Tel *758 459 6000*
W cbayresort.com
Elegant rooms set amid a large garden. The resort offers an array of water and land activities, including children's programs.

GROS ISLET:
The BodyHoliday at LeSport **$$$**
Luxury
Cariblue Beach, Cap Estate
Tel *758 457 7800*
W thebodyholiday.com
This resort places great emphasis on health, exercise, and relaxation, and it is famous for its therapeutic spa.

LABRELOTTE BAY:
Windjammer Landing   **$$**
Beach Resort
Labrelotte Bay
Tel *758 456 9000*
W windjammer-landing.com
A large, luxurious place featuring fully equipped rooms, large villas with private plunge pools, and five restaurants.

MALABAR BEACH:
Rendezvous   **$$$**
Boutique
Malabar Beach
Tel *758 457 7900*
W theromanticholiday.com
A couples-only hotel with beautifully decorated cottages, suites, and rooms. Guests can enjoy a romantic candlelit dinner in their room, on the beach, or in the gourmet restaurant.

MARIGOT BAY: Oasis Marigot **$$**
Villas
117 Seaview Avenue
Tel *758 451 4185*
W oasismarigot.com
Each unit here offers stunning views over Marigot Bay, as well as access to the small palm-fringed beach.

REDUIT BAY: Royal Hotel   **$$$**
Beach Resort
Reduit Beach
Tel *758 425 9999*
W rexresorts.com
Located on the island's most scenic beach, the Royal Hotel

has well-fitted rooms. Amenities include two restaurants, a spa, and a pre-teens' club.

RODNEY BAY: Bay Gardens   **$$**
Modern
Rodney Bay
Tel *758 457 8006*
W baygardenshotel.com
Bay Gardens offers comfortable rooms, some equipped with their own kitchenettes. On occasion, there are entertainment programs by local artistes.

RODNEY BAY:
The Landings   **$$$**
Luxury
Rodney Bay
Tel *758 458 7300*
W thelandingsstlucia.com
Relax in this large oceanfront resort that features suites with full kitchens, making it an ideal choice for families. It also has its own private yacht harbor.

SOUFRIÈRE: Ladera   **$$$**
Beach Resort
Rabot Estate
Tel *758 459 6600*
W ladera.com
Ladera is a small, elegant resort with villas and suites that feature open-air bedrooms and plunge pools. Children under 14 are not allowed.

SOUFRIÈRE: Stonefield
Estate Resort   **$$$**
Luxury
Stonefield Estate
Tel *758 459 7037*
W stonefieldresort.com
Stonefield Estate offers villas built to highlight and maximize views, each with intimate outdoor garden showers, verandas, and hammocks. The restaurant food features organic local produce.

SOUFRIÈRE: Sugar Beach,
A Viceroy Resort   **$$$**
Luxury
Val des Pitons
Tel *758 456 8000*
W viceroyhotelsandresorts.com
The eco-friendly resort Sugar Beach is noted for its spa and fine dining, with each room featuring panoramic views of the Pitons or the Caribbean Sea.

Where to Eat and Drink

CASTRIES: Auberge Seraphine $$$
Caribbean/International
Vielle Bay, Pointe Seraphine
Tel *758 453 2073*
Choose from an exciting menu at this pretty and popular restaurant overlooking a marina. Try the seafood risotto. Great desserts, too.

CASTRIES: The Coal Pot $$$
Caribbean/French
Vigie Cove
Tel *758 452 5566* **Closed** *Sat & Sun*
Relaxing waterfront dining, especially romantic at night. Excellent food, with meals served in locally made pottery.

MARIGOT BAY: Boudreau Restaurant at Discovery $$$
Fine Dining
Capella Marigot Bay Hotel
Tel *758 458 5300*
Creative, French-inspired food is served in a lovely location. The menu constantly changes, but all dishes are exquisite. Boudreau has a tree house for private groups.

REDUIT BAY: Chic $$$
International
Royal St. Lucian Resort & Spa
Tel *758 452 9999*
Head to the elegant, romantic Chic for a special night out. On offer is international cuisine with Caribbean influences to delight the tastebuds. Extensive wine list.

RODNEY BAY: Wingz 'n' Thingz $$
International
Seagrape Avenue
Tel *758 451-8200*
This is a casual spot for a relaxed meal and good company. The varied menu features Cajun, Caribbean, and seafood dishes, as well as the eponymous wings.

RODNEY BAY: Big Chef Steakhouse $$$
International
Rodney Bay Village
Tel *758 450 0210* **Closed** *Mon*
Beautifully prepared hearty portions of steaks and seafood dishes at Big Chef draws locals and tourists alike.

RODNEY BAY: Buzz $$$
Seafood/International
Rodney Bay
Tel *758 458 0450* **Closed** *Mon*
The varied menu here focuses prominently on seafood, but there are also several good vegetarian options. Among the many local favorites are lobster

and crab cakes and Moroccan spiced lamb shanks. Indoor and outdoor seating.

RODNEY BAY: Chef Xavier $$$
Caribbean/International
Bay Walk Shopping Mall
Tel *758 458 2433*
This restaurant enjoys a beautiful waterfront location that makes the most of the fresh sea breezes. It has an interesting menu, with creative takes on Caribbean and international favorites.

DK Choice

RODNEY BAY: La Terasse $$$
French/Caribbean
Rodney Bay Village
Tel *758 572 0389* **Closed** *Tue*
French cuisine melds beautifully with Caribbean flavors at La Terasse. The kitchen uses fresh produce, fish, and meats, and everything is cooked from scratch, even the desserts. Set in an outdoor deck amid a tropical garden, the restaurant is part of a small inn. Lamb cutlets, seafood stew and mahi mahi are all highlights.

RODNEY BAY: Razmataz $$$
Indian
Rodney Bay
Tel *758 452 9800*
This lively open-air restaurant overlooking the marina serves exquisite South Asian cuisine. The dishes can be served mild or hot according to the diner's personal preference.

SOUFRIÈRE: Camilla's $$
Caribbean
Soufrière
Tel *758 459 5379* **Closed** *Mon*
Located in the middle of town, overlooking a busy street, this popular spot specializes in tasty Caribbean cuisine.

The tables at The Coal Pot are laid with hand-painted plates, Castries

---

Price Guide
Prices are based on a two-course meal for one, including tax and service charges and half a bottle of wine.

$	up to $15
$$	$15–40
$$$	over $40

Superb view from the dining area at Dasheene, Soufrière

SOUFRIÈRE: Dasheene $$
Caribbean/Fusion
Ladera Resort
Tel *758 459 7323*
Head to Dasheene for scrumptious, award-winning food and stunning views of the Pitons. An unforgettable experience.

SOUFRIÈRE: Martha's Tables $$
Caribbean
Soufrière
Tel *758 459 7270* **Closed** *Sat & Sun*
Local cuisine featuring seafood, meat, and vegetables is served in a breezy veranda overlooking the ocean.

SOUFRIÈRE: The Treehouse $$$
Caribbean
Anse Chastanet Resort
Tel *758 459 7354* **Closed** *Tue dinner*
Savor wonderful food in a stunning open-air clifftop location. The breakfast buffet is extensive and there is a daily changing dinner menu.

VIEUX FORT: The Reef Beach Café $$
Caribbean/International
Anse de Sables Beach
Tel *758 454 3518* **Closed** *Mon*
The Reef is a chalet-style café right on the beach, with trees and greenery all around. Choose from a wide range of dishes including chicken currey, grilled fish and pizza. Great coffee, too.

Practical Information

St. Lucia's attractions make it a year-round tourist destination. The island is fairly accessible with direct flights arriving from the US and UK, and neighboring islands are easily reached by high-speed ferry. The tourist infrastrucure is top-notch and transport and accommodations are easily available. The island's capital, Castries, has some interesting markets to explore and shop for memorable gifts and souvenirs.

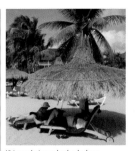

Visitors relaxing under the shade on Reduit Beach

When to Go

St. Lucia has year-round good weather but the high season is between mid-November and March, which are the driest months. Most rain falls between May and October. Average daytime temperatures are around 85º F (29º C). Hurricane season lasts from June to November.

Getting There

The international airport is at Hewanorra just outside Vieux Fort, about 40 miles (64 km) south of Castries. It receives regular scheduled non-stop services from **British Airways** and **Virgin Atlantic** from the UK, **American Eagle**, **JetBlue**, and **Delta** from the US, and **Air Canada** and **West Jet** from Canada. Visitors from Europe and Australia have to connect with one of these carriers. The smaller George Charles Airport at Vigie, just north of Castries, has some international connections, but mostly serves flights to and from other Caribbean destinations. St. Lucia is visited almost daily by cruise ships, and the main terminal is at Pointe Seraphine, just outside Castries. **Caribbean Express** is

a great way to explore nearby islands, and runs a high-speed ferry service between St. Lucia, Martinique, Guadeloupe, and Dominica.

Documentation

A passport is required to visit St. Lucia. An immigration form has to be filled in, one part of which is stamped and returned, and must be handed back at the time of departure. Citizens of the US and of specific Commonwealth nations do not require a visa to enter. Check with the concerned embassies for details. Luggage is often checked, so in case of jewelry or expensive cameras, travel with a copy of the purchase receipt. A departure tax for passengers over the age of 12 is applied at the time of ticket purchase.

Visitor Information

The **St. Lucia Tourist Board** has its main office at Castries, and overseas offices in the UK, USA, Canada, France, and Germany. Tourist information centers are located at La Place Carenage, Pointe Seraphine, Soufrière, and at both airports.

Health and Security

All hotels have doctors on call. **Victoria Hospital**, **St. Jude Hospital**, **Dennery Hospital**, and **Soufrière Hospital** are the island's main medical facilities. Insect repellent is essential, as mosquitoes can be a problem.

St. Lucia has a low crime rate but stick to well-lit, popular areas, and avoid wearing expensive jewelry or carrying large sums of money. It is a good idea to keep valuables in the hotel safe. Vendors are likely to pester visitors, especially on the beach or in town, but a firm "no thanks" should do the trick.

Banking and Currency

Banks are open Monday to Thursday 8am to 2pm, and to 5pm on Fridays. The official currency is the East Caribbean dollar (EC$), but US dollars are accepted almost everywhere. Banks offer a fixed rate of exchange, usually better than the rates offered in hotels and shops. There are ATMs throughout the island and all major credit cards are widely accepted. When arranging for a taxi, guide, or charter, visitors should check which currency they are dealing in.

Communications

The international dialling code for St. Lucia is 1 758. To call the UK, dial 011-44 and the number, and for the US, dial 1 followed by the number. Card and coin-operated public phones are found easily. Cards can be purchased through

Cruise liner viewed from the Morne Lookout, Castries

Cable & Wireless offices which also rent cell phones. Internet access is available at most large hotels, at Pointe Seraphine, and at cyber cafés.

Transport

Car hire is the best way to explore the island. Renters should be over 25 and have a valid driver's license. If they do not have an international driver's license, a temporary one can be purchased from rental firms such as **AVIS**, **Hertz**, **Budget Rent-a-Car**, and **Island Car Rental**. In St. Lucia driving is on the left side of the road. Road signs are rare and some side roads may be potholed. In case of an accident or breakdown in a hired car, call the hire company or the police. An exhilarating means of moving around the island is by helicopter, available at **St. Lucia Helicopters**.

Taxis and island buses are easily available and cheap. Taxi drivers make excellent guides, but negotiate the price beforehand. There are regular bus services between the main towns, but evening services are less frequent, and smaller towns and villages may not be served.

A bustling marketplace, Castries

Shopping

Castries Market and beachside vendors offer local arts and crafts. Pointe Seraphine and La Place Carenage are duty-free shopping centers, and there are many galleries and boutiques in Castries. Most large hotels and resorts have mini-shopping malls.

Language

English is the official language, although many people speak a French-based patois.

Electricity

The usual electricity supply is 220 volts, but most hotels also have 110-volt sockets, which are suitable for US appliances.

Time

St. Lucia is 4 hours behind Greenwich Mean Time (GMT), and 1 hour ahead of Eastern Time in the United States.

Getting Married

It is possible to marry on the day of arrival at an additional cost. Documents required include birth certificate, passport, deed poll in case of name change, divorce papers if any, and parents' notarized consent if under 18 years. Documents must be in English or have an English translation. Besides the cost of the marriage certificate, a registrar fee is also charged. **A Wedding in St. Lucia**, **Tropic Isle Weddings**, and **Weddings in St. Lucia** have special offers.

DIRECTORY

Getting There

Air Canada
ⓦ aircanada.com

American Eagle
ⓦ aa.com

British Airways
ⓦ ba.com

Caribbean Express
Tel 758 452 2211.

Delta
ⓦ delta.com

JetBlue
ⓦ bluejet.com

Virgin Atlantic
ⓦ virginatlantic.com

West Jet
ⓦ westjet.com

Visitor Information

St. Lucia Tourist Board
Sureline Building, Vide Bouteille, Castries.
Tel 758 452 4094 (Castries);
1 800 869 0377 (Canada);
020 7431 3675 (UK);
212 867 2950 (USA).
ⓦ stlucia.org

Health and Security

Ambulance and Fire
Tel 911.

Dennery Hospital
Hospital Road.
Tel 758 453 3310.

Police
Tel 999.

Soufrière Hospital
WC Queenland Street.
Tel 758 449 7258.

St. Jude Hospital
St. Jude's Highway,
Vieux Fort.
Tel 758 454 6041.

Victoria Hospital
Hospital Road, Castries.
Tel 758 452 2421.

Communications

Cable & Wireless
Tel 758 453 9000.

Transport

AVIS
Tel 758 452 2700.

Budget Rent-a-Car
Tel 758 452 0233.

Hertz
Tel 758 452 0679.

Island Car Rental
Tel 758 450 4840.

St. Lucia Helicopters
Tel 758 453 6950.
ⓦ stluciahelicopters.com

Getting Married

A Wedding in St. Lucia
ⓦ aweddinginstlucia.com

Tropic Isle Weddings
ⓦ tropicisleweddings.com

Weddings in St. Lucia
ⓦ weddingsinstlucia.com

Exploring St. Vincent and the Grenadines

With its lush rainforests, waterfalls, black sand beaches, and spectacularly jagged terrain, topped off by La Soufrière volcano in the north, St. Vincent is a dream haven for eco and adventure travelers. To the south, its capital Kingstown is bustling during the day but towards the evening, the action moves to the nearby Villa and Indian Bay areas, where lively bars and restaurants abound. The Grenadines comprises tiny islands stretching between St. Vincent and Grenada and are politically divided between the two. Thirty-two of these exquisite isles belong to St. Vincent, and offer the quintessential Caribbean holiday experience of shimmering sand beaches, gorgeous cays, and turquoise waters.

Locator Map

Palm-shaded Carenage Bay Beach, Canouan Resort, Canouan

Getting Around

There are no direct international flights to St. Vincent and the Grenadines, but connecting flights from other Caribbean islands land at the E.T. Joshua Airport in St. Vincent. There are airstrips on Canouan, Bequia, Mustique, and Union Island as well. Inter-island ferries are a cheap and popular way to travel. Visitors can get to most places by minibus, taxi, or rental vehicle, and there are a number of reliable tour services for sightseeing trips around the islands. The fit and adventurous can opt for bike and scooter rentals.

Key

—— Major road
—— Minor road
– – Track
···· Ferry route
△ Peak

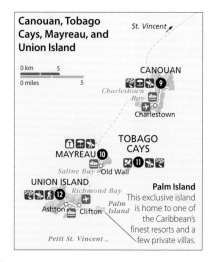

Canouan, Tobago Cays, Mayreau, and Union Island

0 km   5
0 miles   5

St. Vincent

CANOUAN ⑨
Charlestown Bay
Charlestown

TOBAGO CAYS

MAYREAU ⑩
Saline Bay Old Wall ⑪

UNION ISLAND
Richmond Bay ⑫
Ashton Clifton
Palm Island

Palm Island
This exclusive island is home to one of the Caribbean's finest resorts and a few private villas.

Petit St. Vincent

For hotels and restaurants on these islands see p420 and p421

Sights at a Glance

The Botanical Gardens, founded in 1762 – the oldest in the Western Hemisphere

Orange Hill
Four-wheel drives to Bamboo Ridge start from Orange Hill, to go to La Soufrière.

Fancy
Owia Bay
Falls of Baleine
OWIA 5
La Soufrière 4,000 ft
Sandy Bay
Larikai Bay
Sandy Bay

LA SOUFRIÈRE HIKE 6
Richmond
Chateaubelair
Mt Brisbane 3,058 ft
Orange Hill
Rabacca
Langley Park
Richmond Peak 3,523 ft
Troumaca
South Rivers
Georgetown
Cumberland
Rose Hall
Black Point
allilabou Bay
Gordon Yard
St. Vincent
Colonarie
Barrouallie
Grand Bonhomme 3,181 ft
Colonarie Bay
North Union
Peter's Hope
Vermont
Biabou
South Union
Layou Bay
Mt St Andrew 2,413 ft
Grant's Bay
uccament Bay
Layou
MESOPOTAMIA VALLEY 4
Questelles
Green Hill
Mesopotamia
KINGSTOWN 1 2 BOTANICAL GARDENS
Stubbs
3 VILLA
Cane Garden

Man Point

BEQUIA 7
Spring Bay
Admiralty Bay
Port Elizabeth
West Cay
Mount Pleasant
Adams Bay
Paget
Mount Pleasant Bay
Petit Niéves
Bettowia
Quatre
Baliceaux

Lovell Village
Britannia Bay
Macaroni Bay
MUSTIQUE 8

Mustique
Mustique is the hotspot for the rich and famous.

Canouan
Petit Mustique

Yachts moored in Admiralty Bay, Port Elizabeth, Bequia

0 km   5
0 miles   5

For additional map symbols *see back flap*

Arcaded buildings in downtown Kingstown

❶ Kingstown

SW coast of St. Vincent. 🏛 26,000. ✈
🚌 🚐 **i** Ministry of Tourism, Upper
Bay Street, 784 457 1502. 🚢 Fri & Sat.
🎭 Vincy Mas (late Jun).

A busy port city nestled in a
sheltered bay, Kingstown is
known as the City of Arcades,
thanks to the many arched
walkways in its tiny downtown
area. The area features some
of the town's main attractions,
including the three churches
on Grenville Street: the Anglican
St. George's, the more flamboyant St. Mary's Cathedral, and
the Methodist Church, which
was built in 1841 with money
raised by freed slaves. Not far
from downtown is a market
area known as Little Tokyo, so
named because its fish market
was built with Japanese aid.
Situated on a 630-ft (192-m)
ridge, north of the capital, Fort
Charlotte offers expansive views
of the island's leeward coast and
the Grenadines. Built in 1805
to repel invasions from the sea,
it had many of its 34 cannons
pointing inland, as the British
felt their greatest threat came
from the Black Caribs. A few
of its cannons still exist and oil
murals displayed in the fort
depict Black Carib history.

❷ Botanical Gardens

2 miles (4 km) E of Kingstown.
Tel 784 457 1003. 🚐
Open 6am–6pm daily. 🅿 🗲 🏛

The oldest in the Western
Hemisphere, the Botanical
Gardens were founded in 1762

as a station to propagate plants
from all parts of the British
Empire. The gardens have a
wide variety of native and exotic
plants. A famous specimen is
a thriving descendant of a
breadfruit tree, brought here by
the British naval officer Captain
William Bligh. There is a breeding program for rare plants and
the endangered national bird,
the St. Vincent parrot.

❸ Villa

3 miles (5 km) SE from Kingstown,
St. Vincent. 🚐

The liveliest strip in St. Vincent,
Villa is the place to be for those
looking for great nightlife. Villa
and the nearby Indian Bay boast
several good restaurants, bars,
and nightclubs. Some of the
best-known hotels can be
found here as well, both upscale
and the more moderately
priced, while the Young Island
Resort (see p420) is just offshore.

❹ Mesopotamia Valley

8 miles (13 km) NE of Kingstown,
St. Vincent. 🚐 🚗 HazECO Tours.

The Mesopotamia Valley or
"Mespo," regarded as the
bread-basket of St. Vincent, is
a luxuriant valley teeming with
cultivated vegetation: nutmeg,
bananas, breadfruit, and all
varieties of root crops. Encircled
by mountains, including Grand
Bonhomme, the island's highest
at 3,181 ft (970 m), it is a unique
sight in the southern Caribbean.
   Just north of Mesopotamia
Valley, the colorful **Montreal
Gardens** are worth visiting
for the great variety of flowers
and plants grown here.

🌺 Montreal Gardens
Near Richland Park, Windward
Highway. **Tel** 784 458 1198.
Open 9am–4pm Mon–Fri. 🅿
🚹 limited.

❺ Owia

30 miles (48 km) NE of Kingstown,
St. Vincent. 🏛 2,700. 🚐

On the north side of La
Soufrière, Owia is one of the
few Carib villages on the
island's rugged northeastern
coast. It is known for a series
of beautiful tidal pools encircled
by volcanic rock in an area
called Salt Pond. The scenery
here is quite dramatic as waves
of the feisty Atlantic dash
against the surrounding
volcanic rocks.

Black Caribs making cassava
breads outside their huts

Black Caribs

In 1675, a Dutch ship carrying settlers
and African slaves was shipwrecked
off St. Vincent's southern coast.
The sole survivors, the Africans, were
welcomed by the native Caribs. They
intermarried, producing the "Black
Caribs" or "Black Calinagos". During the
wars of possession between the
British and French in the 18th century,
they favored the French. When St.
Vincent was ceded to Britain under
the Treaty of Versailles of 1783, the
Caribs resisted, leading to the Carib
Wars. Finally defeated in 1797, most Black Caribs were deported,
while the rest were sent to Sandy Bay, where their descendants
have settled.

For hotels and restaurants on these islands see p420 and p421

⑥ La Soufrière Hike

The hike up the 4,000-ft (1,219-m) high La Soufrière is a moderately strenuous, approximately four-hour climb. The active volcano can be approached from either side of St. Vincent, though the easier trek is via the Atlantic Coast. The trail leads through varied vegetation such as arrowroot, banana, and coconut plantations, tropical rainforest, and then cloud forest with its stunted growth. The view from the summit is absolutely breathtaking.

Tips for Hikers

Starting point: Bamboo Ridge.
Length: 3 miles (5 km).
Getting there: Minibus from Kingstown to Orange Hill; 4-wheel drive from Orange Hill to Bamboo Ridge.
Note: Ideal to go on a guided tour as novices can get lost. Wear sturdy shoes and carry a change of clothes in case of rain. Bring insect repellent.

④ La Soufrière Crater
The highest peak on the island, La Soufrière dominates the northern part of St. Vincent. In 1970, a new island was formed in its crater lake.

③ Jacobs Well
A dry riverbed, Jacobs Well is surrounded by pristine tropical rainforest.

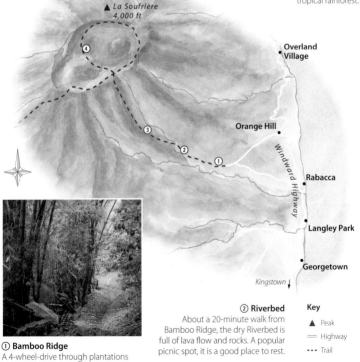

▲ La Soufrière
4,000 ft

Overland Village

Orange Hill

Windward Highway

Rabacca

Langley Park

Georgetown

Kingstown ↓

① Bamboo Ridge
A 4-wheel-drive through plantations ends at Bamboo Ridge, where the foot-trail begins. At 1,300 ft (396 m), this is the point where the mountain climb starts.

② Riverbed
About a 20-minute walk from Bamboo Ridge, the dry Riverbed is full of lava flow and rocks. A popular picnic spot, it is a good place to rest.

Key

▲ Peak
= Highway
--- Trail

0 kilometers   2
0 miles   2

Waterfront restaurant in Port Elizabeth, Bequia

7 Bequia

9 miles (14 km) S of St. Vincent. 5,000. Bequia Tourism Association, Port Elizabeth. Easter Regatta (Mar/Apr). **bequiatourism.com**

The largest of the Grenadine islands at 7 sq miles (18 sq km), Bequia is the northernmost in the Grenadine chain. Its capital, Port Elizabeth, is a picturesque waterfront town set in the natural harbor of the sweeping Admiralty Bay. Lined with hotels, restaurants, bars, and shops, it is a popular stop with visitors and sailors. Bequia's famous model boat-builders have their workshops here and can be seen crafting their intricate, traditional double-ended whalers as well as other contemporary boats.

Bequia has a long tradition of fishing and whaling. The International Whaling Commission now allows the island to kill a quota of two humpback whales a year. The Whaling Museum at Paget chronicles the island's whaling history. The aptly named Mount Pleasant near the east coast offers panoramic views of Bequia's golden beaches, coves, and sparkling waters, which all make it a popular sailing and snorkeling spot. The Old Hegg Turtle Sanctuary on the far northeastern side of the island is worth visiting. It is run by conservationist Orton King, who lovingly tends to hawksbill turtles.

Frangipani flowers, Bequia

8 Mustique

7 miles (11 km) SE of Bequia. 550. Mustique Blues Festival (early Feb). **mustique-island.com**

Mustique has long been associated with British royalty and celebrities. The tiny 1,400-acre (565-ha) island was acquired by a single proprietor, Scottish landowner Colin Tennant, in the 1960s. He developed it into a private resort for the rich and famous. Today, apart from private residences, there are villas available for weekly rental. Visitors can explore the island by scooter or car, or go swimming and hiking. Day trips from St. Vincent to the island are organized by the Mustique Company. The island is best known for the world-famous Basil's Bar.

9 Canouan

14 miles (22 km) S of St. Vincent. 1,200. Canouan Regatta (May). **canouan.com**

Stretching over not more than 5 sq miles (13 sq km), Canouan is home to some of the Caribbean's most spectacular beaches. Its powder-white sands, clear waters, and an impressive coral reef make it excellent for sailing, swimming, and snorkeling. The main town, Charlestown, is in Charlestown Bay, the island's primary anchorage with a long beach. The exclusive Canouan Resort and its 18-hole Trump International Golf Course *(see p418)* and its stylish casinos draw many famous guests.

10 Mayreau

6 miles (10 km) SE of Canouan. 260.

An essential stop on a sailing day trip, Mayreau is the smallest inhabited island in the Grenadines. Most of its population lives at Station Hill, which has a handful of restaurants and bars. Built of stone in 1929, the old Roman Catholic Church is a short uphill walk from Station Hill. It offers great views of the island, across Salt Whistle Bay with its private resort, and the Tobago Cays.

View across Charlestown Bay, Canouan

For hotels and restaurants on these islands see p420 and p421

⓫ Tobago Cays

Sheltered by the aptly named Horseshoe Reef, the Tobago Cays are a group of uninhabited isles. To protect the delicate reefs, the islands have been declared a marine park by the St. Vincent government. The waters are exceptionally clear, and the diverse marine life includes squirrel fish, angelfish, and grouper.

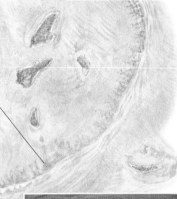

Horseshoe Reef
Although some of the reef has suffered damage from anchors, over-fishing, and removal of black corals, much of it remains in surprisingly excellent condition.

0 metres 700
0 yards 700

Snorkeling
One of the most remarkable sites for snorkeling in the Caribbean, the Tobago Cays become very busy during the high season (Dec to Apr).

Boat Vendors
Locals on boats paddle between the yachts, selling wares that range from fresh fish to jewelry and clothes.

⓬ Union Island

1 mile (1.6 km) SE of Mayreau.
🔺 3,000. ✈ 🚢 🎭 Easterval (Mar or Apr).

In the southern part of the island chain, Union Island is the commercial center of the Grenadines, and also the hub of yachting and airport traffic. Measuring around 3 miles (5 km) long, it is fringed with gorgeous bays, lagoons, and reefs with perfect swimming and sailing waters.

Though many people visit Union Island to catch a yacht charter, there is a lot to do on the island itself. The main town, Clifton, has a few good restaurants, small hotels, main harbor and anchorage, and an open-air market where visitors can buy crafts as well as fresh produce. Mount Taboi, at 1,000 ft (305 m), is the highest point in the Grenadines, and hiking the mountain or any of the island's numerous nature trails is a good way to explore the terrain. The island is also known for its Big Drum dance, a combination of African and French influences, which is performed in times of disaster, but also on joyous occasions such as weddings, or the launching of a new boat.

Yachts anchored at Clifton harbor, Union Island

Outdoor Activities and Specialized Holidays

The tiny islands of St. Vincent and the Grenadines offer visitors a stunning range of activities, including exploring the dramatic terrain, dolphin-watching, and hiking at La Soufrière volcano on St. Vincent. The islands have a good assortment of tour operators, who can organize sightseeing or hiking tours, and are especially well-equipped for sailing, scuba diving, and other watersports. Sports enthusiasts can play tennis, golf, or cycle, and there are some excellent spas for recuperating from the exertion as well.

A beach on Young Island, St. Vincent

Beaches

The beaches on the calm leeward side of St. Vincent are mostly smooth, black- sand beaches formed from volcanic rock that sparkle in the sun. The palest sand can be found on the beaches to the south, especially in Villa and Indian Bay areas where most of the hotels are located. Calliaqua Bay, Blue Lagoon, and the Young Island Cut are among the beautiful beaches in this area.

The Windward coast is rocky with strong currents, making it unsafe for bathing, but the black-sand beaches are impressive and a number of them are popular, including Argyle, where the surf crashes dramatically on to the sand. The Salt Pond at Owia (see p412) is set in a magical landscape and good for a swim while waves break on huge rocks all around the tidal pools. For turquoise sea and dazzling powder-white and golden sands, visitors can head to the Grenadines, where most spend at least a day to experience life on a postcard-perfect Caribbean island. All beaches, except some on Mustique, are public.

Diving and Snorkeling

There are numerous wall diving sites and sunken wrecks in St. Vincent and the Grenadines. Extensive coral reefs with crystal-clear water surround these islands, which makes them among the best for diving and snorkeling in the Caribbean. Rich reef life can usually be found at a depth of 80 ft (25 m), while there is a whole world of marine creatures and abundant tropical fish flourishing at only 25 ft (8 m).

There are several companies that cater to divers. On St. Vincent, **Dive St Vincent** is a popular dive shop. On the Grenadines, diving and snorkeling gear can be hired from **Mustique Water Sports, Bequia Dive Adventures, Canouan Scuba Center,** and **Grenadines Dive.** Divers and snorkelers should take care not to disturb the islands' marine life and corals.

Watersports

There are facilities for all types of watersports, with kayaking off the calm leeward coast of St. Vincent being a special treat. **SVG Multi-Day Adventures** and **Coreas Caribbean Adventures** arrange kayaking excursions. Other operators organize windsurfing and Jet Skiing tours including Dive St Vincent, **Sea Breeze Nature Tours,** and **Fantasea Tours.**

Fishing

Both amateur and experienced fishermen enjoy the islands for their rich sea life and excellent sailing conditions. Many options are offered by dive and watersports companies such as Fantasea and Sea Breeze Nature Tours, which include both deep-sea and shallow water fishing. Fishing is not allowed in protected areas such as the northeast coast of Bequia, all of Palm Island, Mustique, Mayreau, and Tobago Cays. Barrouallie on St. Vincent's leeward coast is a popular center for fishing. The village is known for its "black fish", a small whale species, plentiful in the waters.

Clusters of corals in the waters off St. Vincent and the Grenadines

A catamaran picking up visitors for a sailing tour

Sailing

St. Vincent and the Grenadines have a long-standing seafaring tradition as well as perfect sailing conditions. The first visitors to notice the holiday potential of St. Vincent and the Grenadines were sailors and yachtsmen.

Privately owned yachts need to clear immigration and customs at one of the several designated entry points. These are Kingstown, Chateaubelair, and Wallilabou in St. Vincent, and Port Elizabeth in Bequia, Mustique, Canouan, and Union Island.

Charter agencies such as **Barefoot Yacht Charters** and **Yannis Sail Private Charters** offer some great exploring and allow people with little know-how of sailing to get a taste of the sea as well as experience the active and luxurious life aboard a crewed yacht.

Sea Tours

A good way to experience the seafaring side of St. Vincent and the Grenadines is to join a tour to some of the hidden coves and beaches inaccessible by road.

A sea tour of St. Vincent involves a trip on a speedboat along the leeward side of the island. Fort Charlotte (see p412), overlooking Kingstown, is the first notable landmark, but as the boat skims along visitors can see black-sand beaches, statuesque cliffs, and forest-covered mountains. The route traces the coast, past several pretty villages, all the way to

the Falls of Baleine. The tour will include a stop at the Falls for a swim at its lovely natural pool. The trip also gives a good idea of the fishing culture of these islands, with its colorful boats and quiet coastal villages.

If the trip includes dolphin-watching, the captain goes farther offshore where dolphins are flipping in the water. For whale-watching the boat will go still farther out. Around 20 species of whales and dolphins, including the humpback whale, are found in the the waters off St. Vincent and the Grenadines. Sea Breeze Nature Tours, Fantasea Tours, and **Baleine Tours** are among the reputable operators.

Hiking and Bird-Watching

There are many hiking trails in St. Vincent, ranging from relaxed treks in the Dark View Falls area and through the rolling terrain of the Vermont Nature Trail to challenging hikes to the crater of La Soufrière (see p413). **Sailor's Wilderness Tours** offers hiking trips in St. Vincent and **Ruff and Ready Hiking** on the Grenadine islands. Much of St. Vincent is forested, providing a protected habitat for many bird species, while the Grenadine islands are flatter and drier. This geographical diversity makes for a varied terrain that includes birdlife, rainforest, wetland, and garden. Thrushes, warblers, herons, and hummingbirds, are easily spotted. The Vermont Nature Trail is a good place to see the St. Vincent parrot. Other birding sites are the Falls of Baleine, Trinity Falls, Owia Salt Pond, Buccament Valley, Wallilabou Falls, La Soufrière Volcano trail and Richmond Beach. The **Ministry of Agriculture** has a wealth of information on the birdlife. Sailor's Wilderness Tours and **Richmond Vale Nature & Hiking Centre** organize birding trips.

St. Vincent parrot

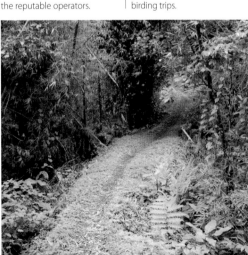
Trail to La Soufrière's summit through verdant rainforest, St. Vincent

Treatment room, Canouan Resort, Canouan

Spas

Seclusion and relaxation can easily be achieved in St. Vincent and the Grenadines. Most major resorts have spas, which offer a range of rejuvenating beauty treatments and relaxing massages to soothe both the body and mind. The Spa Kalina, located in the Young Island Resort (see p420), is one of the best spas on the islands. Day spas such as the **Oasis Spa and Wellness Center** and **Bamboo Spa** are also popular.

Golf

One of the Caribbean's most scenic and challenging golf courses is located in the Canouan Resort. The **Trump International Golf Course** has been designed by the well-known golf course architect Jim Fazio. The only 18-hole championship course on St. Vincent and the Grenadine islands, it is widely regarded as one of the best in the world. It stretches over 135 acres (55 ha) of hill and seashore and showcases the stunning scenery of Canouan. The 13th hole is considered to be the supreme spot with its spectacular views of the Grenadines, Atlantic Ocean, and the Caribbean Sea. Though a haven for professional golfers, it offers lessons for amateurs too. There is a fully stocked golf shop and a clubhouse on the premises as well.

Well-manicured grounds of the Trump International Golf Course, Canouan

DIRECTORY

Diving and Snorkeling

Bequia Dive Adventures
Belmont Walkway, Bequia.
Tel 784 458 3826. [W] bequiadiveadventures.com

Canouan Scuba Center
Tamarind Beach, Canouan.
Tel 784 528 8030.
[W] canouandivecenter.com

Dive St Vincent
Young Island Dock, St. Vincent. Tel 784 457 4928.
[W] divestvincent.com

Grenadines Dive
Clifton, Union Island.
Tel 784 458 8138.
[W] grenadinesdive.com

Mustique Water Sports
1 Watersports Way, Mustique. Tel 784 488 8486. [W] mustique-island.com

Watersports

Coreas Caribbean Adventures
Kingstown, St. Vincent.
Tel 784 456 2158.
[W] coreascaribbeanadventures.com

Fantasea Tours
Villa Beach, St. Vincent.
Tel 784 457 4477.
[W] fantaseatours.com

Sea Breeze Nature Tours
Kingstown, St. Vincent.
Tel 784 458 4969.
[W] seabreezenaturetours.com

SVG Multi-Day Adventures
Bay Hill, St. Vincent.
Tel 784 456 5419.
[W] svgmultidayadventure.com

Sailing

Barefoot Yacht Charters
Blue Lagoon, St. Vincent.
Tel 784 456 9526.
[W] barefootyachts.com

Yannis Sail Private Charters
Clifton, Union Island.
Tel 784 458 8513.

Sea Tours

Baleine Tours
Villa, St. Vincent.
Tel 784 457 4089.
[W] baleinetours.com

Hiking and Bird-Watching

Ministry of Agriculture
Richmond Hill, Kingstown, St. Vincent.
Tel 784 456 1111.
[W] gov.vc

Richmond Vale Nature & Hiking Center
Richmond, St. Vincent.
Tel 784 458 2255.
[W] richmondvalehiking.com

Ruff and Ready Hiking
Bequia.
Tel 784 495 2524.

Sailor's Wilderness Tours
Upper Middle Street, St. Vincent.
Tel 784 457 1712.
[W] sailortours.com

Spas

Bamboo Spa
Caine Hall, St. Vincent.
Tel 784 482 9506.

Oasis Spa and Wellness Center
Villa Flat, St. Vincent.
Tel 784 456 2555.

Golf

Trump International Golf Course
Canouan Resort, Canouan.
Tel 784 458 8000.
[W] canouan.com/golf.asp

Sailing the Grenadines

Fishing, sailing, diving, and boat-making are a way of life in St. Vincent and the Grenadines. It is no surprise then that sailors and yachtsmen were the first to discover their tranquil waters, white sand beaches, and extensive reefs. The Grenadines, along with the Virgin Islands, have the best sailing in the Caribbean because of the many islands at good sailing distance from each other, as well as the infrastructure – the number of marinas, chandlers, anchorages, seaside restaurants, and bars. Sailing here favors seasoned sailors, but there are crewed boats and yacht charters to ensure that amateurs have just as good a time.

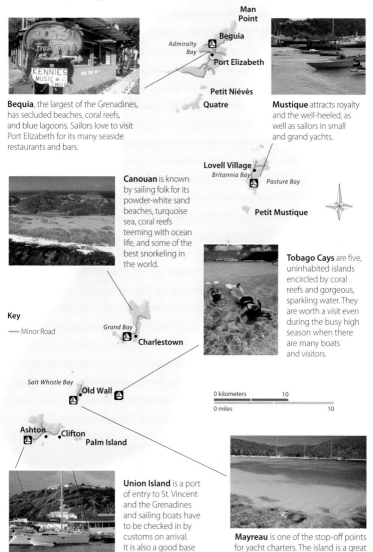

Bequia, the largest of the Grenadines, has secluded beaches, coral reefs, and blue lagoons. Sailors love to visit Port Elizabeth for its many seaside restaurants and bars.

Mustique attracts royalty and the well-heeled, as well as sailors in small and grand yachts.

Canouan is known by sailing folk for its powder-white sand beaches, turquoise sea, coral reefs teeming with ocean life, and some of the best snorkeling in the world.

Tobago Cays are five, uninhabited islands encircled by coral reefs and gorgeous, sparkling water. They are worth a visit even during the busy high season when there are many boats and visitors.

Key

— Minor Road

Man Point

Beguia

Admiralty Bay

Port Elizabeth

Petit Niévès

Quatre

Lovell Village

Britannia Bay

Pasture Bay

Petit Mustique

Grand Bay

Charlestown

Salt Whistle Bay

Old Wall

Ashton

Clifton

Palm Island

0 kilometers 10

0 miles 10

Union Island is a port of entry to St. Vincent and the Grenadines and sailing boats have to be checked in by customs on arrival. It is also a good base for sailing trips around the smaller islands.

Mayreau is one of the stop-off points for yacht charters. The island is a great spot for a swim, snorkeling, or a barbecue on the beach.

For keys to symbols *see back flap*

Where to Stay

St. Vincent

BUCCAMENT:
Buccament Bay Resort $$$
Luxury
Buccament Bay
Tel *855 212 1972*
W buccamentbay.com
A luxury all-inclusive resort with elegantly appointed beachfront villas. There is a choice of watersports, plus whale-watching.

KINGSTOWN:
Hotel Alexandrina $
Modern
Prospect
Tel *784 456 9788*
W hotelalexandrina.com
This cozy, family-run hotel set in a hillside garden offers breathtaking views of the Caribbean Sea and the northern Grenadines.

KINGSTOWN:
The Cobblestone Inn $
Historic
Bay Street
Tel *784 456 1937*
W thecobblestoneinn.com
Originally a sugar warehouse, this delightful hotel is popular with business travelers thanks to its downtown location. Stylish rooms.

VILLA: Beachcombers Hotel $
Boutique
Villa Beach
Tel *784 458 4283*
W beachcombershotel.com
Each of the colorful rooms in this hotel has its own patio. Beach bar and restaurant. Set in a lush botanical garden.

VILLA: Grand View Beach Hotel $
Beach
Villa Point, Colonarie
Tel *784 458 4811*
W grandviewhotel.com
Grand View Beach is one of the oldest and most charming hotels on the island, with breezy rooms and awe-inspiring views.

VILLA: Paradise Beach Hotel $
Beach
Villa Beach
Tel *784 457 4795*
W paradisesvg.com
With standard rooms and self-contained apartments, there are options for all kinds of travelers at the Paradise Beach.

VILLA: Rosewood Apartment Hotel $
Modern
Rose Cottage
Tel *784 457 5051*
W rosewoodsvg.com
A mixture of self-catering and standard rooms are available at Rosewood. Stunning views of the ocean from every room.

VILLA: Young Island Resort $$$
Luxury
1, Young Island Crossing
Tel *784 458 4826*
W youngisland.com
Stay at self-contained delux cottages on a private island just off the coast of St. Vincent. Swim over to the lovely Coconut Bar.

The Grenadines

BEQUIA: Bequia Beach Hotel $$
Beach Resort
Friendship Bay
Tel *784 458 1600*
W bequiabeach.com
Beachfront suites and rooms, some with terraces offering views. The hotel is famous for its restaurant, Bagatelle. Spa, gym, and pool.

BEQUIA: Firefly Plantation Hotel $$
Historic
Spring Estate
Tel *784 488 8414*
W fireflybequia.com
A resort set on the foundations of an 18th-century homestead amid orchards of tropical fruit trees. The beautiful rooms all have balconies.

Price Guide
Prices are based on one night's stay in high season for a standard double room, inclusive of service charges and taxes.

$	up to $200
$$	$200–500
$$$	over $500

DK Choice

BEQUIA:
Sugar Reef Bequia $$
Resort
Main Road, Crescent Beach
Tel *784 458 3400*
W sugarreefbequia.com
One of the most renowned resorts on the island, Sugar Reef is set on a coconut plantation, adjacent to a tropical forest. Featuring rustic decor, this luxurious spot is the perfect place to unwind, and a great base for exploring Bequia.

CANOUAN: Tamarind Beach Hotel and Yacht Club $$
Luxury
Grand Bay
Tel *784 458 8044*
W tamarindbeachhotel.com
Tucked away on a long white-sand beach, this hotel has plush rooms featuring Brazilian walnut wooden paneling and balconies overlooking the Caribbean Sea.

MUSTIQUE: The Cotton House $$$
Luxury
Cheltenham
Tel *784 456 4777*
W cottonhouse.net
This is a full-service resort on the private island of Mustique, with great emphasis on relaxation, comfort, and exclusivity.

PALM ISLAND: Palm Island Resort & Spa $$$
Luxury
Palm Island
Tel *866 237 2157*
W palmislandresortgrenadines.com
Most rooms at this all-inclusive beach resort on an idyllic island are beachfront, with private terraces and deep soaking tubs.

UNION ISLAND:
The Islander's Inn $
Beach
Zion
Tel *784 458 8745*
W theislandersinn.com
This family-run hotel is known for its relaxed atmosphere and warm and friendly service. All rooms offer lovely sea views.

Relaxing outdoor seating at the Firefly Plantation Hotel, Bequia

Where to Eat and Drink

Wallilabou Anchorage in Wallilabou Bay enjoys a wonderful waterfront setting, St. Vincent

WALLILABOU BAY:
Wallilabou Anchorage $$
International
Wallilabou Bay
Tel *784 458 7270*
Set on the bay where scenes from the first *Pirates of the Caribbean* movie was filmed, this eatery offers excellent seafood dishes.

The Grenadines

BEQUIA: De Reef Beach Bar $$
Seafood
Lower Bay
Tel *784 458 3958*
The dishes at De Reef make the most of Bequia's fish and seafood bounty. Enjoy scrumptious food alongside gorgeous ocean views.

BEQUIA: Devil's Table $$
International
Bequia Marina
Tel *784 458 3900*
The pirate-themed decor and superb menu at Devil's Table contribute to a fun evening out. There is a live band on Fridays. Try the lobster appetizer.

BEQUIA: Sugar Reef Café $$
Caribbean
Crescent Beach
Tel *784 458 3400*
Located in an idyllic oceanside setting, this restaurant prides itself on offering the freshest locally sourced organic meats and produce.

BEQUIA: Coco's Place $$$
Caribbean
Lower Bay
Tel *784 458 3463*
The seaside location, lively atmosphere, and varied menu make Coco's Place a perfect spot for a family outing. The soup, fish dishes, and steak are all excellent.

UNION ISLAND:
Big Citi Restaurant $
Caribbean
Clifton
Tel *784 458 8960* **Closed** *Sun*
Veranda-style café on the second floor of the Tourism Information Building. The menu includes pizzas, burgers, and local seafood.

St. Vincent

GEORGETOWN: Ferdi's
Restaurant and Bar $
Caribbean
Commercial Road
Tel *784 458 6433*
A excellent pit stop for those on their way to La Soufrière, Ferdi's offers hearty Caribbean meals.

KINGSTOWN: The Bounty $
Caribbean
Egmont Street
Tel *784 456 1776* **Closed** *Sun*
This café is a good choice for a quick bite – pies, pastries, *rotis* (Caribbean burritos), and juices. On-site gift shop and gallery.

KINGSTOWN: Cobblestone
Rooftop Restaurant $$
Caribbean/International
Upper Bay Street
Tel *784 456 1937*
A charming waterfront restaurant serving up traditional and modern Caribbean cuisine. There are vegetarian specialties, too.

VILLA: Beachcombers
Restaurant & Bar $$
Caribbean/International
Villa Beach
Tel *784 458 4283*
Numerous culinary delights await at this relaxing hotel-restaurant with a great beach setting.

VILLA: Grand View Grill $$
International
Villa Point
Tel *784 457 5487* **Closed** *Mon*
The beachside restaurant of the historic Grand View Beach Hotel has a large menu featuring fresh fish, seafood, and pizzas, as well as a range of vegan dishes.

VILLA: High Tide $$
Caribbean/International
Villa Harbour
Tel *784 456 6777*
An oceanfront eatery with a convivial ambience, High Tide offers a formal dinner menu, as well as pub fare at its popular bar. Lovely place to enjoy an evening drink while watching the sun set.

DK Choice

VILLA: Paradise Beach
Hotel Restaurant $$
Caribbean/International
Villa Beach
Tel *784 457 4795*
In a wonderful setting overlooking the ocean, this excellent restaurant serves up flavorful local specialties including Creole chicken, conch *rotis* (Caribbean burritos), fresh fish, and legendary grilled lobster (when in season). They have popular theme nights, such as Grillin' with the Captain, Latin dancing, and sunset cocktails. Friendly service.

VILLA: Surf Side $$
International
Calliaqua
Tel *784 457 5362* **Closed** *Mon*
Informal restaurant serving pizzas, seafood, grilled steaks, and other tasty dishes. Good views.

VILLA: French Verandah $$$
French/Caribbean
Villa Beach
Tel *784 453 1111*
Located at the Marina Hotel and overlooking Villa Beach, this elegant French restaurant is well known for its exquisite meals and hospitable service.

Practical Information

St. Vincent and the Grenadines have always been a sailor's delight and are gradually becoming a popular tourist destination as well. Visitors to the once British Windwards Islands will find the residents very warm and friendly. Relevant information is available from the Ministry of Tourism and most hotels can also provide useful information for tourists. Taxi drivers are usually knowledgeable and helpful.

E. T. Joshua Airport, Arnos Vale, St. Vincent

When to Go

The average annual temperature in St. Vincent and the Grenadines is 81°F (27°C). The rainy season lasts from May to November, while the coolest months are from November to February. A good time to visit is between December and February, when some of the islands' biggest events and festivals take place.

Getting There

The E. T. Joshua Airport in St. Vincent is a 15-minute drive to the capital Kingstown. There are no direct international services, but same-day connecting flights arrive via Puerto Rico, Barbados, St. Lucia, Martinique, Grenada, and Trinidad on **Caribbean Airlines**, **Air Jamaica**, **Air Canada**, **American Eagle**, **British Airways**, and **Virgin Atlantic**. **LIAT** has scheduled services that link these islands to the rest of the Caribbean. Argyle International Airport is due to open on St Vincent's eastern coast in late 2013.

Canouan, Bequia, Mustique, and Union Island also have airstrips, where **SVG Air**, **Mustique Airways**, and **Grenadine Airways** operate scheduled flights between St. Vincent and the Grenadine islands. SVG Air and Mustique Airways are also available for charter.

Documentation

Visitors must have a valid passport, with the exception of citizens of the Organization of Eastern Caribbean States (OECS) who only need proof of citizenship (driver's license or voter's registration card). Visas are required from citizens of various nations, so check with the respective embassies. All visitors must have an onward or return ticket as well. Jewelry, cameras, and other expensive items are allowed if they are for personal use only. Passengers 18 years and over are allowed free import of 200 cigarettes or 50 cigars and 1 quart of wine or spirits. Drugs, firearms and ammunition and spear fishing equipment are prohibited. A departure tax is to be paid when leaving the island.

Visitor Information

St. Vincent and the Grenadines Ministry of Tourism has its main office on Upper Bay Street in Kingstown and there is an information booth at the airport as well. **Bequia Tourism Association** has an office in Port Elizabeth. Overseas, tourist offices are located in the UK, Canada, and USA.

Health and Security

Milton Cato Memorial Hospital is the largest of the six public hospitals on the islands with smaller ones in Georgetown, Chateaubelair, and Bequia and clinics throughout the islands. **Maryfield Hospital** in St. Vincent is a private hospital. The beaches do not have lifeguards. It is advisable not to leave personal belongings unattended and to avoid walking in unlit areas.

Banking and Currency

The official currency is the Eastern Caribbean dollar (EC$). Bank hours are Monday to Thursday 8am to 1pm and Friday 8am to 5pm. The bank at E. T. Joshua Airport opens Monday to Friday 9am to noon and 3pm to 5:30pm. A few ATMs are located in St. Vincent, Bequia, and Union Island. Major credit cards are accepted everywhere.

Communications

The area code for St. Vincent and the Grenadines is 1 784. Coin and phone card services are found throughout the islands. Cell phone service is available in most places, and visitors can receive and make

Scooters available for hire on St. Vincent and the Grenadines

calls through their roaming service. Local telephone operators include **LIME**, **Caribbean Cellular**, and **Digicel SVG Ltd**.

Transport

If visitors do not have an OECS or international driving license, a local one can be obtained. Taxis and minibuses are readily available and vehicles can be hired at rental agencies, including **AVIS**, **B&G Jeep Rental**, **Rent and Drive**, and **Greg's Auto Care and Rental Services**. On St. Vincent, public buses link major towns and villages.

Shopping

St. Vincent and the Grenadines might not be huge shopping centers but visitors can browse through Kingstown's small town center, where there are locally-made crafts, batik, hand-painted T-shirts, and the famed Sea Island cotton. Some special craft items,

including hand-made dolls, can be found at the nearby **St. Vincent and the Grenadines Craftsmen's Center**. Bequia's model boat-makers sell their amazing creations at workshops in Port Elizabeth and perhaps the most well-known is the **Sargeant Brothers Model Boat Shop**. There are also several duty-free stores including **Vogager**, which has shops on Halifax and Bay streets.

Model boats lined up and ready for sale, Bequia

Language

English is the official language spoken on St. Vincent and the Grenadines.

Electricity

Voltage is 220 volts, 50 cycles, but Petit St. Vincent has 110 volts, 60 cycles.

Time

St. Vincent and the Grenadines are on Atlantic Standard Time (AST), 1 hour ahead of Eastern Standard Time in the US, and 4 hours behind GMT.

Getting Married

Visitors who wish to get married must be residents in St. Vincent and the Grenadines for a minimum of a day. A special Governor General's license (valid for 3 months) is available from the **Ministry of Legal Affairs** for a minimal fee. **A Caribbean Wedding** are wedding coordinators.

DIRECTORY

Getting There

Air Canada
w aircanada.com

Air Jamaica
w airjamaica.com

American Eagle
w aa.com

British Airways
w ba.com

Caribbean Airlines
w caribbean-airlines.com

Grenadine Airways
w caribbeanjet.com

LIAT
w liatairline.com

Mustique Airways
w mustique.com

SVG Air
w svgair.com

Virgin Atlantic
w virgin-atlantic.com

Visitor Information

Bequia Tourism Association
PO Box 146 BQ, Bequia.
Tel 784 458 3286.
w bequiatourism.com

St. Vincent and the Grenadines Ministry of Tourism
Upper Bay Street, St. Vincent. **Tel** 784 457 1502 (Kingstown). **Tel** 212 687 4981 (USA). **Tel** 020 7937 6570 (UK). **Tel** 416 630 9292 (Canada).
w svgtourism.com

Health and Security

Maryfield Hospital
Kingstown, St. Vincent.
Tel 784 457 8991.

Milton Cato Memorial Hospital
Kingstown, St. Vincent.
Tel 784 456 1185.

Police, Fire, and Ambulance
Tel 999/911.

Communications

Caribbean Cellular
Halifax Street, St. Vincent.
Tel 784 457 4600.

Digicel SVG Ltd
Halifax Street, St. Vincent.
Tel 784 453 3022.

LIME
Halifax Street, St. Vincent.
Tel 784 457 1901.

Transport

AVIS
E. T. Joshua Airport, St. Vincent. **Tel** 784 456 6861.

B&G Jeep Rental
Port Elizabeth, Bequia.
Tel 784 458 3760.

Greg's Auto Care and Rental Services
St. Vincent.
Tel 784 457 9814.

Rent and Drive
St. Vincent.
Tel 784 457 5601.

Shopping

Sargeant Brothers Model Boat Shop
O'Car Reform, Bequia.
Tel 784 458 3344.

St. Vincent and the Grenadines Craftsmen's Center
Kingstown, St. Vincent.
Tel 784 457 2516.

Voyager
Kingstown.
Tel 784 456 1686.

Getting Married

A Caribbean Wedding
Bequia. **Tel** 784 528 7444.
w acaribbeanwedding.com

Ministry of Legal Affairs
Granby Street, Kingstown, St. Vincent.
Tel 784 456 1762.

Exploring Grenada

Famously known as the "Isle of Spice," Grenada is a lush, mountainous island carved by deep valleys with beautiful waterfalls and cool freshwater streams. Formed by volcanoes, the island's 133 sq miles (344 sq km) are blessed with both tropical rainforest and a bevy of stunning white- and black-sand beaches. To its northeast are the sister islands of Carriacou and Petite Martinique. Their topography is hilly, rather than mountainous, and much drier. Life on the two islands still moves at a leisurely pace. Seafaring, fishing, and boat-building are the major occupations here. The three islands form part of the Grenadine Islands chain that runs south from St. Vincent to Grenada.

DOMINICA

ST. LUCIA

BARBADOS

ST. VINCENT AND THE GRENADINES

GRENADA

Locator Map

Cruise ships towering over the capital of St. George's, Grenada

Key

━━ Major road

═══ Minor road

– – Trail

···· Ferry route

△ Peak

Getting Around

Island tours are the best way to explore Grenada and its sister isles. On Grenada, visitors can either choose from several tour operators or take a taxi tour. In Carriacou, taxi drivers willing to undertake sightseeing trips await the ferry for prospective customers. Grenada and Carriacou are linked by air (20 minutes), but most visitors prefer taking the ferry. The *Osprey* power-catamaran operates a round-trip passenger service between Grenada and Carriacou. It also plies between Petite Martinique, which is only accessible by boat, and Grenada and Carriacou. Petite Martinique has one taxi service, which offers tours. The *Osprey* runs once daily. Private water taxis are also available.

0 kilometers   5

0 miles   5

Mt Rouge

Point Salines

Cal

Glover Island

Sights at a Glance

❶ St. George's

❷ Grand Etang Forest Reserve

❸ Leapers Hill

❹ Belmont Estate

❺ Carriacou

❻ Petite Martinique

For hotels and restaurants on this island see p434 and p435

Mount Carmel Waterfall, between Port Royal and Carmel villages

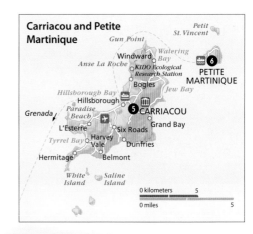

Belmont Estate
Primarily a cocoa plantation, this estate has a chocolate factory in its vicinity and offers day visitors an extensive lunch buffet.

Grenville
Founded by the French in the 1760s, Grenada's second largest town boasts the biggest nutmeg-processing plant on the island.

La Sagesse Nature Center
This former plantation is now an idyllic retreat in proximity to three superlative beaches, which lure visitors with azure waters and golden sands.

Abundance of flavors for sale at St. George's Spice Market

❶ St. George's

SW coast of Grenada. 🄰 36,000.
✈ 🚢 🚌 ℹ Burns Point
(east end Carenage), 473 440 2279.
🅦 grenadagrenadines.com

Grenada's capital, St. George's, is renowned for the most picturesque harbor, if not city, in the Caribbean. Rich in West Indian, English, and French history, the city has many architectural gems from the French and British colonial periods. The horseshoe-shaped harbor is surrounded by pastel warehouses and old Georgian buildings rising up the hills, with distinctive roofs covered with red tiles, which were once the ballasts of ships.

The inner harbor, called the Carenage, is the center of St. George's marine activity, filled with colorful Carriacou sloops, fishing vessels, and tourist boats. Rimming this harbor is Wharf Road, lined with shops and restaurants. Visitors can stroll along the Carenage waterfront and into the hills to capture stunning views from various angles. Lowther's Lane is the vantage point to watch boats coming into the harbor, especially in the morning.

Fort George is another ideal point from which to photograph the Carenage and the city. Sitting high atop St. George Point with its battery of cannons pointing out to sea, it towers above its surroundings. Built in 1706 by the French, it is now the police headquarters. The site where politician Maurice Bishop and many cabinet members were executed in 1983, this fort was bombed by American troops in the infamous military intervention that followed.

Facing the Carenage are the exquisite Georgian-style Houses of Parliament and three of the city's prominent churches, still roofless after horrific Hurricane Ivan (2004): St. Andrew's Presbyterian Kirk, St. George's Anglican Church, and St. George's Roman Catholic Cathedral. Built in 1818, the cathedral's Neo-Gothic tower is the city's most visible landmark. The church itself dates to 1884, built on the site of an older church.

Nearby, just off Young Street, is the **Grenada National Museum**. Housed in a former army barracks and prison, this small but interesting museum covers many aspects of the island's history and culture, ranging from the Caribs to Hurricane Ivan.

Built in 1894, the 340-ft (103-m) Sendall Tunnel connects the Carenage to the Esplanade, which is home to the Esplanade duty-free mall, located at the cruise terminal.

Nearby, the Granby Street leads to Market Square (also called Spice Market). Outdoors, women in traditional Grenadian attire sell spices and produce. In the cooler, new indoor market, a range of souvenirs and products made in Grenada are sold. About 5 miles (8 km) to the east of the city along the Eastern Main Road lies La Sagesse Hotel, Restaurant & Beach Bar (see p434), a former manor house built by Lord Brownlow in 1968 that now functions as an inn.

🏰 **Fort George**
St. George Point. **Open** 9am–5pm Mon–Fri.

🏛 **Grenada National Museum**
Corner Young & Monkton Streets.
Tel 473 440 3725. **Open** 9am–4:30pm Mon–Fri; 10am–1pm Sat. 🖼 ✉

Fort George perched above the colonial warehouses of Carenage Harbor, St. George's

Grand Etang Lake in a volcanic crater, Grand Etang Forest Reserve

❷ Grand Etang Forest Reserve

7 miles (11 km) NE of St. George's.
🛈 Grand Etang Visitors' Center,
473 440 6160. **Open** 9am–4pm
Mon–Fri. 🏤 🚻 💻 📷 Note: open
during weekends if big cruise ships
are in port.

Located high in the central
mountains, this reserve protects
a lush rainforest and several
ecological sub-systems, and is
popular for sightseeing and
hiking, with trails leading to
its many waterfalls *(see p431)*.
The forest was greatly damaged
by Hurricane Ivan, but has
quickly regrown. The visitors'
center's walkway is lined with
spice vendors and musical
entertainers, and visitors
may also get a chance to spot
mona monkeys. The center
has some interpretive displays,
and provides a good view of
Grand Etang Lake in the extinct
volcanic crater.

❸ Leapers Hill

23 miles (37 km) N of St. George's.
Tel 473 444 3222.
Open 10am–4pm daily.
🏤 🚻 💻 📷

A historic landmark (also
called Carib's Leap), this is
where the Carib Indians leapt
off a 100-ft (30-m) cliff into
the sea, rather than surrender

to French colonists in 1651.
This site is a good pit stop
while touring the island. There
is a cemetery, as well as some
recreated petroglyphs on the
rocky wall, and travelers can
enjoy a scenic view of the
Grenadine islands.

❹ Belmont Estate

20 miles (32 km) N of St. George's.
Tel 473 442 9524. **Open** 8am–4:30pm
Sun–Fri. 🏤 🚻 🍴 💻 📷
🔲 **belmontestate.net**

It is possible to get a glimpse
of traditional Grenadian plantation life at this 400-acre (162-ha)
estate dating back to the late
1600s, and owned by the
Nyacks since 1944. Originally
a coffee plantation, the estate
has changed crops over the
years; today, primarily cocoa
and nutmeg are grown here.
Touring the cocoa operation,
visitors learn about the
traditional processing of a
cocoa bean, from its start as a
pod on the tree to fermenting
to drying on wooden trays in
the sun. It is possible to sample
delicious cocoa tea and organic
dark chocolate, produced
by the Grenada Chocolate
Company nearby. A small
museum documents island
history and houses estate
memorabilia. The plantation's
lunch buffet of home-cooked

Creole dishes, including estate-
grown fruits and vegetables,
is a feast.

Environs
Another plantation house in
this area is **Helvellyn House**,
located at the northern tip of
the island. This is a good spot
to enjoy an alfresco lunch of
authentic Caribbean dishes
served in a lovely setting of
gardens with a view of the
Grenadines. The pottery workshop here also offers lessons.

🏛 **Helvellyn House**
La Fortune, St. Patrick. **Tel** 473 442
9252. **Open** Pottery workshop:
9am–5pm Mon–Sat.

Women walking on cocoa beans to aerate
them, Belmont Estate

Beachside stilt house, the northeast coast of Carriacou

❺ Carriacou

23 miles (37 km) N of Grenada.
🏔 5,300. ⛴ 🚌 🚐 *i* Main Street,
Hillsborough, 473 443 7948.
W grenadagrenadines.com

Although covering an area
of just 13 sq miles (34 sq km),
Carriacou is the largest of the
Grenadine islands. It is a popular
destination for a day trip from
Grenada, but also offers
overnight budget accommoda-
tions in a tranquil setting. The
Carib word for Land of Reefs,
Carriacou is ringed by some of
Caribbean's most exquisite reefs.

The Osprey Lines ferry
(*see p437*) arrives daily from
Grenada to the heart of the
main town Hillsborough. In
town, the small **Carriacou
Museum**, set in a restored
cotton gin mill, exhibits
Amerindian and African
artifacts, and traces the early
British and French occupation
of the islands. The museum also
pays tribute to Canute Calliste
(1914–2005), the internationally
acclaimed Grenadian artist.

For a sweeping panoramic
view of Hillsborough Bay,
Carriacou, and the outer islands,
visitors can head northeast
to the 640-ft (195-m) hilltop
site of Princess Royal Hospital
in Belair, framed by seaward-
pointing cannons.

In the east coast village of
Windward, the Carriacou sloops
are still built using the highly
skilled traditional methods of
constructing sturdy wooden
boats originally introduced by
the Scottish colonial settlers
of the island.

On the northern tip, Gun Point
is named after the still standing
cannon erected here by the
British in the 1780s.

Heading south down the
west coast, **KIDO Ecological
Research Station** arranges
guided eco-tours including
hiking through High North
National Park, the isle's highest
point, and turtle-watching.

Nearby, the secluded Anse
La Roche, a wonderfully scenic
beach with offshore coral reefs,
can be reached either by a
water taxi or on foot.

South of Hillsborough on
L'Esterre Bay is the famous
Paradise Beach, an easily
accessible, 1-mile (1.6-km) long
beach with plenty of amenities.
Sandy Island, a lovely islet just
offshore, is popular for
snorkeling and picnics.

Farther south, Tyrrel Bay is a
yachters' haven. Heading east,
water-taxis are available in
Belmont that ferry visitors to
White Island, an islet that has

pristine stretches of fine sandy
beaches and offers great
snorkeling opportunities. It is
also relatively uncrowded and
is ideal for people who want
some solitude.

Carriacou Museum
Paterson Street, Hillsborough. **Tel** 473
443 8288. **Open** 9:30am–4pm Mon–
Fri. **Closed** public hols. 🖼 🖼 🖼

KIDO Ecological Research Station
Sanctuary, Carriacou. **Tel** 473 443
7936. **W** kido.optsoftware.com

❻ Petite Martinique

3 miles (5 km) NE of Carriacou.
🏔 less than 1,000. ⛴

Dominated by a 738-ft (225-m)
volcanic cone that gives it its
conical appearance, the tiny
island of Petite Martinique
(locally called PM) is roughly
1 mile (1.6 km) in diameter.
It is scarcely populated and
most residents are acquainted
with each other. The sea is the
source of livelihood here and
boat-building is the main
occupation of most islanders.

Travelers arrive at the jetty
in Paradise, the sole village on
the islet, with basic amenities.
There is only one main road,
2-mile (3-km) long, so a taxi tour
takes under an hour. The rocky
East Coast is uninhabited and
unreachable by road. While
Paradise has a white-sand
beach, Petit St. Vincent, a
5-minute boat ride away, and
other surrounding cays have
a few good strands and offer
excellent snorkeling.

Volcanic peak rising up from Petite Martinique

Spice Isle

More spices are grown in Grenada per square mile than anywhere else in the world. With the fragrant aromas of cinnamon, ginger, and vanilla wafting through the air, the island has been dubbed the "Isle of Spice" as it is the Caribbean's only spice producer. The most important crop is nutmeg, coined "black gold" by former Prime Minister George Brizan (1995). Spice estates, including the Gouyave and Grenville Nutmeg Processing Stations and Dougaldston Spice Estate, offer tours highlighting the various stages of spice production, and also sell fresh spices and spice products.

Nutmeg and Mace

Grenada is the fifth largest producer of nutmeg in the world. It has been striving to regain its position as second largest producer since Hurricane Ivan hit the island hard in 2004. Nutmeg production has been the backbone of Grenada's economy and agriculture since 1843, when it was brought here from Banda, Indonesia. Along with its twin spice, mace, which grows around the shell of the nutmeg, it is one of the isle's top export crops.

The nutmeg tree grows up to 75 ft (23 m) in height, bearing a yellow fleshy fruit called the pericarp, which contains two spices – nutmeg and mace. When ripe, the fruit splits open and drops to the ground, from where it is gathered by hand.

The nutmeg seed has a dark, thin shell, covered by the lacy, brilliantly scarlet mace.

Mace is separated from nutmeg shells at the processing stations. Cured in wooden bins for four months, the mace gradually assumes a golden tinge.

Nutmeg syrup, jams, liqueur, as well as chocolate bars, soaps, perfumes, and candles are some locally-made spice goods.

Nutmeg shells are dried indoors for six to eight weeks. Their brittle shells are then removed and the nuts washed, graded, polished, and packaged for export.

Other Spices

Grenada's famous spices include cloves, ginger, pepper, pimento, cinnamon, bay leaves, and tonka beans. All over the island, there are plantations as well as spice-processing plants.

The cinnamon bark is peeled during the rainy season. When dried in the sun, it curls to form cinnamon sticks.

Bay leaves have a distinct aroma. They are found on the evergreen bay tree, native to the Windward Islands.

Clove buds when picked have a deep red hue. When dried, they turn dark brown.

Black pepper berries grow on creeping vines. Reddish in color when picked, they turn black after drying.

Outdoor Activities and Specialized Holidays

Grenada and its sister isles are an ideal getaway for the adventurous and with their varied geographical topography, comprising mountains, volcanoes, rainforests, and waterfalls, the islands lend themselves to a wide range of outdoor activities. Guided hikes are the best way of exploring mainland Grenada and Carriacou. Alternatively, a day-sail or a trip on the *Osprey* catamaran is a great way to see the rugged terrain, jutting shorelines, and beautiful beaches from the sea. The islands also offer popular activities such as scuba diving and snorkeling from its numerous offshore reefs.

A relatively uncrowded stretch of Grand Anse Beach, Grenada

Beaches

The tri-island nation of Grenada, Carriacou, and Petite Martinique is blessed with 45 white-sand and nine black-sand beaches, which are among some of the best in the Caribbean. The 2-mile (3-km) long Grand Anse, popular with sunbathers, is by far Grenada's most beautiful beach, while the Morne Rouge also on the southwestern side is quieter and attracts relatively fewer visitors. Other choices include Bathway Beach in the northeast and La Sagesse Nature Center with three beaches to explore.

Paradise Beach in Carriacou has a protective reef, which allows visitors the comfort of swimming in its calm waters. Anse La Roche is accessible only by a steep, well-marked trail or a water-taxi.

Paradise village on Petite Martinique is an excellent base to explore the nearby tiny cays and great beaches. Petit St. Vincent is also just a 5-minute boat ride away.

Diving and Snorkeling

Although Grenada is not as renowned as some other Caribbean isles for diving, it features a larger variety of marine creatures and less-crowded, more intact reefs, many in its five marine parks. Carriacou, known as the Land of Reefs, is a popular dive center. Together, the two islands boast more than 50 sites, most rated easy (except for a few with strong currents), and quickly reached by a 5- to 15-minute boat ride. There are several walls and wrecks with common marine life, including sharks, turtles, lobsters, giant moray eels, soft coral forests, and sponges. Carriacou is famous for its beautiful coral gardens and small marine creatures such as sea horses.

Wreck enthusiasts will get their fill exploring the many shipwrecks, including *Bianca C*, the largest in the Caribbean Sea. Known as the "*Titanic* of the Caribbean," the sunken 600-ft (183-m) cruise ship is only suitable for experienced wreck divers.

In Grenada, the most convenient snorkeling is south of Grand Anse Beach. La Sagesse is another great spot. A new, unique site for both diving and snorkeling is the **Underwater Sculpture Park** in Grenada's Molinière Bay by artist Jason de Caires Taylor. Several day sails and dive operators, including **Aquanauts Grenada**, offer both diving and guided snorkeling trips to the site.

All the Grenadian islands, including Petite Martinique and its neighboring cays, offer good snorkeling opportunities.

Grenada has a few dive shops, most are located on the south coast beaches, and Carriacou has three. For a list, contact the Grenada Board of Tourism (*see p437*) or **Grenada Scuba Diving Association**.

Watersports

Many resorts, watersports centers, and dive shops, mainly on Grand Anse Beach, offer a full array of watersports and rentals including ocean kayaks, Hobie Cats, windsurfing, parasailing, waterskiing, and wake and knee boarding. **Adventure River Tubing** is a fun, wet activity offered in Grenada. Participants don life-jackets and helmets before boarding a large modified rubber tube with handles. With guides to assist along the way, they "whitewater" tube around rocks and down little drops on Balthazar River, in the depths of the rainforest. Also available are combo adventure jeep/ tubing tours.

Riding a banana boat at Grand Anse Beach, Grenada

Waterfalls of Grenada

With its mountainous terrain and lush tropical rainforest, Grenada boasts several idyllic waterfalls, some amongst the most beautiful in the Caribbean. Grand Etang Forest Reserve *(see p427)*, has the highest number of falls in any one geographic region. Rosemount Falls, in the western parish of St. John, is privately owned and only open to visitors lunching at Rosemount Plantation House. Farther north, Victoria Falls (also called Tufton Hall), is the island's tallest waterfall, and is relatively difficult to reach. Visiting one or all of these cataracts is a highlight of a trip to the island.

Tropical plants, including banana, are abundant near the Seven Sisters Falls.

The Seven Sisters range from small cascades to 70-ft (21-m) falls.

Pools, formed at the base of the Seven Sisters, are ideal for a refreshing dip.

Waterfalls of Grand Etang Forest Reserve

Grand Etang harbors five waterfalls within the reserve or on its fringes: Concord, Honeymoon, Annandale, Seven Sisters, and Royal Mt. Carmel. Trails pass through rainforest, citrus groves, and plantations growing fragrant spices and fruits.

Annandale Falls is one of the easiest to reach. A lovely garden of labeled trees, such as nutmeg and flowering plants, lines the path to the falls.

Concord Falls consists of three waterfalls of which the first is the most accessible and popular.

Flora and Fauna

Trails around the waterfalls are lined with huge mahogany, gommier trees, and endemic plants such as Grand Etang fern. Wildlife includes nine-banded armadillos and iguanas.

The mona monkey, introduced from Africa three centuries ago, is one of the most easily spotted animals near Rosemount Falls.

Water hyacinths, among other plants such as balisier, wild fuchsia, and hibiscus, thrive near Grand Etang's waterfalls.

Selaginella and fungi are widespread in the forest around Victoria Falls.

Day sail boats at the lagoon in St. George's marina

Hiking

Grenada's mountainous terrain, reaching 2,757 ft (840 m) atop Mount St. Catherine, provides one of the Caribbean's loveliest and most varied hiking environments, and a good variety of flora and fauna. To protect its natural environment, the island has set aside one-sixth of its landmass as wildlife sanctuaries and parks.

One of the most popular hiking areas, Grenada's Grand Etang Forest Reserve (see p427) has hikes ranging from easy 15-minute jaunts to rigorous expeditions. All trails are cleared and maintained by the Forestry Department of the Ministry of Agriculture. However, it is always a good idea to hire a hiking guide.

Expert **Telfor Bedeau**, who knows the island intimately, assesses visitors' interests and abilities and then creates tailor-made hikes or mountain climbs anywhere on the island.

Other popular operators include **Edwin Frank's Tours and Services**, **Henry's Safari**, **Kennedy Tours**, **K&J Tours**, and **Mandoo Tours**.

Hilly, but not mountainous, Carriacou is ideal for walking. KIDO Ecological Research Station (see p428) can arrange a guide for hikers.

Day-Sails and Boat Trips

Thanks to its many bays and sheltered anchorages, Grenada is is one of the main yachting centers of the Eastern Caribbean. For a day out on the water, there are some good options. **Carib CATS**, a 60-ft (18-m) sailing catamaran, offers full- and half-day snorkeling and sunset cruises, as does **Shadowfax**. **First Impressions** runs whale and dolphin-watching tours, four sailing tours (minimum six guests), fishing trips, and evening karaoke tours aboard catamarans. **Spice Kayaking & Eco Tours**,

launched by the same operator, offers guided eco tours by kayak and pedal-boat in some of Grenada's most untouched spots, including sunset and moonlight trips. **Grenada Seafaris** takes visitors on a high-speed Zodiac tour of Grenada's west coast. The 2-hour tour includes snorkeling at the Underwater Sculpture Park (see p430) and fun lessons on the isle's history, ecology, and geography. The UK-based **Carib Tours** is another operator that runs luxury yachts near Grenada. In Carriacou, KIDO runs catamaran trips.

Fishing

Marine life is plentiful in Grenada and a wide range of fish, billfish, blue and white marlin, sailfish, wahoo, yellowfin tuna, and a common dolphin fish, called dorado or mahimahi, populate its waters. Plenty of charters offer half- and full-day deep-sea fishing, including **True Blue Sportfishing** aboard the 31-ft (9-m) Yes Aye. The agency believes in conserving billfish stocks and regularly tags and releases all marlin and sailfish. Skipper Stewart's **Wayward Wind Fishing Charters** offers discounts to groups.

A visitor with her catch

Hurricane-damaged forest in the Grand Etang Forest Reserve

Gardens

With such a profusion of tropical flora, it is no surprise that Grenada has some spectacular gardens to tour. On a guided walking tour through pleasant **Laura Herbs and Spice Garden**, visitors can see all the herbs and spices grown on the island, such as thyme, cinnamon, and basil, and learn about their medicinal uses.

Just 15 minutes from St. George's is **Sunnyside Garden**. At this garden, Jean Renwick shares her passion by showing the beautiful 3-acre (1-ha) gardens around her home, which comprise a gorgeous koi pond, native flora, tortoises, a citrus grove, and themed gardens including a Japanese one. The view from here, 600 ft (183 m) above sea level, is stunning.

A leatherback turtle laying eggs

Turtle-Watching

Historically the Grenadians relied upon sea turtles for food and income. **Ocean Spirits**, a non-profit organization that is engaged in protecting the endangered leatherback turtles by demonstrating their higher value as nesting turtles, is the first to offer turtle-watching tours. These are entirely run by two local communities. With a trained turtle guide, visitors witness the spectacle of massive leatherbacks nesting on remote Levera Beach, home to one of the Caribbean's top three largest nesting populations. All profits go to sea turtle or other conservation initiatives in the local communities, providing them with an economic stake in saving turtles. Those interested can book for this program, available from April to July, with **Discover Grenada**.

Hibiscus in Sunnyside Garden

In Carriacou, leatherbacks and critically endangered hawksbills nest at Petite Carenage Beach from March to October. Guests can join night nesting patrols that protect turtles from illegal hunting and egg poaching. For more information visitors can contact KIDO.

DIRECTORY

Diving and Snorkeling

Aquanauts Grenada
True Blue Bay Resort and Spice Island Beach Resort, Grenada.
Tel 473 444 1126.
W aquanautsgrenada.com

Grenada Scuba Diving Association
W grenadascubadivingassociation.com

Underwater Sculpture Park
Tel 776 282 9173.
W underwatersculpture.com

Watersports

Adventure River Tubing
St. George's, Grenada.
Tel 473 444 5337.
W adventuregrenada.com

Hiking

Edwin Frank's Tours and Services
Grenada.
Tel 473 407 5393.

Henry's Safari
Grenada.
Tel 473 444 5313.
W henrysafari.com

Kennedy Tours
Grenada.
Tel 473 444 1074.
W kennedytours.com

K&J Tours
St. Pauls, Grenada.
Tel 473 440 4227.
W grenadaguide.com/kjtours/hikes.htm

Mandoo Tours
St. George's, Grenada.
Tel 473 440 1428.
W grenadatours.com

Telfor Bedeau
Grenada.
Tel 473 442 6200.

Day-Sails and Boat Trips

Carib CATS
St. George's, Grenada.
Tel 473 444 3222.
W travelgrenadagrenadines.com

Carib Tours
The Point, 210 New Kings Road, London SW6 4NZ.
Tel 020 3131 0174.
W caribtours.co.uk

First Impressions
St. George's, Grenada.
Tel 473 440 3678.
W catamaranchartering.com

Grenada Seafaris
Grenada.
Tel 473 405 7800.
W grenadaseafaris.com

Shadowfax
True Blue, St. George's, Grenada.
Tel 473 437 3737.
W bananaboattoursgrenada.com

Spice Kayaking & Eco Tours
Allamanda Hotel, Grand Anse, St. George's, Grenada.
Tel 473 440 3678.
W spicekayaking.com

Fishing

True Blue Sportfishing
St. George's, Grenada.
Tel 473 444 2048.
W yesaye.com

Wayward Wind Fishing Charters
Grenada Yacht Club, St. George's, Grenada.
Tel 473 538 9821.
W grenadafishing.co.uk

Gardens

Laura Herbs and Spice Garden
Perdmontemps, St. David, Grenada.
Tel 473 443 2604.

Sunnyside Garden
St. Paul's village, St. George's, Grenada.
Tel 473 440 2747.

Turtle-Watching

Discover Grenada
Tel 473 435 5958.

Ocean Spirits
St. George's, Grenada.
Tel 473 442 2341.
W oceanspirits.org

Where to Stay

CARRIACOU: Bogles Round House Cottages $
B&B
Bogles
Tel *473 443 7841*
W *boglesroundhouse.com*
Stay in an intimate self-contained cottage in an idyllic village. Watersports and tours available.

GRAND ANSE, ST. GEORGE: Jenny's Place $
Beach
Grand Anse Bay
Tel *473 439 5186*
W *jennysplacegrenada.com*
Jenny's Place is a cozy seaside guesthouse with self-contained apartments. It offers lots of activities, including kayaking, snorkeling, and hiking.

GRAND ANSE, ST. GEORGE: Blue Horizons Garden Resort $$
Boutique
Grand Anse
Tel *473 444 4316*
W *grenadabluehorizons.com*
A beach resort set in a large tropical garden that is home to over 20 species of birds. There are deluxe one-bedroom suites, as well as studios with kitchenettes.

GRAND ANSE, ST. GEORGE: The Flamboyant Hotel and Villas $$
Modern
Morne Rouge
Tel *473 444 4247*
W *flamboyant.com*
This is a casual hotel, with each room offering breathtaking views of Grand Anse Beach and Grenada's capital city. It has a beachside restaurant and bar.

The La Sagesse Hotel, Restaurant & Beach Bar in St. David is located on this beautiful cove

PETITE MARTINIQUE: The Palm Beach Guest House $
Modern
Petite Martinique
Tel *473 443 9103*
W *petitemartinique.com*
Two apartments on a tiny island, close to the beach. Easy access by ferry from the mainland.

ST. DAVID: La Sagesse Hotel, Restaurant & Beach Bar $
Boutique
La Sagesse Beach
Tel *473 444 6458*
W *lasagesse.com*
Set on a picturesque cove, this small intimate hotel is perfect for a romatic getaway. Most rooms have ocean views.

ST. DAVID: Petite Anse $$
Beach Resort
Prospect Road, Sauters
Tel *473 442 5252*
W *petiteanse.com*
This beachfront property set amid hillsides and waterfalls offers tasteful cottages and suites.

ST. GEORGE'S: Le Phare Bleu Boutique Hotel $$
Boutique
Petite Calivigny Bay
Tel *473 444 2400*
W *lepharebleu.com*
Choose between beach villas and apartments in a charming village-style hotel.

DK Choice
ST. GEORGE'S: True Blue Bay Resort $$
Beach Resort
Old Mill Road, True Blue
Tel *473 443 8783*
W *truebluebay.com*
Specializing in wedding and honeymoon packages, this resort is also perfect for families, with facilities such as pools, kids' playgrounds, and babysitting. Fun activities for grown-ups include cooking classes, rum tasting, and mermaid swimming. The modern accommodations have colorful touches.

ST. GEORGE'S: Calabash Hotel $$$
Luxury
L'Anse Aux Epines Beach
Tel *473 444 4334*
W *calabashhotel.com*
An intimate resort featuring beautiful rooms and a gem of a spa. Live entertainment most nights at the in-house restaurant.

Price Guide
Prices are based on one night's stay in high season for a standard double room, inclusive of service charges and taxes.

$	up to $200
$$	$200–500
$$$	over $500

ST. GEORGE'S: Laluna $$$
Luxury
Portici Beach, Morne Rouge
Tel *473 439 0001*
W *laluna.com*
Laluna is a small, and romantic boutique resort, set on a secluded bay. Each suite has a private plunge pool, and there is a wellness spa and yoga classes.

ST. GEORGE'S: Mount Cinnamon $$$
Beach Resort
Morne Rouge
Tel *473 439 4400*
W *mountcinnamon grenadahotel.com*
Stay in beautifully appointed villas featuring contemporary decor at this luxurious beach resort. The beachside open-air massage cabana is divine.

ST. GEORGE'S: Sandals LaSource Resort and Spa $$$
Luxury
Pink Gin Beach, Point Salines
Tel *888 726 3257*
W *sandals.com*
Sandals features opulent design and all the facilities imaginable, including rooms with butler service. Private plunge pools, infinity pools, cascading waterfalls, and nine restaurants.

ST. GEORGE'S: Spice Island Beach Resort $$$
Luxury
Grand Anse Beach
Tel *473 444 4258*
W *spiceislandbeachresort.com*
Elegant tropical decor and breathtaking views are just two reasons to head to Spice Island. All suites are beachfront, with a private lawn garden.

ST. JOHN: Mango Bay Cottages $
Resort
Woodford
Tel *473 444 3829*
W *mangobaygrenada.com*
Mango Bay Cottages offers its guests the perfect hideaway. Each well-equipped cottage has a private veranda with sea views and a hammock. Facilities include snorkeling and kayaking, a vegetarian restaurant, and yoga classes.

Where to Eat and Drink

CARRIACOU:
Slipway Restaurant **$$**
Caribbean
Tyrell Bay, Hermitage
Tel *473 443 6500*
Great location and atmosphere.
The menu varies according to
the freshest available ingredients.
Good Sunday brunch.

PETITE MARTINIQUE: Palm
Beach Restaurant & Bar **$$**
Caribbean
Petite Martinique
Tel *473 443 9103*
Enjoy fresh seafood and idyllic
panoramic views of other
palm-fringed Grenadine islands.
Palm Beach has an extensive list
of cocktails, including a number
of original concoctions.

ST. DAVID: La Sagesse
Nature Centre **$$**
Seafood/International
La Sagesse Beach
Tel *473 444 6458*
Amid a beautiful setting, La
Sagesse offers a menu featuring
fresh fish and seafood, with
vegetables and herbs from their
organic garden.

ST. GEORGE'S: BB's Crabback
Caribbean Restaurant **$$**
Caribbean
Progress House, The Carenage
Tel *473 435 7058*
Sample local cuisine prepared
with flair at this eatery located
at the waterfront in St George's.
Try the signature Crabback dish.

ST. GEORGE'S: Carib Sushi **$$**
Sushi
16 Le Marquis Complex, Grand Anse
Tel *473 439 5640* **Closed** *Sun*
Expert sushi chefs make use
of the fresh local fish and seafood
at this popular restaurant. Range
of sushi, *nigiri*, and sashimi, as
well as mains.

ST. GEORGE'S: Museum Bistro **$$**
International
Young Street
Tel *473 444 4371* **Closed** *Sun*
Delicious food and fresh juices in
the cozy, leafy courtyard of the
Grenada National Museum.

DK Choice

ST. GEORGE'S: Patrick's
Homestyle Cooking **$$**
Caribbean
Lagoon Road
Tel *473 440 0364*
At this charming restaurant,
the staff bring tapas-like dishes
of local delicacies to the table.
The feast offers 20 Grenadian
dishes, plus soup and dessert,
and usually includes *coo-coo*
(made of cornflour and okra),
stir-fried rabbit, *lambi* (conch),
and tannia cakes with shrimp.
Reserve ahead.

ST. GEORGE'S: Victory Bar
and Restaurant **$$**
International
Port Louis Marina, Lagoon Road
Tel *473 435 7263*
This casual, convivial eatery is
great for lunch or dinner. Serves
hearty American-style food.

ST. GEORGE'S:
Whisper Cove Marina **$$**
Steak house
Woburn Street, Grand Anse
Tel *473 444 5296*
The menu here includes delicious
local organic steaks. Popular Roast
Chicken Night on Thursdays.
Great waterside location.

ST. GEORGE'S: Dodgy Dock
Restaurant **$$$**
Caribbean/International
Old Mill Road, True Blue Bay
Tel *473 443 8783*
Set on a deck overlooking the
ocean, the Dodgy Dock has a
menu that runs from local
seafood to Mexican cuisine.
The Sunday brunch is popular.

ST. GEORGE'S:
Savvy's Restaurant **$$$**
Caribbean/International
Morne Rouge, Grand Anse
Tel *473 439 4400*
Enjoy sophisticated cuisine on
a terrace or a beach cabana with
stunning ocean and city views.
Don't miss the fish shish kebob.
Vegetarian options available.

ST. GEORGE'S:
The Aquarium Restaurant **$$$**
Caribbean/European
Magazine Beach, Point Salines
Tel *473 444 1410* **Closed** *Mon*
A wonderful cliffside setting and
delicious Caribbean-influenced
European cuisine. There is a
beach barbecue on Sundays.

ST. GEORGE'S: The Beach
House Restaurant & Bar **$$$**
International
Portici Bay
Tel *473 444 4455* **Closed** *Sun*
This restaurant has a varied menu,
with favorites such as seared
tuna, grilled vegetables, and *rotis*.

ST. GEORGE'S: The Red Crab **$$$**
Caribbean
L'Anse Aux Epines
Tel *473 444 4424* **Closed** *Sun*
Great spot for casual dining and
English-style pub fare. Fresh local
fish and seafood, and a Lobster
Fest on Saturdays.

ST. PATRICK: Aggies
Restaurant and Bar **$$**
Caribbean
Bathway Beach
Tel *473 442 2336* **Closed** *Mon*
A pleasant, friendly option while
touring the island's northeast.
Aggies specializes in simply
prepared, delicious seafood.

ST. PATRICK: Belmont Estate **$$**
Caribbean
Belmont Estate
Tel *473 442 9524* **Closed** *Sat*
The lunch buffet at this working
cocoa and spice estate is very
popular. The fish and meat dishes
are prepared with local vegetables
and herbs. Tasty soups.

Casual outdoor seating, with lovely views at the Whisper Cove Marina, St. George's

Practical Information

The Western Hemisphere's second smallest independent country, Grenada has had a relatively slower rate of growth in tourism and infrastructure development than its larger Caribbean cousins. After Hurricane Ivan (2004), however, the island rebuilt quickly, attracting several international hotel and vacation property developers. Today, visitors can find luxury accommodations and tourist amenities here. The laid-back tranquil atmosphere makes it a great destination for a relaxed holiday.

When to Go

Most people visit Grenada between December and April. Year-round temperature ranges from 75 to 85°F (24 to 30°C), with November to February being the coolest and January to May the driest season. June to December is humid, although there are hardly any prolonged spells of rainfall. Hurricane season lasts from June to November, with September the peak month.

Getting There

All flights arrive at Maurice Bishop International Airport (GND). From the UK, **British Airways** and **Virgin Atlantic** have weekly direct flights to Grenada. **Caribbean Airlines** connects London's Gatwick to Antigua, Barbados, and Trinidad with daily direct flights and has connections via **LIAT** that arrive the same day. From Toronto, weekly direct flights between December and April are offered by **Air Canada**, which also has year-round flights to Barbados, with LIAT connections. **Conviasa Airlines** has twice-weekly flights from Venezuela.

Documentation

A valid passport for British, and US citizens or a proof of citizenship bearing a photograph for Canadians, and a return ticket are required. The citizens of the USA, Canada, British Commonwealth, Japan, South Korea, most Caribbean and European countries, do not require a visa. A departure tax is mandatory at Maurice Bishop International Airport and there is no ferry service to Grenada. Contact the **Immigration Department** or visit the **Grenada Tourism Authority** website for a list of countries requiring, and those exempt from, visas.

Visitor Information

The Grenada Tourism Authority has offices in Canada and the UK. Its head office is in Grenada and a branch in Carriacou. The **Carriacou and Petite Martinique Tourism Association** also provides information concerning transportation and accommodations on Grenada's sister islands.

Health and Security

The **General Hospital** in St. George's, **Princess Alice Hospital** in St. Andrew's Parish, and **Princess Royal Hospital** in Carriacou are public hospitals. Visitors should have medical insurance. All hotels have doctors on call. In case of hurricanes and other emergencies, evacuation to a larger center is common.

Grenada is generally safe for traveling. However, muggings and purse snatchings may occur after dark, so it is best to keep valuables in the hotel safe and to exercise caution when walking and traveling in local buses or taxis. Often found on beaches, the tiny green fruit of the manchineel apple trees contains poison, which can blister the skin.

Banking and Currency

The official currency is the Eastern Caribbean dollar. Most places accept US dollars, but banks have the best currency exchange rates. Traveler's checks are accepted everywhere, and major credit cards are accepted by most hotels, car rental companies, and shops. Banking hours are usually Monday to Thursday 8am to 3pm, and Friday 8am to 4pm. ATM machines are available on Grenada and Carriacou.

Communications

Public phones are available throughout the islands. There are coin phones for local calls and prepaid card phones for both local and overseas calls. International Direct Dialing is available from most hotels, but can be expensive. The country code for Grenada is 473, followed by a seven-digit number. Mobile service is available from **LIME** and **Digicel**. Roaming service is available to AMPS-compatible cellular owners. Local cell phones can also be rented from the LIME and Digicel offices. Most hotels have wireless and/or business centers with Internet. There are a few cyber cafés.

Transport

Taxis and minibuses for hire are readily available and are denoted by an "H" license plate.

Cruise ships docked at the cruise liner terminal, St. George's, Grenada

Between 6pm and 6am, there is an additional charge. Private minibuses provide an inexpensive service. Buses display route numbers, and fares are fixed according to distance. The bus terminus is on Melville Street in St. George's. In Carriacou, buses run from about 7am to 5pm. Water taxis are available in St. George's, Carriacou, and Petite Martinique.

To hire cars, visitors need to be over 21, with a driving license and a local driving permit, issued by car rental firms such as **Dollar Rent-A-Car**, **AVIS** and **Martin & Wayne's Auto Rental**. Grenada has about 650 miles (1,050 km) of paved roads in decent condition. However, most have blind corners, with narrow or no shoulders. Driving is on the left and all occupants must wear seat belts.

Osprey Lines Ltd. has a daily ferry service connecting Grenada, Carriacou, and Petite Martinique. **SVG Air** has a daily 20-minute flight from Grenada to Carriacou's Lauriston Airport.

Shopping

The best buys are spices, jellies, jams, syrups (especially nutmeg), rum, batik and screen-printed textiles, locally made handicrafts and art. Most duty-free shops selling jewelry, alcohol, perfumes, and so on are on the Carenage and Esplanade Shopping Mall in St. George's, or at Maurice Bishop International Airport.

Language

Grenada's official language is English but a French-African patois is also spoken.

Souvenir stall displaying locally-made food products

Electricity

Grenada operates on 220 volts but 110-volt appliances also work if used in conjunction with adaptors.

Time

Grenada is on Atlantic Standard Time (AST), which is 4 hours behind Greenwich Mean Time (GMT).

Getting Married

Visitors need to be on the island three days before applying for a marriage license. (The government is working on legislation to change this period to one day.) On the third day, apply in person at the Prime Minister's office after paying stamp duty and license fees. Generally, the license is ready within two working days, but it may take a little longer if either partner is divorced. View the wedding section on the Grenada Board of Tourism website for details.

DIRECTORY

Getting There

Air Canada
w aircanada.com

British Airways
w ba.com

Caribbean Airlines
w caribbean-airlines.com

Conviasa Airlines
w conviasa.aero

LIAT
w liatairline.com

Virgin Atlantic
w virgin-atlantic.com

Documentation

Grenada Tourism Authority
Tel 473 440 2279 (St. George's), 473 443 7948 (Carriacou), 416 595 1339 (Canada), 020 8877 4516 (UK). w grenadagrenadines.com

Immigration Department
Tel 473 440 2456.

Visitor Information

Carriacou and Petite Martinique Tourism Association
Tel 473 443 7882.
w carriacoupetitemartinique.com

Health and Security

General Hospital
Grand Etang Road, St. George's, Grenada.
Tel 473 440 2051.

Police and Fire
Tel 911.

Princess Alice Hospital
Mirabeau, St. Andrew's, Grenada.
Tel 473 442 7251.

Princess Royal Hospital
Carriacou.
Tel 473 443 7400.

Communications

Digicel
Tel 473 439 4500.
w digitalgrenada.com

LIME-Grenada
Tel 473 440 1000.
w lime.com

Transport

AVIS
Corner Paddock and Lagoon Roads, St. George's, Grenada.
Tel 473 440 3936.

Dollar Rent-A-Car
Maurice Bishop International Airport, St. George's, Grenada.
Tel 473 444 4786.
w dollargrenada.com

Martin & Wayne's Auto Rental
Hillsborough gas station, Carriacou.
Tel 473 443 7204.

Osprey Lines Ltd.
Queen's Jetty on the Carenage, St. George's, Grenada.
Tel 473 440 8126.
w ospreylines.com

SVG Air
Tel 784 457 5124.
w svgair.com

Exploring Barbados

A tiny island of 166 sq miles (430 sq km), Barbados has beautiful beaches surrounded by clear waters and coral reefs, and year-round good weather. The island has a rich and diverse cultural background with vibrant festivals and fine historic buildings especially in its capital, Bridgetown. The island's biggest asset, however, is its population. The Bajans love to share their island's history, folklore, and traditions. Visitors will have a vast choice of things to do, including exploring the hidden waterfalls and underground rivers in Harrison's Cave. Restaurants serving the island's traditional dishes are found on most beaches.

Locator Map

Brightly colored shops selling local crafts and souvenirs, Holetown

Getting Around

Buses are a great way to get around. They operate throughout the island and there is a set fare irrespective of the distance. It is advisable to carry the exact fare or use tokens which can be bought at bus stations. Taxis are plentiful and reasonably priced. However, they are not metered and it is best to negotiate a price before setting off. Registered taxis have the letter "Z" on their number plate. Taxi drivers also make knowledgeable guides for either a half-day or one-day tour. A hired car is the best way to explore the island independently. A good map can be helpful but many roads are not signposted and secondary ones are often pot-holed.

West Coast
The prime resort area in Barbados, the west coast also has some of the safest beaches for swimming in the Caribbean.

Bridgetown
Cosmopolitan Bridgetown has a wide range of duty-free shops and bars.

0 kilometers   5

0 miles   5

One of the massive boulders dotting the coastline, Bathsheba

Sights at a Glance
1 Bridgetown
2 Garrison Historic Area
3 South Coast
4 Oistins
5 Barbados Concorde Experience
6 Sunbury Plantation House
7 Gun Hill Signal Station
8 Harrison's Cave
9 Bathsheba
10 Barbados Wildlife Reserve
11 Holetown
12 *St. Nicholas Abbey p445*

Barbados Wildlife Reserve
The ideal place to catch a glimpse of the shy Barbados green monkeys, brought to the island from West Africa.

Bathsheba
This popular spot for surfers offers dramatic views of the Atlantic breakers crashing against the rugged shoreline.

Key
— Major road
— Minor road
⋯ Ferry route
— Administrative border

For keys to symbols *see back flap*

Parliament Buildings in the capital, Bridgetown

❶ Bridgetown

SW coast of Barbados. 🏛 96,500. ✈
🚌 🚢 ℹ️ Barbados Tourist Office,
Bridgetown Harbor Road, 246 427
2623. 🎭 Crop Over Festival (Aug).

Founded in 1628, Bridgetown
is a fascinating combination
of the old and new. The town
center is compact and any
walking tour typically starts in
the National Heroes Square with
its statue of Lord Nelson. Adjacent is the colorful Careenage,
where in the early days ships
would be careened – turned
over to have barnacles scraped
off their sides. A busy marina
today, it is packed with luxury
yachts and surrounded by
restaurants, bars, and shops.

Broad Street has been the
main shopping street in
Barbados since the start of the
18th century. It is dominated by
the impressive Mutual Building,
with its twin white domes,
dating back to 1895.

At the end of Broad Street are
the Italian-Renaissance-style
Parliament Buildings, the third
oldest in the English-speaking
world. The Parliament was
founded in 1637 and has met
regularly since 1639. The west
wing houses the Museum of
Parliament and the National
Heroes Gallery.

Nearby, in Synagogue Lane,
is the **Bridgetown Synagogue**
and cemetery. The synagogue,
founded in 1654, is the oldest
in the western hemisphere.
It has been restored and is open
to the public, and contains the
Nidhe Israel Museum.

Bridgetown Harbor hosts the
modern cruise ship terminal

and is encircled by upscale
duty-free shops, bars, and restaurants. Along the waterfront
is the Pelican Village, an arts
and crafts center amid beautiful
gardens. Visitors can watch artists at work and buy their wares.

🏛 **Parliament Buildings**
Broad Street. **Tel** 246 427 2019.
Open 10am–4pm Mon–Fri. 📷

✡️ **Bridgetown Synagogue and
Nidhe Israel Museum**
Synagogue Lane. **Tel** 246 436 6869.
Open 9am–4pm Mon–Fri. 📷

❷ Garrison Historic Area

2 miles (3.2 km) SE of Bridgetown. ⓘ

The first garrison in the West
Indies was located in the
Garrison Historic Area. More
than 70 original buildings and
forts still stand. Most of the
garrison buildings date from
1789 onwards, when Barbados
became the British army's headquarters in the Windward and
Leeward Islands. However,
Charles Fort, the first on the

island, was built in the 1650s,
while St. Ann's Fort can be
traced to 1688. The tombstones
in the restored Military
Cemetery graphically depict
the history and hardships of
the garrison. Today, Garrison
Savannah is the island's main
horse racing track and is used
for parades and celebrations.

Barbados Museum is set in
what was the garrison's prison.
Built around 1818 and an example of West Indies Georgian
architecture, it is a great place to
learn about the island's history,
culture, and people. The exhibits
are displayed in a series of galleries, set in former cells.
Different galleries realistically
re-create lifestyles from various
periods in the island's history.

Environs
About 3 miles (5 km) northwest
of the Garrison Historic Area is
Mount Gay Distillery, which
has been officially producing
rum since 1703 making it the
world's oldest. A visitors' center
is set in a chattel-style house
next to the warehouses where
aged rums are stored. Guided
tours take visitors through the
process of rum-making and end
in the tasting room. Nearby, the
West Indies Rum Distillery
houses the Malibu Visitors'
Center. One of the most
modern refineries in the
Caribbean, its main products
are Cockspur rum and Malibu
Coconut rum. Guests can tour
the distillery, enjoy lunch and
rum cocktails at the Malibu
Beach Club, and then laze away
the afternoon on the club's
beautiful beach.

Display of Arawak artifacts in the Barbados Museum, Garrison Historic Area

For hotels and restaurants on this island see p450 and p451

Shops and restaurants in the lively St. Lawrence Gap on the South Coast

Close by, Kensington Oval has been the home of Barbados cricket since 1982 and the venue for international test matches. The islanders are passionate about the sport and matches tend to take on a carnival atmosphere.

🏛 Barbados Museum
Tel 246 427 0201. **Open** 9am–5pm Mon–Sat, 2–6pm Sun. 🌐 📷

🏭 Mount Gay Distillery
Spring Garden Highway, St. Michael. **Tel** 246 425 8757. **Open** 9:30am–3:30pm Mon–Fri. 🌐 📷 📱
w mountgayrum.com

🏭 West Indies Rum Distillery
Black Rock. **Tel** 246 425 9301. **Open** 9am–4pm Mon–Fri. 🌐 📷
w westindiesrum.com

❸ South Coast

5 miles (8 km) SE of Bridgetown. 🚌

The south coast is built up all the way from Bridgetown to Oistins, but still boasts some marvelous stretches of sand such as the Accra, Rockley, and Dover beaches. A well-signposted detour off the main coast road leads to **St. Lawrence Gap**, which is the party capital of Barbados. It has restaurants offering a wide range of cuisines, but the local Bajan dishes, especially the fresh fish, are superb. Towards the evening, fast-food stalls serving cheap but delicious fare spring up along the road. Local vendors also set up stalls selling hand-made jewelry and other crafts. Bars play live music and the nightlife continues until the early morning hours. St. Lawrence has a small police post but late-night revelers should still take care and avoid walking in areas with poor lighting.

The Gap is also worth visiting during the daytime, for the impressive Chattel House Village, a collection of shops selling tropical fashions, handicrafts, and souvenirs.

❹ Oistins

7 miles (11 km) SE of Bridgetown. 🚌 🎣 Fish Festival (Mar or Apr).

Named after Austin, the area's first landowner, Oistins is the island's main fishing port and boasts a modern jetty and busy fish market. It has a long history, and in 1652, a treaty was signed at its Mermaid Tavern which led to Barbados accepting the authority of Oliver Cromwell, Britain's military commander and Lord Protector.

The village is well worth a visit as it has many interesting historic buildings that are now protected, as well as several rum shops. Visitors can also watch the bright and colorful fishing boats return at the end of the day and unload their catch. Oistins is renowned for its annual Fish Festival which celebrates the local fishing industry. During the festival, stalls are set up on the streets selling salt fish cakes and fried fish, drinks, and local goods amid much music and dancing.

❺ Barbados Concorde Experience

Grantley Adams International Airport, 10 miles (16 km) E of Bridgetown. **Tel** 246 420 7738. ✈ 🚌 **Open** 9am–5pm Tue–Sat. 📷 🎫 📱 📷
w barbadosconcorde.com

Barbados was one of the few places in the world where the supersonic British Airways Concorde G-BOAE aircraft touched down. The Concorde Experience features the legendary aeroplane, as well as other aviation exhibits, in a popular tour. The tour shows how the technology was developed and includes an interactive flight demon-stration. Visitors are invited to walk the red carpet into the Concorde and to experience how it felt to fly in this incredible plane.

An aviation exhibit, Barbados Concorde Experience

Classic interiors and exquisite furnishings in the lounge area, Sunbury Plantation House

❻ Sunbury Plantation House

10 miles (16 km) NE of Bridgetown.
Tel 246 423 6270. ▦ **Open** 10am–5pm daily. 🎨 🎫 🎨 🏛

Built around 1660 by one of the island's first settlers, Matthew Chapman, Sunbury Plantation House is among the oldest and grandest of the great houses in Barbados. Chapman was apparently granted lands on the island because he was related to the Earl of Carlisle. The house was built to withstand hurricanes with walls more than 30 inches (76 cm) thick.

Restored after a fire in 1995, the Great House recreates the lifestyle and ambience of the 18th and 19th centuries. Its original furnishings have been replaced by antiques from other houses on the island. Look out for the Barbados mahogany furniture, some of which has been made from trees grown on the plantation. It is the only great house with all rooms open for viewing. A unique collection of horse-drawn carriages is displayed in the cellars, and plantation vehicles and machinery are scattered around the land-scaped grounds. There is also a bar, restaurant, and gift shop in the plantation complex. The Planter's Candlelit Dinner is a five-course feast around the 19th-century mahogany table where the notorious pirate Samuel Hall Lord is said to have dined. After dinner, guests are taken on a tour around the house.

Environs

About 2 miles (3 km) south from Sunbury Plantation House, the **Four Square Rum Factory and Heritage Park** is located on the site of a former sugar plantation that dates from 1636. The island's most modern distillery offers free daily self-guided tours and tastings.

Farther east, **Crane Beach** nestles beneath cliffs that overlook the fabulous white and pink coral sands. This isolated stretch of sand along the south coast is among the most stunning beaches on the island. In olden times, ships would anchor in the bay and a crane set on top of the cliff would load or unload their cargo. Protected by a coral reef, Crane Beach provides for safe swimming inshore.

❼ Gun Hill Signal Station

5 miles (8 km) NE of Bridgetown. 🚌
Open 9am–5pm Mon–Sat.

Gun Hill Signal Station is part of a chain of signal stations built across the island by the British in 1818. Signaling mirrors were used to flash warnings about approaching enemy ships from one station to the next. Standing at 700 ft (213 m) above sea level, the station has been carefully restored by the Barbados National Trust (see p448). It offers great views over most of the island and has a small museum housing military memorabilia. From its tower, the statue of a large white lion is visible below the station. This British military emblem was carved from a single boulder in 1868 by Henry Wilkinson, a British officer.

Entrance of the Gun Hill Signal Station

❽ Harrison's Cave

7 miles (11 km) NE of Bridgetown.
Tel 246 438 6640. 🚌 ℹ️ Welchman
Hall, St. Thomas, 246 438 6640.
Open 9am–3:45pm Wed–Sun. 🅿️ 🛍️
📷 📸 🌐 harrisonscave.com

A magnificent attraction, this cave was carved out over millions of years by seeping surface water. It comprises a series of crystallized limestone subterranean caverns with underground rivers, waterfalls, and uniquely shaped stalagmites, stalactites, and columns. The cave is named after Thomas Harrison, who owned the land in the 1770s. Although several expeditions ventured into the caves, it took almost 200 years before it was fully explored and mapped by Danish engineer and cave adventurer, Ole Sorensen. Conducted tours through the floodlit caverns aboard small electric trams are available.

Environs
About 3 miles (5 km) north of Harrison's cave, the Old Richmond Plantation is the setting for the 50-acre (20-ha) **Flower Forest**. It was planted by a group of islanders who wanted to preserve an area of tropical beauty for future generations. A map available at the visitors' center provides information about the tropical fruit trees, exotic plants, and flowers. The area is also rich in wildlife and includes green monkeys and chattering birds. There is wheelchair access throughout although some of the nature trails are uneven. There is an information center and refreshments are available.

Home to 200 species of tropical plants, flowers, and fruits, the **Welchman Hall Gully**, 2 miles (3 km) north of Harrison's Cave, is owned by the Barbados National Trust. It is named after General William Asygell, a Welshman whose plantation included the gully. The remnants of a colossal cave whose roof collapsed thousands of years ago are still visible. There used to be an entrance from the gully into Harrison's Cave. Asygell introduced tropical

Lilypond and palm trees in Andromeda Gardens, near Bathsheba

plants from around the world in 1860, and today there are mature trees and towering bamboo groves. The grapefruit, once called the forbidden fruit of Barbados, is said to have originated here. The aim is to introduce more native plants so that the Gully's flora and fauna resembles that of the island in the 18th century.

❾ Bathsheba

11 miles (18 km) NE of Bridgetown. 🚉

As travelers approach this small, pretty fishing village on the rugged Atlantic coast, they are met with spectacular views of the huge boulders offshore that line its dramatic landscape.

Bottles of locally produced white rum

The crashing waves makes Bathsheba a popular spot for surfers and it hosts many international surfing events. Swimmers must be wary of the powerful waves and undercurrents.

Environs
On the outskirts of Bathsheba is **Andromeda Gardens**, one of the most remarkable and varied botanical gardens in the Caribbean. Created by Iris Bannochie in 1954, it was bequeathed by her to the Barbados National Trust. The gardens showcase spectacular botanical displays including hibiscus, orchids, bougainvillea, and heliconia.

Rum Production

Barbados has been a rum producer for centuries and continues to manufacture many of the world's finest rums. By the end of the 17th century, rum had become an important commodity and figured prominently in the infamous Triangle Trade in which slaves from Africa were sold for rum in the West Indies, which was then sold in Europe to raise more money to buy more slaves. Rum is produced from sugarcane which is grown throughout the island. The cane is crushed to extract sugar which is boiled to obtain the sticky molasses. This is then fermented and distilled into a clear liquid. Light or white rums can be bottled immediately or aged for only a few months until they are smooth, while dark or gold rums are usually aged for many years in oak barrels as they develop their color, richness, and flavor. Two of the world's best gold rums found on Barbados are Mount Gay Eclipse and Mount Gay Extra Old.

Trail through the mahogany forest, Barbados Wildlife Reserve

⑩ Barbados Wildlife Reserve

14 miles (22 km) N of Bridgetown. **Tel** 246 422 8826. 🚌 **Open** 10am–5pm daily, monkey feeding at 2pm. 🏠 🍴 🖥 🐾 🗺 **barbados.org**

The Barbados Wildlife Reserve is a wonderful place to see the island's wildlife in its natural surroundings. The reserve was founded in 1985 by Canadian primatologist Jean Baulu to protect the Barbados green monkey. These monkeys originally came from West Africa in the mid-17th century, but are now found throughout the island.

Agouti inside an enclosure, Barbados Wildlife Reserve

Over time, other Caribbean animals such as iguanas, agoutis, deer, armadillos, and the rare red-footed tortoise, have also been introduced into the reserve's mahogany woods.

There are several imported animal species, a walk-through aviary, and also a collection of snakes. The reserve has an information and education center, built from coral stone gathered from the nearby fields, while the pathway bricks come from 17th- and 18th-century sugar mills.

Environs

Nearby, a delightful 3-mile (5-km) trail gently winds through a natural forest to the restored 19th-century **Grenade Hall Signal Station**. The signal tower was one of six straddling the island, designed to get news back to the Garrison in Bridgetown as quickly as possible. During the restoration of the tower, more than 6,000 artifacts were found, including pre-Columbian tools. Many of these are now on display in the tower alongside old military equipment, including the semaphore flags once used to signal messages from tower to tower. These were in use until 1883 when telephones were introduced in Barbados. The tower offers stunning views over the island.

There are interesting signs along the nature trail explaining the medicinal, culinary, and other uses of the various trees, herbs, and shrubs growing in the forest.

⑪ Holetown

6 miles (10 km) N of Bridgetown. 🏠 35,000. 🚌 🎉 Holetown Festival (Feb).

Located on the west coast, Holetown was first named Jamestown (after the British monarch, James I) by Captain John Powell who led a band of English sailors ashore in 1625. Two years later, the first English settlers arrived here and began calling the place Holetown; the inlet where they anchored reminded them of a stretch of the Thames in London called the Limehouse Hole. A memorial in the center of town marks the first British landing on Barbados.

A short distance away from the town center, **St. James Parish Church** is one of the oldest churches on the island and parts of its lower levels are believed to be from the original stone structure built in 1660. The south entrance and porch are over 300 years old.

Today, Holetown is a busy center with a few good restaurants, bars, and shops. During the Holetown Festival, the place comes alive with street parades and entertainment such as sporting events, exhibitions, and concerts.

Environs

Driving out of Holetown, visitors will see long stretches of

Impressive façade of St. James Parish Church, Holetown

palm-fringed, white sand beaches along the west coast. The safe, shallow turquoise Caribbean waters are in sharp contrast to the crashing Atlantic surf on the eastern side of the island. The extensively developed coastline is home to many of the island's high-end resorts and private homes, and is dotted with bays, most with cafés and bars for refreshment.

Just north of Holetown, the **Folkstone Marine Park** was officially designated a marine reserve and park in 1981. It was created in 1976 when the Greek freighter *Stavronikita*, previously destroyed by fire, was deliberately sunk to create an artificial reef. The ship lies at a depth of 120 ft (37 m), making this site suitable only for experienced divers. However, the shallow waters off Folkstone Beach feature a marked underwater trail through the Dottins Reef, suitable for all levels of experience. A wide range of fish and other oceanic creatures can be spotted. A small aquarium and interpretive center onshore has exhibits on the reef and its marine life.

Lifeguard station on Folkstone Beach, near Holetown

⑫ St. Nicholas Abbey

Set in a former sugar plantation, St. Nicholas Abbey is a magnificent stone great house built in the mid-17th century by a wealthy planter, Colonel Berringer. The grounds are spectacular and feature several labeled plants and a herb garden. A film shot in 1935 by Colonel Cave, another former owner of the Abbey, is screened daily and vividly depicts the house and plantation life at that time.

Old sugar factory and rum distillery

Great House
The Jacobean great house is the oldest building in Barbados.

Interiors
The house has some classic porcelain and china, as well as antique pieces of furniture, some of which were made with local Barbados mahogany.

Windmill
The old windmill and other out-buildings including the sugar syrup factory have been restored.

Outdoor Activities and Specialized Holidays

White and pink coral sands, palm tree-fringed beaches and warm, clear turquoise waters make Barbados a fabulous destination for those who want to sun, swim or enjoy a host of watersports ranging from scuba to water skiing. Cricket is the national game and there are scores of teams throughout the island. It is a great spectator sport, but for visitors seeking something more energetic there is no shortage of opportunities from cycling to golf and hiking to horseback riding.

Coastline at Bathsheba, eastern Barbados

Beaches

There are more than 70 miles (112 km) of beautiful beaches around Barbados. The west coast beaches have warmer waters and safer swimming. Mullins Beach is a superb white-sand strip close to Speightstown. The popular Paynes Bay Beach has all amenities including cafés, restaurants, and watersports outlets. The east coast beaches are great for sunbathing but the strong Atlantic rollers can be dangerous for young and inexperienced swimmers. The island's southern coast has a few good beaches too. The lively Accra Beach, also known as Rockley Beach, attracts both locals and visitors. On the southeast coast, the reef-protected Crane Beach is good for body-surfing. All beaches are public with free access although visitors have to pay to use facilities such as beach chairs and umbrellas.

Yachting and Day Sails

The island's offshore waters attract yachts from around the world and there are a number of international regattas including the annual Mount Gay Regatta every December. Many hotels and watersports centers offer day cruises – either bare-board or crewed. The best sailing is off the west and south coasts. Some of the reputable concessionaires that offer yachting and sailing services include **Small Cats, Shasa, Shamon Too, El Tigre Catamaran Cruises,** and **Jolly Roger.**

Pirate Ship Cruises

Pirate ship cruises are fun, noisy, and an opportunity, for those who wish, to consume large quantities of free rum. Organized by agencies, such as

Jolly Roger, they offer a chance to see what the west coast of Barbados looks like from the sea, though there are usually lots of distractions such as walking the plank and a pirate wedding.

Recreational Submarine

Visitors can join the tender at Bridgetown for the 15-minute journey out to the *Atlantis*, part of the world's first recreational submarine operation, taking guests on dives to 130 ft (40 m). Organized by **Atlantis Submarines (Barbados)**, the underwater trip over reefs and shipwrecks lasts almost an hour. It is possible to get eye-to-eye with the fishes through the large portholes.

Glass-Bottom Boats

For those who are not good swimmers, glass bottom boats are a great way to safely explore the wonderful world of reefs, especially with a good guide to point things out. Many companies offer glass-bottom boat tours and most will pick up visitors from their hotels and drop them back.

Watersports

There are opportunities for watersports all around the island. Jet Skis are provided by the many hotels and resorts on the west coast. The best surfing, both body and board, is off the east coast although the waves can be rough. Rental and surfing lessons are available through agencies

Hobie Cats for hire lined on a beach, western coast of Barbados

Windsurfing at Silver Sands Beach on the south coast

such as **Surf Barbados** and **Zed's Surfing Adventures**. International events are held at Bathsheba's Soup Bowl *(see p443)*, named after the foaming water. There is good parasailing along the west coast and excellent windsurfing as well, especially in Little Bay near South Point. The best water skiing is along the west coast, particularly early or late in the day when there are fewer people in the water. Many companies such as **Good Times Barbados** and **The Boatyard** specialize in watersports and offer a large number of activities.

Scuba

The shallow, warm, clear waters, pristine reefs with teeming marine life, and many shipwrecks make Barbados a world-class diving site with dives to suit all levels of experience. Carlisle Bay, on the west coast, is one of the most popular sites because of the many wrecks, but it also has caves, deep trenches and drop-offs for the more adventurous. It is estimated that since 1666 more than 200 ships have foundered offshore. Others have been deliberately scuttled to create artificial reefs. Popular dive sites include Bright Ledge, Clarkes Reef, Fisherman's Reef, and Speightstown Reef. There are several licensed dive centers offering certification, equipment rental, as well as diving trips. The popular outfits offering scuba diving activities include **Reefers and Wreckers**, **Barbados Blue**, and **Hightide**.

Fishing

There is great deep-sea fishing for world-record breaking fish in Barbados. The best fishing is off the north and south coasts because of the stronger currents. Local records include blue marlin (505 lbs/230 kg), yellow fin tuna (167.5 lbs/76 kg), and wahoo (74 lbs/33 kg). Most hotels and resorts offer fishing trips and there are many boats available for half- or full-day charters. **Cannon Charters**, **IOU Charters**, Outdoors Barbados, and the **Barbados Game Fishing Association** can be contacted for organizing fishing trips.

Guided Walks

There are many trails and a number of organizations offer guided walks, many of which are free. Most of the trails are along the coast but there are some inland hikes. The **Welchman Hall Gully** *(see p443)* is another place where visitors can walk through a tropical forest with innumerable exotic plants. It is advisable to walk very early in the morning before the sun gets too high. The **Barbados National Trust** organizes free rural walks on Sundays from January to March. They attract a large number of people, making for a very convivial amble. The walks start at 6am and 3:30pm, and there is also moonlight walks that begin at 5:30pm. **Hike Barbados** and **Xtreme Hikers Barbados** offer longer hikes for varying levels of fitness.

Fishing boat at Oistins on the south coast of Barbados

Off-Road Tours

Many operators such as **Out Back 4x4** and **Island Safari** offer off-road tours in specially equipped, four-wheel drive vehicles. The tours take visitors to parts of the island that they may not visit on their own and include a stop for lunch or a dip in the sea. Knowledgeable guides make the trips more enjoyable.

Visitors enjoying a special jeep safari tour of Barbados

Riding tour through the Bajan countryside

Horse-Riding

There are several stables and riding is available in all the resort areas with scenic trails. Those with little or no experience can take a gentle trot while adventure rides are available inland for those with more experience. Stables such as the **Caribbean International Riding Center** and **Ocean Echo Stables** normally pick up visitors from the hotel and drop them back.

Spas

After all that physical activity a little pampering is welcome. Most large resorts and hotels have spas such as The Spa at Sandy Lane, Yin Yang at the Savannah hotel, the **Sugar Cane Spa**, and the **Centre for Wellbeing**, that all offer a range of beauty treatments.

Mountain Biking

Mountain bikes are available at several locations and there are long stretches of side roads and trails to explore. Although not mountainous, some of the hills are very steep. The views are magnificent and there is always a bar, restaurant or beach to stop at. **Highland Adventure Center** and **Flex Bicycle Tours** provide equipment and assistance. Insurance is also available.

DIRECTORY

Yachting and Day Sails

El Tigre Catamaran Cruises
Tel 246 417 7245.
W eltigrecruises.com

Jolly Roger
Tel 246 430 0900.
W tallshipcruises.com

Shamon Too
Tel 246 233 6089.
W westwater-adventures-barbados.com

Shasa
Tel 246 433 8274.
W shasacatamarancruises.com

Small Cats
Tel 246 421 6419.
W smallcatscruises.com

Recreational Submarine

Atlantis Submarines (Barbados)
Tel 246 436 8929.
W atlantissubmarines.com

Watersports

The Boatyard
Tel 246 436 2622.
W theboatyard.com

Good Times Barbados
Tel 246 422 1900.
W goodtimesbarbados.com

Surf Barbados
Tel 246 256 3906.
W surfing-barbados.com

Zed's Surfing Adventures
Tel 246 428 7873.
W zedssurftravel.com

Scuba

Barbados Blue
Tel 246 434 5764.
W divebarbadosblue.com

Hightide
Tel 246 432 0931.
W divehightide.com

Reefers and Wreckers
Tel 246 422 5450.
W scubdiving.bb

Fishing

Barbados Game Fishing Association
Tel 246 230 2684.
W barbadosgamefishing.com

Cannon Charters
Tel 246 424 6107.
W fishingbarbados.com

IOU Charters
Tel 246 429 1050.
W ioucharters barbados.net

Guided Walks

Barbados National Trust
Tel 246 426 2421.
W funbarbados.com

Hike Barbados
Tel 246 230 4818.
W hikebarbados.com

Welchman Hall Gully
Tel 246 438 6671.
W welchmanhallgullybarbados.com

Xtreme Hikers Barbados
Tel 246 262 0935.

Off-Road Tours

Adventure 4x4
Tel 246 418 3687.
W adventurelandbarbados.com

Island Safari
Tel 246 429 5337.
W islandsafari.bb

Mountain Biking

Flex Bicycle Tours
Tel 246 419 2453.

Highland Adventure Center
Tel 246 438 8069.

Horse-Riding

Caribbean International Riding Centre
Tel 246 422 7343.
W funbarbados.com

Ocean Echo Stables
Tel 246 433 6772.
W barbadoshorseriding.com

Spas

Centre for Wellbeing
Tel 246 422 2291.
W cobblerscove.com

Sugar Cane Spa
Tel 246 422 5026.
W sugarcaneclub.com

Golf Courses of Barbados

There are seven golf courses on Barbados, more than on any other Caribbean island of comparable size. The island's first course, the 9-hole Rockley Golf Club, was laid out as early as 1946. Sandy Lane Resort has three courses – Old Nine, Green Monkey, and Country Club, all of which are different in style and difficulty, while Royal Westmoreland is set within a gated luxury community. Barbados Golf Club is located inland from Oistins, and the Apes Hill Golf Club has stunning views. Most of these are private clubs, so tee time for outsiders is limited. Many of the resorts offer special non-member deals for their guests.

Old Nine Course at the Sandy Lane estate was constructed in the early 1960s. This is where world-renowned golfer Tiger Woods got married in 2004. At 3,345 yards (3,059 m) and par 36, the Old Nine has small greens and tight fairways providing a real challenge to golfers.

The Country Club Restaurant is welcoming after a round of golf at the Country Club, designed by Tom Fazio. The club hosted the 2006 World Golf Championships World Cup.

Green Monkey Course is an exclusive par 72 course spread over 7,343 yards (6,715 m). It is aptly named after the monkeys that can be seen around, though they can occasionally be a hazard.

Barbados Golf Club has a par 72 course stretching over 6,805 yards (6,222 m). Restyled in 2000 by Ron Kirby, the 18-hole championship course has a challenging "Amen corner" on holes 15 and 16.

Royal Westmoreland championship course was designed by Robert Trent Jones Jr. The par 72 course has magnificent ocean views from every hole. Some of the holes can be challenging, with one green bordering a ravine.

GOLF CLUBS

Apes Hill Golf Club
Tel 246 432 4500.

Barbados Golf Club
Tel 246 428 8463.
W barbadosgolfclub.com

Rockley Golf Club
Tel 246 435 7873.
W rockleygolfclub.com

Royal Westmoreland
Tel 246 422 4653.
W royal-westmoreland.com

Sandy Lane
Tel 246 444 2000.
W sandylane.com/golf

Where to Stay

CHRIST CHURCH: Accra Beach Hotel $
Beach
Rockley
Tel *246 435 8920*
W accrabeachhotel.com
One of the most popular hotels on the island, Accra Beach Hotel has tasteful rooms, a full-service spa and two pools. Complimentary Wi-Fi.

CHRIST CHURCH: Coconut Court Beach Hotel $
Beach
The Garrison Historic Area, Hastings
Tel *246 427 1655*
W coconut-court.com
Situated on a small, beautiful white-sand beach, this hotel boasts modern, well-equipped accommodation. Free Wi-Fi, lively bar, and good food.

CHRIST CHURCH: Divi Southwinds $
Beach
St. Lawrence Main Rd.
Tel *246 428 7181*
W diviresorts.com
Conveniently located in the heart of St. Lawrence Gap, this hotel offers everything visitors need, from watersports to hiking tours. Spacious suites with kitchens.

CHRIST CHURCH: Pirate's Inn $
Value
Browne's Gap
Tel *246 426 6273*
W piratesinnbarbados.com
Cozy studio suites and one-bedroom apartments with well-equipped kitchenettes. Good for families. Free Wi-Fi.

CHRIST CHURCH: Barbados Beach Club $$
Beach Resort
Maxwell Coast Rd.
Tel *246 428 9900*
W barbadosbeachclub.com
All-inclusive resort that is known for its wedding packages. Ideal for big families or groups. Pool and mini-golf facilities. Rooms with ocean, pool, or garden views.

CHRIST CHURCH: Bougainvillea Beach Resort $$
Beach Resort
Maxwell Coast Rd.
Tel *246 418 0990*
W bougainvillearesort.com
This resort offers loads of amenities, two white-sand beaches, three pools with swim-up bars, and a tropical garden. There is also a kids' club.

Attractive pool and swim-up cave bar at the Crystal Cove, St. Jamese

CHRIST CHURCH: Little Arches $$
Boutique
Enterprise Beach Rd.
Tel *246 420 4689*
W littlearches.com
A beautiful adults-only hotel that is known for its privacy. Little Arches is famous for its Café Luna. Elegant rooms and mini-spa.

ST. JAMES: Europa – All Seasons $
Beach
Palm Avenue, Sunset Crest
Tel *246 432 5046*
W allseasonsresort.bb
With a relaxed ambience, a calypso-themed decor, and a freshwater pool, All Seasons is the quintessential island getaway.

ST. JAMES: Coral Reef Club $$$
Luxury
Porters
Tel *246 422 2372*
W coralreefbarbados.com
Elegant hotel with rooms, suites, and cottages set amid beautifully landscaped, expansive gardens.

ST. JAMES: Crystal Cove $$$
Beach Resort
Appleby
Tel *888 996 9948*
W crystalcovehotelbarbados.com
All-inclusive beach resort that features three lagoon-like swimming pools, spacious rooms, and modern tropical decor.

ST. JAMES: Mango Bay $$$
Beach Resort
2nd Street, Holetown
Tel *246 432 1384*
W mangobaybarbados.com
Beachfront, all-inclusive resort, with excellent dining and

Price Guide
Prices are based on one night's stay in high season for a standard double room, inclusive of service charges and taxes.

$	up to $200
$$	$200–400
$$$	over $400

recreational activities. All rooms are modern and come with either a balcony or patio. Mini-gym and spa on site.

ST. LUCY: Little Good Harbour $$$
Boutique
Shermans
Tel *246 439 3000*
W littlegoodharbourbarbados.com
This small hotel has lovely, comfortable cottages and lush gardens. Its sensational Fish Pot Restaurant, is a regular favorite with both locals and vacationers.

ST. MICHAEL: Barbados Hilton $$
Modern
Needham's Point
Tel *246 426 0200*
W hiltonbarbadoshotel.com
Chain hotel with a contemporary design, offering private balconies and scenic views from each guest room. Business services, a conference center, and a range of recreational activities are available.

ST. MICHAEL: Island Inn Hotel $$$
Boutique
Aquatic Gap, Garrison Historic Site
Tel *246 436 6393*
W islandinnbarbados.com
Built in 1804 as a rum storage facility, this simple yet charming hotel offers most amenities and facilities of larger hotel chains. The tastefully furnished rooms all have splashes of colour.

DK Choice

ST. PHILIP: The Crane Residential Resort $$
Luxury
Crane Beach
Tel *246 423 6220*
W thecrane.com
Perched on a cliff overlooking the pink sand of the famous Crane Beach, this full-service resort is famed for its breath-taking views and fantastic dining options. The Caribbean's first-ever resort hotel, it has sumptuous guest rooms, some featuring private pools, gardens, and rooftop terraces.

Where to Eat and Drink

AQUATIC GAP: Brown Sugar $$
Bajan/Caribbean
Bay Street
Tel *246 426 7684*
Creole cooking at its best in the elegant surroundings of a traditional "gingerbread" house. Sunday brunch and Monday Bajan buffets are favorites.

DK Choice

BRIDGETOWN: Waterfront Café $
Caribbean
The Careenage
Tel *246 427 0093* **Closed** *Sun*
Situated on the banks of the Bridgetown Marina this eatery is a favorite with locals and visitors. The food is fresh and tasty, featuring Caribbean specialties like Bajan flying fish, and cou cou and pepperpot, as well as pasta, steaks, and seafood. Great ambience, and there is live entertainment Thursday to Saturday nights. Buffet on Tuesday nights.

CHRIST CHURCH: 39 Steps Bistro & Wine Bar $$
Caribbean
The Chattel Plaza, Hastings
Tel *246 427 0715* **Closed** *Sun*
International and Caribbean menu, with "blackened" fish as its signature dish. Features jazz every other Saturday night.

CHRIST CHURCH: Champers $$
Seafood/International
Skeetes Hill, Worthing
Tel *246 434 3463* **Closed** *Sun*
Overlooking Rockley Bay, this excellent restaurant offers a beautifully crafted menu. Don't miss the coconut shrimp starter.

CHRIST CHURCH: Harlequin $$
Seafood/International
St. Lawrence Gap
Tel *246 420 7677*
Bistro-style dining in the heart of lively St. Lawrence Gap. The eclectic menu includes seafood, grill, vegetarian, and children's choices.

CHRIST CHURCH: Pisces $$
Seafood/International
St. Lawrence Gap
Tel *246 435 6564*
Fish and seafood have pride of place in this fine restaurant, which overlooks the ocean at St. Lawrence Bay.

ST. JAMES: Cariba $$
Bajan/Caribbean
1 Clarke's Gap, Derricks
Tel *246 432 8737* **Closed** *Mon*
Set in a beautifully appointed chattel house, this is a friendly spot for superb cuisine. The meat dishes are succulent. Great cocktails.

ST. JAMES: Elbow Room Grill $$
2nd Street, Holetown
Tel *246 432 1927* **Closed** *Sun*
Come here for a laid-back atmosphere and stone-grilled meals on lava stones, served at the table. Weekends are especially lively.

ST. JAMES: Cin Cin By the Sea $$$
International
Prospect
Tel *246 424 4557*
Equisite Mediterranean cuisine with a Caribbean twist. Ultra-chic decor and stunning ocean views make for a wonderful night out. Very popular, so reserve ahead.

ST. JAMES: The Cliff $$$
Seafood/International
Derricks
Tel *246 432 1922*
With a romantic cliff-top setting, and a menu featuring fine cuisine with an Asian touch, The Cliff is a great place for special occasions. Dishes are beautifully presented.

ST. JAMES: Daphne's $$$
Italian
Paynes Bay
Tel *246 432 2731* **Closed** *Sun*
Daphne's offers a sophisticated ambience and an innovative Italian-Caribbean fusion menu, which also features vegetarian and gluten-free options.

Price Guide		
Prices are based on a two-course meal for one, including tax and service charges, and half a bottle of wine.		
$	up to $50	
$$	$50–70	
$$$	over $70	

ST. JAMES: The Tides $$$
International/Vegetarian
Balmore House, Holetown
Tel *246 432 8356*
One of the finest restaurants on the west coast, The Tides specializes in seafood. The intimate oceanfront setting makes it a favorite for weddings.

ST. LUCY: The Fish Pot $$$
Caribbean/Seafood
Shermans
Tel *246 439 2604*
Part of the luxury Little Good Harbour resort and located in a small 18th-century seaside fort, this restaurant offers a varied menu of Caribbean favorites. The fish platter is a highlight.

ST. PHILLIP: Zen $$$
Japanese/Thai
The Crane Residential Resort
Tel *246 423 6220* **Closed** *Sat & Sun*
This chic restaurant is highly rated for its authentic Thai and Japanese cuisine, excellent sushi bar, and spectacular ocean views.

ST. THOMAS: Chatters Tea Room $
British
Bagatelle Great House
Tel *246 438 7403* **Closed** *Mon & Tue*
Savor full English afternoon tea in the charming environs of a traditional plantation house and garden. Tours of the historic house are also offered.

The idyllic, picturesque setting of The Cliff, St. James

Practical Information

With good weather year round and small enough to explore easily, Barbados is the perfect place for an effortless holiday. It is well connected to both North America and Europe, has a well developed infrastructure and generally excellent service, although prices can be on the expensive side. Rental cars are widely available and the local buses are also a great way to see the island.

Grantley Adams International Airport, near Bridgetown

When to Go

The high season is from December to April but Barbados has year-round good weather with an annual average temperature of 27°C (80°F). The best time to visit is from January to April which are the coolest months. It tends to get very hot between July and September. There are lots of activities throughout the year but the Holetown Festival in February and Crop Over Festival in July and August are always exciting times to visit.

Getting There

Grantley Adams International Airport is 8 miles (13 km) east of Bridgetown and is served by several major airlines from the US and Europe, including **American Airlines**, **Air Canada**, **JetBlue**, **British Airways**, **LIAT**, **Virgin Atlantic**, and **Caribbean Airlines**.

Documentation

All visitors need a valid passport and a return ticket to enter Barbados. A visa is not required from citizens of the US, Canada, UK, most Caribbean and European countries, and Japan. Travelers should contact the **Ministry of Foreign Affairs and Foreign Trade** for a list of countries requiring, and exempted from, visas. Officials may also ask travelers to show adequate funds to cover their visit.

Visitor Information

All tourist information, including brochures and maps, is available from the **Barbados Tourism Authority**, which has an office in Warrens, St Michael, as well as two smaller branches at the Bridgetown Port and at Grantley Adams International Airport.

Health and Security

There are no serious health problems but visitors should protect themselves from the sun and insects. The main hospital is **Queen Elizabeth** on the outskirts of Bridgetown. The island also has a number of private, modern health centers such as **Bayview Hospital** and **Sandy Crest Medical Center**.

Barbados has a low crime rate but it still pays to take sensible precautions. It is advisable not to wear expensive jewelry or flash large sums of money. Keep valuables out of sight in parked cars or when on the beach and avoid straying into unfamiliar areas late at night. In case of theft or any crime, report to the police.

Banking and Currency

Most major credit cards are widely accepted in all the island's cities but may not be welcomed in small places such as cafés. Bridgetown, Holetown, and Speightstown have many banks and they also have branches scattered across the island. There are 24-hour ATM facilities at a number of locations around the island. However, ATM machines dispense only local currency. Banks are open from 8am to 3pm Monday to Thursday and from 8am to 1pm and 3 to 5pm on Friday. The airport bank is open from 8am to midnight daily.

The official currency is the Barbados dollar (BDS$) which is tied to the US dollar at US$1=Bds$2. It comes in bills of 2 (blue), 5 (green), 10 (brown), 20 (purple), 50 (orange), and 100 (gray) dollars.

Building of the Barbados National Bank in Holetown

Communications

The international dialling code for Barbados is 246. There is direct international dialling from hotels and pay phones, which also accept phone cards. **Digicel** and **LIME** are among the most popular phone operators on the island.

Most major US and European newspapers and magazines are available. Satellite television is widely accessible and most large hotels offer Internet. Cyber cafés are found in most towns.

Transport

Visitors must have a valid driver's license or international license and purchase a temporary Barbados one. The license is valid for a year. There is a government tax of 12.5 percent on all rentals. Rental cars have an H on the number plate. Check the condition of the car, especially the tyres, before accepting it and make sure there is a good spare. Cars drive on the left and the speed limit is 25 mph (40 kph) in towns, 40 mph (60 kph) on rural roads, and 50mph (80 kph) on sign-posted highways. Many service stations only accept cash. The main operators are **ABC Rentals**, **Courtesy Car Rentals**, **Double J Car and Moke Rentals**, and **Drive-A-Matic Car Rentals**. Buses are the cheapest mode of transport and ply everywhere. They are also a good way to meet the locals. Taxis are easily available as well and they are identifiable by Z on their number plates. There are no meters so visitors are advised to agree a fare before the trip.

Shopping

Broad Street is the main shopping district in Bridgetown but there are small shopping malls throughout the island and many hotels have gift shops selling local arts, crafts and souvenirs. Outside the capital, there is the Sky Mall in Haggatt Hall, Lanterns at Hastings, the Vista Complex in Worthing, and Sheraton Centre in Sergeants Village, as well as the West Coast Mall, the Chattel House Village, and Limegrove Lifestyle Centre, all in Holetown.

Language

The official language is English, but a local Bajan patois – a combination of old English and West African languages – is widely spoken.

Electricity

The electricity supply is generally 110 volts/50 cycles; All European appliances will need adapters.

Time

Barbados is on Atlantic Standard Time (AST), 4 hours behind Greenwich Mean Time (GMT). Daylight savings is not observed.

Getting Married

New laws make it even easier to get married in Barbados. Couples can get married on the day they arrive. Apply to the **Ministry of Home Affairs** in person to get a marriage license. Visitors will need to present a valid passport or birth certificate, proof of divorce or death, return tickets, and money for the license and revenue stamp. Many hotels have their own wedding consultants who can make all the arrangements and most offer special honeymoon packages.

Crafts and souvenirs shopping area in Holetown

DIRECTORY

Getting There

Air Canada
W aircanada.com

American Airlines
W aa.com

British Airways
W ba.com

Caribbean Airlines
W caribbean-airlines.com

JetBlue
W jetblue.com

LIAT
W liatairline.com

Virgin Atlantic
W virgin-atlantic.com

Documentation

Ministry of Foreign Affairs and Foreign Trade
Bridgetown.
Tel 246 431 2200.
W foreign.gov.bb

Visitor Information

Barbados Tourism Authority
Bridgetown.
Tel 246 467 3600.
W barbados.org

Health and Security

Ambulance
Tel 511.

Bayview Hospital
Bridgetown.
Tel 246 436 5446.

Fire
Tel 311.

Police
Tel 211.

Queen Elizabeth
Martindale's Road,
St. Michael.
Tel 246 436 6450.

Sandy Crest Medical Centre
St. James.
Tel 246 419 4911.

Communications

Digicel
W digicelbarbados.com

LIME
W lime.com

Transport

ABC Rentals
Tel 246 420 4648.

Courtesy Car Rentals
Tel 246 431 4160.

Double J Car and Moke Rentals
Tel 246 423 8135.

Drive-A-Matic Car Rentals
Tel 246 422 3000.

Getting Married

Ministry of Home Affairs
Tel 246 228 8950.

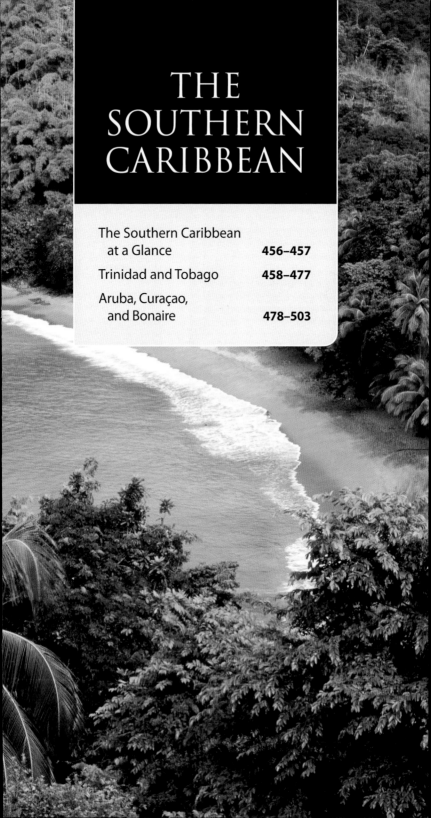

THE SOUTHERN CARIBBEAN

The Southern Caribbean at a Glance

The islands of the Southern Caribbean have lovely coastlines, diverse landscapes, and stunning underwater reefs with abundant marine life. Each island – from Aruba, Curaçao, and Bonaire, to Trinidad and Tobago – has developed its own unique personality since settlement by various European nations about 500 years ago. Islanders place high value on music, art, fine cuisine, and jubilant celebrations, and visitors quickly fall into the sensual style and leisurely pace of the region.

A blue gray tanager found in Trinidad and Tobago

Aruba's entire eastern coast is a stretch of picture-perfect white-sand beaches. High-rise resorts line up along Palm Beach and low-rise accommodations pepper Eagle Beach.

Bonaire is still the Caribbean of old and strives to remain so with restrictions in its underwater parks and reluctance to court land developers.

ARUBA, CURAÇAO, AND BONAIRE
(See pp478–503)

Oranjestad

Willemstad

Kralendijk

Curaçao's charming capital, Willemstad, is a UNESCO World Heritage Site and served as the seat of government for the entire Netherlands Antilles prior to its dissolution in 2010.

◀ Beach at Little Englishman's Bay near the village of Castara, on the coast of Tobago

Locator Map

Trinidad is a highly industrialized island with a population of approximately one million people, mostly of African or East Indian descent. The island is known for its vibrant nightlife, unparalleled in the pre-Lenten Carnival, and its thrilling soca music.

0 kilometers   100

0 miles   100

TRINIDAD
AND TOBAGO
(See pp458–77)

● Scarborough

● Port of Spain

Tobago is an eco-paradise for nature lovers who can spend their time hiking through the Forest Reserve, driving back roads that wind through craggy hills, climbing to picturesque waterfalls and seeking hidden bays with white-sand beaches.

A PORTRAIT OF TRINIDAD AND TOBAGO

As culturally diverse as it is physically varied, the twin-island republic of Trinidad and Tobago makes for a fascinating place to visit. The most southerly of the Caribbean chain, Trinidad and Tobago have wild Atlantic beaches as well as calm Caribbean shorelines and an incredibly rich array of flora and fauna.

As holiday destinations, Trinidad and Tobago are not as developed as some of their regional neighbors, which makes a refreshing change. In Trinidad, particularly, the beaches and attractions are equally shared by locals and visitors. Tobago, on the other hand, is well geared up for holidaymakers, with a host of hotels, restaurants, and places to drink and dance, but even here, the beaches away from the busy Crown Point are either completely undeveloped or have a few pleasantly laid-back places to stay and eat. Its central forest reserve is the oldest protected rainforest in the Western Hemisphere.

Trinidad is more industrialized, its southern half characterized by the trappings of the oil and natural gas industries that have long ensured the country's thriving ecomoy. Central Trinidad has a gorgeous palm-fringed beach along much of its east coast, while the north is dominated by the Northern Range rainforest, peppered with hiking trails and waterfalls and the habitat of more than 400 bird species

People and History

Many of the festivals of Trinidad and Tobago are rooted in the ethnic traditions of the two islands' residents, collectively known as "Trinbagonians". Forty percent of the population are of East Indian origin, 38 percent African, and the rest a mix of European, Middle Eastern, and Chinese, a result of the influx of slaves and immigration that took place after the original inhabitants, the Carib Indians, were almost wiped out when the Spanish settled in Trinidad in 1592. Encouraged by land grants, French settlers followed, and a nascent plantation economy

Maracas Bay surrounded by lush green mountains, Trinidad

Stiltwalkers on parade, Trinidad Carnival

Culture and Festivals

Trinidad and Tobago have many occasions to celebrate throughout the year. The original home of the West Indian Carnival, the islands' dedication to good times can seem exhausting to even the most determined of party animals. Swinging into action just before Lent, but with a couple of months of pre-event parties, the Carnival is the highlight of the festival calendar. It starts with the pre-dawn Jouvert – in which revellers slink through the streets covered in mud and body paint – and culminates in the Parade of the Bands, with several thousand costumed masqueraders dancing to pounding soca. Hindus celebrate Phagwa, in which participants color each other with dye, called *abir*, and Diwali, when thousands of oil lamps and electric displays light up the nation. In Tobago, crab and goat races are held after Easter, while in summer a number of parties take place from the Great Race to the Fishermen's Festivals.

developed, dependent on African slave labor. Between 1592 and 1814, when it was ceded to the British, Tobago ricocheted between Dutch, French, and British control, changing hands 31 times. In the late 1950s calls for independence from Britain began in earnest; it was finally granted in 1962, with the nation led by Dr. Eric Williams, who remains an iconic political figure.

The discovery of vast oil reserves in the 1970s boosted the economy, which remains one of the most stable in the region. Over the last few decades, political power has oscillated between the two main parties, the United National Congress (UNC) and the People's National Movement. In May 2010 the country elected its first female Prime Minister, Kamla Persad-Bissessar, who contested the general election with a UNC-led coalition, the People's Partnership.

Dusk view of the Hindu Temple in the Sea, Waterloo, Trinidad

Exploring Trinidad and Tobago

Trinidad, the largest island of the Lesser Antilles, was named by Christopher Columbus in honor of the three peaks, crowning the southeastern coast, now known as Trinity Hills. While Trinidad's capital, Port of Spain, bustles and throbs with city life, the island's quiet interior is a haven for turtle- and bird-watchers. The much-smaller Tobago is best known for its long stretches of powdery white beaches, excellent diving spots, and lush rainforests.

Caribbean Sea

ARUBA, CURAÇAO, AND BONAIRE

TRINIDAD AND TOBAGO

VENEZUELA

Locator Map

Trees lining the lagoon at Blanchisseuse, on Trinidad's north coast

Getting Around

Apart from a reliable bus service connecting the major towns on both islands, transport is run privately. Trinidad has maxi taxis (color-coded minibuses) and route taxis (cars running on short, set routes). Tobago has only buses and route taxis. The best way to get around the islands is to take a tour or rent a car. The two islands are also linked by air and ferry. Airports are at Piarco and Crown Point, while ferries run between Port of Spain and Scarborough.

Blanchisseuse
This peaceful village is a favorite retreat for local people.

0 kilometers   15
0 miles   15

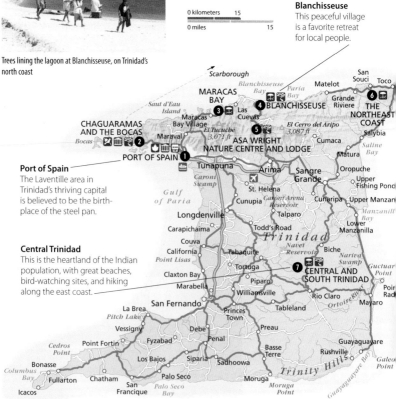

Port of Spain
The Laventille area in Trinidad's thriving capital is believed to be the birthplace of the steel pan.

Central Trinidad
This is the heartland of the Indian population, with great beaches, bird-watching sites, and hiking along the east coast.

A typical grocery shop near Castara, Tobago

Charlotteville
Located at the tip of Tobago, this small town has a remote feel, pretty beaches, and some lovely places to stay and dine.

Castara
Known for its yellow-sand beaches, this is a charming laid-back little village.

The idyllic setting of Mount Irvine, Tobago

Sights at a Glance

1. Port of Spain
2. Chaguaramas and the Bocas
3. Maracas Bay
4. Blanchisseuse
5. The Northeast Coast
6. Central and South Trinidad
7. Crown Point
8. Pigeon Point Beach
10. Buccoo
11. Mount Irvine
12. Kimme Museum
13. Castara

14. Englishman's Bay to Bloody Bay
15. Scarborough
16. The Windward Coast
17. Tobago Forest Reserve
18. Speyside *pp466–7*
19. Charlotteville

Featured Hotels and Resorts

5. Asa Wright Nature Centre and Lodge

Key

━━━ Highway
━━━ Major road
──── Minor road
– – Track
····· Ferry route
△ Peak

For additional map symbols *see back flap*

Old planters' mansions along the Queen's Park Savannah, Port of Spain

❶ Port of Spain

NW coast of Trinidad. 🏔 35,000.
✈ 🚢 🛈 Tourism Development
Company, 29 Tenth Avenue, Barataria,
868 675 7034. 🎭 Carnival *(pre-Lent)*,
Diwali (Oct/Nov).

Gridlocked with traffic but bubbling with life, Trinidad's capital is home to the island's best restaurants and nightlife, as well as a vibrant cultural scene. The centerpiece of downtown Port of Spain is Independence Square, a shop-lined boulevard with the Brian Lara Promenade in the middle. To the north, Frederick Street is busy with shoppers, and threads up past Woodford Square, a grassy little park, home to an impromptu speakers' corner known as the University, where locals debate current affairs. On the square's western side is the Red House, the imposing Neo-Renaissance parliament building. At the northern end of Frederick Street, the **National Museum and Art Gallery** houses a collection of local history and geology, an excellent art gallery, and the imposing **National Academy for the Performing Arts (NAPA)**, the venue for concerts and other cultural events.

Past the museum are the wide open spaces of the **Queen's Park Savannah**, the city's largest open area and the focal point of the annual Carnival parade. At the northern edge of the Savannah, the **Botanical Gardens** are home to some 700 trees and many exotic plants. Next door, the **Emperor Valley Zoo** is one of the largest in the Caribbean and a good place to view local species.

🏛 National Museum and Art Gallery
Corner Frederick & Keate Streets.
Tel 868 623 5941. **Open** 10am–6pm
Tue–Sat, 2–6pm Sun. 🛗

🌿 Botanical Gardens
Circular Road. **Tel** 868 622 1221.
Open 6am–6pm daily. ♿

🦓 Emperor Valley Zoo
Circular Road. **Tel** 868 622 3530.
Open 9am–6pm daily. 🛗 ♿ 🖥

❷ Chaguaramas and the Bocas

6 miles (10 km) W of Port of Spain,
Trinidad. **Tel** 868 634 4227. 💬 🛈
Chaguaramas Development Authority
(CDA), off Western Main Road. 📷
🅦 **chagdev.com**

Port of Spain's playground and a haven for yacht owners, the Chaguaramas area occupies the island's western tip. To the

Yachts moored at Crews Inn Marina, Chaguaramas

north is a national park centered around Tucker Valley, with its bamboo groves, rainforests, and hiking trails. On the southern coast, where US troops had built a base during World War II, the **Military History and Aerospace Museum** chronicles the island's military history. Spreading into the Gulf of Paria, the Bocas islands are a favored spot for palatial holiday homes. Gaspar Grande holds the **Gasparee Cave**, a huge cavern with a few impressive stalactites and a pool at its base.

🏛 Military History and Aerospace Museum
Western Main Road, Chaguaramas.
Tel 868 634 4391. **Open** 9am–5pm
daily. 🛗 📷 ♿ 🖥 📷

🕳 Gasparee Cave
Gasparee Island. 🛗 📷 with CDA

View of Maracas Bay on the north coast of Trinidad

❸ Maracas Bay

🚗 7 miles (11 km) NE of Port of Spain,
Trinidad. 🏖 🛶

The closest beach with amenities from Port of Spain, Maracas Bay is a sweep of fine yellow sand, pounded by waves, lined with palms, and backed by forested hills. Quiet during the week, Maracas becomes the place to be on weekends, when locals set up camp under beach umbrellas and enjoy drinks and food. Vendors in the car park sell bake and shark, a delicious fish sandwich slathered with local sauces, and salads.

Environs
Around 4 miles (6 km) east of Maracas, is another lovely spot

for swimming at **Las Cuevas**, the north coast's longest beach. Quieter than Maracas, with gentler surf but the same facilities, its only downside is the sandfly population.

❹ Blanchisseuse

17 miles (27 km) NE of Port of Spain, Trinidad. 🚐 800. 📷

The closest thing to a resort on the northern coast is Blanchisseuse. With its upper and lower villages, this quiet, rural area is backed by a string of wild beaches that are favored by surfers. It offers peace and quiet, a few appealing places to stay and dine, and swimming in the sea and the sparklingly clean Marianne River. The river also has a number of waterfalls upstream, reached by an easy 30-minute walk. It is possible to hike from Blanchisseuse along the undeveloped coastline to the east, toward spectacular Paria Bay and waterfall without a guide.

❺ Asa Wright Nature Centre and Lodge

🚗 Arima Valley, Arima–Blanchisseuse Road, Trinidad. **Tel** 868 667 5162. 📷 ♿ 🌐 **asawright.org**

High in the rainforested hills of the Northern Range, the Asa Wright Nature Centre is a renowned eco-lodge that offers some of the best bird-watching in the Caribbean. Spread out

Bird-watching at the Asa Wright Nature Centre

around a colonial great house, the 2-sq-mile (5-sq-km) pristine forest is home to a multitude of birds and animals. Bird-watchers can see up to 159 species of birds, some with stunning plumages. Non-guests can visit during the day to tour the immediate grounds and for lunch.

❻ The Northeast Coast

🚐 to Arima, then taxi to Sangre Grande and to the coast.

The northeast coastline is among Trinidad's most beautiful. Matura, a windswept sretch of beach, is favored by leatherbacks as an egg-laying site; it is a great spot for beachcombing, but the waters are too rough to swim. Visitors can take a dip some 2 miles (3 km) north at Salybia, where Rio Seco Waterfall, surrounded by greenery,

tumbles about 26 ft (8 m) down into a wide and deep pool. For proper beachlife, it is best to head another 12 miles (19 km) along the main road to Toco, a peaceful fishing village with a white-sand beach, whose calm waters are protected by a reef.

The only good resort area along the northeast coast is Grande Riviere, a wonderfully laid-back spot around the rugged beach with a few staying and eating options. To the west, Shark River offers freshwater bathing.

❼ Central and South Trinidad

📷

Home to the majority of the island's East Indian population, Central and South Trinidad have some stunning natural attractions. Lining the east coast is the spectacular 14-mile (22-km) Manzanilla Beach, backed with a dense coconut plantation that gives the area its name, The Cocal. Southern Trinidad is oil country, and roadside derricks and offshore rigs are part of the scenery. The geological richness bubbles up to the surface at La Brea, site of the largest **Pitch Lake** in the world, covering an area of 10 acres (4 ha).

On the northern outskirts of Trinidad's second city, San Fernando, visitors can observe rare birdlife at the **Point-a-Pierre Wildfowl Trust**. There is more fabulous birdwatching farther north at the **Caroni Swamp Bird Sanctuary**, a dense network of mangroves providing shelter for the scarlet ibis.

Pitch Lake
Southern Trunk Road. **Tel** 868 648 7697. **Open** 9am–5pm daily. 📷 📷

🦜 **Point-a-Pierre Wildfowl Trust**
Off the Southern Main Road. **Tel** 868 658 4200. **Open** 8am–5pm Mon–Fri, 10am–5pm Sat & Sun. 📷 📷 ♿ limited. 📷 🌐 **pointeapierrewild fowltrust.org**

🦜 **Caroni Swamp Bird Sanctuary**
Uriah Butler Highway. **Tel** 868 645 1305. **Open** 9am–4pm daily. 📷 📷

Stunning view of the coastline, northeast coast of Trinidad

❽ Crown Point

SE coast of Tobago. ✈ 🚌
ℹ ANR Robinson International
Airport, 868 639 0509.

Tobago's most touristy area,
Crown Point holds a wealth of
restaurants and hotels, as well
as some great beaches. Within
walking distance of the airport,
Store Bay Beach is a compact
sretch of white sand with gentle
surf, clear waters and several
craft shops; there is also a line
of restaurants that serve some
delicious takeaway lunches
and breakfasts.

🏖 **Store Bay Beach**
Store Bay Local Road. 🚻 🖥 📷
Note: lifeguards and changing facilities
available from 10am–6pm daily.

❾ Pigeon Point Beach

🏖 Pigeon Point Road, Crown Point.
👤 🏨 🚤 🛶 🏖 ⚓ 🚴

Hyped as Tobago's best beach,
Pigeon Point is certainly the
island's most quintessentially
Caribbean seashore, its white
sand overhung by palm trees
and lapped by turquoise
water; controversially, it is also
the only one in the island to
charge an entrance fee. It is a
great place to spend the day,
especially for families with kids,
as there is a playground and
the calm waters remain
shallow almost up to the
distant reef. There are places
selling food and drinks, while
Jet Skis and Hobie Cats buzz
around offshore.

Houses in the fishing village of
Buccoo, Tobago

❿ Buccoo

4 miles (6 km) NE of Crown Point,
Tobago. 🚌 📷 glass-bottom boat
tours to the reef from Buccoo, Pigeon
Point, and Store Bay.

Northeast of Crown Point,
Shirvan Road shoots off the
main Milford Road toward
Buccoo, a faded fishing village
that plays host to the Sunday
School outdoor party each
Sunday night. Just offshore,
Buccoo Reef is the island's most
heavily visited patch of coral,
with double-decker glass-
bottom boats making regular
sorties from all the beaches in
the area. Though the 40-odd
species of coral have suffered a
lot of damage from storms and
human encroachment, there
is still some color to be seen
alongside a host of gorgeous
tropical fish such as butterfly
and parrot fish. To the south
of the reef is the crystal-clear
water of the Nylon Pool
sandbar where swimming
is a refreshing treat.

⓫ Mount Irvine

5 miles (8 km) NE of Crown Point,
Tobago. 🚌

The next coastal village after
Buccoo is Mount Irvine, home
to Tobago's first golf course.
Past Buccoo, Shirvan Road
cuts through the middle of
the 18-hole **Mount Irvine Golf
Course** and swings on past
Mount Irvine Bay Beach, a
stretch of yellow sand overhung
by sea grape and palm trees,
and with covered gazebos for
picnicking. The waves here are
some of the best in Tobago,
making it a surfer's paradise.
At the other side of the beach
is a sandy area that offers lovely
swimming and good snorkeling
over the rocks and coral. Beyond
Mount Irvine, the coast road
sweeps past two more excellent
places to swim, Grafton and
Turtle Beaches. Both are wide
and long and are perfect for
a day by the sea.

🏌 **Mount Irvine Golf Course**
Shirvan Road. **Tel** 868 639 8871.
🚻 🖥 🌐 mtirvine.com

🏖 **Mount Irvine Bay Beach**
♿ 🚻 Note: changing facilities are
available on-site.

⓬ Kimme Museum

5 miles (8 km) NE of Crown Point,
Tobago. **Tel** 868 639 0257. 🚌
Open 10am–2pm Sun; at other times,
call to arrange a viewing. 📷 📷
🌐 luisekimme.com

Just past the Mount Irvine Golf
Course, the right-hand turnoff
on to Orange Hill Road leads

The palm-fringed powdery white sand of Pigeon Point Beach, Tobago

For hotels and restaurants on these islands see p474 and p475

View of Parlatuvier Bay, on the north coast of Tobago

up into the hills and to the intriguing Kimme Museum, the turreted, mural-decorated former home and studio of German sculptor Luise Kimme, who lived in Tobago for some 30 years, until her death in 2013. Inspired by local life and folklore, her stunning pieces are each sculpted from a whole oak trunk, and depict everything from the mythical La Diablesse to Nijinski dancers, and dancing couples.

⑬ Castara

18 miles (29 km) NE of Crown Point, Tobago.

Past the diminutive town of Plymouth, the coast is paralleled by the Northside Road, a twisting and picturesque route that affords some lovely glimpses of interior villages and inaccessible coastline.

The first point of interest is Castara, a beautiful mini-resort that has grown up around a placid fishing village and a gorgeous curve of beach. It is a laid-back and attractive spot, and is ideal to spend some time relaxing, with a couple of great places to eat right on the beach and a sprinkling of low-key guesthouses overlooking the bay. There is enough space so it rarely feels crowded, however, if need be, it is possible to head for the adjoining Little Bay for some solitude. Castara is also one of the points from which boat tours *(see p470)* are available for the various excellent beaches and snorkeling spots located nearby.

⑭ Englishman's Bay to Bloody Bay

20 miles (32 km) NE of Crown Point, Tobago.

The countryside beyond Castara becomes noticeably less developed, with the Northside Road twisting through jungle-smothered hillsides with hardly a building in sight. The first place to stop is Englishman's Bay, a delightful and stunning horseshoe of yellow sand that lies between untouched rainforest on one side and deep emerald waters on the other. The offshore reef here offers good snorkeling opportunities.

Just above the fishing village of Parlatuvier, some 2 miles (3 km) farther along the coastal road, people can stop off at a roadside parking spot for some pretty views of the bay below, with fishing boats bobbing in the turquoise waters and terraced smallholdings rolling up the hillside.

About 2 miles (3 km) from the village is Bloody Bay, offering some fine coastal views, with the spectacular Sisters Rocks lying just offshore. At the bay's rough, yellow-sand beach, a turnoff swings inland leading to the Tobago Forest Reserve *(see p467)*. Moving east along the coast, visitors pass through the pretty village of L'Anse Fourmi and finally reach Charlotteville *(see p467)* at the island's northeast tip.

Sunday School

An enduring Tobago tradition that remains popular with both locals and visitors, Sunday School is a huge outdoor party that overtakes Buccoo each Sunday evening. From around 8pm, the Bucconeers steel band play under the stars one block from the beach facilities for a predominantly older crowd, who take to the dance floor to display some killer moves. After the live music, DJs take over, playing dancehall, hip-hop, and R&B for a younger crowd – the drinks flow and everyone lets their hair down. The sandy "dance floor" in front of the beach facilities becomes a great place to dance and mingle. Vendors sell crafts and jewelry, all night long, along the roadside leading to Buccoo. Dinner options include a full-fledged fish menu as well as lighter snacks such as corn soup. If not driving, it is best to arrange for a taxi pickup at the end of the night.

Steel pan band playing at Sunday School, Buccoo, Tobago

⑮ Scarborough

7 miles (11 km) NE of Crown Point, Tobago. 🄰 20,000. 🚢 ℹ Cruise ship complex, 868 635 0934.
🌐 gotrinidadandtobago.com

Tobago's capital, Scarborough is a hotbed of activity compared to the rest of the island, with taxis and shoppers crowding the streets, vendors setting up their stalls at the roadside, and plenty of traffic to and from the busy ferry port. The best place for shopping is the market, set back from the seafront and accessed from Gardenside Street. It is busiest on Fridays and Saturdays, but visitors will always find piles of exotic fruits and vegetables and other assorted general goods. On the other side of Gardenside Street is the

Signage at Fort King George, Scarborough

18-acre (7-ha) Botanical Gardens, its smooth lawns and fishponds offering quiet respite from the clamor. It is open on all days.

Scarborough's other main draw is Fort King George. A collection of handsome restored colonial-era brick buildings surrounding the modern light-house, the complex features many cannons and offers sweeping views down the wind-ward coast and Scarborough. The fort is also home to the small but interesting **Tobago Museum**, which has some absorbing exhibits on the island's local history.

🏛 **Tobago Museum**
Fort King George. **Tel** 868 639 3970.
Open 9am–4:30pm Mon–Fri. 🏷

⑯ The Windward Coast

9 miles (14 km) NE of Scarborough, Tobago. 🚌

In comparison to the tranquil leeward side of the island, bordered by the calm Caribbean Sea, the windward coast is a lot more rugged, washed by pounding Atlantic waves and with strong currents that make some beaches out of bounds for swimmers. The best place to experience the sea is King's Bay, bordered by a forest of palms and with calm water and fine volcanic sand. To the southwest there is another chance to get wet at Argyle Waterfall, the island's highest three-tiered 177-ft (54-m) cascade with several pools. Otherwise, the windward coast is best appreciated as a scenic – if winding – drive, its pretty villages with board houses teetering at the edge of the

⑱ Speyside

A short drive from Charlotteville, over the island's central spine and onto the east coast, Speyside offers some of Tobago's best diving and snorkeling. The viewing area above town on the Scarborough road gives a bird's-eye view of the brightly-painted village and the offshore islands, including Little Tobago rising from the blue seas. Glass-bottom boats make regular trips out to the reef from the beach; visitors can also don a mask and flippers and just swim out themselves.

Jemma's Sea View Kitchen, built around a tree at the Speyside seashore

Diving is great in Speyside with several wonderful scuba sites nearby and a teeming reef just offshore between the mainland and the nearby Goat and Little Tobago Islands.

Pirate's Bay · 🏕 · Charlotteville
Man O'War Bay
🏕 · Cambleton
Northside Road · 🛫
Eastern Tobago National Park · Tyrrel's Bay
Speyside · 🏕 · Goat Island
L To

Lucy Vale Bay

Windward Road

Delaford · King's Bay · 🏕 Delaford Beach

Roxborough

Prince's Bay · Queen's Bay · Queen's Island

Key
▬▬ Major road
═══ Minor road

For hotels and restaurants on these islands see p474 and p475

cliffs or spreading out on either side of the road running along the coast.

🦋 Argyle Waterfall
Windward Road. **Open** 9am–5pm daily; last tour 4pm. 🅿️ 🚻 🖥️
Note: changing facilities are available on-site.

⓱ Tobago Forest Reserve

17 miles (27 km) NE of Scarborough, Tobago. 🅣 🚻

The oldest protected rainforest in the Western Hemisphere, the Tobago Forest Reserve comprises 22 sq miles (57 sq km) of densely forested land in the northern half of the island, accessible via a scenic road. Much of the area is inaccessible, but from Gilpin Trace – marked by a huge rock by the roadside – visitors can follow a trail into the dense forest, with its

A gazebo at Cambleton Battery, Charlotteville

towering trees and greenish light filtering through the thick canopy. Guides are available at the entrance to the reserve.

⓲ Charlotteville

27 miles (43 km) NE of Scarborough, Tobago. 🚌

Tucked into a protected bay at Tobago's extreme northeast tip, Charlotteville is a slow-paced place, with tourism and fishing co-existing easily as the main industries. Tumbling down a steep hillside, the village meets the sea at the yellow sands and calm waters of Man O'War Bay. Overlooking the Man O'War Bay to the west is the British-built Cambleton Battery, while to the east, via a rough track around the headland, is Pirate's Bay, perhaps Tobago's prettiest beach, completely undeveloped and with excellent snorkeling spots.

Panoramic view of Speyside with the village's beach just seen to the left and Goat Island in the lee of the larger Little Tobago. This is among the most photographed spots on the island.

0 kilometers 2

0 miles 2

Speyside's Wildlife

Enriched by nutrients from Venezuela's Orinoco River, the reefs around Speyside are some of Tobago's best. It is possible to see incredibly diverse marine life and corals, including, at the Kelleston Drain site, one of the largest brain corals in the world, measuring 13-ft (4-m) high and 20-ft (6-m) wide. The island's position at the confluence of the Caribbean Sea and Atlantic Ocean also makes it a great place to spot deep-water pelagic species, most notably the huge, graceful manta rays that are a common sight here. Above ground, there is also some great bird-watching on Little Tobago, a protected sanctuary since 1924 and a good place to spot species such as boobies, frigates, and the red-billed tropic-bird. Specialist guides (see p470) lead trips to the island.

Two divers approaching a gigantic brain coral

VISITORS' CHECKLIST

Practical Information
Around 20 miles (32 km) NE of Scarborough. 🚤 glass-bottom boat tours with snorkeling are available from Frank's at Blue Waters Inn (868 660 5438), and from Fear Not at Jemma's Sea View Kitchen (868 660 4654). 🚻 🖥️ 🏊

Transport
🚌 from Scarborough.

Speyside's Beach is best at the village's western end, around the Blue Waters Inn hotel (see p474), and to the east, where there are changing facilities adjacent to the football field.

For keys to symbols see back flap

Outdoor Activities and Specialized Holidays

Trinidad and Tobago offer plenty of activities that take place beyond their beaches. With a wide range of habitats, ranging from swamp to savannah to rainforest, they provide some of the Caribbean's best hiking and bird-watching. Tour operators arrange trips or entire holidays based around birding or diving. Along with guided hikes or mountain-bike rides, visitors can watch millions of bats exit from their daytime roost in a cave, kayak through the swamps in search of manatees, and take in the unforgettable sight of a huge leatherback turtle hauling herself up a beach to lay eggs in the sand.

One of the secluded beaches at Blanchisseuse, north coast of Trinidad

Beaches

Of the two islands, Tobago boasts of better beaches. However, the north coast of Trinidad with its wide curves of yellow sand and clean waters, features some great spots for swimming. Maracas Bay (see pp462–3) has excellent facilities and cool green waters. Popular with both locals and visitors, it tends to get crowded during weekends. For quieter alternatives to the buzzing northeast coast, it is best to head to the secluded One Thousand Steps at La Filette or the deserted and wild Yarra. Accessible only on foot or by boat from Blanchisseuse, Paria Bay has a waterfall with a deep pool and a generous stretch of untouched yellow sand.

Tobago's leeward coast boasts a couple of sublime beaches. Pigeon Point Beach (see p464) lures visitors with its soft white sand and azure waters. A boat trip around the island allows access to beaches that might not be reached on foot or by car. These include the picture-perfect No Man's Land and the lovely Stingray Beach, where people can swim with the friendly rays.

Diving and Snorkeling

Trinidad and Tobago's reefs are impressively rich and diverse, as they are fed by sediments from the great South American rivers. In Trinidad, visibility ranges from just 6 ft (2 m) to a depth of 50 ft (15 m). Though there is some interesting diving around the Bocas islands, most prefer Tobago's waters, where the visibility is better and the Guyana Current makes for some exciting drift diving. Tobago is also one of the few places in the world where divers can swim alongside manta rays and spot the unusual toadfish and short-nose batfish. The best dive sites are around Speyside (see pp466–7), but there are some prime spots along the north coast, at Man O'War Bay in Charlotteville and the St. Giles Islands off the northwest tip. Buccoo Reef, Arnos Vale Bay Beach, Pirate's Bay, and Speyside also have good snorkeling. Diving and snorkeling gear can be hired from dive shops such as **R & Sea Divers**, **Aquamarine Dive**, and **Tobago Dive Experience**.

Watersports

The more visited Tobago has the bulk of the available watersports, with most outlets in Crown Point, with a particular concentration at Pigeon Point Beach, including **Radical Sports**. From there visitors can enjoy banana boat rides, kitesurfing, waterskiing,

Diver approaching a cluster of stunning corals in the waters around Tobago

A watersports center at Pigeon Point Beach, Tobago

and parasailing. Jet Skis and Hobie Cat catamarans can also be rented. Watersports agencies also include **Tobago Surf & Kite Camp**, in Mt. Irvine Bay.

Boat Tours

With its jungle-covered hillsides tumbling down to deserted, inaccessible beaches and a host of offshore islands, Tobago's coastline is best seen by boat. Many operators such as **Frankie Tours** and **Alibaba Tours** offer trips that include lunch, drinks, and stops for snorkeling and swimming, along with a bit of line fishing. Trips from the western end of the island tend to go up to Englishman's Bay for snorkeling and then head back for lunch at the gorgeous No Man's Land Beach. From places such as Castara, it is possible to reach secluded hard-to-reach shores, while spotting dolphins, turtles, and flying fish along the way. **Plantation Beach Watersports** (better known as Island Girl) has crafts that accommodate up to 30 passengers and offer freshwater showers and a buffet lunch.

In Trinidad, boat tours around the Bocas islands give an insight into the fascinating local history. Tourists can enjoy swimming at secluded beaches or in a cave on Gasparee Island, and hiking through dry scrub forest as part of the tour. **In Joy Tours**, located in Petit Valley, also organizes boat trips.

Fishing

The waters of Trinidad and Tobago promise some good game fishing, with the main catches being marlin, tuna, and wahoo. Chartering an entire sportfishing boat to head out to the deep-sea waters might make for an expensive day out. It may be a better idea to hire a local fishing pirogue and try line fishing for kingfish, mahimahi, barracuda, and jack. **Hard Play Fishing Charters** and **King David Tours** on Tobago are reputable fishing charters.

Kayaking

With just a few inland rivers, kayaking in Tobago is mostly restricted to the sea. **Tobago Sea Kayak Experience** in Charlotteville offer guided paddles that provide a gentle

and unique way to see the undeveloped coastline. They also offer a trip from Pigeon Point that includes lunch and snorkeling at No Man's Land.

In Trinidad, **Chaguaramas Kayak Centre** is a kayak rental outlet. From here visitors can paddle around the sheltered waters of Williams Bay, or take a guided tour around the Bocas islands. It is also possible to paddle up the Marianne River from Blanchisseuse. On the east coast, the protected wetland of Nariva Swamp is a habitat for birds and animals, and offers some fantastic kayaking through calm waters choked with water hyacinth and lilies. Kayaking trips on Trinidad are arranged by companies such as Caribbean Discovery Tours and Paria Springs Eco Community (see p471).

Mountain Biking

Though mountain biking is a relatively new sport in Trinidad and Tobago, there are several operators on both islands who take visitors on exciting trails and can provide excellent guided rides for amateurs and aficionados. It is better to ride early in the morning and stick to shaded forest trails to avoid the tropical sun. However, many trails end with a cool dip in the sea or at a waterfall. Interested visitors can contact **Mountain Biking Tobago** in Tobago and Paria Springs Eco Community in Trinidad.

Kayaking in the calm waters of Williams Bay, Trinidad

Hiking through the verdant trails of the Tobago Forest Reserve

Hiking

Although Tobago has plenty of splendid trails, particularly through the Tobago Forest Reserve (see p467) and along undeveloped portions of the leeward coast, it is Trinidad that offers the nation's best hiking. The Northern Range mountains are laced with trails that take in waterfalls, rivers, gorges, and lush rainforest. Climbs up Trinidad's highest peaks, El Tucuche at 3,071 ft (936 m) and El Cerro del Aripo at 3,087 ft (941 m), are challenging. Others may prefer the short trek up Mount Tamana to watch the spectacular dusk exit of a colony of resident bats. Paria Springs

Eco Community and Caribbean Discovery Tours arrange guided hikes. **Harris' Jungle Tours** and Peter Cox Nature Tours (see p471) offer excursions in Tobago.

Bird-Watching

Ranking among the world's top ten destinations in terms of the number of species, with around 460 recorded, Trinidad and Tobago are a bird-watchers' paradise. Alongside the common cowbirds and bananaquits, it is possible to spot bay-headed tanagers, channel-billed toucans, and the very rare nocturnal oilbirds. The islands boast the full spectrum of iridescent hummingbirds. In fact, the Taíno name for Trinidad was *lere*, or "land of the hummingbirds." The Northern Range is home to the birders' mecca – the Asa Wright Nature Centre and Lodge (see p463). Other great places for birding include the Caroni Swamp, where scarlet ibis roost each evening, and the Cocal at Manzanilla, which serves as a nesting site for red-bellied macaws.

Birding trips are arranged by Paria Springs Eco Community and Caribbean Discovery Tours in Trinidad, and **NG & Company Nature Tours** and Peter Cox Nature Tours in Tobago.

Golf

The islands have a few great golf clubs. In Tobago, the 18-hole Mount Irvine course (see p464) offers sea views from every hole. The Plantations course is another 18-hole option. In Trinidad, the 9-hole Chaguaramas Golf Club, the 18-hole St. Andrew's, and Millennium Lakes have fine courses. The **Trinidad and Tobago Golf Association** provides all details.

Golfers at the Mount Irvine Golf Course, Tobago

DIRECTORY

Diving and Snorkeling

Aquamarine Dive
Speyside, Tobago.
Tel 868 639 4416.
W aquamarinedive.com

R & Sea Divers
Crown Point, Tobago.
Tel 868 639 8120.
W rseadivers.com

Tobago Dive Experience
Speyside, Tobago.
Tel 868 660 4888.
W tobagodiveexperience.com

Watersports

Radical Sports
Pigeon Point Heritage Park, Tobago.
Tel 868 631 5150.
W radicalsportstobago.com

Tobago Kite & Surf Camp
Mt. Irvine Bay, Tobago.
Tel 868 313 1260.
W surfcamp-tobago.com

Boat Tours

Alibaba Tours
Castara, Tobago.
Tel 868 635 1017.
W alibaba-tours.com

Frankie Tours
Mount Irvine Bay Beach, Tobago.
Tel 868 631 0369.
W frankietours.com

In Joy Tours
Petit Valley, Trinidad.
Tel 868 633 4733.
W injoytours.com

Plantation Beach Watersports (Island Girl)
Bon Accord, Tobago.
Tel 868 639 7245.
W sailtobago.com

Fishing

Hard Play Fishing Charters
Old Grange, Tobago.
Tel 868 639 7108.
W hardplay.net

King David Tours
Castara, Tobago.
Tel 868 660 7906.

Kayaking

Chaguaramas Kayak Centre
Williams Bay, Trinidad.
Tel 868 633 7871.

Tobago Sea Kayak Experience
Tobago. **Tel** 868 660 6186.
W seakayaktobago.com

Mountain Biking

Mountain Biking Tobago
Bon Accord, Tobago.
Tel 868 639 9709.
W mountainbikingtobago.com

Hiking

Harris' Jungle Tours
Crown Point, Tobago.
Tel 868 639 0513.
W harris-jungle-tours.com

Bird-Watching

NG & Company Nature Tours
Speyside, Tobago.
Tel 868 660 5463.
W newtongeorge.com

Golf

Trinidad and Tobago Golf Association
St. Andrew's Golf Club, Moka, Trinidad.
Tel 868 629 7127.
W trinidadandtobagogolfassociation.com

Turtle-Watching

Each year during the March–July season, thousands of turtles draw themselves up onto the beaches of Trinidad and Tobago to lay their eggs. The most common species in local waters is the leatherback turtle, with up to 50 visiting the more well-known beaches on a good night. There are several places where environmental groups have set up turtle watches to protect the animals from human and animal predators, and at many of these, visitors too can take in the amazing spectacle. In Trinidad, the main beaches for turtle-watching are at Matura and Grande Riviere, while in Tobago there are occasional nestings at Turtle Beach.

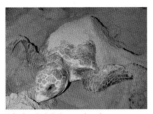

A hole, slightly larger than her own body, is dug by the female. Decoy nests are also made to confuse predators.

The Nesting Process

Female leatherbacks may lay up to nine times during the season. They usually come ashore at night during the high tide to lay their eggs, which are deposited well beyond the waterline. This is done to ensure that tides do not erode the nests and uncover the eggs.

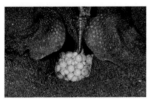

The eggs, laid over a period of approximately two hours, number between 80 to 100. The leatherback turtle sheds tears to protect her eyes against the sand. After depositing the eggs, she covers the nest with sand and returns to the sea.

Powerful flippers are used to remove the surface sand and dig the nest.

Visitors can observe the turtle at close quarters due to the trance-like state she enters while laying eggs.

Hatchlings, fully-formed but tiny, emerge from the eggs after an incubation period of around 60 days. The eggs usually hatch during the night.

TOUR OPERATORS

Caribbean Discovery Tours
Trinidad. **Tel** 868 624 7281.
W caribbeandiscovery tours.com

Grande Riviere Nature Tour Guide Association
Trinidad. **Tel** 868 670 4257.

Nature Seekers
Trinidad. **Tel** 868 668 7337.

Paria Springs Eco Community
Trinidad. **Tel** 868 622 8826.
W pariasprings.com

Peter Cox Nature Tours
Tobago. **Tel** 868 751 5822.
W tobagonaturetours.com

Newborn turtles head for the sea upon hatching. During the early stages, hatchling populations are very vulnerable and most fall prey to large fish, birds, and crabs. Once in the sea, the males never return to shore, while the female turtles visit the same beach where they hatched to lay their own eggs.

Where to Stay

Trinidad

ARIMA: ASA Wright Nature Centre and Lodge $$$
Eco Lodge
7 3/4 mm Blanchisseuse Road
Tel *868 667 4655*
W asawright.org
A world-famous nature sanctuary and bird-watching lodge tucked away in the rainforest of Trinidad's Northern Range. Simple rooms.

BLANCHISSEUSE: Laguna Mar $
Guesthouse
65 ½ Mile Marker, Paria Main Road
Tel *868 669 2963*
W lagunamar.com
This long-established place offers basic rooms in a stunning location.

GRAND RIVIERE: Mt. Plaisir Estate $$
Eco Lodge
Grande Riviere
Tel *868 670 1868*
W mtplaisir.com
The rooms at the rustic Mt. Plaisir are furnished using items made by local craftsmen.

PORT OF SPAIN: Monique's $
Guesthouse
114/116 Saddle Road, Maraval
Tel *868 622 3232*
W moniquestrinidad.com
This guesthouse has spacious rooms and is located within easy reach of the north coast beaches.

DK Choice

PORT OF SPAIN: Hilton Trinidad and Conference Centre $$
Modern
Lady Young Road
Tel *868 624 3211*
W hiltontrinidadhotel.com
Trinidad's "upside-down hotel" (the lobby is on the top floor) has played host to world leaders, royalty, and international entertainers, and is known for its family-friendly hospitality. The rooms are stylish and modern. Sundays are popular as guests and locals often follow the lavish brunch with a swim in the pool.

PORT OF SPAIN: Kapok Hotel $$
Modern
16–18 Cotton Hill, St. Clair
Tel *868 622 5765*
W kapokhotel.com
This family-run hotel is renowned for its restaurants, good accommodation, facilities, and service.

PORT OF SPAIN: Courtyard Marriott $$$
Modern
Invaders Bay, Audrey Jeffers Highway
Tel *868 627 5555*
W marriott.com
This full-service hotel is located close to good shopping and entertainment facilities. Stylish and comfortable rooms.

PORT OF SPAIN: Hyatt Regency $$$
Modern
1 Wrightson Road
Tel *868 623 2222*
W trinidad.hyatt.com
Luxurious downtown chain hotel, popular with business travelers. Bright, contemporary rooms.

Tobago

CROWN POINT: Bananaquit Apartments $
Guesthouse
Store Bay Local Road
Tel *868 368 3539*
W bananaquit.com
Beach lovers will appreciate the great location of these well-equipped self-catering apartments.

DK Choice

CROWN POINT: Kariwak Village $$
Boutique
Store Bay Local Road
Tel *868 639 8442*
W kariwak.com
A few minutes' walk from Store Bay, Kariwak is a welcoming oasis. Guests stay in comfortable cabanas. The food is delicious and uses vegetables mainly from their garden. Morning yoga and tai chi classes, hammocks and massages (plus a waterfall, Jacuzzi, and plunge pool) all encourage relaxation.

Price Guide
Prices are based on one night's stay in high season for a standard double room, inclusive of service charges and taxes.

$	up to $100
$$	$100–200
$$$	over $200

CROWN POINT: Coco Reef Resort $$$
Coconut Bay
Tel *868 639 8571*
W cocoreef.com
This all-inclusive resort offers complimentary watersports and a private white-sand beach.

CULLODEN BAY: Footprints Eco Resort $
Eco Lodge
Golden Lane, Culloden Road
Tel *868 660 0416*
W footprintseco-resort.com
An isolated, peaceful sanctuary rich with wildlife. There are nature trails for hiking and bird-watching.

MT. IRVINE: Mt. Irvine Bay Hotel and Golf Club $$
Resort
Scarborough
Tel *868 639 8871*
W mtirvine.com
Near the beach and an 18-hole golf course, this hotel has a freshwater pool with a swim-up bar.

SCARBOROUGH: Bacolet Beach Club $$$
Boutique
73 Bacolet Street
Tel *868 639 2357*
W bacoletbeachclub.com
Small and intimate, with a beach bar, an infinity pool, and a wooden deck to soak up the sun.

SPEYSIDE: Blue Waters Inn $$$
Beach Resort
Batteaux Bay
Tel *868 660 4341*
W bluewatersinn.com
A small, elegantly designed place with lots of outdoor activities.

Relaxing, attractive pool area at Kariwak Village, Crown Point, Tobago

Where to Eat and Drink

Simple, colorful interior at the Veni Mange, Port of Spain, Trinidad

Trinidad

**PORT OF SPAIN:
Femmes Du Chalet** $
Caribbean
Wrightson Road
Vendors at this shed serve hearty local specialties for breakfast and lunch. Take-out is also available.

PORT OF SPAIN: Veni Mangé $$
Caribbean
67A Ariapita Avenue, Woodbrook
Tel *868 624 4597* **Closed** *Sat & Sun*
This eatery is famous for its friendly hospitality, Caribbean art, and superb West Indian cuisine.

DK Choice

PORT OF SPAIN: Aioli $$$
Mediterranean
Ellerslie Plaza, Boissiere
Tel *868 222 3291* **Closed** *Sun*
Stylish, modern decor complements an innovative menu by a young and gifted Trinidadian chef. The dishes would delight any foodie, right down to the mouth-watering desserts to end the meal. The service is impeccable and enthusiastic. Aioli is popular with couples looking for a romantic evening, as well as families out for a special night.

PORT OF SPAIN: Apsara $$$
Indian
13 Queen's Park East
Tel *868 623 7659*
Enjoy authentic South Asian cuisine in a luxurious, evocative setting. On the menu are classic North Indian dishes, as well as many vegetarian choices.

PORT OF SPAIN: Chaud KM $$$
French/Caribbean
2 Queen's Park West
Tel *868 623 0375* **Closed** *Sun*
The chef brings fresh Caribbean flavors to French gourmet cuisine. Try the fish soup to start and the oven-roasted chicken for main. Save room for dessert. Good, reasonably priced lunch menu.

Tobago

BLACK ROCK: The Fish Pot $$$
Caribbean/Seafood
Pleasant Prospect
Tel *868 635 1728* **Closed** *Sun*
The menu at this unassuming, delightful eatery changes daily. Choose your meal from the list on the chalkboard.

**BLACK ROCK: The Seahorse
Inn Restaurant & Bar** $$$
Caribbean/International
Grafton Beach Road
Tel *868 639 0686*
Seafood, meat, and salads are all on the menu at this elegant spot. Brilliant sunsets add to the charm.

DK Choice

BUCCOO: El Pescador $$$
Seafood
14 Miller's Street, Buccoo Village
Tel *868 631 1266*
Facing the picturesque Buccoo Bay, El Pescador specializes in fresh fish and seafood. The chef offers a Caribbean fusion menu, which includes wonderful desserts. The relaxed setting makes this a fine spot for a leisurely dinner.

BUCCOO: La Tartaruga $$$
Italian
Buccoo Bay Road
Tel *868 639 0940* **Closed** *Sun*
Classic Italian dishes, including vegetarian options, as well as an award-winning wine list.

**CASTARA: The Boat House
Restaurant** $$
Caribbean
Depot Road, Little Bay
Tel *868 483 0964* **Closed** *Sat*
A casual seaside eatery known for fresh lobster. Wednesday is entertainment night, usually with drumming and limbo dancing.

CROWN POINT: La Cantina $$
Italian
Milford Road, Store Bay
Tel *868 639 8242*
This popular family restaurant with a fun atmosphere offers authentic Italian pizza and pasta.

**LAMBEAU: Shore Things
Café and Craft** $$
Caribbean
Red Point, 25 Milford Road
Tel *868 635 1072* **Closed** *Sat & Sun*
Admire the view at this seaside café with a garden. Serves local specialties and pizza, as well as fresh juices.

SCARBOROUGH: Blue Crab $$
Caribbean
Corner Robinson and Main streets
Tel *868 639 2737* **Closed** *Sat & Sun*
Popular family-run restaurant offering a very good local menu, with afternoon tea on Tuesdays.

SCARBOROUGH: Ciao Café $$
Italian
Burnett Street
Tel *868 639 3001*
This casual Italian café features authentic Neapolitan pizza, pasta dishes, panini, and a range of delicious home-made *gelati*.

**SPEYSIDE: Jemma's Tree
House Restaurant** $$$
Caribbean
Main Street
Tel *868 660 4066* **Closed** *Sat*
A favorite with visitors, Jemma's kitchen serves fresh fish and seafood, complemented by beautiful ocean views.

Practical Information

Trinidad and Tobago are easy islands to travel to. Public transport is relatively reliable, with several options to choose from, including maxi taxis, which are unique to the two islands. The infrastructure is also quite good. The two islands are comparatively less expensive than the others in the region. This is particularly true for Trinidad, where restaurant prices and the like are geared more to locals than to tourists. Shopping is a pleasant experience on both islands as there are a variety of places to visit, each selling interesting souvenirs.

When to Go

The best time to visit is between January and May, when the weather is most pleasant. By May, the dry season has parched the landscape. June to December is the rainy season. Visitors also come during September when there is a dry spell known as the Indian summer and the air fares dip.

Getting There

The islands are served by international flights which land at Piarco International Airport and ANR Robinson International Airport in Trinidad and Tobago respectively. The main airlines are **American Airlines**, **Caribbean Airlines**, **Continental**, **Delta**, **Condor**, **British Airways**, **Virgin Atlantic**, and **WestJet**. Ferries and cruise ships dock at King's Wharf in Trinidad, and Scarborough in Tobago.

Documentation

Citizens of the European Union (plus Switzerland and Norway), the US, and Canada do not need a visa for stays of less than three months. Citizens of other countries must apply for a visa from the nearest Trinidad and Tobago embassy or consulate. Visitors are allowed to import 200 cigarettes, 50 cigars, or 9 oz (250g) of tobacco, 3 pints (1.5 l) of spirits, and gifts worth TT$1,200.

Visitor Information

The **Tourism Development Company**, Trinidad and Tobago's tourist board, operates booths at both international airports.

Health and Security

There are no major health hazards on the islands. Tap water is safe to drink. Both islands have good hospitals such as the **Port of Spain General Hospital** and **Tobago Regional Hospital**.

Crime is a problem in inner city areas of Port of Spain, and visitors have been victims of robberies in both Trinidad and Tobago. Be especially alert if leaving Piarco International Airport after dark, as travelers have been accosted in the airport parking lot, on the highway, and outside residences on arrival. Avoid maxi taxis and arrange a taxi pick-up through your hotel. To stay safe, avoid walking alone at night in deserted areas, and lonely beaches.

One of the many ATMs located on Trinidad

Banking and Currency

The local currency is the TT dollar (TT$). Banks, found in all towns and cities, offer the best exchange rates. ATMs are widespread; those at Crown Point and Piarco airports dispense US dollars and local currency. Credit cards are widely accepted.

Communications

Both islands' code is 1 868. There are card phones dotted around the two islands, but many are out of service. Phone cards are available from supermarkets and small stores, which sell cheap-rate international calling cards. These cards can be used from any landline. Tri-band mobiles will work in the two islands, and local pay-as-you-go SIM cards are also widely available.

Transport

All buses in Trinidad leave from the City Gate terminus in downtown Port of Spain, as do maxi taxis (20-seater buses), color-coded yellow (Port of Spain and the west), red (east-west corridor), green (central and south), black (around Princes Town), and brown (San Fernando). In Tobago, buses depart from the depot

Passengers boarding a plane at ANR Robinson International Airport

Maxi taxi, Port of Spain, Trinidad

on Sangster Hill Road in Scarborough. Route taxis running on set routes are great for short trips. It is best to ask locals for help with the routes.

There are numerous car rental companies on both islands as well. Visitors renting a car need to be over 25 and should hold a valid driving license. Major international companies such as **Thrifty** and **Hertz** have franchises on both islands. Other car rental companies include **Econo-Car**, **Auto Rentals**, **Rattan's**, and **Sheppy's**. It is advisable to check the condition of the vehicle before hiring it.

Shopping

Both the islands offer a wide variety of souvenirs and crafts. Specialties include pretty woven palm hats, local handicrafts such as fine carvings from driftwood, and jewelry made from shells and beads. Both islands also have a rich musical tradition and music CDs are available at most shops. A good selection of fabric can be bought in Port of Spain on Charlotte Street.

Shops are open from around 8am to 5:30pm on weekdays, and from 8am to 5pm on Saturdays. Large shopping malls tend to stay open until 9pm Monday to Saturday. On Sundays, they remain open from 1pm to 5pm.

Language

English is the main language spoken on both islands but French Creole (or patois) is still spoken among elders in Trinidad.

Electricity

The electric current is 110 or 220 volts, 60 cycles. Plug sockets take two flat prongs.

Time

Both islands are 4 hours behind GMT (5 behind British Summer Time) and 1 hour ahead of EST.

Getting Married

To get married in Trinidad and Tobago, both parties must have been on the island for three or more days before the ceremony; on the fourth day one can apply for a marriage license for which the person will need ID, Decree Absolute or death certificate if divorced or widowed, and proof of any name change. There are many companies, such as **Tobago Weddings**, who can sort out the formalities for the couple.

Souvenir stall on the Northside Road, Tobago

DIRECTORY

Getting There

American Airlines
W aa.com

British Airways
W ba.com

Caribbean Airlines
W caribbean-airlines.com

Condor
W condor.com

Continental
W continental.com

Delta
W delta.com

Virgin Atlantic
W virgin-atlantic.com

WestJet
W westjet.com

Visitor Information

Tourism Development Company
29 Tenth Avenue, Barataria, Trinidad.
Tel 868 675 7034.
W gotrinidadandtobago.com

Health and Security

Fire and Ambulance
Tel 990.

Police
Tel 999.

Port of Spain General Hospital
Port of Spain, Trinidad.
Tel 868 623 2951.

Tobago Regional Hospital
Scarborough, Tobago.
Tel 868 639 2551.

Transport

Auto Rentals
Tel 868 675 7368 (Trinidad); 868 639 0644 (Tobago).

Econo-Car
W econocarrentalstt.com

Hertz
W hertz.com

Rattan's
Tobago.
Tel 868 639 8271.

Sheppy's
Tel 868 639 1543.
W tobagocarrental.com

Thrifty
W thrifty.com

Getting Married

Tobago Weddings
Tel 868 660 8063.
W tobagoweddings.com

A PORTRAIT OF ARUBA, CURAÇAO, AND BONAIRE

The islands of Aruba, Curaçao, and Bonaire line up along the north coast of Venezuela, well outside the Atlantic hurricane belt. These Dutch isles provide an amazing mix of desert landscapes, awesome beaches and coves, spectacular underwater reefs brimming with marine life, and heritage architecture, as well as world-class shops and casinos.

Each of the islands – Aruba, Bonaire, and Curaçao – is a jagged scrap of rocky land that broke away from South America before dinosaurs roamed the earth. Over time, reefs began growing around the islands' stone cores. Today, the underwater coral acts as a protective barrier for the numerous beaches, as well as a habitat for marine creatures and a playground for divers.

History

The Caiquetio tribe, a subtribe of the Arawaks, were the inhabitants of these islands when Christopher Columbus and subsequent European explorers arrived in the late 15th century. The Spanish had expected to find gold on the islands, but when they discovered that there was none and that fresh water was scarce, they

captured the natives and sent them to work on their plantations in Hispaniola and abandoned their claim to these islands.

The Dutch West India Company took over the islands in the 1630s, established successful plantations and began a thriving export business that included importing African slaves, training them for domestic and farm labor, then reselling them throughout the Caribbean and the Americas. During these years, the Papiamento language began to evolve, incorporating Dutch, Spanish, Portuguese, and several African dialects. Today, it is the preferred language, even though the official language is Dutch. In the early 18th century, the islands' ports and favorable location attracted European settlers who were interested in valuable trade routes

Dutch-style buildings with outdoor cafés lining the waterfront in Willemstad, Curaçao

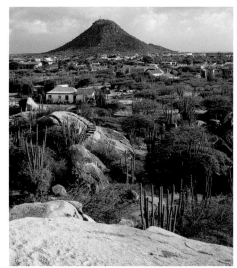
Landscape of cactus and shrubs, typical of Aruba

though oil transport, local construction, and financial services also contribute a significant income. Unemployment is low and the people enjoy a standard of living that is relatively higher than in many other Caribbean islands, mainly because of good education, steady employment, and a stable government.

Culture and the Arts

Music, dance, and the visual arts are a vital part of island life. The Dutch heritage is a strong presence, but well mixed with English, Spanish, and African influences. Local artists draw international attention with dramatic sculptures, often depicting African and Dutch characters, and paintings splashed with the vivid Caribbean colors. All the islands hold annual carnivals showcasing their music, a combination of traditional calypso and drum-pounding tumba that produces unique spirit-lifting beats, as well as street dances called jump-ups.

and military strongholds. Ownership of the islands changed regularly in the early 1800s, but the Dutch regained control by mid-century. When Venezuela discovered oil off its northern coast in 1920, Aruba and Curaçao became distilling centers, and immigrant workers arrived from around the world. The Dutch developed Curaçao into one of the Caribbean's most important ports, bred horses on Aruba, and produced salt from the saline pits of Bonaire. After World War II, the islands were granted partial autonomy.

The Islands Today

The official status of Aruba, Curaçao, and Bonaire is complicated, even to its residents. All are part of the Netherlands, which is a Commonwealth and includes Holland, the former Netherlands Antilles (Bonaire, Saba, and St. Eustatius, now referred to as the BES Islands), and Aruba, Curaçao, and Sint Maarten. Aruba was part of the Antilles group until 1986, and Curaçao until 2008, when they became autonomous countries within the Commonwealth. About 75 percent of the islands' GDP comes from tourism-related businesses,

Children dressed in colorful, traditional costumes at the Carnival, Curaçao

Exploring Aruba, Curaçao, and Bonaire

Aruba, Curaçao, and Bonaire are all part of the Kingdom of the Netherlands, and have been since the Dutch took them from the Spanish in 1634. While there is non-stop action in glamorous resorts and casinos on the beaches along Aruba's coast, world-class scuba diving thrives in the unspoiled waters surrounding Bonaire. The quietest of the three, Curaçao, is famous for its UNESCO World Heritage Site, Willemstad, lined with pretty old Dutch buildings.

Locator Map

Christoffel National Park
Ruins of plantation buildings are surrounded by nature trails in this eco-park.

Arikok National Park
This arid area provides a home for desert-loving wildlife and migrating birds.

Footpath leading to Kunuku Arikok, Arikok National Park

Sights at a Glance
1. Oranjestad
2. California Dunes and Lighthouse
3. Palm Beach
4. Eagle Beach
5. Arikok National Park
6. *Willemstad pp484–5*
7. Curaçao Sea Aquarium
8. Christoffel National Park
9. Kralendijk
10. Rincón
11. Washington Slagbaai National Park
12. Kaminda Goto
13. Pekelmeer

The wide Queen Emma Bridge in Willemstad, Curaçao

0 kilometers   10
0 miles   10

Washington Slagbaai National Park
This is the oldest nature sanctuary of the Netherlands Antilles and comprises two of the largest plantations on the island – Washington and Slagbaai.

Curaçao Sea Aquarium
The Curaçao Sea Aquarium is a large complex featuring at least 400 saltwater species.

Pekelmeer
Located on the south end of Bonaire, Pekelmeer is a protected sanctuary for flamingos. These birds fly in from Venezuela to lay eggs and hatch them.

0 kilometers   10
0 miles   10

Key

━━━ Major road

═══ Minor road

△ Peak

Getting Around

Aruba's Reina Beatrix International Airport, Curaçao's Hato International Airport and Bonaire's Flamingo International Airport are large airports with daily flights to and from other Caribbean islands, as well as international services. Ferries are not practical due to the long distances between the islands, and unpredictable sea conditions. Aruba has a good bus service that connects the airport, Oranjestad, and resorts along the west coast beaches. Bonaire has no public transportation, and Curaçao has limited bus and van service. Visitors must rely on tours or rental cars to explore the countryside. Taxis are also available on all three islands.

For additional map symbols see back flap

Cannons at Fort Zoutman, Oranjestad, Aruba

❶ Oranjestad

W coast of Aruba. 🏔 30,000. ✈ 🚌
🚢 cruise ship port. ℹ L.G. Smith
Boulevard, 297 582 3777. 🏪 daily
along waterfront. 🎭 Bonbini Festival
(Thu). 🌐 **aruba.com**

At the center of Aruba's capital,
Oranjestad, lies the Yacht Basin
and cruise ship port fronted
by brightly painted shops and
restaurants built in Dutch
colonial style. Lloyd G. Smith
Boulevard, the main roadway,
runs along the waterfront and
connects the town to the
popular tourist areas along the
northwest coast. Although the
town lacks major attractions,
it offers a pleasant diversion
from the beach.

At the south end of the town
lies Fort Zoutman, constructed
in 1796 and named for an
admiral in the Dutch navy.
Adjoining the fort is Willem III
Tower, which was built in 1868.
It is the best-preserved part and
used to serve as a lighthouse.
Across from the fort, on the

waterfront, is the Renaissance
Mall and marketplace, with
more than 100 upscale shops.
A couple of blocks inland, the
small **Archaeological Museum**
displays stone tools from 4,500
years ago found at Arikok and
Sero Muskita, and human bones
unearthed from the ruins of the
island's first Arawak inhabitants,
the Caiquetio. The **Numismatic
Museum** of Aruba houses a
coin collection that is far more
interesting than it sounds. There
are approximately 40,000 pieces
from 400 countries in this
treasury owned by the Mario
Odor family, who were avid
coin collectors, and each piece
is displayed with a written
account of its significance.

🏛 **Archaeological Museum**
Schelpstraat 42. **Tel** 297 582 8979.
Open 8am–noon & 1–4pm
Mon–Fri. 🈂

🏛 **Numismatic Museum**
Weststraat 7. **Tel** 297 582 8831.
Open 9am–4pm Mon–Thu, 9am–1pm
Fri, 9am–noon Sat. 🈂 🈂

❷ California Dunes and Lighthouse

7 miles (11 km) N of Oranjestad,
Aruba. 🈂 🈂

The main west coast highway
leads north to the California
Lighthouse at the tip of the
island. Just past the town of
Malmok is an elevated stretch
of isolated land known locally
as *hudishibana* (in the native
language once spoken by
the Caiquetio), but often
called the California Dunes.
Here, rolling mounds of white
sand spread across a desert
landscape, surrounding the
lighthouse which was designed
by a French architect in 1910
and constructed on the island
between 1914 and 1916.
The name comes from the S.S.
California, a wooden-hulled ship
with five masts that sank just
offshore in the late 1800s and
now is a popular dive site. The
lighthouse is closed to visitors,
but the views from its elevated
base are spectacular and include
the dunes, beaches, and the
greens of Tierra del Sol Country
Club *(see p494)*. Late in the afternoon, the view gets even more
breathtaking as the sun sets.

❸ Palm Beach

🚌 4 miles (6 km) NW of Oranjestad,
Aruba. 🈂 🈂 🈂

Ranked among the best in
the world, Palm Beach is a
long stretch of white sand lined
with luxurious upscale resorts,
restaurants, beach bars, and
watersports operators. Among

The California Lighthouse, surrounded by rolling dunes

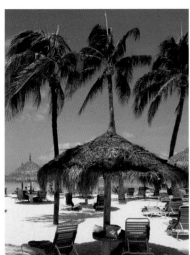
The immaculate Palm Beach, Aruba

the extravagant resorts, three Marriott complexes anchor the north end of the beach and sprawl across the landscaped grounds, which provide a flowering habitat for tropical birds. At the southern end, Divi Aruba Phoenix Beach Resort occupies the last bit of sand before a rocky outcrop that separates Palm from Eagle Beach.

Just opposite the resort is the **Butterfly Farm** featuring 40 species of butterflies *(see p488)*. There are interesting guided walks exploring the lifecycle of a butterfly. Just south of the high-rise Palm Beach hotels is an open marsh where birds are protected in Bubali Bird Sanctuary. The sanctuary attracts hundreds of migratory birds and bird-watchers.

Butterfly Farm
J. Irausquin Boulevard, Oranjestad.
Tel 297 586 3656. **Open** 9am–4pm daily. 🅿 🕙 🆆 **thebutterfly farm.com**

❹ Eagle Beach

🚏 2 miles (3.2 km) NW of Oranjestad, Aruba. 🅼 🚻 🛥

Eagle Beach is separated from Palm Beach by a rocky over-grown stretch of coastline. While Palm Beach is known

for non-stop action, Eagle Beach is more relaxed; motor-ized water-sports are not allowed offshore and shaded picnic tables draw many local families as well as guests from nearby low-rise resorts. The white-sand beach is wide and the water is calm and perfect for swimming. There are fewer bars and restaurants than on Palm Beach and the hotels reach no higher than the shady palm trees. Many pro-perties participate in the Green Globe Program signifying that they adhere to environmental-friendly policies and sustainable tourism standards.

❺ Arikok National Park

8 miles (12 km) E of Oranjestad, Aruba. 🅣 🅘 National Park Office, Santa Cruz, 297 585 1234. **Open** 7am–5pm daily (entrance hut); park open 24 hr daily. 🚗 at the entrance to caves. 🅿

The entrance to this ecological park is off Highway 7 A/B, east of the town of Santa Cruz. The park protects a large portion of land bordered on

the east by the sea. Within its boundaries are 21 miles (33 km) of marked hiking trails that wind through native flora, including divi-divi trees, rare cacti, aloe plants, and flowering bushes. Wildlife includes *conejos* (rabbits), indigenous *kododo blauw* (whiptail lizards), and the *cascabel* (rattlesnake).

A walking path beyond the entrance leads to Cunucu Arikok, a semi-restored farm at the foot of Cero Arikok, a 500-ft (150-m) tall hill that is the base of the airport's radar station. The farm has a typical country house made of mud-and-grass adobe and protected by the remains of a cactus fence and stone wall.

Heading east from the road at the entrance is a 2-mile (4-km) trail that leads to the highest point on the island, Mount Jamanota at 630 ft (189 m). The same road also leads visitors to the coastline which begins with sand dunes. The Dos Playa beach here is not ideal for swimming due to strong currents, but photographers will enjoy snapping shots of the unique landscape and sea vistas. There is a small snack bar here for a picnic.

From the snack bar, a road takes people to the Fontein Caves, where beautiful Indian rock paintings decorate the walls and ceilings. Near the caves is the Fontein Garden, which has a 19th-century plantation house. It is also the site for a museum displaying old tools.

Gigantic cacti growing in Arikok National Park

⊙ Street-by-Street: Willemstad

Designated a UNESCO World Heritage Site in 1997, historic
Willemstad is the capital of Curaçao. Its older area is made
up of distinct districts, with their architectural styles
reflecting the 17th-century Dutch colonization of the islands.
Sint Annabaai, a channel linking the sea to the inner harbor,
divides the central city into Otrobanda, a primarily residential
area, and Punda, the commercial hub. The much photographed
floating pontoon bridge, Queen Emma Bridge, spans the
channel and swings open to allow passage for ships.

Centuries-old Dutch style
buildings, Punda

Philatelic Museum, located
in a restored colonial building,
displays a large collection of
Netherlands Antilles stamps.

★ **Queen Emma Bridge**
One of the major landmarks
in Willemstad, the bridge was
designed by US businessman
Leonard B. Smith in 1888.

0 meters 50
0 yards 50

HANDELS KADE

HEERENSTR

KEUKENSTRAAT

BREEDESTRAAT

WATERFOR   TSTRA   A

★ **Fort Amsterdam**
Dating from 1635, Fort Amsterdam now houses a government
complex. It is painted in traditional bright colors of Dutch colonial
architecture. A small museum, set in the old fort church, still has
an English cannonball embedded in its southwestern wall.

For hotels and restaurants on these islands see pp496–8 and pp499–501

Floating Market
Merchants from Venezuela sell various products including fresh fish, meat, tropical fruits, vegetables, and spices from their boats at the Floating Market.

Key

— Suggested route

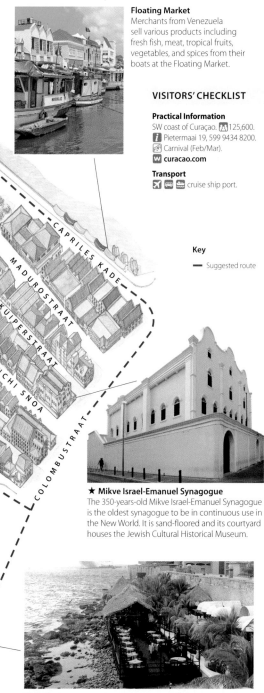

★ **Mikve Israel-Emanuel Synagogue**
The 350-years-old Mikve Israel-Emanuel Synagogue is the oldest synagogue to be in continuous use in the New World. It is sand-floored and its courtyard houses the Jewish Cultural Historical Museum.

Waterfort
Built in 1634 and renovated in 1827, the Waterfort is now a lively area with shops and restaurants overlooking the sea. Many of the fort's original turrets and vaults are still visible.

❼ Curaçao Sea Aquarium

3 miles (5 km) SE of Willemstad, Curaçao. **Tel** 599 9461 6666.
Open 8:30am–5:30pm daily.
🔗 **curacao-sea-aquarium.com**

Located on a large beach, this complex includes exhibits of more than 400 saltwater species in their natural environment. Touch tanks allow direct contact with sea stars, conchs, and urchins. Participants of all ages can snorkel or dive with rays, sharks, and turtles in the Animal Encounter program. Visitors can also touch, feed, and swim with dolphins and sea lions. The kids' programs include instruction on preserving reefs, and allow contact with endangered species. The adjoining Seaquarium Beach has sports outlets that rent watersports gear.

❽ Christoffel National Park

25 miles (40 km) NW of Willemstad, Curaçao. **Tel** 599 9864 0363.
Open 7am–4pm Mon–Sat, 6am–3pm Sun. 🔗 **carmabi.org**

Spread over what was once three plantations, Christoffel National Park now serves as Curaçao's prized eco-preserve. At the entrance, the Savonet Museum showcases the island's natural features and history through geological and archaeological exhibits. Four marked hiking trails wind through the 4,500-acre (1,821-ha) park. Hikers take on the challenge of the 1,240-ft (370-m) Mount Christoffel, that offers views of the rugged countryside. Color-coded driving routes lead to various areas of the sprawling park including the windward coast, noted for its ancient rock drawings and cave-riddled cliffs. Another route begins at Piedra de Monton, from where it winds past hillsides covered with wild orchids, to the coves of Santa Marta Bay and Seru Bientu.

Waterfront of Kralendijk, capital of Bonaire

❾ Kralendijk

W coast of Bonaire. 🚹 12,000. ✈️ 🚢 cruise ship port. ℹ️ Tourism Corporation Kaya Grandi 2, 599 717 8322. 🛍️ produce market at the pier & crafts market at Wilhelmina Park. 🌐 infobonaire.com

Bonaire's capital, Kralendijk, is a large, easygoing village about midway along the island's sharply-curved leeward coast. The town's main road runs parallel to the sea, so orientation and navigating is simple. The best way to get around is on foot. When a cruise ship is in port, the narrow streets transform into an outdoor marketplace and mini-festival. Artists, craftsmen, and cooks set up booths offering West Indian specialties and performers put their heart into island-style dance and cultural shows backed by local musicians. A daily produce market takes place in an open-air building near the town pier. Most of the permanent shops and restaurants line the two main roads, Kaya Craane, with a pretty waterfront promenade, and Kaya Grandi, a block inland.

Fort Oranje stands guard at the southern end of the town center. It is one of the oldest structures on Bonaire, built by the Dutch in 1639 and allotted four cannons to defend against the English, Spanish, and French. The stone tower was added in 1932, and the fort now houses government offices. Next door, the lovely two-story white-trimmed golden-yellow building also dates from the 19th century and is a fine example of Dutch-Caribbean architecture. The raised front porch and staircase is particularly attractive. Various government offices are located in the building, known as the Bestuurskantoor (government office). Neither of these two historic buildings is open to the public, but the **Museo Boneriano**, located a short walk from the town center, welcomes visitors. This beautifully restored plantation home was built at the end of the 19th century and has the original architectural plans on display inside. Other exhibits include a shell collection, ancient maps, and bits of island memorabilia, but the most interesting display is the building itself.

Signage, Kralendijk, Bonaire

🏛️ Museo Boneriano
Kaya J.C. van der Ree 7, at the junction of Kaya Sabana. **Tel** 599 717 8868. **Open** 8am–noon, 1:30–5pm Mon–Fri. 📷

❿ Rincón

11 miles (18 km) NW of Kralendijk, Bonaire. 🚹 1,800. 🛍️ first Sat of the month. 🎭 Dia de Rincón (Apr 30).

The oldest town on the island, Rincón (Spanish for corner), is rich in local flavor. It was founded by the Spanish late in the 1500s as an inland safe haven hidden from view of pirate ships. Later, the village became a community of former slaves and is the birthplace of many of the island's political and business leaders. There is little to see here, except on festival days, which occur with amazing frequency. Tradition and culture are important to the residents, and the town annually hosts a jubilant Dia de Rincón (Rincón Day) to celebrate the official birthday of the Queen of the Netherlands. At the center of the town, the impressive San Luis Bertran Church is considered a historical monument, even though the present structure was completed in 1984. Originally built in 1861, the church was destroyed by a hurricane in October 1907. The present church was rebuilt around the ruins beginning in 1977. On Market Day (Marshe Rincón), dozens of booths are set up along the main road to sell fresh fruits, plants, colorful handicrafts, and locally made foods.

San Lodovico Bertran Catholic Church in Rincón, Bonaire

For hotels and restaurants on these islands see pp496–8 and pp499–501

Renovated aloe oven, Washington Slagbaai National Park

⓫ Washington Slagbaai National Park

16 miles (26 km) NW of Kralendijk, Bonaire. 🚉 ℹ️ park entrance, 599 717 8444. **Open** 8am–5pm daily. **Closed** Christmas & New Year's Day. 📷 🚻 🏪 🏛 🅦 **washington parkbonaire.org**

Extending over 16,358 acres (6,620 ha), the Washington Slagbaai National Park covers about 20 percent of the northern part of the island. Dive sites, hiking trails, salt pans, a lake, and driving routes are within the boundaries of what originally comprised two of the largest plantations on the island, Washington and Slagbaai. The plantations, called *kunukus* in the local Papiamento language, grew the distinctive divi-divi trees for their pods, which were processed into tannin for use in tanning animal hides, and aloe plants for their sap, which was used as a laxative.

The Washington *kunuku* became a public park in 1969, and when the Slagbaai property was added in 1979, the area became the first nature sanctuary in the Netherlands Antilles. Parrots, flamingos, iguanas, and parakeets are a few of the many endemic species that live within the park. The beaches provide nesting grounds for all four species of Caribbean sea turtles, and the park is part of the Ramsar Convention, an international treaty that protects wetlands and their inhabitants. The Visitors' Center, located at the park entrance, has many of the original plantation-era structures still intact and is a good place to pick up maps and information. A museum, set in the former main house, displays historical, archaeological, and geological information about the island and its native plants and wildlife. Highlights of the park include the 784-ft (238-m) Brandaris Hill, the highest point on the island; Pos di Mangel, a key area for bird-watching; Boca Chikitu, a rocky cove backed by sand dunes; Playa Funchi and Boca Slagbaai, the prime snorkeling beaches. Two dirt driving tracks wind through the park: Yellow, making a 21-mile (33-km) sweep along the north coast and Green, a 14-mile (24-km) stretch connecting sites in the middle of the park. Nature lovers will want to spend time on the walking paths starting at the Visitors' Center and the hiking-biking trails up to Brandaris and Pos di Mangel. The fresh water lake at Pos di Mangel attracts large flocks of birds.

⓬ Kaminda Goto

9 miles (15 km) NW of Kralendijk, Bonaire.

Kaminda Goto is a road that follows the shores of Lake Goto (Gotomeer), on the southwest border of the national park. The road up to the landlocked saltwater Lake Goto offers excellent close-up views of flocks of flamingos that nest and feed around the water. The birds are shy, but are most interested in food and preening, so patient watchers have a good chance of getting a proper look at these fascinating creatures. Benches at the paved and bricked Salina Grande viewing area provide a good place to sit and watch the birds.

⓭ Pekelmeer

13 miles (21 km) S of Kralendijk, Bonaire.

At the far south end of Bonaire, Pekelmeer is a protected sanctuary for Southern Caribbean flamingos. Many of them come from Venezuela, 50 miles (18 km) away, to breed and tend their young. During hatching season, as many as 2,500 chicks are born. The nests are easy to spot, as they are 1 ft (0.3 m) tall and about 2 ft (0.6 m) wide.

Other birds also nest and feed here, including heron, osprey and other marine birds. Morning and late afternoon are the best times to see the birds in flight, but visitors are advised to stay in their cars to avoid disturbing the birds.

The rocky coastline at Boka Chikitu, Washington Slagbaai National Park, Bonaire

Driving on Aruba, Curaçao, and Bonaire

Aruba, Curaçao, and Bonaire are each small enough to tour by car in a single day. Cruise-ship passengers can see all the highlights and be back on the ship in time for dinner, but visitors with more time may stop at key attractions. Tour operators offer around-the-island excursions and many taxi drivers are knowledgeable guides. However, the best way to discover the islands' unique features is on a self-guided driving tour. The main roads are paved but secondary roads may be rough and some pass through rugged terrain.

ARUBA, CURAÇAO, AND BONAIRE

ARUBA CURAÇAO BONAIRE

Caribbean Sea

⑦ The mysterious Casibari Rock Formations, Aruba

Aruba

Aruba is a two-faced beauty with glamorous west coast beaches and a high-energy downtown area while its sunburned interior is strewn with curious rock formations. About 3 miles (5 km) from Oranjestad lies **Butterfly Farm** ①, a mesh-enclosed garden teeming with butterflies from all over the world *(see p483).* A visit in the morning is best as the butterflies are most active and newborns emerge.

Another 2 miles (3 km) away is Noord village, inland from Palm Beach. Its little **Santa Anna Church** ② is where brides often choose to be married. The solid oak altar was carved in Neo-Gothic style by Dutch craftsman Hendrik van der Geld in the 1870s. Some 2 miles (3 km) from Noord stands the **Chapel of Alto Vista** ③. Known as the pilgrim's church, this tiny yellow chapel is one of the most photographed buildings on the island. Constructed by native Indians and Spanish settlers, it was rebuilt in 1952. The tranquil site is on a spectacular bluff above the sea with white

crosses lining its narrow paved road. At 6 miles (10 km) from Noord are the **Bushiribana Gold Mine Ruins** ④. A rock heap and a crumbling stone wall is all that remains of the Aruba Island Gold Mining Company, but the views from here are great. **Boca Andicuri Natural Bridge** ⑤ is 2 miles (3 km) east of Bushiribana. The famous long stretch of limestone at Boca Andicuri unexpectedly collapsed in 2005 but still holds the curiosity of visitors. Another natural bridge is still standing on the southern curve of Andicuri Bay. About 2 miles (3 km) inland from Andicuri are the **Ayo Rock Formations** ⑥. These boulders resemble images from a space fantasy and geologists cannot explain how they came to be on the otherwise flat island. Nearby caves have pictographs left by native inhabitants. Similar boulders are also found at **Casibari Rock Formations** ⑦, located about 2 miles (3 km) farther inland.

③ The charming Chapel of Alto Vista, overlooking the north coast

Palm Beach
① **Noord** ②
Oranjestad · **Calbas**
Boca Wariruri
③
④
Boca Mahos
Aruba
Andicuri Bay
⑤
Paradera
⑦
⑥

Key to all Maps

— Minor road

— Major road

0 kilometers   2

0 miles   2

Curaçao

Locals call the eastern part of Curaçao Banda Riba, which means upwind. The countryside is dotted with developments, yacht-filled harbors, and a few

③ Dinah Veeris in her Botanic and Historic Garden

tourist sites. About 70 *landhuizen* (old plantation homes), with Dutch colonial architecture, sit on hill tops. In Salina Ariba, 2 miles (3 km) east of the capital, Willemstad, is the **Senior Curaçao Liqueur Distillery** ①. Housed in the 17th-century Landhuis Chobolobo, this distillery still uses 19th-century equipment to make the famous cordial from dried orange skins. Guided tours include an overview of the production process. The liqueur is sold in quaint bottles at the adjacent gift shop. About 3 miles (5 km) from the capital are **Spanish Water and Caracasbaai** ②.

Curaçao liqueur bottle

These trendy developments are popular with young locals and yacht owners. Visitors can enjoy a meal at the Landhuis Brakkeput Mei Mei in Spanish Water and a tour of Fort Beekenburg at Caracasbaai. **Dinah's Botanic and Historic Garden (Den Paradara)** ③ lies 6 miles (10 km) east of the capital. The scent of herbs lures visitors to this garden featuring local plants that have been used for centuries as folk medicines. It has a model village and lodge built by Amazon Indians and the owner Dinah Veeris tells visitors about it. The largest farm of its type outside Africa, the **Ostrich and Game Farm** ④ is 7 miles (11 km) from Willemstad. Tours on zebra-striped jeeps let visitors watch the world's largest birds closely and feed them. Hand-crafted products from Africa are on sale at the African Art Shop. To the north of the capital lie the **Hato Caves** ⑤, 4 miles (7 km) away. These caves were formed millions of years ago, when Curaçao was underwater. There are underground waterfalls, a lake, and chambers with stalagmites, stalactites, and hundreds of bats.

Bonaire

Bonaire's sun-drenched, quiet countryside has many natural attractions. Eco-tourists treasure the protected areas and a drive around the island reveals long stretches of desert landscape punctuated by surprising beauty. **Donkey Paradise Safari Park** ① lies 2 miles (4 km) south of Kralendijk. When donkeys become old, injured, or orphaned, they find refuge here and live along with an assortment of iguanas, turtles, and birds. About 4 miles (7 km) east of Kralendijk is **Rooi Lamoenchi Kunuku Park** ②. Plantation estates are called *kunuku* in Bonaire, and this is one of the best

preserved. Guided tours include a visit to the historic plantation house, aloe fields, and gardens filled with native plants and wildlife. On Lac Bay the **Mangrove Information Center** ③, 4 miles (7 km) southeast of the capital, works with The Netherlands's Rotterdam Zoo to investigate the endangered environment of mangrove forests. Guided kayak or boat tours take visitors through this site. Small stone huts that once served as quarters for African slaves are located at **Witte Pan** ④, 7 miles (11 km) south of the

main coastal road from Kralendijk. During the 1800s, Dutch companies used slave labor to process and export salt to Europe. The workers were housed in the tiny huts where five or six people slept on the floor.

Outdoor Activities and Specialized Holidays

Visitors to Aruba, Curaçao, and Bonaire often plan their holiday around specific outdoor activities. While Aruba draws people who prefer to just lie on the beach with a good book, Curaçao appeals to those who love sightseeing and exploring the island to break up the beach time. Bonaire attracts adventurous scuba divers and snorkelers. The tour operators on the three islands also offer thrilling inventive eco-tour packages such as night kayaking through mangroves or snorkeling through coastal caves, and sightseeing on a motorcyle.

Palm Beach, Aruba, one of the busiest beaches on the three islands

Beaches

Aruba has the best beaches and liveliest beach life. Palm and Eagle Beaches *(see pp482–3)* are the most well-known. To the north, Arashi and Malmok are less crowded while Hadicurari, between Malmok and Palm, is the site of an annual windsurfing competition. In the south, Sereo Colorado is popular with families. On the windward side of the island, most of the beaches are rocky and strong currents make it risky for swimming.

Curaçao's beaches on the windward side also have strong tides, making swimming dangerous. On the leeward side, the sand is often mixed with coral. Mambo Beach, near Willemstad, has a long stretch of white sand while Jan Thiel Beach has little sand but people can relax along the cement quays along the bay.

Signage on Palm Beach, Aruba

At the far northwest end of the island, Westpunt Beach is well-known for its towering cliffs. The area is dramatic but better sand is found to the south at Knip Bay Beach.

Bonaire is known for fantastic diving, though the beaches are not-so-fantastic as most are rocky. Boca Cocolishi has lovely black sand, and is ideal for snorkeling. Playa Funchi has a strong current far out from the shore, but a shallow shelf closer in has fine coral that draws hundreds of fish. Lac Cai is piled high with conch shells and is popular with locals on weekends, while Pink Beach is often named as one of the most spectacular of the Caribbean due to its pink hue in the late-afternoon sunlight, which comes from its sand being mixed with bits of red coral. Out on Klein Bonaire, an island off Kralendijk, is a pleasant palm-shaded beach called Turtle Beach. The beach can be reached by water taxis.

Diving and Snorkeling

Bonaire is recognized as the best scuba and snorkeling destination in the Southern Antilles, mainly due to its protected marine parks. Beaches slope steeply and drop off into deeper waters, which makes it easy for divers to enter the ocean from the shore. Curaçao also has protected virgin sites with large coral formations sheltering an abundance of marine life, and some of its most popular dive locations feature shallow reefs that slope to magnificent walls. Aruba is known for its sunken wrecks that include several ships which were torpedoed during World War II and two airplanes that were deliberately sunk to create artificial reefs.

Each island has various programs to sustain and improve the growth of their coral reefs and protect underwater wildlife. Visitors are told to avoid stepping on the coral or anchoring boats in protected waters. In addition, all marine life is protected, so fishing and shell collecting is not allowed. Visibility is routinely high throughout the area, and snorkelers can often see underwater reefs and fish at depths of 50 ft (15 m). Divers report visibility of 100 ft (30 m) or more, except during and right after a storm. All three islands offer snorkeling and scuba excursions. Rental operators are **Bonaire Dive & Adventure**, **Ocean Encounters**, **Red Sail Sports**, and **Dive Aruba**.

Scuba divers getting ready to explore the waters off Aruba

Diving off Bonaire

Bonaire's National Marine Park protects some of the healthiest reefs in the world, and scuba divers enjoy exploring more than 80 named sites, many accessible after a short boat ride. Water off the leeward side is sheltered by the island's reverse-C-curve shape, providing excellent conditions for learners and novice divers, while the more exposed sites near the north and south coasts present plenty of challenges for experienced divers. With little rainfall and virtually no tropical storms to stir up the sea, underwater visibility is consistently 100 ft (30 m) or more. Several sites have pretty reefs that extend to depths of about 200 ft (60 m), making Bonaire a popular destination for experienced divers.

Under the Sea

Thriving coral formations grow close to the shore in fairly shallow water, which allows snorkelers fabulous opportunities to observe a wide variety of tropical fish, rays, and other marine life.

Caribbean reef octopuses are easy to spot at night as their blue-green skin is reflective, and they feed in shallow coastal seagrass beds.

BONAIRE

KLEIN
BONAIRE

*Caribbean
Sea*

Elkhorn coral gets its name from antler-like branches that grow up to 4 inches (10 cm) per year; one of the fastest growing corals.

Site map

☐ Novice divers
■ Experienced divers

Yellow goatfish are night feeders.

Scuba divers use flashlight to observe fish.

Brain coral grows in a spherical shape.

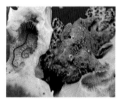

Frog fish which changes colors to camouflage itself crawls along the sea floor using its bottom fins as feet.

Diving Resorts

Diving resorts serve as one-stop destinations for vacationers who want to spend most of their time in or under water.

Diving lessons begin in shallow water near the shore. Even beginners may dive with an instructor during a discovery class.

Buddy Dive Resort is one of the several hotels in Bonaire that cater to divers with packaged vacations.

Windsurfing in Aruba

Sportfishing

The islands of Aruba, Bonaire, and Curaçao offer many choices to the fishing enthusiasts. Charter boats locate large schools of tuna, dolphin, and bonito, while fishermen catch tarpon and snook using squid and sardines for bait. Most charter fishing is on a catch-and-release basis. Fresh fish cannot be brought back into most countries and the islands prohibit visitors from selling their catch. On Aruba and Curaçao, charter boats have fishing licenses that cover their clients, so individuals need not apply for their own non-commercial license. Everyone who uses the waters of Bonaire's National Marine Park must pay a nature fee and receive a usage tag, which also allows complimentary admission to Washington Slagbaai National Park. The tags are available through watersports operators, marinas, and most hotels. The main operators are **Mahi Mahi**, **Piscatur Fishing Charters**, **Multifish Charters**, **Curaçao Activities**, and **Captain Boots**.

Wind Surfing

Bonaire is a popular vacation destination for surfers, with windsurfing as the dominant sport followed by kiteboarding. Lightweight kites and sails, safety release systems and high-tech boards make surfing sports fun for all skill levels. While Curaçao is still in a nascent stage, Aruba is rapidly gaining recognition as a world-class surfing destination. All three islands have full-service operators that offer expert advice and top-of-the-line equipment rentals. Aruba's Hi-Winds Pro Am Windsurfing Competition is a windsurfing event for all skill levels held at Hadikurari Beach each summer, with contestants coming from more than 30 countries. On Bonaire, Lac Bay is one of the best-known spots among international windsurfing and kiteboarding enthusiasts due to its clear water, consistent on-shore breezes, and excellent facilities.

Curaçao has a loosely organized surfing club and a couple of shops that set up events, give lessons, and rent equipment. Locals usually meet at secluded coves on the eastern end of the island, while surfing operators are located at Caracas Bay on the south shore and St. Joris Bay on the north shore. The operators are **Jibe City**, **Aruba Active Vacations**, **Kitesurfing Aruba**, and **Windsurfing Curaçao**.

Windsurfing sign at Sorobon Beach, Bonaire

Watersports

Jet Ski rentals, parasailing, waterskiing, and wakeboarding are all centered on Palm Beach in Aruba. On Curaçao, outfitters specialize in providing the latest water-based activities. On Bonaire, motorized watersports are almost nonexistent, due to restrictions within the marine park and visitors tend to be interested in underwater and wind-powered sports.

The islands have ideal conditions for kayaking in the swampy mangroves, and various operators lead eco trips. Instruction is also available for sea kayaking. Operators are **Pelican Watersports**, **Aruba Watersport Center**, and **Caribbean Sea Sports**.

Boating and Sailing

There is no better way to see the coastal areas than by boat. Day sails and theme cruises give visitors a chance to explore sites that are inaccessible from land. Day-sail tours include **Jolly Pirates**, **Bounty Adventures**, and **Samur Sailing Charters**. Long-term private charters are possible and when booking a trip, ask how many passengers will be on board as the difference between a good and a fantastic cruise is the amount of open space on the boat. Party boats are popular on Aruba, and all three islands offer sunset cruises.

Motorboats, Hobie Cat sailboats, and other small watercraft may be rented for sightseeing. The rental agencies are **Adrenaline Tours** and **Insulinde** in Curaçao, **De Palm Tours** in Aruba, and **Woodwing Sailing** in Bonaire.

Watersport equipment for hire on Palm Beach, Aruba

Sailing Trips

Aruba, Curaçao, and Bonaire have been a safe harbor for sailors for more than 500 years. The islands are outside the hurricane belt and rarely experience tropical storms, so the calm seas surrounding the coasts are perfect for day sails that include snorkeling off remote islands, such as Klein Curaçao, and sunset cruises offering elaborate snacks and drinks. Some outfitters also offer an adventure aboard a pirate ship, Asian junk, or multi-mast schooner. Crews often dress to match the ship's design or the sailing theme and even add themed music and entertainment to fit the occasion. Night cruises are also a wonderful experience not to be missed.

Themed cruises with Jolly Pirates include one-day sailing tour. It is a day of fun aboard a finely-crafted 85-ft (26-m) gaff-rigged sailing yacht, designed like a pirate ship.

Activities such as snorkeling are common on day-sails. Visitors are assisted by knowledgeable crew members who point out amazing underwater sights.

Night cruises are a unique experience. Diving or snorkeling after dark is fantastic as sea creatures slumber, graze, and hunt in secret after the sun goes down.

Passengers aboard Samur wait to watch the green flash, a phenomenon that sometimes appears in the sky at sundown in Bonaire.

Shipwrecks along the shore of Klein Curaçao are a fascinating sight. Many leading tour operators offers day trips to see the wrecks.

Fantastic buffets are usually served to daytrippers on private charters, either aboard the boat or at a private beach. Some of these are included in the price.

Cyclists taking a break on the northwest coast of Bonaire

Hiking

With national parks and good hiking conditions on all three islands, hiking and related activities such as climbing, rappeling, and caving are becoming more common. On Aruba, Arikok National Park (*see p483*) is great for hiking, and trail maps for self-guided hikes are available at the visitors' center. On the eastern point of the island, the cliffs in the Grapefield area are popular with climbers and explorers. Curaçao has more than three dozen marked trails and outfitters such as **Curaçao Actief** offer guided hikes. Christoffel National Park (*see p485*) provides information on all activities available in the park, such as hiking and climbing. On Bonaire, Washington Slagbaai National Park (*see p487*) has 21 miles (33 km) of dirt road and three signed trails, including a moderately rigorous trek up Brandaris, the highest point on the island. Hiking companies are **Sensitive Hikers**, **Bonaire Dive & Adventure**, and **Outdoor Bonaire**.

Cycling

Mountain bikers often use the same trails as hikers on the islands, and guided tours are available through operators such as **Pablito's Bike Rental**, and **Wanna Bike**. Washington Slagbaai Park on Bonaire does not have any rental facilities for bikes, but visitors may bring their own gear rented from operators such as **De Freewieler**. All biking begins early morning as the park staff recommends it. Christoffel on Curaçao has several moderate to difficult bike

routes that go past secluded coves, caves with ancient drawings on the walls, and the island's highest peak, Christoffelberg. Rangers at Arikok on Aruba provide information about touring the dirt trails by mountain bike. The routes start near the entrance and go on to Kunuku Arikok and Cero Arikok.

Jeep and ATV Tours

Jeeps and All Terrain Vehicles (ATVs) can reach remote places where cars and buses cannot. Group and private excursions offer trips into the countryside and along the windward coasts on all three islands. Those who want to let someone else do the driving can sign on for a jeep tour while joining a guided ATV tour offers a bigger thrill. On Aruba, Four Wheelin't at **Rancho Daimari**, **Aruba Jeep Safari**, and **ABC Tours** schedules jeep excursions. There are 4-hour and full-day trips on Curaçao arranged by **Eric's ATV Adventures** which includes trips to caves. Contact **Rento Fun Drive** for exciting tours to remote sites on Bonaire.

Visitors on ATVs near Bushiribana Gold Mine Ruins, Aruba

Golf

Bonaire does not have a golf course, but Curaçao and Aruba have lovely 18-hole courses. On Curaçao, the **Blue Bay Golf** course and the **Old Quarry Golf Course** (both on the grounds of plantations) offer fantastic views overlooking the sea. At **Tierra del Sol Country Club** on Aruba, the 18-hole golf course, designed by owner Robert Trent Jones II highlights the dramatic contrast between desert landscapes and ocean vistas.

Horseback-riding at a ranch in Aruba

Horse-Riding

Guided tours through the countryside and along the coasts are offered on all three islands. Hotels and multi-activity operators, **The Riding Academy Club** can make arrangements for visitors, and stables such as **Rancho Alegre** also may be contacted directly. Some rides include a seaside picnic or trips along secluded beaches.

Tennis

Many resorts on the islands have tennis courts for use by registered guests, and some allow non-guests for a fee. On Aruba, courts can be found at resorts such as Occidental Grand Aruba, Divi Village Golf & Beach Resort, and Tierra del Sol Resort, Spa & Country Club (*see p496*), **Aruba Tennis Academy** also welcomes visitors. On Bonaire, the best courts are at **Harbor Village Beach Club Tennis Center**. Most of the upscale resorts have courts for visitors on Curaçao.

DIRECTORY

Diving and Snorkeling

Bonaire Dive & Adventure
Kaya Gobernador N
Debrot 77A, Kralendijk,
Bonaire.
Tel 599 717 2229.
W bonairedive
andadventure.com

Dive Aruba
Renaissance Marina,
Oranjestad, Aruba.
Tel 297 582 7337.
W divearuba.com

Ocean Encounters
Seaquarium – Mambo
Beach, Curaçao.
Tel 599 9461 8131.
W oceanencounters.
com

Red Sail Sports
L.G. Smith Boulevard 17,
Oranjestad, Aruba.
Tel 297 586 1603.
W aruba-redsail.com

Sportfishing

Captain Boots
Kimi Kalki Marina,
Curaçao.
Tel 599 513 2747.
W captainboots.com

Curaçao Activities
Willemstad, Curaçao.
Tel 599 9465 1664.
W curacaoactivities.
com

Mahi Mahi
Seaport Marina,
Oranjestad, Aruba.
Tel 297 587 0538.
W aruba-mahimahi.
com

Multifish Charters
Harbor Village Marina,
Bonaire.
Tel 599 786 1228.
W multifish.com

Piscatur Fishing Charters
Kaya J. Pop 4, Kralendijk,
Bonaire.
Tel 599 717 8774.
W bonairefishing.com/
piscatur

Wind Surfing

Aruba Active Vacations
Fisherman's Huts,
Hadikurari Beach, Aruba.
Tel 297 586 0989.
W aruba-active-
vacations.com

Jibe City
Lac Bay, Bonaire.
Tel 599 717 5233.
W jibecity.com

Kitesurfing Aruba
Fisherman's Huts,
Hadikurari Beach, Aruba.
Tel 297 733 1515.
W kitesurfingaruba.
com

Windsurfing Curaçao
Caracasbaai, Curaçao.
Tel 599 9738 4555.
W windsurfingcuracao.
com

Watersports

Aruba Watersport Center
J.E. Irausquin Boulevard
81b, Palm Beach, Aruba.
Tel 297 586 6613.
W arubawatersport
center.com

Caribbean Sea Sports
John F. Kennedy
Boulevard, Marriott
Resort, Curaçao.
Tel 599 9462 2620.
W caribseasports.com

Pelican Watersports
J.E. Irausquin Blvd 232,
Oranjestad, Aruba.
Tel 297 587 2302.
W pelican-aruba.com

Boating and Sailing

Adrenaline Tours
Jan Thiel Beach, Curaçao.
Tel 599 767 6241.
W adrenalinetours
curacao.com

Bounty Adventures
W bountyadventures.
com

De Palm Tours
Oranjestad, Aruba.
Tel 297 582 4400.
W depalmtours.com

Insulinde
Punda, Curaçao.
Tel 599 9560 1340.
W insulinde.com

Jolly Pirates
W jolly-pirates.com

Samur Sailing Charters
W samursailing.com

Woodwind Sailing
Kaya Seminole 3,
Bonaire.
Tel 599 786 7055.
W woodwindbonaire.
com

Hiking

Bonaire Dive & Adventure
Kaya Gobernador N.
Debrot 77A, Kralendijk,
Bonaire.
Tel 599 717 2229.
W bonairediveanda
dventure.com

Curaçao Actief
Willemstad, Curaçao.
Tel 599 9433 8858.
W curacao-actief.com

Outdoor Bonaire
Road to Lac Bay
Kralendijk, Bonaire.
Tel 599 791 6272.
W outdoorbonaire.com

Sensitive Hikers
Oranjestad, Aruba.
Tel 297 594 5017.
W sensitivehikers.com

Cycling

De Freewieler
Kaya Grandi 61,
Kralendijk, Bonaire.
Tel 599 717 8545.

Pablito's Bike Rental
L. G. Smith Boulevard,
Oranjestad, Aruba.
Tel 297 587 8655.

Wanna Bike
W wannabike.com

Jeep and ATV Tours

ABC Tours
Tel 297 582 5600.
W abc-aruba.com

Aruba Jeep Safari
Oranjestad, Aruba.
Tel 297 582 5600.
W abc-aruba.com

Eric's ATV Adventures
Kaya Serafin 63,
Willemstad, Curaçao.
Tel 599 9524 7418.
W curacaoatv.com

Rancho Daimari
Noord, Aruba.
Tel 297 748 4559.
W arubarancho
daimari.com

Rento Fun Drive
Kaya Grandi 47,
Kralendijk, Bonaire.
Tel 599 717 2408.
W rentofunbonaire.com

Golf

Blue Bay Golf
Landhuis Blauw, Curaçao.
Tel 599 9868 1755.
W bluebay-curacao.com

Old Quarry Golf Course
Santa Barbara Plantation,
Nieuwpoort, Fuik, Curaçao.
Tel 599 9840 6886.
W oldquarrygolf
curacao.com

Tierra del Sol Country Club
Tel 297 586 0978.
W tierradelsol.com

Horse-Riding

Rancho Alegre Club
Landhuis Groot,
St. Michiel.
Tel 599 868 1181.

The Riding Academy Club
Kunuku Warahama,
Bonaire.
Tel 599 560 7949.
W infobonaire.com/
ridingacademy/

Tennis

Aruba Tennis Academy
Oranjestad, Aruba.
Tel 297 583 7074.
W tennisaruba.com

Harbor Village Beach Club Tennis Center
W harbourvillage.com

Where to Stay

Impressive exterior of the Westin Resort & Casino, Palm Beach, Aruba

Aruba

EAGLE BEACH: Manchebo Beach Resort & Spa $$
Beach Resort
JE Irausquin Boulevard 55
Tel *888 673 8036*
w manchebo.com
Enjoy a Caribbean-Balinese spa and yoga classes at this peaceful resort on the beach. Guests are welcomed with mojitos. Elegant rooms with dark wood furnishings.

DK Choice

EAGLE BEACH: Bucuti & Tara Beach Resorts $$$
Beach Resort
LG Smith Boulevard 55B
Tel *888 428 2884*
w bucuti.com
An award-winning, eco-friendly, adults-only retreat set on a lovely beach. Luxurious amenities include pillow-top mattresses and upmarket toiletries. The oceanfront Tara Suites have the best views. There is a champagne welcome, complimentary breakfast, and romantic beachside dining.

NOORD: My Aruban Home $
Apartments
Bakval 15A
Tel *297 593 3367*
w myarubanhome.com
Tastefully furnished one-bedroom units with living areas and kitchenettes, close to the beach.

NOORD: Caribbean Palm Village Resort $$
Apartments
Noord 43E, Palm Beach Road
Tel *297 526 2875*
w cpvr.com
An inland resort with studios and one- and two-bedroom units with kitchens. Free beach shuttle.

NOORD: Tierra del Sol Resort, Spa & Country Club $$$
Boutique
Caya di Solo 10
Tel *297 586 7800*
w tierradelsol.com
A collection of luxury villas, suites, and condo units adjacent to an 18-hole golf course. Pool, access to Arashi Beach, tennis courts.

ORANJESTAD: Aruba Harmony Apartments $
Apartments
Palmitastraat 9
Tel *297 593 7661*
w arubaharmony.com
This apartment complex offers modern studios and suites with kitchens and terraces. In a central location, near the airport, shops, beaches, and restaurants.

ORANJESTAD: Paradera Park Apartments $
Apartments
Paradera 203
Tel *297 582 3289*
w paraderapark-aruba.com
A complex with one- and two-bedroom units, lush gardens, and a pool. Close to Oranjestad shops and sightseeing.

ORANJESTAD: Divi Village Golf & Beach Resort $$
Beach Resort
JE Irausquin Boulevard 93
Tel *800 367 3484*
w diviresorts.com/divivillage
In addition to studios and one- and two-bedroom suites, Divi Village offers restaurants, a tennis court, and a golf course. A white-sand beach is across the street.

ORANJESTAD: Tamarijn Aruba All-Inclusive $$$
Beach Resort
JE Irausquin Boulevard 41, Druif Beach
Tel *800 554 2008*
w tamarijnaruba.com
A low-rise resort on the harbor with basic accommodations and a good beach. Meals and drinks included. Guests can use facilities at Divi Village at no extra charge.

PALM BEACH: Amsterdam Manor Beach Resort $$
Beach Resort
JE Irausquin Boulevard 252
Tel *297 527 1100*
w amsterdammanor.com
Ideal for families, this low-rise Dutch Colonial resort has suites with kitchenettes. There is a pool with waterfall, plus a kids' pool on the beach and two restaurants.

Price Guide	
Prices are based on one night's stay in high season for a standard double room, inclusive of service charges and taxes.	
$	up to $200
$$	$200–400
$$$	over $400

PALM BEACH: Brickell Bay Beach Club & Spa $$
Boutique
JE Irausquin Boulevard 370
Tel *297 586 0900*
w brickellbayaruba.com
Right across from the beach, this hotel offers stylish rooms and luxury touches such as nightly turndown service, free calls to the US and Canada, and complimentary bottled water.

PALM BEACH: Occidental Grand Aruba $$$
Luxury
JE Irausquin Boulevard 83
Tel *297 586 4500*
w occidentalhotels.com
A self-contained resort with restaurants, pools, tennis courts, a casino, a shopping arcade, and a kids' program. All rooms have views. Complimentary breakfasts.

PALM BEACH: Riu Palace Aruba $$$
Luxury
JE Irausquin Boulevard 79
Tel *297 586 3900*
w riu.com
Staying at this hotel right on the beach is like being on a cruise ship, with all meals, drinks, and activities included. There are five restaurants, three pools, a spa, and watersports.

PALM BEACH: Westin Resort & Casino $$$
Luxury
JE Irausquin Boulevard 77
Tel *297 586 4466*
w westinaruba.com
Amenities at this large resort include a beach, a spa, a casino, a selection of restaurants, a kids' program, and a theater with nightly magic shows. Island. All rooms have balconies.

SAVENETA: Club Arias Bed & Breakfast $$
B&B
123-K Saveneta
Tel *297 593 3408*
w clubarias.com
Located in the oldest town on the island, this small inn offers personal service by the owners. Suites with kitchenettes. A short walk to Saveneta Beach

Bonaire

BELNEM: Bellafonte Chateau de la Mer $
Modern
EEG Boulevard 10
Tel *599 717 3333*
W bellafontebonaire.com
An elegant oceanfront resort with a boardwalk leading to the sea, this is ideal for snorkelers and divers. Studios, plus one- and two-bedroom suites.

BELNEM: Hotel Roomer $
Modern
EEG Boulevard 97
Tel *599 717 7488*
W roomerbonaire.com
A small inland hotel offering simple but comfortable rooms, a good restaurant, and plenty of facilities for divers. Excellent service by the owners.

BELNEM: Belmar Oceanfront Apartments $$
Apartments
EEG Boulevard 88
Tel *599 717 7878*
W belmar-bonaire.com
Oceanfront complex with one- to three-bedroom apartments with contemporary decor. All terraces offer great ocean views. Dive packages are available, and there is a dive shop on site.

KRALENDIJK: Auriga Ecolodge $
Eco Lodge
Rancho San Miguel 100, Bara di Carta
Tel *599 785 6272*
W ecolodgebonaire.com
An environment-friendly two-bedroom lodge in the countryside east of the town. There are hammocks and a sky-gazing platform. Hiking tours and activities are offered through Outdoor Bonaire *(see p495).*

DK Choice

KRALENDIJK: Eden Beach Resort $
Beach Resort
Kaya Gobernador N Debrot 73
Tel *599 717 6720*
W edenbeach.com
A serene property with one of the best beaches on the island, Eden Beach Resort offers studios, one-bedroom suites, and two-bedroom apartments. Instruction in free diving is a highlight. There are facilities for divers and a dive center right on the property, along with an oceanview fitness center and spa.

KRALENDIJK: Sonrisa Boutique Hotel $
Modern
Kaya Finlandia 1/3
Tel *599 717 6633*
W sonrisabonaire.com
In the heart of town, but close to the beach, this comfortable hotel has pleasant rooms and apartments with kitchens. Complimentary breakfasts.

KRALENDIJK: Bamboo Bali Bonaire Resort $$
Modern
Kaya Gobernador N Debrot 86
Tel *599 700 6933*
W bamboobalibonaire.com
Intimate resort with one-bedroom Asian-style bungalows amid lush tropical gardens. Truck rental is included in the rate. Close to dive shops, restaurants, and shopping.

KRALENDIJK: Captain Don's Habitat $$
Beach Resort
Kaya Gobernador N Debrot 103
Tel *599 717 8290*
W habitatbonaire.com
Hotel rooms, suites, bungalows, and apartments are available at this eco-friendly oceanfront resort. A dive operator offers tours and shore diving.

KRALENDIJK: Coral Paradise Resort $$
Beach Resort
Kaya Gobernador N Debrot 107
Tel *877 267 2572*
W coralparadise.com
A warm welcome awaits guests at this small, but charming resort on the beach. Adjacent to a dive shop. Truck rental included in the rate.

KRALENDIJK: Divi Flamingo Beach Resort and Casino $$
Beach Resort
JA Abraham Boulevard 40
Tel *599 717 8285*
W diviresorts.com
Called a "diver's paradise," this resort is heavily oriented toward

divers, with daily trips, instruction, gear, and excellent shore diving and snorkeling facilities. Rooms have ocean or garden views.

KRALENDIJK: La Pura Vista $$
Modern
Kaya Turkesa 7
Tel *599 717 6582*
W lapuravista.com
This luxurious five-bedroom hillside villa is available for adults only. There is one studio, three deluxe guest rooms, and one suite with a Jacuzzi, as well as a communal kitchen and barbecue area.

KRALENDIJK: Harbour Village Beach Club $$$
Beach Resort
Kaya Gobernador N Debrot 71
Tel *800 424 0004*
W harbourvillage.com
A luxury beachfront resort on the peninsula, Harbour Village has a marina, tennis courts, a center for watersports, with diving equipment and instruction, and a spa. One- and two-bedroom suites have sofa beds and kitchens.

KRALENDIJK: Bonaire Sunset Villa $$$
Modern
Hamlet Oasis
Tel *599 786 8602*
This five-bedroom oceanfront villa has a sun deck near the ocean, a roof terrace for sunbathing, a large kitchen, and outdoor dining areas. Minimum four-person rental.

LAC BAY: LacBaai Apartments $
Apartments
Kaminda Sorobon 64
Tel *599 717 5369*
W lacbaai.com
A small complex of tastefully decorated studios and one- and two-bedroom apartments with full kitchens and balconies overlooking Lac Bay. There is also a small beach with cabanas.

The bright, white building of Bonaire Sunset Villa, Kralendijk, Bonaire

LAC BAY: Sorobon Beach Resort $$
Beach Resort
Sorobon 10
Tel *599 717 8080*
w sorobonbeachresort.com
Stay in one-bedroom cottages on a sandy beach looking out to Lac Bay and coral reefs. Sorobon teams up with Wannadive Bonaire for daily dives and equipment, and good windsurfing.

Curaçao

JAN THIEL: B&B Sombre di Kabana $
B&B
Kaya Beethoven 62
Tel *5999 520 7790*
w bnb-sombredikabana.com
This pleasant bed-and-breakfast offers rooms in the main house or a delightful garden cottage. There is a pool with Jacuzzi.

JAN THIEL: Landhuis Jan Thiel $$
Historic
Caracasbaaiweg z/n
Tel *5999 747 1068*
w landhuisjanthiel.com
Four charming guesthouses on the Jan Thiel Country Estate, a former plantation, are available for couples or groups. The estate has a tennis court, a pool, and a small pitch-and-putt course.

JAN THIEL: Papagayo Beach & Lounge Resort $$
Beach Resort
Jan Thiel Village
Tel *5999 747 4333*
w papagayo-beach.com
A complex of elegant two- and four-bedroom villas, with fully equipped kitchens, set in lush tropical gardens with sea views.The living room has wooden partitions.

DK Choice

JAN THIEL: Santa Barbara Beach & Golf Resort $$
Beach Resort
Porta Blancu, Nieuwpoort
Tel *855 590 2266*
w santabarbararesort
curacao.com
Relax on the white-sand beach, or take a dip in the swimming lagoon at this sprawling resort on a nature preserve, located away from the main town. There is also an 18-hole Pete Dye-designed golf course, four restaurants, a spa, and pools. Choice of water- or resort-view rooms, and luxury or spa suites.

JAN THIEL: Villa Boca $$$
Luxury
Boca Gentil B-04
Tel *5999 514 6305*
w villaboca.nl
A deluxe villa overlooking Caracas Bai and the sea, with a tropical landscaped garden and an infinity pool. Gourmet fare.

SABENA WESTPUNT: Marazul Dive Resort $
Apartments
Westpunt z/n
Tel *5999 516 9640*
w cometocuracao.com
An oceanside collection of apartments and bungalows, most with ocean views. The reef just offshore is good for diving.

SABENA WESTPUNT: Nos Krusero Apartments $
Apartments
Westpunt z/n tegenover kv 20, Playa Kalki
Tel *5999 524 9454*
w noskrusero-apartments.com
Close to the beach and dive shop, this colorful building with furnished apartments overlooking the sea. Pool and free Wi-Fi.

WILLEMSTAD: PM78 Urban Oasis Curacao $
Modern
Pietermaai 78
Tel *5999 528 6118*
w pietermaai78.com
This chic townhouse has a stylish apartment with a private pool, a city apartment, and a junior suite.

WILLEMSTAD: Royal Sea Aquarium Resort $
Beach Resort
Bapor Kibra z/n
Tel *888 721 4432*
w royalreservations.com
A collection of villas on an island just off the town center. Adjacent to the Sea Aquarium, admission to which is included in the rate.

WILLEMSTAD: Scuba Lodge & Suites $
Boutique
Pietermaai 104
Tel *5999-465-2575*
w scubalodge.com
A beautiful contemporary resort offering rooms, suites, and villas. PADI dive operator on site, with dive/room packages available.

WILLEMSTAD: Villa Tokara $
Historic
Penstraat 55
Tel *5999 461 0674*
w villatokara.com
Set in a beautiful 18th-century home, this inn has four rooms, including a family room. High standards of service and comfort.

WILLEMSTAD: Avila Hotel $$
Beach Resort
Penstraat 130
Tel *5999 461 4377*
w avilahotel.com
Elegant resort in the town center, with man-made lagoons creating two white-sand beaches. A spa offers treatments and classes.

WILLEMSTAD: The Strand $$
Apartments
Penstraat z/n
Tel *5999 671 5927*
w thestrandcuracao.com
An apartment complex on the beach, with lots of amenities, such as fully equipped kitchens and iPod docking stations.

WILLEMSTAD: Baoase Luxury Resort $$$
Beach Resort
Winterswijkstraat 2
Tel *5999 461 1799*
w baoase.com
Situated on a lagoon and white-sand beach, this resort has created a garden paradise with Asian accents. Choice of rooms, suites, and villas.

The pleasant waterfront path behind the Avila Hotel, Curaçao

Key to Price Guide *see page 496*

Where to Eat and Drink

Aruba

EAGLE BEACH:
Carte Blanche $$$
International
LG Smith Boulevard 55G
Tel *297 586 3339* **Closed** *Sun & Mon*
The chef creates a five-course dinner for up to 16 patrons at an oval bar. Guests can interact with him as he works his magic in front of them.

NOORD: Bingo! Café $$
International
Palm Beach 6D
Tel *297 586 2818*
A typical Dutch bar, with top-notch and reasonably priced fare, including lots of grilled entrées, burgers, brochettes, and salads. Large terrace seating.

NOORD: Wacky Wahoo's $$
Seafood
33B Palm Beach
Tel *297 586 7333* **Closed** *Sun*
The focus at this small eatery in a strip mall is on amazingly fresh Caribbean seafood entrées. The portions are generous, and the catch of the day comes right from the docks.

DK Choice

NOORD:
2 Fools & A Bull $$$
International
Palm Beach 17
Tel *297 586 7177* **Closed** *Sat & Sun*
"A fools' dinner party with two crazy hosts" is the way the owners describe the unique dining experience they offer – a five-course dinner with only 18 diners enjoying the evening at a communal table. The carefully thought out menu changes daily. Guests are welcomed with a glass of champagne. This diner is not to be missed. Online reservations are required, to be then reconfirmed 24 hours ahead.

ORANJESTAD: Amadeus
Restaurant $$
International
Tanki Leendert 249
Tel *297 587 3644* **Closed** *Mon*
Continental cuisine from an Austrian chef in a two-story European setting. Entrées include Stroganoff, schnitzel, and goulash, as well as West Indian ribs. Don't miss their signature Lost Symphony liquor.

ORANJESTAD: Barefoot
Restaurant $$
Seafood/Caribbean
LG Smith Boulevard 1
Tel *297 588 9824*
This beachfront restaurant offers elegant dining with a casual ambience. The specialties are fish and seafood, but they also serve beef and veggie entrées. There is a long list of luscious desserts, and a good wine list, too.

ORANJESTAD: Gostoso
Restaurante $$
Portuguese/Aruban
Caya Ing Roland H Lacle 12
Tel *297 588 0053* **Closed** *Mon*
A favorite neighborhood eatery, Gostoso offers daily specials and a selection of beef, seafood, and chicken entrées, as well as pasta. The Black Angus steak in red wine sauce is popular.

ORANJESTAD: Passions
on the Beach $$$
International
JE Irausquin Boulevard 252
Tel *297 527 1129*
Toes-in-the-sand dining on a beautiful beach is accompanied by gorgeous sunset views. The menu features lots of seafood, plus meat and pasta dishes.

ORANJESTAD: Windows
on Aruba Restaurant $$$
American
J E Irausquin Boulevard 93
Tel *297 523 5017*
This elegant restaurant in the golf clubhouse at Divi is noted for its steak and seafood entrées, and the fixed-price champagne Sunday brunch. Sea views over the golf course.

ORANJESTAD: Yemanja
Woodfired Grill $$$
Caribbean/Grill
Wilhelminastraat 2
Tel *297 588 4711*
Yemanja boasts the only wood-fired grill on the island, which produces outstanding seafood and meat entrées. The appetizer shrimp in puff pastry is not to be missed. There is a gluten-free menu as well.

PALM BEACH: Bavarian
German Restaurant $
German
Palm Beach 186 #3
Tel *297 736 4007* **Closed** *Sun*
Those with a taste for Wiener schnitzel, bratwurst, or *Sauerbraten* (pot roast) will not be disappointed at this welcoming

Price Guide
Prices are for a two-course meal for one, including tax and service charges and half a bottle of wine.
$ up to $50
$$ $50–70
$$$ over $70

Dine under a palapa at the Barefoot restaurant, Oranjestad, Aruba

restaurant. There is an extensive list of German beers, plus wines and German liquors to complement the food.

PALM BEACH: Linda's
Dutch Pancakes & Pizza $
Dutch/International
Palm Beach 6D
Tel *297 586 3378* **Closed** *Sun*
Sweet or savory, Dutch pancakes are perfect for breakfast, lunch, or dinner. They are served with lots of toppings, including fruit, ice cream, cheese, and bacon. Also pizzas, sandwiches, and salads, plus some Dutch entrées.

PALM BEACH: Scott's Brats $
American
Palm Beach
Tel *N/A* **Closed** *Sun*
This beachside spot serves up bratwurst from Wisconsin done in several ways, along with beers, sodas, and Bloody Marys. Good prices and friendly service.

PALM BEACH: Texas de
Brazil Churrascaria $$$
Brazilian
JE Irausquin Boulevard 382
Tel *297 586 4686*
Part of an international chain, this steakhouse has servers walking around with large skewers of grilled meats that are carved at the table. The fixed-price menu includes entrées, salads, and side dishes.

**SAVANETA: The Flying
Fishbone** $$$
Seafood
Savaneta 344
Tel *297 584 2506*
The tables here aren't just in the
sand, but in the surf, offering a
unique dining experience. Good,
fresh seafood, with a signature
Seafood History Soup entrée that
combines daily local catches.

Bonaire

**KRALENDIJK:
Dive Hut Bonaire** $
Internationali
Kaya Dialma 11
Tel *599 701 0404*
Small, popular restaurant with
special nights, including Swiss
food on Tuesdays, Thai on
Wednesdays, and barbecue on
Thursdays. Reservations required.

KRALENDIJK: Pasa Bon Pizza $
Italian
Kaya Gobernador N Debrot
Tel *599 780 1111* **Closed** *Mon & Tue*
In addition to traditional pizzas,
there are fresh fish pizza specials
here. Salads, pastas, and desserts
are also available. Take out or eat
in. Basic decor.

KRALENDIJK: Plazita Limena $
Peruvian
Kaya Grandi
Tel *599 717 8080* **Closed** *Sun*
Generous portions of authentic
Peruvian food, including *seviche*
(raw fish in citrus juices), fresh sea-
food, and meat entrées. Cash only.

KRALENDIJK: Ribs Factory $
Mexican
Kaya Grandi 51
Tel *599 717 4600* **Closed** *Wed*
Come here for finger-licking good
baby-back ribs served by the half
or full rack, plus seafood, frozen
drinks, and specialty cocktails.
There is also a children's menu.

DK Choice

KRALENDIJK: Appetite $$
International
12 Kaya Grandi
Tel *599 717 9535* **Closed** *Sat*
Innovative appetizers and
entrées are made using culinary
styles from around the globe.
Guests can choose from a daily-
changing selection of seafood,
meats, and vegetarian plates.
The chef designs three-, four-,
and five-course fixed-price
menus each day. Good wines
and sumptuous desserts.

KRALENDIJK: Bistro de Paris $$
French
Kaya Gobernador N Debrot 46
Tel *599 717 7070* **Closed** *Sun*
A classic French bistro offering
traditional meals accented with
Caribbean flavors. Freshly made
croissants, soups, and desserts.

**KRALENDIJK:
Chez Madeleine** $$
French
*Yachtclub Apartments, Kaya
Gobernador N Debrot 54*
Tel *599 782 1714* **Closed** *Tue & Wed*
A Michelin-starred chef creates
superb French and Belgian dishes
with artistic flair. The goat cheese
salad, and duck and lamb entrées
are especially good.

KRALENDIJK: It Rains Fishes $$
Seafood
Kaya Jan NE Craane 24
Tel *599 717 8780* **Closed** *Sun*
This oceanfront restaurant has its
own boat that brings in the catch
of the day. The seafood is superb,
but the menu also has steaks and
a good selection of salads.

**KRALENDIJK: Paradise Moon
Bar & Restaurant** $$
International
Kaya Gobernador Debrot 71
Tel *599 717 5025* **Closed** *Sun*
Paradise Moon has something for
every mood: entrées range from
a decadent seafood thermidor,
to coconut curry, pasta dishes,
fish 'n' chips, and tacos.

**KRALENDIJK: Spice
Beach Club** $$
International
*Bulevar Gobernador Nicollas
Debrot 73*
Tel *599 717 8080*
Enjoy a sophisticated, cool decor
in a beachside setting. Entrées
include seafood, steaks, and
pasta. Couples can reserve a
romantic Cabana Dinner.

KRALENDIJK: Unbelievable $$
Seafood
Kaya JA Abraham Boulevard 29
Tel *599 717 3000* **Closed** *Sat*
A highly rated restaurant offering
fresh seafood, as well as steaks
and pasta. Home-made desserts.
Dine on the rooftop terrace while
enjoying the sea views.

KRALENDIJK: At Sea $$$
International
Kaya CEB Hellmund 25
Tel *599 701 0134* **Closed** *Sun & Mon*
Often cited as one of the best
eateries on the island, this chic
oceanfront restaurant offers an
ever-changing four-course fixed-
price menu, plus à la carte entrées.

Fun, colourful paintings decorate the exterior
walls at It Rains Fishes, Kralendijk, Bonaire

**KRALENDIJK: Capriccio
Il Ristorante** $$$
Italian
5 Kaya CEB Hellmund
Tel *599 717 7230* **Closed** *Tue*
Italian cooking with a Caribbean
twist, plus traditional pizzas,
pastas, bread, *gelatos*, and
desserts. They also have the most
extensive wine cellar on the island.

**KRALENDIJK: La Guernica
Fish & Tapas** $$$
Spanish
Kaya Bonaire 4C
Tel *599 717 5022*
A wide selection of tapas, fresh
fish, and *gazpacho* (Spanish soup)
sets this seaside eatery apart.
There are meat and vegetarian
entrées, and a children's menu
as well. Wines from Spain, France,
and Chile.

**SOUTH END: Cactus Blue
on the Beach** $
International
Kite Beach, Atlantis
Tel *599 786 0816*
This food truck appears on
Atlantis when the wind is up
and the kitesurfers are out.
It serves outstanding burgers
and lionfish sandwiches, plus
beer and snack foods.

Curaçao

**CARACASBAAI:
Pincho Garden** $
Barbecue
Caracasbaaiweg 216A
Tel *5999 28 1234*
Pincho Garden may look slightly
seedy from the outside, but this
eatery serves the best grilled
skewers on the island, with
Portuguese salad and grilled
bread included. Cash only.

JAN THIEL: Zanzibar Beach $$
International
Jan Thiel Beach
Tel *5999 864 0126*
An upscale beach bar offering a range of tastes in appetizers, entrées, and desserts, plus specialty pizzas. There is a romantic four-course dinner on beach loungebeds for couples.

JAN THIEL: Boathouse Food & Marina $$$
International
Brakkeput Ariba z/n
Tel *5999 767 2221* **Closed** *Tue*
This relaxed eatery, set on a hill and overlooking Spanish Waters, offers tasting menus (such as Tasting Curaçao and Tasting Asia), plus seafood and grilled meats.

SABENA WESTPUNT: Jaanchies Restaurant $
Caribbean
Westpunt 15
Tel *5999 864 0126*
A long-established favorite, this eatery serves tasty local fare in a pleasant open-air setting. The owner, Jaanchie, greets guests and verbally presents the varied menu. Don't miss the iguana stew.

SABENA WESTPUNT: Landhuis Misje $
Caribbean
Weg Naar Westpunt
Tel *5999 515 6888* **Closed** *Sun*
Simple surroundings, basic good local food, and the warmth of the staff set this place apart. Menu favorites include *keshi yena* (stuffed cheese) and baked pasta with beef stew, raisins, spices, and cheese.

SABENA WESTPUNT: Sol Food $
American
Sunshine Getaway on the Weg Naar Playa Kalki
Tel *5999 864 0005* **Closed** *Mon–Thu*
A laid-back, environmentally conscious restaurant near the beach, with great food. Pizzas, grilled fish, hamburgers, hot dogs, and amazing brownies often feature on the weekly changing menu. The lionfish dish is a must.

WILLEMSTAD: Ginger $
Asian/Caribbean
Nieuwestraat 32
Tel *5999 465 1666*
The Asian-fusion cuisine here combines flavors from India, China, and Thailand with Caribbean spices and fruits. There are good noodle and rice dishes, and the three-course fixed-price menu changes on a regular basis.

WILLEMSTAD: Playa Porto Mari $
Caribbean
Porto Mari, West Coast
Tel *5999 864 7558*
As part of a public beach complex, this good-value seaside eatery offers Dutch pancakes, satays, fish and meat entrées, sandwiches, salads, and snacks.

WILLEMSTAD: Karakter Curacao $$
International
Coral Estate, Rif St. Marie
Tel *5999 864 2233*
This beachfront café near Coral Estate offers sandwiches, smoothies, and salads during the day, and fine dining at night. Good range of meat, seafood, and vegetarian entrées, plus a tapas menu. Good wine list, too.

DK Choice

WILLEMSTAD: Kome $$
International
Johan van Walbeeckplein 6
Tel *5999 465 0413* **Closed** *Sun*
Kome is the Papiamentu word for "eat", and there is lots to try here. The ever-changing imaginative menu features fried chicken and kimchi, chicken and waffles, and homemade sausages, plus great desserts including the Salty Dog – a combination of chocolate tart, ice cream, caramel sauce, and pretzels. Lengthy menu of martinis and house cocktails. Tapas on Wednesday nights.

WILLEMSTAD: L'Aldea Restaurant BV $$
South American
Sta Catharina 67
Tel *5999 767 6777*
A South American restaurant with a fixed-price menu that includes a main course of

20 distinct grilled meats brought to the table for selection. There is also a salad bar, as well as delicious side dishes, and desserts.

WILLEMSTAD: Mundo Bizarro $$
Latin
Nieuwestraat 12
Tel *5999 461 6767*
Excellent food is complemented by a hip Latino vibe and a quirky interior design. Try the three-course surprise menu, seafood and meat entrées, and desserts such as *tarte tartin* (fruit tart) or baklava.

WILLEMSTAD: Tempo Doeloe $$
Asian
La Vista Resort, Piscaderaweg
Tel *5999 461 2881*
A mix of the best Asian cuisines, offering *lumpia* (fried spring rolls), satays, sushi, an Indonesian rice table (for two or more), and a varied range of entrées.

WILLEMSTAD: Bistro Le Clochard $$$
French
Rif Fort, Otrabanda
Tel *5999 462 5666*
Fine dining in a historic setting overlooking Punda and the harbor. There are classics like *foie gras* and onion soup on the menu, plus interesting seafood dishes and a great cheese fondue. Extensive wine list.

WILLEMSTAD: The Wine Cellar $$$
French
Ooststraat at Concordiastraat
Tel *5999 461 2178* **Closed** *Sun*
Dine amid a welcoming atmosphere at this delightful restaurant, which offers French cuisine with a Caribbean flair. The chef designs multicourse dinners with an emphasis on fresh ingredients.

The pleasant dining area at Kome, Willemstad, Curaçao

Practical Information

Aruba, Curaçao, and Bonaire are linked by location and politics, both past and present, but each one is fiercely independent and unique. Accommodations are varied with Aruba being the most expensive, Bonaire catering to divers, and Curaçao, with the most number of budget hotels. The tourist organizations on each island have a friendly staff willing to help organize and promote comforts, entertainment, and attractions for visitors. An immense amount of information is available at tourist offices including maps and magazines, for those planning a trip to the region.

Terminal of the Curaçao International Airport, Hato

When to Go

Aruba, Curaçao, and Bonaire are well out of the hurricane belt, and though storms can occur, warm temperatures and cool breezes can be found all year round. Summer and fall are the best time to visit the three islands, when many cultural events are held.

Getting There

Aruba and Curaçao have daily direct air service from North America and Amsterdam. Bonaire has weekly non-stop service from North America and Amsterdam and one-stop daily service from North America. Flights land at the international airports of Queen Beatrix on Aruba, Flamingo on Bonaire, and Hato on Curaçao. **Delta** flies non-stop to all islands from Atlanta. **American Eagle** flies to Aruba and Curaçao from the US, and to Bonaire from Puerto Rico. **US Airways** and **United Airlines** have flights to Aruba from the US. Flights from Amsterdam to all three islands are on **KLM**. Regional airlines such as **Divi Divi** fly within the

islands, and **Insel Air** connects Curaçao with Jamaica. There is no scheduled ferry service to the islands.

Documentation

Citizens of the EU nations as well as all other nationalities, including Canadians and Americans must show a passport to enter the islands. Visits may extend to three months without a visa. In addition, immigration officials may ask for an onward or return ticket, proof of sufficient funds for the planned stay, and an address where travelers plan to reside on the islands. Visitors can also check with their concerned embassies.

Visitor Information

Tourist information kiosks are located at the airports on all three islands. Government Tourist Boards including the **Aruba Tourism Authority**, **Tourism Corporation Bonaire**, and **Curaçao Tourist Board** have offices on each island as

well as public relations agents overseas. Websites run by the official tourism offices give all the details about planning a vacation and provide links to a number of tourist-oriented businesses.

Health and Security

Crime is rare on the three islands, with crimes against tourists among the lowest in the Caribbean. Still, precautions should be taken, especially against theft from rental cars. Visitors should also avoid leaving valuables unattended. Drug-related crimes occur occasionally, so avoid secluded roads and alleys after dark. Any crime must be reported with a request for a written report. Tap water here is safe to drink. **Dr. Horacio Oduber Hospital** in Aruba, **San Francisco Hospital** in Bonaire, and **St. Elizabeth Hospital** in Curaçao are among the best hospitals.

Banking and Currency

US dollars and major credit cards are widely accepted on the islands. The official currency on Aruba is the Aruban Florin (AF or Afl), which is divided into 100 cents, and Curaçao uses the Netherlands Antillean Florin (NAFI or FI). The NAFI is also known as the Netherlands Antillean Guilder (ANG). Bonaire uses the US dollar. Banks and ATMs are located throughout the islands. Banking hours are Monday to Friday from 8am to 3:30pm.

Communications

The country codes for Aruba, Bonaire, and Curaçao are 297, 599, and 5999 respectively followed by the seven-digit local number. To call from outside the Caribbean, dial the international code (011 from the US) plus the area code, and the local number. For example, dial 011, then area code 297, and the seven-digit number for Aruba. Internet access is provided at major resorts and airports, and there are many Wi-Fi hotspots. Local SIM cards are available at **Digicel** offices.

Transport

Taxis are easily found at the airports, cruise ship terminals, hotels, and major tourist attractions. The international airports have car rental agencies on-site. A valid driver's license and major credit card are needed to hire a car. Driving is on the right side, and all the islands have a network of paved roads connecting the main towns. Dirt roads run through the countryside, and a four-wheel drive vehicle is practical for independent travelers touring outside major tourist areas. **AVIS**, **Hertz**, **AB Carrental**, **Amigo Rent-A-Car**, and **Michel Car Rental** are popular car rental companies. Aruba and Curaçao also have public bus systems.

Shopping

Curaçao offers the best shopping experience. Cheese, chocolates, and Delftware are popular items. The goods in Aruba and Curaçao

Market stalls awaiting cruise ship passengers in Brionplein, Willemstad

are cheap due to a low import duty. Dutch goods are of particular interest on these two islands. On Bonaire, Kralendijk offers art, jewelry, and beachwear. Look out for Aruba's **Strada complex**, **Island Fashions** in Bonaire, and **Riffort Village** in Curaçao.

Language

Dutch is the official language, but locals speak a dialect called Papiamento, as well as English, and Spanish.

Electricity

On Aruba, the voltage is 110 AC, 127/120 AC on Bonaire, and 110/130 AC on Curaçao. Most outlets accept US plugs.

Time

The islands are on Atlantic Standard Time, 4 hours behind Greenwich Mean Time.

Getting Married

On Aruba, couples need to submit their documents at the **Office of Civil Registry** at least 14 days prior to the wedding date. On Bonaire, either party needs to become a temporary resident of the island. Check the Bonaire tourism website for details. Paperwork on Curaçao begins two months in advance, and both the bride and groom must be temporary residents for at least 3 days. Contact **Wedding Services Curaçao** for assistance.

DIRECTORY

Getting There

American Eagle
ⓦ aa.com

Delta
ⓦ delta.com

Divi Divi
Tel 599 9839 1515.
ⓦ flydivi.com

Insel Air
ⓦ fly-inselair.com

KLM
ⓦ klm.com

United Airlines
ⓦ united.com

US Airways
ⓦ usair.com

Visitor Information

Aruba Tourism Authority
ⓦ aruba.com

Curaçao Tourist Board
ⓦ curacao.com

Tourism Corporation Bonaire
ⓦ infobonaire.com

Health and Security

Ambulance
Tel 911 (Aruba),
119 (Bonaire),
912 (Curaçao).

Dr. Horacio Oduber Hospital
Tel 297 587 4300.

Police
Tel 100 (Aruba),
911 (Bonaire),
911 (Curaçao).

San Francisco Hospital
Tel 599 717 8900.

St. Elizabeth Hospital
Tel 599 9462 5100.

Communications

Digicel
ⓦ digicelaruba.com
ⓦ digicelbonaire.com
ⓦ digicelcuracao.com

Transport

AB Carrental
ⓦ abcarrental.com

Amigo Rent-A-Car
ⓦ amigocar.com

AVIS
ⓦ avis.com

Hertz
Tel 297 588 7570 (Aruba),
599 717 7221 (Bonaire),
599 9888 0188 (Curaçao).

Michel Car Rental
ⓦ michelcarrental.com

Shopping

Island Fashions
5 Kaya Grandi, Kralendijk.

Riffort Village
Otrobanda, Willemstad.

Strada Complex
Caya G.F. Betico Croes, Oranjestad, Aruba.

Getting Married

Office of Civil Registry
Oranjestad, Aruba.
Tel 297 583 4400.

Wedding Services Curaçao
Piscadera Bay, Curaçao.
Tel 599 9463 6207.
ⓦ weddingscuracao.com

General Index

Acknowledgments

Dorling Kindersley would like to thank the many people whose help and assistance contributed to the preparation of this book.

Contributors

Christopher P. Baker, winner of the 2008 Lowell Thomas Award as the Travel Journalist of the Year, is a Caribbean specialist and an authority on Cuba travel. He has contributed to more than 200 publications worldwide, including Caribbean Travel & Life, Islands, Maxim, and National Geographic Traveler. He has been named Travel Writer of the Year by the Caribbean Tourism Organization and the Jamaican Tourist Board.

James Henderson has been visiting the Caribbean for more than 20 years, contributing words and images to travel guides and the press. He has written for many leading UK publications and magazines and is the founder-editor of definitivecaribbean.com, an on-line guide to the islands.

Skye Hernandez is a writer and editor living in Trinidad and Tobago. She has traveled widely in the Caribbean and is a former editor of Caribbean Beat and MACO Caribbean Living magazine.

Lynda Lohr moved to the Caribbean seeking an adventure 25 years back. A resident of St. John (US Virgin Islands), she regularly writes articles for many news organizations, travel publications, and has contributed to many guidebooks on the Caribbean.

KC Nash, an American freelance writer who has been visiting the Caribbean for over 20 years, now lives in Antigua. A former editor of a daily newspaper, she has also written for many regional magazines and publications.

Don Philpott, a writer for more than 40 years, has authored about 90 books on many subjects including travel. More than 5,000 of his articles have been published in US and UK newspapers and magazines.

Theresa Storm, a Canadian freelance travel journalist, author, and photographer, has contributed to well-known magazines such as Reader's Digest, Islands, and Caribbean Escapes. She has also won several awards for her travel writing.

Lynne Sullivan, an American freelance journalist, writes extensively about Caribbean destinations. She is a member of the Society of American Travel Writers and the American Society of Journalists and Authors.

Polly Thomas lives in Trinidad and is a freelance writer and editor who first visited the Caribbean aged 17, when she traveled around Jamaica. Since then, she has explored most of the islands, and is the author of guidebooks to Jamaica, Trinidad and Tobago, St. Lucia, and Antigua.

Fact Checkers

Lynda Lohr, Textosdom (Santo Domingo), Rukmini Tilara

Proofreader

Stewart Wild

Indexer

Cyber Media Services Ltd.

Design and Editorial

Publisher Douglas Amrine
List Manager Vivien Antwi
Managing Art Editor Jane Ewart
Project Editor Alastair Laing
Project Art Editors Kate Leonard, Shahid Mahmood
Editorial Assistance Vicki Allen
Senior Cartographic Editor Casper Morris
Managing Art Editor (Jackets) Karen Constanti
Jacket Designer Tessa Bindloss
Senior DTP Designer Jason Little
DTP Designer Natasha Lu
Picture Researcher Ellen Root
Production Controller Liz Cherry

Revisions Team

Emma Anacootee, Christopher P. Baker, Kate Berens, Hilary Bird, Cobalt Id, Imogen Corke, Jane Ellis, Fay Franklin, Skye Hernandez, Shobhna Iyer, Taraneh Ghajar Jerven, Claire Jones, Sumita Khatwani, Priya Kukadia, Jude Ledger, Hayley Maher, Alison McGill, Casper Morris, KC Nash, George Nimmo, Lucy Richards, Sands Publishing Solutions, Susana Smith, Anna Streiffert, Priyanka Thakur, Rukmini Tilara, Priyansha Tuli, Janis Utton, Conrad Van Dyk, Lisa Voormeij, Tanveer Abbas Zaidi

DK Picture Library

Romaine Werblow

Additional Photography

Max Alexander, Andy Crawford, Ian Cummings, Mike Dunning, Lydia Evans, Neil Fletcher and Matthew Ward, Trish Gant, Heidi Grassley, Frank Greenaway, Dave King, Cyril Laubscher, Martin Norris, Ian O'Leary, Gary Ombler, Martin Richardson, Tim Ridley, Lucio Rossi, Rough Guides / Ian Cummings,/ Lydia Evans,/ Roger Mapp,/ Anthony Pidgeon,/ Martin Richardson, Karl Shone, Tony Souter, Jon Spaull, Polly Thomas.

Photography Permissions

Dorling Kindersley would like to thank the following for their assistance and kind permission to photograph at their establishments:

Ajili Mójili, Puerto Rico; Altar de la Patria, Santo Domingo; Anse Chastanet, St. Lucia; Apple Bay, British Virgin Islands; Barbados Golf Club; Cindy Corbin at Barbados Museum; Belmont Estate, Grenada; Biras Creek; Calle San Sebastián, Puerto Rico; Captain Oliver's Resort Hotel, Sint Maarten; Caribelle Batik, St. Kitts; Catedral Primada de América; Creighton Estate Coffee Farm and Great House; Daphne's, Barbados; Decker's Grille & Lounge; Diamond Casino; Discovery at Marigot Bay; Firefly; Grace Bay Club, Turks & Caicos; Mr Bob Betton at Greenwood Great House; Half Moon Club, Jamaica; Harbour Lights, Barbados; Annabella Proudlock at Harmony Hall; Hotel El Convento, Puerto Rico; Jobean's Hot Glass Studio; Jump Up Casino; La Cathédrale Saint-Louis, Martinique; Le Plein Soleil, Martinique; Le Sereno; Grand Cul-de-Sac, St Barthélemy; Matilde Restaurant & Historic Monument, Guadeloupe; Carlos I. Ayala at Museo de Arte de Puerto Rico; Museo de Arte e Historia de San Juan; Old Gin House; St. Eustatius; Parque de Bombas; Pati de St. Barth; Pedro St. James National Historic Site; Pyrat Rum Factory, Anguilla; Raffles Canouan; Rainforest Restaurant at Papillote, Dominica; Rawlins Plantation Inn; RockHouse; Negril; Royal Westmoreland; Sacred Heart Church, a Roman Catholic Church; Frank Costin at Savannah Gallery, Anguilla; Marietta Norville at St. Nicholas Abbey, Barbados; Sunbury Plantation House; The Blue Haven Hotel, Tobago; The Cove, Antigua; The Edge, St. Lucia; The Fort Young Hotel, Dominica; The Grenadines Resort; The Hermitage Plantation Inn, Nevis; The Jaipur Restaurant; The Rhodes Restaurant; The Roman Catholic Cathedral, St. Lucia; Westin Dawn Beach Resort Casino, St. Martin; Young Island Resort, St. Vincent & the Grenadines; Zurra, Anguilla.

Picture Credits

Key: a-above; below/bottom; c-centre; f-far; l-left; r-right; t-top.

Every effort has been made to trace the copyright holders, and we apologize in advance for any unintentional omissions. We would be pleased to insert the appropriate acknowledgments in any subsequent edition of this publication.

The publisher would like to thank the following individuals, companies, and picture libraries for their kind permission to reproduce their photographs:

Works of art have been reproduced with the kind permission of the following copyright holders:

Figura Ecuestre in Plaza de la Revolución © Alberto Lescay Merencio 91c; Sam Sharpe Monument in Montego Bay © Kay Sullivan 137tl; Maternity at the Galeria de Arte Cándido Bidó © Cándido Bidó 166bl; Girafo in San Juan © Jorge Zeno 194c; The Resurrection and Ascension mural in the Sacred Heart Church, a Roman Catholic Church, Saba © Heleen Cornet 282bl

4Corners: Larsen Collinge 58tr; Guido Cozzi 335br, 493crb, 494tl, 494cr; Devaux Danielle 388-389c; SIME / Dutton Colin 351cr,/ Romiti Fabrizio 118br,/ Damm Fridmar 479br,/ Grafenhain Gunter 29crb, 30-31c, 245tr, 456cl, 479tl, 493br,/ Mehlig Manfred 46cr,/ Ripani Massimo 266b,/ Schmid Reinhard 5tr, 29br, 40bc, 73br, 84tl, 90bl, 92tr, 102cl, 132b, 133tl, 152br, 461tl.

Aguaviva restaurant: 218tc.

Alamy Images: Rolf Adlercreutz 338cl; John Anderson 491c; Arco Images GmbH 87cra, 181cla, 325c; Bill Bachmann 253tr; Mark Bassett 31br; 145clb; Henry George Beeker 485tl, 493bl; John Bentley 52clb; Blaine Harrington III 54cr; blickwinkel 31bl; Steve Bly 498bl; Brandon Cole Marine Photography 48clb; George Brice 427t; Caribbean 131tr; Maria Grazia Casella 54tr; Heeb Christian 189br; Robert Clay 433tr; Thornton Cohen 34-35c; Content Mine International 55cb, 297br; Chris A Crumley 339tr; Stuart Crump 58crb; CuboImages srl 82tl, 155br; Tim Cuff 44crb, 120bc, 130tr; Danita Delimont 1c, 106clb, 110bc, 121tr, 127tl, 130cl, 303bc, 349br, 353cl, 383bl, 485c, 494bc, 500tr; Susan E. Degginger 244cl, 401cla; Delfini Int Ltd (UK) 245tl; Reinhard Dirscherl 48tr, 180br; Don Despain / www.rekindlephoto.com 106tr; Alissa Everett 41br; Fabian Gonzales Editorial 401clb, 401br; FAN travelstock 95tc; Waldhaeusl Franz 192br; Robert Fried 48cla, 137cl, 207tr; Dan Galic 37bl, Geogphotos 112br, 113cl; David Giral 372br; Jeff Greenberg 44tr, 126tl, 126b; Guillen Photography / UW / Bonaire 491cl; Nick Hanna 44bl, 105cr, 183cl; Headline Photo Agency 147br; Bill Heinsohn 104bl; Gavin Hellier 49tl, 295t, 448tl; Hemis 84br; John Henshall 78bl; Wesley Hitt 140bl; Tryphosa Ho 441br; Peter Horree 338clb; ImageGap 157tr; ImageState 61tr; Imagestate Media Partners Limited - Impact Photos 55bl; Ingolf Pompe 452crb; Ingolf Pompe-8 349tl, 353br; Ingolf Pompe-32 52cla, 464tc; Isifa Image Service s.r.o 87tc, 89cl; James Davis Photography 319cla; Andre Jenny 227br, 244bl; Matthew Johnston 431clb; Jon Arnold Images Ltd 79tl, 296cr; JTB Photo Communications, Inc 86clb; Karen & Ian Stewart 33cr, 49cr; Kim Karpeles 200cl, Jim Kidd 258br; David Kilpatrick 447br; Dan Leeth 31tl; Mark Lewis 37tl, 121tl, 237cl; LH Images 296bl, 297crb; Randy Lincks 285bc; Melvyn Longhurst 78cl, Lordprice Collection 52tr; Iain Lowson 456tr; MagicSea.com / Carlos Villoch 241br, 245bl, 280br; Stephen Mallaby 86cl; Mark Summerfield 232bl, 232br, 233crb; Marka 98tl; Mary Evans Picture Library 398br; mediacolor's 34bl; Michael DeFreitas Caribbean 36crb, 127cr; MJ Photography 477cr; Mountain Light / Galen Rowell 259bl; Steve Murray 41cr; nagelestock.com 136bl;

Martin Norris 86tr; Brian North 431bc; North Wind Picture Archives 143crb; M. Timothy O'Keefe 40cb, 40br, 48bl, 109cl, 124cl, 179c, 179br, 192cl, 300tl, 383crb, 389br; Paul Thompson Images 437c; Peter Arnold, Inc. 203br; Photoshot Holdings Ltd 461cr; Photov.com / Hisham Ibrahim 138t; David Pick 58cr, 312br, 326cra; Walter Pietsch 346br, 353clb; Kristjan Porm 338br; Reimar 271br; Robert Harding Picture Library Ltd 75br, 465br; Helene Rogers 328tr, 476cra, 477tl; Grant Rooney 54cl; Rough Guides 315bl; Kevin Schafer 213c, 431bl; James Schwabel 237clb, 263br; SCPhotos 228c; Alex Segre 78cb, 79crb; Antony Souter 100b; Stephen Frink Collection 32cr, 125br, 248bc, 416br; Stock Connection Blue 53tr; Stockfolio 353cr; Lee Karen Stow 179tr; Rick Strange 236tl; Mark Sykes 338bc; Steve Taylor ARPS 386tr; Terry Harris just Greece photo library 45tl; Terry Smith Images Turks and Caicos Collection 124crb; Topcris 162tr, 163bl; Travelib Asia 47br; Travelshots.com 313br, 432cr; Kirk Treakle 237bl; Bob Turner 476bl; Eye Ubiquitous 445clb; Tom Uhlman 31tr, 39tr; V1 54crb; Landrin Valerie 421tl; Michael Ventura 423c; Visual&Written SL 33crb; Nik Wheeler 39tl; Poelzer Wolfgang 429ca; Andrew Woodley 42cb, 316cl, 322tr, 338tr; World Pictures 435bl, 444br; WorldFoto 111cl; Ruchan Ziya 49br.

The Alexander Hotel: 114tl.

Amanyara hotel: 128tc.

Axiom Photographic Agency: 389bl; Gardel Bertrand 35tl; Chris Caldicott 40–41c; Ian Cumming 133br, 145tl, 151tl, 153tl; Hemis 330b.

Bananas Restaurant: www.taraleighphotography.com 307br.

Barefoot: 499cr.

Louis N Batides: 45tr.

El Beaterio: 189tr.

Biras Creek Resort: 251bc.

Blue Bubbles Watersports & Dive Center: 274tl.

Bonaire Sunset Villa: 497br.

Bonito: 341tl.

The Bridgeman Art Library: Plan of Drake's attack on Santo Domingo, c.1595 (engraving) 65tr, Sir Henry Morgan (c.1635-88) (coloured engraving) 65bc, Eruption of a Volcano on Martinique, from 'Le Petit Parisien', 15th May 1902 (colour litho) 366crb.

Cayman Brac Lost City of Atlantis: Elisa Buller 111bc.

The Champs: 391br.

Anne Chopin: 367br.

Christopher Baker: 93cra.

Chukka Caribbean Adventures: 155cra, 155c.

Philip Chung: 63cl.

Coal Pot: 407bc.

Coco Beach Resort: 356bl.

Corbis: 412bc; C.I. Aguera 269tc; Tony Arruza 67br; Yann Arthus-Bertrand 413cl, 415cla; Atlantide Phototravel 58bl, 71br, 194b, 458b; Tom Bean 38br, 195br; Bettmann 40tr, 67tr; Blaine Harrington III 5crb, 459tl, 472–473; Tibor Bognar 88tl; Gary Braasch 471br; Diane Cook & Len Jenshel 181br; Reinhard Eisele 145bl; EPA / Alejandro Ernesto 20bl; Macduff Everton 59br, 419br; Ales Fevzer 41bl; Stephen Frink 111crb, 285cl, 467bc; Goodlook Pictures / Philippe Giraud 38–39c, 63br, 365br, 379br; Rose Hartman 41crb; Gavin Hellier 378bl; Hemis / Bertrand Gardel 165br / Du Boisberranger Jean 26–27; Dave G. Houser 53cra, 54br, 259t, 260bc, 287br, 429cla; George H.H. Huey 383cra; image100 456cr; J.Garcia / photocuisine 429cb; JAI / Doug Pearson 68–69; Catherine Karnow 38tr; Layne Kennedy 153br; Keren Su 454–455; Bob Krist 35bl, 232cl, 243cr, 303cl, 385cl, 429clb; Liu Dawei / Xinhua Press 43bl; Buddy Mays 233bl; Joe McDonald 47cr; MedioImages 123clb, 388cl; Minden Pictures / Norbert Wu 222–223; Amos Nachoum 493cl; Neil Emmerson / Robert Harding World Imagery 314bl / Sergio Pitamitz 376–377; Onne van der Wal 36cl; Mark Peterson 139bc; Reuters / Jorge Silva 54cb; Bill Ross 29cra; Rykoff Collection 67bl; Bob Sacha 52–53c; Sygma / Philippe Giraud 334t; Liba Taylor 43br; Troy Wayrynen / NewSport 43tr; Michele Westmorland 120t; Nik Wheeler 281t; Hein van den Heuvel / zefa 36clb.

Crescent Moon Cabins: 390tl.

Cuisinart Golf Resort & Spa: 262tc.

Danita Delimont Stock Photography: Bill Bachmann 491br; Walter Bibikow 5clb, 331tl, 486tl, 491bl; Robin Hill 45cr; Greg Johnston 302cl; Jon Arnold Images 28br; Scott T. Smith 331br, 365tl, 374cl; Nik Wheeler 303clb.

Dirk Dijkhuizen: 485bl.

Dorling Kindersley: Courtesy of the Meson de la Cava, Santo Domingo / Jon Spaull 191t.

Dreamstime.com: Donyanedomam 184–185; Roxana González 12tr; Sean Pavone 13b; Tim Ridgers 404–405; Zhukovsky 17tc.

The Fairmont Royal Pavilion: 58br.

Firefly Plantation: 420bl.

FLPA: SA TEAM / FN / Minden 471cl.

Geejam: 159bl, 161tl.

Getty Images: AFP / Juan Barreto 43cra / Jacques Demarthon 43clb / Adrian Dennis 42cl; Axiom Photographic Agency / Ian Cumming 141tr; Shaun

Botterill 42–43c; Gustavo Caballero 53bl; David Cannon 40cla; Jeff R Clow 246–247; Digital Vision / Stephen Frink 32crb; Horst Tappe / Hulton Archive 397br; The Image Bank / Michele Westmorland 56cl; Darrell Jones 32bl; Ross Kinnaird 40clb; Medioimages / Photodisc 29tl; Philippe Merle 53crb; Michael Ochs Archives 151clb; Donald Miralle 37cr; Photodisc / Stuart Gregory 379tr; Photographer's Choice / Jeff Hunter 111c; Photodisc / Chel Beeson 2–3; Photonica / Daniel Allan 41bc; Premium Archive / Alan Oxley 85bc; Redferns / Ian Dickson 52bc / JM International 53br / David Redfern 53tl, 53bc; Riser / Jeff Hunter 93cl; Robert Harding World Imagery / Richard Cummins 456bl; Roger Viollet / Harlingue 347bc; Stringer 42crb / Brian Kersey 43crb / Phil Inglis 449bl; Taxi / Richard Bradbury 57tl; Michele Westmorland 467c.

GoldenEye: 158tl.

The Granger Collection, New York: 64cr, 64bl, 64br, 65cb, 66tl, 66bc, 67cb.

Hotel Nacional de Cuba: 97tr.

Houserstock: Ellen Barone 31cr, 419cb; Dave G. Houser 419cla.

Grete Howard: South West Regional Development Agency 155clb.

IBEROSTAR Hotels & Resorts: 99b, 186cr.

Island Exposure Inc: 325br.

iStockphoto.com: Susanna Pershern 237crb.

Jacobson Associates, Inc: 125cl, 125cr, 125clb.

Jolly Harbour Golf and Country Club: 321t.

jupiterimages: Don Hebert 233tr.

Kariwak Village: Skene Howie 474br.

Mikko Karvonen: 55tr.

Kome : 501br.

La Guarida: 101tr.

La Sagesse Hotel: 434bl.

La Samanna: 276bl.

La Yola: 190bl.

Lonely Planet Images: Jerry Alexander 489cl; Richard Cummins 489c; Richard l'Anson 34tr, 338cr; John Elk III 213cla; Wayne Walton 317br.

Lucio Rossi: 59tr, 89bl, 91tr, 92cr, 273clb

Malliouhana Hotel & Spa: 44clb

Mary Evans Picture Library: 299bc

Masterfile: Jean-Yves Bruel 342cl; Mark Downey 145cb; Steve Fitzpatrick 36cr;

Greg Stott 54bl.

Christopher Mazz: 285crb, 285br

Mike Messina: 213clb

Mille Fleurs: 161bc

National Geographic Stock: Cotton Coulson 415cl; Melissa Farlow 46cb; Michael Melford 51bl; Minden Pictures / Gerry Ellis 419cl / Laus Meyer 51cr / Mike Parry 93crb; Joel Sartore 213bc; Rex Stucky 4br, 35cb; Steve Winter 50cla, 50cr, 50clb.

naturepl.com: Nigel Bean 50crb; Brandon Cole 122br; George McCarthy 303cb; Rolf Nussbaumer 46crb, 47cra, 144tr, 213bl, 213br; Pete Oxford 50bl,123bc, 289cl; Doug Perrine 50tr, 210bc, 211tl; Mike Potts 47cla, 50cl, 50c; Jean E. Roche 47bl; Shattil & Rozinski 47tr; Lynn M. Stone 47c; Kim Taylor 46bl; Doug Wechsler 46cl, 123c; Rod Williams 123cl.

Paul F. Neumann: 237ca.

Nisbet Plantation Beach Club: 59cl.

Odyssey Productions, Inc.: Robert Frerck 195tl; James Quine 72b.

Ondeck Group: 34cl, 319clb, 319crb, 319br.

Ottley's Plantation Inn: 59crb, 60cl, 60bl, 306tc.

The Peninsula House: 188bl.

Peter Island Resort & Spa: 250tr.

Photographer's Direct: Alan Weaver Photography 46clb.

Photolibrary: age fotostock / Alvaro Leiva 389cr / Georgie Holland 106br / Gonzalo Azumendi 366tl / P Narayan 346tl, 493clb / Terrance Klassen 267cr / Walter Bibikow 486br / Angelo Cavalli 245br; Animals Animals / Hamman / Heldring 471cr; Bill Bachmann 135tl; Dan Barba 70br; Bibikow Bibikow 119bl; Walter Bibikow 351bl; Imagestate / Greg Johnston 33cl; John Warburton-Lee Photography / Paul Harris 388bl; Jon Arnold Travel / Walter Bibikow 34br; Joyce & Frank Burek 49tr; JTB Photo 70clb; Mark M Lawrence 71tl; Alvaro Leiva 429cl; Japack Photo Library 46tr; Mauritius / Walter Bibikow 486c; Wendell Metzen 71cr; moodboard 471cla; Roberta Parkin 429cr; PhotoLink / T OKeefe 135br; Photononstop 354tc; J-C&D. Pratt 370b; PureStock 268b; Alex Quesada 37tr; Robert Harding Travel / Ellen Rooney 28bl / J Lightfoot 28tr / Richard Cummins 380b, 442bc, 478b, 481t; Lothar Schulz 73tl; Paul Thompson 35br; WaterFrame / Reinhard Dirscherl 32tr, 32cl, 491clb, 491crb / Manuela Kirschner 92bl, 468br.

Photoshot: Authors Images 365cr; Eye Ubiquitous 42tr; Jean-Marc Lecerf 355tc, 371tc, 374br; NHPA / Jany Sauvanet 471cb; World Pictures 28clb, 42bl, 364c, 368br, 415cr; WpN 55tc.

Redferns: David Sinclair 52br.

Reflexstock: PhotoNonStop / Van Osaka 55cl.

Reuters: Jorge Silva 457tr.

Robert Harding Picture Library: Walter Bibikow 422br, Bruno Morandi 57c.

Sandy Lane: 449cl, 449cr, 449crb.

Seven Stars Resort: 129bl.

Steve Simonsen - Marine Scenes: 8–9, 59bl, 109tl, 224cl, 288cla, 299crb, 303bl, 304t, 402tl, 402b, 403cr; Spain Pix 59tl.

Sonesta Maho Beach Resort & Casino, St. Maarten: 44br.

SuperStock: Angelo Cavalli 121br.

Sweet Plantains: 252bc.

The Bay at Nonsuch: 327br.

The Casino Royale at Sonesta Maho Beach Resort & Casino: 273cl.

The Mangrove Information Center: 36br.

The Ocean Adventure: 2008 Wayne & Karen Brown / Brown & Co. Photography 369cla.

TopFoto.co.uk: The Image Works 353crb.

Tortuga Bay: 187bl.

The Travel Library: Erik Schaffer 63tl.

Travel Pictures: PCL Travel / Terry Harris 431crb, Spain Pix 37clb.

Travel-Images.com: 55tl, G. Friedman 62clb, M.Torres 171br, 177br; 2006 David Smith 272bc.

Tropic Isle Weddings: 60tr, 61cl.

Tropical Ties: Celia Sorhaindo 388tr.

Tropicasub Plongee: 369cl, 369cr, 369clb, 369bl, 369br.

Veni Mange: 475tl.

Westin Resort and Villas: 249tr, 496tl.

Front Endpaper: Corbis: JAI / Doug Pearson tl, Keren Su br, Minden Pictures / Norbert Wu tc, , Robert Harding World Imagery / Sergio Pitamitz bc

Jacket Images: Front: Getty Images: Jeff Hunter, **DK Images:** Linda Whitwam bl; **Spine: Getty Images:** Jeff Hunter tl.

All other images copyright © Dorling Kindersley.

For further information: **www.dkimages.com**

Caribbean Inter-island Air Routes

UNITED STATES
OF AMERICA

Gulf of Mexico

BAHAMAS

A t l a

CUBA

Havana

Cayo Coco

Nueva
Gerona

Camagüey

Holguin

TURKS A
CAICO
ISLAND

Providenciales

Baracoa

Santiago
de Cuba

HAITI

CAYMAN
ISLANDS

George
Town

Montego
Bay

JAMAICA

Kingston

C a r i

COLOMBIA

Key

— Aero Caribbean

--- Air Antilles

— Air Caraïbes

— Air Turks and Caicos

— American Eagle

— Caribbean Airlines

— Cayman Airways

— Cubana

— Insel Air

— JetBlue

— LIAT

— Winair

0 kilometers   200

0 miles   200